D0341704

GREAT
FOOTBALL
WRITING

SPORTS ILLUSTRATED
1954–2006

EDITED BY ROB FLEDER
SPORTS ILLUSTRATED BOOKS

GREAT
FOOTBALL
WRITING

CONTENTS

Inside Football

Down by Contact

Game Time

Higher Powers

All-Everything

Outside the Lines

INTRODUCTION

Introduction

BY PETER KING

E HAVE SO MANY CHERISHED VERITIES IN life—and in sports—that we accept without question. The Ivies are the best colleges in America. California girls are the cutest girls in the world. Seattle espresso is the tastiest. Roger Clemens's repertoire is the nastiest. Baseball writing is better than football writing.

Well, I say, Not so fast. Reasonable men could argue about Dartmouth versus Notre Dame, and I would argue that Pennsylvania girls are the best, having married a great one. Also, I know a great latte place in Houston, and I wouldn't be surprised if a poll of baseball players concluded that Pedro Martinez, at his peak, was tougher to hit than Clemens. And with regard to the writing, well, you're about to have that verity knocked off its perch as well.

Over the years, it's been carved in stone that the greatest sports journalism, indeed, the only writing in sports worthy of being called "literature," has come from baseball's best chroniclers—Ring Lardner, Bernard Malamud, Robert Creamer, Roger Angell and David Halberstam among them. Not sure why that is. Maybe it's because baseball has been around longer and was king of the American sports scene in the twenties and thirties while pro football was a couple of notches below professional wrestling; baseball had the mythic Babe Ruth and had its greatest team in New York City, not a frosty little town in Wisconsin, and . . . well, you get the idea.

It has gotten to the point that even football writers concede the battle without a fight, humbly shuffling our feet everytime somebody corners us in a bar to rave about the latest Roger Kahn exegesis on playing pepper. I've heard the same rant from NFL p.r. types a dozen times in my 23 years covering football: Why aren't there more stories and more books about what a wonderful game football is? When I wrote a book 15 years ago about the inner lives of some of the NFL's biggest names, I got a letter from the league's relatively new commissioner, Paul Tagliabue. "The game needs more writing like this," he said.

I'm not going to keep theorizing about the reasons why this myth persists about the relative superiority of baseball writing; I'm just going to set the record straight while I whet your appetite for this great collection of stories from SPORTS ILLUSTRATED. Football writing is every bit the equal of the prose that rhapsodizes about baseball. The proof is this book.

Here's George Plimpton on playing quarterback in front of a large crowd during a Lions scrimmage in 1963, a story he later expanded into a book, *Paper Lion.*

Opposite me across the line the linebackers were all close up, shouting, 'Jumbo! Jumbo! Jumbo!' which is one of the Lion code cries to rush the quarterback. When the snap came I fumbled the ball, gaping at it, mouth ajar, as it rocked back and forth gaily at my feet, and I flung myself on it . . . as I tried to draw myself in like a frightened pill bug, and I heard the sharp strange whack of gear, the grunts—and then a sudden weight whooshed the air out of me. It was Dave Lloyd, a 250-pound linebacker, who got through the line and got to me. A whistle blew and I clambered up, seeing him grin inside his helmet, to discover that the quick sense of surprise that I had survived was replaced by a pulsation of fury that I had not done better. I swore lustily at my clumsiness, hopping mad, near to throwing the ball into the ground, and eager to form a huddle to call another play and try again. . . .

I've always felt—having read the two books a year apart in the early seventies—that *Ball Four* and *Paper Lion* were equally captivating. It's just that Jim Bouton's book was sexier. Sexier, but not better.

This is how Dan Jenkins started his story on the USC-UCLA battle for national supremacy in 1967.

Here is the way it was in that college football game for the championship of the earth, Saturn, Pluto and Los Angeles: UCLA's Gary Beban had a rib cage that looked like an abstract painting in purples and pinks, and USC's O.J. Simpson had a foot that looked like it belonged in a museum of natural history, but they kept getting up from these knockout blows, gasping, coming back, and doing all these outrageously heroic things. So do you know what? In the end, the difference in the biggest game of the 1967 season and one of the best since the ears of helmets stopped flapping, was that this guy with a name like a Russian poet, Zenon Andrusyshyn, couldn't place-kick the ball over this other guy with a name like the president of the Van Nuys Jaycees—Bill Hayhoe . . . .

Knowing that I inhabit the same masthead Jenkins once did gives me chills.

And here is a taste of Myron Cope—a Pittsburgh-based writer—on life after football for Sammy Baugh at his ranch in Texas, 1969.

On a vast plain in west Texas, an hour north of Sweetwater, Baugh lives at the foot of Double Mountain, which in the dusk of late winter wears a grayish coat, rising out of the flatlands like two great mounds orphaned from an alien topography. The ranch house, comfortably but inexpensively furnished, belies Baugh's substantial holdings, for he now runs his cattle on 25,000 acres. He came to the door wearing blue jeans and a Western-style shirt of country-store quality. There was a Gary Cooper flavor to his appearance. Six-feet-two and rawboned, he was a leathery man with hips that were remarkably lean. At 55, he weighed only 170 pounds—at least five pounds under his football weight. But incongruously—and perhaps partly this was because he wore bedroom slippers— he walked with the sort of swishing gait associated with chorus boys . . .

You know why that's such a great paragraph? Because in those few sentences, you get a vivid picture of one of the 20 or 30 best football players of all time, brought fully to life by the evocation of his home and by that compelling and incongruous detail: his unmasculine walk. Cope went on to national fame as the Steelers' radio color guy, but boy, could he write.

Finally, here's another titan from the SI staff—Paul Zimmerman, Dr. Z, in a 1990 profile of Joe Montana:

Here's the thing about scouting college football players for the NFL draft: It's based on fear. Scouts cover their tracks. They hedge their bets. Their evaluations all read, 'Yes, but. . . . ' Yes, he can move the team down the field, but he doesn't have an NFL arm. If the player makes it, the scout will say, 'Well, I told you he had potential,' or if he's a bust, the scout will shake his head and say, 'See, the arm didn't hold up, just like I said.'

There are more negatives than positives in most scouting reports. It's a wonder the teams can find enough people to play . . . . It's easy to be wrong, and that's what terrorizes the scouts—the fear of being wrong all by themselves, the big error, the No. 1 pick that was a total bust. And on draft day 1979, a lot of scouts were wrong about Joe Montana. Eighty-one choices were made before the San Francisco 49ers took him near the end of the third round . . . .

What I've always loved about Zimmy is that you know exactly where he stands on any issue. When I read this part of his fine Montana piece, I recalled the legion of scouts I watched closely the time I covered a college pro day at the University of Michigan—the hardworkers and diggers (about 85%), the bull-slingers and doughnut-eaters (the other 15%)—and it made me think, as I so often do while reading his stories: Zim's got 'em pegged.

I hope you'll agree, when you turn the last page of this amazing collection, that I've got football writers pegged, too: These guys are good. Really good.

DISTANT REPLAY

| | | | | |

The Game That Was

BY MYRON COPE

Sharing their vivid memories of pro football's early days, the pioneers of the game evoke an era of American sport—and a way of life—that is gone forever.

I

NDIAN JOE GUYON
(1919–1927: Canton Bulldogs, Cleveland Indians, Oorang Indians, Rock Island Independents, Kansas City Cowboys, New York Giants)
The late Ralph McGill, the distinguished Atlanta newspaper publisher and author, once wrote, "There is no argument about the identity of the greatest football player who ever performed in Dixie. There is a grand argument about second place, but for first place there is Joe Guyon, the Chippewa brave."

JIM THORPE was the one that hired me for my first pro job in football. I had put in two years at Carlisle, which was really nothing but a grammar school, and made second-team All-America. Then I had to go to prep school in order to get enough credits to go to college, see? So I did, and Georgia Tech grabbed me, and I made All-America again. Then, in 1919, a group of people who sponsored a pro football team in Canton, Ohio, hired Jim to coach it and play in the backfield. So he called me over there. I guess I was 26 or 27 by then.

I played halfback on offense, and on defense I played sideback, which I suppose is what they later started calling defensive halfback. I had more damn tricks and, brother, I could hit you. Elbows, knees or whatchamacallit—boy, I could use 'em. Yes, and it's true that I used to laugh like the dickens when I saw other players get injured. Self-protection is the first thing they should have learned. You take care of yourself, you know. I think it's a sin if you don't. It's a rough game, so you've got to *equip* yourself and know what to do.

The games that were real scraps were the ones in Chicago. George Halas was a brawler. There'd be a fight every time we met those sons of biscuits. Halas knew that I was the key man. He knew that getting me out of there would make a difference. I was playing defense one time, and I saw him coming after me from a long ways off. I was always alert. But I pretended I didn't see him. When he got close I wheeled around the nailed him, goddam. Broke three of his ribs. And as they carried him off I said to him, "What the hell, Halas? Don't you know you can't sneak up on an Indian?"

ED HEALEY

(1920–1927: Rock Island Independents, Chicago Bears)
When Chicago Bears owner George Halas, in 1922, purchased Ed Healey's contract from the Rock Island Independents for $100, Healey became—so far as is known—the first pro football player to be sold.

IN 1922 the Rock Island Independents sold me to the Chicago Bears following a game that I remember as clearly as if it were just played today. We had a great team! We had lost just once. And on the Sunday prior to Thanksgiving we played the Bears at Wrigley Field.

Now understand, in Chicago the officialdom was such that on occasion it made it a little difficult for the outsider to win. On this day the game was really a tight one. In fact it was going along 0–0. George Halas, who along with Dutch Sternaman owned the Bears and played for them, was at right end, the opponent for myself, who was the left tackle. Halas had a habit of grabbing ahold of my jersey, see? My sleeve. That would throw me a little off my balance. It would twist me just enough so that my head wasn't going where I was going.

I didn't enjoy being the victim with reference to this holding, so I forewarned him of what I intended to do about it. Likewise it was necessary for me to forewarn the head linesman, whose name was Roy. I said, "Now, Roy, I understand to start with that you're on the payroll of the Bears. I know that your eyesight must be failing you, because this man Halas is holding me on occasion and it is completely destroying all the things that I'm designed to do." I said, "Roy, in the event that Halas holds me again I am going to commit mayhem."

Now bear in mind, please, that we had a squad of about 15 or 16 men. Neither Duke Slater, our right tackle, nor I had a substitute on the bench. So I said, "Roy, you can't put me out of the game, because we don't have another tackle. And I can't really afford to be put out of this ball game because of your failure to call Halas's holding. I have notified him, and now I am about to commit mayhem."

Well, the condition of the field was muddy and slippery—a very unsafe field. Halas pulled his little trick once more, and I come across with a right, because his head was going to my right. Fortunately for him he slipped, and my fist went whizzing straight into the terra firma, which was soft and mucky. My fist was buried. When I pulled it out it was with an effort like a suction pump.

This was on a Sunday, and on the following Tuesday, I believe it was, I was told to report to the Bears. George Halas had bought me for $100.

Two days later I played 60 minutes on Thanksgiving Day against the Chicago Cardinals and learned a lot about Chicago and the atmosphere that existed there. In that game Halas raced downfield on a punt to tackle Paddy Driscoll, the Cardinals star, but Halas wasn't holding on to him very well. Driscoll was one of my dear friends—I had a lot of friends on the Cardinals team—but I was going in to give him an affectionate enclosure, don't you know. I was going to make him secure. And then, holy cow! Out from the Cardinals bench poured a group of men with rods on! They were going out there to protect their idol, Paddy Driscoll.

As you may recall, the vogue at that time was that all the gangsters in the world were functioning in Chicago. Immediately I stopped in my tracks. I stood there in amazement. All I could think of was that a couple of days before I'd signed up for 100 bucks, and now I was liable to be killed. I said, "Jesus, Mary and Joseph! For a hundred bucks?" Luckily, George Halas hung on and completed the tackle of Paddy Driscoll by himself.

I performed for the Bears from 1922 through 1927, and did you know that one year we played eight games in 12 days? As I recall, we won five out of the eight, but it was a schedule fit for neither man nor beast. It came about as a result of the club signing none other than the Redhead—Red Grange.

Three years later, on a Saturday prior to Thanksgiving, 1925, Red performed in his last game for Illinois. He played against Ohio State at Columbus, then took the sleeper to Chicago and the next day he joined the Bears. And then, with Grange as the main attraction, we set out on a trip and exploded the Eastern Coast, playing by day and hopping to the next city by overnight sleeper. Of course, we did not always play up to our capability, because the human body can stand just so much. But the Redhead broke away in Philadelphia on a Saturday. He broke away in New York on Sunday.

With Red Grange, a gentleman and a scholar, we exploded not only the Eastern Coast but likewise the Western Coast and the South with the introduction of professional football. . . .

RED GRANGE
(1925–1934: Chicago Bears, New York Yankees)
Alone among all the players of the pro football decades that preceded television, Grange earned from football the six-figure income that stars of the 1960s were to realize. Behind his early financial success was that unique operator, C.C. (Cash & Carry) Pyle, probably the first players' agent known to football. It was the Roaring Twenties, the Golden Age of Sport, and with Pyle calling the shots Grange became the plutocrat of football.

CHARLIE PYLE was about 44 years old when I met him. He was the most dapper man I have ever seen. He went to the barbershop every day of his life. He had a little mustache that he'd have trimmed, and he would have a manicure and he'd have his hair trimmed up a little, and every day he would get a rubdown. He wore a derby and spats and carried a cane, and believe me, he was a handsome guy. The greatest ladies' man that ever lived.

Money was of no consequence to Charlie.

At this particular time he owned three movie theaters—two in Champaign, Ill., and one in Kokomo, Ind. One night during my senior year at Illinois I went down to the Virginia Theater in Champaign and one of the ushers told me, "Mr. Pyle wants to see you in his office." Well, the first words Charlie Pyle said to me were, "Red, how would you like to make $100,000?" I couldn't figure what he was talking about. But he said, "I have a plan. I will go out and set up about 10 or 12 football games throughout the United States."

Of course I was flabbergasted. But Charlie made good his word. He lined it up for me to play with the Bears and then went out on the road and set up the whole program.

I'll never forget the game we played in Coral Gables outside of Miami, at a time when Florida was swinging. In 1925 everybody there was selling real estate and building things. Three days before the game we looked around, and there was no place to play a football game, so we said, "Where are we going to play?" The people told us, "Out here in this field." Well, there wasn't anything there except a field. But two days before the game they put 200 carpenters to work and built a wooden stadium that seated 25,000. They sold tickets ranging up to $20 apiece, and the next day they tore down the stadium. You'd never know a ball game had taken place there.

One thing about Charlie was that he always thought pro football had a future. I didn't. When I played, outside of the franchise towns nobody knew anything about pro ball. A U.S. Senator took me to the White House once and introduced me to Calvin Coolidge and said, "Mr. President, I want you to meet Red Grange. He's with the Chicago Bears." I remember the President's reply very well. He said, "Well, Mr. Grange, I'm glad to meet you. I have always liked animal acts."

CLARKE HINKLE
(1932–1941: Green Bay Packers)
Oldtimers say he may well have been the toughest man who ever played professional football—tougher, if not stronger, than Bronko Nagurski. "Clarke Hinkle was near the end of the line when I first played against him," says Bulldog Turner, "but he was still the hardest runner I ever tried to tackle. . . . When you hit him it would pop every joint all the way down to your toes." Fullback, linebacker, sometimes passer, placekicker and punter, Hinkle performed with a wondrous sense of dedication and, though he weighed only 207 pounds, he left big men shattered.

A LOT of people today think Green Bay was never a great football town until Vince Lombardi built all those winners in the 1960s. This kind of annoys me. They talk like we were a bunch of guys that got together on weekends. Listen, Curly Lambeau was a great administrator. He won six championships, and in his early days he was just as tough and mean as anybody else. You think Lombardi's tough? Lambeau was tougher.

We were kings in Green Bay. We traveled in the best of society. Whenever they had the charity balls that people attended in evening gowns and all that, we were invited. The best society would invite you to their homes for dinner. And women! When the Packers came back to Green Bay to begin training for another season the gals would say, "The Depression's over!"

Of course you knew everybody in town, so when you lost a ball game you didn't want to face anybody. You'd keep pretty much to the alleys.

Lambeau used to allow us to smoke, but he kind of frowned on us smoking in public, because he thought it created a bad image. We were very strict in our training habits. Lambeau gave us a written diet to follow. No fried foods of any kind. Chocolate drinks were out, because in those days we felt they built fat around the lungs. Coca-Cola was out—we were told that it took 48 hours to digest a bottle of Coke and that the sugar wasn't good for your wind. I'll tell you one thing, you had to be strong in those days. It was 60-minute football, no platoons.

I think I began to get my reputation as a tough player as a result of a famous collision that Nagurski and I had. I was back to punt on third down. In those days it was common to punt on third down, but sometimes I would fake a punt and run with the ball or throw to Don Hutson. It was an option play, really. Well, this time I ran with the ball to my right and I got through a hole. I started upfield and out of the corner of my eye I could see Nagurski coming over to really nail me to the cross. He was edging me to the sideline. Bronk outweighed me by about 20 or so pounds, and what he would do instead of tackling you was run right through you.

So just before I got to the sideline I cut abruptly, right back into him. I thought, I might as well get it now as any other time. I caught him wide-open and met him head-on. The collision knocked me backward, and I sat there for a few seconds to see if I was all right. Then I looked over at Bronk. His nose was over on the side of his face. It was bleeding and broken in two places, I think. His hip was cracked, they say. Whether it was or not, I don't know. But he was out cold. They took him off the field, and that's the first time he'd ever been jolted. After that, people began to want to see Hinkle.

OLE HAUGSRUD
(1926–1927: Owner, Duluth Eskimos)

Originally the Duluth club was a fine semipro outfit called the Kelley-Duluths, having been named for the Kelley-Duluth Hardware Store. The Kelley-Duluths' opposition came largely from teams in nearby towns in the iron-ore range. But in 1923, in order to obtain a professional schedule, Dan Williams and three others—the trainer and two players—put up $250 apiece and bought a National Football League franchise for $1,000. Even then, the renamed Duluth Eskimos were able to arrange no more than seven, and sometimes as few as five, league games a season. Bills piled up. Finally the four owners offered to make a gift of the franchise to Ole Haugsrud, the club's secretary-treasurer. To make the transaction legal, Haugsrud handed them a dollar, which the four men immediately squandered drinking nickel beer. The dollar they paid for those 20 beers would be a dollar Dan Williams and his colleagues would never forget.

The year was 1926, and the struggling NFL was fighting for its life. C.C. Pyle had Red Grange under contract and with Grange as his box-office attraction was formulating his new nine-team league, to be known as the American Football League. Pyle spread the word that he also had signed the celebrated All-America back, Ernie Nevers, a handsome blond who, though just emerging from Stanford, had captured the nation's fancy. The NFL knew Nevers to be the only big name with whom the league could salvage its slim prestige, but NFL club owners took Pyle at his word, and they made no effort to sign Nevers.

Alone, Ole Haugsrud, a mild-looking little Swede, was skeptical. He had been a high-school classmate of Ernie Nevers in Superior, Wis. When he paid a dollar for the Duluth franchise he had it in the back of his mind to travel to St. Louis, where Nevers was pitching for the St. Louis Browns, to see for himself if Pyle actually had Nevers under contract.

ERNIE WAS very glad to see me, and I was glad to see him. I met with him and his wife at their apartment, and Ernie showed me a letter he had from C.C. Pyle. Ernie told me, "Ole, if you can meet the terms Pyle is offering in this letter, it's O.K. with me. I'll play for Duluth." And, really, that's all there was to it. I would have to pay Ernie $15,000 plus a percentage of the larger gates. I didn't pay him five cents to sign. Oh, maybe I gave him a dollar to make it legal, but really a handshake was all Ernie wanted. A handshake with an old friend was good enough for Ernie.

The league meeting was at the Morrison Hotel, and it was getting on close to August, I believe. See, they didn't hold meetings way ahead of the season, because a lot of teams didn't know if they could operate for another year, and they had to get some funds behind them before they could go to a meeting.

In Chicago the first fellows I got hold of were Tim Mara of the New York Giants and George Halas of the Bears. I had called Mara prior to that, and he was the only one who knew about the contract I had with Ernie Nevers.

This was kind of a historic point for the National League, because here everybody was, with the threat that Pyle had hanging over them, and the league really didn't know if it was going to operate again. So Mara said to me, "Wait till I highball you, and then you go up to the league president with your option on Nevers." Well, I waited and watched Mara, and when he signaled I took the option up to Joe Carr, who was being paid $500 to be league president. He read that little document and then looked up and said: "Gentlemen, I got a surprise for you!" He read the option paper aloud, and some of them out front got up and yelled like a bunch of kids. Carr said to me, "You've saved the league!"

There was almost a celebration right there. But Tim Mara said, "Gentlemen, we got to make a league out of this, so we'll start all over by first rehiring the president and paying him a salary that means something."

Then Mara said, "Now let's start over and get a new schedule." Well, we started putting down that 1926 schedule, and now everybody wanted to play me. I had 19 league games as fast as I could write them down. Before I got back to Duluth I had 10 exhibition games, too, which made a total of 29. And all because I had Nevers.

Mr. Mara got up and said, "What we've got to do is to fill the ballparks in the big cities. So we've got to make road teams out of the Duluth Eskimos and the Kansas City Cowboys." He knew we would draw the big-city crowds with Ernie, and the Kansas City Cowboys were good at drawing crowds because they had a gimmick. When they arrived in a town they'd borrow a lot of horses and ride them down the main street. They rode horseback down Broadway and drew 39,000 people in New York.

So we had only two home games—one in Duluth and one over in Superior, where the ballpark had railroad tracks on both sides. The railroad men would leave boxcars lined up there. We drew 3,000 or 4,000 at the box office in Superior, but there were just as many standing on the box-cars watching free.

I believe it was September 6th that we hit the road, and we didn't get back until February 5th. We traveled by train and occasionally by bus, and one time we took a boat from New York to Providence. During one stretch we played five games in eight days, with a squad of 17 men.

All along, Ernie Nevers was everything we had hoped for. Against the Pottsville Maroons he completed 17 consecutive passes. In all the games we played in 1926 Ernie sat out a total of just 27 minutes. He'd get insulted if you told him to rest. He knew the people were paying to see him, and he made sure they did.

One problem we ran into all the time was getting publicity. The news media as a whole were afraid to publicize professional football, because college ball was big and the colleges frowned on us. In fact, they had a rule that if you played professional ball you could never get a college coaching job. I remember a time a little later, around 1930, I took a trip East with the Chicago Cardinals and we were on the same train as the University of Chicago football team. They were going East to play Princeton. The two teams were in adjoining coaches, and Amos Alonzo Stagg, the Chicago coach, locked the doors between the coaches. He thought the pros would contaminate his players. He had a rule that if after a boy was graduated from Chicago he played pro ball his letter would be recalled. I remember going out on the platform during a stop in Ohio. Stagg was out on the platform, too, and I said, "How do you do, Mr. Stagg?" I must have said it 10 times, but he never answered.

After that '27 season, I put the club in mothballs, and then I sold the franchise for $2,000.

But I didn't do so bad by selling. You see, we negotiated the deal at a league meeting in Cleveland, and the fellows from the other clubs were anxious to see it settled and get away, because they didn't always have money enough to stay three, four days in a high-priced hotel. I wanted $3,000 but the fellow wanted to give me $2,000. The others said to me, "Come on, Swede. We got to get going home."

So I said, "All right, but with one stipulation. The next time a franchise is granted in the state of Minnesota I will have the first opportunity to bid for it."

In 1961, when the Minnesota Vikings were created, I got 10% of the stock. The franchise cost $600,000, and I paid $60,000. Since then we've had offers of between $12 million and $15 million for the franchise. So I guess you would have to say that as result of originally buying a franchise for a dollar, and later investing $60,000, I now own stock that is worth about a million and a half.

BULLDOG TURNER
(1940–1952: Chicago Bears)

In 1941, only a year after he had turned pro with the Chicago Bears, he became the first man in nine years to unseat the great Mel Hein of the New York Giants as the NFL's All-League center. Men who played against Turner say that among his virtuosities must be included exquisite stealth in the art of holding.

I GUESS you'd say my pro career really started one day in 1939 when I was a senior at Hardin Simmons. We rode out to play Loyola of Los Angeles in Gilmore Stadium, Los Angeles, and it held about 20,000 people. Well, we had a sellout crowd. I mean, I never saw so many people in my life. Anyway, I had a super game against those Loyola guys, and boy, we smoked 'em. Now at that time George Richards, who owned the Detroit Lions, had a house in Los Angeles, and a guy phoned him at halftime and said, "George, you better come out here to the game. There's a guy you ought to be watching." So when the game was over, George Richards was right there, and he said, "Would you be interested in playing pro football?"

I said, "You bet." And so George Richards said, "Well, I'd like to have you on my team, the Detroit Lions." I'd never heard of the Detroit Lions or anybody else, except I had seen a film on the Green Bay Packers. "We're going to see that you get to play with the Lions," George Richards told me.

George Richards told his head coach, Gus Henderson, to draft me No. 1. And he told me that if any of the other teams wrote to me about playing football, I should tell them I'm not interested. So when the draft came up, Detroit had about the third pick, but instead of picking me, Gus Henderson picked some quarterback that nobody ever heard of. Some guy named Doyle Nave from Southern California that never even showed up. Harry Wismer, who was the broadcaster for Detroit games at that time, told me later that he ran to the phone right quick and called George Richards and told him, "Gus Henderson didn't pick Bulldog Turner, and the Chicago Bears picked him." So George said, "I can't get anyone to run things the way I want them to," and he fired Gus Henderson.

Richards didn't give up on me. He said, "You're still going to be with the Lions. You just tell the Bears you're not going to play pro football. I'll make you a coach at a high school out here in California for the first year, and after George Halas gives up on you, you come with the Lions."

So I went along with that, but then Halas invited me to fly up to Chicago on an expense-paid trip. Being the country boy that I was, I had never been on an airplane before, so I couldn't say no. It took all day to fly to Chicago then. George and his wife met me at the airport, which George Halas don't do normally. But I didn't sign a contract. I was grateful for the trip, but I kind of strung Halas along, you might say. However, Richards found out I went up there, and he was mad.

He came down to Abilene, Mr. Richards himself did, and registered incognito. Now I had a friend on the newspaper, Hershell Schooley, and I told Hershell, "George Richards that owns the Detroit Lions is in town and he wants to talk to me tonight." Well, you can't tell a newspaperman secrets. Hershell said, "I'm going with you," and carried a pad and pencil. We went up there to the room, and Mr. Richards came out of the shower with a towel wrapped around him and he said, "Who is this?" I said, "A reporter!" And man, he hit the ceiling. He said, "I've come all the way from California incognito, and you bring a newspaperman here?" Hershell said, "Why, you old s.o.b.," and I had to step in and cool the smoke down. Anyway, we finally worked it out that Mr. Richards was going to send me $100 a month until something happened on the high school coaching job. But real soon after that I asked them to quit sending me the $100. Mr. Richards promised me the world, and I'm sure he would have kept his promise, but I signed with the Bears. I didn't want to lay out a year.

Then the league found out that George Richards had been trying to get me, and they fined him $5,000 for tampering with me after I was drafted by the Bears. They said Mr. Richards had spent $500 getting my teeth fixed. Well, that wasn't the truth. He never spent anything on my teeth. He sold his ball club and got out of football, and it was an injustice, because he had never spent a nickel on my teeth.

Here was George Halas's method of operation in practice. First he'd say,

"Give me a center!" Then he'd say, "Bausch!" He'd say, "Give me two guards!" Then he'd say, "Fortmann and Musso!" Well, the first time I heard Halas say, "Give me a center!" I didn't wait for nothing more and ran out there and got over the ball. I noticed he looked kind of funny at me, but I didn't think anything about it. I found out later that Pete Bausch was the center—a big, broad, mean ol' ballplayer, a real nice German from Kansas. But all I knew was George had drafted me No. 1 and I had signed a contract to play center, and I thought when it come time to line up I should *be* at center. From the beginning I was overendowed with self-confidence. I feared no man. So I just went out there and got over that ball, and I was there ever since. They didn't need Pete no more.

I was such a good blocker that the men they put in front of me—and some of them were stars that were supposed to be making a lot of tackles—they would have their coaches saying, "Why ain't you making any tackles?" They'd say, "That bum Turner is holding!" Well, that wasn't true. I held a few, but I was blocking them too. I used to think I could handle anybody that they'd put in front of me.

One guy I remember was big Ed Neal. There in the late 1940s he played at Green Bay, and by this time they had put in the 5–4 defense. They put the biggest, toughest guy they had right in front of the center, and I was expected to block him either way. Well, Ed Neal weighed 303 pounds stripped. His arms was as big as my leg and just as hard as that table. He could tell when I was going to center the ball, and he'd get right over it and hit me in the face. You didn't have a face guard then, and so Ed Neal broke my nose seven times. Yes, that's right. No—he broke my nose *five* times. I got it broke seven times, but five times *he* broke it.

Anyway, I got where I'd center that ball and duck my head, so then he started hitting me on top of the headgear. He would beat hell out of my head. We had those headgears that were made out of composition of some kind—some sort of fiber—and I used to take three of them to Green Bay. These headgears would just crack when he'd hit 'em—they'd just ripple across there like lightening had struck them. So one day, every time Neal went by me I'd grab him by the leg, and I began to get him worried. He said, "You s.o.b., quit holding me!" I said, "If you'll quit hitting me on the head, I'll quit holding you." And Neal said, "That's a deal, 'cause I ain't making no tackles." So the second half of that game we got along good, and later I got Halas to trade for him.

I don't know if you want to put this in your book, and I don't care if you do, but I originated the draw play, along with a lot of other plays. I discovered the draw play because Buckets Goldenberg, who played for Green Bay, could read our quarterback, Sid Luckman, real well. Somehow he could tell when Sid was going to pass. As soon as that ball was snapped, Buckets Goldenberg would pull back and start covering the pass. So I said, "Let's fake a pass and give the ball to the fullback and let him come right up here where I am, 'cause there's nobody here but me." The next year we put that play in, and it averaged 33 yards a try. The fullback would run plumb to the safety man before they knew he had the ball.

I also originated a play that got me even with Ed Neal for beating my head off. I said to Halas one day, "You can run somebody right through there, 'cause Ed Neal is busy whupping my head." I suggested that we put in a sucker play—we called it the 32 sucker—where we double-teamed both of their tackles and I would just relax and let Neal knock me on my back and fall all over me. It'd make a hole from here to that fireplace. Man, you could really run through it, and we did all day. Later Ralph Jones, who had once been a Bears coach and was coaching a little college team, told me he brought his whole team down to watch the Bears play the Packers that day, and he told them, "Boys, I want you to see the greatest football player that ever lived, Bulldog Turner. I want you to watch this man on every play and see how he handles those guys." But ol' Ralph didn't know about that sucker play, and later he said to me, "Damn if you wasn't flat on your back all day!"

ART ROONEY
(1933– : Owner, Pittsburgh Steelers)
The down-to-earth, ward-loving, last-hurrah millionaire president of the Pittsburgh Steelers, Arthur J. Rooney is one of the supreme contradictions in sport. Perhaps the most successful horseplayer America has ever known—he is said to have won a quarter of a million dollars in a single day—he is professional football's champion loser. In 35 years his team has never earned so much as a divisional title.

Like George Halas, Rooney once played as a pro. His team was called Hope-Harvey. He founded it, owned it, coached it and even halfbacked it against the likes of Jim Thorpe and the Canton Bulldogs. Sometimes he was a winner in his Hope-Harvey days, but then. . . .

IN 1933 I paid $2,500 for a National Football League franchise, which I named the Pirates because the Pittsburgh baseball team was called the Pirates. It wasn't until 1940, when we held a contest for a new name, that we became the Steelers. Joe Carr's girlfriend—Joe's been our ticket manager all along—won the contest. There were people who said, "That contest don't look like it was on the level."

I bought the franchise because I figured that eventually professional football would be a big sport. The reason I bought at that particular time was that we knew Pennsylvania was going to repeal some of its blue laws, which had prevented Sunday football. The laws were changed, but a couple of days before our opening game the mayor phoned me and said, "I got a complaint here from a preacher that this game should not be allowed. The blue-law repeal hasn't been ratified yet by the city council."

The mayor told me he didn't know what I could do about it, but that I should go see a fellow named Harmar Denny, who was director of public safety and over the police department.

But this Denny was pretty much of a straitlaced guy. All he would say was that he was going away for the weekend. "Good," I told him. "You go away." Then I went to see the superintendent of police, a man named McQuade, and told him my problem.

"Oh, that there's ridiculous," he said. "Give me a couple of tickets and I'll go to the game Sunday. That'll be the last place they'll look for me if they want me to stop the thing." So McQuade hid out at the game, and Pittsburgh got started in the NFL.

The biggest mistake I've made was that, although I understood the football business as well as anybody, I didn't pay the attention to it that some of the other owners did. I still believe that John Blood could have been a tremendous coach if he would have just paid attention. We once played a game in Los Angeles and John missed the train home. John was known to enjoy a good time, of course, so we didn't see him the whole week. On Sunday he stopped off in Chicago to see his old team, the Green Bay Packers, play the Bears. The newspaper guys asked him, "How come you're not with your team?" And John said, "Oh, we're not playing this week." Well, no sooner did he get those words out of his mouth than the guy on the loudspeaker announced a score: Philadelphia 14, Pittsburgh 7. You really couldn't depend on John a whole lot.

We've had a lot of great ballplayers, you know. Just think of the quarterbacks. We've had Sid Luckman, Earl Morrall, Len Dawson, Jackie Kemp, Bill Nelsen. I'd say we were experts on quarterbacks at Pittsburgh. We had them all, and we got rid of every one of them. We had Johnny Unitas in for a tryout, but our coach then, Walter Kiesling, let him go. Kies said, "He can't remember the plays. He's dumb." You had to know Kies. He was a great coach, but he thought a lot of ballplayers were dumb. We were arguing about a guy one day, and I said, "I don't care how dumb he is. He can run and he can pass and he can block. If he can do those three things, he don't have to be a Rhodes scholar." But all Kies said to that was, "He's dumb."

SAMMY BAUGH

(1937–1952: Washington Redskins)

Although professional football has been intensively souped up since his time, Slingin' Sammy Baugh's name still appears in the record book in more than a dozen places. Starting in 1937, he lasted 16 years and is held by many to have been the finest passer of his or any other time. In one season ('45) he completed 70.3% of his passes. In addition, his leg was as potent as his arm; he holds almost every punting record in the book. But above all, he gave to pro football a radical concept that he had learned from his college coach at Texas Christian, Dutch Meyer—namely, that the forward pass could be more than just a surprise weapon or a desperation tactic. Sammy Baugh made the pass a routine scrimmage play.

On a vast plain in west Texas, an hour north of Sweetwater, Baugh lives at the foot of Double Mountain, which in the dusk of late winter wears a grayish coat, rising out of the flatlands like two great mounds orphaned from an alien topography. The ranch house, comfortably but inexpensively furnished, belies Baugh's substantial holdings, for he now runs his cattle on 25,000 acres. He came to the door wearing blue jeans and a Western-style shirt of country-store quality. There was a Gary Cooper flavor to his appearance. Six-feet-two and rawboned, he was a leathery man with hips that were remarkably lean. At 55, he weighed only 170 pounds—at least five pounds under his football weight. But incongruously—and perhaps partly this was because he wore bedroom slippers—he walked with the sort of swishing gait associated with chorus boys. . . .

THE THING that hurt when I first came into pro football in 1937 was that the rules didn't give any protection to passers. Those linemen could hit the passer until the whistle blew. If you completed a pass and somebody's running 50 yards with the ball, well, that bunch could still hit you. In other words, a passer had to learn to throw and move. You would never see him just throw and stand there looking. You had to throw and start protecting yourself, because those linemen were going to lay you flatter than the ground every time.

If you were a good ballplayer—a passer or whatever—they tried to hurt you and get you out of there. We had only 22 or 23 men on a squad, and your ballplayers were playing both ways—offense and defense—so if you lost two good ones, you were dead. Well, every now and then they'd run what they called a "bootsie" play, and everybody'd hit one man and just try to tear him to pieces. The object was to get him out of there. I don't mean they ran this kind of play very often, but if they came up against a guy that was giving them a lot of trouble, along would come the bootsie.

Pro football was changing by then. Back in the '30s it was more of a defensive game. In other words, when you picked your starters, they usually had to be good on defense first. Take the New York Giants. They had such a good defensive ball club that they wouldn't mind punting to you on third down from practically anywhere. They'd kick the ball to you 'cause they didn't think you were ever going to move it.

The fact is, most men played pro football in those days because they liked football. A lot of players today say they only play for the money, but even now, it's not all money. I don't care if salaries went back down, they'd still play. Of course nobody was making a lot of money out of football in the '30s. That's why I'll always think a lot of George Marshall and George Halas and Art Rooney and those kind of people—they stayed in there when it was rough. They made a great game out of it.

| | | | | | |

The Day World War II Kicked Off

BY S.L. PRICE

*On Dec. 7, 1941, the Redskins and Eagles played a football game, not knowing
that the U.S. had joined the rest of the world at war.*

VERYONE IN WASHINGTON, D.C.'S GRIFFITH STADIUM THAT
day knew his role. The wives walked in together, chattering
like a flock of birds. The 27,102 fans shoved through the
turnstiles, ready to shout and clap, to watch and feel. The
press box filled with reporters, prepared to scribble their notes.

On the field the players tried to keep warm. Some were stars, some weren't.
It was the final pro football game of the season for the Washington Redskins
and the Philadelphia Eagles. It was quite cold. People stamped their feet. They
could see their breath.

No one was thinking yet about Pearl Harbor. Kickoff was at 2 p.m.—9 a.m.
in Hawaii. Bombs had already fallen on the U.S. fleet, men had died, war had
come. In the stands, no one knew: The game was still everything.

Philadelphia took a 7–0 lead on its first drive. Then announcements began
to pour out of the P.A. system. *Admiral Bland is asked to report to his office. . . .
Captain H.X. Fenn is asked to report. . . . The resident commissioner of the*

Philippines is urged to report. . . . "We didn't know what the hell was going on," says Sammy Baugh, the Redskins' quarterback that day. "I had never heard that many announcements, one right after another. We felt something was up, but we just kept playing."

Only the boys in the press box had any idea. Just before kickoff an Associated Press reporter named Pat O'Brien got a message ordering him to keep his story short. When O'Brien complained, another message flashed: *The Japanese have kicked off. War now!* But Redskins president George Marshall wouldn't allow an announcement of Japan's attack during the game, explaining that it would distract the fans. That made Griffith Stadium one of the last outposts of an era that had already slipped away.

The crowd oohed and cheered. When the game—and season—ended with Washington a 20–14 winner, a few hundred fans rushed the goalposts. No one took much notice of Eagles rookie halfback Nick Basca. He hadn't played much all year, making his mark mostly as a kicker and punter, and on this day he'd converted just two extra points. Baugh, with three touchdown passes, was the game's hero.

Then everyone walked out of the stadium: the wives, the future Hall of Famer, the crowd. Outside, newsboys hawked the news. The world tilted; football lost all importance; roles shifted. Women began fearing for their men. Reporters and fans would be soldiers soon. The world would not be divided into players and spectators again for a very long time. "Everybody could feel it," Baugh says.

Baugh went home to Texas and waited for a call from his draft board that never came; he was granted a deferment to stay on his ranch and raise beef cattle. During the war he flew in on the weekends for games.

Nick Basca, meanwhile, had played his final game. A native of tiny Phoenixville, Pa., and a standout at Villanova, Basca enlisted in the Army three days after Pearl Harbor with his younger brother Stephen, who left Europe with three Purple Hearts. Nick was piloting a tank in Gen. George Patton's celebrated Fourth Armored Division in France, when, on Nov. 11, 1944, the tank hit a mine and was blown apart.

In later years no one talked much about Nick's short pro football career. Then, in 1991, 50 years after events had rendered it meaningless, that game between Philadelphia and Washington became everything again. Stephen Basca Jr. says, "My father was lying 60 miles away in a hospital bed when

Nick was killed. They recorded on his chart that he had gotten up screaming about the time Nick's tank blew up. [In 1991] my father and I were sitting watching TV, and they showed a clip of that old game. My dad froze in his chair. It was the first time I'd ever seen him cry."

| | | | | |

0:00 to Go

BY GARY CARTWRIGHT

Time finally ran out on the Southwest Conference, but what a time it was.

L ET'S BURY THE OLD DEAR WITHOUT GETTING MAUDLIN. Date the obituary for the end of the 1995 college football season, football being the Southwest Conference's raison d'être and the only thing anyone will remember about it— except that at least one of its member schools was usually on probation and the majority of its players free on bond. Those of us who paid attention see now that the conference was a goner that night in December 1976 when both Darrell Royal, coach of the University of Texas, and Frank Broyles, his good friend and counterpart at the University of Arkansas, submitted their resignations before facing off for the final time.

For nearly two decades the rivalry between Royal's Longhorns and Broyles's Razorbacks had been the fiercest in the conference, maybe in all of college football. Together the teams had won or tied for 15 Southwest Conference championships in 18 seasons, and 13 times one or both had finished among college football's Top 10. But backstabbing, cheating and mollycoddling increasingly thuggish athletes was becoming acceptable behavior to many conference coaches. So be it. Royal and Broyles, two of the best coaches of modern times, would devote their considerable talents to golf. From that moment the SWC began to expire.

Those of us who grew up with the Southwest Conference shed no tears for what it became but remember fondly what it was. From the time it was founded in 1915 until it began to fall apart in the '70s, the conference shaped our world and gave us stature. Until the second half of this century, Texas was a largely rural, largely homogeneous society. Whites ruled, and blacks lived on the other side of the tracks and drank out of separate water fountains. In those days diversity meant that someone was lefthanded or had red hair. Despite our image of boisterous self-confidence, we Texans weren't sure if outsiders viewed us as rugged individualists or just hayseeds. We didn't think of ourselves as racists, though of course we were. The SWC was the penultimate major conference to integrate, and it was only after a talented receiver named Jerry Levias led SMU to a conference championship in '66 that every school in the conference saw the wisdom of recruiting African-Americans.

For all of our rustic shortcomings, however, nobody played better football. Texas had the finest high school players in the country, and until the 1970s most of them stayed to play in the Southwest Conference. In the '30s SMU, TCU and Texas A&M each won a national title, and from '63 to '70, Royal's Texas teams won three. Those were the two golden eras of SWC football—the '30s and the Royal years—but there were two others nearly as good: the postwar '40s, when SMU and Doak Walker battled Texas and Bobby Layne for state and national supremacy, and Abe Martin's TCU teams of the mid- and late-'50s.

It would be hard to exaggerate the excitement that the first kiss of autumn generated at all levels of Texas society. As early as 1934 the air was literally filled with Southwest Conference football, thanks to the Humble Radio Network, the nation's first broadcast network. You couldn't visit a drugstore or barbershop or even walk along a sidewalk without hearing the roar of the crowd and the boom of the marching bands at Kyle Field or the Cotton Bowl—or the voice of Humble's master of word pictures, Kern Tips, saying, "They give the ball again to little Jimmy Swink, and this time he rides the back of big Norman Hamilton down to the four-, make that the three-yard line, where it's first-and-*goal* for the Froggies!"

You didn't have to be college-educated to have a favorite team. Service stations operated by Humble Oil & Refining Company (now Exxon), which also owned the radio network, gave out pennant-shaped window decals, each with the colors and name of a conference school. Bank presidents with degrees from SMU and pipe fitters who hadn't finished third grade displayed their choice on the rear window of their cars. Millions of Texans from Beaumont to Laredo to Amarillo never saw a game but lived and died from Saturday to Saturday with the Frogs, the Mustangs, the Bears, the Longhorns, the Aggies, the Owls, the Hogs—and later the Red Raiders and the Cougars. In our division of loyalty we discovered unity: Everyone loved the Southwest Conference.

The flavor of the conference came not so much from the coaches and the teams as from the customs and folk wisdom imparted by different groups of fans. It was said that TCU fans wore jeans and white socks and called each other Bubba and Betty Bob. SMU fans drank Chardonnay and lived off their trust funds. Baylor fans did not make love standing up, lest God mistake the act for dancing. Longhorn fans sipped tea and were insufferably high-handed. Aggies were zealots, superpatriots and bumpkins.

On the day he arrived at Texas A&M in 1954, Bear Bryant won the undying adoration of a mob of supporters around the traditional Aggie bonfire by stripping off his sport coat, slamming it to the ground and yelling, "I'm ready to fight them right now!" Bryant remains the most-beloved figure ever to coach at College Station, despite the fact that his recruiting excesses were the first black mark on the conference. The attitude of University of Texas supporters, on the other hand, was best exemplified by the legendary Frank Erwin, autocratic chairman of the university's board of regents in the '60s, who drove an orange Cadillac around campus and personally supervised the bulldozing of ancient oak trees to clear the way for additions to the stadium.

Even the cheerleaders matched their institutions. Texas's best-known cheerleaders from the 1950s and '60s were Kay Bailey Hutchison, Texas's first female senator, and Harley Clark, inventor of the "Hook 'em, Horns" sign and later a judge. SMU's best-known cheerleader was Aaron Spelling, now the titan of trash TV.

I'm not old enough to remember the 1930s, but I grew up on the legends. Sammy Baugh and John Kimbrough were more meaningful to me than Davy Crockett and Jim Bowie. Words like *discipline, obedience* and *sacrifice* weren't abstractions, they were football terms. Coaches Dutch Meyer of TCU and Matty Bell of SMU were good friends who fished together in the spring and tried to beat each other's ears off in the fall. Their '35 game was for the national championship, which SMU won.

The conference's second national champion was Meyer's 1938 TCU team, with the great Davey O'Brien at quarterback, but my favorite stories involved the Southwest Conference's third champions of that decade, the 1939 Aggies. I heard about them from my old granny, who had become addicted to Texas A&M football as a girl when she watched the Fightin' Texas Aggie Band parade down Fort Worth's Main Street before a game at TCU. Though she never saw a game, Granny could recite plays from every Aggie season. "When time was a-runnin' out," she would tell me as I lay curled at her feet, "we give the ball to Jarrin' John Kimbrough, and he went and followed Marshall Robnett's block, bodies going this-a-way and that-a-way, plumb to the end zone." In the '40s and '50s, Granny and I listened to Aggie games on radio. Before each game she would kill a chicken and study the entrails, then place an appropriately colored candle in the window. When the Aggies scored, we would march around the room, waving maroon-and-white pennants and singing the *Aggie War Hymn*.

My first Southwest Conference game was SMU versus Texas in Dallas in 1947, which was the second and final meeting between Walker and Layne, who had been teammates at Dallas's Highland Park High. Their rivalry took SWC football to its highest level. Layne was primarily a passer and leader but also played defense. Walker did it all—ran, passed, caught, kicked, played defense—and was the most graceful and indomitable player I ever saw.

That was not only the first major college game I ever saw, it was also the best. After SMU took the lead on a backward reverse from Walker to wing-back Paul Page, the Longhorns tied it with a plunge by running back Tom Landry—you'll remember that name, though probably not from his days as a Longhorn—but SMU struck again when Walker caught a 54-yard pass in front of Landry, now playing defensive halfback. Layne's passing pulled Texas to within a point, 14–13, but the Longhorns missed the extra-point attempt. The Mustangs' margin of victory was Walker's second extra point. Walker accounted for 125 of SMU's 199 yards on offense. Layne passed for 120 of Texas's 196 yards.

In the 1950s I became directly involved with the Southwest Conference, first as a student at TCU, then as a sportswriter for the *Fort Worth Press*. I was in the stands as a cheering undergraduate in '55 when Jim Swink led TCU to a conference championship. Swink was a fluid runner, dashing through defenders like a mountain stream rushing past boulders. The Frogs won the title again in '58 and tied for it in '59.

The best team of the 1950s may have been Bryant's '56 Aggies, who included John David Crow, Bobby Joe Conrad, Jack Pardee, Charlie Krueger and an unheralded defensive end who would become better known as a coach, Gene Stallings. Unfortunately, as the conference's first major pay-for-play scandal enveloped a number of the players, the Aggies became best known as the finest team money could buy. They went 9-0-1 that season but went nowhere on New Year's Day because they were on probation.

One other thing I remember about the 1956 season is a song that several writers for the *Fort Worth Press* composed in the press box after the Frogs lost a 7–6 heartbreaker to the Aggies in a rainstorm. Sports editor Blackie Sherrod had hired the editor of the TCU student newspaper to cover the Frogs' dressing room, but when the game ended, the kid said he couldn't face those valiant boys. Sherrod reminded the lad that his attitude was less than professional, but the student stood his ground with this immortal reply: "You never went to that school, buddy!" That's why, anytime I watch the Frogs play football, I remember this opening verse:

> *You never went to that school, buddy!*
> *You never walked down Tom Brown Hall.*
> *You never had no dealings with M.E. Sadler.*
> *You never attended a Howdy Week Ball.*
> *(No, you never went to that school, buddy*
> *And you don't know nothing at all!)*

FOR MOST of us living in Dallas, two events in the fall of 1963 affected us profoundly: the assassination of President Kennedy and the weekly struggle of Royal's Longhorns in their drive for a national championship. I was with the *Dallas Morning News*, sharing an apartment with fellow sportswriter Bud Shrake. In the evenings we hung out in smoky bars like Jack Ruby's Carousel Club, sometimes partying all night. My day job was covering the

Cowboys and occasionally the Longhorns. Two days after the assassination, Shrake told me in the parking lot of Cleveland's Memorial Stadium that the man arrested for shooting Kennedy had himself just been shot in the basement of the Dallas police station. Shrake asked me to guess the name of the gunman. I guessed Jack Ruby. I still don't know why that name popped into my head, except it was the wildest thing I could think of.

A few days later I was standing in the mud and cold at Kyle Field, watching the Longhorns try desperately to salvage the season and their No. 1 ranking against fired-up A&M. In the dying minutes defensive back James Willenborg appeared to intercept a Texas pass in the end zone, which would have ended Royal's dream of a national title. But Willenborg was juggling the ball as he fell over the end line, and it was ruled that he did not have possession. The ball went to Texas, which scored and won 15–13. The Longhorns were on their way to the Cotton Bowl against second-ranked Navy and its Heisman Trophy-winning quarterback, Roger Staubach.

In the days before that game Shrake and I spent time in Austin, eating Mexican food with our new friend Darrell and writing about how he was preparing his team to contain the scrambling Staubach. We didn't realize that Royal was also putting a wrinkle in his three-yards-and-a-cloud-of-dust attack. The 1963 Longhorns had a defense that was among the best in the country. It included linebacker Tommy Nobis, the most efficient predator since Vlad the Impaler. But the Eastern press was unimpressed. One sportswriter called the Longhorns "the biggest fraud ever perpetrated on the football public" and wrote that Texas linemen had "skinny legs like centipedes or girls and high rear ends."

Navy never had a chance. The Longhorns not only contained Staubach, but their journeyman quarterback Duke Carlisle also outgained him as Texas won 28–6. A few weeks later the American Football Coaches Association named Royal its Coach of the Year. In the winter of 1964, when he was in Dallas, Royal would hide out at our apartment. "I need to get away from the media," he told us with a wink. I also remember him telling us, "Great players make great coaches, but great coaches make champions."

In 1968 Royal and his offensive coordinator, Emory Bellard, introduced the wishbone offense and transformed college football. With James Street at quarterback, the Longhorns built a 30-game winning streak, the most memorable game of which was the Big Shoot-out—a.k.a. the Game of the

Century—a heart-stopping 15–14 victory over Arkansas in December 1969. Played in an icy fog at Fayetteville, this game had everything: It was the climactic game of college football's 100th year, No. 1 Texas versus No. 2 Arkansas, with war protesters outside the stadium and President Richard Nixon, accompanied by the Reverend Billy Graham, inside to bestow on the winner a national championship plaque. With 6:10 remaining, Texas trailed by six points and faced fourth-and-three from its own 43. Royal told Street to call "right 53 veer pass" to tight end Randy Peschel, a play that hadn't worked all year. Street asked Royal if he was sure, and Royal said he was: He'd noticed that the Razorback secondary was crowding the line to stop the triple option and ignoring the tight end. Street heaved the ball, and Peschel ran under it and was tackled at the Arkansas 13. Two plays later the Longhorns scored, then kicked the winning point after. A few weeks later Texas beat Notre Dame in the Cotton Bowl to finish Royal's second perfect season. Great coaches make champions.

After Broyles and Royal quit, the University of Houston under Bill Yeoman emerged as a power for a time, then sank out of sight under the stigma of recruiting violations. Starting in the mid-1980s, SMU, TCU, Texas A&M, Texas Tech, Texas and Houston were found to have committed violations and were placed on probation. The Mustangs suffered the ultimate punishment when the only "death penalty" ever assessed by the NCAA, in 1986, shut down their program for two years. The conference crimes and misdemeanors covered a wide and imaginative range—paying players, fixing test results and even, in one case, editing clips from porn movies into game film for the edification of student athletes.

How they handled problems with the NCAA said a lot about the schools and the coaches. TCU coach Jim Wacker blew the whistle on himself when he learned in 1985 that some of his players, including Heisman candidate Kenneth Davis, were taking money from a group of oilmen. Most Frog followers believed this was the honorable thing to do; others felt Wacker was a fool. A&M's Jackie Sherrill, on the other hand, stonewalled the NCAA in '88, in effect telling investigators, "I don't understand the question," and escaped unscathed.

SMU produced the most egregious display of mendacity the conference ever witnessed. An NCAA investigation turned up evidence that a group of Mustang alumni had set out to buy a national title or the players to provide one. By the time SMU began serving its sentence in 1987, the former head of SMU's board of governors, Bill Clements, was the governor of Texas. Initially he denied approving payments, but later he admitted his part in the scheme. Asked why he lied, Clements replied, "Well, there wasn't a Bible in the room. . . . "

In the 1990s the only nationally recognized conference team has been the Aggies, who won 29 consecutive SWC games before Texas Tech upset them on Oct. 7. The league's dismal level of competition has assured the Cotton Bowl of consistently mediocre host teams: With A&M on probation in '94, five SWC teams finished as runners-up, at 4–3. Texas Tech went to the Cotton Bowl and was routed 55–14 by Southern Cal.

A lot of factors contributed to the demise of the conference: Arkansas's pulling out to join the Southeastern Conference; the rising cost of tuition, which made it difficult for the private schools (Baylor, Rice, SMU and TCU) to compete with schools subsidized by the state; having eight schools in one state competing for fans and media with eight major pro teams; the saturation of sports on TV. Like a senile old man, the conference seemed only dimly aware of its own history. There was no sadder illustration of this than at the SWC's Hall of Honor ceremony last summer. Among the 12 former players and coaches inducted was Yeoman, on whose watch Houston began to drag the conference to the bottom. Worse, whoever selected the honorees forgot Broyles. Maybe he'll be named posthumously.

Oh, one other thing. The late Bobby Layne was also inducted. As a gesture to the University of Texas, a replica of his trophy was cast for display at the Longhorns' Memorial Stadium. It's a fine replica, except for this: Somebody misspelled the name of Texas's greatest quarterback, engraving it as BOBBY LANE.

| | | | | |

Frozen in Time

BY JOHNETTE HOWARD

*Lambeau Field is the NFL's holy ground, treasured as much
for what it has (community spirit, sacred memories)
as for what it doesn't have (plastic grass, a roof).*

HERE WAS A TIME WHEN THE GREEN BAY PACKERS'
Lambeau Field wasn't the quaint anomaly it is today. Every-
one played football on grass, and there were no Teflon roofs
to shut out the midday sun, no domes to block the late-
autumn wind. When mud-spattered linemen Forrest Gregg and Jerry Kramer
hoisted coach Vince Lombardi on their shoulders in 1961 for his first NFL
title ride, only God's gray sky hung overhead.

Franchise free agency didn't exist back then either. There was no threat
of the Packers' being wooed away by some Sun Belt city offering a percentage of the revenue generated from the sale of personal seat licenses.
Why, the world hadn't even heard of turf toe when Lombardi stalked Lambeau's frozen sidelines in his trademark overcoat, shrieking, "Hey! Whad-
daya doin' out there?" in his best Brooklynese. "With Lombardi it was never
cold here," says former All-Pro Fuzzy Thurston, who played guard for Green
Bay from 1959 to '67. "Before games he'd just say something like, 'Men, it's
a little blustery out there today.' Blustery, see? Then he'd say, 'It's our kind
of day. Now get out there and strut around like it's the middle of July.'"

The Packers were a league power then, and Lambeau Field was the NFL's answer to Boston Garden or Yankee Stadium—hallowed ground where dynasties were born. During Lombardi's nine-year stay the Packers won five league championships, including the first two Super Bowls. Twenty-nine winters have passed since Green Bay last had a championship team, yet within the magical space of Lambeau Field it still seems to be 1967.

Once the ball is kicked off and pads start to clatter, the Titletown past and the promising present almost become one on the floor of the old stadium. The sight of defensive end Reggie White barreling into an opponent's backfield conjures up memories of Hall of Famer Willie Davis. Quarterback Brett Favre's 1992 burst from anonymity—he led the Packers to an electrifying, come-from-behind victory over the Cincinnati Bengals in relief of starter Don Majkowski during coach Mike Holmgren's first season—wasn't all that different from Bart Starr's midseason ascension in 1959, Lombardi's first year.

Visitors from far and wide still stop by Lambeau and ask to be shown the spot in the south end zone where, in the 1967 NFL championship game, better known as the Ice Bowl, Starr made the one-yard touchdown plunge that gave the Pack a 21–17 win over the Dallas Cowboys. Grainy black-and-white photos show Starr burrowing across the goal line with 13 seconds to play, his arms hugging the football as if he were protecting a newborn from the -46° windchill.

For four decades Lambeau Field has been a landmark moored on the southwest edge of Green Bay, its underside sunk into a gently sloping hill, making it look like a ship run aground, never to leave. But, says Packers president and chief executive officer Bob Harlan, "it's not so much what the stadium looks like; it's what happened here that makes this place unique. A story like this will never happen in professional sports again."

FOOTBALL HISTORY isn't learned in Green Bay as much as it's lived and touched and felt. Linebacker Ray Nitschke, who played from 1958 to '72, isn't just one of the 19 members of the Pro Football Hall of Fame whose names form a ring at skybox level around the inside of Lambeau: Nitschke is in the Green Bay phone book, and he still attends home games, often eschewing a skybox for a seat in the stands. Call Nitschke at home and ask for an audience, and he's likely to reply, "Let's talk over the phone. I might scare ya in person."

Starr and Kramer still come back to Lambeau for the Packers' annual fantasy camp, and numerous players return for alumni day and the opportunity to walk along the hash marks one more time as applause rains down, as it always has. Thurston, who has survived throat cancer and two hip replacements, still owns and operates Shenanigan's, a neighborhood bar on the southeast fringe of town. On one wall he has begun a collection of mostly out-of-state license plates given to him by patrons; all are vanity plates bearing some expression of support for the Packers (GO PACK, for example, or GBP FAN) "Forget Dallas," Thurston says. "The Green Bay Packers are America's Team."

Martha's Coffee Club, a feisty group of 40 or so fans, some of whom have been meeting since 1947, convenes in a diner near Lambeau at 9 a.m. every weekday year-round to discuss the Packers' fortunes. In accordance with a set of arcane rules the club levies 25-cent fines for transgressions such as talking about something other than football, and the members roll dice to see who picks up the check—visitors not excepted.

When the Packers return from an important road game, win or lose, townspeople leave their porch lights on as a show of support. When a heavy snowfall hits the area in the days leading up to a game, the front office puts an announcement in the *Green Bay Press-Gazette* asking fans to show up at Lambeau, shovel in hand. For six dollars an hour citizens come by the dozens to clear the stands. (More than 150 people showed up the weekend before Christmas after a storm dumped 10 inches of snow on Green Bay.) "It's like a time warp here," says Packers wideout Robert Brooks, who has been with the Packers since 1992. "There's an aura. It's almost like you're still back when Lombardi was here. It's just that the names on the jerseys have changed."

IN THIS era of extortionist owners, Packers fans needn't worry about getting jilted. "We're a nonprofit, public corporation whose only business is football," Harlan says. The owners of the team are 1,915 stockholders from all walks of life, most of whom live in Wisconsin. (However, there are stockholders from all 50 states and three foreign countries.) When the team, which was founded in 1919, was on the brink of bankruptcy in 1950, about

5,000 shares of stock were offered to the public at $25 apiece. No dividends have ever been paid; all profits have been plowed back into the franchise. According to the Packers' bylaws, anyone wishing to sell shares must first turn them over to the executive committee of the team's board of directors, who then decide to either reissue the shares or buy them back. No individual can own more than 200 shares, and if the shareholders ever vote to sell their investment (the Packers' estimated worth is $166 million), the profits will go to the Sullivan-Wallen American Legion Post on Sal Street in Green Bay.

The Packers, who draw from all around Wisconsin and are sold out on a season-ticket basis, have played before 175 consecutive sellouts at Lambeau, dating back to 1960. A Lambeau-record crowd of 60,787 witnessed last Saturday's 35–14 divisional playoff win over the San Francisco 49ers. There were all of three no-shows. This season a game-day scalping zone was established one block from the stadium, and the action there has been fierce: A $28 end-zone seat goes for between $125 and $200, depending on the opponent. The waiting list for season tickets stands at more than 28,000, and only eight people from last year's list received tickets for this season. In 1985, when the Pack announced plans to construct 72 skyboxes, the suites were all leased within 24 hours. Lambeau now has 198 skyboxes, and the waiting list for them exceeds 230.

The easiest way to get season tickets is through the death of an immediate family member who leaves the prized objects behind in his or her will. Green Bay ticket manager Mark Wagner says he has heard every ruse in his 19 years on the job—sob stories, bald-faced lies, even offers of bribes—from Packers fans determined to get season seats. Inevitably, some impatient fans suspect that others have come by their tickets by less-than-ethical means, even though the transfer of the title to tickets requires notarization. Some fans have even blown the whistle on others who have renewed the tickets of a relative who died without bequeathing the tickets to them. And then? "Well," Wagner says, "then we have to call them and, well, you know." Ask them why they're not dead? "Yeah," he says with a laugh.

People go out of their way to stop at Lambeau, even when it's empty. In 1996 more than 29,000 visitors took the 90-minute tour of the place. President Clinton dropped in after a Labor Day campaign speech in nearby De

Pere. Harlan recalls leaving work one day last August when a van bearing Kansas plates pulled into a stadium parking lot. The driver jumped out, fell to his knees and began bowing with his arms outstretched while his passengers laughed and snapped pictures. "Pilgrimages, that's what they are," says Char Sievert, a tour guide who has had season tickets since 1956, the year she graduated from high school. "Last year a man on one of my tours said, 'I saw the Colosseum in Rome last year. Now this!' "

Many Packers say there's nowhere they'd rather play than in Green Bay. When more than 4,000 fans showed up for a training-camp workout last summer, awestruck rookie center Mike Flanagan asked a teammate, "Doesn't anybody in Green Bay have a job?" Wideout Don Beebe spent six years playing before the rabid fans of the Buffalo Bills, yet he says, "I'd give a little edge to the people here. I mean, we had 45,000 people in the stadium for our first intrasquad scrimmage this year. It was unbelievable."

Brooks popularized the Lambeau Leap, the ritual in which a Packer who scores a TD vaults into the end-zone stands like a salmon swimming upstream. He says the idea came to him before the 1995 season. Sterling Sharpe, Green Bay's career receptions leader, had been forced into retirement with a neck injury, and Brooks was entering his first year as Sharpe's replacement. Rather than slink onto center stage, Brooks says he wanted to ingratiate himself with the Lambeau crowd by doing something "crazy, out of the ordinary, to get the fans' confidence." He remembered how safety LeRoy Butler had tried to leap into the seats after returning a fumble for a touchdown in a December '93 victory over the Los Angeles Raiders, which clinched a playoff spot for Green Bay. "Except LeRoy didn't get all the way in," Brooks says with a chuckle. "He stuck to the wall like Velcro. I said, When I score at Lambeau, I'm jumping all the way in."

Which is exactly what Brooks did on Sept. 17, 1995, after catching a 19-yard touchdown pass from Favre during the second quarter of a 14–6 win over the New York Giants. The fans loved it. By the end of last season most of the Packers' scorers were jubilantly mimicking him. "The first time I did it and saw the TV highlights, I thought, Man, that is so much fun! It's just the best," Brooks says. "You can dance and do all that other stuff in the end zone. But this, it's like you're a rock star, and you're trusting your fans completely, and you dive off the stage, and they throw you back on. It's the best feeling in the world. And I don't think you could do it anywhere but here."

THE IRONY? For all the memories that Lambeau has provided, it's not much to look at. Its beauty is in its throwback simplicity. There are no flourishes, certainly nothing like the grand pillars that adorn Chicago's 73-year-old Soldier Field. Lambeau's exterior is a serviceable skin of steel sheeting painted in the Packers' colors of forest green and stoplight yellow.

Steve Sabol, president of NFL Films, has been coming to Green Bay for 30 years, or ever since he and his dad, Ed, used to preview their work for Lombardi on a bedsheet hung on the basement wall of Lombardi's house. While Sabol agrees that Lambeau is the "holy ground of the NFL," he adds, "When I think of NFL stadiums, there are so many other more eccentric places that come to mind.

"At Giants Stadium you've got the Hawk—that terrible wind. And Phil Simms can tell you how three-fourths of his touchdown passes there came in the north end zone, where Jimmy Hoffa is supposedly buried. Texas Stadium has its shadows. Al Davis used to always complain that his Oakland Raiders could never beat those great Pittsburgh Steelers teams at Three Rivers because the sidelines freeze before the middle of the field, so Cliff Branch could never get open deep. To me, those are the stadiums that have a sense of mystery. Lambeau is just a nice, friendly, intimate place to watch a game."

The Packers had outgrown their previous home—City Stadium, a 25,000-seat bandbox so primitive that it didn't have women's rest rooms and players used the locker rooms at adjacent East High—and had to ask Green Bay voters to underwrite construction of a new one. At a rally the weekend before the balloting on whether to build the stadium, George Halas, the legendary owner and coach of the rival Chicago Bears, told voters that the only way the Packers could continue to compete in the NFL was with a new facility. The bond issue passed by a 2-to-1 margin, and the stadium was built on a shoestring budget of $960,000. It opened at the start of the 1957 season.

A game-day walk around Lambeau's main concourse reveals no-frills concession stands, cinder-block rest rooms and metal framing that supports the grandstands. Over the past 15 years Green Bay has poured $40 million into stadium updates such as skyboxes, club seating and JumboTron replay boards. Seating has been expanded seven times since 1961, increasing Lambeau's capacity from the original 32,150 to 60,790. The stadium's single-level, bowl-shaped configuration assures that there are no obstructed views, but all the outdoor seats are backless aluminum bleachers.

Inside the home locker room there's no cracking Naugahyde sofa on which notorious playboy halfback Paul Hornung might've slept off a hangover, no battered oak desk on which Lombardi could've propped up his cleats. Instead there's the usual wall-to-wall carpet, walk-in dressing cubicles and players-only lounge with a mammoth TV. Action photos line the walls of the Green Bay executive offices, and the Packers celebrate their 11 title seasons by listing the years in the southeast corner of Lambeau, at the same level as the names of their Hall of Famers.

And there aren't any claims of helpful gremlins blowing field goal attempts wide right or ghosts haunting Lambeau—though it has been pointed out that many fans have asked the Packers if their ashes could be scattered on the field after they die. "We always say no," says head groundskeeper Todd Edlebeck, "but, you know, it could've happened. Some mornings you can just tell someone's been on the field overnight. Carts that we left out will be moved. Equipment has been handled."

Lambeau's most famous feature—the Frozen Tundra—isn't all that it's cracked up to be. In the summer of 1967 Lombardi had the field equipped with a then newfangled underground heating system, which works something like an electric blanket. About 14 miles of plastic-covered cables, spaced one foot apart, run sideline to sideline and are buried six inches beneath the surface. A General Electric press release touting the system promised "September-like playing conditions throughout the season. Instead of a frozen field, the Wisconsin contests will be played on a green, soft, frost-free turf."

Meaning the Frozen Tundra isn't really frozen? "Well, the system doesn't do much good when the air temperature drops below 20," Edlebeck says. "But the field's not frozen nearly as often as it's said to be. I guess it sounds cute to say *frozen tundra*. And at least when ESPN's Chris Berman says it, he says it as a joke. What bugs you is when TV announcers say it's a frozen tundra and they haven't even been on the field. My mother used to watch all the games on TV, and, you know, that really used to burn her up."

IT HAS BEEN 40 years since quarterback Babe Parilli and tight end Gary

Knafelc made opening day (Sept. 29, 1957) at Lambeau a success for the Packers, combining on a fourth-quarter touchdown pass that clinched a 21–17 win over the Bears. It has been 32 years since the name of the facility was changed from City Stadium to honor team founder and longtime coach Curly Lambeau, the bon vivant who won seven championships during his 31 seasons in Green Bay, married three times and in 1922 paid the club's $250 league entry fee with money he got from the sale of a friend's car.

Just as the 1967 championship game is rarely called anything but the Ice Bowl, some other games have been so compelling that Packers fans have slapped titles on them, too. The Snow Bowl was an '85 game against the Tampa Bay Buccaneers; a 16-inch snowfall blanketed the city, and many fans drove their snowmobiles to the stadium, where, predictably, the Packers whipped their warm-weather opponents 21–0. The Instant Replay Game? That was the one in '89 during which Bears coach Mike Ditka went ballistic after officials reversed themselves and announced that Majkowski hadn't been over the line of scrimmage when, on the last play of the game, he'd tossed a game-winning touchdown pass to Sharpe. The hard feelings run so deep that the Chicago media guide still carries an asterisk next to the result of that game.

From 1973 through '92 the Packers languished, qualifying for the playoffs only in the 1982 strike-shortened season. But Green Bay fans still laugh about the 1980 season opener at Lambeau in which the Bears blocked Chester Marcol's overtime field goal attempt, only to see Marcol catch the ricochet and scoot 25 yards for the winning score. Marcol looked like an accountant in his thick, black-frame glasses, and he ran as if he had pails on his feet.

Nitschke's finest Lambeau moment came in the 1965 NFL title game against the Cleveland Browns. He was assigned to shadow the great Jim Brown, who finished with just 50 yards rushing on 12 carries, and his diving, fingertip deflection of a sure touchdown pass intended for Brown sealed the Packers' 23–12 win. Hornung outdid Brown with a scintillating 105-yard performance. After scoring a third-quarter touchdown, Hornung ran to the sidelines shouting, "It's just like the good old days!" That led Lombardi to crow, "Did you hear that? Just like the good old days, boys!"

WHEN HARLAN, a member of the Packers' front office since 1971, looks at the sports world today, he notes that the Bears are talking about abandoning Soldier Field, that Boston Garden is no more and that if George Steinbrenner has his way, Yankee Stadium may soon follow. "Every time I see another old ballpark bite the dust, I think, That's too bad," Harlan says. "There will never be another Yankee Stadium. Regardless of what you name the new one, it will never be *the* Yankee Stadium. It's the same with Lambeau Field. There have been just too many world championships and glory times here. I think for the NFL to lose a story like the Green Bay Packers would be a disaster."

"We know there could come a time when, first, we just won't have the money to stay competitive," Harlan says. "And, well, I can't sit here and say that for 10, 15 or 20 years this stadium is going to be fine. Because I'm not sure it is."

In the 1970s some businessmen approached the Packers' board of directors with plans for a dome. Smiling bemusedly, Harlan says, "The idea didn't go over very well." And he doubts it would now. "When you go out in our stadium and sit in the stands for a game, you just get the feeling this is football the way it's supposed to be played," he says. "Somehow those voices just sound louder in that terrible chill."

When Thurston is asked what Lombardi would think of playing in a dome, his eyebrows arch like those of a startled cat. He smirks. "Lombardi would say, 'No dome—no, no, no,' " he says, his chin jutting out. "He'd say, 'Football is meant to be played outdoors. Now and forever.' "

| | | | | |

Mr. Inside & Mr. Outside

BY RON FIMRITE

Doc Blanchard made his yards up the middle and Glenn Davis picked up his around end for Army's fabled teams of the 1940s.

I T IS HOMECOMING WEEKEND AT WEST POINT. THE LEAVES are turning, and though the October days have been unseasonably mild and sunny along the Hudson, there is at dusk the suggestion of an autumn chill. It is almost nightfall as the little van driven by U.S. Military Academy athletic director Carl Ullrich pulls up alongside the football practice field. Joe Steffy, a squarely built man who was an All-America guard on the great Army teams of the '40s, is there to meet Ullrich and his passengers, with a smile on his ruddy face as wide as the river.

Steffy, who has recently retired, lives just up the road from West Point, in Newburgh, N.Y. He hasn't missed an Army football home game in 35 years. The two old friends Steffy has driven over to meet, who are now disengaging themselves from the van with theatrically exaggerated difficulty, live far away—one in California near Palm Springs, the other in San Antonio. And though he visits both of them from time to time, Steffy is happy to have them back on his own turf. Of course there was a time, so many years ago, when it was their turf too. Theirs for sure.

"Doc! Glenn!" Steffy bellows, jogging over to the three-foot-high fence that borders the practice field. The visitors are equally joyous, the smaller of the two actually vaulting the fence—no mean feat for a 63-year-old man recently recovered from prostate surgery. The larger man, heavier by many pounds than in his robust playing days, takes the longer way around, but he, too, hurries over to embrace his old teammate. "How's it goin', you old duffer!" he says. The Army team is still practicing, so the older men confine their friendly scuffling and noisy reminiscences to the edge of the field. An errant punt bounces within a few feet of them.

"They can sure as hell kick that ball these days," says Steffy.

"Aw, Joe," says Doc, "they just blow the ball up tighter."

"But they are *big*," says Glenn. "We'd look like termites out there."

Jim Young, the Army coach, soon joins the group. Young is 53, but he addresses the two visitors as if he were a mere schoolboy in the presence of idols, which, certainly to his way of thinking, he is.

"Could you two possibly say a few words to the team?" the coach inquires. "It would be important to them if you could. They've all seen you plenty of times. We show the highlight films from '45 and '46 before our games."

Doc and Glenn cheerfully agree, following Young, who whistles his team to assembly in the middle of the field. It is growing dark, and the damp grass has a velvet sheen. The Hudson River beyond looks like a long black ribbon. There is the smell of sweat in the evening air. The players gather in a semicircle around their coach and his two guests.

"Men," Young begins, "I want you to meet the two greatest football players Army ever had, the two best backs ever to play on the same college football team—Glenn Davis and Doc Blanchard." Applause and cheers. The years now are peeling away from the returning heroes, and, embarrassed by this rush of sentiment, they hastily wish these new Black Knights of the Hudson good luck and Godspeed.

As the two greatest football players Army ever had walk away from this scene so hauntingly familiar to them, Blanchard turns to Davis and says in a large gruff voice, "Glenn, what I wanted to tell those boys was that we wore hightop shoes and long-sleeved shirts with elbow pads and we had no face masks, and on the bus down to New York, we'd sing *Barbry Allen* and *John Henry*."

"Doc, I notice you're still smoking."

"Aw, Glenn, I've lived so long that everything from now on is just a bonus."

BLANCHARD AND Davis. They are as different as two men can be, and yet it is almost impossible for those who remember them to say one name without the other. They are the Damon and Pythias, the Chang and Eng, the MacNeil and Lehrer of football. Indeed, though they rarely see each other anymore and live many miles apart, though they have followed entirely separate paths since they left West Point more than 41 years ago and were never really that close—they were in different battalions at the Academy—Doc Blanchard and Glenn Davis are destined to march in lockstep through time, inseparably bound by mutually extraordinary deeds. They will forever be what George Trevor of the old New York *Sun* called them long ago in a moment of matchless inspiration, Mr. Inside and Mr. Outside.

They were running backs who perfectly complemented each other, the one, Blanchard, a battering ram up the middle; the other, Davis, a wraith around end. Together they formed the most devastating backfield combination since the Four Horsemen of Notre Dame 20 years earlier. Individually, they rank among the finest backs ever to play college football. Their coach, Colonel Earl (Red) Blaik, now 91 and living in Colorado Springs, says, "There is no comparing them with anyone else. They were the best."

Ed McKeever, the Notre Dame coach in 1944, said on first watching Blanchard, "I've just seen Superman in the flesh. He wears number 35 and goes by the name of Blanchard." Davis was similarly extolled. "He's better than Grange," said Steve Owen, coach of the NFL New York Giants during the Blanchard-Davis years. "He's faster and he cuts better."

Bill Yeoman, the former University of Houston coach and a Blanchard-Davis teammate, told the *Los Angeles Times* only five years ago, "There are words to describe how good an athlete Doc Blanchard was. But there aren't words to describe how good Glenn Davis was."

Blanchard and Davis were consensus All-Americas in 1944, '45 and '46, the only three-time All-America backfield teammates. They won the Heisman Trophy in successive years, Blanchard in '45, Davis in '46—again the only members of the same backfield to achieve that distinction. In 1945 alone, they scored 37 touchdowns—19 by Blanchard, 18 by Davis—and since Army beat opponents by an average score that year of 45.8–5.1, they played barely half the time; Davis averaged only nine carries a game and Blanchard slightly more than 11.

Their skills were hardly defined by their sobriquets. Mr. Inside had the speed to run outside, and he frequently did. As Yeoman has observed, "Davis was so fast he made the rest of us look slow, so people forget how fast Doc was." Indeed, Blanchard ran 100 yards in under 10 seconds. He was also a superb pass receiver who, though Army seldom threw, caught seven touchdown passes (five from Davis) in his three-year career. Blanchard also punted, kicked off and occasionally kicked extra points. On defense (Mr. Inside and Mr. Outside were two-way players), he was a punishing tackler as a linebacker. He still holds the Academy three-year record for yards returned on intercepted passes (189), and he ran back two interceptions for touchdowns.

Blanchard also returned two punts for touchdowns. The year he won his Heisman, he averaged 7.1 yards on a mere 101 carries. He also won the Maxwell Trophy, and he became the first football player to win the Sullivan Award as the nation's finest amateur athlete. Blanchard is the only man ever to win the Heisman and the Sullivan. He dabbled in track and field his senior year and, with no previous experience in the event, was putting the shot close to 54 feet at a time when the world record was not yet 60 feet.

Blanchard was a superior athlete. Davis was an amazing one. In his four years at West Point, Davis won 10 letters: four in football, three in baseball, two in track and one in basketball. In his time, cadets were required to take a physical-fitness test that included such events as the rope climb, the 300-yard run, the bar vault, the vertical jump, the standing long jump and the softball throw, as well as chin-ups and push-ups. A perfect score was 1,000 points. Before Davis the record score was 901½ points and the average for all cadets not quite 550. Davis scored an unheard-of 962½.

His career batting average on the Army baseball team was .403 for 51 games, and he stole 64 bases in 65 attempts, including second, third and home in an exhibition game against the Brooklyn Dodgers at West Point. Branch Rickey, the Dodgers' president at the time, made him a standing offer of $75,000 to sign, which was a king's ransom in the '40s.

Davis may well have been the fastest football player ever to play the game up to his time. The qualifier is necessary because no one could ever be certain just how fast he was; like Blanchard, he considered track a mere diversion. But in 1947 Davis did beat Barney Ewell, who would win the silver medal at 100 meters in the '48 Olympic Games, in a 6.1 60-yard dash at a meet in Madison Square Garden. Davis's most famous track exploit, though, came after a baseball game against Navy at West Point in '47. The ball game, which started in the morning, was followed that afternoon by the annual Army-Navy track meet. Davis played the full nine innings in centerfield, getting, as he recalls, "a couple of hits." Then, because Army was short of sprinters, he was rushed by car from the diamond to the track, where he changed to shorts and was handed a pair of borrowed track shoes. Davis had not run in an outdoor meet that year, nor had he practiced a single day on the track.

"They held up the dashes for him," says Bobby Folsom, a former football teammate who, from 1976 to '81, was the mayor of Dallas. "I can remember Glenn jogging over to the start of the 100 carrying those borrowed shoes. Well, we all know what happened next."

Davis was called for one false start in the 100-yard dash, and he was so cautious on the next start that he was all but left in the blocks. But he easily caught up with the field and won in 9.7, an excellent time for any sprinter in 1947, an astonishing time for one who hadn't trained and who had just finished playing nine innings of baseball. Then, in the 220, he merely established a meet and an Academy record of 20.9.

But Davis had more than speed on the football field. He was only 5' 9" and 170 pounds, but he ran with unusual power and was one of the shiftiest backs the game has ever known. "He and Doc were both easy to block for," says DeWitt (Tex) Coulter, an All-America tackle on the Blanchard-Davis teams. "You didn't really need to get in a solid lick, because they had this sense of where to go, that great running instinct."

Davis still holds or shares five NCAA rushing and scoring records. His career-average gain of 8.26 yards (2,957 yards in 358 carries) has been the standard for 42 years. He is tied with Pittsburgh's Tony Dorsett for career touchdowns, with 59. Davis had 43 rushing TDs, 14 on pass receptions and two on punt returns. He also scored touchdowns in 31 games, a record he shares with Dorsett and Ted Brown of North Carolina State, and he scored two or more touchdowns in 17 games, a record he shares with Dorsett and Steve Owens of Oklahoma. Together, Davis and Blanchard hold the career record for most touchdowns and points scored by two players on the same team—97 and 585, respectively.

Granted, some of those extraordinary numbers were achieved against weak, wartime opponents, but by 1946 the big boys, older, stronger and more experienced from service football, were back. Mr. Inside and Mr. Outside were equal to the occasion. Although Blanchard missed two games with a knee injury, he still rushed for 613 yards and a 5.2 average. Davis averaged 5.8 yards a carry that year, gained 712 yards and scored 13 touchdowns. It was his turn for the Heisman.

The Blanchard-Davis Army teams of '44 through '46 had only a 0–0 tie with Notre Dame on Nov. 9, 1946, at Yankee Stadium to taint an otherwise unblemished 27-0-1 record. They won 25 straight before coming up empty against the Irish. The '44 team set an NCAA record by averaging 56 points a game and holding opponents to only 3.9.

The '45 team, considered by Colonel Blaik and his two stars to have been the best of the three, set records for average gain per rushing play (7.64) and average gain per play (7.92). That team averaged 459 yards a game. The '46 team, depleted by graduations, dismissals and injuries to Blanchard and quarterback Young Arnold Tucker, and playing against such war-veteran-revived powers as Oklahoma, Michigan and Notre Dame, still went on to finish undefeated, outscoring its 10 opponents 263 to 80.

But the Black Knights of the Hudson would never again ride so triumphantly. "I finally figured out what will stop Blanchard and Davis," Giants coach Owen slyly advised some of his college coaching friends. "Graduation."

And so it did. Blanchard graduated 296th and Davis 305th in a 1947 class of 310, but the Corps of Cadets gave each of them the longest and loudest cheers heard that day. Actually, there was rejoicing all over the country in that second postwar spring. The boys were home again, wartime restrictions had been lifted, and the nation was entering an era of unprecedented prosperity. But at the same time that veterans were shedding their uniforms for civilian clothes, the two most famous football players in the land were getting their marching orders. And all the while, professional football, just entering its own era of prosperity, was offering them a share in the postwar boom.

INA DAVIS had packed a fried chicken lunch for her twin sons, Ralph and Glenn, to take with them on the train trip back to New York that summer of 1944. Glenn was the younger brother by five minutes, so he was called Junior, a nickname that had stuck with him from childhood, in Claremont, Calif. Ralph had been a pretty fair athlete at Bonita Union High, a shot-putter on the track team and a football end. But Glenn was already a legend, a four-sport star who was being hailed as the best athlete ever to come out of Southern California. In his senior year at Bonita, he had scored 236 points in nine football games. "You gave him the ball and he was gone," said Ralph, his biggest fan. Glenn also passed and kicked in coach John Price's single wing.

But, for all of his athletic success—he was All-California Interscholastic Federation in football, baseball and basketball (second team) and a champion sprinter—Glenn was the shy one of the brothers. They lived in a fine old house on a sycamore-lined street in Claremont with Ina and Ralph Sr., a banker, and an older sister, Mary. The boys also worked and played together in the orange orchard the family owned in nearby La Verne. It was altogether a blissful and innocent time in a Southern California that then had open space and more sunshine than smog.

The twins were set to enter USC after graduation in 1943, but Blaik, who had heard of Davis's exploits from a friend, invited Glenn to come east and play for Army. Glenn agreed, but only if Ralph could join him. The brothers were accepted as a package, and they got their appointments from California Congressman Jerry Voorhis, who would later lose his seat to a young lawyer named Richard Nixon, who accused him of being soft on Communism.

The twins went East in the spring of 1943 and lived with Blaik and his wife while studying for the entrance exams, which they passed. Glenn played fullback and right halfback on a '43 Army team that was still adjusting to the T formation Blaik had installed the year before. As a plebe playing varsity, which was permitted then, he gained 634 yards on 95 carries, a 6.7-per-carry average, and scored eight touchdowns. Army won seven games that year but lost 26–0 to Notre Dame and 13–0 to Navy, and was tied 13–13 by Penn. Glenn was named to several All-America teams. Ralph, as he would throughout his West Point stay, played on the B squad.

But Ralph did better academically. Glenn discovered early on that West

Point made few concessions to athletes, and he was simply not prepared for the rigors of classwork, barracks discipline and varsity football. "I just couldn't do it all," he says now. "I was taking five classes every day. I'd get out of the last one at 3:30 and be on the football field at 4:00. I wouldn't get home until 6:30. Then I'd have dinner and study."

The routine was too much for Glenn. He flunked mathematics that spring of his plebe year and went home to Claremont, where he took courses at Webb School for Boys in preparation for reentering the Academy the next fall. Ralph, who would graduate a year ahead of his brother, found this separation "very rough, the saddest time for me. Glenn was my brother, my best friend. To this day, I've never met a finer man."

But now, in July 1944, they were together again, returning by train from San Bernardino to West Point. Glenn had been readmitted as a plebe and would be eligible for the football season.

As the brothers talked, they noticed that a tall, silver-haired man seated across from them seemed to be taking more than a casual interest in their conversation. "My name is Shaughnessy," the stranger finally said, introducing himself. "Clark Shaughnessy." The twins laughed in recognition. Clark Shaughnessy. Why, he'd coached Stanford's 1940 Wow Boys to an undefeated season and a Rose Bowl win. His was the team that ignited the T formation revolution in college football. Shaughnessy, who was coaching at the University of Pittsburgh that year, told them he was a good friend of Blaik's and that, in fact, he had touted to the Army coach a sensational fullback he'd seen play freshman football at the University of North Carolina. "You'll be seeing him this fall," he told the twins. "Remember the name: Felix Blanchard." Glenn said he certainly would.

Shaughnessy had coached Blanchard's father, Felix Anthony Blanchard Sr., at Tulane in 1920. The elder Blanchard had also been a fine fullback, and though he had gone on to medical school and started up a practice in the little town of McColl, S.C., he had never lost interest in the game. He had, in fact, married Mary Tatum, a cousin of Jim Tatum's. Tatum was later the coach at North Carolina, Maryland and Oklahoma. By the time Felix Jr. was three, he was kicking the ball on the front lawn of the Blanchard home.

The Blanchards had moved from South Carolina to Dexter, Iowa, in 1929, but returned two years later to Bishopville, S.C., where Little Doc, as he was known, went to school until he was 13. Then Big Doc enrolled him in the St. Stanislaus prep school in Bay St. Louis, Miss., where he himself had first learned to play football. Little Doc stayed at St. Stanislaus for four years, and in his senior year scored 165 points and led an otherwise so-so football team to an undefeated regular season.

Young Blanchard was besieged with college football scholarship offers, and he settled on North Carolina, where his mother's cousin was the head coach. He starred on the Tar Heel freshman team in 1942 (that year freshmen were still unable to play varsity) and was drafted into the Army the following spring. He played no football in 1943, but West Point became interested in him, and on July 1, 1944, he received his appointment to the Academy from South Carolina Congressman John L. McMillan.

Blanchard reported for the Beast Barracks indoctrination for new cadets. Davis, although technically a plebe, was not there to suffer with him; he had undergone the ordeal a year earlier. Mr. Inside and Mr. Outside did not meet until the first day of football practice, an encounter much dramatized in film and story. But neither of the principals recalls anything significant about their meeting beyond "Pleased to meet you."

Blanchard and Davis were entirely different personalities then. Davis was the more earnest of the two, something of a worrier, a physical-fitness zealot who neither smoked nor drank. He had a round baby face, and a lock of hair that always seemed to be spilling over his forehead. He was photographed more often pouting than smiling.

Blanchard, on the other hand, was something of a good-time Charlie. "I never regarded Glenn as exactly shy, but Doc was looser, less straitlaced," says former teammate Coulter. "He was just a lot of fun. I remember Colonel Blaik asking each of us before our first practice if we drank. Well, most of us dodged that one, but Doc just said, 'Oh, sure.' "

Blanchard was actually closer to Ralph Davis than he was to Glenn. "Doc was such a good guy, always joking, laughing, so easy to get along with," says Ralph, now a real estate appraiser in Joshua Tree, Calif. "The track coach asked me to teach him the shot put. It was something he'd never done before, but he went from 30 feet to almost 54 feet in the same season."

Anyone knowing the two football players then would have guessed that Blanchard would be the one to bridle at West Point restrictions and want to get out of the Army as soon as possible, and that the self-disciplined Davis would be the one to adapt to the regimen. And it would surely be

Blanchard, well-known as a ladies' man, who would date one actress, Elizabeth Taylor no less, and marry another, Terry Moore. It is one of the peculiar paradoxes of the Blanchard-Davis legend that it was exactly the other way around. And now, years after West Point, it is as if they had just switched personalities; Glenn is outgoing and Doc retiring.

Their final season together was the most taxing and, because of the Notre Dame tie and the narrow Navy win, the most disappointing. And yet because the team lacked depth, it was the most rewarding. The team had lost through graduation or dismissal All-America linemen Coulter, John Green and Al Nemetz. And in the opening game, against Villanova, Blanchard tore ligaments in his left knee and missed the next two games, against Oklahoma and Cornell.

He returned, still hurting, to the lineup for the fourth game, against Michigan, a team loaded with stars like Bob Chappuis, Bump Elliott, Jack Weisenburger, Len Ford and Bob Mann. On the fourth play of the game, Army quarterback Tucker, himself an All-America, suffered a shoulder separation and a sprained elbow and wrist in his passing arm. Davis, taking direct snaps through the quarterback's legs or pitchouts on the pass-run option, took over the Army passing game. He completed seven of eight for 168 yards, including a 23-yard toss to Folsom for a touchdown. He also had a 69-yard touchdown run. Blanchard, held to 44 yards for the day, scored the winning touchdown in the 13–10 win on a seven-yard plunge in the fourth quarter.

The Notre Dame game at Yankee Stadium on Nov. 9 was one of the most publicized college football games ever played. The undefeated Irish had a lineup loaded with once and future All-Americas—Johnny Lujack at quarterback with his backups George Ratterman and Frank Tripucka, and All-America linemen George Connor, Bill Fischer and Jim Martin. They were out to avenge successive 59–0 and 48–0 cadet wins over inferior wartime Notre Dame teams.

Notre Dame would eventually be crowned national champion after Army's narrow scrape with Navy. Army was also undefeated, of course, but the Notre Dame game was a bust. "It was the most boring game I've ever played in," says Blanchard. "I think Blaik and (Irish coach Frank) Leahy were more worried about losing than winning." Mr. Inside and Mr. Outside together gained only 82 yards on 35 carries.

In the Navy game two weeks later, they did much better, Blanchard scoring on a 53-yard run and on a 27-yard pass from Davis, and Davis on a 14-yard run, but the cadets had to hold off a second-half comeback by the midshipmen, and the game ended with Navy on the Army five-yard line. The Blanchard-Davis era had ended quietly.

So now what? Both stars were confronted with a three-year military commitment. But there were also tempting pro football offers from teams in both the established National Football League and the new All-America Conference. Davis was drafted by the Detroit Lions and Blanchard by the Pittsburgh Steelers in the NFL. The San Francisco 49ers of the AAC acquired rights to both of them and were prepared to offer them $130,000 apiece—$10,000 in signing bonuses and $40,000 annually for three years—this at a time when the pro game's best players were earning barely $20,000 a year.

Davis and Blanchard appealed to Major General Maxwell Taylor, the West Point superintendent, to have their normal postgraduation 60-day furlough extended another two months so they might at least play the '47 season for the 49ers. They further proposed, and Taylor concurred, that they be given four-month leaves in each of the next three years in exchange for an open-ended military commitment. The request was leaked to the press and became, as it were, a political football. "I thought we sent these boys to West Point to be future officers and not pro football players," fumed Congressman Les Arends of Illinois. Hearst columnist Bill Corum threatened to boycott their games if they ever played pro football. The War Department, sensing a no-win situation, emphatically denied the requests for extended leaves, remarking in a press release that "any other decision would be inimical to the best interests of the service."

Blanchard accepted the decision with a shrug. "I'd like to have had the money," he says now. But Davis, who had concluded after four years at the Academy that the Army was no life for him, was bitterly disappointed. The two spent their postgraduation furlough playing football before the movie cameras in Hollywood, filming *The Spirit of West Point*. It was a turkey, but they were paid $20,000 apiece, partial compensation at least for the lost football income.

Blanchard had a ball in Hollywood. "I met James Cagney, Hopalong Cassidy (William Boyd), Alan Hale and William Bendix," he says. "I found there were actually a few real people out there—not too many, but a few." For Davis the movie-making adventure was a disaster. Filming a football scene on the UCLA campus, he twisted his right knee making a cut and fell to the turf. Davis, who had never been injured in an actual football game, had been hurt in a sham one.

Blanchard was stunned by this freak injury to a player he considered indestructible. "We were just horsing around making that scene," he recalls. "Glenn didn't do anything unusual. He just made a normal cut and . . . well, he was never the same after that."

"It was," says Davis, "the end of me."

Davis reinjured the knee practicing for the annual College All-Star game against the 1946 NFL champion Chicago Bears. He missed that game, then hurt the knee again while playing for another all-star squad in a charity game in New York against the Giants. A few weeks later, he underwent surgery in New York. More than 40 years later his knee is loose and wandering. As a player he found he could not run to his right and cut to his left and that even his straightahead speed was affected by the bandages and braces he needed to wear to keep the knee in place.

But Davis did not give up on football. He worked out with the Rams, who had obtained rights to him, during his furlough in 1948. More significantly, perhaps, he also met a lovely 16-year-old actress named Elizabeth Taylor at her parents' home in Malibu. The next year, a storybook romance seemed to be under way between the All-American boy and the movie beauty. Davis had been assigned to an Army base in Korea, and when he returned on leave to Miami he was met at the airport by both Taylor and LIFE photographers. Their reunion was recorded in the March 21, 1949, LIFE, with Taylor depicted wiping lipstick from "the handsome lieutenant's" face after an embrace.

In December 1947, Davis had asked to be discharged early from the Army, but the request was denied. He served his full three years, with 18 months of the hitch in Korea. He finally resigned in time to join the Rams for the '50 season, but once again his timing, flawless in football, was faulty in the real world. War in Korea broke out in June '50, less than two months after Davis, an infantry officer who had been stationed on the embattled 38th parallel, left there to resume his long-delayed football career. Once more, he became prey for angry politicians and newspaper pundits.

Robert Ruark, the novelist then writing a syndicated column, equated Davis's resignation from the Army at a time of national emergency with the defection to Russia of "avowed Communist" Paul Robeson. Ruark wrote, "Mr. Davis worked for the Army a couple of years of the recent post-war period, to pay off Uncle Sam, quit his commission and is now playing professional football as anticlimax to his romance with Elizabeth Taylor." Dan Parker of the *New York Daily Mirror* rose to Davis's defense: "The Army enrolled Davis for his athletic prowess, not because he looked like General Grant in the bud. He played his role well, and has now put in [his] years soldiering."

The controversy over Davis's efforts to get out of the Army and the mostly embarrassing publicity he had received for his amatory adventures in Hollywood—two years after his fling with Taylor, he was married briefly to Moore—may well have delayed Davis's induction into the National Football Foundation and Hall of Fame. Blanchard was admitted in 1959, and Davis two years later, but only after an intense and angry campaign by Army sports information director Joseph Cahill.

In 1960, Cahill wrote the Foundation: "Contrary to the belief of the uninformed, Glenn fulfilled his military obligation in an honorable manner. . . . This he did without fanfare. That 18 months of this time was served in the dismal atmosphere of Korea is pertinent. As for the small segment who would defame his current status as a respected citizen, I would like to report that he is a happily married man (to his current wife, the former Harriet Lancaster Slack) with two children."

Davis played two years with the Rams. Despite the gimpy knee, he led the team in rushing in 1950 with a 4.28 average per carry and caught 42 passes for 592 yards. In the league championship game that year with the Cleveland Browns, which the Rams lost 30–28, he caught a pass from Bob Waterfield and ran 50 yards with it for the first Los Angeles touchdown.

But Davis's old injury and the three-year layoff had sorely diminished his skills. "It was really tough for me to come back," he says. "It would take me two days or more to recover from a game. I was a mere image of what I had been. I was a better player my senior year in high school than I was with the Rams." In 1951, Davis played sparingly because of injuries, rushing 64 times for 200 yards. He sat out the '52 season, then tried to make a comeback in '53, but the battered knee would not respond. His last game was a Rams exhibition against the Philadelphia Eagles in Little Rock, on Sept. 12, 1953. Mr. Outside was finished. He was not quite 29.

Blanchard never gave pro football a thought after the 49er affair. But he played football in 1947 for Randolph Field, an Air Force Base in Texas, where he was a pilot trainee. He married a San Antonio woman, Jody King, on Oct. 12, 1948, and got his wings at almost the same time. In 1959, while stationed in England, he won a special citation for taking a burning plane in for a safe landing away from a village. He did some coaching, both at West Point and at the Air Force Academy, but he was by that time a full-fledged fighter jock, and in 1967–68 he flew 85 combat missions over North Vietnam and won a Distinguished Flying Cross.

Blanchard retired from the Air Force as a full colonel in 1971 and served for two years as the commandant of the New Mexico Military Institute in Roswell, N.Mex. In 1973, he retired permanently. He was 49. The Blanchards have a son, two daughters and seven grandchildren, one of whom, 15-year-old Mary Ellen Blanchard, swam in the Olympic trials last summer. Blanchard says he lives in virtual anonymity in San Antonio. "People down here don't know you played unless it was for Texas or A & M. Anywhere else, they just say, 'Where's that, boy?' "

Davis took a job as assistant director of special events for the *Los Angeles Times* in 1954 and became the director in '60, responsible for the countless charity athletic events staged by the newspaper, including, for 20 years, the NFL Pro Bowl game. He married Harriet, a war widow, on April 17, 1953, and they have a son, Ralph, as well as her son, John, from the previous marriage.

Davis retired from the *Times* in January 1987 and moved from North Hollywood to a condominium just off the 6th tee at the La Quinta Country Club. He's an eight-handicap golfer whose partners number such neighbors as former President Gerald Ford, Bob Hope, Don Drysdale and George Blanda. Davis is, as publicist Cahill wrote so many years ago, "a happily married man." He is also as affable and approachable now as he was shy and withdrawn years ago. His modesty is genuine, not feigned, and he would as soon talk about his newspaper days as he would the football years. But he has not been forgotten. "It's amazing, but I still get at least a half dozen fan letters every week. People send me cards and clippings and magazine covers—Doc and I were on the covers of both LIFE and TIME—and they're people of all ages, too, not just of my vintage. After all these years, that's really something."

THEY MARCH shoulder-to-shoulder across the broad West Point Plain, past the monuments to Ike and MacArthur, past the stark granite Gothic buildings that nestle between the green hills and the silvery Hudson. The Army band is playing an incongruous medley of *Over There*; *Jesus Loves Me*; *On, Brave Old Army Team*; *Onward, Christian Soldiers*; and *Hail, Hail, the Gang's All Here*. It is, in fact, quite a gang Glenn and Doc are marching with in the alumni parade at this Homecoming celebration.

Major General (ret.) George S. Patton III, son of Old Blood and Guts, is beside them. And in their company are General Roscoe Robinson, Jr., the Army's first black man to achieve four-star rank, and General Sam S. Walker, superintendent of the Virginia Military Institute. The alumni ranks are led by 85-year-old Major General (ret.) Charles E. Saltzman, class of 1925, a brisk and humorous man who walked up to Glenn and Doc before the parade and announced, "I'm going to tell the coach to put you two boys in against Lafayette today."

"Well, if that's the case, you must not like us very much," replied Doc.

The parade comes to rest before the glowering statue of Colonel Sylvanus Thayer, "The Father of the Military Academy." A bugler blows *Taps* and Saltzman places a wreath at the feet of old Thayer. The Academy Glee Club sings *The Corps*.

> *Grip hands—though it be from the shadows—*
> *While we swear as, you did of yore,*
> *Or living, or dying, to honor the Corps,*
> *And the Corps, and the Corps!*

Harriet Davis watches her husband, dapper in a brand new trenchcoat, stand roughly at attention through this ceremony. "You know," she says, "I don't think there's anything Glenn has ever accomplished that he's prouder of than graduating from West Point."

THE VISITING alumni are guests of Lieutenant General Dave R. Palmer, superintendent of the Academy, at a luncheon before the game. Glenn and Doc do their best to blend in with the other old grads, but with little success, for the room is alive with memories of them. "I'm Colonel Al Rushton, director of admissions here," says one smiling man in uniform, "and I just want to tell you that you two have been my heroes since I was in grammar school."

"Grammar school?" asks an abashed Doc. "Glenn, I told you it wasn't gonna get any better. Didn't it used to be high school?" General Palmer calls the large room to attention. "Ladies and gentlemen," he says,"I was unable to get Grant and Lee for you today, or Eisenhower and MacArthur, but we do have another pair of Army heroes here, and I must call them a pair, because that's certainly what they were. Will you please join me in welcoming Glenn Davis and Doc Blanchard."

The guests rise to their feet and the room fairly explodes with applause. Slowly, Mr. Inside and Mr. Outside set aside their luncheon plates to stand in acknowledgment of this thunderous reception. True enough, Blanchard and Davis were never Grant and Lee. The one was a fighter jock, the other a reluctant infantry lieutenant. They're middle-aged now, gone a little gray, a little paunchy. They are both of them humble enough and sane enough to accept with good humor that to new generations of Americans they will be strangers. But their eyes glisten as they stand before this applauding crowd. Here, on the banks of the Hudson, they will always have a place. And as the applause rises, they look at each other with genuine affection and respect, and they share a little smile. Together again. Together forever.

CHARACTER
WITNESSES

| | | | | |

My Career
(So to Speak)

BY ALEX HAWKINS WITH MYRON COPE

The confessions of a pro who played six positions in 10 NFL seasons and did none of them justice.

FEW MORE WEEKS AND IT WOULD BE TIME TO REPORT to training camp—time to get ready for the 1969 season—but something was telling me that I faced a decision. I had awakened with a case of the hives. Whenever I get the hives I know it's time for a change. Usually I solve the problem by going off on a fishing trip or flying up to Baltimore to have a few drinks with my fans (mostly bartenders, petty hoodlums and worthless newspapermen), but lately I had been brooding about my career. Mind you, I had no illusions; I had not expected great things of myself. It's true that the first year a thumbnail sketch of me appeared in the Baltimore Colts' press book, I was described as a "fleet breakaway threat," but, of course, publicity men write press books grimly determined to find a compliment for every player. In my case it was a terrible struggle. Becoming less of a threat each year, I was demoted to "the hard-running blond," then to "the solid-socking blond." Finally, publicist Jim Walker reached the bottom of the barrel. He put

down that I was "loose and fun-loving off the field" and let it go at that.

But no, it was not my station that I brooded about. Actually, you could say my career had been unique. I mean, how many football players can you name who in 10 years in the National Football League played six positions—cornerback, halfback, fullback, split end, flanker and tight end—and did none of them justice?

Although I would be 32 in just a few days, I wasn't worried about being able to take the football grind for another year. On practice days our coach, Don Shula, used to say to me, "Well, Hawk, what are you going to do today?" I'd say, "I think I'll warm up the quarterbacks and later I'll go over and bat the breeze with the kickers." Shula would say, "Good. Just stay out of everybody's way." It was a routine I could live with.

Nor was I worried that I might not be able to retain my position as the No. 6 man in the Colts' six-man corps of receivers. Having risen to the captaincy of the suicide squad, I commanded a certain amount of prestige, and while it's true that Shula's better judgment often told him to release me, he always managed to rationalize his way out of the decision by noting that I knew the plays at six positions and that if I happened to turn up in the right saloon at the right time I usually could talk Lou Michaels out of a fight before the cops arrived. No, Shula wouldn't cut me. But for reasons I'll get to presently, I had become dissatisfied with life as a pro football player. The hives were telling me to take stock. Their message was clear. I decided to quit while I was still on the bottom.

From my home in Atlanta, I telephone Baltimore and called a press conference. The *club* was damn well not going to, but I still had a little Super Bowl money left that would pay for a nice luncheon, so I booked the back room at the Golden Arm, which is owned by John Unitas and Bobby Boyd, and leaked the word that I intended to announce my retirement. The turnout was huge and I might say, enthusiastic. Shula showed up, and so did a number of my teammates. The newspapermen already were charging drinks to my tab before I arrived. Also, there were bellboys and bookies and thieves and even a few thirsty priests. If I shock you by admitting that while playing pro football I associated with hoodlums, let me explain that in Baltimore there is no such thing as a clever hoodlum. One of my good friends, for example, made his getaway from a bank robbery by hailing a cab. After traveling five blocks he was caught, owing to the fact that he had neglected to tell the driver he had robbed a bank and the driver had stopped for a red light.

The speeches were terrific. Bert Bell Jr., the son of the late NFL commissioner, got up and said, "I think the Colts ought to retire the Hawk's jersey. Ball clubs are always retiring the stars' jerseys, but they never do anything for a stiff."

Gussie the Bookie got up and said, "Does anybody know who won the second at Monmouth?"

The sight of all my old pals so touched me that I arose and said, "I can't go through with it. I'm not going to quit." Shula threw down his napkin and stalked out of the room.

When the shouting died away and my resolve to remain active had been vetoed, the celebration began in earnest. The luncheon ended at 9:30 the next morning, at which time I awoke on the barroom floor, knowing that I had gone out in style.

Yes, once upon a time football was fun. The feeling that the fun was ebbing began to creep up on me in 1965, when John Unitas and I fell to reflecting on our training camp that year. We agreed that for the first time the place had no zest. You had to search high and low for a poker game. Players sat around checking their investment portfolios. In the past, if the coach gave the team the weekend off, 30 players would get together for a party, but now, with a free weekend starting, you would see them scattering like quail. The briefcase carriers had taken over. We were now a team during working hours only.

If I seem to be saying that in order to play pro football properly it's necessary that large groups of players hang out in bars, you read me perfectly. Regardless of what the Fellowship of Christian Athletes says, true pro football teams accomplished half of their pregame preparation in bars. Each team had its favorite after-practice hangout, a hangout being any bar where, let's say, six or more players gathered. By the third round of drinks you actually could see them getting themselves up for Sunday's game. For no apparent reason, except that we talked football (and girls) endlessly, you would suddenly hear a lineman say, "I'm going to block that son of a bitch all over the field." Having been immersed in the football talk, he was bringing his own little battle into focus and committing himself.

Confrontations took place at those hangouts. "When the hell are you going to start doing a better job?" a player would demand of another. Players were taken apart pointblank by their equals, and the team was the better for it. Today if you confront a teammate, he becomes highly indignant. When a few players occasionally get together, they talk about their Dairy Queens. If more than two players meet after practice for a beer, the odds are heavy that at least one wife will phone to say, "Now you be sure to be home on time because we're going over to Green Spring Inn with the Braases." I'm not saying it's a crime. I'm saying it's civil. Pro football was not designed to be played by sane or civil men.

The first day I reported to the Colts, in 1959, Bert Rechichar held out his hand and said, "I'm 44. What's your name?" He never thought of himself as Bert Rechichar. Had he been introducing himself to the president, he would have said, "I'm 44." He carried a cigar in the corner of his mouth and, being blind in one eye, which remained closed as he studied me with his good eye, he gave me the feeling that if I hadn't met him in the Colts' dressing room, I would have guessed his occupation as hangman.

He was a mystery man. While no one had ever been inside Raymond Berry's house, no one even knew where Rechichar lived. He carried his entire savings in his pocket, which caused players to refer to him as the First National Bank of Rechichar. In line at the $10 window at Pimlico, our general manager, the late Don Kellett, would find it irritating to see Bert at the $100 window.

A mean football player? He was meaner than hell at high noon. He had played quarterback, fullback, receiver, safety (where he made All-Pro) and linebacker. He was an Alex Hawkins with ability. In his first year at Baltimore, I was told, Bert fooled around in practice, kicking long field goals, although he wasn't the club's regular field goal man. In a game against the Chicago Bears the Colts had the ball on the Bears' 40 with four seconds left in the first half. Bert had started walking to the dressing room when an assistant coach said, "I wonder if Bert can kick a field goal from back there." Then he yelled, "Hey, Bert! Go in there and try a field goal." Bert shrugged and said, "Why the ---- not?" He walked back into the game and, without bothering to hook up his chin strap, booted a line drive that sailed 56 yards through the uprights. Until last week, when Tom Dempsey of New Orleans kicked a 63-yarder, it was a professional record.

When Weeb Ewbank coached the Colts, Bert would walk up to him every now and then and stare down at him with his good eye and say, "Don't you ever trade me." When at last Ewbank released him, Bert asked me to give him a lift in my car—he had to pick up his belongings. I thought I would finally learn where he lived, but instead Bert had me stop at half a dozen places at least—back alleys and side streets where I had never been. He would disappear into a doorway and return a few minutes later with a pair of pants and a jacket. At the next stop he would come out with a couple of shirts and maybe a pair of shoes. I drove him around for an hour before he said, "O.K., that's it." Would you say that Bert Rechichar was a totally sane man?

I'm not saying every pro football player has to be abnormal to perform well at the sport, but it helps.

Just *smelling* security has destroyed brilliant careers. Jim Taylor, the Green Bay fullback, was my idea of a perfect pro football player, which is to say half man, half animal. I knew him briefly at Green Bay, where I spent a few months as a rookie. It seemed to me that Taylor enjoyed talking to himself. This impression was confirmed years later when John Unitas returned from the Pro Bowl and said to me, "I was in the huddle, starting to call a play, when I heard that guy Taylor muttering. I said, 'What's wrong, Jim?' He said, 'Don't pay no attention to me. I'm talking to myself.' " Like Bert Rechichar, Taylor never, to my knowledge, referred to himself by his Christian name. Sometimes he called himself Roy and at other times he called himself Doody. I have no idea why. He called other people Doody, too.

But when I say that Jim Taylor was right for pro football I'm thinking mostly of an incident related to me by an old Baltimore teammate, Wendell Harris. Wendell had played at Louisiana State, where Taylor had played a bit earlier, and one day in the off-season Wendell was exercising a weak knee by running up and down an aisle in the LSU stadium. He thought the stadium was empty, but then he looked down to the field and saw Taylor working out. Taylor was beating his backside against the stadium wall. "Jim!" yelled Wendell. "What are you doing?"

Taylor turned halfway around and patted himself on the backside. "I got the toughest ass in the business!" he barked, and with that he walked proudly out of the stadium.

He was all football player, Jim Taylor was, but then, as the gold began to flow on all sides, he started thinking about security. He played out his option at Green Bay. Vince Lombardi said, "The hell with him." Taylor went to New Orleans on a fat contract, but you'll notice that he instantly turned into a shadow of the player he had been.

Be that as it may, one day toward the end of my career in the NFL, Don Shula was moved to point out just how far *I* had come." You know, I saw you play for South Carolina," he told me, "and I put you down as a surefire pro prospect. I told myself, 'Can't miss, offensively or defensively.' " Shula stroked his chin for a few moments and then said, "Hawk, it just goes to show you how wrong a guy can be."

I PLAYED in the NFL for 10 years, while men who were faster, bigger and stronger than I were cut. Why? A nagging question. I believe the reason was that I was fanatically endowed with intangible qualities. For example, when he was coaching at Baltimore, Don Shula found that I had a better-than-average ability to humor the type of teammate who tends to make Page One by breaking up saloons. Shula knew, too, that if I happened to be broken in half along with the barroom mirror, well, the club would suffer no great loss. Therefore, one summer morning on 1964 he called me to his training-camp office and said, "Hawk, we've just traded with the Steelers for Lou Michaels. How about rooming with him?"

"Absolutely not," I said. Michaels's reputation, which one might summarize as being predictably unpredictable, had preceded him. He's a burly guy with a 5 o'clock shadow on a face that ought to belong to an Arkansas prison guard. As a matter of fact, the Steelers had got rid of him because one night, just as a defensive back named Jim Bradshaw was emerging from the training-camp bathroom whistling a cheerful tune, he walked straight into a left hand thrown by Lou and was put to sleep without having reached bed. I told Shula, "I am not going to room with anyone who's crazier than I am."

"O.K., O.K.," said Shula. "But do this for me—look after him. Sort of keep an eye on him, O.K.?" I gave Shula my word that I'd do what I could.

At a tavern a few days later, as Lou and I sat in a booth drinking a little too much, I began needling him, because I felt intelligent talking to him. I told him he could learn a thing or two from me. This caused him at last to announce, "Let me tell *you* something. I'm going to tear your head off."

"Well, Lou," I said, "you go right ahead and take your best shot." I leaned over the table and stuck out my jaw. While Lou was getting ready, polishing his left fist with his right hand, I said, "By the way, has anybody told you?"

"Told me what?"

"You mean you don't know?"

"Know *what*? What are you talking about?"

"Lord! I guess nobody *has* told you, Lou." I said, "I own the ball club."

"Don't give me that," snapped Lou. "Carroll Rosenbloom owns the club."

"Yes, but I'm a silent partner. I own a piece of it. As a matter of fact, the night before we traded for you, Carroll called me and said, 'Lou Michaels is available. What do you think?' And I said, 'Well, let's take a look at him. I'll be with the team all the time, and if I catch him stepping out of line we'll send him back to Swoyersville, Pa. with no transportation money.' Now, then, Lou," I said, "you just go right ahead and take your best shot."

"You expect me to buy that?" he said. "You think I'm some kind of dummy?"

"Suit yourself. But here's something you ought to think about. In the few days you've been with the Colts, have you seen me do any real work at practice?" It was true that I hadn't, because Shula usually preferred that I stay out of everyone's way, holding myself ready in the event of a man-power crisis. "You see," I went on, "the reasons I get away with loafing is that I'm a player-owner."

Lou unclenched his fist, but he remained unconvinced—confused but still unconvinced. The next day, however, I gathered some of the boys and front-office man Bert Bell Jr. and equipment manager Freddie Schubach to propose a small conspiracy. In the days that followed, Lou began over-hearing interesting remarks in the dressing room. "Well," a voice would say, "it looks like the Hawk's team will be O.K. this year." Later, another voice would say, "I got drunk the other night but it's all right—the Hawk didn't find out about it."

From that point, Lou insisted on paying for my drinks. Furthermore, I found it a cinch to fulfill the mission given me by Shula. One night, for ex-ample, when Lou was about to throw a policeman out of a bar, I gave him a stern shaking and sent him home.

Since I was doing such a good job with Lou, Shula assigned me to the famous rookie Joe Don Looney, who had flattened an assistant coach in college. "No," I told Shula, "I am not going to be in the same room with him with the lights out." As in Lou's case, Shula settled for a promise that I would keep an eye on Looney.

One night I received a phone call from a policeman, who said, "I understand you know how to speak Looney language, is that right?"

"We communicate for time to time," I answered.

"Well, we've got him down here at the station. He worked over a couple of guys pretty good, but apparently they're Colt fans and they can't make up their minds whether to press charges. Meanwhile, Looney is acting very belligerent, and we're thinking that it might be helpful if you talked to him."

Now Joe Don, in all fairness, is a very nice boy, a lad I count as a friend. He rarely drinks. But when he does, only a few beers are enough to put him in the mood to slug a couple of total strangers, which is precisely what he had done on the evening in question. By the time I reached the station, however, he had departed, the cops having neither the papers nor the will to stop him. I phoned the Colts' general manager, the late Don Kellett, figuring that Joe Don might be in deep trouble and need help from the top. "Find him," said Kellett, "and stay with him."

At about 1 a.m., I found Joe Don at his apartment. I tried to engage him in conversation. He began to talk about his "five-year plan." Joe Don, you see, was a physical-culture fanatic. He showed me pictures of an island of Australia, explaining that he was saving to buy it in partnership with our friends who were equally concerned with the advancement of the human physique. "What are you going to do with this island, Joe Don?" I inquired.

"We're going to get some healthy girls and take 'em over on a boat," he said, "and then we're just going to breed." Eyes glazed, he informed me that he intended to breed a super race. I kept myself awake until Joe Don dropped off at 5 a.m. As I had told Shula, there was no way in the world I was going to fall asleep in the same room with that man while he remained mobile.

Established therefore as having a talent in player relations, I had a good thing going for me in Baltimore. But in the spring of 1965, looking ahead to my seventh season with the Colts, I committed a serious mistake. I began to think I had football talent. The notion occurred to me when I started hearing reports that the league intended to put an expansion franchise in Atlanta. If I could get with Atlanta, I thought, I no longer would be hidden in the shadows of Raymond Berry and Jimmy Orr. No longer would I be flip-flopping from one position to another, my place dictated by the injuries of other men. I could concentrate on a single position and bring to it my years of savvy. By God, I could become a starter!

Consequently, when it was announced that Atlanta was in business, I reminded Shula of a promise he had made—namely, that in the event of a new franchise he would place my name in the expansion pool. "Hawk," he said, "you have no idea how much confusion there is with an expansion club. If you insist on holding me to my word, all right, but you're going to be sorry." I shrugged. I could scarcely wait for the day I would report to the Falcons' training camp at Black Mountain, in North Carolina, a place that, in the light of developments, I came to call Camp Runamuck.

This sylvan retreat lay 35 miles from Asheville in a mountainous forest, a perfectly sensible location if you are planning to re-create Fort Leavenworth. Driving out from Asheville, I observed with a certain sense of uneasiness that along the entire 35 miles—at least 10 of them torn up—there appeared to be only one bar, and that one about the size of a small porch. I turned off the highway and climbed a narrow, twisting road that led through the forest until at last I came upon a sun-broiled clearing, Camp Runamuck. Formally, it was known as the Blue Ridge Assembly, a YMCA camp. After taking in the compound of ancient frame buildings, I drove off to find the practice field, following the twisting road through half a mile of forest to another clearing, which the Falcons had created by removing about 300 trees. This was the practice field. I tested the ground and found it harder than Peachtree Street at high noon.

"Hello, Leavenworth," I said. "And good-bye, Leavenworth." I drove straight back to Asheville and phoned Shula. "Sorry, I can't help you now," he said. "Maybe you'll learn to like it."

Norb Hecker had come down from Green Bay to be the Falcons' head coach, and because he was determined to be another Lombardi he decided to establish that he was boss. The way he did it was to tire everybody. When he wasn't holding meetings he was running us through sprints under a blazing sun, players keeling over and gasping like fish washed up on a beach. Each Wednesday, Hecker gave us a holiday, which lasted four hours—from 7 p.m. till 11. Subtracting the almost two hours required to travel to and from Asheville, and knowing that Asheville is not exactly Miami Beach, it hardly paid to turn over the motor. The daily grind began eating at us. Bill Jobko, once a good linebacker, but nearing the end of the trail, keep up an easygoing appearance, at no time complaining, but one day I walked into his room and found him lying in bed gazing at a spider. He turned to me and said, "Alex, I'm in trouble."

"What's wrong, Bill?" I asked.

"Well, for the past three days, off and on, I've been watching that spider spin his web, and you know something? I'm beginning to enjoy it."

Through July and August, Hecker's Camp Runamuck legion plodded on. But come September our food supply began to run out. From the beginning, eating had been a problem. For one thing, an unending series of Protestant religious conferences took place at Runamuck, the result being that at mealtimes we were as apt as not to be locked out of the cafeteria until a lot of little old ladies had put away the last of their tapioca pudding and patted their lips. Also, the dietitian had quit following a run-in with our trainer. And once, after we had sat down to an old North Carolina mountain dish—spaghetti—ballplayers took sick in droves. But now I learned that a true crisis had come upon us. I was approached by a young man who was one of a group of college kids hired to work in the kitchen and cafeteria. "What do you like to eat?" he said.

"Why do you ask that?" I said

"Well, the cooks have left because they agreed to work only for the summer, and the college kids are going back to school. On account of the emergency, four of us have agreed to stay on. I'm the new head cook."

"Can you cook?" I asked.

"No, but I think we can survive if you like canned soup." In the week that remained of camp the players lost, on the average, 15 pounds.

You've heard of people burning their bridges behind them? Well, when we broke camp two of our players went down to a creek bordering the compound and burned a wooden bridge.

Don Shula, to be sure, had warned me about life with an expansion club, and though I had reached my goal, though I had won a job as a starter, I could see he had been right. On the festive day we opened the season against the Los Angeles Rams in Atlanta, a peculiar set of developments occurred that caused me to tell myself, "Yes, this is going to be all uphill."

From the sideline Hecker sent us instructions to run a sweep against Deacon Jones. The play puzzled us, because our game plan called for no sweeps against Deacon's side, but we ran the play anyway and gained about a yard. I noticed that for some reason Hecker appeared pleased. He sent us another messenger, this time with a play none of us had ever heard of. The player knelt in the huddle and drew it on the infield sand. It was then we learned why we had run the sweep. The idea was to move the ball over to the infield base path. That way we would reach sand and the messenger could draw the next play.

Expansion football proved to be everything that its worst critics called it, the proof being that I finished the 1966 season as the Falcons' leading receiver. Knowing how ridiculous it was that I should rank No. 1 in anything but fines paid, I came back to earth. Forced to look at myself on film, I realized just how terrible I was, and I arrived at the conclusion that I would rather be a backup man with a good club than a first-stringer with an expansion team. Three weeks into the next season I celebrated upon learning that Shula had swung a nothing-for-nothing trade that would take me back to Baltimore for my remaining two years of pro ball.

Even knowing my limitations, I saw one last chance to distinguish myself in a small way before calling it a career. In honor of Don Kellett, who had retired from the general manager's office the previous winter, the Colts had established the Don Kellett Award, which carried a prize of $5,000 that at season's end would go to the player who most typified the Colt spirit. Of course, nobody ever doubted that I had spirit. I played recklessly, if not well. I had captained the Colts' suicide squad, had I not? Furthermore, taking into account the character of the members of the three-man board appointed to select the award winner, I had every reason to believe that the $5,000 Don Kellett Award was within my reach. The board consisted of the three Baltimore writers covering the team—Cameron Snyder, Larry Harris and N. P. Clark. I knew the quality they most admired in a player. As soon as I rejoined the Baltimore club, I started buying them drinks.

Within a month the board agreed, informally, that there could be only one choice. Until Halloween night, I was a lock. On that fateful night, while the kiddies of Baltimore were out trick-or-treating and mugging, I sat in the back room of a shopping-center barbershop enjoying a lively game of poker. About 5 a.m. a commotion out front caused us to look up and see a handful of men dressed in woodchopper costumes burst into the back room. They were, it turned out, Baltimore county police. Right away the one in charge blew his opening line, "This is a card game!" he announced. "I mean, this is a raid!"

With that, we all just sat there, wondering if he was joking. "You're all under arrest," he said. "Everybody stay seated, because we got a photographer here who's going to take pictures." We sat for a team picture, but the photographer couldn't get the camera to work. So the head man sent to the station house for another camera.

The second camera wouldn't work, either. The flash wouldn't go off. So the raiders canceled the team picture and started loading us into a paddy wagon, whereupon a new difficulty developed. Nine poker players and a handful of cops were more than the wagon could hold. Three players remained at the curb. "Tell you what," said one of them. "You taking us to a bailiff's office? O.K., I'll drive the rest of us there in my car, but I don't know the way, so I'll have to follow you." The cops agreed, so off we went, me with the boys in the wagon, the overflow following.

Along the way, however, the paddy wagon put on a burst of speed to make a light and left the boys in the car behind. They got lost, and we had to turn back to search for them. All the while, I'm thinking, Story of my life—I can't even get arrested successfully.

Finally we located the others, but when we arrived at the bailiff's office, it was closed; he had gone home. So off we went to a station house. After posting bail, I freshened up and went straight to Shula's office, figuring it would be wise to break the news to him before he saw it in the afternoon papers. "I already heard it on the 7 o'clock news," Shula said, straightaway. "What the hell were you doing in that barbershop at 4:45 in the morning?"

"Look," I said, "you know how I hate to wait in lines."

"This is very serious," Shula snapped. "Rozelle already has talked to Rosenbloom on the phone. You're to call Rosenbloom immediately."

A minute later Rosenbloom was telling me the guy running the card game had 33 arrests for selling parlay cards. Now if he had committed three murders it probably would have been a minor matter, but Pete Rozelle is touchy about known gamblers and the player contract stipulates that we cannot have any association with them.

Anyhow, Rosenbloom advised me to keep my nose clean and refrain from speaking to reporters, which was a ridiculous thing to tell a guy who was relying on three of them for a $5,000 award. First thing after practice that day, Larry Harris of the *Evening Sun* said, "What were you doing up at 4:45 playing cards with a guy with 33 arrests?"

"Jeez!" I shot back, unable to keep my mouth shut. "You're up at 4:45 it's tough enough to get a game going, you can't screen the applicants!"

Later, as I read my words in the paper, I realized that I hadn't helped my case.

The next afternoon Harris and Cameron Snyder approached me. "Hawk," said Larry, "I'm worried. You know how Rozelle came down on Karras and Hornung for associating with gamblers. This looks very serious."

"All right," I said. "You guys have always protected me before, so get busy now. Turn it into a joke."

"Not a bad idea," said Snyder. "It just might work." The next day a picture of me catching a pass appeared in the afternoon paper. The caption read, "Winning Hands!" It went on to say, "Alex Hawkins . . . always at his best when the chips are down . . . especially adept at handling the inside-straight pass routes." In another newspaper my picture bore the caption "Ace in the Hole!" All week the newspaper boys poured it on, until the Alex Hawkins Scandal was practically laughed into oblivion.

On Sunday, against the Packers, we trailed 10–0 with six minutes remaining. The game was lost—nobody beat those Packers when they had a 10-point lead with six minutes to play—so Shula said. "It's all over," and put me into the game. With 2:19 left on the clock, Unitas threw me a touchdown pass. And then, bingbang, we recovered an onside kick and Unitas threw a touchdown pass to Willie Richardson. We had beaten the Packers! Richardson's catch was the big story, of course, but not in the Baltimore papers. The Don Kellett Award board couldn't find enough ink to describe my catch, and as the Colts went on to win their next five games, that catch was remembered in the papers as the play that touched off the winning streak.

So I survived another season, weathering ugly looks from Rozelle's office, and went on to make it an even 10 years in the NFL. Finally, I retired, having concluded that the game is in a sorry condition when the newspaper guys are more fun than the players.

Oh, yes—about the Kellett Award. No, I didn't get it. The front office, knowing of no way to prevent the board from voting me in, canceled the award. The Colts gave the $5,000 to charity. Unwilling to forget the poker game, Shula fined me $500.

| | | | | |

Concrete Charlie

BY JOHN SCHULIAN

*Chuck Bednarik, the last of the 60-minute men, was a pillar of strength at both
linebacker and center for the 1960 NFL champion Philadelphia Eagles.*

E WENT DOWN HARD, LEFT IN A HEAP BY A CRACK-
back block as naked as it was vicious. Pro football was
like that in 1960, a gang fight in shoulder pads, its violence devoid of the high-tech veneer it has today. The
crackback was legal, and all the Philadelphia Eagles could do about it that
Sunday in Cleveland was carry a linebacker named Bob Pellegrini off on his
shield.

Buck Shaw, a gentleman coach in this ruffian's pastime, watched for as
long as he could, then he started searching the Eagle sideline for someone
to throw into the breach. His first choice was already banged up, and after
that the standard 38-man NFL roster felt as tight as a hangman's noose.
Looking back, you realize that Shaw had only one choice all along.

"Chuck," he said, "get in there."

And Charles Philip Bednarik, who already had a full-time job as Philadelphia's offensive center and a part-time job selling concrete after practice,
headed onto the field without a word. Just the way his father had marched
off to the open-hearth furnaces at Bethlehem Steel on so many heartless

mornings. Just the way Bednarik himself had climbed behind the machine gun in a B-24 for 30 missions as a teenager fighting in World War II. It was a family tradition: Duty called, you answered.

Chuck Bednarik was 35 years old, still imposing at 6' 3" and 235 pounds, but also the father of one daughter too many to be what he really had in mind—retired. Jackie's birth the previous February gave him five children, all girls, and more bills than he thought he could handle without football. So here he was in his 12th NFL season, telling himself he was taking it easy on his creaky legs by playing center after all those years as an All-Pro linebacker. The only time he intended to move back to defense was in practice, when he wanted to work up a little extra sweat.

And now, five games into the season, this: Jim Brown over there in the Cleveland huddle, waiting to trample some fresh meat, and Bednarik trying to decipher the defensive terminology the Eagles had installed in the two years since he was their middle linebacker. Chuck Weber had his old job now, and Bednarik found himself asking what the left outside linebacker was supposed to do on passing plays. "Take the second man out of the backfield," Weber said. That was as fancy as it would get. Everything else would be about putting the wood to Jim Brown.

Bednarik nodded and turned to face a destiny that went far beyond emergency duty at linebacker. He was taking his first step toward a place in NFL history as the kind of player they don't make anymore.

THE KIDS start at about 7 a.m. and don't stop until fatigue slips them a Mickey after dark. For 20 months it has been this way, three grandchildren roaring around like gnats with turbochargers, and Bednarik feeling every one of his years. And hating the feeling. And letting the kids know about it.

Get to be 68 and you deserve to turn the volume on your life as low as you want it. That's what Bednarik thinks, not without justification. But life has been even more unfair to the kids than it has been to him. The girl is eight, the boys are six and five, and they live with Bednarik and his wife in Coopersburg, Pa., because of a marriage gone bad. The kids' mother, Donna, is there too, trying to put her life back together, flinching every time her father's anger erupts. "I can't help it," Bednarik says plaintively. "It's the way I am."

The explanation means nothing to the kids warily eyeing this big man with the flattened nose and the gnarled fingers and the faded tattoos on his right arm. He is one more question in a world that seemingly exists to deny them answers. Only with the passage of time will they realize they were yelled at by Concrete Charlie, the toughest Philadelphia Eagle there ever was.

But for the moment, football makes no more sense to the kids than does anything else about their grandfather. "I'm not *one* of the last 60-minute players," they hear him say. "I am the last." Then he barks at them to stop making so much noise and to clean up the mess they made in the family room, where trophies, photographs and game balls form a mosaic of the best days of his life. The kids scamper out of sight, years from comprehending the significance of what Bednarik is saying.

He really was the last of a breed. For 58½ minutes in the NFL's 1960 championship game, he held his ground in the middle of Philly's Franklin Field, a force of nature determined to postpone the christening of the Green Bay Packers' dynasty. "I didn't run down on kickoffs, that's all," Bednarik says. The rest of that frosty Dec. 26, on both offense and defense, he played with the passion that crested when he wrestled Packers fullback Jim Taylor to the ground one last time and held him there until the final gun punctuated the Eagles' 17–13 victory.

Philadelphia hasn't ruled pro football since then, and pro football hasn't produced a player with the combination of talent, hunger and opportunity to duplicate what Bednarik did. It is a far different game now, of course, its complexities seeming to increase exponentially every year, but the athletes playing it are so much bigger and faster than Bednarik and his contemporaries that surely someone with the ability to go both ways must dwell among them. It is easy to imagine Walter Payton having shifted from running back to safety, or Lawrence Taylor moving from linebacker to tight end. But that day is long past, for the NFL of the '90s is a monument to specialization.

There are running backs who block but don't run, others who run but only from inside the five-yard line and still others who exist for no other reason than to catch passes. Some linebackers can't play the run, and some can't play the pass, and there are monsters on the defensive line who dream of decapitating quarterbacks but resemble the Maiden Surprised when they come face mask to face mask with a pulling guard.

"No way in hell any of them can go both ways," Bednarik insists.

"They don't want to. They're afraid they'll get hurt. And the money's too big, that's another thing. They'd just say, 'Forget it, I'm already making enough.'"

The sentiment is what you might expect from someone who signed with the Eagles for $10,000 when he left the University of Pennsylvania for the 1949 season and who was pulling down only 17 grand when he made sure they were champions 11 years later. Seventeen grand, and Reggie White fled Philadelphia for Green Bay over the winter for what, $4 million a year? "If he gets that much," Bednarik says, "I should be in the same class." But at least White has already proved that someday he will be taking his place alongside Concrete Charlie in the Hall of Fame. At least he isn't a runny-nosed quarterback like Drew Bledsoe, signing a long-term deal for $14.5 million before he has ever taken a snap for the New England Patriots. "When I read about that," Bednarik says, "I wanted to regurgitate."

He nurtures the resentment he is sure every star of his era shares, feeding it with the dollar figures he sees in the sports pages every day, priming it with the memory that his fattest contract with the Eagles paid him $25,000, in 1962, his farewell season.

"People laugh when they hear what I made," he says. "I tell them, 'Hey, don't laugh at me. I could do everything but eat a football.'" Even when he was in his 50s, brought back by then coach Dick Vermeil to show the struggling Eagles what a champion looked like, Bednarik was something to behold. He walked into training camp, bent over the first ball he saw and whistled a strike back through his legs to a punter unused to such service from the team's long snappers. "And you know the amazing thing?" Vermeil says. "Chuck didn't look."

He was born for the game, a physical giant among his generation's line-backers, and so versatile that he occasionally got the call to punt and kick off. "This guy was a football athlete," says Nick Skorich, an Eagle assistant and head coach for six years. "He was a very strong blocker at center and quick as a cat off the ball." He had to be, because week in, week out he was tangling with Sam Huff or Joe Schmidt, Bill George or Les Richter, the best middle linebackers of the day. Bednarik more than held his own against them, or so we are told, which is the problem with judging the performance of any center. Who the hell knows what's happening in that pile of humanity?

It is different with linebackers. Linebackers are out there in the open for all to see, and that was where Bednarik was always at his best. He could intercept a pass with a single meat hook and tackle with the cold-blooded efficiency of a sniper. "Dick Butkus was the one who manhandled people," says Tom Brookshier, the loquacious former Eagle cornerback. "Chuck just snapped them down like rag dolls."

It was a style that left Frank Gifford for dead, and New York seething, in 1960, and it made people everywhere forget that Concrete Charlie, for all his love of collisions, played the game in a way that went beyond the purely physical. "He was probably the most instinctive football player I've ever seen," says Maxie Baughan, a rookie linebacker with the Eagles in Bednarik's whole-schmear season. Bednarik could see a guard inching one foot backward in preparation for a sweep or a tight end setting up just a little farther from the tackle than normal for a pass play. Most important, he could think along with the best coaches in the business.

And the coaches didn't appreciate that, which may explain the rude goodbye that the Dallas Cowboys' Tom Landry tried to give Bednarik in '62. First the Cowboys ran a trap, pulling a guard and running a back through the hole. "Chuck was standing right there," Brookshier says. "Almost killed the guy." Next the Cowboys ran a sweep behind that same pulling guard, only to have Bednarik catch the ballcarrier from behind. "Almost beheaded the guy," Brookshier says. Finally the Cowboys pulled the guard, faked the sweep and threw a screen pass. Bednarik turned it into a two-yard loss. "He had such a sense for the game," Brookshier says. "You could do all that shifting and put all those men in motion, and Chuck still went right where the ball was."

Three decades later Bednarik is in his family room watching a tape from NFL Films that validates what all the fuss was about. The grandchildren have been shooed off to another part of the house, and he has found the strange peace that comes from seeing himself saying on the TV screen, "All you can think of is 'Kill, kill, kill.' " He laughs about what a ham he was back then, but the footage that follows his admission proves that it was no joke. Bednarik sinks deep in his easy chair. "This movie," he says, "turns me on even now."

Suddenly the spell is broken by a chorus of voices and a stampede through the kitchen. The grandchildren again, thundering out to the backyard. "Hey, how many times I have to tell you?" Bednarik shouts. "Close the door!"

THE PASS was behind Gifford. It was a bad delivery under the best of circumstances, life-threatening where he was now, crossing over the middle. But Gifford was too much the pro not to reach back and grab the ball. He tucked it under his arm and turned back in the right direction, all in the same motion—and then Bednarik hit him like a lifetime supply of bad news.

Thirty-three years later there are still people reeling from the Tackle, none of them named Gifford or Bednarik. In New York somebody always seems to be coming up to old number 16 of the Giants and telling him they were there the day he got starched in the Polo Grounds (it was Yankee Stadium). Other times they say that everything could have been avoided if Charlie Conerly had thrown the ball where he was supposed to (George Shaw was the guilty Giant quarterback). And then there was Howard Cosell, who sat beside Gifford on *Monday Night Football* for 14 years and seemed to bring up Bednarik whenever he was stuck for something to say. One week Cosell would accuse Bednarik of blindsiding Gifford, the next he would blame Bednarik for knocking Gifford out of football. Both were classic examples of telling it like it wasn't.

But it is too late to undo any of the above, for the Tackle has taken on a life of its own. So Gifford plays along by telling what sounds like an apocryphal story about one of his early dates with the woman who would become his third wife. "Kathie Lee," he told her, "one word you're going to hear a lot of around me is Bednarik." And Kathie Lee supposedly said, "What's that, a pasta?"

For all the laughing Gifford does when he spins that yarn, there was nothing funny about Nov. 20, 1960, the day Bednarik handed him his lunch. The Eagles, who complemented Concrete Charlie and Hall of Fame quarterback Norm Van Brocklin with a roster full of tough, resourceful John Does, blew into New York intent on knocking the Giants on their media-fed reputation. Philadelphia was leading 17–10 with under two minutes to play, but the Giants kept slashing and pounding, smelling one of those comeback victories that were supposed to be the Eagles' specialty. Then Gifford caught that pass. "I ran through him right up here," Bednarik says, slapping himself on the chest hard enough to break something. "*Right here.*" And this time he pops the passenger in his van on the chest. "It was like when you hit a home run; you say, 'Jeez, I didn't even feel it hit the bat.' "

Huff would later call it "the greatest tackle I've ever seen," but at the time it happened his emotion was utter despair. Gifford fell backward, the ball flew forward. When Weber pounced on it, Bednarik started dancing as if St. Vitus had taken possession of him. And as he danced, he yelled at Gifford, "This game is over!" But Gifford couldn't hear him.

"He didn't hurt me," Gifford insists. "When he hit me, I landed on my ass and then my head snapped back. That was what put me out—the whiplash, not Bednarik."

Whatever the cause, Gifford looked like he was past tense as he lay there motionless. A funereal silence fell over the crowd, and Bednarik rejoiced no more. He has never been given to regret, but in that moment he almost changed his ways. Maybe he actually would have repented if he had been next to the first Mrs. Gifford after her husband had been carried off on a stretcher. She was standing outside the Giants' dressing room when the team physician stuck his head out the door and said, "I'm afraid he's dead." Only after she stopped wobbling did Mrs. Gifford learn that the doctor was talking about a security guard who had suffered a heart attack during the game. Even so, Gifford didn't get off lightly. He had a concussion that kept him out for the rest of the season and all of 1961. But in '62 he returned as a flanker and played with honor for three more seasons. He would also have the good grace to invite Bednarik to play golf with him, and he would never, ever whine about the Tackle. "It was perfectly legal," Gifford says. "If I'd had the chance, I would have done the same thing to Chuck."

But all that came later. In the week after the Tackle, with a Giant-Eagle rematch looming, Gifford got back at Bednarik the only way he could, by refusing to take his calls or to acknowledge the flowers and fruit he sent to the hospital. Naturally there was talk that Gifford's teammates would try to break Concrete Charlie into little pieces, especially since Conerly kept calling him a cheap-shot artist in the papers. But talk was all it turned out to be. The Eagles, on the other hand, didn't run their mouths until after they had whipped the Giants a second time. Bednarik hasn't stopped talking since then.

"This is a true story," he says. "They're having a charity roast for Gifford in Parsippany, N.J., a couple of years ago, and I'm one of the roasters. I ask the manager of this place if he'll do me a favor. Then, when it's my turn to talk, the lights go down and it's dark for five or six seconds. Nobody knows what the hell's going on until I tell them, 'Now you know how Frank Gifford felt when I hit him.' "

HE GREW up poor, and poor boys fight the wars for this country. He never thought anything of it back then. All he knew was that every other guy from the south side of Bethlehem, Pa., was in a uniform, and he figured he should be in a uniform too. So he enlisted without finishing his senior year at Liberty High School. It was a special program they had; your mother picked up your diploma while you went off to kill or be killed. Bednarik didn't take anything with him but the memories of the place he called *Betlam* until the speech teachers at Penn classed up his pronunciation. Betlam was where his father emigrated from Czechoslovakia and worked all those years in the steel mill without making foreman because he couldn't read or write English. It was where his mother gave birth to him and his three brothers and two sisters, then shepherded them through the Depression with potato soup and second-hand clothes. It was where he made 90 cents a round caddying at Saucon Valley Country Club and $2 a day toiling on a farm at the foot of South Mountain, and gave every penny to his mother. It was where he fought in the streets and scaled the wall at the old Lehigh University stadium to play until the guards chased him off. "It was," he says, "the greatest place in the world to be a kid."

The worst place was in the sky over Europe, just him and a bunch of other kids in an Army Air Corps bomber with the Nazis down below trying to incinerate them. "The antiaircraft fire would be all around us," Bednarik says. "It was so thick you could walk on it. And you could hear it penetrating. *Ping! Ping! Ping!* Here you are, this wild, dumb kid, you didn't think you were afraid of anything, and now, every time you take off, you're convinced this is it, you're gonna be ashes."

Thirty times he went through that behind his .50-caliber machine gun. He still has the pieces of paper on which he neatly wrote each target, each date. It started with Berlin on Aug. 27, 1944, and ended with Zwiesel on April 20, 1945. He looks at those names now and remembers the base in England that he flew out of, the wake-ups at four o'clock in the morning, the big breakfasts he ate in case one of them turned out to be his last meal, the rain and fog that made just getting off the ground a dance with death. "We'd have to scratch missions because our planes kept banging together," he says. "These guys were knocking each other off."

Bednarik almost bought it himself when his plane, crippled by flak, skidded off the runway on landing and crashed. To escape he kicked out a window and jumped 20 feet to the ground. Then he did what he did after every mission, good or bad. He lit a cigarette and headed for the briefing room, where there was always a bottle on the table. "I was 18, 19 years old," he says, "and I was drinking that damn whiskey straight."

The passing of time does nothing to help him forget, because the war comes back to him whenever he looks at the tattoo on his right forearm. It isn't like the CPB monogram that adorns his right biceps, a souvenir from a night on some Army town. The tattoo on his forearm shows a flower blossoming to reveal the word MOTHER. He got it in case his plane was shot down and his arm was all that remained of him to identify.

THERE WERE only two things the Eagles didn't get from Bednarik in 1960: the color TV and the $1,000 that had been their gifts to him when he said he was retiring at the end of the previous season. The Eagles didn't ask for them back, and Bednarik didn't offer to return them. If he ever felt sheepish about it, that ended when he started going both ways.

For no player could do more for his team than Bednarik did as pro football began evolving into a game of specialists. He risked old bones that could just as easily have been out of harm's way, and even though he never missed a game that season—and only three in his entire career—every step hurt like the dickens.

Bednarik doesn't talk about it, which is surprising because, as Dick Vermeil says, "it usually takes about 20 seconds to find out what's on Chuck's mind." But this is different. This is about the code he lived by as a player, one that treated the mere thought of calling in sick as a betrayal of his manhood. "There's a difference between pain and injury," Baughan says, "and Chuck showed everybody on our team what it was."

His brave front collapsed in front of only one person, the former Emma Margetich, who married Bednarik in 1948 and went on to reward him with five daughters. It was Emma who pulled him out of bed when he couldn't make it on his own, who kneaded his aching muscles, who held his hand until he could settle into the hot bath she had drawn for him.

"Why are you doing this?" she kept asking. "They're not paying you for it." And every time, his voice little more than a whisper, he would reply, "Because we have to win." Nobody in Philadelphia felt that need more than Bednarik did, maybe because in the increasingly distant past he had been the town's biggest winner. It started when he took his high school coach's advice and became the least likely Ivy Leaguer that Penn has ever seen, a hard case who had every opponent he put a dent in screaming for the Quakers to live up to their nickname and de-emphasize football.

Next came the 1949 NFL champion Eagles, with halfback Steve Van Buren and end Pete Pihos lighting the way with their Hall of Fame greatness, and the rookie Bednarik ready to go elsewhere after warming the bench for all of his first two regular-season games. On the train home from a victory in Detroit, he took a deep breath and went to see the head coach, who refused to fly and had one of those names you don't find anymore, Earle (Greasy) Neale. "I told him, 'Coach Neale, I want to be traded, I want to go somewhere I can play,' " Bednarik says. "And after that I started every week—he had me flip-flopping between center and linebacker—and I never sat down for the next 14 years."

He got a tie clasp and a $1,100 winner's share for being part of that championship season, and then it seemed that he would never be treated so royally again. Some years before their return to glory, the Eagles were plug-ugly, others they managed to maintain their dignity, but the team's best always fell short of Bednarik's. From 1950 to '56 and in '60 he was an All-Pro linebacker. In the '54 Pro Bowl he punted in place of the injured Charlie Trippi and spent the rest of the game winning the MVP award by recovering three fumbles and running an interception back for a touchdown. But Bednarik did not return to the winner's circle until Van Brocklin hit town.

As far as everybody else in the league was concerned, when the Los Angeles Rams traded the Dutchman to Philadelphia months before the opening of the '58 season, it just meant one more Eagle with a tainted reputation. Tommy McDonald was being accused of making up his pass patterns as he went along, Brookshier was deemed too slow to play cornerback, and end Pete Retzlaff bore the taint of having been cut twice by Detroit. And now they had Van Brocklin, a long-in-the-tooth quarterback with the disposition of an unfed doberman.

In Philly, however, he was able to do what he hadn't done in L.A. He won. And winning rendered his personality deficiencies secondary. So McDonald had to take it when Van Brocklin told him that a separated shoulder wasn't reason enough to leave a game, and Brookshier, fearing he had been paralyzed after making a tackle, had to grit his teeth when the Dutch-man ordered his carcass dragged off the field. "Actually Van Brocklin was a lot like me," Bednarik says. "We both had that heavy temperament."

But once you got past Dutch's mouth, he didn't weigh much. The Eagles knew that Van Brocklin wasn't one to stand and fight, having seen him hightail it away from a postgame beef with Pellegrini in Los Angeles. Con-crete Charlie, on the other hand, was as two-fisted as they came. He decked a teammate who was clowning around during calisthenics just as readily as he tried to punch the face off a Pittsburgh Steeler guard named Chuck Noll. Somehow, though, Bednarik was even tougher on himself. In '61, for ex-ample, he tore his right biceps so terribly that it wound up in a lump by his elbow. "He hardly missed a down," says Skorich, who had ascended to head coach by then, "and I know for a fact he's never let a doctor touch his arm." That was the kind of man it took to go both ways in an era when the species was all but extinct.

The San Francisco 49ers were reluctant to ask Leo Nomellini to play offensive tackle, preferring that he pour all his energy into defense, and the Giants no longer let Gifford wear himself out at defensive back. In the early days of the American Football League the Kansas City Chiefs had linebacker E.J. Holub double-dipping at center until his ravaged knees put him on offense permanently. But none of them ever carried the load that Bednarik did. When Buck Shaw kept asking him to go both ways, there was a championship riding on it. "Give it up, old man," Paul Brown said when Bednarik got knocked out of bounds and landed at his feet in that championship season. Bednarik responded by calling the patriarch of the Browns a 10-letter obscenity. Damned if he would give anything up.

All five times the Eagles needed him to be an iron man that season, they won. Even when they tried to take it easy on him by playing him on only one side of the ball, he still wound up doing double duty the way he did the day he nailed Gifford. A rookie took his place at center just long enough to be overmatched by the Giants' blitzes. In came Bednarik, and on the first play he knocked the red-dogging Huff on his dime. "That's all for you, Sam," Bednarik said. "The big guys are in now."

And that was how the season went, right up to the day after Christmas and what Bednarik calls "the greatest game I ever played." It was the Eagles and Green Bay for the NFL championship at Franklin Field, where Bednarik had played his college ball, and there would be no coming out, save for the kickoffs. It didn't look like there would be any losing either, after Bednarik nearly yanked Packers sweep artist Paul Hornung's arm out of its socket. But there was no quit in Vince Lombardi's Pack. By the game's final moments, they had the Eagles clinging to a 17–13 lead, and Bart Starr was throwing a screen pass to that raging bull Taylor at the Philadelphia 23. Baughan had the first shot at him, but Taylor cut back and broke Baughan's tackle. Then he ran through safety Don Burroughs. And then it was just Taylor and Bednarik at the 10. In another season, with another set of circumstances, Taylor might have been stopped by no man. But this was the coronation of Concrete Charlie. Taylor didn't have a chance as Bednarik dragged him to the ground and the other Eagles piled on. He kicked and cussed and struggled to break free, but Bednarik kept him pinned where he was while precious seconds ticked off the clock, a maneuver that NFL rule-makers would later outlaw. Only when the final gun sounded did Bednarik roll off him and say, "O.K., you can get up now."

It was a play they will always remember in Philadelphia, on a day they will always remember in Philadelphia. When Bednarik floated off the field, he hardly paid attention to the news that Van Brocklin had been named the game's most valuable player. For nine-of-20 passing that produced one touchdown—an ordinary performance, but also his last one as a player—the Dutchman drove off in the sports car that the award earned him. Sometime later Bednarik caught a ride to Atlantic City with Retzlaff and halfway there blurted out that he felt like Paul Revere's horse.

"What do you mean by that?" the startled Retzlaff asked.

"The horse did all the work," Bednarik said, "but Paul Revere got all the credit."

IN THE mornings he will pick up his accordion and play the sweet, sad "etnik" music he loves so much. As his football-warped fingers thump up and down the keyboard, he often wishes he and Emma and the girls had a family band, the kind Emma's father had that summer night he met her at the Croatian Hall in Bethlehem. Not what you might expect, but then Bednarik is a man of contradictions. Like his not moving any farther than his easy chair to watch the Eagles anymore. Like his going to 8 a.m. Mass every Sunday and saying the Rosary daily with the industrial-strength beads that Cardinal Krol of Philadelphia gave him. "I'm a very religious person, I believe in prayer," Bednarik says, "but I've got this violent temper." Sixty-eight years old and there is still no telling when he will chase some joker who cut him off in traffic or gave him the finger for winning the race to a parking place. If anybody ever thought he would mellow, Bednarik put that idea to rest a few years back when he tangled with a bulldozer operator almost 40 years his junior. As evening fell the guy was still leveling some nearby farmland for housing sites, so Bednarik broke away from his cocktail hour to put in a profane request for a little peace and quiet. One verb led to another, and the next thing Bednarik knew, he thought the guy was going to push a tree over on him. He reacted in classic Concrete Charlie fashion and got a fine that sounded like it came from the World Wrestling Federation instead of the local justice of the peace: $250 for choking.

That wouldn't change him, though. It slowed him down, made him hope that when he dies, people will find it in their hearts to say he was a good egg despite all his hard edges. But it couldn't stop him from becoming as gnarly as ever the instant a stranger asked whether he, Chuck Bednarik, the last of the 60-minute men, could have played in today's NFL. "I wasn't rude or anything," he says, "but inside I was thinking: I'd like to punch this guy in the mouth."

Of course. He is Concrete Charlie. "You know, people still call me that," he says, "and I love it." So he does everything he can to live up to the nickname, helping to oversee boxing in Pennsylvania for the state athletic commission, getting enough exercise to stay six pounds under his final playing weight of 242, golfing in every celebrity tournament that will invite Emma along with him, refusing to give ground to the artificial knee he got last December. "It's supposed to take older people a year to get through the rehab," he says. "I was done in four months." Of course. He is the toughest Philadelphia Eagle there ever was.

But every time he looks in the mirror, he wonders how much longer that will last. Not so many years ago he would flex his muscles and roar, "I'm never gonna die!" Now he studies the age in his eyes and whispers, "Whoa, go back, go back." But he can't do it. He thinks instead of the six teammates from the 1960 Eagles who have died. And when he sees a picture of himself with six other Hall of Fame inductees from 1967, he realizes he is the only one still living. It is at such a moment that he digs out the letter he got from Greasy Neale, his first coach with the Eagles, shortly after he made it to the Hall. "Here, read this out loud," Bednarik says, thrusting the letter at a visitor. "I want to hear it."

There is no point in asking how many times he has done this before. He is already looking at the far wall in the family room, waiting to hear words so heartfelt that the unsteady hand with which they were written just makes them seem that much more sincere. Neale thought he hadn't given Bednarik the kind of introduction he deserved at the Hall, and the letter was the old coach's apology. In it he talked about Bednarik's ability, his range, his desire—all the things Neale would have praised if his role as the day's first speaker hadn't prevented him from knowing how long everybody else was going to carry on.

"If I had it to do over again," he wrote in closing, "I would give you as great a send-off as the others received. You deserve anything I could have said about you, Chuck. You were the greatest."

Then the room is filled with a silence that is louder than Bednarik's grandchildren have ever been. It will stay that way until Concrete Charlie can blink back the tears welling in his eyes.

| | | | | |

'I'll Do Anything
I Can Get Away With'

BY DAPHNE HURFORD

What's a little holding or eye-gouging or biting between NFL players?
For St. Louis's controversial guard Conrad Dobler, "anything" on a
football field seemed to be everything short of nuclear warfare.

NE OF THE QUESTIONS ON THE NFL'S PERSONNEL
survey form is, "Did you take up football for any particu-
lar reason?" Conrad Dobler's answer was, "It is still the
only sport where there is controlled violence mixed with
careful technical planning. Football is still a very physical game."

What Dobler, the All-Pro right guard for the St. Louis Cardinals, means by
controlled violence, careful technical planning and *a very physical game* is:
"I'll do anything I can get away with to protect my quarterback." And according to his opponents, what Dobler gets away with is holding, eye-
gouging, face-mask twisting, leg-whipping, tripping, even biting.

Outside St. Louis, Dobler is considered the dirtiest player in the league.
In one game Dobler's tactics so infuriated Merlin Olsen, defensive tackle
of the Los Angeles Rams, that Olsen swore he would never utter Dobler's
name again. However, there is one player who has good reason to utter
Dobler's name in his prayers—Cardinal quarterback Jim Hart. Thanks to the

protection—legal or otherwise—afforded by Dobler and his linemates, Hart has been sacked only 41 times over the last three seasons, an NFL low. Among others who recognize Dobler's prowess are the NFL coaches, who have twice picked him to start in the Pro Bowl.

Dobler was just another obscure lineman until 1974, his third season in the league, when some Minnesota Vikings jokingly requested rabies shots before a game against the Cardinals. Suddenly Dobler had acquired an image. "What you need when you play against Dobler," said one rival, "is a string of garlic buds around your neck and a wooden stake. If they played every game under a full moon, Dobler would make All-Pro. He must be the only guy in the league who sleeps in a casket." When the camera showed Dobler going through his repertoire during a telecast of a St. Louis-Dallas game, commentator Tom Brookshier wondered aloud, "How does he get away with it?"

Asked the same question, Dobler says that he holds no more than any other player, that he would get caught more often if he did, and that reports of his dastardly deeds have been exaggerated. In the next breath he says that rules are made to be broken and adds, with a slightly superior air, "If you're going to break the rules, you've got to have a little style and class." Asked if he really bites opponents, Dobler usually replies that he would never do such a tasteless thing, believing as he does in good oral hygiene. Of course, he adds, "If someone stuck his hand in your face mask and put his fingers in your mouth, what would *you* do?"

While Dobler insists that he is an aggrieved party as far as holding is concerned, he willingly offers a few hints on the best way to hold a defensive lineman or a blitzing linebacker. "Always keep your hands inside your chest because it's much harder for the referees to see them when they're in there," he says, "and if a guy does get past you, grab his face mask, not his jersey." Dobler also recommends "hooking"—clamping the opponent with your arm and dragging him down—as an effective means of detaining defenders.

"Sometimes I hold by accident," he says. "I get my hand caught in a face mask. But always remember this: At no time do my fingers leave my hand."

Surprisingly, Dobler rarely uses his tongue on rivals. "You have to get just the right comment to make them mad," he says. "Verbal abuse could take all day. A faster and more efficient way to aggravate and intimidate people is to knock the stuffing out of them." Dobler particularly likes to aggravate and intimidate Pro Bowlers, first-round draft choices and players whose salaries are higher than his $50,000 a year. "Of course I'm vindictive," he says. "I was a fifth-round draft choice, and who ever heard of a player from Wyoming?"

Born in Chicago, Dobler grew up in the middle of the Mojave Desert at Twentynine Palms, Calif. There are seven Dobler children—Corrine, Cynthia, Clifford, Conrad, Christopher, Catherine and Cassandra—and Conrad always was considered the "meanest kid" in the family. Catherine, who was unlucky enough to win the starring role in a charming Joan of Arc game devised by her brother, says Conrad "was always mean and ornery and liked to show off his muscles." Conrad's mother Clara says her son was always compassionate and eager to help someone less fortunate, that he is definitely "a winner, not a loser" and that he has always been "just like his father." His father, a former Golden Gloves fighter whom Conrad calls "Big John," says that "Conrad plays pretty good football from what they tell me" and adds that his son "is not quite as mean as they say he is." As proof he offers a tale about Conrad, then nine, escorting his mother to the doctor after she had cut her hand and fainting at the sight of her blood.

Conrad claims he has always been motivated by a lack of peer approval. After attending a Catholic grammar school, where there were only eight students in his graduating class, he went to a large high school where he felt lost and insignificant. To gain acceptance he took up football and basketball. "I never finished a basketball game," he says. "I always fouled out. Something just seemed to come over me. I had more fouls, I think, than the second string had points." A football scholarship took him to the University of Wyoming. Recently he taunted his coach at Wyoming, Jack Taylor, saying, "I'm the only 10¢ player the Cowboys ever had. All it took to recruit me was one letter." At Wyoming, Dobler maintained a B average in his political-science major and child-psychology minor.

Drafted by the Cardinals in 1972, Dobler was released before his rookie season. Luckily for him a number of the Cardinals' linemen were injured early on, and they re-signed Dobler in time for their third game. "When I came back I decided that I'd just play my own game," he says. "I'd do what I do best and make the other guys play into my hands, make them have to beat me."

Jim Hanifan, St. Louis' offensive line coach, says of his right guard, "You'd have to kill him to beat him."

Dobler smiles. "When you're fighting in the dirt for a position, climbing up from the bottom, you know what it is to compete," he says. "If we both wanted it, I'd want it more. I'd mow 'em right down with no compassion, no mercy."

By midseason of 1972 Dobler had become the Cardinals' starting right guard, and he currently has no plans to vacate the position. "I've thrived on criticism," he says. "Tell me I can't do it, and that's all I need. When I started out, no one gave a damn who I was. I had to prove to everyone that they had a fight on their hands. All the bad-mouthing I get is just fuel. If a guy says he doesn't respect me, he just makes my job that much easier." When Olsen accused Dobler of having a tremendous ego, Dobler replied, "If you don't have an ago, you're a wino." When Minnesota defensive tackle Doug Sutherland labeled Dobler a "marked man," Dobler said, "I'd have a lot more fun in this game if more people said they were going to get me. I've been playing dirty a lot longer than they have. Yeah, I'll get mine someday, but when I do, I'll take my portion plus some."

For all his tough talk, Dobler is often astonished when he watches himself on game films. "Sometimes I can't believe what I do, that I can fling my body around the way I do," he says. "Those things happen at the time. I couldn't repeat any one of them." Something certainly does come over Dobler during a game. The Greeks had a word for it: *aristeia*, that special show of valor when great warriors put forth superhuman effort. Diomedes had *aristeia*, so did Hector. What does Dobler call it? "I don't know. Insanity, maybe." Hanifan calls it a mean streak. But Homer and Hanifan would agree that the truly great warriors leave their whatever-you-call-it at the scene of battle, and away from the gridiron Dobler is a charmer.

Intelligent and articulate, he is quick to laugh and has a gentle, polite manner. He lights women's cigarettes, saying, "I once dated a sorority girl," and never forgets to add, "It's just an adjective" when he thinks his language might offend. His intensity shows in his chewed nails and in his restlessness; his hunger for approval shows in his attempts to entertain. He even does magic tricks. Dobler holds strong opinions, speaks his mind freely and then worries that he spoke too freely. When a player complains about Dobler's methods, Conrad simply says, "He'll get over it." But when

Dobler feels he has hurt a friend's feelings, he says, "Oh, he'll get over it. But you know something? I won't."

Dobler's looks belie his 26 years. His dark brown hair is liberally dusted with gray. He limps as a result of arthritis in his knees, and he says he has "the bones of a 65-year-old man." His own private set of harpies keeps him from sleeping well, and when awake he can be described as hyperactive. He skis well, plays racquetball with grace and throws a dart with deadly accuracy.

During the off-season the Doblers—Conrad, wife Linda and 7-year-old son Mark, live in Laramie, Wyo. Dobler owns some property, including a bar called Block 11, in the town of Encampment (pop. 321) high in the Sierra Madres. The bar is so named because of zoning rules, not because Dobler thinks he can simultaneously block all 11 men on a team.

Every June there is a Woodchoppers Jamboree in Encampment, and Block 11 is the center of the boisterous nocturnal activity. Dobler always attends the jamboree, driving up from Laramie in his CB-equipped Mercedes, because it is such fun and, well, because his presence in Block 11 guarantees peace. Things can get rough in Wyoming saloons, most of which have iron bars on the windows to prevent the throwing of furniture and/or people through the glass, but no one is eager to deal with a bouncer of Dobler's size and reputation. The men's room in Block 11 is filled with raunchy graffiti expressing opinions on Dobler's athletic abilities—or lack of them.

Linda Dobler, who was raised on a Wyoming ranch, will receive her bachelor's degree in psychology from the University of Wyoming in December and intends to continue her studies until she gets a doctorate. Despite what others might think, she says she does not need it to handle her husband. She drinks tequila by the shot (no lime, no salt), manages home, family and school with ease and roundly beats her husband at tennis. She admits that Conrad has a mean streak but says it doesn't affect their life together.

Conrad worries that talk of his image as the NFL's dirtiest player will turn the officials against him. Already, he claims, he receives extra scrutiny. "In one game I was called for tripping a guy who was standing up," he says. "Sure I tried to trip him, but I didn't succeed, and attempted tripping is not illegal." He pauses, then adds, "Oh, hell, the officials are only human." Some members of the Dobler clan tend to get upset when Conrad's reputation is discussed, but his mother says that she was told by an official that her son is "an intelligent player who has finesse, knows the rules and uses them to the nth degree." She is unconcerned about his image, saying, "If that helps bring in money to the stadium, well. . . . " Linda Dobler occasionally worries about the effect Conrad's reputation will have on Mark, but the boy seems to be able to differentiate between No. 66 on the field and the person who is his father. Once when Mark was being taunted by a schoolmate about his father's play, Mark ended the discussion by saying, "He's only doing his job."

If Dobler's image has hindered his performance by making the officials more aware of him, Conrad feels it has also helped by making opponents more aware of him. "Sometimes someone will say, 'Watch out, Dobler's behind you,' he says. "The guy stops and turns around, and that gives us the time we need to complete the play."

Dobler wonders whether it will be as easy in the years ahead, for he fears he might be mellowing. "At the Pro Bowl you get to know and like your opponents," he says. "And when you like a guy, you don't step on his fingers or kick him getting up."

Of course, if Conrad Dobler ever does mellow, he can use his own words to bring him back to reality: "If you ever forget that football is a violent game, they'll catch you gazing at the stars and put your lights out."

| | | | | |

Gettin' Nowhere Fast

BY ROBERT F. JONES

Back home in Alabama after leading Oakland to victory in Super Bowl XI, Kenny Stabler never worried about what was on the day's agenda, so long as it involved plenty of Scotch, shrimp scampi and the Wickedly Wonderful Wanda.

HE BLACK CHEVY SILVERADO PICKUP BURBLES DOWN Main Street. Past the sun-faded feed and grain store, where less elegant trucks stand scarred and dusty while their owners dip snoose in the shade, comparing notes on drought damage. Past the sporting-goods store with its display of heavy handguns and shiny fishing lures. Past the church, the high school and the obligatory but somehow anachronistic shopping center, where young housewives in curlers and short shorts stride purposefully through the heat with a baby on one hip and a bag of groceries on the other. The driver of the Silverado studies the scene closely. As if feeling his eyes on them, some of the townsfolk turn and stare at the truck. After a moment, their faces inevitably break into wide country grins.

"Hey there, Kenny!"

"Hoo boy, Snake!"

The driver acknowledges them with a wave of his free hand. Actually, the hand is not fully free. The big knuckles bulge around a beaded can of beer, second of the morning though it is scarcely 9 a.m. "This is home," says Kenny Stabler. "I'll die here."

The flat tone of the statement, issuing as it does from a face masked by a grizzled brown beard and mirrored sunglasses, raises questions. Does the premier quarterback of the NFL, the 1976 MVP, the star of Super Bowl XI, whose deft passes and clever calls eviscerated the Minnesota Vikings, mean that he's outgrown his hometown? That the rustic pleasures of Foley, Ala. (pop. 4,000) are beginning to pall? That he would die of boredom if he had to live here year-round?

Not a bit.

"I love this place," says Stabler, gunning the motor as he hits the edge of town. "It's got everything I'll ever need. Come on, let's get some beer and go for a boat ride."

A week with Stabler shot by like a long wet blur. Through it ran the sounds of Stablerian pleasure: the steady gurgle of upturned beer bottles, the clack and thunk of pool balls, the snarl of outboard motors, the whiny cadences of country music. At the end of it, anyone following in Stabler's wake would be ready for a body transplant: liver and lights, heart and kidneys, eardrums—maybe even a few new teeth.

Since it is virtually impossible to catch Stabler at rest, any portrait of him must convey his nonstop motion. To that extent he epitomizes his nickname: Snake. Try to get, say, a blue racer in repose for an interview. All you'll come away with is an impression of flickering tongue and a sapphirine slithering through the weeds.

IT BEGAN in Memphis, where Stabler was expected to perform in the pro-am of the Danny Thomas-Memphis Classic. Stabler was waiting at the airport. He was, of course, in the bar. He had been there since noon. It was now close to 5 p.m. Surrounded by reeling pals, beautiful girls and an array of empty or partially drained glassware—beer bottles, Bloody Marys, Salty Dogs, Seven and Sevens—he grinned at a newcomer. "You're late," he exulted. "Thank God. Here"—he unwrapped his thick left arm from a petite blonde, who emerged like a bauble from the shadow of his armpit—"meet Wanda." She smiled demurely, then stuck out her tongue.

The next morning a caravan of Continental Mark Vs wound erratically through southeastern Memphis. "Where the *hayull* is the golf course?" snarled a Southern voice. "Danged if *Ah* know," answered another. "Turn on the goldurned *ayer* conditioner," gasped a third. "It's runnin' full blast, you knucklehead," was the response.

"Wayull, shore," continued Bear Bryant, as if he hadn't been interrupted. "Ah remember that boy. He looked like a good 'un but he always left his football game in some parked car the night before we played. Ah remember that Auburn game in. . . . " Bryant, Stabler's coach during his college All-America days at Alabama, was paired with Stabler for the pro-am. His deep, hoarse, mellifluous voice, eroded by hard living and the football wars of a quarter of a century, filled the car with meaningless magic, reminiscence. Stabler giggled like a schoolboy at the great man's mots.

Later, under a scorching sun, Stabler quit short of nine holes. A tremendous roar had gone up moments before his retirement from the golf match. Ex-President Gerald Ford had just shot a hole in one. Playing behind him, Stabler stopped. His own shots were snaking into the rough. He pleaded "migraine."

"Hayull," grumped Bear in mock chagrin as Kenny was departing for the clubhouse. "Ah was gonna pull that one myself but you beat me to it."

The ride back to the motel is a montage of hysterical blasphemies, and hollow pauses while people catch their wind. One of the passengers, a fat man named Philadelphia Phil, pours sweat and outrageous jokes in equal profusion. During one of the lulls, Stabler turns and eyes his entourage. "Let's blow this pop stand," he says. "We'll clear out of here tonight and head back home. We've had three days in Las Vegas and now this. Too much. I want to just lay back and maybe drive my boat some. I'm one of your clean-living NFL quarterbacks and I need to replenish my physical ree-sources."

"Sure you are," says Henry Pitts, Stabler's lawyer and good buddy from Selma, Ala. "Sure you do. I'll have you out of here and home by midnight. But meanwhile let's stop and grab us a six-pack."

Shortly after midnight, emerging from the airport at Pensacola, Fla. On his way home, Stabler is haled to the curb by a traffic cop. He's just made a left turn, the cop informs him, on a red light. Stabler produces his license with decorum—no protest, no mention of who he is or what he'd done to become it. The cop writes him up. "Now take care, heah?" the cop says, smiling.

"Shore," says Kenny. Then he smiles into the dark. "Win a few, lose a few."

STABLER IS eating a fried-oyster sandwich in the Pink Pony Pub. A pitcher of draft beer sweats on the table before him. Both sandwich and beer are disappearing at a remarkable rate. He is clad in a red T-shirt with a silvery cobra silk-screened on the chest, its hood opening and closing to his swallows, white shorts and a pair of battered flip-flops. This is the uniform of the day when he's at home. The Pink Pony Pub dominates the beachfront of Gulf Shores, Ala., a resort-cum-fishing community south of Foley. A rickety string-pier extends into the Gulf of Mexico. Milky blue water laps the dunes of the offshore islands between Mobile Bay and Pensacola. Girls in bikinis bake on the beach, turning slowly, voluptuously. Stabler never misses a move.

Twice divorced and now living just up the coast from Gulf Shores with the blonde girl named Wanda—"Wickedly Wonderful Wanda," as she styles herself, but more prosaically, Wanda Blalock, age 23, from Robertsdale— he eschews the married state or any demanding facsimile thereof. He likes to watch girls. But now his anatomical studies are interrupted by a lean, middle-aged man who plunks himself down at the table to chat. Denzil Hollis was Stabler's baseball, basketball, track and football coach in junior high. "That was when I gave him the nickname Snake," says Denzil. "Back in the eighth or ninth grade. He'd run 200 yards to score from 20 yards out." He slaps Stabler's thick gut. "Skinny as a snake too, back then. Straight up from top to bottom, and when he turned sideways, he weren't no thicker than an airmail letter."

Even in 1968, when Stabler first appeared on the Oakland Raiders' roster, he was snake-slim—6' 3" by 185 pounds. Now he weighs 215. "I've been working with weights," he says. "You can't play quarterback in the league at anything under 200 these days. The stronger you are, the more muscle you got around those joints, the less likely you are to get hurt."

In high school, Stabler actually achieved greater renown as a baseball player than for his football skills. He was a smoking southpaw pitcher who, with a mediocre squad, won nine games in his senior year, racking up 125 strikeouts and five shutouts on speed alone. The only loss that Don Sutton of Clio, Ala. ever suffered in high school was a 1–0 game to Stabler and Foley, with Stabler striking out 16 and Sutton 14. "When I was 17," Stabler says, flatly, not boasting, "the Pittsburgh Pirates offered me $50,000 to sign. But by then I'd gotten to like football. And I wanted to play for Coach

Bryant. If it hadn't been for sports, I wouldn't have gone to college. My dad was a mechanic in a garage, and I'd have followed him, I'm sure. I went to college to play football, not for education. That may have been wrong, but that's the way it was. I always wanted to play pro ball, and I've done it." He finished up the pitcher of beer. "Come on, let's get out on the water."

En route to the Bear Point Marina, where Stabler moors his V-hulled, 150-horsepower outboard racing boat, *Boogie*, he pulls to a stop beside a dank, reed-grown tarn. A chain-link fence surrounds the pond, and a neatly lettered white sign proclaims CHARLIE.

"Charlie's a 12-foot alligator, something of a local celebrity," says Stabler. "We'll see if he's home." He rattles the fence and hoots a few times, but the big gator doesn't appear. "Maybe he's taken a stroll into town for a Big Mac," says Stabler. All that moves in the black water is a soft-shelled turtle the size of a manhole cover. As Stabler is about to climb back into the truck, a police cruiser brakes to a stop behind him. Out jumps Chief James E. Maples of the Gulf Shores heat—the headquarters is located just beside the gator pond. Maples, stout and bouncy, insists on showing Stabler his latest set of pictures.

Inside the office, he produces a sheaf of Polaroids depicting Maples in a soldier suit, armed with an M-16 and various other weaponry, standing before what appear to be blazing bales of hay. "We got 17 tons of grass off that cabin cruiser yesterday," he says. "Buncha damn hippies runnin' it up from Mesko, I do believe. Hayull, I stood right in the middle of it when it was burnin' and didn't feel a thang." As he flashes the photos like a new parent with baby pictures, one wonders what got him so high.

"Shucks, the Chief jest gets high on work," says Stabler as he drives away. "He's a dedicated man, Chief Maples is." There's a wry twinkle in the blue eyes, crow's feet at the corners of the broad, bearded face.

THE INTRACOASTAL Waterway, rimming the Gulf from Texas clear around the Florida Keys, affords Stabler and his boating buddies an all-weather playground. Even when gales are blowing outside the barrier islands that protect the Waterway from the Gulf, the seas inside are flat enough to run wide open at 70 mph. It's hazardous sport, what with mile-long strings of barges being threaded by their tugs through the serpentine, buoy-marked channels, but Stabler loves nothing better than jumping the wakes of the barges or running flat out beside them and making commerce look like it's standing still. He's doing it right now.

"Here he comes," says Bobby Holk, a young, pale-haired engineering grad from Auburn and—despite the rivalry between his school and Stabler's alma mater—a good boating buddy. "Roger's gonna whip him, though, you watch." The two racing boats appear from behind a barge train, Stabler in the lead and Roger Tyndal coming up fast behind him. Roger is a farmer—corn, mainly—but with the spring drought working havoc in the Deep South he has little to do. His corn tassled out at knee height. No ears. Hardly worth saving for silage. So Tyndal might as well spend the day racing.

The boats close rapidly, hulls angled up clear of the water, screws lashing the channel. The sound comes on like a swarm of giant killer bees. Just as Holk had predicted, Tyndal's boat—with an added 50 horsepower—snaps Stabler's up as soon as they reach flat water beyond the barge wake. Stabler shakes a fist in mock frustration, then the two leap each other's wakes as they head for the next marina.

"That's how we do it," Stabler says after he ties up at the Shelter Cove Marina. "We race around on the Waterway, and stop at all the marinas. There's about 10 or 12 of 'em between where I live and the end of the line, down there below Gulf Shores. Good way to travel, gettin' nowhere fast."

The marina is equipped in the uniform fashion of the region: air conditioner, bar, pool table, juke box. The bare essentials, in precisely that order. Tyndal and Holk order a bottle of Tickled Pink flavored wine while Stabler feeds the juke box and racks the balls. As Waylon Jennings extols the virtues of Luckenbach, Texas, Stabler proceeds to whip his buddies in a game of 8-ball. He wins a free beer, of course, and thus must play them another game so they can get revenge. Before they chalk the cues for the last time, Stabler and his partner (a middling player at best) have won all five games. Stabler picks up a tab from a beer can on the way and slips it over his finger. "Looky here, Bobby," he says to Holk. "This is an Auburn class ring. See, it's got a built-in nose picker."

STABLER IS now dining at a Gulf Shores squat-'n-gobble. Wanda at his side, before him his third Scotch of the meal and a heaping plate of scampi in garlic sauce. "Scotch and scampi," he crows between chomps. "I love 'em. Johnnie Walker Red. Namath drinks it. Sonny Jurgensen is a Scotch drinker too. Maybe all the great quarterbacks drink Scotch. And I love seafood, particularly these babies." (Munch, crunch, gulp.) "I told Pete Banaszak last season, just after we beat Pittsburgh in the opening game, that I'd eat scampi for 14 weeks in a row if it would guarantee us winning all our games." Like Proust's madeleine, the jumbo shrimp provoke a remembrance of the season past.

"They were all tough games—that's true in any season—but the only one that was really bad was the Patriots. And that's the only one we lost. New England kicked our butts good and proper, 48–17. I guess we should have been wary when we went up against them again in the first playoff game. But I wasn't. That was stupid. They damn near ended our playoff bid right there."

The waiter brings another plate of scampi, another drink.

"Then we give Pittsburgh a whuppin': 24–7. That felt good. Don't let no one tell you that the Pittsburgh-Oakland rivalry is press hype. We hate them; they hate us. Beating them that bad in the playoffs was sweet indeed. People who'd been saying we couldn't win the big ones had to eat crow. Pittsburgh couldn't say we'd been lucky—the way they were in '72 when Franco picked up the ricochet and won in the final seconds. No, we flat blew them away."

Wanda, bored, utters a pussycat yawn. Stabler chucks her under the chin.

"The thing is, we really didn't know what to expect from the Vikings in the Super Bowl. We knew they were an experienced team, disciplined, and well-coached at all levels, a no-nonsense bunch of guys, straight up, older than us but not necessarily wiser. Some of our guys got up so high that they vomited before the game. I remember Freddie Biletnikoff was tying his shoes over and over again. He'll do it maybe 50 times before a regular-season game, but that day Freddie must have hit 1,000.

"After the game was over, for the first time I felt real happy for myself. I remember thinking that there are only about six quarterbacks who have ever won the Super Bowl, and now I'm one of them. A great feeling, a great release, an ego balloon. Freddie was crying and coach Madden was all red and grinning and guys were hugging each other like a bunch of fruits and pouring champagne over each other and then I suddenly had this tremendous urge for a great big plate of scampi and a bottle of Johnnie Red."

ON FRIDAY night, the mayor of Foley is hosting a barbecue in Stabler's honor—a build-up of sorts for the big festivities of the night to follow. On Saturday, Stabler will submit to a "roast" in the civic auditorium. There, for $12.50 a plate, the local citizenry can watch their favorite son get insulted, maligned, slandered, humiliated and otherwise dumped upon by a panel of experts. The roast is for a good cause, though: a new field house for the Foley Lions high school teams. Anyone with the scratch can attend the roast, but the mayor's barbecue is by invitation only. The mayor of Foley is Arthur Holk, a sprightly slat of a man, an inveterate fisherman and boatman who owns much of the prime real estate in adjacent Gulf Shores. Mayor Holk is the cousin of Bobby Holk, Stabler's boating and 8-ball buddy.

The guests circulate under Japanese lanterns and electric bug-zappers on the spacious grounds of the mayor's house, wreathed in the smoke from sizzling steaks, munching freshly boiled jumbo shrimp and corn on the cob. It's an odd contrast in groups: on the one hand, the Foley upper crust, matronly, Rotarian, with cash-register eyeballs; on the other, the Stabler gang, raffish, sunburnt, hard of hand and piratical of glance. Two new arrivals add another element to the scene. Raiders running back Pete Banaszak and Tony Cline, a defensive end who played six seasons with the Raiders before being traded across the Bay to San Francisco, have showed up for the roast, and they plan to accompany Stabler to his weeklong football camp near Selma. Banaszak and Cline are clearly on their best behavior. They've been in the air most of the day, flying in from the Coast, and are much the worse for wear. "We started drinking before we got on the plane," laments Cline, "and then we had to wait two hours in the Pensacola airport before Kenny remembered to send someone to pick us up. Where's that steak?"

STABLER'S HOUSE, just over the Alabama line at the tail end of the Florida Panhandle, and half an hour's drive from Foley or Gulf Shores, was stripped to the bare minimum of furnishings by his most recent divorce. A painting of a tiger glares from the wall of the empty dining room. A lone couch adorns the living room. The refrigerator is stocked mainly with beer and white wine (the latter for the Wickedly Wonderful one). In the den, things are a bit homier. Team photographs depict him as a Foley Lion, a

'Bama Crimson Tidester and a young beardless Oakland Raider. Thinking back, one realizes that all the photos of Stabler except the candids show him as shy and self-effacing. They do not capture the driven playfulness of the man.

The garage and the yard, though, tell a different story. In the garage are fishing rods, tackle boxes laden with lures, leaders and hooks; a bench rest for the barbells with which he works out three days a week; a Honda MR-250 Elsinore dirt bike; a glossily flaked dune buggy; his four-wheel-drive pickup truck. Out on the Bermuda-grass lawn, resting in its cradled trailer, the *Boogie* looks like it's still moving at 70 mph. And down at the Bear Point Marina, not yet ready for the water, is his latest acquisition, a tunnel-hulled racing boat that should leave the V-hulled *Boogie* gasping in its wake—and Roger Tyndal's boat as well. "I picked up the tunnel-hull cheap from a boy over near Mobile," Stabler says, his voice firing with eagerness. "I'm going to fix her up—needs a little glass work here and there—and paint her real nifty, and then hang a big Merc on her. I reckon she'll go 80 plus."

If a man can be assessed by his possessions, and particularly his attitude toward them, then Ken Stabler is a man in motion. Furious, violent motion. Exultant motion.

"Gettin' nowhere fast," he says. "I like it. As philosophies go, it's as good as any. What counts isn't so much where you're going—I mean, we all end up in the same place—but what counts is the getting there. Kind of simple-minded, maybe, but it's fun."

YOU HEAR the roadhouse before you see it—the amplified four-four beat of country music pounding like surf through the woods, silencing the bullfrogs, setting the beards of Spanish moss dancing on the trees that fringe the two-lane blacktop. The parking lot is jammed with pickups, most of them costly 4-WDs with customized paint jobs. Men reel and glare and slosh beer on themselves as they stagger around the veranda—skinny, sunburnt men in Levi's and workshirts, with scuffed cowboy boots and baseball caps cocked back on their foreheads to reveal the badge of the farmer: that blanched expanse of skin where the cap has shaded the face, babyhood pallor above the sun-blackened snoose-bulging jaws. Half shot with drink, they wear the faces of Confederate dead in Mathew Brady photographs.

Stabler and Wanda disappear into the musical melee. A pair of Stabler's friends belly up to the bar. They are joined by Henry Pitts, Stabler's attorney, who flew in from Selma for the barbecue and roast, and Henry's wife Sister. Pitts is the paragon of Southern hospitality, a witty, well-read man in his late 30s who, from his small country-lawyer office in the heart of the Cotton Belt, handles all the arrangements for Stabler's travel, endorsements, and guest appearances—no easy task with a subject as whimsically peripatetic as Stabler. It's always amusing to watch Pitts introducing his wife to a stranger: "This is mah wife, Sistah." "Your wife's sister?" "No, mah wife—Sistah!" ("It always draws a double take when we check into a motel," he says.) Her real name is Mary Rose.

FOLEY'S KENNY Stabler roast is well-attended. The spacious new civic auditorium is nearly full in anticipation of seeing the local hero who has made it nationwide get his verbal comeuppance. Mayor Holk and Dr. John E. Foster, the master of ceremonies and longtime physician to Foley's athletic teams, are everywhere, planting suggestions for sharp jibes with the forgathered roasters. The most interesting contrast of the evening is between Stabler and Scott Hunter, the Atlanta Falcons' quarterback and Stabler's successor at 'Bama who has journeyed down to Foley to deliver the invocation. Stabler is massive, bearded, almost bearlike in his heavy-shouldered carriage; Hunter, active in the Fellowship of Christian Athletes, is dapper, clean-shaven, very sincere. He could be the president of the Jaycees. Stabler could be a fugitive from the chain gang.

Seated in a high-backed, thronelike chair in front of the stage, Stabler takes the roasters' best shots, wincing with mock outrage at the repeated references to his dubious intellectuality, his unconventional training habits ("Eight beers and two hours' sleep a night," says Banaszak, "that's the way to stardom as an NFL quarterback"), his penchant for monogamy ("He's a one-woman man—one woman a night").

"The other day," says Tony Cline, "my son asked me, 'Daddy, when are they going to roast you?' 'When I get overweight and overpaid,' I told him."

Terry Henley, a former Auburn football player, embroiders on the theme of Stabler's womanizing. "Up at 'Bama, Kenny had a girlfriend who was so ugly that Kenny couldn't bring himself to take her out to dinner. Instead he'd put her in a corner and feed her with a slingshot."

The digs are harsh, hard, biting close to the marrow. The fans love it.

Stabler gives as good as he gets. When all the roasters have had their say, he delivers a brief rebuttal. His voice is once again his public voice, shading to the higher registers, tentative, almost boyish. But in a few words he rips everyone who savaged him, and then some. The good people of Baldwin County, Ala., leave the hall sated with rubber chicken and ribaldry.

"GOOD FOLKS," Stabler says later, driving back toward Gulf Shores. "Yeah, I'll die here. I really haven't given much thought to what I'm going to do when I'm done with football. Something competitive, though. It has to be something with a hard challenge to it. Maybe racing boats, or racing cars. I really get off on high speed. If I was to coach, as a lot of people have suggested, I wouldn't want to coach anything above the high school level. Not college football and certainly not the pros. But my lifestyle is too rough— too much booze and babes and cigarettes—to be a high school coach. I'd hardly be a shining example to the young athletes of the future. The quarterbacks I admire most are Bobby Layne and Billy Kilmer—tough, hard-living guys who don't know how to quit. We've got a lot of that spirit on the Raiders. For the past five or six years we've been the best team, overall, in the game, and yet, until last season, we never quite made it all the way. But we kept on a-truckin', never quitting, never doubting our ability to do it. Al Davis is tough and it rubs off on the rest of us, all the way down the line.

"But Al can be generous, too. Look at this Super Bowl ring—it's got to be the most expensive one any owner has ever given to his team." The crest of the ring glints in the humid darkness—16 small diamonds, one for each of the Raiders' 1976 victories, encircling a large stone that represents the Super Bowl triumph. "The only thing that's missing is a little chip of coal on the bottom of the ring, to represent the shellacking New England gave us early in the season."

Stabler cruises down the main drag of Gulf Shores. A light surf is sloshing in off the Gulf, lit by a fat, white moon. From the Pink Pony Pub come the sounds of revelry—war whoops and rebel yells, the clink of beer pitchers and the whine of the juke box. Kenny Rogers's voice rates through the cooling, wet air, bitter with salt. "You picked a fine time to leave me Lucille, with four hungry children and crops in the field. . . . "

"Sure hope it rains," says Stabler. "The farmers are losing their shirts. Anyway," getting back to his point of departure, "I'll never end up in coaching. Maybe I'll open up a honky-tonk here in Gulf Shores. Or maybe a little marina with a pool table, and a juke box and tanks full of live bait. Honky-tonks and marinas—that's where I spend most of the good time anyway. But whatever it is, I'll die here." He turns the truck toward the sound of the music. "Hell, I'm falling behind in my clean-living campaign. Let's grab us a beer."

| | | | | |

The Way He Was

BY LEIGH MONTVILLE

Genial Cowboy Nate Newton used to be a big bad bully; he's still big but he's no longer a bully—unless you have the misfortune of lining up opposite him.

HE PEOPLE NATE NEWTON ONCE KNEW STILL RUN from him. He will encounter them in an airport sometime or see them on the street or get a glimpse of them across a crowded restaurant as they hurry to gather their possessions and head for the exit. If his eyes somehow make contact with their eyes, he will see a fear that embarrasses him. Was he really that bad? Yes, he was. The legacy of a bully is hard to shake.

"I was terrible," he says. "I was the worst. If you were having a party and I wasn't invited?" he says. "I would walk inside and shut that s--- down. Just shut it down. I was very good at shutting a party down."

Newton is the 6' 3", 335-pound offensive lineman for the Dallas Cowboys. Across the country he is perceived as some kind of enormous, lovable Chia Pet, a big huggy-bear of a man in the NFL's cast of cartoon characters. Two consecutive Super Bowls and two consecutive Pro Bowls and the unabashed *"Whoaaaaaa!"* and *"Heyyyyyyyy!"* of John Madden have lifted Newton above the anonymity of the offensive line. For five straight years—two at tackle, three at guard—he has been named to the

All-Madden Team, an honor earned by get-dirty football traditionalists who seem to enjoy their work. Newton is a big, strong man, as quotable and profane as an MTV comedian as he recounts his battles with a body that has weighed between 297 and 400-plus pounds during his 10-year professional career.

Nate Newton a bully? The idea that he could be anything but this roly-poly, happy warrior is a surprise. "There's a woman who can tell you about me," he says. "Her name is Pam Oliver, and she's a reporter on ESPN. She went to college with me at Florida A&M. She was the girl-friend of my best friend, Tony Hayes. Two years ago we played a pre-season game in Tokyo, and she showed up. I hadn't seen her since college, and there she was. I smiled and started to say hello. I just saw her eyes go real wide. I could see she wanted to run away. I said, 'Pam, wait, I'm not like that anymore. Really, I'm a different guy.' "

Was he really that bad?

"Nate Newton," Oliver says, "was a monster."

HIS BASE of operations on the Florida A&M campus in Tallahassee was a street called the Set. Every campus has a similar place, where everyone hangs around to see and be seen. This place was near the dining hall and en route to the women's dorms, and it drew its name from the fact that everyone approached it with a Hollywood attitude. Newton's attitude came from action movies. He was Jaws, the oversized James Bond villain.

"He was the biggest guy on campus, first of all," says Hayes, now a Dallas policeman. "Second, this was before guys shaved their heads. Nate's head was shaved. Third, he always wore shorts. It could be the coldest day of the year, and he'd be wearing shorts and these business-man's hard-soled shoes and these long black businessman's socks. He was something to see."

What makes a bully? It was hard to figure in his case. He had grown up in Orlando. His father, Nate Sr., ran a filling station that gradually ex-panded to sell food and detergent and all manner of items. His mother, Margret, is a schoolteacher. He had a sister and three brothers, one of whom, Tim, would play defensive tackle for three NFL teams. Nate played football and basketball, wrestled and put the shot at Jones High and worked in his father's store. He remembers that he mostly was a loner and liked to stay home. He never was a neighborhood gang guy, a hang-around guy, a follower. The colleges that approached him in his senior year were big-time places. Arizona State, for one, was very hot in its pursuit. Arizona State? The thought of going so far away and working under, Frank Kush, a coach who made players run up and down a mountain, was not appealing. Newton asked his high school coach to contact A&M, which had not called. The predominantly black school 260 miles away expressed an interest in him, and Newton decided to go there as soon as he saw the campus, which was never the same once he arrived.

"One thing I've always liked to do is curse," he says. "I was cursing once when I was a kid, and my father heard me. He told me that when I was big enough and when I was away from home, I could start cursing, not before. I hit FAMU and I said, 'All right. Here I am. I'm big enough, and I'm away from home.' "

Words were his primary weapon. The happy one-liners of today were dipped in chem-lab acid in college and fired in lethal barrages. No one was safe. Especially women. Woe to the A&M woman who dressed in a morning hurry, mismatching the colors of her skirt and blouse. Woe to the poor soul who was having a bad hair day. Newton was walking his beat. *Hey, wait a minute. Don't they have a f----- comb in your dormitory? Don't they have a hairbrush?*

He was funny, for sure, but the laughter of those around him always was nervous. First, there was relief that someone else was the target. Second, there was fear that the target might change. Third, if there was going to be a physical confrontation, well, the biggest man on campus was ready for that, too, at any time. "Here's how bad it got," Hayes says. "Nate would go to dinner. He would sit by the door. No one would leave the dining hall, because they knew they would have to walk past him. Thirty minutes would go by, an hour. It would be eight o'clock at night, and no one would be leaving. Just because they didn't want to go past Nate."

His mistake, Newton thinks now, was that he considered himself funny. Weren't people laughing? For the longest time he wasn't hearing the nervousness. He knew something was wrong—he didn't have many real friends, and he didn't have as many dates as he wanted—but he wasn't sure what it was. He was the fool, and he didn't know it. "Something happened, though, that got me thinking," he says. "There was this little dude around campus who owed money to this big dude. The big dude told the little dude not to show up at this bar on Saturday night without the money, because he'd hurt him bad. Well, the little dude showed up. Without the money. The big dude came over, and they were talking, and the little dude pulled out a .45. He put the gun under the big dude's chin and blew his brains out. Just like that.

"The whole thing, you see, happened because the little dude was so scared of the big dude. I got thinking about having people afraid of you. It's not a good way to live. I don't care how bad you are, how big you are, there's someone inside who wants to be liked. Nobody wants to be treated like some kind of leper when he comes around." The change had begun.

"I LIKE riding the bike," he says now. "It's the best exercise for me, especially because it keeps the weight off my knees. You should see me out there. I bought the $2,000 bike. I have the helmet. I have the Spandex shorts. I have those funny little shoes that fit in the pedals. The only thing that gets to me is that tiny little seat. You know what I mean? If I get by that, in two years I'll be ready for that f------ Greg LeMond."

(He can be a real panic.)

"I had 14 pit bulls in a pen behind my house until a few months ago," he says. "I got rid of them because I wanted to be ready to move if I went to some other city as a free agent. I didn't want to have to worry about the dogs. I had two fences, a wooden fence and a chain-link fence, so they weren't a danger to anyone. If someone got through those fences, his biggest problem wouldn't have been with the dogs—it would have been with me."

(He can also bring back just a little bit of the old intimidation every now and then.)

Twelve years have passed since A&M and the Set, and for Newton those years have been an upward, successful march. Undrafted by the NFL, cut as a free agent in 1983 by the Washington Redskins, injured in a serious car accident the night he was cut, he landed in the now defunct USFL with the Tampa Bay Bandits, for whom he played for two years. He signed with the Cowboys in 1986 and for a while at first was treated as an overweight curiosity. His nickname was the Kitchen (bigger than the Fridge, get it?), and he had to endure all the fat jokes and the fat pictures in the newspaper articles, which he has carefully saved in a scrapbook.

His breakout came with the arrival of Jimmy Johnson as the Dallas coach in 1989. Johnson didn't care what a player looked like or sounded like or smelled like as long as the player could play the game. That fit fine with Newton. He was always one of the team's strongest players though he had lost weight and gained weight and lost weight and gained weight by following an assortment of plans in search of his best weight (about 335). Then three years ago he discovered the bicycles and off-season trainer Mike Spotts in Orlando. This was the regimen that has worked best of all. He has made himself what he is, traveling from fat-man joke to Pro Bowl starter. A stiffening of league steroid rules has been an obvious help; football has again become a game of naturally huge men.

"You look around the league now, and every team has one of me—every team with a good offensive line, at least," Newton says. "I started out as this big fat guy all by myself, and it turns out I was the f------- prototype."

The Cowboys showed how much they value him when he and fullback Daryl Johnston became the first free agents retained after the departure of Johnson and the arrival of Barry Switzer in this tumultuous off-season. Two other veteran free-agent guards, Kevin Gogan and John Gesek, were allowed to move along to other cities. Newton will be the foundation of a line that has to be rebuilt. This is fine with him. He would have moved for the right money, but he wanted to stay.

"I'm happy," he says. "I'm as happy these past few years as I've ever been. I look back and see that I was nothing but a fool, a clown. You can't live that way."

The bully is gone. Time changes people as much as anything. Time and experience. He is married and financially secure. He and his wife, Dorothy, have a son, Nate III, and his personal life, after having had three children with three different women, has settled. His mind has settled. There still might be public problems here and there—he will appear in court on June 27 on a 1993 charge of driving while intoxicated, and he has gone back to Spotts in Orlando to lose 45 pounds before the start of training camp—but he is certainly no longer the menacing figure of the Set. He has changed that. Oliver saw Newton at the Super Bowl in January 1993. "He was sitting there with a microphone and with his little name card in front of him, talking to all of these people," she says. "He was talking so nice, and everyone was writing down what he said. I said to myself, 'Look at Nate. He's all grown up.' "

| | | | | |

Muddied but Unbowed

BY JEFF MACGREGOR

This was the season he was going to ascend to the cosmology of one-name stars. This was the year his team was going to the Big Show. This was the year it all fell apart . . . yet Keyshawn Johnson continued to shine.

IRST, THE MAN POINTS. THEN, FIVE SECONDS LATER, AS fluid and practiced as a mime, he fans his hand up into a curt wave, the pale palm arcing back and forth from the wrist. Once, twice, thrice. Pause. The arm doesn't move. One. Two. Three. Not frantic, like your mom trying to hail a cab, but slow, stately, like a man buffing the dashboard of a Bentley, the better to see his reflection there. This is the measured celebrity *howdy* that begs reciprocity—especially when accompanied (as this one is) by a great Jaggering of the fiendish eyebrows and a sly semi-wink. Let us now wave at famous men. This is the wave that Charlton Heston undoubtedly used to greet Kirk Douglas from across the street at the Hollywood Christmas Parade. It is a wave that says, "It's me! But then you knew that, didn't you?"

Without pause the famous fingertips are brought quickly to the palm. The fabulous thumb alone remains erect. Thumbs up! The universal benediction of the okey-dokey! The thumb points heavenward, speaks volumes. "Here we are," it says, "and we're both rich and famous! Keep up the good work!" Attached to that happy thumb is billionaire nut-job Donald Trump.

On the receiving end of the thumb's well-wishes is Keyshawn Johnson.

On a damp New York night in September, amid the crudités and snack baskets of a Women's Tennis Association President's Suite at the U.S. Open, Keyshawn acknowledges Le Donald's acknowledgment with a brusque wave and a polite smile. Number 19 came here to watch Serena Williams run Monica Seles ragged in the quarterfinals, as is now happening, not work the crowd. He offers no love, no thumb, in return.

Three presidential boxes over, though—50 feet, give or take—the improbably coiffed plutocrat isn't quite finished. No, no. Keyshawn is, after all, the most famous Jet since Uncle Vanya Namath. With that in mind, Trump spins one of his girlfriends around so hard it looks as if he's trying to start a balky outboard. He whispers to her. Then he gestures to a point in space that may include large parts of Keyshawn Johnson. The double-dizzy spokesmodel does her best to raise a buxom thumb in that direction. She may mistakenly be thumbing Harry Connick Jr. and his wife, Jill Goodacre, who are seated close by. She may be thumbing total strangers for that matter, but she's game, by god, and full of bright prospects and blender drinks, and that thumb remains proudly suspended until an entire quadrant of the U.S Tennis Center has been well and truly thumbed. Keyshawn politely flags a hand back at her.

A minute later John McEnroe enters the Trump box. Trump whispers in his shell-like ear. Johnny Mac turns. Points. Waves. Then launches a thumb Keyward and smiles. This is what it means to be famous in America. You become Fonzie.

Keyshawn again volleys back a small wave, smiling. To the reporter standing behind him trying to conceal a smirk and a fistful of free shrimp he says, laughing, "You're loving this, aren't you?"

Follow Keyshawn long enough and you'll see single fingers raised in several familiar configurations.

KEYSHAWN JOHNSON has to stick his head up over the knot of reporters in front of his locker and yell to the clubhouse guy for a jockstrap. This happens almost every day before practice. Then, still talking—seamless, uninterruptible—he goes back to the questions. Can you? Will you? Did you? Mini-camp, training camp, preseason, real season; this is New York, so there are always questions.

For the past three years he's had answers, too, answers that are by turns funny and incendiary and smart, audacious or elusive or self-congratulatory, right, wrong, contradictory, contentious, sweet, sour, true and false. He is a 72-point banner headline waiting to happen. His relationship with the press is as vivid a part of his life as the game itself. Sometimes it *is* the game.

He'll crack you up. He'll piss you off. He'll ask better questions than you do. If he doesn't think a question makes any sense, he'll repeat it. Slowly. Like he's doing a lab at Berlitz. He'll stand there holding his practice pants— so small they look as if they came from Baby Gap but threaded with that long, swashbuckler's belt—and repeat the question. Eventually it makes sense to no one, not even the blushing knucklehead who asked it. Sometimes he ignores the question and answers a question nobody thought to ask. Sometimes he asks *and* answers the questions. Man!

He is as brash and self-referential as the young Ali, minus the poetry; as irritating and engaging and confounding to conventional wisdom as Ali before he leveled Liston. Is he really as good as he says he is? "I can hurt you all over the field." Who can be that good? "I can carry this team." Nobody's that good! "Reinvent the position?" Who would even say this kind of stuff!

If Keyshawn Johnson didn't exist, the press would have to create him. The way he created himself.

HE IS 6' 3". He weighs 212 pounds. He trains year-round for his day job as a wide receiver for the New York Jets: weights, plyometrics, running. Off-season he runs in the California hills. Or he runs those stairs that lead down to the sand at Santa Monica beach. There are hundreds of them. This might take a couple of hours. He runs until he's ready to puke. Matinee-idol jock millionaire, and he's about to puke in front of tourists on their way to the Santa Monica pier. This is when James Strom, his strength coach, tells him to run some more. That way, when reporters call Strom to ask what sort of shape Keyshawn is in, he can answer in simple declarative sentences: "Nobody works any harder. Pound for pound he's up there with the strongest guys in the league."

The dietary secrets at Keyshawn's training table? No soda, alcohol only on special occasions, don't mess with supplements, eat lots of Popeye's fried chicken.

He is 27 years old. Married to Shikiri Hightower. They have two children, doll-perfect Maia, 4, and chubby-handsome KiKi (Keyshawn Jr.), 15
months. He grew up in South-Central Los Angeles. He is the youngest of six
kids. Didn't know his dad. Still doesn't. He and his mother moved around
a lot, never settled for long in one house, one apartment. His brothers and
sisters often stayed with relatives. He showed up one afternoon at a USC
football practice and started hanging around as a ball boy. He was nine.

Street kid. Smart. Supported the family. Hustled, scammed, scalped
tickets. Did time at two juvenile camps. Moved around, played for three
high schools. Sold dope, carried a gun. Got shot. Went to a couple of junior colleges after he realized he couldn't talk his way past the SATs. Finally got into USC. Played two years, as a junior and a senior, but finished second on the Trojans' alltime list in receptions (176) and receiving
yardage (2,940). Two-time All-America. Was the 1996 Rose Bowl MVP,
with 12 catches for 216 yards. Went first in the NFL draft that spring.
Held out. Missed three weeks of camp. Got a six-year deal with the Jets
worth a reported $15 million.

He is not dead and he is not in prison because he created in his imagination something called Keyshawn Johnson. He carries this invention out
into the world and talks about it. That makes it real.

THIS WAS their year. Seven bookies out of 10 made the Jets the favorites
to go all the way. All the pain and the practice add up to this moment, this
season, right here, right now.

Week 1. Jets versus New England. Quarterback Vinny Testaverde goes
down with a ruptured Achilles tendon while stepping forward no more
quickly than he might have if he were opening a door for his wife. Vinny T.,
earnest as a priest, the physical and spiritual foundation upon which the Jets'
hopes rest, is out for the season.

Still, Keyshawn has eight catches for a career-high 194 yards, and one
touchdown, against cornerback Ty Law, his co-MVP from the 1998 Pro
Bowl. But at the press conference a few hours later he breaks a cardinal
rule of the NFL: Never show any genuine emotion on the podium. Speak
only in upbeat clichés. Soldier on. Cry only if you're retiring. "We're f-----"
won't sell many tickets.

Some papers the next day said he "[came] unglued in a stream of profanity." Someone wrote that he panicked, threw a "temper tantrum." It is no longer their year, their time. But the first half of the first game? This wasn't supposed to happen. In a roomful of sports reporters, with all the cameras and the lights and those eyes looking up at you for answers, how do you say you have a broken heart?

HIS BOOK, *Just Give Me the Damn Ball*, a scathing recapitulation of his '96 rookie season with the 1–15 Jets, was as popular inside the football establishment as a persistent urinary tract infection. The NFL didn't like it, the Jets didn't like it, the sporting press didn't like it, *The New York Times Book Review* didn't like it. The language used to scald it was as inflammatory as anything written inside it. "I have no regrets," Keyshawn says.

That he batted about .750 with his contumely was largely unremarked upon. As John Robinson, Keyshawn's coach at USC says, "Nobody should write a book till they're 70." The book is dedicated to, among others, "The Lord Savior Jesus Christ."

ACCORDING TO Jets coach Bill Parcells, Keyshawn has the best receiver's straight-arm in the game. He is one of the best blocking receivers too, and he's fast enough and has good hands and knows how to use his great size against defensive backs. Parcells goes on to say that he'll only get better. Parcells is not given to exaggeration. He has whitewall tires on his family sedan, for goodness' sake!

In three seasons with the Jets, Keyshawn has caught 216 passes for 2,938 yards and 23 touchdowns. In the divisional playoffs last year he tore up Jacksonville—caught nine passes for 121 yards and a touchdown, ran a reverse for a touchdown, intercepted a pass and recovered a fumble. After that game the radio sports guys who'd called him a bust started using phrases like "Hall of Fame numbers." Those numbers get better every year.

CAN KEYSHAWN make it to the Hall of Fame? John Robinson says yes. Murphy Ruffin thinks so, too. Murphy Ruffin was Keyshawn's probation officer at Camp Miraloma.

HE IS A state-of-the-art postmodern cross-promotional platform. A well-spoken, Gable-handsome, user-friendly content provider at the confluence of the great American data streams of sports and commerce and entertainment. He had the book and shoe deals before he caught a ball in the NFL. Sitcoms, movies, magazines; he's everywhere you are and every place you want to be. Works with Adidas, Coca-Cola. You can't watch one of those nitrous-giddy pregame shows without hearing about him, hearing from him. He attracts *Day of the Locust* crowds now; mothers lean out of the stands in Green Bay (Green Bay!) to snap his picture for the kiddies—Sign for me, Keyshawn, sign for me!

IN THE preseason these Jets were a relaxed and confident bunch. Then, laid low Greek-tragedy-style by a wounded Achilles, they collapsed—they were stunned instead of stunning. What bled from this team in those first few weeks was that confidence.

And for all his bumptious talk about putting this team on his back, what could number 19—or anyone, for that matter—do? Until journeyman backup quarterback Rick Mirer learned a few more pages from the Jets' playbook, not much. But against Denver on Oct. 3, with New York looking down the barrel of a possible 0–4 start, Mirer, cribbing from a teensy playlist taped to his wristband, got Keyshawn the accursed ball. Thus did he catch eight passes for 98 yards and a touchdown from his seventh quarterback in three-plus seasons. He also drew 45 yards' worth of pass interference calls on the game-winning drive. Man!

Since then, though, the Jets have come apart like a cardboard suitcase in a hard rain, losing inventively to Jacksonville, Indianapolis and Oakland. They stagger punch-drunk into their bye week at 1–6, a record roughly the reverse of preseason expectations. Crazy strange too is this: After those first seven games, with little discernible help from his quarterbacks, Keyshawn's numbers are better than they were at this time last year.

The psychology of losing is an elusive thing. There are more ways to shoot yourself in the foot than Barney Fife ever dreamed possible, and the Jets seem determined to explore every variant. Blown coverages or ill-timed interceptions or missed tackles or the wrong play called at the wrong time—failure has many faces; pick one. They've choked up four fourth-quarter leads in seven games. Are their lapses physical? Mental? Spiritual? "I have no idea," answers Keyshawn, genuinely baffled by the high-octane knack this team has shown for self-immolation.

"If we had Vinny, we'd be rollin'," he asserts. "We could be 7 and 0, as close as these games have been." And he's probably right. Even with a quarterback whose ratings read like premature-birth weights.

Keyshawn talks about all this with a tired kind of equanimity, makes it clear that he still has fun playing the game, still thinks the Jets can rise above their injuries and insults. "I just believe different than other people, I guess." There isn't any bluster behind his optimism, though, and he knows this season may play out as a long, slow-motion disaster.

KEYSHAWN, ON his several appearances with the President of the United States on national panels discussing the role of race in athletics: "I'm really proud of that. How many people get to chop it up with the top dog?"

LIKE ITS owner, the restaurant defies most of your expectations. Situated on a quiet, tree-lined street at the moneyed frontier between West Los Angeles and Beverly Hills, Reign is not a sports restaurant. ("Reign," by the way, is a name no one on the Keyshawn, Inc. flowchart takes sole credit for, but it suits the ambitious iconography of the athlete in question.)

Historically, eateries owned and operated by the jockocracy fall into one of three evolutionary epochs. The ancient (e.g., Jack Dempsey's place, the kind of Runyonesque steak house where a man could ogle DiMaggio and live large on redheads, red meat and red liquor in the company of other Broadway swells and touts); the modern (an all-star-style museum and memorabilia outlet, where everything has a price on it and the sweat-stained sanitary socks of Charlie Hustle's youth hang framed and certified just inches from your souvenir minicrock of congealing beer-cheese soup); and the postmodern (a multimedia "themed environment" like the ESPNZone in Times Square, which has nothing to do with eating but, thanks to TV monitors numbering in the dozens, everything to do with the re-education scene from *A Clockwork Orange*).

Reign, though, is just a very nice restaurant in a neighborhood that's flush with very nice restaurants. No framed jerseys or commemorative balls are on display, no buzzing neon beer signs or blaring video games. Rather, it is a model of expensively designed restraint, done up in the chic urban signifiers of blond wood with stainless-steel trim and earth-tone fabrics.

ON A night not long after it opened, the restaurant was bustling, three-quarters filled, loud with people enjoying themselves and the food. Keyshawn was working the room, greeting customers and politely turning away those who didn't meet his dress code, fussing over the details and kibitzing in the kitchen, pinching more filé into the gumbo pot, all the while giving one interview to a television crew in the party room and another to a writer in the dining room. From the decor to the mortgage, from the menu to the personnel to the little gondolas of calamari, he takes responsibility for everything here. It wears you out just watching him.

Weirdly, even more than football, this restaurant may be the truest manifestation of his character. Food and beverage management is something for which he has no formal training, but he had always wanted to own a restaurant, so he simply willed himself to master it.

During the football season he checks in with his boyhood pal Skeats Spalding (one of Reign's managers) by phone two or three times a day—turnover, receipts, breakage. Off-season, if you don't see him out front, stick your head in the kitchen; he's probably showing his dishwashers the most efficient way to scrape a plate.

But the restaurant business is cutthroat, and the common wisdom is that you either make a million or lose a million. There's nothing in between. "I've never failed at anything, and I don't expect to fail at this," Keyshawn says. Making sportswriters with expense accounts pay for their own dinners is a thrifty step in the right direction. [Note to editor: Receipt to follow under separate cover.]

If for some reason keeping wolfish reporters from running a tab isn't sufficient for success and the restaurant doesn't make it, don't worry. He can always lease the space. He owns the building too.

THIS IS how he works: Under a sky as high and hot as scalded milk, Keyshawn is running patterns on a practice field at Hofstra University, catching long, elegant passes.

He comes off the line of scrimmage like Walter Brennan. For the first three steps he's all crotchet and fuss and pistoning forearms, his big feet flapping. Then on the fourth step his feet are under him again, so he unfolds himself and he's daddy longlegs now, football fast, going, pumping—he plants one of those size-13 shoes, cutting, fakes, fakes again with a shake of the head that seems like an angry denial, pumping, going. Part of him is headed upfield now, and the other part isn't. You can see him from every angle at once, a cubist painting of a man running, and the ball is in the air, drilling an arc into those hands as big and soft as oven mitts.

During the worst of this unseasonal heat wave it feels as if you're wearing clothes made out of steel wool, but Keyshawn is running flat out up the sideline, going deep, hitch and go, over and over—fast, as if he's chasing something. Or something's chasing him.

KEYSHAWN USES his shoulder belt nearly every time he drives. His favorite color is blue. He listens to Tupac. He is a "shining star" in a flashlight world. He often refers to himself as "Number 19." He has been known to use the phrase "hunky-dory" in conversation.

DURING THE season Keyshawn and Shikiri and their children live on Long Island in a town house. Nothing palatial, just normal; the neighbors rag him if he leaves the lids off his garbage cans on trash day. This is a seasonal home—they're Californians to the marrow—so the place has a look of impermanence. Nice furniture, but not a lot of it; low knickknack count. A television downstairs the size of a JumboTron, though, and plenty of Pokémon videos. With kids, you don't have to worry much about decorating anyway; they'll take care of it for you. Their real home, the new place they're building in Los Angeles, is almost finished. Many thousands of square feet to decorate and accessorize. If you see young Mr. Johnson often enough at Weeb Ewbank Hall, the Jets' headquarters, he's apt to confront you with a design magazine folded to a picture of an armoire. "I like this. We're doing Mediterranean."

HE FORMED Keyshawn, Inc. in part to organize and operate his charitable enterprises. The two most prominent among these are Key's Kids, a community outreach program for underprivileged children, and the Keyshawn Johnson Education Fund, which provides scholarships.

In a windowless, airless basement auditorium borrowed from the University of Southern California for the Dorsey High senior awards ceremony in June, Keyshawn and Shikiri made one of the last presentations of the evening. Through his education fund he awarded four $5,000-per-year scholarships to exceptional Dorsey graduates. He did this last year, too, and the year before. Next year he'll add two more. Then two more, and so on, for at least as long as he plays.

Eventually, he hopes 100 students will be going to college with money that came from Keyshawn Johnson. When he explains this benevolent academic pyramid scheme to the audience, it gives him a standing ovation. No cameras are present in the small auditorium. Later, when asked about the breadth of the plan, he says, "You gotta give back. So, you comin' to eat?"

IS THE Feud for real? Do Keyshawn Johnson and fellow wideout Wayne Chrebet really hate each other? If so, does it matter?

To the joy of neither, their long-running Alphonse and Gaston routine has become a comic staple of the New York sports pages and radio shows. They are, to the press at least, as necessary to each other as the very air, and as irresistible in their epic spat as Moby and Ahab. That they still share adjoining lockers compounds the comedy. To see them giving separate interviews to separate sets of reporters while studiously ignoring each other from a distance of 18 inches is to witness the rebirth of vaudeville.

In the midst of the Jets' early-season swoon, the *New York Post* found space to feature this headline: CHREBET FIRES A KEY SHOT. The subhead: CALLS JOHNSON 'RETARDED.' (Nobody ever said the NFL was the Algonquin Round Table.) The piece, though riddled with factual errors, recounted a comment laughingly made by Chrebet during a recent radio show on which he was flogging his book, *Every Down, Every Distance.* Johnson responded the next day by taking what was left of the moral high ground and raining football clichés—"I'm just trying to win games," etc.—down on Chrebet's head.

Absent the notoriety he gained by being referred to in Johnson's book as a "team mascot," Hofstra long-shot Chrebet might not have so quickly become the blue-collar folk hero he is today. And without Chrebet as his foil, Johnson and his comments might not have registered quite so brightly on the great tabloid radar screen. Largely ignored is the fact that they have more in common than either will admit. Each works like a draft horse in practice; both have a burning ambition to win; both are fearless going across the middle. Each is a "Parcells guy," a "parking lot player" (i.e., they would play football in the parking lot even if no one were watching). Both are proud and stubborn. Each is as tough as a U.S. Army ham.

As to the true nature of their relationship, the following scene from training camp might be illustrative. Chrebet catches a touchdown pass in the big scrimmage. Cheers erupt. As the offensive unit jogs off the field, Keyshawn touches celebratory knuckles with everyone around him. Chrebet, however, walks right past him but receives no knuckle, gets no love. A few series later, when Keyshawn hauls one down in the end zone, Chrebet has the loving knuckles out for all but Keyshawn. (During the regular season, they knuckle grudgingly, like a long-divorced couple, for the fans.)

While not complimentary, they are certainly complementary. When both are playing—along with Testaverde—the Jets' aerial attack is a thing to be reckoned with. Perhaps more important, Keyshawn and Chrebet play necessary characters in the ongoing drama of our national game. Sports (and sportswriting) has always been about the creation of heroes and villains, the manufacture of mythologies. Fans have a rooting interest not just in the outcome of each game, but also in the eternal, operatic struggle between one-dimensional archetypes of good and evil. Thus a team becomes, as Parcells often calls it in a different context, a "cast of characters." Chrebet satisfies our need for a scrappy underdog, a diminutive overachiever, while Keyshawn is portrayed as the blustering L.A. glamour-puss with awesome physical gifts. (The uglier subtext is racial, with Chrebet as a white, anti-Keyshawn. Sadly, this too is a story that some faction of the Jets' fan base wants to hear.) Thus, both players are done a great disservice.

So, do they hate each other? Probably not. After all, why waste that kind of energy? Contrary to what *Newsweek* said in its recent profile of Keyshawn, teammates do not have to be friends.

But who knows how they feel about each other? Neither would talk about the feud they aren't having. Chrebet refused to be interviewed for this piece, and Keyshawn's last word on the subject was this, "I don't want to help him sell any more books."

J-E-T-S! Jets! Jets! Jets!

TWO PHRASES recur when you talk to people about Keyshawn: "He is the most intensely loyal person I've ever met," and "If I had to go into a dark alley, he's the one I'd want with me."

Why a corporate marketing director would be in a dark alley is anybody's guess.

MAYBE YOU think you know the place from movies or TV or hip-hop, but South-Central Los Angeles is not metaphorical—it is not a jungle or a war zone or a Third World country. Those are literary clichés that obscure the reality of the place and make any responsibility for it seem distant and impossible. South-Central is an American neighborhood of wide streets lined with small pastel houses where American families suffer not just gang violence or institutionalized poverty, but worse still, the failure of hope. That Keyshawn got out testifies to his strength of will. That he comes back says a lot about his heart.

After the riots and fires in 1992, folks in Los Angeles heard a lot of uplifting rhetoric from local politicians and corporate glad-handers about rebuilding the scorched economy of South-Central. Rhetoric looks swell on the op-ed page or in the annual report but doesn't create any actual jobs or lay any actual bricks. Most large companies hid behind the sterile language of cost/benefit analyses. But not all. One of the largest projects, a 26-acre, $50 million retail center, is being undertaken by a consortium made up of three entities: Capital Vision Equities, a residential developer; Katell Properties, a commercial developer; and Keyshawn Johnson, a Pro Bowl MVP. "It's a very important project for Los Angeles," says L.A. city councilman Mark Ridley-Thomas. "It's the first project of this size and sort in the last decade. The residents here are very excited."

Chesterfield Square, as the center will be known, breaks ground this month at the intersection of Western and Slauson avenues. With its opening planned for Christmas, 2000, it will be anchored by a huge Home Depot, a supermarket and a drugstore. (Keyshawn would like to see a McDonald's in there too, and maybe an athletic-shoe store.) The center will create 600 jobs and send millions of dollars through the local economy.

Keyshawn's participation in the enterprise is "substantial" according to those who know. In other words, he doesn't want to be just a face on the prospectus. As Ridley-Thomas puts it, "He hasn't been bashful about getting involved and putting his money where his mouth is."

Keyshawn knows how successful former Lakers colossus Magic Johnson has been with his inner-city investments, like his movie theaters a few neighborhoods away in Baldwin Hills. Make no mistake, this is not, according to the councilman, "a matter of charity. It is not a matter of philanthropy. This is a matter of business." And for Keyshawn, a matter of pride. He well understands that he may make a reasonable return on his investment—in fact, he underscores this in conversation—but his eyes widen only when he talks about doing well by doing good: "It's a good investment. And why wouldn't I want to do something like this in the place where I was born and raised?"

KEYSHAWN TALKS to his mom, Vivian, two or three times a week. She lives in a house Keyshawn bought after he made it to the NFL. They talk about the family, about the restaurant, about the world at large. They also talk about football. "She knows a lot about sports," he says. A long time ago she was the one who threw him the damn ball. What does she say to him about the 1999 Jets? "What's wrong with y'all?"

HE CAN'T get out of New York fast enough for his bye-week break, a chance to fly well away from the blast radius of the tabloid second-guessers and wise-guy finger-pointers. "All they're gonna see is the back of my head gettin' smaller and smaller," Keyshawn tells every paper in town.

SHIKIRI JOHNSON is a stunningly beautiful and well-spoken young woman. She rarely talks to the press. She and Keyshawn are homebodies, protective of their privacy, reluctant to trade away every little bit of themselves the way some famous couples do. Turn around one day, if you're not careful, and all you have left is a promotional device, not a marriage.

She has a degree in journalism and is working on a career in broadcasting. "Not sports television," says Shikiri. "That's way too close to home." She is also taking business classes in anticipation of opening a boutique a few blocks from the restaurant. They met at a party at USC; she thought at first that he was a basketball player. They were married on Valentine's Day, 1998.

"I love that things are going right for him," she says, "but it's hard on our family time. I'm very proud of him, but it's difficult to have my own identity."

KEYSHAWN'S BACKSTAGE at the Letterman show, waiting to go on, watching the monitor in the dressing room: tonight's Top 10 list. He's too big in this little room, has to stand up or hinge himself down onto a too-small couch. His legs are everywhere. Maybe it's all these mirrors. He's in a plaid flannel shirt and baggy jeans; he looks huge, looks like Tupac Bunyan. "Why are those people laughing?" he asks.

Twenty minutes later he's on stage. Dave asks what it was like to lose Vinny. Keyshawn takes a beat—as if he's the tummler at Grossinger's—then asks back, "How would you feel if you lost Paul?" The audience roars. Somewhere in Hollywood telephones start ringing.

SHIKIRI AND Keyshawn sit on a milk crate in their front hallway; behind them is a piece of black velvet hung from the banister. They are having their picture taken. Millions of magazine readers will see them and envy them their youth, their beauty, their love, their talent.

As soon as the photographer leaves, Keyshawn pulls on a coat to run out and get their dinner. It is 11 p.m. He's going to Taco Bell. "Don't forget the sour cream," Shikiri says. It's all about the glamour.

IN THE U.S. Open players' lounge after the Seles-Williams match, Keyshawn makes small talk with Serena and Venus and other members of the Williams family. They've met before. Serena leaves to tidy up; Venus plays with two tiny terriers that are part of her entourage. They live in a carry-on bag. Keyshawn has been briefly abandoned by the friends he brought—they've gone to meet Seles. Venus sits on a table edge and opens up the new Harry Potter book.

Two of the most popular athletes of the age are sitting a few feet from each other on a banquet table in the players' lounge of the U.S. Tennis Center at 10 o'clock at night, slowly swinging their long legs back and forth. Not talking. Just swinging. It is dead quiet, and for some reason, against all logic, it's easy to feel protective of them both. Keyshawn's friends have been gone a long time. "Can we go pretty soon?" he asks no one in particular. This is fame, too.

LETTERS MEN

| | | | | | |

The Tackle

BY JOHN O'HARA

He was an All-America who wanted to forget his football past, and, as the years went by, he tried insult and irony and even a bloody brawl in his effort to escape it.

UGO RAINSFORD'S NAME BECAME PROMINENT IN THE East, back in the Twenties, when he was so often referred to as the giant Harvard tackle, although he was only 6 feet 2 and his playing weight was never more than 220. But he looked big, and he was big against Yale and Princeton, especially in one Yale game in which he blocked a punt and scored a touchdown which won for Harvard; and in a Princeton game in which he tore the ball out of Eddie Gramatan's grasp and literally stole a touchdown from Princeton. You had to be strong and alert to do that. Hugo did not make Walter Camp's First All-America, because there was a tackle at Illinois and another at Wisconsin who were getting the benefit of Camp's fairly recent discovery that Western Conference football was superior to the brand played in the Big Three. Nevertheless Hugo Rainsford as a Second All-America tackle made a bigger and more lasting reputation than the men who played his position in the Western Conference. The Eastern sportswriters had a way of forgetting about those Westerners and remembering anecdotes about Rainsford of Harvard, and he was called the giant tackle by reporters who had never seen him play. More-

over, he got a certain amount of publicity in the news columns, in which his football reputation was a secondary consideration. He was sued for breach of promise by a dancer in *George White's Scandals* (an action which was settled out of court); and he was arrested for punching a policeman outside a cabaret called the Pre Catelan on West 39th Street. Hugo's father, who was one of the Republican friends of Alfred E. Smith, managed to have the matter taken care of. Hugo was sent off to a ranch near Sheridan, Wyoming, where he fell in love with Gladys Tompkins, of Tompkins Iron & Steel (Pittsburgh, Sandusky and Birmingham, Alabama). They were married that fall, in Sewickley, attended by 10 bridesmaids and 14 ushers, and to the music of Mike Markel. To the utter amazement of those who knew him—and thousands who did not—Hugo immediately settled down and vanished from the public prints. If you looked on the financial pages you would see his name and a one-column photograph of Hugo, wearing a starched collar and Spitalfields tie, and the briefest of announcements to the effect that H.B. Rainsford had been admitted to this partnership or elected to that directorate. He was, of course, the same Hugo Rainsford who by coincidence might be mentioned that same day in that same paper as the giant Harvard tackle, but he could not control the sportswriters' reminiscences. Once a year he would go to New Haven or to Boston for the Yale game, and he made his private contributions to the funds for the education of thick-calved high school boys from Brockton and Medford who might otherwise have turned up at Holy Cross. But he was not so impatient to learn the results of the Brown and Dartmouth games that he could not wait for the Sunday papers. Politeness to his friends rather than postgraduate enthusiasm of his own sustained Hugo's interest in football. Downtown in the daytime and at dinner parties in the evening, through the months of October and November, he was expected to comment as an expert, but all he really knew he got from *The Sun* and the *Herald Tribune*. One afternoon on the 5th tee at Piping Rock a man in a suede windbreaker, playing in a foursome behind him, said, "Hugo Rainsford? What the hell are you doing here? Why aren't you at Princeton?"

"Oh, for Christ's sake lay off," said Hugo. The man was older, and Hugo did not know his name, but whoever he was he achieved the distinction of being the first football nut who irritated Hugo to the point of rudeness.

Gladys Rainsford stepped in. "Why don't you people go through?" she said. "I'm a terribly slow player."

The rebuffed suede windbreaker and his companions thanked her and hit their tee shots in silence. They tipped their caps to Gladys and left the tee.

"Well, you know what they're thinking," said Hugo.

"What?" said Gladys.

"They're sure you and I had a fight and that's why I'm so disagreeable."

"Do you know who he is? I think he's the father of that boy that plays for Yale. I'll think of his name in a minute."

"I suppose I ought to apologize to him later, but my heart won't be in it."

"Then don't say anything," she said.

"Oh, I'll tell him I took a 9 on the 4th or something. No use antagonizing him unnecessarily. But suddenly I finally got fed up."

"Oh, I know. I'm on your side," she said. "Don't forget, they bore me too, and I don't even know anything about football."

"You know a damned sight more than most of them do. I only thank God I'm not Red Grange or Bronko Nagurski. I hate to think what they must have to put up with. Oh, boy. I probably could have made the crew, but I didn't like rowing and I did like football. And with my marks I couldn't do both and hope to stay in college. Tough enough as it was."

"Well, Giant, the price of fame," she said.

"Now you cut that out," said Hugo.

"Go on, hit one out and show them how good you are," she said. "Anyway, the season'll be over in a week or two."

But the end of the season did not mean the inauguration of an annual moratorium on football talk. Since he had become—for a lineman—only a little less legendary than Jim Thorpe, he had to accustom himself to surprise recognition, not so surprising to him as to the delighted individuals who were meeting him for the first time; and with the passing of the years they seemed to grow more astonished at his durability. It was hard to reconcile their points of view, held simultaneously, that he had been built of marble and iron, indestructibly, and that he was not only alive but playing golf, swimming and engaged in the daily transactions of financial business. They seemed to believe he had accomplished prodigious feats of agility and strength while existing as a piece of statuary, heroic size. There were times when he wanted to remove his two front teeth, to pull up his pants and let them see a 10-inch scar, to show how vulnerable he had been to the taped fists and the pointed cleats of the gods who had played against him. But by the time he was in his thirties he had learned that the easiest way to handle a football nut was to let him do all the talking.

HUGO AND Gladys had two daughters. "If you had a son would you want him to play football?" was a question that people felt compelled to ask him from time to time. His usual answer was that if the boy wanted to play, that would be all right. But on a trip to Bermuda, in the ship's bar, a woman who almost certainly had been a sociology major at her college asked him the same old question, and Hugo told her that he was bringing up his daughters to play football. "You're not serious," said the woman.

"Well, I should say I am," said Hugo. He thereupon got carried away with his fantasy and for the better part of an hour, as the daiquiris came and went, Hugo described the weekends at his house in Locust Valley, the half-size football field on his place, the regulation goal posts, the tackling dummy, the eagerness with which his two Chapin School daughters were learning to place-kick, forward pass and do the bodybuilding calisthenics that he himself had learned at St. Bartholomew's and Harvard. "It's character building as well as body building," he told the woman. "Naturally I never expect them to really play football, but it's very good for them to learn to protect themselves. The give and take of life, you might say."

"You're not afraid they might hurt themselves?" said the woman.

"A few bruises," said Hugo. "Actually no more dangerous than if they went fox hunting, when you stop to think of it."

"I suppose so," said the woman. "And there's just the two of them."

"Oh, no. I wouldn't go to all that trouble just for my two. They have two teams. The girls from Miss Chapin's on one team, and the other team consists of girls from Spence and Green Vale and Brearley. There're the greens—they're the girls from Miss Chapin's—and the Blues, from the other schools."

"Is that so?" said the woman.

"It's really lots of fun," said Hugo. He looked at his watch. "Lord, I hate to break this up, but I've got to change. And so have you. My wife'll give me hell."

He had no further conversation with the woman, although she made some effort to get some more information. "I think you've made a conquest," said Gladys Rainsford. "That woman from Cleveland."

"Keep her away from me," said Hugo.

"Don't worry, I will," said Gladys.

It was about six months later that Gladys placed a clipping before him and said, "What the *hell* is this?"

The clipping was from a magazine published in Cleveland for local consumption. There was an old photograph of Hugo Rainsford in his football uniform, and a more recent picture of him in business clothes. "Where did this come from?" said Hugo.

"Lydia Williamson sent it to me. Read it," said Gladys.

The article was a reasonably accurate report of the conversation that had taken place in the bar of the Furness liner *Bermuda*, and was signed by Edith Trapnell McGaver. The title of the article was *Football for Girls*, and the subhead was *Ex-Harvard Star Tutors N.Y. Society Girls in Grid Tactics*.

Hugo read the article with horrified fascination. Mrs. McGaver had had to use her imagination to depict the Rainsfords' Locust Valley football field, and she did so. She had expanded Hugo's remark as to the comparative safety of football and fox hunting, and had inserted a few observations of her own on the character-building aspects of contact sport. But in general the interview, as she called it, stuck to Hugo's statements.

"I never should have left you alone with her," said Gladys. "You're going to have a fine time living this down."

"Well—Cleveland," said Hugo. "Nobody around here'll see it."

"You *hope*," said Gladys.

But a Yale man in the Cleveland branch of a stock brokerage sent a dozen copies of the interview to New York friends, and in no time at all Hugo was being greeted as "Coach" Rainsford. Wherever he went—the Lunch Club, the Down Town Association, the Recess—some wisecracker had something to say about the article. They rang all the changes, from the evils of proselytizing young athletes to the fun Hugo must have in the girls' locker room. Inevitably, the Rainsfords' daughters saw the article. Marjorie, the firstborn, was tearful. "Daddy, how *could* you?" she said. The younger one, Mary, said, "Well, I guess there goes the Junior Assembly." So many of Hugo's and Gladys's contemporaries asked to be shown the football field at Locust Valley that Gladys had to warn them beforehand that it was a touchy subject. Hugo put an end to the use of the "coach" nickname by his friends. "Do you want me to swat you?" he would say.

The word got around that Hugo had swatted an unidentified friend, and as no one wanted to be swatted by those ham hands, the joke got to be unfunny. "Hereafter, you'll know better than to get tight with strange women," said Gladys.

"She was strange, all right," said Hugo.

More or less indirectly the episode of the Cleveland interview caused his friends to avoid the whole topic of football. They stifled the impulse to make humorous mention of the interview, and having become overconscious of that restriction they hesitated to speak of football in any connection. Except for rare and casual references to the Yale game and Harvard's prospects they finally had begun to relegate his football exertions to his youth—and he was already in his thirties. The sportswriters continued to celebrate his exploits; he was, after all, a kind of brand name. It was practically a tradition among the writers to compose at least one column a year in which the Golden Age of Sport was recalled, and the basic cast of characters was always the same: Babe Ruth, Walter Hagen, Bill Tilden, Tommy Hitchcock, Earl Sande, Jack Dempsey and Red Grange. (No matter how plainly the writers stated that they were writing about the Twenties, they got angry letters from fans of Bobby Jones, who forgot that Jones's Grand Slam was in 1930, and from admirers of John L. Sullivan, who died in 1918.) Hugo Rainsford was an added starter, but he was legitimately of the glamorous decade, and his was a name that broke the monotony of the traditional list. "I saw your name in Grantland Rice's column the other day," someone would say.

"That's nothing," Hugo would say. "I saw Grantland Rice at the National the other day." He was in his thirties, and he was free.

He was not a very complicated man, and he was married to a woman who did not search for complexities in him. They lived, moreover, in a time when the headshrinker was a South American Indian who had mastered the art of reducing the size of a human skull, posthumously. Gladys Tompkins Rainsford was the well-educated granddaughter of an English immigrant who had established one of the great American fortunes. Her father had gone to Princeton, taken a degree, and was easily persuaded to stay out of the way while Tompkins Iron & Steel was operated by an efficient regency, headed by an uncle. Tommy Tompkins sent his daughter to Foxcroft, and she chose to go on to Bryn Mawr and then chose to resign in the summer before her senior year, when she met Hugo Rainsford. Her mother was a lumpy little woman who traveled to Palm Beach and Bar Harbor by private car, was seldom without her parasol, and paid considerable sums in a hopeless effort to improve her negligible skill at auction bridge. She said that champagne made her acid, but she drank it anyhow. Gladys loved her ineffectual father and from a distance could pity her vulgar, lonely mother; but her feeling for the positive young man with the football reputation and the hinted-at notoriety was never in doubt. He was to be hers on any terms that were necessary, and it happened that he wanted her too. They were very nearly asked to leave the dude ranch where they met, and all parties were greatly relieved when Gladys, on the last night of a pack trip, announced their engagement.

Through the early years of their marriage Gladys frequently observed Hugo's indifferent attitude toward football, which she put down to boredom. He had played it well, but since he could no longer play it, he had lost interest; he was the victim of bores who wanted to talk about something he had graduated from; he wanted to get away from football and make a career for himself in the financial district. But she was not convinced that she had come upon the true reason for his increasingly perfunctory attention to the devotees of the game and the game itself. After his first show of petulance on the Piping Rock golf course she commenced to wonder how important his antipathy to the game had become. His subsequent experience with the Cleveland interview revealed—or so Gladys's believed—a sardonic and deep disgust with the game or some aspect of it.

It took patience, but she finally got the story, and like everything else about him, it was simple enough. "You're wrong about my not liking the game," he said. "I loved it, and I still do. If I had to do over again I wouldn't take back a minute of the playing, or the business of learning the plays, or getting hurt. I didn't like getting my teeth knocked out, but I honestly didn't feel that till the half was over. You should have seen my leg when that son of a bitch jumped on me. The skin damn near came off with my stocking. But don't forget, I was dishing it out, not just taking it. A lot of fellows will tell you that they get the lump before the game starts, and they're all right after the first scrimmage. I don't think I ever did. The only thing I was afraid of was doing something stupid, made to look silly by the opposing end, for instance. And that happened more than once. But the physical part didn't bother me, because I figured I was pretty strong and at least an even match for most of the fellows on the opposing teams. Also, generally speaking, a tackle is more out in the open than the guards and the centers, and he's usually pretty big, so he's easier to keep an eye on. That means he can't get away with as much dirty stuff as some of the others, and I never liked to play dirty. Oh, a little holding, maybe, but that wasn't dirty. If you get away with it, fine. If not, 15 yards. And if you got away with it too often the other team'd run a couple of plays at you to keep you honest. That was how I lost my front teeth. 'Let's get Rainsford,' they said. And they did. Their end, their tackle, and their fullback hit me all at once. Two straight plays. I must have been pretty groggy, but I can remember that referee looking at me. O'Ryan, his name was, and he was a dentist. Little fellow with a mustache, from Tufts. I realized later that he was looking at me professionally. My mouth. Oh, it was a lot of fun, and some of the guys I know through football will be friends of mine for the rest of my life.

"But not all."

"A name you never heard me mention was George Carr. I only mention his name now because I have to. Otherwise you wouldn't be able to understand how I feel about football. I haven't mentioned George Carr's name since the year you and I were married. He was a classmate of mine, both at St. Bartholomew's and Harvard. He came from Philadelphia. His father was and probably still is a corporation lawyer, one of those Philadelphia Club-Fish House-Rabbit Club types and a Harvard man himself. He was very anxious to have George become a good football player, but George never quite made it. He played in prep school, but at Harvard he didn't get his freshman numerals, and in sophomore year he was dropped from the squad before the first game. I suppose that was a great disappointment to his old man, and George took it out on all athletes, but particularly football players and most of all, me. I didn't sweat over that. He bothered me about as much as a gnat, a flea. Athletes were guys with strong backs and weak minds, and I was the prime example. Well, after we were married and I went to work downtown someone repeated a remark that George made. He told somebody that I'd do very well in Wall Street as long as I wore my sweater with the H on it. But that if I had to depend on my brains, I'd soon be like your father—sponging off Tompkins Iron & Steel.

"Now you know how I've always felt about your father. A very sweet man, who couldn't possibly duplicate what your grandfather'd done. In a way, your father was licked from the start. If he went out and made a pile of money on his own, people would still say he hadn't made it on his own. That he had fifty million to begin with. On the other had, if he made a botch of it, he'd be blamed worse than a man that started with nothing. So your father did what he did and let your uncle take over, and I've never known a nicer man than your father. Therefore, when George Carr made that crack I called him up and told him I wanted to see him. He suggested having lunch, but I said I preferred to call on him at his apartment, which I did. Much to my surprise he had another fellow with him. His lawyer, he said but if he was a lawyer he must have earned his way through law school by prizefighting, judging by his appearance. He looked plenty tough. His name was Sherman. I said I didn't think it was necessary to have Sherman hear what I had to say, but George insisted that it was. So I asked him if the cracks I heard were accurately quoted, and he said they were. He repeated them, and included what he'd said about your father. 'All right,' I said. 'I just wanted to make sure. Now do I take on Mr. Sherman first, or both of you two at a time?' Sherman said I'd better not start anything, and while he was saying it I hit him. I went at him as hard as I ever hit anybody. He was used to getting punched, not to being tackled. I drove him against the wall, so he got it both ways. The impact of the tackle, and the impact of the wall. Then I did hit him with my fist and he went down, all the fight was out of him. Then I went to work on George, with my fists, and I said 'See how your brains get you out of this.' You know, I'd been used to that kind of mixing it. Sixty minutes a game, and this wasn't Marquis of Queensberry rules. We wrecked some furniture, but I came through practically un-scathed, and when I saw that the game was over for that day, I put on my hat and coat and went down to the Harvard Club and had a shower and a rubdown and a few drinks. Nothing ever came of it. Obviously George Carr wasn't going to go around town and tell people that I'd beaten up him and his bodyguard single-handed. And I didn't tell anybody either."

"That must have been the first time you didn't show up for dinner," said Gladys.

"It was. I don't remember what excuse I gave, but you accepted it," said Hugo.

"But why did it turn you against football? I don't quite see that," said Gladys.

"I never did turn against football," he said. "But I wanted to get away from football, and people wouldn't let me. In other words, I didn't want George Carr to be right. *You* know I've never worn my sweaters."

"Oh, yes you have," said Gladys. "On the pack trip in Wyoming."

"Oh, did I? I guess I did," said Hugo.

"I *know* you did," said Gladys.

"Yes, it got quite cold at night, as I remember," said Hugo.

"Uh-huh," she said.

| | | | | | |

Vanity on the Gridiron

BY JACK KEROUAC

Years before he became a spokesman for the Beat Generation, the author was a
promising football player. What follows is an excerpt from his novel, Vanity of
Duluoz, *which records his barely fictionalized athletic reminiscences.*

FTER I'VE GIVEN YOU A RECITATION OF THE TROUBLES I
had to go through to make good in America between 1935
and more or less now, 1967, and although I also know
everybody in the world's had his own troubles, you'll understand that my particular form of anguish came from being too sensitive
to all the lunkheads I had to deal with just so I could get to be a high school football star, a college student pouring coffee and washing dishes and scrim-
maging till dark and reading Homer's *Iliad* in three days all at the same time
and, God help me, a W R I T E R whose very "success," far from being a happy
triumph as of old, was the sign of doom Himself.

Look: my anguish, as I call it, arises from the fact that people have
changed so much, not only in the past five years, for God's sake, or past
10 years as McLuhan says, but in the past 30 years, to such an extent that
I don't recognize them as people anymore or recognize myself as a real
member of something called the "human race." I can remember in 1935
when full-grown men, hands deep in jacket pockets, used to go whistling
down the street unnoticed by anybody and noticing no one themselves.

And walking *fast* too, to work or store or girlfriend. Nowadays, tell me, what is this slouching stroll people have? Is it because they're used to walking across parking lots only? Has the automobile filled them with such vanity that they walk like a bunch of lounging hoodlums to no destination in particular?

Autumn nights in Massachusetts before the war, you'd always see a guy going home for supper with his fists buried deep in the side pockets of his jacket, whistling and striding along in his own thoughts, not even looking at anybody else on the sidewalk, and after supper you'd always see the same guy rushing out the same way, headed for the corner candy store, or to see Joe, or to a movie, or to the poolroom, or the deadman's shift in the mills, or to see his girl. You no longer see this in America, not only because everybody drives a car and goes with a stupid erect head guiding the idiot machine through the pitfalls and penalties of traffic, but because nowadays no one walks with unconcern, head down, whistling, everybody looks at everybody else on the sidewalk with guilt and, worse than that, curiosity and faked concern, in some cases "hip" regard based on "Don't miss a thing," while in those days there even used to be movies of Wallace Berry turning over in bed on a rainy morning and saying: "Aw gee, I'm goin' back to sleep, I ain't gonna miss anything anyway." And he never missed a thing. Today we hear of "creative contribution to society" and nobody dares sleep out a whole rainy day or dares think they'll not really miss anything.

That whistling walk I tell you about, that was the way grown-up men used to walk out to Dracut Tigers Field in Lowell, Mass. On Saturdays and Sundays just to go see a kids' sandlot football game. In the cold winds of November, there they are, men and boys, sidelines, some nut's even made a homemade sideline chain with two pegs to measure the downs, that is to say, the gains. In football when your team gains over 10 yards you get another four chances to gain ten more. Somebody has to keep tabs by rushing out on the field when it's close and measuring accurately how much ground is left.

So here comes this mob of carefree men and boys too, even girls and quite a few mothers, hiking a mile across the meadow of Dracut Tigers Field just to see their boys play football in an up-and-down uneven field with no goalposts, measured off for 100 yards more or less by a pine tree on one end and a peg on the other.

But in my first sandlot game in 1935, about October, no such crowd: It was early Saturday morning, my gang had challenged the so-and-so team from Rosemont, yes, in fact it was the Dracut Tigers (us) versus the Rosemont Tigers, Tigers everywhere, we'd challenged them in *The Lowell Sun* newspaper in a little article written in by our team captain Scotcho Boldieu and edited by myself: "The Dracut Tigers, age 13 to 15, challenge any football team age 13 to 15, to a game in Dracut Tigers field or any field Saturday morning." It was no official league or anything, just kids, and yet the bigger fellows showed up to keep measurement of the yardage with their chain and pegs.

In this game, although I was probably the youngest player on the field, I was also the only big one in the football sense of bigness, i.e., thick legs and heavy body. I scored nine touchdowns and we won 60–0 after missing three points after. I thought, from that morning on, I would be scoring touchdowns like that all my life and never be touched or tackled, but the serious football was coming up that following week when the bigger fellows who hung around my father's pool hall and bowling alley at the Pawtucketville Social Club decided to show us something about bashing heads. Their reason, some of them, to show, was that my father kept throwing them out of the club because they never had a nickel for a Coke or a game of pool or a dime for a string of bowling, and just hung around smoking with their legs stuck out, blocking the passage of the real habitués who came there to play. Little I knew of what was coming up, that morning after the nine touchdowns, as I rushed up to my bedroom and wrote down by hand, in neat print, a big newspaper headline and story announcing DULUOZ SCORES 9 TOUCHDOWNS AS DRACUT CLOBBERS ROSEMONT 60–0! This newspaper, the only copy, I sold for 3 cents to Nick Rigolopoulos, my only customer. Nick was a sick man of about 35 who liked to read my newspaper since he had nothing else to do and was soon to be in a wheelchair.

Comes the big game, when, as I say, men with hands-a-pockets came a-whistling and laughing across the field, with wives, daughters, gangs of other men, boys, all to line up along the sidelines, to watch the sensational Dracut Tigers try on a tough team.

Fact is, the "pool hall" team averaged the ages of 16 to 18. But I had some tough boys in my line. I had Iddyboy Bissonnette as my center, who was bigger and older than I was, but preferred not to run in the backfield, liked, instead, the bingbang inside the line, to open holes for the runners. He was hard as a rock, and would have been one of the greatest linemen in the history of Lowell High football later on if his marks had not averaged E, or D-minus. My quarterback was the clever strong little Scotcho Boldieu who could pass beautifully (and was a wonderful pitcher in baseball later). I had another wiry strong kid called Billy Artaud who could really hit a runner and when he did so, bragged about it for a week. I had others less effectual, like Dicky Hampshire who one morning actually played in his best suit (at right end) because he was on his way to a wedding, and was afraid to get his suit dirty so let nobody touch him and touched no one. I had G. J. Rigolopoulos who was pretty good when he got sore. For the big game I managed to recruit Bong Baudoin from the now-defunct Rosemont Tigers and he was strong. But we were all 13 and 14.

On the kickoff I caught the ball and ran in and got swarmed under by the big boys. In the pileup, with me underneath clutching the ball, suddenly 17-year-old Halmalo, the poolhall kickout, was punching me in the face under cover of the bodies and saying to his pals "Get the little Christ of a Duluoz."

My father was on the sidelines and saw it. He strode up and down puffing on his cigar, face red with rage. (I'm going to write like this to simplify matters.) After three downs we have to punt, do so, the safety man of the older boys runs back a few yards and it's their first down. I tell Iddyboy Bissonnette about the punch in the pileup. They make their first play and somebody in the older boys' line gets up with a bloody nose. Everybody's mad.

On the next play Halmalo receives the ball from center and starts waltzing around his left end, long-legged and thin, with good interference, thinking he's going to go all the way against these punk kids. Running low, I come up, so low his interference thinks in their exertion that I'm fallen on my knees, and when they split a bit to go hit others to open the way for Halmalo, I dive through that hole and come up on him head on, and drive him some 10 yards back, sliding on his arse with the ball scattered into the sidelines and himself out like a light.

He's carried off the field unconscious.

I WANTED to go to college and somehow I knew my father would never be able to afford to send me, as it turned out to be true. I, of all things, wanted to end up on a campus somewhere smoking a pipe, with a button-down sweater, like Bing Crosby serenading a coed in the moonlight down the old Ox Road as the strains of alma mater song come from the frat house. This was our dream, gleaned from going to the Rialto Theater and seeing movies. The further dream was to graduate from college and become a big insurance salesman wearing a gray felt hat getting off the train in Chicago with a briefcase and being embraced by a blonde wife on the platform, in the smoke and soot of the big city hum and excitement. Can you picture what this would be like today? What with air pollution and all, and the ulcers of the executive, and the ads in TIME magazine, and our nowadays highways with cars zipping along by the millions in all directions in and around rotaries from one ulceration of the joy of the spirit to the other? And then I pictured myself, college grad, insurance success, growing old with my wife in a paneled house where hang my moose heads from successful Labradorian hunting expeditions and I'm sipping bourbon from my liquor cabinet with white hair I bless my son to the next mess of sheer heart attack (as I see it now).

As we binged and banged in dusty bloody fields we didn't even dream we'd all end up in World War II, some of us killed, some of us wounded, the rest of us eviscerated of 1930s innocent ambition.

THE NEXT step was to pick a college. My mother insisted on Columbia because she eventually wanted to move to New York City and see the big town. My father wanted me to go to Boston College because his employers, Callahan Printers of Lowell, were promising him a promotion if he could persuade me to go there and play under Francis Fahey. They also hinted he'd be fired if I went to any other college. Fahey, as I say, was at the house, and I have in my possession today a postcard he wrote Callahan saying: "Get Jack to Boston College at all costs." (More or less.) But I wanted to go to New York City too and see the big town, what on earth was I expected to learn from Newton Heights or South Bend, Indiana on Saturday nights and besides I'd seen so many movies about New York I was ... well no need to go into that, the waterfront, Central Park, Fifth Avenue, Don Ameche on the sidewalk, Hedy Lamarr on my arm at the Ritz. I agreed my mother was right as usual. She not only told me to leave Maggie Cassidy at home and go on to New York to school but rushed to McQuade's and bought big sports jacket and ties and shirts out of her pitiful shoe shop savings that she kept in her corset, and arranged for me to board with her stepmother in Brooklyn in a nice big room with high ceiling and privacy so I could study and make good grades and get my sleep for the big football games. There were big arguments in the kitchen. My father was fired. He went downtrodden to work in places out of town, always riding sooty old trains back to Lowell on weekends. His only happiness in life now, in a way, considering the hissing of the old radiators in old cockroach hotel rooms of New England in the winter, was that I make good and justify him anyway.

That he was fired is of course a scandal and something about Callahan Printers I haven't forgotten and is another black plume in my hat of "success." For after all, what is success? You kill yourself and a few others to get to the top of your profession, so to speak, so that when you reach middle age or a little later you can stay home and cultivate your own garden in bliss; but by that time, because you've invented some kind of better mousetrap, mobs come rushing across your garden and trampling all your flowers. What's with that?

First, Columbia arranged to have me go to prep school in New York to make up credits in math and French, subjects overlooked by myself at Lowell High School. Big deal, I couldn't speak anything but French till I was six, so naturally I was in for an "A" right there. Math was basic, a Canuck can always count. The prep school was really an advanced high school called Horace Mann School for boys, founded I s'pose by odd old Horace Mann, and a fine school it was, with ivy on granite walls, awards, running tracks, tennis courts, gyms, jolly principals and teachers, all on a high hill overlooking Van Cortlandt Park in New York City. Well, since you've never been there why bother with the details except to say it was at 246th Street in New York City and I was living with my stepgrandmother in Brooklyn, New York, a daily trip of one hour and a half by subway each way.

Nothing deters young punk kids, not even today; here's how I managed a typical day:

First evening before first day of school I'm sitting at my large table set in the middle of my high-ceilinged room, stately erect in the chair, with pen in hand, books ranged before me and held up by noble bronze bookends found in the cellar. It is completely formal beginning of my search for success. I write: "Journal. Fall. 1939. Sept. 21. My name is John L. Duluoz, regardless of how little that may matter to the casual reader. However, I find it necessary to give some pretense of explanation for the material existence of this Journal" and other such schoolboy stuff.

This done, I go downstairs to the basement where my great stepmother Aunt Ti Ma has fixed up her place like a combination of gypsy with drapes and hanging beads in doorways and lace doilies Victorian style, a thousand dolls, comfort, beautiful, clean, neat chairs, reading her paper, big fat happy Ti Ma. Her husband is Nick the Greek, Evangelakis, whom she met and married in Nashua, N.H., after the death of my own mother's Pa. Her daughter Yvonne, blue-eyed, companion of her mother, married to Joey Robert who comes home every night at 11 with the *Daily News* from a trucking warehouse job and gets in his T shirt at the kitchen table and reads. Down there they have for me all the time great vast glasses of milk and beautiful sand tart cakes from Cushman's of Brooklyn. They say "Go to bed early now, Jacky, school and practice tomorrow. You know what your Mama said, gotta make good." But before I got to bed, full of cake and ice cream, I make my lunch for the next day: always the same: I butter one sandwich plain and the other peanut butter and jam, and throw in a fruit, either apple or banana, and wrap it up nice and put it in bag. Then Nick, Uncle Nick, takes me by the arm and says, "When you have more time I tell you some more about Father Coughlin. If you want some more books, there are many more in the cellar. Look this one." He hands me a dusty old Jules Romains novel called *Ecstasy*, no I think it was *Rapture*. I take it upstairs and add it to my library. My room is separated from Aunt Yvonne's by nothing but a huge double glass door but the gypsy drapes are there. My own room has a disusable marble fireplace, a little sink in an alcove, and a huge bed. Out the vast Brooklyn Thomas Wolfe windows I see exactly what Wolfe always saw, even in that very month: old red light falling on Brooklyn warehouse windows where men lean out of sills in undershirts chewing on toothpicks while taking a break.

I set up my neatly pressed pants, sports jacket, school books, shoes in place together neatly, socks over that, wash and go to bed. I set the alarm clock for, listen to this, 6 a.m.

At 6 a.m. I groan and get out, wash, dress, go downstairs, take that lunch bag and rush to into the pippin' red snippy streets of Brooklyn and go three blocks to the IRT subway at the El on Fulton Street. Down I go and push into the subway with hundreds of people carrying newspapers and lunch bags. I stand all the way to Times Square, threequarter solid hour, every blessed morning. But what does young dughead do about it? I whip out my math book and do all my homework while standing, lunch between feet. I always find a corner where I can sorta guard my lunch between feet and where I can lean and turn and study with face to lurching car wall. What a stink in there, of hundreds of mouths breathing and no air; the sickening perfume of women; the well-known garlic breath of Old New York; old men coughing and secretly spitting between their feet. Who lived through it?

Everybody.

By the time we're at Times Square, or maybe Penn Station at 34th just before that, most people rush out, to midtown work, and ah, I get the usual corner seat and start in on the physics studies. Now it's easy sailing. At 72nd Street we pick up another slew of workers headed for uptown Manhattan and Bronx work but I don't care anymore, I've got a seat. I turn to the French book and read all those funny French words we never speak in Canadian French. I have to consult and look them up in the glossary in back. I think with anticipation how Professor Carton of French class will laugh at my accent this morning as he asks me to get up and read a spate of prose. The other kids however read French like Spanish cows and he actually used me to teach them the true accent. Now you'd think I'm close to school but from 96th Street we go past Columbia College, we go into Harlem, past Harlem, way up, another hour, till the subway emerges from the tunnel (as though by nature it was impossible for it to go underground so long) and goes soaring to the very end of the line in Yonkers practically.

Near school? No, because there I have to go down the elevated steps and then start up a steep hill about as steep as 45 degrees or a little less, a tremendous climb. By now all the other kids are with me, puffing, blowing steam of morning, so that from 6 a.m. when I got up in Brooklyn till now, 8:30, it's been 2½ hours of negotiating my way to actual class.

Now the football field. Practice. We don our regalia, as Don Regalis, the sports writer, always says in *The New York Sun*, and we come out. Of all things and lo and behold, the coach of Horace Mann, Ump Mayhew, is going to let me start every game and is going to let me do the punting and even a little passing. It seems he thinks I'm okay. . . .

We showered after practice, dressed up and went our various ways, me down the hill to the subway with my books, bone weary of course, dark over the roofs of upper Manhattan, the long El ride dipping down in the subway, zoom down through old Manhattoes, me thinking "What's up there above this hole? Why, it's sparkling Manhattan, shows, restaurants, newspaper scoops, Times Square, Wall Street, Edward G. Robinson chomping on a cigar in Chinatown." But I had to stick to my guns and ride all the way to Brooklyn and get off there, trudge to Ma's rooming house and there was my huge steaming supper, 8:30, almost time for bed already and of course no time to do any homework.

ON ARMISTICE Day, my Pop, Emil Duluoz, came down all the way from Lowell just to see me play against Garden City, in Long Island, and also to check on how my studies were going, how the situation was in the boarding house in Brooklyn, to go see a few shows, eat a few New York steaks, take me out to see the town and generally amuse himself. Naturally I wanted to show off for Pop. Funny man that he is, and used to locker rooms as a former wrestling *and* boxing promoter around Lowell, he hung around as we changed and joked with us, and the coaches didn't mind one bit; and my father's presence amused the rest of the team. "That kooky Dulouse's got a hell of a nice father." None of their own fathers ever dared to come in the locker room. We went out and took the field against poor Garden City and somewhat hurt them, if you ask me. For instance at one point, after throwing a block for Bill Quinlan, I look up from the ground and see his big feet plowing onward about 20 yards with his head down, over the goal line, knocking kids aside in every direction. And a few plays later, to show off to my father and remind him again, some poor Garden City kid is waltzing around his left end precisely as Halmalo had done, but he a stranger in this case, I pull the same trick, come up full speed, low, get inside his interference and hit him head on in a legitimate and clean tackle at the knees that knocks him back 10 feet. Off the field on a stretcher.

Now I begin to feel bad about football and war. And showing off. But after the game (HM 27, Garden City 0) my father is beaming and all delighted. "Come on Jacky me boy, we're going out and hit the town tonight." So we go down to Jack Delaney's steak restaurant on Sheridan Square, myself little knowing how much time I was destined to spend around that Square, in Greenwich Village, in darker years, but tenderer years, to come.

COME GRADUATION time I had no money to buy a white suit so I just sat in the grass in back of the gym and read Walt Whitman with a leaf of grass in my mouth while the ceremonies were going on in the field, with flags. Then when it was over I came over and joined everybody, shook hands all around, graduated with a 92 average, and rode downtown with Mike Hennessey and his mother to his apartment on Columbia campus, 116th and Broadway, which was going to be my campus in the fall after a summer in Lowell.

SOME OLD buddies, the Ladeau brothers, proposed to drive me to New York for my freshman year at Columbia because they were going to see the World's Fair at Flushing Meadow and might as well take me along for the ride and I could help with the gas instead of taking a bus. And who comes along, riding in the rumble seat in back of the old 1935 coupe, hair blowing in the wind, singing "Whoooeee here we come New York!" if it wasn't my old Pop himself, Emil. Me and 350 pounds of Pop and baggage in a rumble seat, all the way with the car veering here, veering there, I guess from the unsuitable disposition of weight in the back, all the way to Manhattan, 116th Street, Columbia campus, where me and Pa got out with my gear and went into my dormitory, Hartley Hall.

What dreams you get when you think you're going to go to college. Here we stood in this sort of dreary room overlooking Amsterdam Avenue, a wooden desk, bed, chairs, bare walls, and one huge cockroach suddenly rushing off. Furthermore, in walks a little kid with glasses wearing a blue skull cap and announces he will be my roommate for the year and that he is a pledge with the Wi Delta Woowoo fraternity and that's the skull cap. "When they rush you you'll have to wear one too," But I was already devising means of changing my room on account of that cockroach and others I saw later, bigger.

NEVER IN my life have I ever seen such a bum team as the Columbia freshmen. The coach was Rolfe Firney who had made his mark at Columbia as a very good back who'd made a sensational run against Navy that won the game in 1934 or so. He was a good man, I liked Rolfe, but he seemed to keep warning me about something all the time and whenever the big coach, famous Lu Libble, went by, all sartorial in one of his 100 suits, he never even gave me the once-over.

The fact of the matter is, Lu Libble was very famous because in his very first year as coach of Columbia, using a system of his own devised at his alma mater, Georgetown, he won the bloody Rose Bowl against Stanford. It was such a sensational smash in the eye all over America nobody ever got over it, but that was 1934, and here it was 1940 and he hadn't done anything noteworthy since with his team and went clear into the 1950s doing nothing further either. I think it was the bunch of players he had in 1934 who carried him over: Cliff Montgomery, Al Barabas, et al., and the surprise of that crazy KF-79 play of his that took everybody a year to understand. It was simply . . . well I had to run it, anyway, and you'll understand it when we run it.

So here I am out with the Columbia freshman team and I see I'm not going to be a starter. Will admit one thing, I wasn't being encouraged, and psychologically this made me feel lackadaisical and my punting, for instance, fell off. I couldn't get off a good kick anymore and they didn't believe in the quick kick. I guess they didn't believe in touchdowns either. We practiced at Baker Field in the old field in back. At dusk you could see the lights of New York across the Harlem River, it was right smack in the middle of New York City, even tugboats went by in the Harlem River, a great bridge crossed it full of cars, I couldn't understand what had gone wrong.

ONE GREAT move I made was to switch my dormitory room from Hartley Hall to Livingston Hall where there were no cockroaches and where b'God I had a room all to myself, on the second floor, overlooking the beautiful trees and walkways of the campus and overlooking, to my greatest delight, besides the Van Am Quadrangle, the library itself, the new one, with its stone frieze running around entire with the names engraved in stone forever: "Goethe . . . Voltaire . . . Shakespeare . . . Molière . . . Dante." That was more like it. Lighting my fragrant pipe at 8 p.m. I'd open the pages of my homework, turn on station WQXR for the continual classical music, and sit there, in the golden glow of my lamp, in a sweater, sigh and say "Well now I'm a collegian at last."

Only trouble is, the first week of school my job began as a dishwasher in the dining room cafeteria sinks: this was to pay for my meals. Secondly, classes. Thirdly, homework: i.e., read Homer's *Iliad* in three days and then the *Odyssey* in three more. Finally, go to football practice at four in the afternoon and return to my room at eight, eating voracious suppers right after at the training table in John Jay Hall upstairs. (Plenty of milk, plenty of meat, dry toast, that was good.)

But who on earth in his right mind can think that anybody can do all these things in one week? And get some sleep? And rest war-torn muscles? "Well," said they, "this is the Ivy League son, this is no college or group of colleges where you get a Cadillac and some money just because you play football, and remember you're on a Columbia University Club scholarship and you've got to get good marks. They can't feed you free, it's against the Ivy League rules against preference for athletes." In fact, though, the entire Columbia football gang, both varsity and freshmen, had B averages. It was true. We had to work like Trojans to get our education and the old white-haired trainer used to intone "All for glory, me boys, all for glory."

It was the work in the cafeteria that bothered me, because on Sundays it was closed and nobody who worked got to eat anything. I s'pose in this case we were s'posed to eat at the homes of friends in New York City or New Jersey or get food money from home. Some scholarship.

THE OPENING game of the season the freshman team traveled to New Brunswick, N.J. for a game against Rutgers freshmen. This was Saturday, October 12, 1940, and as our varsity defeated Dartmouth 20–6, we went down there and I sat on the bench and we lost 18–7. The little daily paper of the college said: FRESHMEN DROP GRID OPENER TO RUTGERS YEARLINGS BY 19–7 COUNT. It doesn't mention that I only got in the game in the second half, just like at Lowell High, the article concludes with: "The Morningsiders showed a fairly good running attack at times with Jack Duluoz showing up well . . . . Outstanding in the backfield for the Columbia Frosh were Marsden (police chief's son), Runstedt and Duluoz, who was probably the best back on the field."

So that in the following game, against St. Benedict's Prep, okay, now they started me.

After the Rutgers game, and coach Libble'd heard about my running, and now his backfield coach, Cliff Battles, was interested, everybody came down to Baker Field to see the new nut run. Cliff Cattles was one of the greatest football players who ever lived, in a class with Red Grange and the others, one of the greatest runners anyway. I remember as a kid, when I was 11,

Pa saying suddenly one Sunday "Come on Angie, Ti Nin, Ti Jean, let's all get in the car and drive down to Boston and watch the Boston Redskins play pro football, the great Cliff Battles is running today." Because of traffic we never made it, or we were waylaid by ice cream and apples in Chelmsford, Dunstable or someplace and wound up in New Hampshire visiting Grand'mère Jeanne. And in those days I kept elaborate clippings of all sports and pasted them carefully, among my own sports writings, in my notebooks, and I knew very well about Cliff Battles. Now here all of a sudden the night before the game with St. Benedict and we freshmen are practicing, here comes Cliff Battles up to me and says "So you're the great Dulouse that ran so good at Rutgers. Let's see how fast you can go."

"What do you mean?"

"I'll race you to the showers, practice is over." He stood there, 6 feet 3, smiling, in his coach pants and cleated shoes and sweat jacket.

"Okay" says I and I take off like a little bird. By God I've got him by five yards as we head for the sidelines at the end of the field but here he comes with his long antelope legs behind me and just passes me under the goalposts and goes ahead five yards and stops at the shower doors, arms akimbo, saying:

"Well can't you run?"

"Aw heck your legs are longer than mine."

"You'll do all right kid," he says, pats me, and goes off laughing. "See you tomorrow," he throws back.

This made me happier than anything that had happened so far at Columbia, because also I certainly wasn't happy that I hadn't yet read the *Iliad* or the *Odyssey*, John Stuart Mill, Aeschylus, Plato, Horace and everything else they were throwing at us with the dishes.

Comes the St. Benedict game, and what a big bunch of mugs you never saw, they reminded me of that awful Blair team a year ago, and the Malden team in high school, big, mean looking, with grease under their eyes to shield the glare of the sun, wearing mean-looking brown-red uniforms against our sort of silly looking (if you ask me) light blue uniforms with dark blue numerals. (*Sans Souci* is the name of the Columbia alma mater song, means "without care," humph. And the football rallying song is *Roar Lion Roar*—sounds more like it.) Here we go, lined up on the field, on the sidelines I see that coach Lu Libble is finally there to give me the personal once-over. He's heard about the Rutgers game naturally and he's got to think of next year's backfield. He'd heard, I s'pose, that I was a kind of nutty French kid from Massachusetts with no particular football savvy like his great Italian favorites from Manhattan that were now starring on the varsity (Lu Libble's real name is Guido Pistola, he's from Massachusetts.)

St. Benedict was to kick off. They lined up. I went deep into safety near the goal line as ordered, and said to myself, "Screw, I'm going to show these bums how a French boy from Lowell runs, Cliff Battles and the whole bunch, and who's that old bum standing next to him? Hey Runstedt, who's that guy in the coat next to Cliff Battles there near the water can?"

"They tell me that's the coach of Army, Earl Blaik, he's just wiling away an afternoon."

Whistle blows and St. Benedict kicks off. The ball comes wobbling over and over in the air into my arms. I got it secure and head straight down the field in the direction an arrow takes, no dodging, no looking, no head down either but just straight ahead at everybody. They're all converging there in midfield in smashing blocks and pushings so they can get through one way or the other. A few of the red Benedicts get through and are coming in straight at me from three angles but the angles are narrow because I've made sure of that by coming in straight as an arrow down the very middle of the field. So that by the time I reach midfield where I'm going to be clobbered and smothered by 11 giants I give them no look at all, still, but head right into them: they gather up arms to smother me: it's psychological. They never dream I'm really roosting up in my head the plan to suddenly (as I do) dart off, bank to the right, leaving them all there bumbling for air. I run as fast as I can, which I could do very well with a heavy football uniform, as I say, because of thick legs, and had trackman speed, and before you know it I'm going down the sidelines all alone with the whole 21 other guys of the ball game all befuddling around in midfield and turning to follow me. I hear whoops from the sidelines. I go and I go. I'm down to the 30, the 20, the 10, I hear huffing and puffing behind me. I look behind me and there's that self-same old long-legged end catchin' up on me, like Cliff Battles, done, and by the time I'm over the 5 he lays a big hand on the scruff of my neck and lays me down on the ground. A 90-yard rushback.

I see Lu Libble and Cliff Battles, and Rolfe Firney our coach too, rubbing their hands with zeal and dancing little Hitler dances on the sidelines. But naturally by now I'm out of breath and that dopey quarterback wants me to make my own touchdown. I just can't make it. I want to controvert his order but you're not supposed to. I puff into the line and get buried on the five. Then he, Runstedt, tries it, and the big St. Ben's line buries him, and then we miss the next two downs too and are stopped on the three and have to fall back for the St. Benedict punt.

By now I've got my wind again and I'm ready for another go. But the punt that's sent to me is so high, spirally, perfect, I see it's going to take an hour for it to fall down in my arms and I should really raise my arm for a fair catch and touch it down to the ground and start our team from there. But no, vain Jack, even though I hear the huffing and puffing of the two downfield men practically on my toes, I catch the ball free catch and practically say "Alley Oop" as I feel their four big hands squeeze like vices around my ankles, two on each, and puffing with pride I do the complete vicious twist of my whole body so that I can undo their grip and move on. But their St. Benedict grips have me rooted to where I am as if I were a tree, or an iron pole. I do the complete turnaround twist and hear a loud crack and it's my leg breaking. They let me fall back deposited gently on the turf and look at me and say to each other "The only way to get *him*, don't miss (more or less)."

I'm helped off the field limping.

I go into the showers and undress and the trainer massages my right calf and says "Oh, a little sprain won't hurt you. Next week it's Princeton and we'll give them the old one-two again Jacky boy."

But it was a broken leg, a cracked tibia, like if you cracked a bone about the size of a pencil and the pencil was still stuck together except for the hairline crack, meaning if you wanted you could just break the pencil in half with a twist of two fingers. But nobody knew this. The entire week they told me I was a softy and to get going and run around and stop limping. They had liniments, this and that, I tried to run, I ran and practiced and ran but the limp got worse. Finally they sent me off to Columbia Medical Center, took X-rays, and found out I had broken my tibia in the right leg and that I had been spending a week running on a broken leg.

You just can't run off a broken leg. Of course, old Lu Libble didn't know that the leg was broken, but even so I felt he had some kind of bug against me. He was always hinting I was a no-good and with those big legs he ought to put me in the line and make "a watch charm guard" out of me.

THAT NEXT next summer came the time when my father, who'd been working out of town as a linotypist, sometimes at Andover, Mass., sometimes Boston, sometimes Meriden, Conn., now had a steady job lined up at New Haven, Conn., and it was decided we move there. My sister by now was married. As we were packing, I went about and wrote sad songs about "picking up my stakes and rolling." But that wasn't the point.

One night my cousin Blanche came to the house and sat in the kitchen talking to Ma among the packing boxes. I sat on the porch outside and leaned way back with feet on rail and gazed at the stars for the first time in my life. A clear August night, the stars, the Milky Way, the whole works clear. I stared and stared till they stared back at me. Where the hell was I and what was all this?

I went into the parlor and sat down in my father's old deep easy chair and fell into the wildest daydream of my life.

As Ma and Cousin talked in the kitchen, I daydreamed that I was now going to go back to Columbia, for my sophomore year, with home in New Haven, maybe near Yale campus, with soft light in room and rain on the sill, mist on the pane, and go all the way in football and studies. I was going to be such a sensational runner that we'd win every game, against Dartmouth, Yale, Princeton, Harvard, Georgia U., Michigan U., Cornell, the bloody lot, and wind up in the Rose Bowl. In the Rose Bowl, worse even than Cliff Montgomery, I was going to run wild. Uncle Lu Libble for the first time in his life would throw his arms around me and weep. Even his wife would do so. The boys on the team would raise me up in Rose Bowl's Pasadena stadium and march me to the showers singing. On returning to Columbia campus in January, having passed chemistry with an A, I would then idly turn my attention to winter indoor track and decide on the mile and run it in under 4 flat (that was fast in those days). So fast, indeed, that I'd be in the big meets at Madison Square Garden and beat the current great milers in final fantastic sprints bringing my time down to 3:50 flat. By this time everybody in the world is crying "Duluoz! Duluoz!" But, unsatisfied, I idly go out in the spring of the Columbia baseball team and bat home runs clear over the Harlem River, one or two a game, including fast breaks from the bag to steal from the first to second, from second to third, and finally, in the climactic game, from third to home, zip, slide, dust, boom. Now the New York Yankees are after me.

They want me to be their next Joe DiMaggio; I idly turn that down because I want Columbia to go to the Rose Bowl again in 1943. Hah. But then I also, in mad midnight musings over a Faustian skull, after drawing circles in the earth, talking to God in the tower of the gothic church steeple of Riverside cathedral, meeting Jesus on the Brooklyn Bridge, getting friend Sabby a part on Broadway as Hamlet (playing King Lear myself across the street), I become the greatest writer that ever lived and write a book so golden and so purchased with magic that everybody smacks their brows on Madison Avenue. Even Professor Claire is chasing after me on his crutches on the Columbia campus. Mike Hennessey, his father's hand in hand, comes screaming up the dorm steps to find me. All the kids of HM are singing in the field. "Bravo, bravo, author!" they're yelling for me in the theater where I've also presented my newest idle work, a play rivaling Eugene O'Neill and Maxwell Anderson and making Strindberg spin. Finally, a delegation of cigar-chewing guys come and get me and want to know if I want to train for the world heavyweight boxing championship fight with Joe Louis. Okay, I train idly in the Catskills, come down on a June night, face big tall Joe as the referee gives us instructions, and then, when the bell rings, I rush out real fast and just pepper him real fast and so hard that he actually goes back bouncing over the ropes and into the third row and lays there knocked out.

I'm the world heavyweight boxing champion, the greatest writer, the world's champ miler, Rose Bowl and (pro-bound with New York Giants football nonpareil) now offered every job on every paper in New York, and what else? Tennis anyone?

I woke up from this daydream realizing that all I had to do was go back on the porch and look at the stars again, which I did, and still they just stared at me blankly.

I BEGAN to see that good old Lu Libble wasn't going to start me my sophomore year but let me sit on the bench while Liam McDiarmid and Spider Barth, who were seniors, wore out their seniority. Now they were shifty and nifty runners but not as fast or strong as I was. That didn't matter to Lu Libble. He insulted me in front of everybody again by saying "You're not such a hot runner, you can't handle the KF-79 reverse deception"—as if I'd joined football for "deception" for God's sake—"first thing you know, you with your big legs"—they weren't that big—"I'm going to make you lineman. Now run and do that reverse."

With my eyes I said "I can't run any faster these first two days, my legs are sore."

Never mind, he said with his eyes, putting me in mind of the time he made me run on a broken leg for a week.

At night, after those meaningless big suppers of steak and milk and dry toast, I began to realize this: "Lu Libble won't let you start this year, not even in the Army game against your great enemy Art Janur (who pushed me out of the shower when I was a kid in Lowell High), and not even maybe next year as a junior, he wants to make a big hero out of his Italian Mike Romanino, well Mike is a great passer, but he runs like an old cow. And Hank Full's leaving. The hell with it. What'll I do?"

I stared into the darkness of the bunk rooms thinking what to do.

"Ah shucks, go into the American night, the Thomas Wolfe darkness, the hell with these big-shot football coaches, go after being an American writer, tell the truth, don't be pushed around by them or anybody else or any of their goons. . . . The Ivy League is just an excuse to get football players for nothing and get them to be American cornballs enough to make America sick for a thousand years. You shoulda stuck to Francis Fahey. . . . "

Well I can't remember what I was thinking altogether but all I know is that the next night, after dinner, I packed all my gear in my suitcase and sauntered down the steps right in front of Lu Libble's table where he was sitting with his assistant coaches figuring out plays. My bones were rasping against my muscles from the overtraining; I limped. "Where are you going Dulouse?"

"Going over to my grandmother's house in Brooklyn and dump some of this clothes."

"It's Saturday night. Be back by tomorrow at eight. You gonna sleep there?"

"Yeh."

"Be back by eight. We're going to have a light calisthenics, you know the part where you get on your back and turn your skull to the grass and roll around so you won't get your fool neck broken in a game?"

"Yes sir."

"Be back by eight. What you got in there?"

"Junk. Present from home, dirty laundry. . . . "

"We got a laundry here."

"There's presents, letters, stuff, Coach."

"Okay, back at eight."

And I went out and took the subway down to Brooklyn with all my gear, whipped out a few dollars from the suitcase, said goodbye to Uncle Nick saying I was going back to Baker Field, walked down the hot September streets of Brooklyn hearing Franklin Delano Roosevelt's speech about "I Hate War" coming out of every barbershop in Brooklyn, took the subway to the 8th Avenue Greyhound bus station, and bough a ticket to the South.

I wanted to see the Southland and start my career as an American careener.

| | | | | |

Zero of the Lions

BY GEORGE PLIMPTON

*In the brief career of a professional amateur who had the chance
to play quarterback for Detroit, there were many telling moments
but none more harrowing than his first foray into the pit.*

RIDAY MACKLEM, THE EQUIPMENT MANAGER OF THE
Detroit Lions, was waiting by my locker. "Two hours to go,"
he said. I was about to find out what it felt like to quarterback a professional football team in an actual game. I was
going to do it without much confidence, not being a football player but a
writer, a weekend athlete who had been a lanky and ineffective end 15 years before, playing haphazardly and never proficiently enough to make a first team.
But it was worth recording, perhaps, what would happen to the amateur inserted in the world of the professional. My participation had been arranged with
the Detroit Lions. In late July last year, I arrived along with the new crop of rookies for three weeks of preseason workouts at the Lion training camp at Cran-
brook, a Michigan boys' school. I had hoped to preserve the fiction that I had
enjoyed experience as a quarterback—on a semipro team known as the New-
foundland Newfs—but a few clumsy maneuvers on the practice field had given
me away. Yet I had tried, never treating the opportunity flippantly, and I had
prepared intently, learning a series of plays that I would call in the big intrasquad scrimmage in Pontiac, Mich. A large crowd would be on hand, Fri-

day told me, overflowing the stadium to get a first look of the year at the Lions, particularly the new rookies.

They're going to see some strange ones out there," Friday said, looking at me. He handed me my game jersey of tearaway material, in the deep blue of Detroit—Honolulu blue, it was called—with my number in silver, which was 0 on both the back and front and on the sleeves.

"You feel all right?" he asked.

"Oh sure," I said. I sat down on the bench and took off my street shoes, setting them carefully in the locker. The plan was to dress at the training camp and ride in game uniform to Pontiac, a half-hour trip by bus, rather than change in the stadium there.

"You better jump to it," Friday said. "Most everyone's dressed."

Sam Williams, who was a first-string defensive end, came by, and looked down my aisle of lockers. "Nerves?" he asked. "How are the nerves?"

"Well, I've got them, Sam," I said. "I feel them in the stomach."

He was in his fifth year of professional football, and I asked him if nerves still affected him.

"Sure," he said. "In the feet and hands—heavy feet, heavy hands, so's I can barely move around."

"Heavy feet!" I said. "Think of that." I took a breath, a deep one, to relieve the tension, and went back to dressing, putting on the paraphernalia of the uniform slowly, item by item, overfastidious to get them set right. Williams's locker was in the next aisle, and when I was ready I went around and he pulled the blue jersey down over my shoulder pads, something difficult to do alone, and he cuffed the pads into place.

"That's a good number you're wearing," Williams said. "Johnny Olszewski's—Johnny O's."

Olszewski had been a Detroit back on the 1961 team.

"It indicates my talent," I said. Friday Macklem had either Hopalong Cassady's old number available, which was 40, or Johnny O's zero, and he thought the zero had more—well, distinction.

I went back to my locker. My football shoes were up on top, next to the big silver helmet with the blue Lion decal, and when I took the shoes down they seemed astonishingly heavy to the hand. "Hey!" I said.

I spotted Friday coming by again.

"Hey, Friday, what's happened to my shoes?"

He came over. He looked very busy. "What's trouble?" he asked briskly. "Boy, you'd better hop to it. You're going to miss the bus."

"Well," I said, "these shoes seem, well, sort of heavy, that's what they seem."

"Your shoes seem heavy?" said Friday, quite loudly, so that I moved toward him and I said softly, "Well, look here, Friday, heft them for yourself."

He did so, and he looked surprised. "There's nothing wrong."

"Somebody's put something in them," I said stubbornly.

Friday called out loudly: "Hey, the rookie thinks somebody's weighted his shoes. What'd anyone want to do that for?" I looked carefully at the corners of his mouth for a turn that would suggest that a joke was being played. There was no such indication. Sam Williams came around the lockers with Joe Schmidt, the All-League linebacker.

"Feet seem heavy?" Williams asked.

"Hell no, Sam," I said. "It's the shoes. Someone's stuck weights in them."

"Who'd want to do that?" asked Schmidt. He leaned over and hefted the shoes. "They seem all right to me."

A number of players were standing around by then, dressed for the bus ride, holding their helmets by the chin straps.

"Try them on," Schmidt suggested.

I slipped the shoes on, laced them up, and clomped around the locker room floor in front of my bench.

"What do you think?" Friday asked.

"Well, I don't know," I said, "I mean, I can walk and all, but they still seem all-fired heavy."

"That's not surprising," said Sam Williams. "Look, you got a big night coming up, quarterbacking your first game, and you got a real case of heavy feet, that's all. Perfectly natural. Nothing to be blamed for."

He had a grin on his face, but I began to wonder if it wasn't one of sympathy. Around the circle of faces there was not a glimmer—even on that of Night Train Lane, whose manner was so easy he was always laughing—to suggest that they weren't all being perfectly serious.

"Aw, come on now," I said. "I haven't got heavy feet, for godsake! Come on now," I said again, watching them, particularly Night Train's eyes, waiting for the laughter to dissolve them and give them away. They all remained solemn. At the edge of the circle players just arriving, who couldn't see past the big phalanx of shoulder pads, wanted to know what was going on.

"Someone fainted?" I heard a voice ask.

"It's his nerves," someone said. "He's got heavy feet."

Friday suddenly said: "I'll tell you something about those shoes. The cleats are worn thin. Hand 'em over and I'll get one of the boys to screw in a new set for you."

I sat down on the bench and took the shoes off, hefting them once more, and shaking my head. Friday disappeared with them.

Someone said, "D'ja ever see such a case of nerves?"

The players began drifting away—those who were dressed heading for the buses out in the parking lot, their cleats crashing against the locker room floor. Someone came by as I waited and said I was wanted—and quick—for the quarterback meeting.

[After the meeting] I hurried off to the equipment manager's room to retrieve my football shoes. Friday's assistant was still screwing cleats into them. "Hey, Friday!" I said. "Those cleats look awful long. Those aren't *mud* cleats you're sticking in there?"

Friday came over. "What'd I want to stick mud cleats in there for?" he said. "The day's fine outside. Going to be a lovely night. What do you want mud cleats for?"

"I don't want mud cleats, dammit, Friday, but those things being put in there are long enough to bring up, well, oil, and as for the shoes themselves, Friday, they got to have weights in them."

Friday began hefting them again, but then suddenly he grinned and broke—with a thin wheeze that left him struggling for breath. "O.K., O.K.," he said. "Look at this." He tugged at the inside sole of the shoe, straining against the glue that had hardened fast, and he skinned out a thin metal strip. It weighted at least a pound.

"What do you think of that?" he asked. "They were put in this morning."

"Look at those things," I said.

Friday explained that players who wanted to strengthen their leg muscles often wore the metal plates in their shoes in the early part of training. You could tell when they came in from running with them—sort of like gimpy hens," he said.

"Great," I said. "You mean to say they would have let me play the game tonight wearing those things?"

"Probably not," said Friday. "They'd all like to see you do well, but it's hard for them not to kid around. They'd have had a good laugh afterwards, and if you didn't do so well you would have had a good excuse. Now you haven't got an excuse."

I laced on the shoes and hurried out to the parking lot, where the bus was waiting.

"DON'T FORGET to put on your helmet," he said. "This is for real and there's not going to be any fooling around."

I said: "How much time is there before . . . ?"

"Ten minutes," he said. "There'll be an award ceremony after the contests and then the game will start."

I looked for my helmet, relieved to see it lying in the grass a few yards away. My impulse was to put it on. From the beginning I'd had trouble getting into the helmet. The procedure was to stick the thumbs in the helmet's ear holes and stretch the helmet out as it came down over the head—a matter of lateral pull, and easy enough if you practiced isometrics, but I never had the strength to get my ears quite clear, so they were bent double inside the helmet once it was on. I would work a finger up inside to get the ears upright again, a painful procedure, and noisy, the sounds sharp in the confines of the hard shell of the helmet as I twisted and murmured until it was done, the ears ringing softly. Then quiet would settle in the helmet, and I would look out beyond the bars of the nose guard—the "cage," the players call it—to see what was going on outside, my eyes still watering slightly. It was even more difficult to get the helmet off. The first helmet Friday Macklem had given me was too small—a helmet is supposed to fit snugly to afford the best protection—and when I tried it on in front of my locker I yelled as it came down over my ears. Wayne Walker, the big linebacker, happened to be chatting with me at the time.

"How'd she feel?"

"Feels fine. Snug," I said. "Once you get the thing on."

I tried to take it off. Got my thumbs in the ear holes and tried to budge the helmet loose. "I'm stuck in here," I said, simply.

Walker began to grin. He looked down the locker room aisle for other players who would have enjoyed the dilemma. Mercifully, none were on hand.

"Damn!" I said. "I can't budge this thing."

"You'll get used to it," Walker said.

"Jeez!" I was straining to get it off.

"You're truly married to pro football," said Walker. "After a while you'll never know you got it on."

The helmet came away finally, leaving my ears inflamed and raw, the side of my head furrowed. "Enough to make one quit the game," I said.

I soon got in the habit of putting the helmet on when there was even the slightest chance of entering a scrimmage, rather than face the awkward possibility of being called suddenly by coach Wilson and either not having a helmet at all (players were supposed to keep their helmets at hand, but it was easy enough to leave them lying in the grass while you tossed a ball back and forth) or having difficulty getting into it: the strain, and getting the ears straight, all that procedure, while running out to take over the offensive huddle.

So when Wilson said there were 10 minutes to go, I stared at him wildly, retrieving my helmet from the grass and fidgeting with it.

I turned away, got my thumbs into the helmet ear holes and, ducking my head, I wrenched the helmet on. When I'd got my ears straight I clicked the chin strap fast to a little punch-on snap—which sounds sharply in the helmet, pop!—and I wandered over to the bench and sat down.

One of the troubles with wearing the helmet was that it closed off the outside world, the noise of the crowd, the cheering as the contests wore on—all of this just a murmur—leaving my mind to work away busily inside the amphitheater of the helmet. Voices, my own, spoke quite clearly, my lips moving in the security of the helmet, offering consolation, encouragement and paternal advice of a particularly galling sort: "The thing to be is calm, son, and remember not to snatch back from the ball until you get it set in your palm."

"I'll hang on to the ball," I murmured back.

"But"—the portentous voice came again like Ghost's in *Hamlet*—"you must not dally, son. On the handoffs you must get the ball to the halfbacks with dispatch."

These pronouncements were accompanied by short, visual vignettes, subliminal, but which seemed to flash inside the helmet with the clarity of a television screen in a dark room—tumultuous scenes of big tackles and guards in what seemed a landslide, a cliff of them toppling toward me like the slow-moving object in a dream, as I lay in some sort of a depression gaping up in resigned dismay. Raymond Berry, the knowledgeable Baltimore end, once told me that I would survive a scrimmage if I played his position (out on the flank) and was sure to stay out of what he referred to as the "pit"—a designation that often came to mind just before my participation in scrimmages. It was an area, as he described it, along the line of scrimmage, perhaps 10 yards deep, where at the centering of the ball the Neanderthal struggle began between the opposing linemen. The struggle raged within a relatively restricted area that was possible to avoid. Berry himself, when he told me this, had wandered into the pit only three times in his career—coming back to catch poorly thrown buttonhook passes falling short—and he spoke of each instance as one might speak of a serious automobile accident. The particulars were embalmed in his memory in absolute clarity; that year, in that city, at such-and-such a game, during such-and-such a quarter, when so-and-so, the quarterback, threw the ball short, his arm jogged by a red-dogging linebacker, so that Berry had to run out of his pattern back toward the scrimmage line so many yards to catch it, and it was so-and-so, the 290-pounder, who reached an arm out of the ruck of the pit and dragged him down into it.

"One thing to remember when you do get hit," Berry told me in his soft Texas accent, "is to try to fall in the foetus position. Curl up around the ball, and keep your limbs from being extended, because there'll be other people coming up out of the pit to see you don't move any, and one of them landing on an arm that's outstretched, y'know, can snap it."

"Right," I said.

"But the big thing is just stay out of that area."

"Sure," I said.

But when I arrived to train with the Lions I disregarded his advice. What I had to try to play was quarterback, because the essence of the game was involved with that position. The coaches agreed, if reluctantly, and after the front office had made me sign some papers absolving them of any responsibility, I became the "last-string" quarterback, and thus stood in Berry's pit each time I walked up behind the center to call signals. He was right, of course. One of the first plays I called landed me in the pit. It was a simple handoff play. Opposite me across the line the linebackers were all close up, shouting, "Jumbo! Jumbo! Jumbo!" which is one of the Lion code cries to rush the quarterback. When the snap came I fumbled the ball, gaping at it, mouth ajar, as it rocked back and forth gaily at my feet, and I flung myself on it, my subconscious shrilling "Foetus! Foetus!" as I tried to draw myself in like a frightened pill bug, and I heard the sharp strange whack of gear, the grunts—and then a sudden weight whooshed the air out of me.

It was Dave Lloyd, a 250-pound linebacker, who got through the line and got to me. A whistle blew and I clambered up, seeing him grin inside his helmet, to discover that the quick sense of surprise that I had survived was replaced by a pulsation of fury that I had not done better. I swore lustily at my clumsiness, hopping mad, near to throwing the ball into the ground, and eager to form a huddle to call another play and try again. The players were all standing up, some with their helmets off, many with big grins, and I heard someone calling, "Hey, man, hey, man!" and someone else— John Gordy, I think, because he said it all the time—called out, "Beautiful, real beautiful." I sensed then that an initiation had been performed, a blooding ceremony. Wayne Walker said, "Welcome to pro ball." Something in the tone of it made it not only in reference to the quick horror of what had happened when I fumbled but in appreciation that I had gone through something that made me, if tenuously, one of them, and they stood for a while on the field watching me savor it.

| | | | | | |

Bang, You're Dead

BY DON DeLILLO

In this selection from End Zone, *which was first excerpted in* SI *in 1972, one of America's best young writers had college football squarely in his crosshairs.*

AFT ROBINSON WAS THE FIRST BLACK STUDENT TO BE enrolled at Logos College in West Texas. They got him for his speed. ¶ By the end of that first season he was easily one of the best running backs in the history of the Southwest. In time he might have turned up on television screens across the land, endorsing $8,000 automobiles or avocado-flavored instant shave. His name on a chain of fast-food outlets. His life story on the back of cereal boxes. A drowsy monograph might be written on just that subject, the modern athlete as commercial myth, with footnotes. But this doesn't happen to be it. There were other intonations to that year, for me at least, the phenomenon of anti-applause—words broken into brute sound, a consequent silence of metallic texture. And so Taft Robinson, rightly or wrongly, no more than haunts this story. I think it's fitting in a way. The mansion has long been haunted (double metaphor coming up) by the invisible man.

But let's keep things simple. Football players are simple folk. Whatever complexities, whatever dark politics of the human mind, the heart—these are noted only within the chalked borders of the playing fields. At times strange visions ripple across that turf; madness leaks out. But wherever else he goes, the football player travels the straightest of lines. His thoughts are wholesomely commonplace, his actions uncomplicated by history, enigma, holocaust or dream.

A passion for simplicity, for the true old things, as of boys on bicycles delivering newspapers, filled our days and nights that fierce summer. We practiced in the undulating heat with nothing to sustain us but the conviction that things here were simple. Hit and get hit; key the pulling guard; run over people; suck some ice and reassume the three-point stance. We were a lean and dedicated squad run by a hungry coach and his seven oppressive assistants. Some of us were more simple than others; a few might be called outcasts or exiles; three or four, as on every football team, were crazy. But we were all—even myself—we were all dedicated.

We did grass drills at 106° in the sun. We attacked the blocking sleds and strutted through the intersecting ropes. We stood in what was called the chute (a narrow strip of ground bordered on two sides by blocking dummies), and we went one-on-one, blocker and pass-rusher, and hand-fought each other to the earth. We butted, clawed and kicked. There were any number of fistfights. There was one sprawling free-for-all that the coaches allowed to continue for about five minutes, standing on the sidelines looking pleasantly bored as we kicked each other in the shins and threw dumb rights and lefts at caged faces, the more impulsive taking off their helmets and swinging them at anything that moved. In the evenings we prayed.

I was one of the exiles. There were many times, believe it, when I wondered what I was doing in that remote and unfed place, that summer tundra, being hit high and low by a foaming pair of 240-pound Texans. Being so tired and sore at night that I could not raise an arm to brush my teeth. Being made to obey the savage commands of unreasonable men. Being set apart from all styles of civilization as I had known or studied them. Being led in prayer every evening, with the rest of the squad, by our coach, warlock and avenging patriarch. Being made to lead a simple life.

Then they told us that Taft Robinson was coming to school. I looked forward to his arrival—an event, finally, in a time of incidents and small despairs. But my teammates seemed sullen at the news. It was a break with simplicity, the haunted corner of a dream, some piece of forest magic to scare them in the night.

Taft was a transfer student from Columbia. The word on him was good all the way. 1) He ran the 100 in 9.3 seconds. 2) He had good moves and good hands. 3) He was strong and rarely fumbled. 4) He broke tackles like a man pushing through a turnstile. 5) He could pass-block—when in the mood.

But mostly he could fly—9.3 speed. He had real sprinter's speed. Speed is the last excitement left, the one thing we haven't used up, still naked in its potential, the mysterious black gift that thrills the millions.

(EXILE OR outcast: distinctions tend to vanish when the temperature exceeds 100°.)

Taft Robinson showed up at the beginning of September, about two weeks before regular classes were to start. The squad, originally 100 bodies, soon down to 60, soon less, had reported in the middle of August. Taft had missed spring practice and 20 days of the current session. I didn't think he'd be able to catch up. I was in the president's office the day he arrived. The president was Mrs. Tom Wade, the founder's widow. Everybody called her Mrs. Tom. She was the only woman I had ever seen who might accurately be described as Lincolnesque. Beyond appearance, I had no firm idea of her reality; she was tall, black-browed, stark as a railroad spike.

I was there because I was a Northerner. Apparently they thought my presence would help make Taft feel at home, an idea I tended to regard as laughable. (He was from Brooklyn, having gone on to Columbia from Boys' High, a school known for the athletes it turns out.) Mrs. Tom and I sat waiting.

"My husband loved this place," she said. "He built it out of nothing. He had an idea, and he followed it through to the end. He believed in reason. He was a man of reason. He cherished the very word. Unfortunately he was mute."

"I didn't know that."

"All he could do was grunt. He made disgusting sounds. Spit used to collect at both corners of his mouth. It wasn't a real pretty sight."

Taft walked in flanked by our head coach, Emmett Creed, and backfield coach, Oscar Veech. Right away I estimated height and weight, about 6' 2" and 210. Good shoulders, narrow waist, acceptable neck. Prize beef at the county fair. He wore a dark gray suit that may have been as old as he was.

Mrs. Tom made her speech. "Young man, I have always admired the endurance of your people. You've a tough row to hoe. Frankly I was against this from the start. When they told me their plan, I said it was bushwa. Complete

178

bushwa. But Emmett Creed is a mighty persuasive man. This won't be easy for any of us. But what's reason for if not to get us through the hard times? There now. I've had my say. Now you go on ahead with Coach Creed, and when you're all through talking football you be sure to come on back here and see Mrs. Berry Trout next door. She'll get you all settled on courses and accommodations and things. History will be our ultimate judge."

Then it was my turn.

"Gary Harkness," I said. "We're more or less neighbors. I'm from upstate New York."

"How far up?" he said.

"Pretty far. Very far in fact. Small town in the Adirondacks."

We went over to the players' dorm, an isolated unit just about completed but with no landscaping out front and WET PAINT signs everywhere. I left Taft in his room and went downstairs to get suited up for afternoon practice. Moody Kimbrough, our right tackle and offensive captain, stopped me as I was going through the isometrics area.

"Is he here?"

"He is here," I said.

"That's nice. That's real nice."

In the training room Jerry Fallon had his leg in the whirlpool. He was doing a crossword puzzle in the local newspaper.

"Is he here?"

"He is everywhere," I said.

"Who?"

"Supreme being of heaven and earth. Three letters."

"You know who I mean."

"He's here all right. He's all here. Two hundred and fifty-five pounds of solid mahogany."

"How much?" Fallon said.

"They're thinking of playing him at guard. He came in a little heavier than they expected. About 255. Left guard, I think Coach said."

"You kidding me, Gary?"

"Left guard's your spot, isn't it? I just realized."

"How much does he weigh again?"

"He came in at 255, 260. Solid bronze right from the foundry. Coach calls him the fastest two-five-five in the country."

"He's supposed to be a running back," Fallon said.

"That was before he added weight."

"I think you're kidding me, Gary."

"That's right," I said.

WE RAN through some new plays for about an hour. Creed's assistants moved among us yelling at our mistakes. Creed himself was up in the tower studying overall patterns. I saw Taft on the sidelines with Oscar Veech. The players kept glancing that way. When the second unit took over on offense, I went to the far end of the field and grubbed around for a spot of shade in which to sit. Finally I just sank into the canvas fence and remained more or less upright, contemplating the distant fury. These canvas blinds surrounded the entire practice field in order to discourage spying by future opponents. The blinds were one of the many innovations Creed had come up with—innovations as far as this particular college was concerned. He had also had the tower built, as well as the separate living quarters for the football team. (To instill a sense of unity.) This was Creed's first year here. He had been born in Texas, in either a log cabin or a manger, depending on who was telling the story, on the banks of the Rio Grande in what is now Big Bend National Park. The sporting press liked to call him Big Bend. He made a few All-America teams as a tailback in the old single-wing days at SMU and then flew a B-29 during the war and later played halfback for three years with the Chicago Bears. He went into coaching then, first as an assistant to George Halas in Chicago and then as head coach in the Missouri Valley Conference, the Southeastern Conference and the Big Eight. He became famous for creating order out of chaos, building good teams at schools known for their perennial losers. He had four unbeaten seasons, five conference champions and two national champions. Then a second-string quarterback said or did something he didn't like, and Creed broke his jaw. It became something of a national scandal, and he went into obscurity for three years until Mrs. Tom beckoned him to West Texas.

It was a long drop down from the Big Eight, but Creed managed to convince the widow that a good football team could put her lonely little school on the map. So priorities were changed, new assistants were hired, alumni were courted, a certain amount of oil money began to flow, a certain number of private planes were made available for recruiting purposes, the team name was changed from the Cactus Wrens to the Screaming Eagles—and Emmett Creed was on the comeback trail. The only thing that didn't make sense was the ton of canvas that hid our practice sessions. There was nothing out there but insects.

The first unit was called back in, and I headed slowly toward the dust and noise. Creed up in the tower spoke through his bullhorn.

"Defense, I'd appreciate some pursuit. They don't give points for apathy in this sport. Pursue those people. Come out of the ground at them. Hit somebody. Hit somebody. Hit somebody."

On the first play Garland Hobbs, our quarterback, faked to me going straight into the line and then pitched to the other setback, Jim Deering. He got hit first by a linebacker, Dennis Smee, who drove him into the ground, getting some belated and very nasty help from a tackle and another linebacker. Deering didn't move. Two assistant coaches started shouting at him, telling him he was defacing the landscape. He tried to get up but couldn't make it. The rest of us walked over to the far hash mark and ran the next play.

It all ended with two laps around the goalposts. Lloyd Philpot Jr., a defensive end, fell down in the middle of the second lap. We left him there in the end zone, on his stomach, one leg twitching slightly. His father had been All-Conference at Baylor for three straight years.

That evening Emmett Creed addressed the squad.

"Write home on a regular basis. Dress neatly. Be courteous. Articulate your problems. Move swiftly from place to place, both on the field and in the corridors of buildings. Don't ever get too proud to pray."

ROLF HAUPTFUHRER coached the defensive line and attended to problems of morale and grooming. He approached me one morning after practice.

"We want you to room with Bloomberg," he said.

"Why me?"

"John Billy Small was in there with him. Couldn't take the tension. We figure you won't mind. You're more the complicated type."

"Of course I'll mind."

"John Billy said he wets the bed. Aside from that there's no problem. He gets nervous. No doubt about that. A lot of tension in that frame. But we figure you can cope with it."

"I object. I really do. I've got my own tensions."

"Harkness, everybody knows what kind of reputation you brought down here. Coach is willing to take a chance on you only as long as you follow orders. So keep in line. Just keep in line—hear?"

"Who's rooming with Taft Robinson?" I said.

"Robinson rooms alone."

"Why's that?"

"You'll have to ask the powers that be. In the meantime, move your stuff in with Bloomberg."

"I don't like tension," I said. "And I don't see why I have to be the one who gets put in with controversial people."

"It's for the good of the team," Hauptfuhrer said.

I went upstairs to my room. Bloomberg was asleep, on his belly, snoring softly into the pillow. He was absolutely enormous. It was easy to imagine him attached to the bed by guy wires, to be floated aloft once a year like a Macy's balloon. His full name was Anatole Bloomberg, and he played left tackle on offense. That was all I knew about him, that plus the fact that he wasn't a Texan. One of the outcasts, I thought. Or a voluntary exile of the philosophic type. I decided to wake him up.

"Anatole," I said. "It's Gary Harkness, your new roommate. Let's shake hands and be friends."

"We're roommates," he said. "Why do we have to be friends?"

"It's just an expression. I didn't mean undying comrades. Just friends as opposed to enemies. I'm sorry I woke you up."

"I wasn't asleep."

"You were snoring," I said.

"That's the way I breathe when I'm on my stomach. What happened to my original roommate?"

"John Billy? John Billy's been moved."

"Was that his name?"

"He's been moved. I hope you're not tense about my showing up. All I want to do is get off to a good start and avoid all possible tension."

"Who in your opinion was the greater man?" Bloomberg said. "Edward Gibbon or Archimedes?"

"Archimedes."

"Correct," he said.

In the morning Creed sent us into an all-out scrimmage with a brief inspirational message that summed up everything we knew or had to know.

"It's only a game," he said, "but it's the only game."

Taft Robinson and I were the setbacks. Taft caught a flare pass, evaded two men and went racing down the sideline. Bobby Iselin, a cornerback, gave up the chase at the 25. Bobby used to be the team's fastest man.

THROUGH ALL our days together my father returned time and again a favorite saying.

"Suck in that gut and go harder."

He never suggested that this saying of his ranked with the maxims of Teddy Roosevelt. Still, he was dedicated to it. He believed in the idea that a simple but lasting reward, something just short of a presidential handshake, awaited the extra effort, the persevering act of a tired man. Backbone, will, mental toughness, desire—these were his themes, the qualities that insured success. He was a pharmaceutical salesman with a lazy son.

It seems that wherever I went I was hounded by people urging me to suck in my gut and go harder. They would never give up on me—my father, my teachers, my coaches, even a girlfriend or two. I was a challenge, I guess, a piece of string that does not wish to be knotted. My father was by far the most tireless of those who tried to give me direction, to sharpen my initiative, to piece together some collective memory of hard-won land or dusty struggles in the sun. He put a sign in my room:

WHEN THE GOING GETS TOUGH
THE TOUGH GET GOING

I looked at this sign for three years (roughly from ages 14 to 17) before I began to perceive a certain beauty in it. The sentiment of course had small appeal, but it seemed that beauty flew from the words themselves, the letters, consonants swallowing vowels, aggression and tenderness, a semiself-re-creation from line to line, word to word, letter to letter. All meaning faded. The words became pictures. It was a sinister thing to discover at such an age that words can escape their meanings.

My father had a territory and a company car. He sold vitamins, nutritional supplements, mineral preparations and antibiotics. His customers included about 50 doctors and dentists, about a dozen pharmacies, a few hospitals, some drug wholesalers. He had specific goals, both geographic and economic, each linked with the other, and perhaps because of this he hated waste of any kind, of shoe leather, talent, irretrievable time. (Get cracking. Straighten out. Hang in.) It paid, in his view, to follow the simplest, most pioneer of rhythms—the eternal work cycle, the blood hunt for bear and deer, the mellow rocking of chairs as screen doors swing open and bang shut in the gathering fragments of summer's sulky dusk. Beyond these honest latitudes lay nothing but chaos.

He had played football at Michigan State. He had ambitions on my behalf, and more or less at my expense. This is the custom among men who have failed to be heroes; their sons must prove that the seed was not impoverished. He had spent his autumn Saturdays on the sidelines, watching others fall in battle and rise then to the thunder of the drums and the crowd's demanding chants. He put me in a football uniform very early. Then, as a high school junior, I won All-State honors at halfback. (This was the first of his ambitions, and as it turned out the only one to be fulfilled.) Eventually I received 28 offers of athletic scholarships—tuition, books, room and board, $15 a month. There were several broad hints of further almsgiving. Visions were painted of lovely young ladies with charitable instincts of their own. It seemed that every section of the country had much to offer in the way of scenery, outdoor activities, entertainment, companionship, and even, if necessary, education. On the application blanks I had to fill in my height, my weight, my academic average and my time for the 40-yard dash.

I handed over a letter of acceptance to Syracuse University. I was eager to enrich their tradition of great running backs. They threw me out when I barricaded myself in my room with two packages of Oreo cookies and a girl named Lippy Margolis. She wanted to hide from the world, and I volunteered to help her. "For a day and a night we read to each other from a textbook on economics. She seemed calmed by the incoherent doctrines set forth on those pages. When I was sure I had changed the course of her life for the better, I opened the door.

At Penn State, the next stop, I studied hard and played well. But each day that autumn was exactly like the day before and the one to follow. I had not yet learned to appreciate the slowly gliding drift of identical things; chunks of time spun past me like meteorites in a universe predicated on repetition. For weeks the cool clear weather was unvarying; the girls wore white knee-high stockings; a small red plane passed over the practice field every afternoon at the same time. There was something hugely Asian about those days in Pennsylvania. I tripped on the same step on the same staircase on three successive days. After this I stopped going to practice.

The freshman coach wanted to know what was up. I told him I knew all the plays; there was no reason to practice them over and over; the endless repetition might be spiritually disastrous; we were becoming a nation devoted to human xerography. He and I had a long earnest discussion. Much was made of my talent and my potential value to the varsity squad. Oneness was stressed—the oneness necessary for a winning team. It was a good concept, oneness, but I suggested that, to me at least, it could not be truly attractive unless it meant oneness with God or the universe or some equally redoubtable superphenomenon. What he meant by oneness was in fact elevenness or twenty-twoness. He told me that my attitude was all wrong. People don't go to football games to see pass patterns run by theologians. He told me, in effect, that I would have to suck in my gut and go harder. He mentioned, 1) A team sport. 2) The need to sacrifice. 3) Preparation for the future. 4) Microcosm of life.

"You're saying that what I learn on the gridiron about sacrifice and oneness will be of inestimable value later on in life. In other words, if I give up now I'll almost surely give up in the more important contests of the future."

"That's it exactly, Gary."

"I'm giving up," I said.

It was a perverse thing to do—go home and sit through a blinding white winter in the Adirondacks. I was passing through one of those odd periods of youth in which significance is seen only on the blankest of walls, found only in dull places, and so I thought I'd turn my back to the world and to my father's sign and try to achieve, indeed establish, some lowly form of American sainthood. The repetition of Penn State was small stuff compared to that deep winter. For five months I did nothing and then repeated it. I had breakfast in the kitchen, lunch in my room, dinners at the dinner table with the others, meaning my parents. They concluded that I was dying of something slow and incurable and that I did not wish to tell them in order to spare their feelings. This was an excellent thing to infer for all concerned. My father took down the sign and hung in its place a framed

photo of his favorite pro team, the Detroit Lions—their official team picture. In late spring, a word appeared all over town, MILITARIZE. The word
was printed on cardboard placards that stood in the shop windows. It was
scrawled on fences. It was handwritten on loose-leaf paper taped to the
windshields of cars. It appeared on bumper stickers and signboards.

I had accomplished nothing all those months, and so I decided to enroll
at the University of Miami. It wasn't a bad place. Repetition gave way to
the beginnings of simplicity. (A preparation thus for Texas.) I wanted badly
to stay. I liked playing football, and I knew that by this time I'd have trouble finding another school that would take me. But I had to leave. It started with a book, an immense volume about the possibilities of nuclear war—
assigned reading for a course I was taking in modes of disaster technology.
The problem was simple and terrible: I enjoyed the book. I liked reading
about the deaths of tens of millions of people. I liked dwelling on the destruction of great cities. Five to 20 million dead. Fifty to 100 million dead.
Ninety percent population loss. Seattle wiped out by mistake. Moscow demolished. Airbursts over every SAC base in Europe. I liked to think of huge
buildings toppling, of fire storms, of bridges collapsing, survivors roaming
the charred countryside. Carbon 14 and strontium 90. Escalation ladder
and sub-crisis situation. Titan, Spartan, Poseidon. People burned and unable to breathe. I became more fascinated, more depressed, and finally I
left Coral Gables and went back home to my room and to the official team
photo of the Detroit Lions. It seemed the only thing to do. My mother
brought lunch upstairs. I took the dog for walks.

In time the draft board began to get interested. I allowed my father to
get in touch with a former classmate of his, an influential alumnus of
Michigan State. Negotiations were held, and I was granted an interview
with two subalterns of the athletic department, types familiar to football
and other paramilitary complexes, the square-jawed bedrock of the corporation. They knew what I could do on the football field, having followed my high school career, but they wouldn't accept me unless I could
convince them that I was ready to take orders, to pursue a mature course,
to submit my will to the common good. I managed to convince them. I
went to East Lansing the following autumn, an aging recruit, and was
leading the freshman squad in touchdowns, yards gained rushing, and
platitudes. Then, in a game against the Indiana freshmen, I was one of

three players converging on a safetyman who had just intercepted a pass. We seemed to hit him simultaneously. He died the next day and I went home that evening.

I stayed in my room for seven weeks this time, shuffling a deck of cards. I got to the point where I could cut to the six of spades about three out of five times, as long as I didn't try too often, abuse the gift, as long as I tried only when I truly felt an emanation from the six, when I knew in my fingers that I could cut to that particular card.

Then I got a call from Emmett Creed. Two days later he flew up to see me. I liked the idea of losing myself in an obscure part of the world. And I had discovered a very simple truth. My life meant nothing without football.

WE STOOD in a circle in the enormous gray morning, all the receivers and offensive backs, helmets in hands. Thunder moved down from the northeast. Creed, in a transparent raincoat, was already up in the tower. At the center of the circle was Tom Cook Clark, an assistant coach, an expert on quarterbacking, known as a scholarly man because he smoked a pipe and did not use profanity.

"What we want to do is establish a planning procedures approach whereby we neutralize the defense. We'll be employing a lot of play action and some pass-run options off the sweep. We'll be using a minimum number of sprint-outs because the passing philosophy here is based on the pocket concept and we don't want to inflate the injury potential, which is what you do if your quarterback strays from the pocket and if he can't run real well, which most don't. We use the aerial game here to implement the ground game whereby we force their defense to respect the run, which is what they won't do if they can anticipate pass and read pass and if our frequency, say on second and long, indicates pass. So that's what we'll try to come up with, depending on the situation and the contingency plan and how they react to the running game. I should insert at this point that if they send their linebackers, you've been trained and briefed and you know how to counter this. You've got your screen, your flare, your quick slant-in. You've been drilled and drilled on this in the blitz drills. It all depends on what eventuates. It's just 11 men doing their job. That's all it is."

Oscar Veech burst into the circle.

"Guards and tackles, I want you to come off that ball real quick and pop, pop, hit those people, move those people out, pop them, put some hurt on them, drive them back till they look like sick little puppy dogs squatting in the mud."

"The guards and tackles are over in that other group," I said.

"Right, right, right. Now go out there and execute. Move that ball. Hit somebody. Hit somebody. Hit somebody."

Garland Hobbs handed off to me on a quick trap, and two people hit me. There was a big pileup, and I felt a fair number of knees and elbows and then somebody's hand was inside my face mask trying to come away with flesh. On the next play I was pass-blocking for Hobbs and they sent everybody including the free safety. I went after the middle linebacker, Dennis Smee, helmet to groin, and then fell on top of him with a forearm leading the way.

Whistles were blowing, and the coaches edged in a bit closer. Vern Feck took off his baseball cap and put his pink face right into the pileup, little sparks of saliva jumping out of his whistle as he blew it right under my nose. Creed came down from the tower.

ONE DAY in early September we started playing a game called Bang, You're Dead. It's an extremely simpleminded game. Almost every child has played it in one form or another. Your hand assumes the shape of a gun, and you fire at anyone who passes. You try to reproduce, in your own way, the sound of a gun being fired. Or you simply shout these words: Bang, you're dead. The other person clutches a vital area of his body and then falls, simulating death. (Never mere injury: always death.) Nobody knew who had started the game or exactly when it had started. You had to fall if you were shot. The game depended on this.

It went on for six or seven days. At first, naturally enough, I thought it was all very silly, even for a bunch of bored and lonely athletes. Then I began to change my mind. Suddenly, beneath its bluntness, the game seemed compellingly intricate. It possessed gradations, dark joys, a resonance echoing from the most perplexing of dreams. I began to kill selectively. When killed, I fell to the floor or earth with great deliberation, with sincerity. I varied my falls, searching for the rhythm of something imperishable, a classic death.

We did not abuse the powers inherent in the game. The only massacre took place during the game's first or second day when things were still shapeless, the potential unrealized. It started on the second floor of the dormitory, just before lights-out and worked along the floor and down one flight, everyone shooting each other, men in their underwear rolling down the stairs, huge nude brutes draped over the banisters. The pleasure throughout was empty. I guess we realized together that the game was better than this. So we cooled things off and devised unwritten limits.

I shot Terry Madden at sunset from a distance of 40 yards as he appeared over the crest of a small hill and came toward me. He held his stomach and fell, in slow motion, and then rolled down the grassy slope, tumbling, rolling slowly as possible, closer, slower, ever nearer, tumbling down to die at my feet with the pale setting of the sun.

To kill with impunity. To die in the celebration of ancient ways.

All those days the almost empty campus was marked by the sound of human gunfire. There were several ways in which this sound was uttered— the comical, the truly gruesome, the futuristic, the stylized, the circumspect. Each served to break the silence of the long evenings. From the window of my room I'd hear the faint gunfire and see a lone figure in the distance fall to the ground. Sometimes, hearing nothing. I'd merely see the victim get hit, twisting around a tree as he fell or slowly dropping to his knees, and this isolated motion also served to break the silence, the lingering stillness of that time of day. So there was that reason above all to appreciate the game; it forced cracks in the enveloping silence.

I died well and for this reason was killed quite often. One afternoon, shot from behind, I staggered to the steps of the library and remained there, on my back between the second and seventh steps at the approximate middle of the stairway, for more than a few minutes. It was very relaxing despite the hardness of the steps. I felt the sun on my face. I tried to think of nothing. The longer I remained there, the more absurd it seemed to get up. My body became accustomed to the steps, and the sun felt warmer. I was completely relaxed. I felt sure I was alone, that no one was standing there watching or even walking by. This thought relaxed me ever more. In time I opened my eyes. Taft Robinson was sitting on a bench not far away, reading a periodical. For a moment, in a state of near rapture, I thought it was he who had fired the shot.

At length the rest of the student body reported for the beginning of classes. We were no longer alone, and the game ended. But I would think of it with affection because of its scenes of fragmentary beauty, because it brought men closer together through their perversity and fear, because it enabled us to pretend that death could be a tender experience, and because it breached the long silence.

IT'S NOT easy to fake a limp. The tendency is to exaggerate, a natural mistake and one that no coach would fail to recognize. Over the years I had learned to eliminate this tendency. I had mastered the dip and grimace, perfected the semi-moan, and when I came off the field this time, after receiving a mild blow on the right calf, nobody considered pressing me back into service. The trainer handed me an ice pack, and I sat on the bench next to Bing Jackmin, who kicked field goals and extra points. The practice field was miserably hot. I was relieved to be off and slightly surprised that I felt guilty about it. Bing Jackmin was wearing headgear; his eyes, deep inside the face mask, seemed crazed by sun or dust or inner visions.

"Work," he shouted past me. "Work you substandard industrial robots. Work, work, work, work."

"Look at them hit," I said. "What a pretty sight. When Coach says hit, we hit. It's so simple."

"It's not simple, Gary. Reality is constantly being interrupted. We're hardly even aware of it when we're out there. We perform like things with metal claws. But there's the other element. For lack of a better term I call it the psychomythical. That's a phrase I coined myself."

"I don't like it. What does it refer to?"

"Ancient warriorship," he said. "Cults devoted to pagan forms of technology. What we do out on that field harks back. It harks back. Why don't you like the term?"

"It's vague and pretentious. It means nothing. There's only one good thing about it. Nobody could remember a stupid phrase like that for more than five seconds. See, I've already forgotten it."

"Wuuuuurrk. Wuuuuurrrrrk."

"Hobbs'll throw to Jessup now," I said. "He always goes to his tight end on third and short inside the 20. He's like a retarded computer."

"For a quarterback, Hobbs isn't too bright. But you should have seen him last year, Gary. At least Creed's got him changing plays at the line. Last year it was all Hobbsie could do to keep from upchucking when he saw a blitz coming. Linebackers pawing at the ground, snarling at him. He didn't have what you might call a whole lot of poise."

"Here comes Cecil off. Is that him?"

"They got old Cecil. Looks like his shoulder."

Cecil Rector, a guard, came toward the sideline, and Roy Yellin went running in to replace him. The trainer popped Cecil's shoulder back into place. Then Cecil fainted. Bing strolled down that way to have a look at Cecil unconscious.

Later we watched Bobby Hopper get about 18 on a sweep. When the play ended, a defensive tackle named Dickie Kidd remained on his knees. He managed to take his helmet off and then fell forward, his face hitting the midfield stripe. Two players dragged him off, and Raymond Toon went running in to replace him. The next play fell apart when Hobbs fumbled the snap. Creed spoke to him through the bullhorn. Bing walked along the bench to look at Dickie Kidd.

I watched the scrimmage. It was getting mean out there. The players were reaching the point where they wanted to inflict harm. It was hardly a time for displays of finesse and ungoverned grace. This was the ugly hour. I felt like getting back in. Bing took his seat again.

"How's Dickie?"

"Dehydration," Bing said. "Hauptfuhrer's giving him hell."

"What for?"

"For dehydrating."

I went over to Oscar Veech and told him I was ready. He said they wanted to take a longer look at Jim Deering. I watched Deering drop a short pass and get hit a full two seconds later by Buddy Shock, a linebacker. This cheered me up, and I returned to the bench.

"They want to look at Deering some more."

"Coach is getting edgy. We open in six days. This is the last scrimmage, and he wants to look at everybody."

"I wish I knew how good we are."

"Coach must be thinking the same thing."

Time was called, and the coaches moved in to lecture their players. Creed climbed down from the tower and walked slowly toward Garland Hobbs. He took off his baseball cap and brushed it against his thigh as he walked.

Hobbs saw him coming and instinctively put on his helmet. Creed engaged him in conversation.

"It's a tongue-lashing," Bing said. "Coach is hacking at poor old Hobbsie."

"He seems pretty calm."

"It's a tongue-lashing," Bing hissed to Cecil Rector, who was edging along the bench to sit next to us.

"How's the shoulder?" I said.

"Dislocated."

"Too bad."

"They can put a harness on it," he said. "We go in six days. If Coach needs me, I'll be ready."

Just then Creed looked toward Bing Jackmin, drawing him off the bench without even a nod. Bing jogged over there. The rest of the players were standing or kneeling between the 40-yard lines. Next to me, Cecil Rector leaned over and plucked at blades of grass. I thought of the Adirondacks, chill lakes of inverted timber, sash of blue snow across the mountains, the whispering presence of the things that filled my room. Far beyond the canvas blinds, on the top floor of the women's dormitory, a figure stood by an open window. I thought of women. I thought of women in snow and rain, on mountains and in forests, at the end of long galleries immersed in the brave light of Rembrandts.

"Coach is real anxious," Rector said. "He knows a lot of people are watching to see how he does. I bet the wire services send somebody out to cover the opener. If they can ever find this place."

"I'd really like to get back in."

"So would I," he said. "Yellin's been haunting me since way back last spring. He's like a hyena. Every time I get hurt, Roy Yellin is right there grinning. He likes to see me get hurt. He's after my job. Every time I'm face down on the grass in pain, I know I'll look up to see Roy Yellin grinning at the injured part of my body. His daddy sells mutual funds in the prairie states."

Bing came back, apparently upset about something.

"He wants me to practice my squib kick tomorrow. I told him I don't have any squib kick. He guaranteed me I'd have one by tomorrow night."

They played for another 15 minutes. On the final play, after a long steady drive that took the offense down to the eight-yard line, Taft fumbled the handoff. Defense recovered, whistles blew and that was it for the day. The three of us headed back together.

"Hobbsie laid it right in his gut, and he goes and loses it," Rector said. "I attribute that kind of error to lack of concentration. That's a mental error, and it's caused by lack of concentration. Coloreds can run and leap, but they can't concentrate. A colored is a runner and leaper. You're making a big mistake if you ask him to concentrate."

A very heavy girl wearing an orange dress came walking toward us across a wide lawn. There was a mushroom cloud appliquéd on the front of her dress. The dress was brightest orange. I thought she must be a little crazy to wear something like that with her figure. I recognized the girl; we had some classes together. I let the others walk on ahead, and I stood for a moment watching her walk past me and move into the distance. I was wearing a smudge of lampblack under each eye to reduce the sun's glare. I didn't know whether the lampblack was very effective, but I liked the way it looked and I liked the idea of painting myself in a barbaric manner before going forth to battle in mud. I wondered if the fat girl knew I was still watching her. I had a vivid picture of myself standing there holding my helmet at my side, left knee bent slightly, hair all mussed and the lampblack under my eyes.

INSIDE FOOTBALL

| | | | | | |

How Does It Really Feel?

BY ROY BLOUNT JR.

The pain and glory of pro football are exemplified by the players' hands, so vulnerable to injury, so vital to victory. And the ravaged hands of the Pittsburgh Steelers were close to grasping the ultimate prize when the author spent a season with them.

NE AFTERNOON DURING PRACTICE I WAS WATCHING the linemen pound away at each other—wump, clack. Guard Bruce Van Dyke paused to say, "What are you doing?" ⟨ "Trying to get a feel for this," I said. ⟨ "If you really want to get a feel for it you should put on some pads and get out here and get blocked," he said.

"Well," I said, "I thought I would get a feel for it by asking you how it feels."

"I try not to notice how it feels," he said. "If you felt it, you wouldn't do it."

I admired head coach Chuck Noll's response when a reporter came up to him after the Steelers' loss to Cincinnati and asked, "How do you feel?"

"It hasn't changed," said Noll. "I still feel with my hands." Often, you had to hand it to Noll.

So I thought I might try treating the question of how pro football feels by asking players about their hands. One conclusion I was led to from that line of questioning was that pro football feels terrible.

On the backs of their hands and on their knuckles many of the players had wounds of a kind I have never seen on anyone else: fairly deep digs and gouges that were not scabbed over so much as dried. They looked a little like old sores on horses. The body must have given up trying to refill those gouges and just rinded them over and accepted them. During the year, at Noll's suggestion, the offensive line did the backs of their hands a favor by adopting the thick black leather gloves that fighters use for punching a heavy bag. Before he started wearing these gloves, Van Dyke said, the backs of his hands were so sore all season from banging into defensive linemen's ribs that he hated to shake hands.

Different Steelers taped their hands all different ways: the middle two fingers together; the last two together; or just one or more jammed fingers taped singly for support. A jammed finger hurts less after it is taped. Craig Hanneman boasted that he and Mean Joe Greene were the only two defensive linemen on the Steelers who didn't tape and pad their hands and forearms heavily. I asked him why he didn't. "Just to be tough," he said in a self-deprecating way. But he did tape each of his fingers, because they were always jammed or broken from catching on opponents' helmets. Lloyd Voss, a Steeler defensive tackle who retired after the '72 season, used to tape all his fingertips, because otherwise he often would have his nails jerked out. (He also used to bring his small daughter into the dressing room, causing some consternation.)

"I've never broken a finger," said Greene. "I had 'em stepped on, twisted, but not broken. One time I grabbed at Jim Plunkett and my little finger caught in a twist of his jersey and he ran for a ways dragging me that way, by my little finger. That turned my little finger around, but it didn't break it."

Most of the defensive linemen had broken many fingers. "You can't play football, I don't care what position, without hands," said defensive end Dwight White. "I used 'em to pull, knock down, grab. Hands are as important as eyes."

He glanced down at his. "See this fanger," he said. "I got it jammed five years ago, and it's just started to straighten out. See that fanger? Can't wear a ring on it. I got some of the ugliest fangers in the world. They get bloodshot from licks. Come in with the whole end of it brown from hitting."

In '72 L.C. Greenwood looked down in the midst of a play to see the upper two-thirds of his middle finger completely twisted around backward and crossed over the ring finger. "I couldn't figure out what had happened. So

I fixed it right there in the middle of the play and went on." He had it splinted and played with the splint on, and now that finger sticks out at a grotesque angle. He said he would get it straightened after he was out of football; no point doing it until then. It hurt in cold weather, he said.

Fats Holmes, a tackle, pounded the insides of his wrists—where the veins and tendons that suicides slit are—in sand to toughen them up.

Safety Mike Wagner said he broke three fingers his first year in the pros from grabbing at receivers, so now he tried to keep his hands out of his tackles. It is good tackling technique in the open field to use your shoulder and body instead of your hands anyway, he pointed out.

Receivers, running backs and quarterbacks could hardly keep their hands out of play, and they had to use them too subtly to be able to tape their fingers. "My fingers stay jammed," said quarterback Joe Gilliam. "Stepped on. Pop 'em on helmets. Holding on to the ball while people are trying to pull it away. Every time one gets jammed you have to alter your grip, and that makes you anticipate your throw. Makes you think about it. That's bad. My two little fingers never will be the same. I jammed the right one in camp last year and it's still bothering me. Imagine what somebody like John Brodie or Sonny Jurgensen's hands are like, who's been playing so long."

"I don't hold," maintained guard Sam Davis. "If I know a guy's going to beat me and get the quarterback, then I'll hold. Otherwise I use my fists. Hit him with my fists—catch him on the side, uppercut him in the ribs. Make contact with your shoulder and then come up with your hands; it's like a second man coming in to hit him. You ball your hands up so you have a firm type fist situation." But Davis got called for holding a number of times during the year. Noll put together a film to send to the league office, showing Davis getting called for clean licks and other linemen holding blatantly without getting called.

"There isn't a play run," maintained punter Bobby Walden, "when holding couldn't be called."

"That's an old wives' tale," said center Ray Mansfield. "But if I'm holding on purpose, there's no way I'm going to be caught at it."

Things fall apart if the center cannot hold.

"Hands are all in your head," said wide receiver Glenn Scolnik of the concept *good hands*. "A great receiver is totally relaxed from the waist up.

The receiver's face is not all tight. He relaxes so his jowls hang, he eases, and he takes it real soft."

Some of the receivers worked putty in their hands to keep them strong, or squeezed rubber balls, or just spent a lot of time carrying a football around and tossing it from hand to hand. "In the off-season I spend 10 minutes a day with each hand dropping the ball and catching it," said wide receiver Ron Shanklin, a great man for getting *at* the ball as well as for hauling it in.

That is not easy, holding a ball out in front of you in one hand, releasing it and then catching it in the same hand. Wide receiver Barry Pearson, the player you would think of first if you thought *sure-handed*, said his hands weren't big enough to do that. He relied on concentration. "I watch the ball all the way in. You can't let the point hit either of your hands; it should come between them."

"Lots of guys have good hands and nobody knows it," says receiver coach Lionel Taylor, "because they don't have the concentration." He put the Steeler receivers through a number of drills to make them concentrate on the ball.

He would throw them knuckleballs, floaters, end-over-ends. "I learned a lot of hard-catch drills when I was playing. You'd go out for a pass and they'd wave a towel at you, even throw weeds at you. Big handful of brush! You'd say, 'What was *that*!' But then in a game you're used to distractions and you don't flinch.

"Another thing about receivers is when they get hit by somebody when they're coming over the middle. They come through the middle next time, they're *short*-arming it. They don't *want* to catch it. I always thought about two things when the ball was coming: catching the football and getting hit. Always expected to get hit when I caught the football. Expected somebody to tear my head off. Then I wasn't surprised."

You never get far from contact in discussing any aspect of football. But the contact of ball on good hands is a special kind. The ball is hard and the receiver's hands are also hard. But a pass goes *snk* at the end, or even *sk* or, more softly, *ft* or *p* or *pth*—instead of *splack*—when the right touch gets ahold of it. "You don't fight the football," someone said. Iron hands in velvet gloves.

"See those hands," said Kansas City scout Lloyd Wells as we watched a college receiver go out for a practice pass. "Those are board hands. You be scouting long enough you can tell. The sound of 'em. Ball bounced off before he caught it. Plus the fact that the ball made him waver, it made him stride, it made him start to go raggledy-dedaggledy."

Wells said Jimmy Hines, the track star drafted by the Chiefs, "could fly on a pattern. Thought he was going to be another Bob Hayes. Run fast, fast, *fast*. But he could not catch the ball. Not with a basket could he catch the ball. Hank Stram did everything he could to make him a wide receiver. Used to take him out and throw him 200 and 300 passes. Made him walk around with the ball. He could not catch it."

Players who handle the ball frequently develop a connoisseur's hands. Field-equipment manager Jack Hart said he could spin a ball and tell whether it was balanced. Referees would reject a game ball if it had a little bulge around the laces or if the black stitching around the laces didn't follow exactly the black line around them. "Guys claim the night ball is fatter because the white stripes make it look that way," said Hart, "so we use those in practice a few days before a night game. A dark ball is better to grip. A lighter-toned ball is slippery."

"When you can get a good ball," said quarterback Terry Hanratty, "you just want to stay with it. Some are slick and some are fatter than others. Noll will look at it and say no, that ball's not fatter, but unless you've thrown the ball as long as a quarterback has you can't tell."

Terry Bradshaw and Gilliam both have big hands, like most quarterbacks and baseball pitchers. I told Bradshaw I'd seen a picture of him and President Nixon comparing hands, palm to palm, in some White House ceremony, and it looked like their fingertips matched exactly. "Nixon must have big hands," I said.

Bradshaw said, well, Nixon had cheated up on him a little bit from the bottom.

Wide receiver Chuck Dicus said he'd had to stop working on cars, which he loved to do, because it cut up his hands too much and it was bad for a receiver's hands to hurt. I asked him, "Can you do anything special with them because they're a receiver's hands?"

"I can do this," he said, and he crossed his middle finger over his forefinger and his ring finger over his little finger at the same time, without using any of his other fingers to help them into place.

Now that, I thought, is a good little index to a receiver's hands. I was talking to one of the linemen about hands and I said, "Dicus can do this." And I did it.

Oddly enough I could only do it with my left hand. Still, it must not be much of a hallmark of receivers' hands. Unless . . . unless . . . . One afternoon during a Steelers practice, when I was all dressed up in sweat pants and a yellow jersey and shoes with lots of short plastic cleats for artificial turf, placekicker Roy Gerela started lofting me passes and I looked marvelous. I don't think any other part of my body could conceivably make it in the NFL. Once I scrambled down a gravelly hill in front of a scout and at the bottom I said, "Pretty good feet, huh?" and he said, "Yeah. If you had one more of 'em you might be a player." Once in the dressing room the trainer came up behind me and kneaded me at the base of the neck. He acted as though I didn't have any muscles there. "We don't get many in here like you," he said. That made me feel wonderful.

But my hands were nearly as big as Bradshaw's (about the size, then, of Nixon's). I am a third baseman in Central Park softball, and playing third base requires quick hands. I was catching passes from Gerela and a wave of competence came over me. Not only was I catching the ball neatly with my fingers—*ft, pth*—but I actually felt I was *moving* well. I was catching the ball at the sidelines and putting both feet down deftly in bounds.

"Hmmm, SPORTS ILLUSTRATED, eh?" said Gerela, and it sounded vainly like an acknowledgement. I trotted off the field and Dan Rooney said, "You looked like you knew what you were doing out there." The man who directed the club! I think I may have told him as modestly as possible that I caught the only forward pass completed all season by my dorm floor in freshman intramurals in college.

Still I had a great reluctance about asking the quarterbacks to throw to me. Once when Bradshaw was working his arm back into shape I ran out and he *underthrew* me. I may be the only person of my speed ever to be underthrown by Terry Bradshaw. I think he was afraid I would fly apart if he hit me. Or maybe I looked even slower than I was. At any rate I knew it wasn't doing his timing any good, throwing to me. So I never asked him to throw to me again. Photographer Walter Iooss did, though, and he barely got his hands up in time. "All of a sudden the ball was just *there*," he reported. "The ball came in a *line*."

IN PALM Springs preparing for the playoff game with Oakland, the Steelers were very loose. They were usually loose, but in Palm Springs there was a lassitude, almost, in the air. Which Noll, as you can imagine, did not approve of. When guard Moon Mullins pulled too slowly for his taste, though the rest of the offensive line thought Moon was pulling hard, Noll said in a very hard voice, "If you can't run any faster than that, maybe we've got the wrong people out here."

But generally the tone of things was very relaxed in Palm Springs, and I was spending even more time than usual with the players, since they didn't have homes to go to. One afternoon in practice I found myself catching for Bradshaw. When quarterbacks warm up, they have someone else catch the ball when it is thrown back, so as not to take a chance on hurting their fingers. Bradshaw was throwing to someone next to Hanratty and Hanratty was throwing to me.

One problem was that I was wearing street clothes, including a shoe whose crepe sole was loose and flapping. Another problem was that I have never been able to throw a football very well. I have a good arm in softball. Ask anybody. But I throw a wobbly pass.

So when I tossed the ball to Bradshaw after Hanratty threw it to me, I looked bad from the beginning. I admit that. And the fans got on me for it.

There were fans watching. Local people who had nothing better to do on a weekday afternoon (I don't think anybody in Palm Springs has much to do; everybody looks rich; I hate Palm Springs) were clustered around the field watching practice.

But, hey, I was catching the ball. I would run a little pattern in the end zone and Hanratty would pop it to me and I would catch it with just my hands. "Great hands, terrible arm," laughed Hanratty once. I disdained the use of my arms and body, in part, perhaps, because I was mindful that Chris Speier, the San Francisco Giants' shortstop, had caught passes from the Steeler quarterbacks one afternoon and the next day the insides of his arms were black and blue. I wasn't going to wrap the ball up desperately, I was going to flick my hands out there like magnetized rags and just *snk* that ball. I did that. Twice. That pebble grain feels good, like living skin on the whorls of your fingers.

Twice. Or maybe three times. Then my hands gave out on me. I may have been *noticing* too much, and therefore became self-conscious. But it was also true that my hands got numb and leathery. I would put them out like before and there would be a sort of splutter, or splatter, as the ball struggled in them as though frightened and squirted through. Once, trying not to tighten up, I overeased and the ball just tipped my fingers and went zooming way beyond me. "How did I ever catch something like that?" I began to think.

Bradshaw was taking part by coming up heavily behind me like a defender. Footsteps. Like a coward, I would shy away and reach out at the ball awkwardly. Now I am not thoroughly frightened of running into big strong people. I wasn't afraid of bumping into Bradshaw. It was just that I didn't feel I belonged there anyway, and if Bradshaw wanted to be somewhere my instinct was to get out of his way.

But I should have flung my body at the ball if I couldn't get my hands to perform. Stop it *some* way. The ball, though, is hard, and it has that blunt point, like an unsharpened stake. For the first time in my life I had balls coming at me which, if I missed them, would smash my face.

"Sacrifice your body," cried a still small voice in my head.

"How about my pride?" cried a louder, more vibrant one.

And the fans' voices did me no good at all. They were groaning and yelling and hooting, especially when I tripped over the pitcher's mound deep in the end zone and went sprawling, tearing the knee of my pants. "Here! Let me do it! He can't do it!" several adolescent boys cried out. "Oh, God!" some witness cried in perverse delight.

"Now you know what we have to put up with," Bradshaw said softly.

I persisted raggedly, and finally Hanratty and Bradshaw were through warming up. I took a nice soft one from Hanratty over my shoulder, spiked the ball to spite the crowd and trotted hangdog over to the sidelines. Dan Rooney looked away.

There was an 18-year-old girl around the pool at the Gene Autry Hotel, where we were staying, who was so wonderful-looking it made you mad. I'm not even going to try to describe her. She wore a terry-cloth bikini, which you could not have dried off a little mouse with. I think she was why the Steelers lost, if she bothered them as much as she did me. She was there with her mother. A Steeler went out with her one night. It was a chaste evening— her mother and a teammate were along—but the next morning a nonplayer made a funny, disparaging, indelicate comment on the Steeler's ineptitude, socially and athletically.

I relayed the remark to linebacker Any Russell shortly before my receiving experience began. He didn't really laugh. "That's cold-blooded, as the guys say," he said. When I came to the sidelines in disgrace Russell was standing there. I was filled, as I approached him, with the realization that as tight as I might be with the Steelers, for a scribe, I didn't have the license to exchange cold-blooded talk with them concerning on-the-field matters. I shifted the focus of my cold-bloodedness. "The fans hate me," I said. "I hate the fans."

"You loved that, didn't you?" said Russell, smiling.

Loved it? I was startled. I felt terrible. I had *dropped* all those passes. . . .

"Journalistically," I conceded.

As I was getting some faint measure of feel for the game, the Steelers were losing theirs; it is hard to be intense in Palm Springs. Some interesting things happened. Art Rooney, the owner, used the term "bikinkies"—as in bikinky bathing suits; Joe Greene ate hot sauce until, according to some observers, steam rose from his head; a Steeler got a free massage at a local parlor by telling his masseuse she was under arrest; Van Dyke exemplified cold-blooded football humor by saying companionably to Bobby Walden, who'd been having an uneven season punting and was getting up in years, "Well, this is about it for you, huh, Bo?"

Van Dyke also confessed doubts on the part of the offense: "When we get down close to the goal, we're wondering if we can score. You're not just doing your job, you're asking yourself if you can score."

A sobbing anonymous father called the hotel from a Pittsburgh hospital to ask whether Greene and linebacker Jack Ham would talk to his dying young son. They strained to hear the boy's weak voice. "We're going after those Raiders," Ham told him. "Are you going to watch the game?" The boy said he didn't know whether he would live long enough. "Joe and I will come and watch you play football when you get better," Ham said. The boy's answer was inaudible. Ham and Greene were shaken.

"The Raiders are just like any other bunch of kids who like to beat up another bunch of kids," said their great receiver, Fred Biletnikoff. But they were also the kids on whom the Steelers had perpetrated the Immaculate Reception in the playoffs the year before. And Oakland was where things had been so favorably wild for the Steelers six weeks before. On the way out onto the field Bradshaw slung his golden arm over my shoulder and sang a country song he said he'd written: "Hello, trouble . . . Come on in . . . Ain't had no trouble since you know when . . . . " Whatever the sideline equivalent of being on the edge of your seat is, the Steelers were. I found myself sort of bouncing in place like the players, and stopped, feeling silly. The fans were primed. They were holding signs that said MURDER FRANCO and MEAN? JOE GREENE WEARS PANTY HOSE.

Just before the half Bradshaw hit Barry Pearson for a four-yard touchdown pass to make the score Oakland 10, Pittsburgh 7, and Van Dyke exclaimed, "We've got them now! And they know it. Oh, they may make it look good for the fans, but they know it." Surely the Steelers' winning nature would assert itself. Or the Raiders would choke. Somehow things would fit together.

They fit together for Oakland. During halftime Bradshaw nodded his head, "Yeah, yeah, yeah," as Noll tried to tell him what to do. In the third quarter the Raiders kicked two quick field goals and the Steeler offense didn't move. "We're trying to *lose*!" said Barry Pearson, as if he were a fan. "No sense in that!"

"We're getting beat across the board," said defensive tackle Steve Furness. "Offense and defense." The defense had been saving the offense all year; finally they both had gone flat.

"Could be a sad ending to your book," said Craig Hanneman.

"It isn't over yet," I said absurdly.

Franco Harris was pacing back and forth like a zoo lion whose knee hurt. L.C. Greenwood was sitting on the bench with his hands and arms swathed in thick, peeling, stained bandages like those on besieged Marines at Dak To in pictures in LIFE. His head was down. Linebacker Loren Toews got in a fight on the field, came off and was hit with a chocolate ice cream cone from the stands. Ice cream was all over the back of his head, mingling with sweat and grass and dirt and running down the cords of his neck. The fans whooped and laughed.

Bradshaw threw a touchdown pass, but he also threw three interceptions and the final score was 33–14 Oakland. Bradshaw dressed hurriedly and left. He didn't go back to Pittsburgh. Joe Greene sat in the dressing room. On the floor around his feet were scattered jockstraps, dirty towels and battered empty tape husks that had been cut away from hands and still looked grasping. "We're one of the best teams in the country with one of the best coaching staffs." He said. "But something was missing. Today that special ingredient was missing."

Then he sagged. "Now I got to go out and probably fight. 'Cause somebody's going to say something I don't agree with. You gonna help me?" he asked me.

I told him I'd be somewhere behind him, but all the bellicose fans seemed to have gone home. On the plane back, Ham and Wagner jocularly blamed various teammates. "It was your fault."

"It's a game of inches," Ham said.

"Sometimes it's a game of feet," said Wagner.

Rocky Bleier did his chicken imitation. He brushed his hair up like a comb and hunched down with his chest out huge and walked like a hen and clucked.

Sam Davis looked pent-up and desolate. I asked him a dumb scribe's question: How did he feel now compared to the way he felt after the last game in '72?

"Same," he said.

"Does it always feel the same after you lose the last one?"

"It does. To me."

Art Rooney was playing gin with line coach George Perles, in apparent equanimity. "Wait till next year," he said.

"A guy like me," said defensive back Dennis (Kamikaze) Meyer, meaning a marginal recklessly-disregard-your-small-body guy, "I don't know whether I'll have a next year."

"I'd call it a predictable ending," said cornerback John Rowser. "With our offense, anything we got was a bonus." Several other defensive men agreed. They grumbled about Bradshaw's thinking, and Noll's.

"The terrible thing," said Mansfield later, "is that the defense didn't die on the beaches with their bayonets. They ran into the water and drowned. I think that's basic to the success of humanity—don't quit. What if the United States laid down in World War II?"

"It's like what Adlai Stevenson said after Eisenhower beat him so bad," Hanneman said. "He said he felt like a little boy who had stubbed his toe in the dark. He said he was too old to cry, but it hurt too much to laugh."

Players were taking belts out of various things to augment the two free beers. "Watch out for Noll," someone said. "He won't venture back into the pit," said someone else.

In the dressing room after the game, in his last '73 address to the team, Noll had been brief: "We're too good a team to be losing. We're going to take a long concentrated look at the season. We're going to find out where the mistakes came and why. All I can say is Merry Christmas." He didn't smile. "Merry Christmas," he said. Now he sat wordless up front staring straight ahead. He had lost. He would be criticized by fans and scouts and scribes.

When we reached Pittsburgh I said goodbye to people, as though it were a high school graduation. "I can't drive back to Oregon in time for Christmas," Hanneman said blearily, solemnly. "Can't buy gas on Sunday. Hell, Christmas is just like any other day to me. It'll be the 12th year in a row I'll have Christmas by myself." His face was grim. "You know what I said about Stevenson . . . not crying? I said that, but I will. I'll break down before I take off in the car."

What kind of end was this for a year with hard-rolling men of contact? Something missing. Something missing. In a plane crowded with 250-pound people, not one image of fullness.

"Sometimes," Bradshaw had said earlier, "you'd like to go out there and really give them something to boo: have 20 interceptions, hand off to the wrong people, lose 100 to 0. Come off the field and the coach is laughing, everybody's hugging everybody, just having a good time."

Later Mansfield ate his eggs, and then some of my eggs, in a late-night hash house in Pittsburgh and told me this: "In college they'd say, 'Mansfield, you're fat and last.' They wanted me to run hard all the way, but I'd hang back and beat everybody in the last minute. They had guys built like Greek gods who couldn't block, and I got stomach hanging over my belt and I knock hell out of people. I didn't get the MVP my senior year—a guy who was nice did. That's what I like about myself: coaches don't like me. I like to have a good time. But I do the job anyway.

"I'm getting at the stage now where I have to worry about losing my physical ability. My neck hurts so bad sometimes I think about killing myself. I know I'll be a cripple by the time I'm 50. But if that's what it takes, all right. When I was growing up my family never had anything. I want to enjoy life. Next to love, football is the thing I like most."

And right after the playoff loss, in the dressing room before his sweat was dry, I talked to Russell. Russell, who used to be one of the game's great hunch-playing blitzers, but who had sacrificed much of his abandon to Noll's disciplined team-play system. Russell, who surely can't be playing for money, because he makes twice as much in business as in football. Russell, who on a tour of Vietnam, finding himself in a barracks vulnerable to attack, spent the night on its steps with a rifle and a martini.

That was the Russell who after the playoff defeat spoke literally of ecstasy: "I was *into* that game. There was no other world outside it. There was *nothing*. That's the thrill."

"Does that make it hard to lose?"

"No—easier. You know you gave it all you had. Some games you're distracted by an injury or something, and you get down on yourself, question your character. This game—I was *into* the game. We lost. But all I could think afterward was 'Goddam, I had fun.' "

And so I guess did all of that frothing crowd, and maybe even Noll, and so—journalistically and personally—did I, the detached scribe, who had thrown my arm around Russell's shoulder pads on the sidelines as defeat loomed, and so did the fan back home in Pittsburgh, who wrote:

Dear pittsBurgh

I like your team. I watched all of your games, pittsBurgh when you lost to Oklalang I think it was are right and Because you Bet them 3 times so what well pittsBurgh I am very glad that I am a fan of your team well pittsBurgh I am glad I wrote this letter well I guess Id, Better go well Bye. Bye.

Love your fan
Steve

(PS) I love your team.

"It's some game," Russell said. "It's a great game. It's not like going to play a game of squash."

| | | | | | |

Bottom's Up

BY AUSTIN MURPHY

*No wonder long snappers are the game's oddballs: The world they view between
their legs is upside down.*

HEY ARE ANONYMOUS EXCEPT IN TIMES OF DISASTER, FOR
which they are invariably blamed. They are paid to per-
form an act that gives them an upside-down perspective
on the world and leaves them in an absurdly vulnerable
position that cries out to opponents: Clobber me! Is it any wonder that
there is an inordinately high incidence of strangeness among NFL long
snappers?

Among their number we find a poet, a pilot, the owner of a boutique
cookie business, a singer in a group called Toe Jam and a heavily tattooed
heavy-metal junkie who has sported a Mohawk. And you thought kickers
were flakes.

Our question for Trey Junkin is this: Does long-snapping lead to eccen-
tricity, or are the eccentric drawn to long-snapping? Junkin, a 14-year veteran believes it is the latter. "Not every kid grows up and says, 'Mommy, I
want to put my head between my legs and let other guys beat on me while
I snap a football,' " he says.

When Junkin and Dave Binn of the San Diego Chargers got together in a hotel coffee shop to swap anecdotes and insights about long-snapping, it looked like a Hell's Angels' chapter meeting. Binn showed up with shoulder-length hair and a goatee; Junkin was sporting a goatee and a black leather jacket with a Harley-Davidson pin. Security eyed them nervously.

Tell us, guys. Has anyone tried to sabotage a long snap by putting a foreign substance on the ball? "My rookie year a guy threw dirt on the ball," says Binn. "That wasn't too cool."

Junkin has a longer list: "I've had Stickum. I've had Vaseline, which some defensive linemen put under their arms, so you can't hold 'em. I've had packing grease on the ball. I've had guys spit on the ball. One time a guy spit on my hands while I was snapping the ball."

"How was the snap?" asks Binn.

"The snap was good," says Junkin, "but I got fined for punching the guy."

These two occupy opposite ends of the long-snapping spectrum. Binn was a walk-on at Cal who eventually received a scholarship to do nothing but long snap; in 1994 the Chargers signed him as a free agent solely to snap. Junkin didn't snap at all at Louisiana Tech, where he was a linebacker with 4.3 speed in the 40. The Buffalo Bills took him in the fourth round of the '83 draft. "That was 13 years and six knee operations ago," says Junkin, who doubles as a tight end. He took up long-snapping in 1990 to make himself more valuable. Smart move. For the last six or seven years long-snapping has paid the mortgage.

Only a few long snappers double as regular players. They don't need long-snapping. Those guys constitute a smug minority. Probably a quarter of NFL teams split the long-snapping duties: a deep snapper for punts and a short snapper for field goals and extra points.

Which is tougher? Though shorter, the snap-for-placement is often more pressure-packed, since points—and sometimes victory—are at stake. This explains why, according to Adam Schreiber, a 13-year vet who does both short- and deep-snapping for the New York Giants, "you find a lot of spitting in field goal situations."

The center on kick placements makes two adjustments: He has to take something off the ball—"You're not trying to knock the holder over," says Schreiber—and he has to "snap laces." That means the snapper must deliver the ball so that when the holder catches it his top hand is on the laces. "That way when he puts it down, the laces are facing the goalpost," Schreiber adds.

The punt snap is "more of an aggressive snap, with speed," says Schreiber. The ball must reach the punter in .8 of a second. How fast is that? Faster than his wife, Dalene, thought. At a picnic several summers ago, Adam felt "the itch to snap" and asked Dalene if she would catch a few. "What do I do?" she asked. "You say 'set,' and I snap the ball at my convenience," he replied.

"The first one was a nice, tight spiral," recalls Schreiber. "It wasn't high, but then again she's only about five foot four." The ball broke a couple of her fingernails.

Usually it is the snapper who absorbs the abuse. When Junkin thought a Cleveland Browns player was diving at his knees two years ago, he started brawling with him. Junkin was in turn set upon by his own teammate, Kevin Mawae, who, as he tried to save Junkin from being ejected, shouted, "I'm not snapping!" Mawae was Seattle's backup snapper.

In addition to dabbling in motorcycles and martial arts, Junkin writes poetry. The following minimalist, arbitrarily capitalized lines are from *The Snap*:

> *Get a Look*
> *Defense, Ball, Punter*
> *Feel movement*
> *Hear the call*
> *Adjust the Ball*
> *everything comes to*
> *zero*
> *stillness you feel the Line*
> *you to punter*
> *15 yards*
> *perfect snap*
> *Block*
> *Some can;*
> *some can't.*

Some can appreciate timeless verse, some can't. After zipping through Junkin's poem, Binn merely says, "Cool."

To fill the uncomfortable silence, I compliment Junkin on his economical style. Junkin mentions that he has also tried to write haiku. "But that form, like Japanese society, is highly restrictive," he says.

So the poet laureate of long snappers has no snapping-related haiku for us. Emboldened by his example, I give it a whirl:

> *This jerk waits until*
> *I'm helpless, then cleans my clock.*
> *I hate the noseguard.*

By the end of last season Junkin estimates that he had bent over the ball 1,040 times in succession without making a bad punt snap. When he reached the 1,000 mark last season, in a game against the New York Jets, play was not stopped; Cal Ripken–like festivities did not erupt. Junkin staged his own little celebration. "I ran down and snatched the ball from the official," he says. "The guy thought I'd lost my mind."

Ingratitude comes with the territory. As Brad Banta, who handles long-snapping duties for the Indianapolis Colts, says, "The more unnoticed you are, the better you must be doing."

Just because I'm anonymous at work doesn't mean I have to be anonymous in life. This seems to be the philosophy of many of today's deep snappers, none of whom enjoys a higher profile than Minnesota Viking Mike Morris, who stands 6' 7" when his Mohawk has been teased to its full height. No long snapper has cultivated his minor celebrity more assiduously or shrewdly than Morris, who last season got several minutes of face time on *Six Days to Sunday,* a TNT documentary about a week in the life of two pro football teams. He co-hosts a sports talk radio show and has his own fan club, which Morris fondly describes as "my rednecks—a bunch of biker-slash-taxidermists in black T-shirts. They love ball, and they've chosen me as their leader."

Morris acts as a kind of self-appointed shop steward of long snappers. Don't use the expression "long-snapping chores" around him. "Do you hear people calling them 'the quarterbacking chores'?" he says. This reminds him of another slight: "They ought to take a long snapper to the Pro Bowl. They bring a return man, they even bring some goofball who blows up the wedge on kickoffs. But they don't take a long snapper. That's a lot of money out of someone's pocket."

Your pocket, Mike? "Hey, I'll take my name off the list," he says. "That's how strongly I feel about this."

One man doesn't buy it. "If self-promotion was an art, he'd be Michelangelo," Junkin says.

In issuing the following warning to his fellow snappers, the martial artist echoes the wisdom of Master Po, the blind Shaolin sage from the *Kung Fu* TV series. "You've got to be a little strange—that's part of the job description," Junkin says. "But you can't be weird when you're *doing* the job. If you miss a block or roll one back there, you've hurt the team, and it's time for you to leave."

It's also time to meet the press. Long snappers do not get interviewed unless something has gone badly awry. The Atlanta Falcons' Harper Le Bel recalls a game in which he triggered a "jailbreak"—snapper-speak for the anarchy that ensues when the ball sails over the punter's head. After the game reporters crowded around his locker. Feigning compassion but looking for blood, they asked, "What happened?"

"I wanted to say, 'What does it look like happened? I snapped it over his head!'" says Le Bel. Instead he explained, as if to a group of second-graders, "I . . . held . . . on . . . to . . . the . . . ball . . . too . . . long."

Not all NFL snappers bend over and peer back at an upside-down punter. Junkin is one of the few who snap "blind." Another is Trevor Matich of the Washington Redskins. The advantage of this technique is that it enables the center to pick up a rusher more easily. As a result, says Redskins special teams coach Pete Rodriguez, "a lot of teams don't even bother trying to pressure us." The skill is even more impressive considering that Matich, a licensed pilot, did not start snapping until 1990, his sixth season in the league. It was easy to pick it up, he says, "because I didn't have a paradigm to unlearn."

We'll take your word for that, Trevor.

When he was with the Arizona Cardinals, Rodriguez once coached another blind snapper, a Hawaiian named Kani Kauahi. In 10 NFL seasons Kauahi earned a reputation as one of the league's finest snappers. Unfortunately he stuck around for an 11th. Kauahi played one game in 1993, and Rodriguez remembers it well. Kauahi's first snap in the opener, in Philadelphia, was a peach. "But Kani blocked the wrong way," says Rodriguez, "and the kick was almost blocked." His next snap was somewhere over the rainbow. The play resulted in a safety. Kauahi bounced the next snap to punter Rich Camarillo, who kicked the ball sideways. "Kani almost put *another* one over Rich's head," says Rodriguez. "All of a sudden Kani couldn't snap, and he knew it. That was his last game in the NFL."

We feel a haiku coming on:

> *The punter should not*
> *need an eight-foot stepladder.*
> *Good luck on waivers.*

How does a deep snapper go off the deep end? When does a long snapper . . . snap? "You get the mental spins," says Adam Lingner, a 13-year long-snapping veteran who retired from the Bills last spring. "You're thinking, Should I snap it now? Yes—no! Don't! I'm not ready. Once you start thinking over the ball, you're doomed. That's why I used to crack jokes at the line of scrimmage. To keep myself from thinking."

A bad back, rather than the mental spins, forced the retirement of Lingner, who attributes the first poor snap of his career—it came in 1989, during his seventh NFL season—to his inability to come up with a timely put-down. "We were playing the Jets, and [New York's] Troy Benson looks across at John Davis, our tackle, and says, 'Hey, John, nice gut.'

"I was trying to think of a snappy retort when John Kidd, who is holding for the extra point, gives me the signal to snap. I wasn't ready, and I put it over his head."

So why volunteer for such unappreciated duty? Because it is the best way for a mediocre athlete to sneak into the NFL. Do great athletes gravitate to long-snapping? Dale Hellestrae of the Dallas Cowboys thinks not. Hellestrae, who owns and operates a Cookie Bouquet in Phoenix, has survived for 12 years in the league primarily as a long snapper and special-teamer. "If you're a pretty good athlete in ninth, 10th, 11th grade, you're thinking, Why would I ever want to do that?" he says.

As a 10-year-old, Greg Truitt came to that realization too late. One day at a practice for a traveling all-star team in Sarasota, Fla., the coach was auditioning long snappers. The word had spread among the boys: If you don't want to do it, just hike the ball over the punter's head.

"But I'd already gone," says Truitt, "so I got the job." His skill eventually earned him a scholarship to Penn State, and he handled the deep-snapping during the Nittany Lions' 14–10 Fiesta Bowl upset of Miami at the end of the 1986 season. That was his junior year. Truitt took the next season off. "I was disillusioned with the reality of life," he says. Spoken like a true long snapper.

After working two years as a restaurant manager Truitt grew disillusioned with the reality of the job. So he made a crude long-snapping video and sent it to a few NFL teams. To eat, he drove a limo, waited tables, mowed lawns.

He tried out with the Redskins and the Miami Dolphins. Zilch. His agent suggested Truitt head to State College, Pa., during the week that the scouts would be on the Penn State campus. "I went to a corner of the field house and started long-snapping," he says. He caught the eye of a Cincinnati Bengals scout; the team offered him a tryout and, soon thereafter, a contract.

While negotiating the two-year deal, Senior had the temerity to ask about a signing bonus. As Truitt recalls, "They said, 'The guy's been out of football for six years!' "

Thus in 1994 did Truitt become, at 28, the oldest rookie to play in the NFL in 48 years. Last season he made $150,000. He has teamed up with the Bengals' kicking specialists to form an a cappella group called Toe Jam. Truitt says that he feels blessed, but not lucky. "Everyone has the same opportunity," he says. "It's just a matter of who wants to take it."

As a poet of our acquaintance once wrote: Some can, some can't.

| | | | | |

One Play

BY PETER KING

Ever wonder what's going on in the mind of a quarterback between snaps?
Here are 40 heart-pounding Super Bowl seconds, as seen
through the eyes of the Packers' Brett Favre.

I N THE METICULOUSLY TIME-MANAGED WORLD OF THE NFL, in which months of off-season preparation are followed by weeks of training camp and then a daily regimen leading to each game, the culmination of all that planning is compressed into 40-second segments. That's how much time there is between the end of one play and the start of the next. Here's an account of one play in the life of the Packers' offense, as seen through the eyes of three-time league MVP Brett Favre. It's Green Bay's ball, first-and-10 at the Denver 22, with about 11 minutes left in the first quarter of a scoreless Super Bowl XXXII. The play clock behind each end zone resets to. . . .

:40 After landing hard at the end of a 13-yard catch, Packers wideout Antonio Freeman rises and shakes out the cobwebs. Green Bay coach Mike Holmgren stares at the field, looking to see where the ball will be spotted.

:38 Favre strides upfield, looking to the sideline for quarterbacks coach Andy Reid. Reid, who's wearing a headset, relays the plays from Holmgren to the quarterback by way of a tiny speaker in Favre's helmet.

:37 Once he knows the down and distance, Holmgren begins seven seconds of decision-making, determining which one of the 120 plays on his plastic-coated game plan is the best for this situation. All week he had been speaking to Favre about stretching the red zone a few yards; the Broncos have allowed a generous 65% completion rate between the 15 and 20 all season. Holmgren could also run Dorsey Levens, who has shredded the Denver defense for 28 yards on his first four carries. Even if Green Bay lines up three or four wideouts, Denver must respect the run.

:34 Reid pushes the red button on his right hip, opening communications with Favre. "First-and-10 at the plus-22," Reid says. "Think red zone." Favre is excited. He thinks Holmgren is going to call a pass.

:30 "Two Jet All Go," Holmgren says, speaking into his mike to Reid. The Packers will go for the touchdown. Four wideouts will spread across the field and streak toward the end zone.

:29 The Packers make two substitutions: wide receivers Derrick Mayes and Terry Mickens for fullback William Henderson and tight end Mark Chmura.

:28 "Two Jet All Go," Favre hears in his helmet. Reid then tells him the formation—"Spread Right"—but Favre already knows it. It's the only formation Holmgren would use with Two Jet All Go.

:25 "Spread Right, Two Jet All Go, on one," Favre says in the huddle. As the players break, Freeman looks to Mayes, who will line up outside him, on the far right, and says, "Remember to keep our spacing right."

:24 The four wide receivers move to their positions: Robert Brooks split wide left, a step off the line of scrimmage; Mickens on the line, three paces outside of left tackle Ross Verba; Freeman in the right slot; Mayes split wide. The only player in the backfield with Favre is Levens, who excels at picking up blitzes.

:19 Favre cranes to see the play clock. Good, he thinks, plenty of time. Next he starts looking over the defense as he settles in at the line.

:15 Favre is on his own now. Electronic communication between the bench and the quarterback, introduced exclusively for play-calling, is cut at the 15-second mark by an NFL official in the press box.

:14 Most quarterbacks check the safeties first for clues to the defense's plans. Favre is no different. Broncos safeties Steve Atwater and Tyrone Braxton are 12 yards off the line. Even with the four-wideout set, neither appears to be cheating toward any receiver or to be thinking blitz. Zone coverage more than likely, Favre reasons.

:13 The cornerbacks are five and 10 yards back—giving up the underneath ball, Favre thinks, but there's no reason to call an audible. He likes the play.

:12 As he stands behind center Frank Winters, Favre guesses that the anxious-looking outside linebacker to his left, John Mobley, will blitz. That means Favre must change the blocking assignment for Levens, who in Two Jet was to have picked up any blitzer coming from the right side.

:11 Favre turns and shouts to Levens, "Three Jet! Change to Three Jet!" Levens now knows to look for any blitzer coming from his left.

:09 Now Favre barks the count, "Three 19! Three 19! Set! Hut!"

:08 The ball is snapped. Favre's right leg drives backward as he begins a five-step drop. (The play clock is turned off at the snap, but here is a second-by-second account as the play unfolds.)

:07 Two steps into his drop, Favre glances left and sees Brooks and Mickens running into traffic. Mobley drops to cover Mickens, so Favre thinks that Freeman or Mayes might be open on the right before Atwater, lined up on the left, can get across the field. On the third step, Favre's head swivels slightly right. Mayday!

:06 Out of the corner of his right eye Favre sees number 39, cornerback Ray Crockett, steaming in. Four steps into his drop all Favre can see is that 39 getting bigger and bigger. Favre knows he'll get hit, because Levens is helping Winters pick up blitzing linebacker Bill Romanowski. ("I blew it," Favre thinks of his change in Levens's blocking assignment.)

:05 As he takes the fifth step and plants, Favre looks past Crockett while cocking his arm. He sees Braxton crouch, as though he's expecting Freeman to run a quick hook or out. Bad move, Favre thinks. But it makes sense: Braxton knows Crockett is blitzing. That leaves an open area in the middle of the field, so Braxton figures that Favre will surely dump the ball there before he gets smacked.

:04 Get rid of it quick, is all Favre is thinking now. Freeman accelerates past Braxton. Favre figures Freeman will beat Braxton to the back of the end zone, so he aims for the end line. Standing on the Denver 29, he throws a perfect 39-yard spiral.

:03 Crockett gives Favre a shove, not the jarring shot the quarterback expected to receive.

:02 Behind Braxton now, Freeman looks over his left shoulder and sees the pass coming. Out of the corner of his eye he also sees Atwater closing fast from the left. "Like a freight train," Freeman says later.

:01 The ball nestles into Freeman's hands, and as he plants his right foot just inside the end line, Atwater delivers a wicked shot with his right forearm to Freeman's left shoulder. Too late. For the 38th time in five months, Favre thrusts two fists into the air to celebrate a touchdown pass. "No feeling in the world like it," he says later.

| | | | | |

Six-Shooters

BY JOHN ED BRADLEY

A half-dozen players to a side is the rule in the wild and woolly brand of football played at tiny high schools in the rural West.

ONE AFTER ANOTHER, THE BOYS FROM ZEPHYR DRAG themselves out of the dark and into Mary's Place. It's Friday morning, the first game day of the season, and it seems all the bugs in Texas are screaming. ¶ Mary's stands hard by the Brady Highway in Brownwood, a town of about 20,000, some 12 miles up the road from Zephyr, in the central part of the state. Zephyr counts only about 200 residents, too few to support a restaurant. And so today the boys got up before dawn and came here in a long, headlamps-lit procession, sharing rides in old bombs and pickups, watching out the window as the black land moved past.

The 7 a.m. breakfast they've come to attend has been dubbed the Meet the Bulldogs Breakfast, but except for a radio crew and a local newspaperman, no one is waiting to meet the Bulldogs but the Bulldogs themselves. "How're your boys lookin' today?" somebody asks the coach.

Gary Bufe, 42, stares long and hard before responding. "Some look ugly, some look sleepy," he says. "I don't know if they're ready or not."

Bufe is only joking, but even at this hour of the morning the boys have their game faces on, and nobody laughs. This makes Bufe reconsider. "The boys have come a long ways, and I'll say right now if you have confidence in a group, it's this one." He seems to mean what he's saying, but at the same time he might just be trying to persuade himself and to persuade the boys. Gordon, the Bulldogs' opponent tonight, won't be easy, after all.

Gordon has Jim Ed Kostiha, an all-state linebacker and the starting quarterback, and Jason Sizemore, an all-state running back. Gordon has Jesus Tijerina, a feisty little two-way player with a ponytail and shaved sidewalls and bad attitude galore. Gordon also has that kid John Leven, a running back who, they say, stands 6' 5" and weighs 270 pounds and covers the 40 in 4.8 seconds, and when you hit him it's like meeting the stubborn end of a cement wall.

From the way he's looking at his boys, Bufe seems to be trying to read their minds. He's a tall, thin fellow with a prominent Adam's apple and styled hair, and today he's wearing a crisply starched white dress shirt and a necktie. In addition to coaching, Bufe teaches math at Zephyr High, and this time of year he reports to school at 7:30 in the morning and doesn't get home until after 9 at night. To be close to him, his wife and kids sometimes show up at the football field and watch him work out with the boys under the lights. It's either that or try to catch him rushing out the door in the morning.

Now Bufe says, in a stronger voice, "I feel when the boys step out on the field, they'll be ready to play. I really do. They're going to play hard."

All this heat and worry, and when you come down to it, the game they play isn't something most people have ever heard about, let alone seen. Zephyr is a six-man town, which is to say, it's a town whose high school is too thinly populated to field a regular 11-man football squad. In Texas a school can't have more than 85 students if it wants to participate in the six-man public league. Zephyr High, with an enrollment of 76, has 40 male students, 34 of them varsity and jayvee football players.

By last count there were 89 six-man public schools in Texas, 21 in Nebraska, 16 in Colorado, 14 in Montana, 10 in New Mexico, three in Kansas and two in Arizona. In Canada, too, where spaces are vast and the talent pool shallow, six-man schools abound. This year at least one preseason poll is saying that Gordon has the best team of them all.

This, of course, has been weighing heavily on the minds of the Zephyr boys, who are an inexperienced lot and weren't included in most of the rankings. They are quiet as they form a line and take trays and silverware and decide on breakfast.

"Where's Torrey?" Bufe says. "What's Torrey got on his head? You got some paw prints, Torrey?"

Torrey McClain runs a hand over his nearly naked scalp, which was shaved by a teammate just this week. "Nosuh," he says. "Just some nicks."

"Nicks," Bufe says, giving his head a shake. "We need to look up in the *Guinness Book of World Records* to see the record for the number of nicks on a head."

Zephyr means gentle breeze, Bufe will tell you. The word comes from some foreign language he's not familiar with. And, yes, Zephyr seems the sort of town you breeze through on your way someplace else, with only a caution light to signal its existence and with only one store, Petty's Grocery & Feed, to satisfy its needs. Zephyr is not unlike most other six-man towns around Texas: dirt-poor and down around the mouth, wounded by a depressed ranching economy but still limping along. The most interesting thing to have happened there lately occurred 95 years ago when a tornado went through and flattened everything in sight, including the high school, which was later replaced by a clunky stone structure that bears an uncanny resemblance to the Alamo.

"We might be small, but we do have cable TV in Zephyr," says lineman Jeremy King. "We watch football from all over."

"Personally, I got no use for 11-man," says Mark Schwartz, a cornerback. "It's boring. I can't stand it."

"I honestly don't know what 11-man's like," says linebacker Dusty Miller. "I seen it, but I don't know nothing about it."

"Me, I never even been out of Texas," says McClain, the kid with the nicked head. "As a matter of fact, I never even been farther than San Antone. My mom works at the Red Wagon restaurant in Brownwood. My dad, I don't talk to him. I went to Fort Worth before. I had eye surgery once, and it might've been in Dallas. That's what they tell me, anyway."

The boys eat biscuits and white gravy and sausage wheels and bacon and hash browns and scrambled eggs and toast and milk and juice, and some of them eyeball the ice-box pie but don't say anything. They are wearing their white game jerseys with maroon lettering, and some already have on their black rubber cleats, even though they still have classes today and the game is 12 hours away.

When breakfast is over they file outside and stand in the parking lot, trying to decide how to feel. The sun has come up, and the bugs have gone quiet, and not one of the boys wants to believe that a kid as big as John Leven can run that fast and hit that hard.

IT'S STEPHEN EPLER they all have to blame—Stephen Epler, who in 1934 decided that the boys at his school in little Chester, Neb., deserved a chance to play organized football. Epler is 87 now, retired and living in Sacramento. Over a distinguished career he served as president of four colleges, but everybody remembers him as the guy who invented six-man football. It's a fact that leaves him slightly bemused. Sometimes when he answers the phone he's asked to recount the story of how it all began.

"Well, I was 24 years old and just out of college," he says. "Chester is on the Nebraska-Kansas line. There were about 80 students in the high school, half of them boys, most too little to play football. They'd tried 11-man and had to give it up because of injuries and lack of students. The kids still wanted to play, so one day I said to my superintendent, 'Why don't we have football here?' He told me all the reasons we didn't, and I blurted out, 'Then why don't we have a team with fewer than 11?' He said, 'O.K., you invent the game, and I'll see that it gets a try.' "

First Epler decided how many players to put on each side of the ball. He chose six because he figured he could count on rounding up the five players who started on the basketball team, all of them good-sized, athletic boys. Also, with six you could put three on the line and three in the backfield. Next he devised a set of rules, most of which still apply today. Six-man is played on a field 80 yards long and 40 yards wide. All players are eligible to receive a forward pass, but the quarterback can't run the ball unless a teammate handles it first. After a touchdown a kicked conversion counts for two points, while a pass or a run is good for only one. (A field goal earns four points.) A team must cover 15 yards for a first down.

Epler says the first six-man game, in '34, featured consolidated Nebraska teams from Chester and Hardy on one side, Belvidere and Alexandria on the other. They played under lights on a college field in Hebron, and the final score was 19–19. About a thousand people showed up to watch, a couple of wire-service reporters among them. The oddball slant of the story appealed to newspaper editors nationwide, and by running an account of the game they helped spark interest in little nowhere towns across the country. In that first year, Epler says, he sent out mimeographed copies of his rules to about 50 schools. Over the next decade thousands of schools would field six-man teams, and around 1954 an eight-man version of football would emerge. Eight-man survives today, but with fewer programs than six-man.

Six-man has been enjoying a resurgence in the heartland because a drop-off in enrollment has forced some schools to change from 11-man to six-man teams and because other schools that did not play football at all have caught six-man fever. Elsewhere the game continues to thrive because small towns have found in these teams a repository for all their hopes and dreams and yearnings. The oil patch might run dry, and the bank might foreclose on the family farm, but the football team isn't going anywhere, not as long as there are a half-dozen young male bodies to suit up. Six-man is the temple where the isolated come together and celebrate their smallness.

On top of that, the game's a hoot and an even greater spectacle to watch than 11-man. With only a handful of defensive players to elude, a speedy back or receiver can break one tackle and be in the clear. Long gainers are the rule rather than the exception. It is not uncommon for six-man teams to trade touchdowns throughout a game. In 1991 Zephyr beat Strawn 92–66. And last year May toppled Sidney to the tune of 90–82 in another Texas matchup. "In six-man the game is never boring," says Terry Pophan of Strawn, a town about nine miles from Gordon. Pophan, a partner in a building-materials company, is a charter member of a group that calls itself Six-Man Central. Each week he and some friends attend as many six-man games as possible, occasionally catching four in three days.

"Something's always happening in six-man," Pophan says, "and everyone is involved. All the boys are receivers, which makes it interesting, since you don't have five guys up front just blocking while somebody's trying to throw the ball. Instead you might have five guys going out and trying to get open for a pass. A lot of people who watch six-man for the first time and see all the hitting say, 'My gosh. This is wild, and, well, yeah, it is still football, isn't it?' "

"Six-man distinguishes itself from 11-man in that it's a game where a little guy can be successful," says Wendell Bradley, the coach at Strawn. "Guys like that kid John Leven at Gordon are the exception rather than the rule. Most guys that big are too slow. In six-man you tell the fat boys to go to the sideline, and you play with the skill people. It's all about speed and quickness."

"You'd be amazed at the size of some of the kids who've been all-state," says Doug Hopkins, a member of Six-Man Central. "Not many years ago, a kid from Guthrie was 5' 4" and 130 pounds, and he made second team all-state. That sonofagun was hard to tackle—little tiny fella, ran straight ahead."

In Texas six-man is popular enough to have spawned a couple of publications dedicated to covering the games, ranking the teams and anointing the stars. Joe Nash and Tommy Wells of Ranger put out an annual called *Six-Man Illustrated* and advertise it as "North America's only international six-man magazine," whose mission is "to preach the word of six-man football." Nash and Wells show up at games wearing shirts made to resemble the U.S. flag, and they confess that six-man changed their lives. Wells met his wife at the first six-man game he ever saw, and Nash says six-man is practically all he thinks about, day and night. "I've been married 10 years, and I do love my wife," he says, "but you know how you hear about love at first sight? Well, I gotta admit it, six-man was like that for me."

Although the passion these men feel for the game might run to the extreme, to love six-man is to love a way of life that other places in this country have outgrown or discarded. Six-man celebrates an America that didn't die with the social revolutions of the 1960s but hid out in forgotten little towns in big spaces, waiting for Friday night. "People generally have two opinions of small towns," says Granger Huntress of San Antonio, who publishes *The Huntress Report*, a weekly newsletter devoted to the game. "They either think small towns are innocent and pure and wonderful, which is my view, or they think they're ignorant, mean and backward. But go to any six-man town, and what you'll find there is wonderful. All that talk from politicians about family values? They're wherever six-man is played."

Wonderful, too, are the names of the towns, some of them too little for the map, enduring like a secret: Groom and Rule and Ropesville and Ira and Ackerly and Loop and Paint Rock and Star and Buckholts and Cranfills Gap and Blum and Fruitvale and New Home and Maple. The schools in these towns are "the heart and soul of the community," says Phil Watts, owner of KXYL, a Brownwood radio station that broadcasts six-man games. "Everything revolves around them, economically and socially. And so at this time of year the football team becomes the heart and soul of the town. Everybody goes to the games."

Jack Pardee is the most famous name to break out of the six-man orbit, and his high school career ended 44 years ago. He came from the West Texas town of Christoval, just south of San Angelo, and went on to star at Texas A&M and to play and coach in the NFL. "I was hit as hard in six-man as I was ever hit—college or pro," Pardee once told *USA Today*.

However, few six-man players ever advance to major college ball. Just last year a running back named Raul (Petey) Salaiz finished a historic career at Mullin (Texas) High, where he rushed for 10,468 yards, the second-highest total ever by a U.S. schoolboy. Salaiz received a handful of letters from Division I-A colleges, but alas, none offered a scholarship.

"Kids in six-man don't get scholarships because college coaches can go to bigger schools and pick kids of the same size and ability who've already been exposed to 11-man programs," says Bradley, the Strawn coach. "The six-man kids just don't get the recognition they deserve, no matter how good they are."

The folks in Zephyr can't remember their last football player to receive a free ride to play major college ball, but those in Gordon remember theirs: Nelson Campbell, the coach and principal at the high school. In 1967 Campbell led the Gordon Longhorns to victory in the six-man regional championship, the furthest a school could advance back then. Texas Christian and Southern Methodist came calling, and recruiters from both universities took Campbell to a restaurant for a steak dinner, hoping to cast a spell. Campbell chose Texas Christian, but he never got much respect there.

"Maybe in my coach's mind I was disadvantaged," says Campbell, who lettered two years but played sparingly on the offensive line. "They used to ask me, 'Do they play three-man basketball in Gordon?' There was a bias against me, I think."

After college Campbell went home and coached first at Strawn and then at Gordon, where he has been head man since 1981. Campbell might've been slighted in 11-man, but this year in six-man he's as big as they get. "Nelson and Gordon," says Bradley. "I hesitate to tell you how good they really are in fear I may intimidate myself."

IT'S EARLY afternoon now, and the Zephyr boys pile into a yellow school bus and commence the 110-mile journey to Gordon, with Bufe behind the wheel. Accompanying the bus is a pickup truck, its bed packed with helmets, shoulder pads and other gear. Most of the boys have cottonmouth and fluttering stomachs that nothing but a little physical contact can cure. An uncertain fate awaits them at the end of this road, and here is the lesson: Life is hard, but not compared with six-man.

With a population of 516, Gordon is more than twice the size of Zephyr. Gordon doesn't have a red light either, but it does have street signs, shiny things that were the talk of the town when they went up a couple of years ago. It also has a dry-goods store, a grocery, a video store, a fire hall, a post office, a Ford dealership, a filling station, a bank branch, a barbershop, a hardware store, three churches and a dominoes hall. Empty buildings bracket Main Street, but all things considered, Gordon—with its vital little business district and its proximity to Fort Worth—is prospering compared with Zephyr.

While the Bulldogs are journeying over vast stretches of mesquite-choked terrain, a pep rally begins in the WPA-era gymnasium at Gordon High. Kostiha and Sizemore and Tijerina and Leven are all in attendance, looking eager to get the prelims over with, none of them wanting to crack a smile lest that show weakness.

For the football team, what's happening in the Gordon gym is proof that all those miserable hours of pumping iron and driving the two-man sled and running wind sprints were worth the doing. You hear the applause and see the crowd come to its feet, and it's almost as nice as being kissed for the first time. Both the Longhorns and the Shorthorns—the name for Gordon's junior high six-man team—run out and circle the shiny pine floor before taking seats in the bleachers. Two groups entertain the student body: the cheerleaders, led by Stacie Crain, and the drill team, with Terra Golden in front.

Both girls possess the kind of pure, unsullied beauty that makes your heart squeeze tight in your chest, and that explains why the state of Texas occasionally mops up at Miss America pageants. Mamas from town have come to see their girls perform this afternoon, but all the daddies have stayed away, proud of their precious little sweethearts but not *that* proud.

Gordon High is too small to have a band, so the girls dance to music from a jam box, and nobody trips and falls, and this delights Terra no end. She couldn't sleep the night before in fear of just such an accident. "If I fell, I'd just lay there on the floor and cry," she says. "We're supposed to get right back up, but I don't think I could."

Toward the end of the pep rally the boys spill out onto the floor and stand around looking spooked as the girls dance the macarena. Eventually a few of the team clowns join in, but the real players know to keep still. Kostiha and Sizemore wear sullen faces, the mask of the assassin before he clocks in for a hit. "Nervous?" somebody asks Kostiha.

He gives his head a shake. "Ready."

It was his father, Jimmy Ray Kostiha, a teammate of Campbell's on the '67 championship team, who once said, "Jim Ed's always been a good kid, but then he went and grew his hair out long. Some little girl told him he looked like James Dean, and you know what it did? It ruined him."

In the eyes of his schoolmates Jim Ed is anything but ruined, and the cheers that find him are meant to prove that. Boys are boys until they strap it on come Friday night. Then they become heroes, every one.

"Y'all make sure to wear long pants to the game tonight," Stacie tells a couple of visitors as she leaves the gym. "Mosquitoes'll eat you alive if you don't."

When Stacie's not leading cheers or running cross-country or playing basketball, she likes to ride her horse, Duke. Except when she goes off to college, she plans never to live anywhere but in Gordon. One day she wants to have babies and send them to Gordon High, and she wants her girls to cheer and her boys to play six-man. "I'm mainly just a cowgirl," she says. "I wear pants and boots and a cowboy hat everywhere I go. I couldn't live in a big city. In big cities they beat you up if you don't wear the right clothes. What do you think they'd do to me, wearing what I wear?"

The pep rally ends, and everybody but the coaches goes home. The coaches head out to the field and hit the fire-ant mounds with another lick of spray. Before the ant and mosquito problem, there were armadillos to contend with. Seems they liked to root around in the soft earth of the end zone. Campbell and his assistants finally ran them off. "When those fire ants bite you, they leave a little blister," Campbell says, showing what one did to his finger. "I guess they should be a concern, but I don't think when the boys fall on the ground they'll be staying down very long."

Gordon's field, called Longhorn Stadium, might be the finest six-man facility in all the world. It has metal bleachers with enough room to seat 2,000
and a field house under construction that promises to be as good as any at
small-town schools that play 11-man. The current field house is a little metal
building divided into two spaces: The varsity dressing room, the weight
room, the laundry room and the showers occupy one area, and the smaller jayvee dressing room occupies the other. Campbell himself made the
lockers and now says, "You can see I'm not much of a carpenter. But it's
better than when I played here. When I played here they had hooks on the
wall for your clothes."

Visiting teams suit up in the jayvee room, and that's where the Zephyr
boys congregate upon arriving at Gordon. The wall separating the two
dressing rooms ends with a panel of chicken wire up by the ceiling, and
one side can hear everything said on the other. So everyone speaks in hushed
tones and makes sure to self-edit when discussing the game plan.

During the jayvee game the boys on the Zephyr varsity sit on benches and
in the grass in front of the field house. Not five feet away stand Leven and Tijerina and other members of the Gordon team, but neither side speaks to
the other. The players do, however, share whispered observations with teammates. "We judge 'em by lookin' at 'em," says Jon Temple, a Zephyr running
back. "And I can tell you right now, that big guy ain't so big. He's little. Not
no 6' 5" and not no 275 or whatever, and definitely not no 4.8 in the 40."

Leven, who is in fact 6' 5" but closer to 250 pounds, stands silently by,
unaware that he's the object of so much attention. He lives on his family's
1,400-acre cattle ranch just outside Gordon, and what he likes almost as
much as football is showing heifers, in particular Sarah, a black Angus that
recently won grand-champion honors at a state competition. Leven, everybody says, needs to get meaner if he wants to become a really good player.
He's too kindhearted. "I wish we could make him mad just once," his step-
father, Joey Swain, says. "But I don't think you can do it. He's not the mad
type. John's little brothers, on the other hand, they'll go outside and run
into trees just to show how tough they are."

If you could put Tijerina's aggressiveness in Leven's body, everybody says,
you'd have one of the best football players ever to play the game. "That
Mexican kid is cut pretty good," one of the Zephyr boys allows, glancing
over at Tijerina.

"Yeah, pretty good," says another. "But can he hit?"

Tijerina stands there with his shirt off, letting Zephyr and the world have a look. Except for a few girls, he's the only kid in Gordon with a ponytail and rings in both ears, but he's not the kind of person you would want to say that to. At 5' 7" and 145 pounds, Tijerina is small in size; in terms of heart, they don't come any bigger. He lives with his mother in Palo Pinto, a town about 20 minutes from Gordon. Elaina Tijerina cleans condos and sells tamales to the county jail, and Jesus learned from watching her work that not a thing comes easy in this life. His body, for instance, is the result of years of cutting wood. Handle a chain saw all day in the hot heat of a long Texas summer and see what kind of muscles you get.

The Gordon boys aren't all the Zephyr players talk about. They rate the Gordon girls, too, giving Stacie and Terra high marks. And they can't get over the bleachers, the field house going up, the black rubber track encircling the field. This is big-time. Their place back home is pretty primitive, almost an embarrassment, but typical of most six-man schools. Zephyr's playing field abuts a pasture, where a rancher used to keep several head of buffalo. Whenever games got dull, the fans turned their attention to the action on the other side of the fence: the exotic animals moving under the wild pecans and scrub oaks. The rancher finally got rid of the buffalo and replaced them with llamas, which occasionally looked over the fence but didn't seem to know the difference between the six-man and 11-man games. There are no metal bleachers at Zephyr, only eight long steps of cement in a small hillside. The Bulldogs dress in the school's locker room, and the visiting team uses the weight room off the gym.

Asked to compare Gordon with Zephyr, the Bulldogs' McClain says, "They got a bank and a car dealership in Gordon, so that right there makes them huge compared to us."

"WE'RE GOING to start a new tradition here tonight," Bufe tells his boys shortly before the start of the 7:30 p.m. game. He sounds the way he did earlier, at the Meet the Bulldogs Breakfast, less certain than hopeful. Twelve hours have passed, and it's time to get this thing over with. "You ready to play?" he says. When no answer comes, he says, "That's good. I know you're ready."

Night is starting to fall, and with it comes the smell of barbecue commingled with mosquito repellent. Down on the sideline in front of the home stands Stacie is cheering, "Two bits . . . four bits . . . six bits . . . a dollar," and out in front of the drill team Terra's sequined uniform shivers under the tall electric lights. It is quite a beautiful thing, this night. It is 1996 and 1946. It is today and yesterday and what you hope tomorrow will be. And it is a few other things besides.

It's a Gordon spirit leader dressed up in a velour longhorn costume, and it's little kids playing rough-and-tumble behind the seats, and it's the hills all around colored a mix of pewter and blue, and it's a radio tower way off in the distance beating red lights in the gloaming. It's good old boys in cowboy hats and Wrangler jeans and big-buckled belts talking a language that no untrained ear can make out. It's the U.S. flag hardly stirring over by the scoreboard and a knot of nervous daddies standing on the sidelines, following the movement of the ball as it advances from one end of the field to the other. It's all the mamas, too, wincing at the hard hits and the soft ones, laughing to show they aren't afraid. It's a long train roaring through town just as Gordon's Chris Chamberlain scoops up a fumble and runs it in 25 yards for the game's first score. And it's the mosquitoes and the ants and the armadillos, wherever they've gone.

It's the endless beauty of a night in Texas when nothing happened in town but a six-man football game. Tonight there's a crowd of about 1,200, including 200 who made the trek from Zephyr, Brownwood and neighboring towns. The series between the two schools dates back 10 years, and Gordon barely leads, 4-3-1. Because the Bulldogs and the Longhorns traditionally meet early in the season, when play is still ragged, their games tend to be unusually low-scoring by six-man standards.

Both Bufe and Campbell call plays from the sidelines, but given the chaotic look of things, the boys could be drawing diagrams in the dirt, doing it all on their own. There is a reckless, freelance quality to the action that makes it seem as if anything is possible, that keeps your jaw slack from start to finish. Up and down the field the boys go, playing what amounts to a glorified version of sandlot football, delivering blows that smack like firecrackers. "We aren't exactly performing like ourselves tonight," Campbell says at halftime, though his team leads 14–8.

"The mosquitoes are a distraction," Bufe says. "But nobody's complained yet about the little ants. Heck, if little ants are the only pain they've got, they shouldn't be out there."

In pads Leven looks like a pro, but he doesn't handle the ball much tonight, and he's hardly a factor. In the end it's Kostiha and Sizemore who prove to be as good as their hype. Kostiha completes eight of his 15 passes for 148 yards and one touchdown, and Sizemore runs for three second-half touchdowns. As yellow-haired eight-year-olds they had vowed to be two things: buddies forever and world champs of six-man football. Magic has come to Gordon and to that pair of dreamers, and the Longhorns roll 34–8.

"I'm disappointed in how it all had to end," Bufe says. "Guess I'll stop up the road at the truck stop and let the boys buy themselves some snacks. Then we're going home."

One after another the Zephyr boys take their pads off and put them in the back of the pickup and climb into the bus. They sit steaming in the dark with their wet uniform pants and undershirts still on and with grass and mud clinging to their cleats. "What were they, Number 1 in the world or something?" says Todd Jordan, a senior wide receiver. "We'll see them again. We'll be ready for them when the playoffs come around."

After the Zephyr bus leaves, Campbell hangs around the stadium for a while accepting congratulations from the proud people of Gordon and remembering things about the game that were special or that will require some attention at practice next week. By now most of his boys have headed either to the teen dance at the Gordon fire hall or to the nearby town of Mingus for pizza and root beer and games of pool.

The lights go out, and Campbell is a lone figure moving through the night, his black cap pushed way back on his head, his shoes crunching the ground. He swats a mosquito and looks up at the stars and seems altogether pleased. "Well," he says in a voice gone hoarse from yelling, "I guess I'll go home now and pop a top and relax a little. Anybody want to join me, they're welcome. You remember where I live, don't you?"

Campbell lifts a hand, points to a place not a football field away: "Double-wide right up there on the corner."

| | | | | |

Hang Time

BY TIM LAYDEN

With his future up in the air, Purdue's Drew Brees, like many top prospects, lived in a maddening limbo from New Year's to draft day: working out for NFL teams, watching his stock rise and fall, never knowing which pro jersey he'd wear.

HERE IS NO SOUND QUITE LIKE THE TRILLING OF A telephone on draft day, a beautiful noise with the power to transform anxiety into fulfillment. When the call came for Drew Brees at 3:30 last Saturday afternoon, the former Purdue quarterback was washing dishes in his kitchen, trying to distract himself from the torture of waiting. The cordless handset chirped twice before Brees's girlfriend snatched it off the living-room floor and shouted, "Drew, the phone's ringing!" On the television screen disembodied voices informed viewers that the San Diego Chargers were next on the draft clock, with the first pick of the second round, the 32nd overall. The room became a still-life.

This is how the waiting ends. Nearly 16 weeks after playing his final college game, Brees would at last find out where football would take him next. It had been a strange and tumultuous time, spent in a no-man's land between collegian and professional, where a player's stock rises and falls, buoying him one week, mocking him the next. For Brees the ride had been measured in increments as short as an eighth of an inch in height and as long as the 70 yards a ball sails when thrown by a passer with an NFL-approved arm. He had juggled the demands of a college curriculum and those of 31 NFL teams, and never had he felt in control.

JANUARY I, PASADENA

Brees's college career ends on the pristine grass of the Rose Bowl, where Purdue loses 34–24 to Washington. Brees completes 23 of 39 passes for 275 yards and two touchdowns, but his counterpart, Huskies senior Marques Tuiasosopo, completes 16 of 22 for 138 yards and a touchdown, runs for 75 yards and another touchdown and is named the game's MVP.

Brees could be deflated, but he's not. When he decided a year earlier to return for his senior season, he set his mind on winning the Big Ten and playing in the Rose Bowl. Purdue had done neither in 32 years. "How many players can set goals like that and achieve them?" Brees says. In the locker room, and outside the stadium, he implores teammates to take pride in the season. "Don't let this ruin what we did this year," he tells them.

Brees leaves Purdue as the most productive quarterback in Big Ten history, with league records for career passing yards (11,792) and touchdown passes (90) among his 34 school, conference and NCAA marks. He threw for only 232 yards as a freshman, yet only three college quarterbacks have amassed more total yards than Brees. "No regrets," he says. "I wouldn't do a thing differently."

JANUARY 3–5, AUSTIN

Brees's transition from amateur to professional is almost instantaneous. He is home in Austin to deliberate with his parents on the choice of an agent. Mina and Chip Brees, who are divorced, are both attorneys. Agents have chased Drew since his sophomore year, when he became Purdue's starting quarterback and passed for 3,983 yards and 39 touchdowns. Player representation is a cutthroat business; there are more than 1,100 NFL-approved agents, far more than players entering the league each year. Brees's parents shielded him from overtures. By the start of his senior year, only three suitors remained in the race: Tom Condon of IMG, Texas-based Vann McElroy, and Leigh Steinberg.

Brees met with Steinberg at a motel near the Purdue campus in West Lafayette, Ind., in August, one week before the start of fall practice. Steinberg showed him the rookie contracts he negotiated for Drew Bledsoe, Jake

Plummer and Ryan Leaf. "It was impressive," Brees says. "The guy seemed pretty innovative in the way he structured things." Brees also saw McElroy last summer but did not sit down with Condon until November, after Purdue's last regular-season game.

In the end Brees chooses Condon, with whom he feels he has a better personal connection than with McElroy or Steinberg. Brees is also swayed by the fact that IMG has 35 offices around the country—"Wherever I play, they'll be close," he says—and by the agency's commercial connections, but his decision is based largely on instinct. "I got a good feel from the IMG guys," he says. It will be widely speculated that Brees chose Condon because Condon represents Peyton Manning, who is a friend of Brees's. Not true. "I haven't talked to Peyton in months," says Brees. "He got a new cellphone, and I don't have the number."

JANUARY 12, WEST LAFAYETTE

It is common for potential early-round draft picks to leave college after the fall semester and relocate to a training center to cram for the NFL scouting combine and for personal workouts. "I'm training to be a professional football player," Missouri defensive end Justin Smith will say at the combine, in February. "I can't mess around with something else at the same time."

Most agents offer comprehensive training as part of their representation package, and IMG has one of the best programs. Players are housed and fed at the IMG Academies in Bradenton, Fla., where they often become efficient workout animals, rising in the draft and increasing their contract value as a result. Former NFL assistant coach Larry Kennan works there with quarterbacks. In 1998 Charlie Batch came to Bradenton as an unknown out of Eastern Michigan and worked himself into the upper half of the draft's second round, passing Michigan's Brian Griese, who'd won a national championship. By early January many of Condon's top clients are in Bradenton, but Brees is still at Purdue. He is enrolled for the spring semester to graduate on time, in four years. It wasn't an easy decision for him to make. He is projected as a mid- to low first-round draft choice, but draftniks and NFL scouts have questions about him: Were his big college numbers a product of Purdue's spread offense? Is Brees, barely 6-feet tall, gifted enough to overcome his size? Does he have quick feet and passable sprinting speed? The combine will be important, and Brees would benefit from boot camp. Instead, he will train alone at Purdue. This is a source of minor frustration for IMG, but, Condon says, "How can you criticize a guy for wanting to graduate?" Brees intends to be every bit as prepared for the combine as the prospects who train in Bradenton, but it will be hard.

"I'd love to be down there working out all day, every day, because this is the only time in my life that I'm going to be drafted by the NFL," he says. But he's also a 3.42 student, majoring in industrial management, and an NCAA postgraduate scholarship winner whose good citizenship has resulted in the naming of a street, Brees Way, in his honor in West Lafayette. "Hopefully, I can set an example," he says. "I can show that it's possible to play football at a high level, graduate and still go on to the NFL."

He will have a busy winter. He will soon leave for a week in Maui to play in the Hula Bowl, the first of many diversions from his academic quest. As he walks toward the glass doors of the Mollenkopf Athletic Center, Purdue's football complex, he reaches for the bronze bust of former Boilermakers coach Jack Mollenkopf and touches the brim of the old man's fedora, as he did for good luck all season. "Going to be a wild ride," says Brees, stepping into the cold air.

JANUARY 14–20, MAUI

If it weren't for the presence of scouts, the Hula Bowl would be the alltime postseason boondoggle: exotic locale, great weather, free afternoons and nightly luaus. All a college player has to do in return is show up for practice every morning and, on Saturday, play in a glorified scrimmage at a high school stadium. However, the 60 NFL scouts and personnel executives turn this week from Club Med into *Survivor*.

Most players in Maui are marginal draft fodder. "The talent level is just O.K.," says the Dallas Cowboys' director of college and pro scouting, Larry Lacewell. "Most agents put their best kids in the Senior Bowl." (That's why more than 800 NFL reps are in Mobile the same week.) Brees is the only college star in Maui. He is here as a favor to his Purdue coach, Joe Tiller, who is one of the Hula Bowl coaches, and game organizers used Brees's name to sell tickets. Brees calls the visit "a business trip," and on the first day of practice he snaps teammates out of their island reveries by barking at Ohio State wideout Reggie Germany for dropping a pass. "Wow, talk about presence," says coach Bob Ford of Division I-AA Albany in New York. "One series after we started, you knew every kid on that offense would follow Brees anywhere."

Mostly, though, it's scouts who follow him. On the flight out, Brees took four hours' worth of inane written tests. (Sample question: *Choose A or B: A) I'm a competitive person. B) I like to win.* "What's that about?" asked Brees.) In Maui NFL people interview him ceaselessly. "He's the one guy here who everybody wants to get on paper," says Tampa Bay Bucs scout Ruston Webster.

After one practice each player is weighed and measured. This is a big moment for Brees. He was listed at 6' 1" throughout his college career. The height question hangs over him like a dark cloud because the NFL treats short quarterbacks like the Ebola virus. Inside a dank youth recreation center near the practice fields, a parade of players walks across a stage. Scouts sit at tables, like patrons at a Las Vegas revue. Heights are shouted in succession. The scouts scribble.

When Brees is measured, the attendant pauses before barking, "Five-eleven-seven [5' 11⅞"]." The audience groans. Brees steps back and stares at the scale and its operator. He asks to be measured again. "Six even!" bellows the attendant. Scouts applaud. "He's a good kid; we all want him to be a 6-footer," says Lacewell.

Most scouts in Maui have seen Brees play many college games and watched miles of tape featuring him. "What I'm seeing here [in practices] reaffirms what we already know," says the Miami Dolphins' director of college scouting, Tom Braatz. "The guy is totally accurate, smart, avoids the rush, and he's a gamer. He's not big, but if you like him, that doesn't matter."

Who likes him? Cincinnati Bengals president Mike Brown, whose team has the fourth pick in the draft, has sent assistant coach John Garrett to meet and watch Brees, even though the Bengals took quarterback Akili Smith with the third choice of the draft two years ago.

The Seattle Seahawks' director of player personnel, John Schneider, spends hours talking to Brees in Maui. "We need a quarterback, and there aren't many in the draft," Schneider says. "But just because there's only one girl at the party, you don't have to ask her to dance, right? I like Drew, I really do. Still, we have to decide, how high do you take him?"

On a splendid tropical Saturday, Brees throws for a modest 119 yards and one touchdown in his team's 31–23 win in the Hula Bowl. By 10 p.m. he is on a plane back to the mainland.

JANUARY 26–29, TAMPA

A taste of the big time. IMG flies its top prospective draftees into Tampa for the Super Bowl. On the day before the game Brees signs autographs in a booth at a fan fest, the first time he has been paid for writing his name. For three hours' work he earns $2,500, and he's paid on the spot. "I know it doesn't sound like a lot of money," Brees says, "but it's the biggest check I've ever seen."

On Sunday evening Brees sits in Raymond James Stadium, nine rows from the field on the 25-yard line, as the spectacle of the Super Bowl unfolds. It is intoxicating for a college senior who plans to play in the NFL. "I had to pinch myself," Brees says. "We were on the Giants' side of the field, and when they came out of the tunnel, I imagined myself out there someday."

FEBRUARY 8, WEST LAFAYETTE

On an unseasonably warm winter afternoon, Brees stands with Purdue strength and conditioning coach Jim Lathrop on the sidewalk of North University Drive, which runs between Mackey Arena, where the Boilermakers play basketball, and Ross-Ade Stadium, where Brees set all those passing records. After a group of runners passes, Brees breaks into the first of a half-dozen uphill 100-meter sprints. Passing students rubberneck from car windows, shocked at seeing Mr. Purdue in this setting.

Four times a week Brees lifts in the Purdue weight room, with an emphasis on maintaining strength, not building muscle mass. Often he has trouble finding a partner to spot his lifts because Purdue players are lifting as a team at times that conflict with his schedule. Five times a week he runs sprints and does exercises to improve his sprint technique because he knows he can't afford a slow 40 time at the combine. Last year Louisville quarterback Chris Redman's plodding 5.35-second 40 spooked teams into dropping him from the bottom of the first round into the third.

Brees doesn't lack speed. In three seasons he ran for 891 yards, including 521 as a senior. Trouble is, he doesn't run as fast for a stopwatch as he does on the field. "In a game he's plenty quick," says Lathrop. "Drew's problem is that when he's running for time, he gets his arms up high and tightens up, which causes him to slow down. I'm trying to get him to keep his arms loose."

Almost every day Brees throws. "He probably throws too much," says Condon. Often his arm is sore and tired.

Brees is carrying a full load of five classes. Two of them, Wine Appreciation (taught by, no lie, Dr. Vine) and Job Design, are jokes. But three others—Strategic Management, Labor Relations and Database Systems—are upper-level management classes. They require attention and preparation. "I'm just hoping to make C's this semester," says Brees. "I want to graduate, but pro football is my future, so I'm compromising in some areas. I have to."

FEBRUARY 9–12, LAS VEGAS

Brees spends a long weekend in Vegas for the ESPY Awards. The following Saturday he will be in Ohio to receive the Big Ten MVP award from the Touchdown Club of Columbus, and three days after that he'll be in Philadelphia to accept the Maxwell Award as the country's top college football player. "It's hard to say no," he says of the various invitations. "The ESPYs are a great time, the people in Columbus have invited me three years in a row, and the Maxwell Award is very prestigious."

The combine begins two days after the Maxwell presentation.

FEBRUARY 14, DAVIE, FLA.

In his office at the Dolphins' complex, Rick Spielman, Miami's vice president of player personnel, pops in a videocassette of the 2000 Purdue-Minnesota game. He draws a nine-square grid on a white board and begins charting Brees's throws. Short, medium, long. Right, center, left. "That's a catch, nice release," Spielman says. "That's a drop. That's underthrown a little." After only three series, Spielman's grid is full of notations.

January and February are video months for NFL personnel staffs. They sit in front of TV monitors charting the top college players in almost lunatic detail. If a guard scratches his butt before pulling on sweeps to the left, they will know it.

Brees started 37 games and threw 1,678 passes at Purdue. "At least three people on our staff have seen every snap in his career," says Spielman. The Dolphins do medical and security checks and personality tests on the top 100 players available for the draft and give each a grade: A, B or C. "We will have a substantial file on Brees before we interview him at the combine," says Spielman. To illustrate, he takes a writer into a meeting room. One wall is filled with loose-leaf binders labeled by year. There are at least 15 pages of notes on each player, plus pictures. Most teams have as much. They may make mistakes in drafting, but not for lack of preparation.

With less than two weeks to go before the combine, a leaguewide consensus on Brees has formed: good head, decent feet, average arm. He will need to run reasonably fast and throw well in Indianapolis to improve his file.

FEBRUARY 25, HIGHWAY 65 NORTH, INDIANA

The 1997 Chevy Tahoe, a gift from Chip Brees to his son when he won a scholarship to Purdue, blasts through the darkness on the way from Indianapolis back to West Lafayette. Drew is talking on his cellphone to his mother: "It wasn't great, Mom. . . . It wasn't like I expected. . . . I'm tired, really tired. . . . I'm glad it's over." Brees tells his mother he loves her, flips the phone shut, swings into the left lane and pushes the speedometer past 80 mph. It's been a lousy day, and the sooner it ends, the better.

Brees went to the NFL scouting combine with high expectations and specific targets.

Forty-yard dash: 4.79 seconds, .07 faster than Marshall quarterback Chad Pennington ran in the 2000 combine. (Brees's actual time: somewhere between 4.73 and 4.83. Not bad.)

Five-10-five-yard shuttle: 4.15 seconds. (Actual time: 4.19. Acceptable.)

"L" shuttle: 7.05 seconds. (Actual time: 7.09. Also acceptable.)

Vertical jump: Low 30s. (Actual height: 32 inches. Right on.)

Bottom line: Brees proved himself a good enough athlete to satisfy most doubters, and he delivered under pressure. He even measured a hair taller, 6' ¼". That's the good news. The bad news: Brees had one other goal for Indianapolis—"I don't want any incompletes in the passing drills"—but he didn't come close.

SI was allowed to watch a day of drills at the five-day combine, which is usually off-limits to journalists. The scene inside the RCA Dome was surreal as several hundred NFL scouts, executives and coaches were scattered among the 56,127 seats. The hum of the fans that keep the dome inflated was punctuated only by a buzz from onlookers when something significant happened, as when Nebraska defensive end Kyle Vanden Bosch ran a scorching 4.68-second 40. The atmosphere was that of an SAT exam rather than a football game. "It's totally disorienting," said Heisman Trophy winner Chris Weinke of Florida State.

The heart of the quarterbacks' workout was a series of 20 throws: two pass attempts on each of 10 patterns. Brees was prepared to work at full speed, taking a hard drop and throwing on rhythm, before the receiver broke. However, Seahawks quarterbacks coach Jim Zorn, who ran the session, told the passers, "Just ease up and complete balls. Don't worry about anything else."

Brees was confused. Some quarterbacks took Zorn's advice and threw three-quarter-speed spirals to wideouts long after the receivers came out of their breaks. Balls like those would get picked off in a game, but they were safe passes in this arena. Brees stuck with his game plan and threw on rhythm. Some wideouts made sharp breaks, others didn't. Of Brees's 20 balls, 11 were solid throws and nine were poor. He one-hopped a simple out-cut and overthrew another. His long throws—the post-corner and the streak—were wobbly, setting off alarms throughout the league.

Hours later, Brees sits in the Tahoe, idling in the parking lot of a West Lafayette hotel. During his three days in Indianapolis, almost all teams in the league interviewed him. The Bengals, the Dolphins, the Buffalo Bills, the Oakland Raiders and the Washington Redskins, most of whom are unsettled at quarterback, had long sessions with him. Seahawks coach Mike Holmgren interviewed Brees for more than an hour. The two men seemed to connect. "I'd love to play for coach Holmgren," Brees says. He is silent for a long time. This is familiar territory for him. He was lightly recruited in high school and had to establish himself at Purdue. "Now," he says, "I have to prove myself all over again."

FEBRUARY 27, KANSAS CITY, MO.

At IMG football headquarters, reaction to Brees's combine performance is swift. "He took a step back, no question," says Condon. "I don't think he hurt his status as the Number 2 quarterback in the draft, but he didn't have a good day." If Brees held his draft position, it's because there is little else to choose from at quarterback after the presumed No. 1, Michael Vick. Mel Kiper Jr., who ranked Brees No. 16 before the combine, drops him out of his top 25 prospects.

Brees wants to audition again soon. Purdue seniors will work out for

NFL scouts on March 8, and Brees wants to throw on that day, as well as in a private workout on March 21. Condon puts his foot down and tells Brees to channel all his energy into preparing for the March 21 session. They also make plans to get Brees to Bradenton during his spring break to work with Kennan. "I wish it were tomorrow," says Brees.

MARCH 8, WEST LAFAYETTE

Even though Brees and Condon have faxed, called and e-mailed all NFL teams several times to remind them that he will not work out during the Boilermakers' pro day, Jacksonville Jaguars coach Tom Coughlin wants to see Brees throw. Coughlin is none too happy. Midway through the afternoon, he sidles over to Brees. "Come on, just throw a couple," Coughlin jokes.

"Sorry, Coach," says Brees.

MARCH 9, WEST LAFAYETTE

NFL free-agent signings are giving Brees a headache. On March 2 the Seahawks acquired Matt Hasselbeck from the Green Bay Packers in a trade. Does that mean Seattle won't pick Brees? He is disappointed. "Does Holmgren think Hasselbeck is the guy?" Brees asks. "I could see him and me fighting for the job. Then again, Jim Zorn was running my drills in Indy, and I stunk, so maybe they're not interested in me. I don't know. Nobody calls to tell you. There's no feedback."

Three days after the Hasselbeck deal, Brad Johnson signed with the Buccaneers. Yesterday the Bengals picked up Jon Kitna, who had been with Seattle. It looks as if the Chargers will sign Doug Flutie, whom the Bills let go in favor of Rob Johnson. Should Brees scratch all these teams? "It's crazy," he says. "I'm trying to keep an open mind, but every signing seems to affect my future."

In two days he will leave for Bradenton, and he can't wait. Randall Lane, who played with Brees in '98 and '99 and was hanging around the campus, has gone off to prepare for NFL Europe. Senior wideout Vinny Sutherland went to Cancun for spring break. "There's nobody for me to throw to," says Brees.

MARCH 11–18, BRADENTON

Over 15 years Kennan was an offensive coach for six NFL teams. The last was the New England Patriots, in 1997. He is now executive director of the NFL coaches' association, but for three years he has also been a hired gun for IMG. Brees spends a week in Bradenton rehearsing with Kennan. "I'm not changing anything Drew does," Kennan says. "I'll give him some drills he can use or not use, but mostly he'll practice throwing the routes he'll throw in his workout next week."

They work on a high school's practice field across a highway from the IMG Academies. Brees and Weinke throw routes to Charlie Jones, a four-year NFL veteran who is looking to sign as a free agent. To rest Jones, Kennan has three high school players run patterns for Brees and Weinke. One of them slips and slides on the short grass in shiny spit-and-polish ROTC shoes, yet he moves with grace and speed. "Florida athletes," says Brees. "Incredible."

The two quarterbacks throw for an hour, more than 100 balls apiece. They run and lift every afternoon too, but the emphasis here is on throwing the patterns that NFL people want to see. "They're going to want to see the deep comeback, even though no team in the league uses it," says Kennan. "They're going to want to see the skinny post, the deep post-corner, and they're going to want to see Drew fling it 60 yards, just to be sure he's got enough arm." After five days Kennan and Brees sit down and script his workout for the pros. Kennan will fly to Purdue to conduct the session, and Jones will be one of Brees's two receivers.

"I expect to have butterflies next Wednesday, but that's good," Brees says, sitting on a trainer's rubbing table in the IMG complex. He pounds the table with his fist. "I want the chance to perform!"

MARCH 21, WEST LAFAYETTE

By 10:45 a.m. representatives of seven NFL teams are at one end of the Mollenkopf Center's 100-yard indoor practice field. Almost the entire brain trust of the Kansas City Chiefs is here: president Carl Peterson, coach Dick Vermeil, offensive coordinator Al Saunders and quarterbacks coach Terry Shea. This stands to reason, because the Chiefs have lost Elvis Grbac to free agency and haven't succeeded in trading for Trent Green. San Diego, which has the first pick in the draft, is represented by coach Mike Riley and offensive coordinator Norv Turner. Garrett and offensive coordinator Ken Anderson are in from Cincinnati. The Bills, the Cowboys, the Atlanta Falcons and the Carolina Panthers are also here. Peterson walks over to IMG's Ken Kremer and says, "Well, we all wish he were a couple inches taller, but what can you do?"

At 11:06 Kennan says, "We'll start now. Drew is going to make 75 or 80 throws, and I think you'll all see everything you need to see." The tension is palpable: A player's future is on the line.

Brees will throw the same pattern twice, once to Jones and once to Purdue senior Keith Dawson, and then jog to the other end of the field and throw the same pattern in the opposite direction. He begins with short outs and slants and progresses to modest fades and skinny posts. Every throw is on target, and Brees runs quickly from end to end. Eleven minutes into the workout, Kennan calls for Jones to run a 17-yard comeback to the left sideline. Brees takes a seven-step drop as Jones runs 20 yards, turns and peels back toward the line of scrimmage while veering toward the sideline. The ball must be released before Jones turns, and it must travel nearly 40 yards in the air. It's a long, tough pass that requires timing and arm strength—a litmus-test throw. Brees uncoils a spiral so tight and hard that you can hear the football hum in the dead air. It hits Jones in the hands at nose level, a perfect pass. Somebody whistles softly in approval.

For the next 20 minutes, Brees is in an ungodly zone. He throws a total of 74 balls, and only two hit the ground by his doing. (Dawson drops several others.) He finishes by launching two 70-yard bombs, hitting the receivers in stride. "He threw the s--- out of it, in case you couldn't tell," Kennan says. "It was about the best individual workout I've ever seen."

NFL reps would sooner cut off their thumbs than tip their hands, but they don't disguise their response today. "Now I know why he threw for nine million yards in college," says Turner.

"Very impressive," says Garrett. "He's a solid guy. I think of him as like a baseball player who's going to play 10 years and never hit under .290. Just very, very efficient."

Vermeil and his Kansas City cohorts have been on a quarterback tour, visiting Josh Booty at LSU, Josh Heupel at Oklahoma and Sage Rosenfels at Iowa State before Brees. "Ideally, Drew would be a little bigger," says Vermeil, "but in terms of development and skills, he's well ahead of everybody else we've seen. Well ahead."

Long after the brass leave, Brees flops onto a weight bench and gives a zillion-watt smile. "That was me out there," he says. "Throwing on rhythm, moving back and forth. I feel like 1,000 pounds got lifted off my shoulders."

Whatever damage was done at the combine has been undone here. Brees is back in the mix.

MARCH 26, WEST LAFAYETTE

During Purdue's third pro day for senior players, Jaguars representatives run Brees through a series of deep routes and comebacks. They spend several minutes on one of Jacksonville's pet routes, a deep out-cut off a seven-yard drop. Brees throws every pass that's asked of him. He does fine.

MARCH 29, WEST LAFAYETTE

The Chargers want another look. They will conduct private workouts for only two players: Brees and Vick.

At 10 a.m. Brees is joined in a meeting room at Mollenkopf by Riley, Turner and quarterbacks coach Mike Johnson. For nearly two hours Turner stands at a white board with a black grease pencil and goes over the San Diego pass offense, rapid-fire. He draws up 20 plays, each of which can be run out of five formations, with multiple pass-protection schemes. "No time to study," Brees says later. Then the tables are turned. Brees stands, and Turner tells him to go through any four Chargers plays, including formation and protection permutations. "I guess I did O.K.," Brees will say. "It wasn't easy." (Turner later tells Condon that Brees did well on the board.)

The group eats lunch at a sandwich shop and returns to the indoor practice field, where Turner runs Brees through the entire San Diego offense. He demands many of the same throws that Brees made a week earlier but confuses Brees by asking him for more touch on some difficult throws. On the skinny post Turner tells Brees to imagine a linebacker dropping back into the pattern, forcing Brees to arc the ball. Brees struggles, bouncing several throws. "For three months people have been telling me, 'Show them the big arm, throw it hard,' " he says later. "Now Norv asks for something different. It's frustrating."

The next afternoon Vick will dazzle the Chargers' crew with his athletic skills and cannon arm, and survive in the classroom. What's more, nobody is offering enough for San Diego to trade the top pick. Brees is convinced that the Chargers will draft Vick.

APRIL 7, ATLANTA

The Falcons bring in 20 prospective first-round draft choices to meet the coaches and tour their complex. Atlanta has the fifth pick in the draft and an aging quarterback, Chris Chandler. On the visit Brees hangs out with friends like Steve Hutchinson and Jeff Backus of Michigan. "It was relaxing," he says of the test-free, workout-free trip. "No pressure."

APRIL 14, WEST LAFAYETTE

A week until the draft. No workouts left. No interviews left. A week to listen to more rumors. Is it true that Miami coach Dave Wannstedt told somebody at the NFL meetings that he'd love for Brees to fall to the Dolphins at No. 26? What about the rumor that Seattle, at No. 7, has not lost interest in Brees? Will Dallas try to trade into the first round? Just the other day the Pittsburgh Steelers called to confirm Brees's draft-day phone number. The Steelers? They didn't even watch him work out. "It's all misinformation from now until the draft," Condon tells Brees.

Schoolwork is under control. Final exams aren't until after the draft, and Brees thinks he will escape the semester with a 3.0. "There are no obstacles left," he says. "All I can do is wait."

APRIL 20, WEST LAFAYETTE

One day left. Brees bounds down the concrete steps into Mackey Arena for a photo shoot. "Three weeks ago I thought the draft would never get here," he says. "Now I'm pretty calm." That won't last. Minutes later Purdue sports information director Jim Vruggink finds Brees and tells him, "San Diego traded the first pick to Atlanta for Atlanta's number five, Tim Dwight and some other picks. The Chargers say they want Tomlinson."

Brees's eyes are like saucers. "Woooooo," he says. This changes everything. He tries to figure out how San Diego can take him. "Come on, somebody, take L.T. before the Chargers!" Brees howls. Somebody suggests the Chargers will take Brees in the second round. "I want to be a first-round pick," he says. That night Kansas City will finally get Trent Green, eliminating Brees as a possible pick for the Chiefs. Another part of his career is already in place: IMG has signed him to $980,000 worth of sponsorship and endorsement deals, most of it payable in the first year.

Brees and Brittany Dudchenko, his girlfriend of more than two years, go to dinner with a party of 14. A long meal is garnished with hilarious reminiscences. On the way home Brees talks nonstop. "Three months ago I had no idea who would pick me," he says, "and I still don't. But I've got a funny feeling about San Diego." It will be 2 a.m. before he falls asleep.

APRIL 21, WEST LAFAYETTE

At 6 a.m. Brees rises and makes himself bacon and eggs. By 7:45 he is playing golf, battling periodic rain and high, swirling winds on Purdue's Kampen Course. He shoots a scrambling 42 for nine holes. "Didn't think about the draft once, just my golf," he says. "Now I'm thinking about it." Yet for the first hour of the draft he is on the sideline at the Purdue spring football game.

Brees is home in time to see the Chargers take Tomlinson with the No. 5 pick. He shows no emotion. NFL officials invited him to New York City for the draft, but he refused. "Don't want to be the last guy in the green room," he says. Instead he watches with his younger brother, Dudchenko and a couple friends. Brees has a project to occupy him: deep-frying shrimp and fish fillets on the apartment's patio. "My mind is in there," he says, pointing to the TV, "but I can't sit and watch."

Just before Miami picks at No. 26, Dudchenko walks into the kitchen. "It's getting stressful," she says. Brees moves the phone in front of the television. "Ring, baby, ring!" he shouts. The Dolphins take Wisconsin cornerback Jamar Fletcher.

Twenty-nine minutes later Brees is on the phone with San Diego general manager John Butler. "Yessir, it's me," Brees says. Then: "I'm comin' to play, baby." When ESPN announces his name, Brees shoots his right fist into the air. Dudchenko cries.

The Chargers are thrilled. "We wanted Drew with our second pick," Riley says later. "We tried to make a trade with Miami for its pick at 26, but it didn't happen, so we held our breath." Last year's 32nd pick, Arizona wideout Dennis Northcutt, signed a seven-year, $5.3 million contract that included a $1.5 million signing bonus. Brees, as a quarterback widely considered to have first-round talent, should get significantly more.

Meanwhile, the calm in the Brees-Dudchenko apartment explodes into delirium. Four cell phones are ringing. Brees does a quick teleconference with the San Diego media, agrees to jump on an 8:55 p.m. flight to California and begins throwing clothes into a garment bag. "Man, I'm excited," he says. "I'm already visualizing the plays that Norv and I went over when he was here."

Exactly 63 minutes after Butler's call, Brees climbs into the Tahoe in the parking lot outside his apartment. He points it toward the Purdue campus for one last press conference in Mollenkopf Center before the long, sweet flight west.

DOWN BY CONTACT

| | | | | |

A Name on the Wall

BY WILLIAM NACK

Bob Kalsu had just finished a stellar rookie year in the NFL when he chose to serve in Vietnam—and became the only active U.S. pro athlete to die there.

T HE FEELING HAD GONE OUT OF EVERYTHING. IT WAS LIKE *we were zombies. You didn't care anymore. July was terrible. The [North Vietnamese] whacked Ripcord, that hill we were on, with mortars and rocket fire. Day after day, night after night. I was getting shell-shocked. I didn't care if I got out. At night you could hear the [enemy] yelling from the jungles all around, "GI die tonight! GI die tonight!" This was our deathbed. We thought we were going to be overrun.* —SPC. 4TH CLASS DANIEL THOMPSON, wireman at Firebase Ripcord, Vietnam, July 1970

THERE WERE always lulls between the salvos of incoming mortars, moments of perishable relief. The last salvo had just ended, and the dust was still settling over Firebase Ripcord. In one command bunker, down where the reek of combat hung like whorehouse curtains, Lieut. Bob Kalsu and Pfc. Nick Fotias sat basting in the jungle heat. In that last salvo the North Vietnamese Army (NVA), as usual, had thrown in a round of tear gas, and the stinging gas and the smoke of burning cordite had curled into the

bunkers, making them all but unbearable to breathe in. It was so sweltering inside that many soldiers suffered the gas rather than gasp in their hot,
stinking rubber masks. So, seeking relief, Kalsu and Fotias swam for the
light, heading out the door of the bunker, the threat of mortars be damned.
"Call us foolish or brave, we'd come out to get a breath of fresh air," Fotias
recalls.

It was Tuesday afternoon, July 21, 1970, a day Kalsu had been eagerly
awaiting. Back home in Oklahoma City, his wife, Jan, was due to have their
second child that very day. (They already had a 20-month-old daughter,
Jill Anne.) The Oklahoma City gentry viewed the Kalsus as perfectly matched
links on the cuff of the town. Jan was the pretty brunette with the quick
laugh, the daughter of a successful surgeon. Bob was the handsome, gre-
garious athletic hero with the piano-keys grin, the grandson of Czech immigrants for whom America had been the promised land and Bob the
promise fulfilled. As a college senior, in the fall of 1967, the 6' 3", 220-pound
Kalsu had been an All-America tackle for Oklahoma, a team of overachievers
that went 10–1, beating Tennessee in the Orange Bowl. The next season,
after bulking up to 250 pounds, Kalsu had worked his way into the starting
offensive line of the Buffalo Bills, and at season's end he had been named
the Bills' rookie of the year.

While in Vietnam, Kalsu rarely talked about his gridiron adventures.
Word had gotten around the firebase that he had played for the Bills, but he
would shrug off any mention of it. "Yeah, I play football," he would say.
What he talked about—incessantly—was his young family back home. Jan
knew her husband was somewhere "on a mountaintop" in Vietnam, but
she had no idea what he had been through. In his letters he let on very little. On July 19, the day after a U.S. Army Chinook helicopter, crippled by
antiaircraft fire, crashed on top of the ammunition dump for Ripcord's battery of 105-mm howitzers, setting off a series of explosions that literally
sheared off one tier of the hill, the bunkered-down lieutenant wrote his
wife. He began by using his pet name for her.

Dearest Janny Belle—
How're things with my beautiful, sexy, lovable wife. I love & miss you so very
much and can't wait till I'm back home in your arms and we're back in our
own apartment living a normal life. The time can't pass fast enough for me

until I'm back home with all my loved ones and especially you Jan and Jilly and Baby K. I love and need you so very much.

The wind has quit blowing so hard up here. It calmed down so much it's hard to believe it. Enemy activity remains active in our area. Hopefully it will cease in the near future.

I'm just fine as can be. Feeling real good just waiting to hear the word again that I'm a papa. It shouldn't be much longer until I get word of our arrival....

I love you, xxx-ooo.

Bob

Kalsu was, in fact, involved in the gnarliest battle going on at the time in Vietnam: an increasingly desperate drama being played out on the top of a steep, balding shank of rock and dirt that rose 3,041 feet above sea level and 656 above the jungle floor. From the crest of this two-tiered oblong promontory, on a space no bigger than two football fields, two artillery batteries—the doomed 105s and the six 155-mm howitzers of Battery A, Kalsu's battery—had been giving fire support to infantrymen of the 101st Airborne Division, two battalions of which were scouring the jungles for North Vietnamese while pounding the ganglia of paths and supply routes that branched from the Ho Chi Minh Trail in Laos, 12 miles to the west, spiderwebbing south and east around Ripcord through Thuathien Province and toward the coastal lowlands around Hue.

Atop that rock, Kalsu was caught in a maelstrom that grew stronger as July slouched toward August. On July 17, four days before his baby was due, Kalsu was made the acting commander of Battery A after the captain in charge was choppered out to have a piece of shrapnel removed from a bone in his neck. Kalsu and his men continued their firing missions as the NVA attacks intensified. With a range of 13 miles, Battery A's 155s were putting heavy metal on enemy supply lines as far off as the A Shau Valley, a key NVA logistical base 10 miles to the southwest, helping create such havoc that the enemy grew determined to drive the 300 or so Americans off Ripcord. As many as 5,000 NVA soldiers, 10 to 12 battalions, had massed in the jungles surrounding Ripcord, and by July 21 they were lobbing more than 600 rounds a day on the firebase, sending the deadliest salvos whenever U.S. helicopters whirled in with ammo and soldiers raced for the helipad to carry the shells on their shoulders up the hill.

Kalsu humped those 97-pound explosive rounds along with his men, an officer exposing himself to fire when he could have stayed in the bunker. "A fearless guy, smart, brave and respected by his troops," recalls retired colonel Philip Michaud, who at the time was a captain commanding the ill-fated battery of 105s. "Rounds were coming in, and he was out there. I told him a few times, 'It's good to run around and show what leadership is about, but when rounds are blowing up in your area, you ought to hunker down behind a gun wheel. Or a bunker.' The guy thought he was invincible."

The grunts loved him for it, and they would have followed him anywhere. David Johnson always did. Kalsu and Johnson, by most superficial measures, could not have been more different. Kalsu was white and the only child of middle-class parents—city-bred, college-educated, married, a father, devoutly Catholic. Johnson was black and the seventh of 11 children raised on a poor farm outside of Humnoke, Ark. He was single and childless, a supplicant at the Church of God and Christ. What the two men shared was a gentleness and childlike humanity that reached far beyond race. So James Robert Kalsu, 25, and Spc. 4th Class David Earl Johnson, 24, became inseparable. "They just clicked," recalls former sergeant Alfred Martin. "You saw one, you saw the other."

That lull in incoming fire on July 21 nearly brought the two friends together again. Johnson was standing outside Kalsu's bunker on the pock-marked hill. Cpl. Mike Renner, a gunner, was standing by his 155 with a sergeant who was dressing him down because the jack on the gun had broken, leaving the crew unable to raise it to a different azimuth. At that moment Kalsu and Fotias rose out of the bunker. They stood at the door for a moment, Fotias with his back to it, and Kalsu started reading to him from a piece of paper in his hand. "[It was] a letter he had received from his wife," Fotias says. "I remember the joy on his face as he read the letter to me. He said, 'My wife's having our baby today.'"

Some rounds you heard falling, some you didn't. Fotias did not hear this one. Jim Harris, the battalion surgeon, was across the firebase when he heard the splitting crack and turned his head toward it. The 82-mm mortar landed five feet from the bunker door. "I can still feel the heat of the blast coming past me and the concussion knocking me over," says Renner. "It flipped me backward, my helmet flew off, and the back of my head hit the ground."

Johnson fell sprawling on the ground. Fotias, at the mouth of the bunker, saw the sun go out. "I remember this tremendous noise," he says, "and darkness. And being blown off my feet and flying through the door of the bunker and landing at the bottom of the steps, six feet down, and this tremendous weight crushing me. I couldn't see. I couldn't hear. I had dirt in my eyes, and my eyes were tearing. I rubbed them, and then I could see again. I pushed off this weight that was on top of me, and I realized it was Bob."

KALSU WAS really a boy trapped inside a large man's body—a player of pranks whose high-pitched cackle would fill a room. He laughed so heartily that he drooled, the spittle coursing from the corners of his mouth down around his dimpled chin and on down his chiseled neck. Once, on hearing the punch line of an off-color joke, he slammed a fist so hard on an adjoining barstool that the stool broke into pieces. He had the appetite of a Komodo dragon, but he loved kids even more than food. Some valve must have been missing in his psyche: His ego, unlike that of most jocks, was not inflatable. He always favored the underdog (he arranged the selection of one girl as high school homecoming queen because no one paid her much mind), and he turned down a high school sports award on grounds that he'd already received too many. "It'll mean more to somebody else," he told his mother, Leah.

Kalsu was born in Oklahoma City on April 13, 1945, and he came of age in the suburb of Del City at a time when coach Bud Wilkinson was leading Oklahoma through its gilded age. From 1953 into '57 the Sooners won 47 consecutive games, still a record for a Division I school, and finished three straight seasons ('54 to '56) undefeated. Twice during that run, in '55 and '56, they were national champions. Like every other 18-year-old gridiron star in the state, Kalsu aspired to play in Norman. Even as Wilkinson's program faltered in the early 1960s—the Sooners were 16-14-1 in the first three years of the decade—the coach's aura was so strong that there was only one place for a local kid to go. When Wilkinson recruited Kalsu out of Del City High in '63, Kalsu signed on.

He was not the first in his family to make the big time in Oklahoma college sports. Bob's uncle, Charles Kalsu, played basketball at Oklahoma State for Henry Iba, whose legend in college hoops was writ as large as

Wilkinson's was in football. The 6' 6" Charles was a second-team All-America in 1939 and played pro ball with the old Philips 66 Oilers. Charles's brother Frank Kalsu, three inches shorter and two years younger, yearned to follow him to Oklahoma State. "Frank and Charles were extremely competitive," recalls their younger brother, Milt. "Frank went to Stillwater thinking he could play. He lasted half a semester and came home." Frank married Leah Aguillard, of French Canadian ancestry, became a sheet-metal worker at Tinker Air Force Base in Midwest City, Okla., and settled in Del City.

Frank saw in his son, Bob, an open-field run at fulfilling the dreams that he had left behind in Stillwater. "That's what made him drive his son to be a college athlete," Milt says. "He'd wanted to play basketball for Iba." Frank put the teenage Bob on a rigorous conditioning program long before such regimens were common. Milt still remembers Bob chuffing through four-mile cross-country runs among the tumbleweed and jackrabbits while Frank trailed behind him in the family car.

Early on, the boy began to live for the playing of games, for competition, and he approached everything as if it were a last stand. "He played every kind of ball imaginable," says Leah. "He was even on a bowling team. He loved to play cards—canasta, hearts. We'd play Chinese checkers head-to-head. We played jacks when he was seven or eight. He played jacks until he was in *high school*. He'd never quit when he lost. He'd say, 'Mom, let's play another.' "

Bob liked football well enough—the butting of heads, the grinding contact, the fierceness of play in the trenches—but the game he loved most was golf. He was a four or five handicap. On Sundays, Bob would go to 7 a.m. Mass at St. Paul's Church so he and Uncle Milt could make an 8:30 tee time. They sometimes got in 54 holes in a day, and they spent hours behind Bob's house hitting balls, always competing. "We'd see who could get [the ball] closest to a telephone pole," Milt recalls.

Kalsu never played a down for Wilkinson, who resigned after his freshman season. However, over the next four years, including a redshirt season in 1964, Kalsu matured into one of the best offensive linemen ever to play for the Sooners. He also developed his talent for leading men, which was as natural as the stomping, pounding gait that would earn for him the nickname Buffalo Bob. Steve Campbell, three years behind him at Del City High, remembers summers when Kalsu, preparing for the next Oklahoma season, would call evening practices for high school players and run them as if he were a boot-camp sergeant. He simply put out the word that he would be working out at the high school and that all Del City players should be there.

Kalsu would appear in a jersey cut off at the sleeves, in shorts and baggy socks and cleats, and begin sending the young men through agility and running drills, racing up and down the field with the players and finally dividing them up for a game of touch football. "We were ready and willing followers," Campbell says. "He had a very commanding air about him."

Fact is, in his comportment on and off the field, Kalsu rarely put a cleat down wrong. "He did everything the way you're supposed to," says former Sooners defensive end Joe Riley, who was recruited with Kalsu. "He didn't cut classes. He never gave anybody a minute's trouble. He became the player he was because he believed everything the coaches told him. He didn't complain. We'd all be complaining through two-a-days, and he'd just walk around with a little smirk on his face. He was a little too goody-goody for some of us, but we respected him. And once you got to know him, you liked him."

By his third year of eligibility, 1966, Kalsu was starting on a squad that was showing signs of a pulse. The year before, in Gomer Jones's second season as coach, the Sooners had gone 3–7, and Gomer was a goner. In '66, under new coach Jim Mackenzie, Oklahoma went 6–4. When Mackenzie died of a heart attack in the spring of '67, Chuck Fairbanks took over, and his rise to the practice-field tower presaged the sudden ascension of the team, which would have one of the wildest years in Sooners history.

The '67 Sooners had not been expected to win their conference, much less make a run at the national title. For guards Eddie Lancaster and Byron Bigby, the tone of the season was set on the first play of the first game, against Washington State in Norman on Sept. 23, when they double-teamed a defensive lineman and rolled him seven yards down the field, springing tailback Steve Owens for a 12-yard gain. Next thing Lancaster knew, Kalsu was standing over him and Bigby and yelling, "Good god, awright! Look at this! Look at what you did!"

Bigby turned to Lancaster and said, in some amazement, "You know, we can do this." The Sooners won 21–0. They kept on winning too and nearly pulled off the whole shebang, losing only to Texas, 9–7. Kalsu was smack in the middle of it all. Elected team captain, he took the job to be more than that of a figurehead. He took it to mean that he should lead, which he did in the best way, by example.

Steve Zabel, an Oklahoma tight end at the time, recalls the day Buck Nystrom, the offensive line coach, got peeved at the taxi-squad players who were going against his linemen in the "board drill," in which two players lined up at opposite ends of an eight-foot-long plank and ran into each other like mountain goats, the winner being the one left standing on the board. Disgusted by what he saw as a lack of intensity, the 215-pound Nystrom—"the meanest coach I was ever around," says Zabel—got on the board and turned his cap backward. Without pads or a helmet, he took on all his linemen, one by one. Finally Kalsu got on the board.

Kalsu, at 220 pounds, had become the biggest hammer on the Sooners' offensive line. He took off down the board. "He hit Buck so hard that he lifted him off the board and planted him on the ground with his helmet on Buck's chest," says Zabel. "Everybody was running around yelling, 'Kalsu killed him! Kalsu killed Buck!' "

That night Zabel and center Ken Mendenhall were walking into a Baskin-Robbins when Nystrom came out, holding an ice cream cone in one hand and his two-year-old son, Kyle, in the other. He was wearing the same T-shirt he'd worn at practice, and his arms were discolored. "Zabel! Mendenhall!" Nystrom blurted. "Wasn't that the greatest practice you ever saw?" He handed his cone to Zabel, the boy to Mendenhall, and raised the front of his shirt, revealing the black-and-blue imprint of a helmet. "Look at this!" he said gleefully. "Boy, ol' Bob Kalsu liked to kill me!"

On the field that year Kalsu was everywhere, urging the troops on, picking them up off piles. Every time Owens, the tailback, looked up from the ground, there was Kalsu. Owens would win the Heisman Trophy in 1969, but in '67 he was an unbridled galloper who often ran up the backs of Kalsu's legs. One day the exasperated captain took Owens aside. "Listen, Steve, I'm on your side," he said. "Find the hole!"

Owens was in ROTC, and he remembers Kalsu, a cadet colonel, marching his battalion around the parade grounds like so many toy soldiers. "He was all over us all the time," says Owens. "He took *that* job seriously too."

Before Kansas State played Oklahoma, Wildcats coach Vince Gibson, who had been studying film of the Sooners, approached Fairbanks on the field. "Kalsu is the best blocking lineman I've ever seen," Gibson said. In fact, after the Sooners' coaches studied all their game film of 1967, Fairbanks said that "our average gain on all plays going over Kalsu, including short yardage and goal line plays, is 6.2 net yards rushing. . . . This is what we coaches grade as . . . near perfection."

Kalsu "wasn't better than other players because of his ability," Fairbanks recalls. "He was better because he was smarter and technically better. He was a little more mature in his evaluation of what was happening on the field. There were no problems coaching him. You didn't have to try to motivate him. He came to practice every day with a smile on his face."

At season's end Kalsu appeared to have it all. An appearance in the Orange Bowl. All-America honors. A solid chance at a pro football career. And his marriage, after the Orange Bowl, to Jan Darrow. She and Bob had had their first date on Oct. 15, 1966, and she knew that very night she'd found her mate. "A really cute guy who made me laugh," she says. "I came home, threw myself on my sister Michelle's bed and said, 'I just met the man I'm going to marry.'"

Jan was the third of nine kids—five girls and four boys—and by the summer of 1967 Kalsu had been embraced as the 10th sibling in the Darrows' seven-bedroom house on Country Club Drive. "I always wanted brothers and sisters, and now I got 'em," he told Ione Darrow, the mother of the brood. Kalsu may have been a fearsome lineman, but what the Darrows discovered was a large, lovable kid who liked to scare trick-or-treaters by jumping from behind trees and who failed grandly in his experiments as a pastry chef. Diane Darrow, four years older than Jan, walked into the kitchen one day and saw Bob with his huge hands in a mixing bowl, squashing the batter. She asked him what on earth he was doing. He said he was making an angel food cake for Ione's birthday. Diane wondered why he wasn't using a wooden spoon. "The box says mix by hand," he said.

Around the Darrows' dinner table, everyone would stop to watch the spectacle of Kalsu's eating. Whole salads disappeared at two or three stabs of a fork. Glasses of orange juice vanished in a single swallow. Kalsu could devour a drumstick with a few spins of the bone, stripping it clean. He also played games endlessly with his new siblings, cheerfully cheating at all of them.

Bob and Jan were married on Jan. 27, 1968, and when they returned from their honeymoon in Galveston, Texas, during spring break, the Darrow family sang the news: "Buffalo Bob, won't you come out tonight?" He had been drafted in the eighth round by the Bills of the American Football League. The NFL's Dallas Cowboys and the AFL's Denver Broncos had also shown interest, but both had backed away, leery of Kalsu's military commitment. Having completed ROTC, he would be commissioned a second lieutenant after graduation in May. He was not immediately called to active duty, however. By the time he reported to the Bills that summer, Jan was six months pregnant.

Within a few weeks with the Bills, Kalsu had worked his way into the lineup, taking the place of the injured Joe O'Donnell at right guard and starting nine games that season. No one watched Kalsu more closely than Billy Shaw, Buffalo's left guard and a future Hall of Famer. Shaw was 29 in '68, nearing the end of his career, and he saw Kalsu as a threat to his job. "Bob had a lot of talent," says Shaw. "He had real good feet, and he was strong, good on sweeps. In those days we had only one backup, and he was Joe's and my backup. Our forte was foot speed, and Bob was right there with us. He really fit in with how we played, with a lot of running, a lot of sweeps, a lot of traps."

Shaw and O'Donnell were mirror images of each other—both 6' 2" and about 252 pounds—and when Kalsu joined them, the three looked like triplets. At the Bills' urging, the 6' 3" Kalsu had gained weight by lifting weights and devouring potatoes and chicken ("His neck got so big that even his ties didn't fit him anymore," says Jan), and he was listed at 250 pounds on the Bills' roster. "The thing I noticed is that he was so mature for a young player," says Shaw. "He wasn't your normal rookie. He wasn't in awe."

Bob Lustig, the Bills' general manager at the time, says Kalsu "had a good future in pro football." Lustig recalls something else: "He not only had the talent, but he also had the smarts. He didn't make the same mistake twice."

Kalsu also brought to Buffalo the same love of horseplay and mischief that had marked his days in Oklahoma. He and one of his rookie roommates, John Frantz, a center from Cal, filled a trash can with water and carried it into the head at training camp. They thought their other roommate, rookie tackle Mike McBath, was sitting on the toilet in one of the stalls. They lifted the can and dumped the water into the stall. They heard a thunderous bellow that sounded nothing like McBath. It was six-year veteran Jim Dunaway, Buffalo's 6' 4", 281-pound defensive tackle, who rose from the dumper like Godzilla and screamed, "Whoever did that is dead!"

Kalsu and Frantz bolted in a panic and hid in the closet of their room until Hurricane Dunaway had blown over, and they laughed every time they saw the big tackle after that. "Bob was always stirring the pot," says Frantz. "As good an athlete as he was, he was an even better person."

Frantz and McBath used to hit the night spots, chasing girls, but no amount of coaxing could get Kalsu to go along. "Some of the married guys chased around, but Bob, never," says Frantz. "He loved his wife and his kid. He was totally at ease with himself, confident in who he was. We'd go out, and he'd laugh at us: 'You guys can do what you want. I've got what I want.' "

Only seven active pro athletes would serve in Vietnam: six football players and a bowler. Most other draftable pro athletes elected to serve in the reserves. Kalsu's family and friends urged him to go that route. "I'm no better than anybody else," he told them all. It was early 1969. The Vietnam War was still raging a year after the Tet Offensive, and there was no hope of its ending soon. Frantz pleaded with Kalsu to seek the Bills' help in finding a slot in the reserves. "John, I gave 'em my word," Kalsu said, referring to his promise, on joining ROTC, to serve on active duty. "I'm gonna do it."

"Bob, it's hell over there," Frantz said. "You've got a wife, a child."

Kalsu shook his head. "I'm committed," he said.

THAT SEPTEMBER, after nearly eight months at Fort Sill in Lawton, Okla., Kalsu went home one day looking shaken. His uniform was soaked with sweat. "I have orders to go to Vietnam," he told Jan.

They spent his last weeks in the country at her parents' house, with Jan in growing turmoil over the prospect of losing him. They were in the laundry room washing clothes when she spoke her worst fear. "What if you die over there?" she asked. "What am I to do?"

"I want you to go on with your life," he said. "I want you to marry again."

She broke down. "I don't want to marry again," she said. "I couldn't."

"Jan, I promise you, it'll be all right."

They had been married in the St. James Catholic Church in Oklahoma

City, and a few weeks before he left, they went there together. Jan knelt before the altar. "If you need him more than I do," she prayed silently, "please give me a son to carry on his name."

Bob was gone before Thanksgiving. In one of her first letters to him, Jan gave Bob the good news: She was pregnant again.

If his letters didn't reveal what he was facing in Vietnam, Jan got a sense of it in May 1970 when, seven months pregnant and with Jill in tow, she met him in Hawaii for a week of R and R. Bob slept much of the time, and he was napping one day in their room when fireworks were set off by the pool. "He tore out of that bed frantic, looking for cover," Jan says, "terror and fear on his face. I got a glimpse of what he was living through."

At the end of the week they said goodbye at the airport. "Bob, please be careful," she said.

"You be careful," he said. "You're carrying our baby."

Jan returned to Oklahoma, Bob to Vietnam—and soon to Firebase Ripcord. For the last three weeks he was on that rock, it was under increasing siege, and his men saw him as one of them, a grunt with a silver bar working the trenches of Ripcord and never complaining. "He had a *presence* about him," says former corporal Renner. "He could have holed up in his bunker, giving orders on the radio. He was out there in the open with everybody else. He was always checking the men out, finding out how we were, seeing if we were doing what needed to be done. I got wounded on Ripcord, and he came down into the bunker. My hands were bandaged, and he asked me, 'You want to catch a chopper out of here?' " Renner saw that Kalsu had been hit in the shoulder. "I saw the bandage on him and saw he was staying. I said, 'No, I'm gonna stay.' "

The men of Battery A, trapped on that mountaintop, bonded like cave dwellers in some prehistoric war of the worlds. "Our language and behavior were pitiful," says Renner. "We behaved like junkyard dogs. If you wanted to fight or tear somebody else up, that's what you did. It was the tension. But I never heard Lieutenant Kalsu cuss. Not once. He was such a nice guy."

As was the other gentle soul of the outfit, David Earl Johnson. "A kind, lovable person," recalls his sister, Audrey Wrightsell. Growing up in their little Arkansas community, David played most sports. His junior high coach Leo Collins says that David was good at just about everything and best at basketball and track. "One of the best athletes you could ever wish for in a small school," says Collins. "He was so easy to manage, a coach's dream."

Like Kalsu, Johnson did not take the easy way out of the war. He was paying his way through Philander Smith College in Little Rock, majoring in business administration, when he decided not to apply for another student deferment. "I'm tired of this," he told Audrey. "I'm gonna serve my time."

So it was that Johnson landed on Ripcord with Kalsu, in the middle of the most unpopular war in U.S. history. In May 1970, during a protest against the war at Kent State in Ohio, National Guardsmen had fired on student protesters, killing four. Criticism of the war had become so strong that as the NVA massed to attack Ripcord, the U.S. command in Vietnam decided not to meet force with more force, which would have put even more body bags on the evening news. So Ripcord was left twisting in the boonies.

The men made the most of their fate. Kalsu tried to make a game of the darkest moments. He and Big John, as Johnson was known, "were always laughing and joking," says former sergeant Martin. "For [them], everything was a challenge." When the sling-loads of ammunition would arrive by chopper, Kalsu would call out, "Let's get that ammo off the pads!" He and Johnson would take three of those 97-pound shells apiece and hump them up the hill together. The contest was to see who could carry the most. "Johnson was the biggest man we'd seen until Kalsu came along," says Martin.

They died together at five o'clock that summer afternoon. Fotias rolled Kalsu off him and saw the flowing wound behind the lieutenant's left ear. Kalsu was pulled out of the bunker, not far from where Johnson lay dead, and Doc Harris came running over. He looked down at Kalsu and knew that he was gone.

Renner, dazed from the concussion, saw that Kalsu was dead and picked up Beals, wounded in the blast, and started to carry him to the aid station. "Lieutenant Kalsu has been killed," Renner said. "I don't know what the hell we're gonna do now."

In a hospital where he had been flown after taking shrapnel, Martin got word that Kalsu and Big John were dead. "I sat there and cried," he says.

That evening, the battalion commander on Ripcord, Lieut. Col. Andre Lucas, learned of Kalsu's death. Lucas would die two days later, as the firebase was being evacuated, and for his part in defending it, he would win the

Congressional Medal of Honor. As battle-hardened as he was, he seemed stunned by the news about Kalsu. "The tone went out of the muscles on his face, and his jaw dropped," Harris says.

On July 21, 1970, James Robert Kalsu thus became the only American professional athlete to die in combat in Vietnam.

AT 12:45 A.M. on July 23, at St. Anthony Hospital in Oklahoma City, Jan Kalsu gave birth to an eight-pound, 15½-ounce boy, Robert Todd Kalsu. When Leah Kalsu visited her that morning, Jan fairly shouted, "Bob is going to jump off that mountain when he finds he has a boy!"

That afternoon, as the clan gathered in the Darrow house to head for a celebration at the hospital, there was a knock at the front door. Sandy Szilagyi, one of Jan's sisters, opened it, thinking the visitor might be a florist. She saw a uniformed Army lieutenant. "Is Mrs. James Robert Kalsu home?" he asked.

Sandy knew right then. "She's at St. Anthony Hospital," she said. "She's just given birth to a baby."

The young lieutenant went pale. Turning, he walked away. Sandy called Philip Maguire, the doctor who had delivered the baby, and told him who was coming. At the hospital, the lieutenant stepped into Maguire's office and sat down. He was shaking. "Do you think she'll be able to handle this?" he asked. "I don't know what to do. I'm not sure I can do this."

Maguire led the officer to Jan's room, slipped into a chair and put his arm around her. "Jan, there's a man from the Army here to see you," he said.

"Bob's been killed, hasn't he?" she said.

The officer came in and stood at the foot of the bed. He could barely speak. "It is my duty. . . . " he began. When he finished, he turned and left in tears.

Jan asked to leave the hospital immediately with her baby. She did one thing before she left. She asked for a new birth certificate. She renamed the boy James Robert Kalsu Jr.

The funeral, a week later at Czech National Cemetery, brought people from all around the country, and the gravesite service was more anguished than anything Byron Bigby, Kalsu's old Sooners teammate, had ever seen. "I looked around," he says, "and there was not a dry eye. We walked out of there biting our lips."

Barry Switzer, who had been a young assistant under Fairbanks during the '67 season, was walking to his car when he turned and looked back. What he saw haunts him still. "Bob's daddy got his wife and Jan back to the car," Switzer says. "After everyone was gone from the gravesite, he went back and lay down on the casket."

THREE DECADES have passed since Kalsu died. Jan has sought ways to deal with the void, but times were often difficult. She struggled financially, frequently living from one government check to another, determined to remain at home while raising her kids.

She did not have a serious relationship with a man until the mid-'80s, when she began seeing Bob McLauchlin, an Oklahoma businessman. In 1986 they visited the Vietnam Veterans Memorial in Washington, D.C. They found Kalsu's name on the wall, and McLauchlin shared Jan's bereavement. They married in 1988. Last fall McLauchlin took Jill and Bob Jr. to a reunion of Ripcord survivors in Shreveport, La. Her children persuaded Jan not to go. They didn't want to see her cry as she had for so many years.

Jill and Bob Jr. have suffered a keen ambivalence for years. From all they have heard about their father from Jan and the Darrow clan, they have grown to love and admire him without having known him. They are proud of all he accomplished and the honorable way he conducted his life, but they are angry at him too. They grew up fatherless, after all, having to comfort a lonely, grieving mother whose pain and struggles continually touched them.

The children turned out well. Jill, outgoing and warm, is a housewife in Oklahoma City, the mother of three with a fourth on the way. Bob, soft-spoken and reflective, is an aviation lawyer in Oklahoma City and the father of two. Asked what he would say to his father, Bob says, "I would embrace him and tell him I love him. It would not be derogatory, and it would not be mean, but I would ask him, 'Did you fully contemplate the consequences of your decision? I feel like I lost out, and I wish you had not made the decision to go.' " Bob Jr. considers what he's said for a moment, then goes on, "I'm equally proud he made the decision. That's the kind of man I want to be, to have the integrity that he had." That, of course, is the rub. Bob Kalsu made that decision precisely because he was the kind of man he was.

All who knew him remember him in different ways. The clan, as a family man. The football players, as a tough jock. Then there are those who knew Kalsu on that terrible hill. They have the most painful and poignant memories of him. Fotias has trouble talking about Kalsu, his voice soft and filled with sorrow. So does Renner. He walked over to Kalsu's body lying outside the bunker and peered into his motionless face. He would see that face for years. Now, however, "I can't see the face anymore," Renner says. "I can see his silhouette. I can't see a lot of their faces, only their silhouettes."

Renner is having trouble getting out the words. They come in a whisper. "I've thought of him every Memorial Day," he says. "In my heart, I pay homage to him. And Johnson. They are all very important." He closes his eyes and bows his head and quietly weeps.

| | | | | |

A Life after Wide Right

BY KARL TARO GREENFELD

Thirteen years after missing a Super Bowl–winning field goal for the Bills,
Scott Norwood viewed his worst moment as a step in the right direction.

THIS STOCKY MAN, IN BROWN, RUBBER-SOLED SHOES, gray Dockers and a tan polo shirt, walking across the narrow street from his car, the white Chevy Prism with the cracked windshield, he is a failure. An abject, wretched failure. And yet he is, incontrovertibly, a winner, a success. He stands there in his wraparound sunglasses and breathes the wet spring air and talks to you about interest rates and square footage and backyard park adjacencies and finished basements in this northern Virginia suburb. Houses. Condominiums. A nice parcel out by Centreville. In Chantilly. *Mortgage rates are low. Now is the time to buy.* He speaks in a quiet, slow, gravelly voice. Thoughtful. You lean in to hear him. His steady monotone wins out over your urge to interrupt.

He finishes talking and looks away, at the waving poplars and the unweeded grass, the mini mall in the distance and the Mobil station where kids are filling their bike tires with air. You look at him and you know you know him. He hands you his card. This is an upscale area, he explains, comfortable, a bit pricey perhaps, but great for families. A strong sense of community. The card says SCOTT NORWOOD, REALTOR, and it is red, white and blue. He looks at you to see if you recognize the name. He lives with this, a combination of burden and opportunity. A salesman needs any edge he can get, and he knows that merely being recognized as a former NFL kicker can help win over the husbands but rarely the wives. The wives must be reminded that this is the guy who blew that kick, who, you know, lost that Super Bowl for the Buffalo Bills; then there is understanding and sympathy. And that could help cajole a couple into bidding on that split-level colonial at the end of the cul-de-sac.

But he never asks for the pity. He has known anger and disappointment. Has felt responsible for a city's stifled aspirations. But he will not accept pity.

We are a fickle nation, quick to dismiss failure and embrace success. Prove yourself a champion, and we will love you forever, overlooking spousal abuse and drug busts and murder raps. But fall short on the field, and we may never forgive, no matter how you conduct yourself away from the game. So consider how it would feel to live as the answer to a trivia question, the punch line to a joke, a synonym for misses and muffs and screwups, or, perhaps even more humiliating, the MacGuffin in a Vincent Gallo movie *(Buffalo '66)*. That is the burden Scott Norwood has borne since Super Bowl XXV. And you know what? He has not only survived, but he has also thrived—and not as some lovable loser, a Throneberry or Uecker who uses his haplessness as a huckster's tool.

The measure of a man should no more be his worst moments than it should be the color of his skin or the cut of his suit. It is how we deal with those moments that make us who we are, and that is the most American measure of success: to fail, to pick yourself up and try again. We are a nation of losers made good, descendants of those who settled here in search of a second chance. To fail is not American, it is *human*. But it *is* American to overcome that failure.

It took years for Scott Norwood to get here. To walk down this sidewalk and point to this house and say that it will go in the mid-4s. To raise his three children, who have his blue eyes and his beautiful wife's blonde locks, and to take up his position as man of the house. This man, in his journey, has transformed himself from taciturn failure to stolid hero. It is a small sort of heroism, quotidian, really—the heroism of failing at something and still persevering. Of missing a field goal wide right in the most televised sporting event in the country, and then having to get up the next morning and continue to live your life. We've all known moments of failure—of blowing an exam, of being fired, spurned, disgraced—yet these moments are seldom public. How do you go on when every time you walk into a liquor store or a gas station, there is someone pointing at you, reminding you of your worst moment? You see, this is also a particular kind of American heroism—the simple, quiet heroism of continuing to be a dad and a husband despite knowing, deeply, that life can be a bitch.

THE PATH to Scott Norwood's failure, and the redemptive success of overcoming that setback, begins at Thomas Jefferson High in Alexandria, Va., where a stocky, 5' 10", 17-year-old sweeper is heading back to the locker room after soccer practice. The football coach, Mike Weaver, stops him and says, "Hey, son, I hear you can really kick the ball."

Scott is a quiet boy, the discomfort of adolescence reinforcing his taciturn nature so that when he speaks it is as surprising as a voice coming from a statue. "I'm O.K., sir."

"We need a kicker, son," says coach Weaver, "Why don't you come out for the team this season?"

Scott nods. He's been a standout soccer player since he was old enough to tie his shoes and would make the All-Metropolitan team twice at Thomas Jefferson. But such is the straightforwardness of his world view that he has never thought about applying his skill at kicking a ball to another sport.

At dinner that night at the Norwoods' house in Annandale, his father, Del, who will later be inducted into the Virginia High School Hall of Fame as a baseball coach, listens as Scott recounts his conversation with Weaver. A Maine native and the coach at Washington-Lee High School in Arlington, Va., Del pitched in the minor leagues and was invited to camp with the Boston Red Sox, but never made it to the majors. Yet as much as he once dreamed of the big leagues, he now enjoys playing with and coaching his three children in baseball and soccer. Scott's older brother, Steve, is a pitcher and outfielder for the University of Virginia who will later be drafted by the Milwaukee Brewers. His younger sister, Sandra, is a standout in field hockey, basketball and soccer. Del had been a little disappointed that Scott, when he reached high school, had chosen soccer over baseball, but the nature of Del's commitment to his children was that he would have supported Scott if he had chosen ballet. So when Scott mentions the possibility of kicking for the football team, Del asks him if this is something he wants to do.

"You know, Dad," Scott says, swallowing a bite of chicken-fried steak, "I think I do."

Del nods and tells Scott that he will be happy to help out any way he can.

That summer the father and son spend every morning at Thomas Jefferson, teeing it up and catching kickoffs. The two chart the accuracy of Scott's field goals and the distance of his kickoffs. They don't talk much about their progress, but there is a sense that things are going well. Scott, because of his soccer background, has an intuitive feel for how to approach the ball. Del's books tell him that Scott should take three steps back and two to the left, but Scott just sort of backs up at an angle and sets up, arms swinging, and then makes the smooth run up to the ball followed by the stiff sound of the stuffing being knocked out of the Wilson, which travels 45 yards through the uprights.

"It just felt good," Scott recalls. "I was comfortable with it pretty quickly."

He goes out for the football team, and the coach, of course, is grateful to have a real kicker instead of a backup quarterback who kicks because he doesn't get to play as much as he would like. For Scott—shy, reserved—the position offers an assured place in the universe. There is a simplicity to this role that appeals to him: He scores points. By increments of one and three he becomes the leading scorer on the team, in the county and, finally, in the region. The steadiness of the accretion is pleasing, like interest accumulating in a bank account, and by the time he makes the winning field goal in a game against archrival Annandale High, college scouts who have come to see other players are making notes about this kicker.

EVERY OFF-SEASON, Scott comes home to Annandale. After every year at James Madison University, where he earns a football scholarship. And then, after he graduates with a degree in business in 1982, and Del and Scott blanket the NFL with videotape, and after he signs with the Atlanta Falcons—and is cut. After an upstart league called the USFL is formed and he wins a job with the Birmingham Stallions and kicks 25 field goals in '83. After he tears some cartilage in his knee in his second season with the Stallions and is released. After successes and after failures, he comes back to work out with his father at the same old high school field. They never speak of what it feels like to be cut by an NFL team. Or how it feels to drive from Atlanta back to Fairfax County in the light-blue Riviera and move back in with your folks. Or what it is like to be a guy a few years out of college still practicing field goals with your dad. They never talk about how life isn't fair, or how, no matter what happens, you keep showing up. Del will occasionally express displeasure with the Falcons for cutting his son, or with the NFL or USFL for not appreciating what a good kicker they passed up. And then Del and Scott will jog down the field to retrieve the half-dozen balls and stuff them into the sack and drag them back upfield and set 'em up again, five yards deeper. And when Scott's knee heals, they don't talk about how excited they are when the Bills invite him to camp. He is one of 10 kickers they're bringing in. That doesn't matter, Del tells him. You just keep showing up.

The weather in Buffalo drives other kickers mad, but it suits Norwood. The wind, the cold, the rain, the spartan practice facilities. Norwood has been through worse. He's been cut, injured and overlooked, and compared with that, kicking in rain or a harsh wind blowing from the north is almost a pleasant diversion. He's comfortable with the elements, and from his career as a soccer player he knows how to control the ball in inclement weather, to keep it down in the wind, to improvise. The other kickers are cut, one by one, and finally Scott shows up and looks around the locker room one morning and he's the last kicker left.

Before you belittle the placekicker or make light of him as an athlete, ask yourself: Are you among the 28 best in the world at *anything*? Scott Norwood is in that exclusive club. In 1988, his fourth season with the Bills, he makes the Pro Bowl. In '89 he becomes the alltime leading scorer in Bills history, taking the record from O.J. Simpson. "I felt like I fit into that team," Norwood recalls. "That's one of the special things about sports, the camaraderie." His teammates treat him not as a kicker but as a fellow football player. "Everybody looks at kickers as being a little sissy," says quarterback Jim Kelly. "But Scott was one of us. He had that mean face, that linebacker face. I loved that guy."

The Bills are winning games, the division title and playoff games. Coach Marv Levy and general manager Bill Polian have assembled a remarkable group of football players, starting with Kelly, Thurman Thomas, Andre Reed, Bruce Smith and Cornelius Bennett and extending all the way to

Norwood. He meets Kim Burch, a salesgirl in domestics at a J.C. Penney in Buffalo. She sells him bedding. She smiles. She is slender, strawberry blonde and beautiful. They are married three years later.

And still, Scott comes home, every off-season, though now he's driving a black Ford Bronco that he gets from a dealer in Virginia in exchange for a few ads and personal appearances. Do you know how good that feels, to get something just because you are you? A pro football player, a Pro Bowler, and you make six figures a year? You're on a winning team? You've married a beautiful woman?

Of course you don't. Very few of us do. But it feels like this: You are in the flow of life, not trying to wrestle it down or beat it into submission or twist it and forge it and shape it, but you are instead riding along and each bend or turn reveals a pleasant surprise. And still, Scott keeps coming home, to kick with his dad. Some of the commuters returning from Washington along Annandale Avenue point to the kicker on the grass and the older man holding the ball and say, See that guy? He's the kicker for the Buffalo Bills. And Scott could never imagine a time when that recognition, the same recognition that wins you free automobiles, could make it hard for you to leave your own house.

AS THE ball goes wide right, the instant it is passing the upright, before the official has even signaled, Kim is in the stands thinking, Oh, this is going to be tough for Scott. She has come to Tampa to watch the game with Del, Sandra and Scott's aunt and uncle, and all of them at that instant think some version of that same thought. Kim winds her way down the stands and into the tunnel and then around the stadium to the players' entrance, this petite bobbed blonde in a white sweater, slacks and pumps, darting between cursing Bills fans and elated New York Giants fans, wending through dense clusters of elation and despair as palpable as parade floats. She desperately wants to be there for Scott, to hold him and tell him that it will be O.K., that it was just a kick, that it's just a game, all things he knows, but in the aftermath of the biggest miss in Super Bowl history it might be easy for him to lose perspective.

She waits near the players' entrance—the wives are not allowed into the locker room—and she waits and she waits.

In the Buffalo locker room there is a mixture of anger, disbelief and confusion. The emotional rush of that last drive, in which Kelly took the Bills down to the 30-yard line with eight seconds left, was such that even after Norwood's miss it's hard for the players to absorb what has happened. Some of the Bills are still milling around near the coach or standing near the entrance, as if this is some sort of second halftime and the team will soon be going on to play a third half. Levy tells his team that he has never been more proud of any group of men, and that he could not have asked for anything more from his team—well-intentioned banalities that can't begin to heal the hurt. Then he surveys his team and watches as Reed begins to pull off his jersey and Kelly wipes his face with a towel. Levy wants to talk to his kicker. He finds Norwood and walks over to sit down with him on the wooden bench in front of his locker, between him and wide receiver Steve Tasker.

"I didn't know what to say to him," says Levy. "I was searching for words to buck him up, but I knew how he felt. We engineered that drive to get him in field goal range. It was a 47-yard kick off natural grass. Fewer than 50% of those are made. He had been such a great kicker for us over the years, and he won a few games for us with his leg, but you don't think about things like that at a time like that."

As Levy is trying to console his kicker, linebacker Darryl Talley and cornerback Nate Odomes approach Norwood and explain that if they had made a crucial tackle in the third quarter on a third-and-13 pass play, then the Bills would have never been in the position where they needed to make that kick. Then Reed comes over and says that if he had hung on to a few key passes in the second quarter, then the Bills could have put the Giants away. Teammate after teammate visits with Norwood and reinforces the message that this was a team loss. Fellow special teams player Tasker, who watches all this from his locker next to Norwood's, recalls, "None of the players on that team blamed him. They knew you could take back any one play and the game might have been different."

Then the reporters are let into the locker room. They've rarely bothered to speak with Norwood. But today, of course, he is trapped in the incandescent TV lights and on the business end of three dozen microphones. His special teams coach, Bruce DeHaven, stands by him as he answers every single question from every single reporter. He will stay in the locker room a full hour after most of his teammates have gone. *How does it feel, Scott? Were you nervous? Did you feel like you hit it good? What are you going*

*to do now? What do your teammates think? How does it feel to miss that kick
and lose the Super Bowl?*

DeHaven asks him every few minutes, "Have you had enough? Do you
want me to get rid of these guys?" And Scott shakes his head and replies, "I
think I owe it to the fans to answer some questions."

Sports psychologists will tell you that openness is the first step to healing
from this sort of loss. They use words like *process* and *grieving* and *cleansing*,
but Scott just sees it as his duty. His father would simply call it showing up.

"The biggest thing about that kick," says Norwood, "was not how it im-
pacted me, but how it let the team down. But I had prepared as well as I
could. I had done the best I could. I could look at myself in the mirror."

IN THE 1998 film *Buffalo '66*, a placekicker named Scott Wood misses
the field goal that costs Buffalo the Super Bowl. Billy, the character played
by Vincent Gallo, loses a $10,000 bet on the game and comes to view the
kicker as the cause of all his frustrations and shortcomings. He goes looking for the kicker, intending to murder him. In the movie the kicker in retirement becomes the owner of Scott Wood's Solid Gold Sexotic Dancers—
a shirtless, sequined, bow-tie-wearing fat man who offers up naked women
as a palliative for Buffalo residents devastated by his missed field goal.

Norwood was offered what he calls a "large sum" of money to play himself in *Buffalo '66*. He turned it down and says he has never seen the movie.
"I think if he saw that film, he would be hurt by it," says Gallo, a Buffalo
native. "I love Scott Norwood, but I used the kicker character because Scott
became symbolic of all of Buffalo's problems." While there is no doubt that
Buffalo fans suffered with Norwood after his kick, Buffalo is one of the few
cities where Scott is remembered for the totality of his career and the great
character he showed both before and after that Super Bowl. When he returned to Buffalo after the game and appeared at a post-Super Bowl rally,
25,000 fans showed up and cheered for Norwood almost as loudly as they
did for Levy and Kelly, chanting, "We love Scott!" The fans understood,
perhaps subconsciously, that Norwood's failure could become either an al-
batross or an opportunity, just as their city's rust-belt decline had prompt-
ed them to find hidden depths of character and strength.

"Scott Norwood is one of my three or four favorite Buffalo Bills," says
Gallo, "because of what he went through." Buffalo has not won a major

sports championship since 1965, the third-longest such streak of futility for any city that has at least two major sports franchises. Only San Diego (1963) and Cleveland ('64) have suffered longer. As Buffalo would return to three more Super Bowls in the greatest run of NFL title-game appearances since the Browns of the '50s and then get blown out each time, Norwood's wide right would take on even greater significance. It became clear those few feet between the ball and the right upright were as close as those Bills would ever get to a Super Bowl championship.

"Look, a lot of things happened out there," says Scott. "A lot of other players didn't make plays, but that doesn't excuse me. I'm a player and I'm paid to perform, and I failed in that instance."

AFTER THE 1991 season the Bills sign a promising new kicker, Steve Christie of the Tampa Bay Buccaneers, and waive the 31-year-old Norwood. If he was not associated with that missed field goal, Scott believes, he would get a call from another team looking for a kicker. But the phone never rings. He no longer bothers to show up at the Washington-Lee High School field to practice his placekicks.

The first years out of football are the hardest. He refuses to discuss the Super Bowl with reporters, and when he returns to Fairfax County, he becomes almost a recluse, avoiding the media. "An experience like that has to be a blow to his ego," says Kim, "and then he's out of football and he has to find his place. It was very hard for him to talk about it." Scott retreats into his family, moving into a house with Kim in Clifton, Va., near his parents. He goes hunting with Del and Steve, the three of them heading out to Kmart before every deer season, buying ammunition and camping equipment, new boots and camouflage vests before setting out for Long Island, off the coast of Maine, where Del has hunted since he was a boy. They seldom shoot at anything, the three of them, instead taking long walks through the wilderness. Del doesn't really like the act of killing deer, but the ritual of pitching tents, setting up camp, making a fire and spending time with his boys in the woods keeps him coming back season after season. The laconic talk around the fire is reassuring to Scott, the crackle of burning wood and the chirping of crickets an aural reminder that life still has meaning and purpose and fine moments.

Scott seeks to put his business degree to work selling insurance, mortgages, annuities and trusts. It's hard work, especially the cold-calling, having to dial his way through a list of phone numbers every day and say, "Hi, I'm Scott Norwood, and I have a great opportunity today for you to take care of your family." It takes weeks and months of cajoling to get a prospective policy buyer or annuity purchaser to write that check. For the first time in his life, he finds that just showing up isn't enough.

Everywhere they go, to movie theaters, to doctor's offices, to restaurants, Scott knows what everyone is thinking: *He's the guy who missed.* "I would try to talk to him about other things," Steve says, "but you just knew it was on his mind."

"I saw him working through it," says Sandra. "He would come and tell me, 'This is real tough for me, but I'll get through it.' And we would all tell him, 'Scott, it's football. There are other things out there in life.' "

Scott wants children, suspects that he may find some distraction in the richness of family life, but there, too, he is disappointed as he and Kim struggle to conceive. "They had some problems having kids," explains Steve. "Who knows; maybe that was related to all that stress?"

There are moments when, after returning home from work, he confides to his wife that he doesn't understand why he has been put on this particular path. Why should this have happened to him? And Kim stops him right there and says, "Look, life is full of so many different moments—yes, that was awful what happened—but you were an All-Pro. If someone said, 'We'll take back that kick, but you also have to lose everything you accomplished in football,' would you do it? No way. So you take the good with the bad, only our bad is just really, really bad."

But the good is so very, very good. Twins, Carly and Connor, are born in 1995, and then Corey is born in '96. Still, this healing is a gradual process. The missed kick appears in his consciousness at odd times, and suddenly, in the middle of a phone conversation, *wide right* will replay itself, and every time it is a sickening moment. Then, over a few seasons—but he no longer calls them *seasons*; they're *years* now—thanks to the continued good health of his children and the love of his wife and family, he begins to understand that without that failure, that defeat, he might not have everything he now has. It is an obvious truth but one that comes to him with a most unlikely feeling: gratitude.

"I like the people we've become," he tells his wife at one point, not smugly, but in wonder. How can you measure the health and happiness of three beautiful children against a field goal? Three kids versus three points? "If everything always worked out for you, then you don't have that sense of appreciation," Norwood says. "You can always think you understand what it means to have things not work out, but until you live it, you don't really know."

Scott dusts off his Pro Bowl jersey and has it framed, along with a complete set of his football cards, over the big screen RCA in his wood-paneled den. There's a leather sofa and two chairs, and a desk with a computer where sometimes, in the evening, after he and Kim have gotten the kids bathed and into bed, he will sit and listen to the house settle and consider his future. Everyone seems to be buying, selling, moving. There's a real estate boom afoot, every baby boomer in America seems to be in escrow, making a bid, securing a second mortgage, adding on, remodeling, and he thinks maybe that's for him. He likes the implied optimism of offering people a stake, rather than the pessimism of selling insurance or annuities. Through a friend, a Bills fan, he hears about an opening and then, just like that, he leaves his career in financial planning in 2002 and joins Re/Max, the real estate brokerage.

Stolid and squinty-eyed, he makes an unlikely real estate agent. You arrive at an open house, you don't expect the kicker who missed in the Super Bowl. But years have passed, and now those who don't remember or who never knew outnumber those who do, and even for those who recall the missed kick, it is no longer a source of embarrassment or disappointment but rather a curiosity, like finding an old letter from a girl you once liked but thought you'd completely forgotten. In this housing market, though, in this era of low interest rates and buoyant real estate prices, there is room for even a taciturn, thoughtful broker in his little Chevy Prism. He's not a great financial success, but he has a feeling that things are about to turn around. A few more listings, another handful of referrals. Every day potential buyers are calling him, and he takes them out in the Prism and shows them properties, a few listings south of Clifton, a new development out in Chantilly. And when he talks about life, he nods and leans forward a little, because he is now looking ahead, not back.

Del stands by him, recognizing that his son is finally getting over the missed kick, but he never mentions it; that's not his way. He takes the grandchildren to Orioles and Redskins games, begins to teach and coach them the way he taught and coached his own children. And he can take pride in the man his son is today, a fellow who keeps showing up. It is a tribute to the closeness of the family that all three siblings, Sandra, Steve and Scott, settle within 20 miles of the Annandale home in which they grew up and where Del and his wife Anne still live. Del, at 74, drives himself to ball games, and on a humid July night arrives early at Camden Yards to watch the Orioles take batting practice. After the game, as he's cruising home on the beltway, heading south into the suburban incandescence of Fairfax County, his black Maxima rear-ends a tow truck, stopped in the fast lane without hazard or brake lights. Del dies on impact.

Scott gets the call from Steve the next morning. He gets dressed and heads to his mom's house in Annandale. "That's a lot harder than any missed kick," Scott says. "You realize what matters pretty quickly."

NORWOOD LINES up for the kick with just a few seconds left. The rest of the team is gathered on the sidelines, holding hands, panting, exhausted. The gray-haired coach kneels down, watching with squinted eyes. The kicker stands in place for a moment, at an angle to the ball, and then charges, putting cleated foot to the ball and sending it soaring over the defense.

The Boomerangs have managed to salvage a tie, and Carly Norwood, who takes many of her team's free kicks, runs off the field as dad, assistant coach Scott Norwood, scratches his chin and worries that he didn't evenly divide the playing time. It's hard keeping the nine-year-old soccer players shuttling on and off the field, and often he'll forget to remove a girl who has been in for a while. Parents can usually be counted on to complain if their daughters have been out for too long, but sometimes even they lose track. The scarlet-uniformed Boomerangs gather around for their "two-four-six-eight, who do we appreciate" chant, and then Scott and Kim and the rest of the parents join hands in a tunnel as the girls run through. Several other children join in and run through after the team, and there is some discussion among the players about whether the tunnel is actually more fun than the game.

A few yards away from the sidelines, Connor and Corey are playing in the shade of a crab tree, the purple blossoms taking flight from the boughs in the spring air and wafting across the field to where Scott and the rest of the parents are gathering cones and coolers. These are the games that represent, somehow, American sport at its best. Of course we are a million miles from the sleek arenas and enormo-domes of big-time professional sports, but this Southeastern Youth Soccer league game is part of a cultural continuum connected to those playoff games and Super Bowls, and no one knows both ends of that spectrum better than Scott Norwood. And he will tell you that these sweet afternoons coaching kids or playing pickup soccer are the soul of our athletic obsession, the part that all of us can and do share. And as Corey runs up to Scott and tells him that some kid named Hunter just hit him—"Then don't play with Hunter anymore," is Scott's answer—he thinks about what he had to endure just to get here, with all the rest of us, coaching our kids on a Saturday afternoon.

American sports, Scott will tell you, will break your heart. But they will also, in their most basic form, nurture your soul. He thinks about Del, and about showing up. That's how you really win in life. Not by kicking Super Bowl–winning field goals or covering yourself in glory, but by showing up. And as you look at this life, at Carly sipping from a juice box as Kim braids her hair and Connor and Cory climbing all over Scott as he walks in his steady gait toward the family's Plymouth Voyager, you think, *I know this guy. He's sort of like me.*

THE CHILDREN draw pictures. Crude, stick-figure football players in navy-blue-and-white jerseys and Crayola crimson helmets—the kids find it difficult to render the Bills' charging buffalo logo—in field goal formation. The holder kneeling down. The kicker following through. And in these revisionist drawings by Carly, Connor or Corey Norwood, the kick is never wide right. It is always straight down the middle. It is always good. They represent a portal into one possible alternate universe. A *Mr. Destiny* retake in which the goat becomes the hero, the failure a success.

The pictures are a jumping-off point for a thousand what-might-have-been conversations, thoughts and musings on how the life of the Norwoods could have been different if Scott had made that kick in Super Bowl XXV. Kim sits the kids down and says to them, "It's all right that your father missed that kick. Your dad went out there and did his best—and sometimes, even when you do your best, things don't work out. And you know what?" She looks at each of them.

Three expectant faces gaze back.

She smiles. "That can be O.K., too."

| | | | | |

Where Have You Gone, Joe Namath?

BY MARK KRIEGEL

From star quarterback and world-class bachelor to hard-drinking pitchman and devoted father, the life of Broadway Joe took unlikely turns that even he couldn't have predicted. An excerpt from a revealing biography.

HAT ABOUT JOE NAMATH?" ¶ HE REPEATS the words, announcing himself again and again, reciting the line as both declaration and question, as if he were hearing his name for the first time. He varies the cadence, the accent, the timbre. He says it slow and sly and with an extra dollop of that southern syrup. He tries different styles: first, an anchorman; next, a color commentator; then, with the enthusiastic baritone of a game show host. *What about Jo-o-o-o-e Namath?*

Now he eyes the sportswriter suspiciously. This rehearsal, preparation for a voice-over, will not be part of the story. The sportswriter will gladly agree to these terms. They always do. The sportswriter belongs to the generation that adores him most. Even as a president once listed him as an enemy of the republic, kids rushed to buy popcorn-makers and chocolate milk on his say-so. This sportswriter had been one of those kids. With each passing year, they love him more, but know him less.

The interview is to take place here, in a vacant locker room at the Orange Bowl. He had always been great in January in the Orange Bowl. In 1963, as a sophomore, with John F. Kennedy in attendance, he began by throwing a touchdown pass in a shutout of Oklahoma. In '65, he made his debut in living color, becoming MVP of the first prime-time bowl game. The night served as a pilot for a new kind of action series. He was cast as its leading man, Broadway Joe, a role that culminated in its greatest glory on Jan. 12, 1969, in Super Bowl III. They called him an antihero. But really, there's no such thing. Antiheroes morph into heroes. It's the American way.

Still, little in Namath's current appearance suggests such heroism. As standing can be painful, even on artificial knees of metal and plastic, he sits on a folding chair. The famous stoop in his shoulders seems more pronounced. He slouches, shirtless, a tuft of gray protruding from his chest. He is tan and thin. There is less of him than the sportswriter imagined. He doesn't look like Broadway Joe. Rather, he looks not unlike the sportswriter. He looks like somebody's father.

So what about Joe Namath?

At the height of his fame, he made—or rather, had made for him—a cult of his bachelorhood. Broadway Joe was a high priest of the lush life, his affections sought by a sugar-frosted society of starlets and stews, all of whom sought to worship at an altar adorned with llama-skin rugs.

But now, the star seems a bit unsure at the sound of his own name. He's still practicing his voice-over. For what, the sportswriter does not know, doesn't care. Namath is selling something. Of course he is. This is the Super Bowl, the game he made, that highest sabbath in the American religion, the annual consecration of corporate culture, an event that celebrates 30-second spots as sagas and bookmakers as theologians. The Super Bowl evokes a star-spangled yin and yang, all those equal but opposing forces that create a prime-time culture: Coke and Pepsi, Miller and Bud, McDonald's and Burger King, Disney and Fox, Bloods and Crips, AFC and NFC. Only two things you can do here at the Super Bowl: You're buying, or you're selling.

The sportswriter understands his end of the transaction. He's purchasing another piece of the Guarantee. Thirty years have passed since the New York Jets were 18-point underdogs to the Baltimore Colts. Namath was high on scotch when he promised a Jets victory. *I guarantee it.*

For a generation raised on canned laughter, the Guarantee qualifies as a kind of performance art. He was bigger news than the astronauts returning from the moon. At least that's how they make it sound today. In fact, the Guarantee didn't even make the New York City papers. Not until *after* the game. But, hey, what do you want from sportswriters? Now they come around like pilgrims. Each year they become more devout.

They all want to know about the Good Old Days. They must have been good, a time before clogged arteries and enlarged prostates, before secondhand smoke, before pills to keep you happy and hard.

Broadway Joe was the coolest kid in America, an object of affection for girls and gangsters, a source of bafflement for bookmakers everywhere. He made a debonair comedy of most likelihoods. He walked off with Jagger's girls. He spilled drinks on Sinatra. He grinned his way through it all. The Raiders broke his face, and he caught a flight to Vegas, came back the next week, and set a single-season passing record. Namath had a concussion when he hit Don Maynard in the AFL Championship Game. He was still drunk the day he threw three touchdown passes against the Patriots in '66.

But that's not the stuff for a family newspaper. It's better to play along with these writers and their need for nostalgia. "I get a special feeling when I'm here," he says, quite unconvincingly. His tone is glum, but it's the best he can do.

The sportswriter leaves feeling deceived. But this regret won't last long. He'll give his editor what he wants, what the readers want, what everybody wants: the Guarantee and the Good Old Days. It's Super Bowl week. It's all good, and it's all on the house.

But what about Joe Namath?

He was advertised as a man who told it like it was. In fact, Namath didn't tell much at all. He didn't surrender intimacies. Sure, he'd be happy to rehash the Guarantee, especially for a fee. But his emotional life—family life—was never part of the deal. He'd show the famous scars on his knees. He'd even let you touch that grapefruit-sized ball of mangled tissue on his hamstring. But he'd give not a glimpse of the internal scar tissue. He'd talk about concussions and broken bones. But never the broken heart, his original wound. Years later, at the beginning of a new millennium, this is as much as he would allow: "I can remember as a three- or four-year-old, to this day, hearing [my mother and father] downstairs, talking or arguing about something. I was upstairs and I came to the top of the steps and I was crying because it got me scared."

Perhaps the fear was in his bones, something from his own father's boyhood lodged in the marrow, the knowledge that separation is inevitable. Families fracture. You can get left behind. "His daddy left him when he was in the seventh grade," says Jack (Hoot Owl) Hicks, for many years a devoted friend of Namath's. "He told me that was the saddest day of his life."

He survived, just as he would survive fame and drink and orthopedic ruin. He became a husband and a father. The standard-bearer for booze and broads had become an apostle of family values, even as the first baby boomer president was hustling an intern down the hall from the Oval Office.

Salvation through fatherhood, that's what Joe Namath had come to believe in. That's *all* he believed in. Try explaining that to a sportswriter.

THERE WAS, it turned out, life after football. A decade after Super Bowl III, the edgier aspects of his image had all but worn away. He was softer, cornier, unobjectionable, ubiquitous. He was often seen in the vast wasteland of television: selling corn poppers and fryers, appearing as a guest star on such fare as *The Dean Martin Celebrity Roast* and *The Love Boat*. He also undertook intensive vocal training to forge a stage career, becoming a regular on the dinner-theater circuit.

It was his voice coach, Arthur Joseph, who made the introduction in 1983, in the waiting room outside his studio. The space was adorned with photographs of famous students, among them Joe Namath, who arrived for his lesson just as Deborah Lynne Mays was finishing hers. Joe called her the next day, and they started dating.

Arthur's wife, Rebecca, was upset. "She's just a child," she told her husband. "Why are you introducing her to Joe?"

Deborah was, in fact, 21; Namath was now 40. But the voice coach did not share his wife's misgivings. "I trusted Joe's values," he says. He trusted Deborah, too. She was just starting out, keen and full of ambition, a striking girl with brown hair and brown eyes. "One had a sense about Deborah," says Arthur. "She was a very determined person. She was intense. She wanted what she wanted in life. And she went after it."

Deborah had spent most of her childhood in Ligonier, Pa., where her father was a partner in a plant that manufactured toner for copy machines. Ligonier is horse country; the Mayses belonged to the Pony Club. Deborah, the middle child, showed great talent as an equestrienne, riding English style, foxhunting and eventing. In 1977 her father sold his interest in the toner plant, and the family moved to the Outer Banks of North Carolina. Deborah attended Northeastern High School in Elizabeth City, where she was known as Debbie.

If Shirley Mays had misgivings about her daughter's dating a world-famous ladies' man, she got over them soon enough. "I could not speak for Broadway Joe," says Shirley. "That playboy person, I did not know." But Joe Namath was a darling. And there was something else Shirley liked. "Joe's a lot like my son—his mannerisms and his laid-back attitude," she says. "My son was extremely handsome. He had dark hair. He kept a lot of stuff inside, just like Joe." Deborah was very close to her brother, Jeffrey. "She worshipped him," says Shirley. Jeffrey liked to fish and have a drink, too. He and Joe probably would've gotten along famously.

But on Nov. 13, 1980, not long after Deborah moved to L.A., Jeffrey set out with a friend from Cape Hatteras in a fishing boat. At 6:30 p.m., the men were reported missing. Although they had no radio or flares, the 23-foot *Sea Ox* was a sturdy craft, built to float like a Boston Whaler. "We've got some encouraging news in that the boat is supposedly unsinkable," said Lieut. Tom Blisard, a spokesman for the local Coast Guard station.

The Coast Guard sent out C-130 planes and H-3 helicopters, which were soon joined by Air Force, Marine Corps and Navy aircraft, including E-2 radar surveillance planes that scanned 220,000-square miles without any sign of the boat. But nothing was ever recovered, not a trace of the boat or the young men. The search was called off after seven days.

"You can't fill a void," says Shirley, who remains haunted by the idea that her son is still alive. "It's very difficult to live with the unknown. . . . Each of us is handling it in our own way, the best way we can."

By *we*, she means her family, each member of whom is defined by the missing son, the missing brother. "That is who we are. That is on our minds when we wake up at night. That creates the emotional fallout. . . . We were the all-American family. That blew us apart."

NAMATH'S COURTSHIP of Deborah was a quiet one, his intentions remaining unknown even to his oldest and closest friends. Joe had been in love before. But Deborah had something the others did not—good timing.

Even the astrologer she had begun to see after her brother's disappearance predicted that Deborah would be married in 1984. "He was looking for a wife. He was ready to settle down," says Hoot Owl.

For all but 16 guests, including best man Jimmy Walsh, Joe's old friend and longtime agent, the wedding remained a secret. It took place on Nov. 7. "I took my time to find the perfect girl," Namath said afterward. "I've always said I'm going to get married only once. This is my first and last wedding."

Arthur Joseph learned of the nuptials in the newspaper. The voice coach might have once considered Joe and Deborah like family, but the more the couple saw of each other, the less he saw of them. After a while, they stopped their voice training entirely. He never heard from Joe or Deborah as to why. "I found it so mean," says Joseph.

He wasn't alone in his misgivings. For some the first meeting with Deborah would be the last. Marv Fleming, a friend of Joe's since their USO trip to Vietnam in 1969, recalls meeting Deborah at the Namath football camp. Later he was walking across the practice field toward the locker room when Joe asked if he had called Deborah "Randi" (one of Joe's old girlfriends) by mistake.

"No," said Marv. "I did not. I'll apologize to her if she thinks I did."

No need, said Joe. "Just be cool."

Marv felt regret wash over him as they walked to the locker room. "I could see she was creating a problem, getting rid of everybody," he says, referring to Deborah. "I didn't want to be a problem. So I just faded away."

Joe's old friends Mort and Carol Fishman also met Deborah—Walsh had instructed them not to call her "Debbie"—at the football camp. Namath came off the practice field and was clearly happy to see them. Joe gave Carol a kiss on the cheek and a big hug, almost twirling her around. At Joe's insistence, they made plans for lunch and dinner that same day. Just then, Deborah approached. "You could see," says Mort, "she was boiling over."

She asked to have a word with Joe, and the two of them stepped away. When Joe returned a few minutes later, he told Mort and Carol, "Gotta take a pass on dinner tonight. Matter of fact, I won't be able to have lunch, either."

Mort went home thinking Joe would phone to apologize. He waited, but no call ever came. "Just like that," he says, "never talked to the guy again. I was brokenhearted."

Shirley Mays has heard some of this before, how her daughter drove off

Joe's friends, but protests, "She's getting a raw deal all the way around." Deborah, she explains, didn't like big drinkers, or hangers-on. Having married a man who was famous for not marrying, Deborah also became acutely aware of all the women who had been cast in bit parts and supporting roles in the Broadway Joe story. She couldn't turn on the television without wondering whom he had been with. Even strangers spoke to him with a degree of intimacy.

Old friends and old fans had staked their claim on Joe long before Deborah came into his life. She was only six when he won the Super Bowl, but now she was left to consider the question of his identity, to reconfigure borders between man and myth, public and private, between her husband and Broadway Joe.

"She got hurt from so many remarks," says Shirley. Her daughter wanted a new life, as did Joe. "But he didn't have the courage to do it," Shirley says. "He doesn't like to do distasteful things. He'd been a star so long. He would let someone else be the bad guy, and she became it."

THE COUPLE made their stage debut in a Wilmington, N.C., production of *Cactus Flower*, a romantic comedy about a philandering dentist, played by Joe. Deborah played his young girlfriend. "They were very affectionate, very lovey-dovey," recalls Chuck Kinlaw, one of the actors. "All Deborah talked about was how Joe was a god in New York."

He was big in Atlantic City, too, where the Claridge signed him for another musical, *Bells Are Ringing*. Originally, Namath and his bride were to appear together, but then Deborah decided against it. She was pregnant. The baby was due in October 1985.

With her career on hold, Deborah took charge of Joe's. It was plain to see from the way he watched all those games on TV that he missed football. He would question the coaches. He would disagree with the announcers. The blood rushed to his face as he provided his own spontaneous, unexpurgated color commentary.

Do it, she told him.

Soon thereafter, Jimmy Walsh spoke with Roone Arledge, in charge of news and sports at ABC. Although *Monday Night Football* was about to head into its 16th season, Arledge's infatuation with Namath had hardly diminished.

The network boss had his reasons. Howard Cosell had left after the 1983 season. Don Meredith, whose "Dandy Don" act now seemed less dandy than bored, departed the following year. With ratings down 22% over three seasons, commercial time had been discounted. ABC was now owned by Capital Cities, a bottom-line outfit, which meant that the very survival of *Monday Night Football* was in doubt.

In Namath, Arledge saw the telecast's salvation. The man who saved a league could surely save the show. Joe, who had never broadcast a game, might have been a risk. But so what? Risk was at the core of Broadway Joe. "It was worth the gamble," said Arledge.

Namath would provide color in a booth with Frank Gifford and O.J. Simpson. Walsh got him huge money, two years guaranteed at a reported $850,000 per. A press conference was held at 21, and the writers couldn't have been more impressed with Joe's wife. Who'd have thought? The girl had a good head on her shoulders. "I'm the one," said Deborah, then midway through her pregnancy. "I pushed him into going for this. Blame me."

ON AUG. 3, 1985, Namath went on the air wearing a yellow blazer with the logo of ABC SPORTS. He was broadcasting live from the annual exhibition contest in Canton, Ohio, where earlier that day he had been inducted into the Pro Football Hall of Fame. Larry Bruno, his high school coach, made the speech introducing him. Joe accepted the praise with great gratitude for everyone, especially God: "He was kind enough to Old Joe to let me find my wife, Deborah."

To hear "Old Joe" (as he now called himself) tell is, Deborah completed him.

The *Monday Night* booth now featured a Hall of Fame backfield—Gifford, Simpson and Namath—with unmatched endorsement power. Unfortunately, they didn't make much of a broadcast team. Gifford was ever the straight man. Simpson did his best work shilling for rental cars. As for Namath, the years had taught him something about humility. But humility was of little use to him now. In fact, it was a detriment.

The network didn't offer him a lot of tutelage, as Arledge didn't want his man sounding too polished. The ABC boss, an otherwise shrewd judge of talent, had convinced himself that a 42-year-old expectant father could again become the kid he used to be, as if it were still 1969. But instead of

Broadway Joe, Arledge got Old Joe, this curiously deferential character who insisted on addressing him (as he always addressed his employers) as "Mister."

Old Joe Namath was not the character people liked to remember. Perhaps his misgivings should have been apparent. "I have to convince myself I know what I'm doing," he said.

Deborah went out and got him books on how to speak. "She wanted him not to make mistakes," says Hoot Owl. Joe studied diligently, but Hoot Owl could never understand why Joe Namath of all people was worrying himself sick over his diction and his grammar. "The greatest announcer that ever was, was Dizzy Dean," Hoot Owl told him. Diz was just a hillbilly from Arkansas, who barely spoke a word of proper English.

But Joe didn't want to be Dizzy Dean, or even Dandy Don. For that matter, he didn't want to be Broadway Joe either. Speaking properly became a point of honor. There was a problem with this approach, however: It wasn't him. "If he'da have just been Joe Namath, they would've loved it," says Hoot Owl. Hoot Owl could notice the change every time his friend went on one of those TV shows: "Joe don't act like himself."

FROM THE *New York Post*, April 11, 1987: BROADWAY JOE AND FIJI DEBBIE: *Joe Namath isn't asking people he meets what their sign is, but he did go to the Fiji Islands last month because it was "in the stars." Broadway Joe and baby daughter Jessica were accompanying Joe's wife, Deborah Lynn [sic] Mays, who was making her annual "solar return." And what is a solar return? "Every year on your birthday, the planets line up in the exact same configuration as on your original birthday," Debbie said. But the lineup takes place in a different part of the world each year. And to derive maximum astrological benefit, you have to go to that place. "Astrology is kind of like religion," Deborah told PAGE SIX. . . . "I'm not a flaky kind of person. . . . Astrology doesn't monopolize my time. It's kind of like going to a therapist."*

Joe, for his part, didn't need a therapist or an astrologer to experience happiness or fulfillment; he had his girls, Deborah and Jessica Grace. The baby was born on Oct. 12, 1985, at Lenox Hill Hospital in New York. Joe was present for the birth, the miracle of blood blessed with light. "A love never felt before," said Namath. There was nothing Joe wouldn't do for his girls. He was theirs to have and to hold, to serve and protect, to die for, if necessary. Deborah and Jessica were his stars, the constellations by which he was guided, the basis for his system of belief.

Unfortunately for Joe, a happy home life didn't translate into professional success. ABC fired him after that disastrous first season, opting to pay the remaining year on his contract rather than put him back on the air. A month later, Fabergé officially dropped him as well, fearful that the scent of Brut would become associated with failure. In fact Namath hadn't done a Brut commercial since 1984, but sales had increased 16% without him. As an endorser, Old Joe just didn't have the requisite sex appeal.

Joe wasn't exactly out of business. There were television spots for *USA Today* and Olympic Airways, the national airline of Greece. Namath also did some guest-starring on episodes of *The A-Team* and *ALF*, a show about a furry alien living with an average American family. But he had no steady work, no real job, and spoke of his disappointment and boredom. He spent his days playing golf and fishing. And he drank. Later Deborah complained to an old acquaintance of his how Joe would come home, fill a large glass with vodka, and drink until he slept.

Deborah didn't drink. She hadn't liked it when her brother drank, and now she didn't like it in her husband. "You act foolish when you drink," says Shirley Mays. "It was disappointing to Deborah."

She finally gave him an ultimatum, which Joe preferred to regard as "a bet." Joe would never welsh on a bet, especially not with Deborah. Welshing on your wife would be a form of infidelity. "If I lost," he said, "I was going into rehab."

"She couldn't save my son," says Shirley. "But she certainly saved Joe. He stopped drinking because of her."

Abstinence from drink became another token of his devotion to the family. For more than a year, Namath wrote in a journal, each entry marking another sober day. The first entry was dated March 24, 1987, not long after the family returned from Fiji.

CAROL WEISMAN had never seen her husband so nervous, pacing the lobby in the Century Plaza as he waited for Joe Namath. Michael Weisman was regarded as among the brightest talents in sports television, having already produced the World Series and the Super Bowl. Now, at 37, he was the executive producer of NBC Sports and looking to hire one of his childhood idols. It was Namath who should have been nervous. "Joe was damaged goods at the time," says Weisman. "He had been so beaten up at ABC."

Still, Weisman was a wreck. It was Joe. *Joe.* And now Namath was coming to pick *him* up at the hotel. Namath had insisted on taking him and Carol to dinner. "I had these fantasies that he would arrive in a Maserati or something," says Weisman. "But he came in a four-seat family car, nothing flashy. It was above a Buick but less than a Mercedes."

Joe chose Mr. Chow's. They talked over dinner. Weisman explained that before Namath went back on air, he wanted him to work with someone, like a coach, but for broadcasting. Unlike *Monday Night Football*, where three announcers fought for airtime, this would be only a two-man booth. Namath wouldn't be on big national games, either. Weisman would start by assigning him to the Jets, who weren't very good but afforded Namath the luxury of playing to an audience that already loved him.

This was all to Namath's liking. For once, the matter of salary never came up, as Walsh had already assured Weisman: "Money won't be an issue." Joe, who couldn't have been nicer or more receptive, made it clear he just wanted another shot.

But Joe's cordiality is not what stands out in Weisman's recollection of the evening. Rather, it's Deborah, or as Carol called her once by mistake, "Debbie."

"My name is not Debbie," she said. "It's Deborah."

The severity in her tone caused conversation to come to a momentary halt. "It got our attention," says Weisman. "She was very serious." Weisman thought Joe might say something to break the tension; after all, it had been an honest mistake. But Joe remained silent.

Later that evening, Deborah mentioned that she met her husband at a class. "Oh," said Weisman, trying to make conversation, "you're going to be an actress."

"No," she said sternly. "I *am* an actress."

Then followed another awkward lull, which Joe again ignored until the small talk resumed. Before the evening was over, though, Weisman made it clear to Joe how much he had meant to him, growing up in Queens.

"Mike," said Joe, "you're telling me these stories, I'm getting goose bumps."

As he spent more time with Joe, Weisman discovered that there were a lot of guys who felt as he had. How many times had he seen it happen? A dozen? A hundred? And in how many cities? They felt a need to tell Namath where they were, who they were with, how they felt, what it meant, that they, too, had predicted it. They had been with him. They had been young. "You're giving me goose bumps," Joe would say.

At first, Weisman was taken aback by Namath's apparent insincerity, but with time he came to think differently. Joe could have told these people, "That's nice," or simply have said nothing at all. But goose bumps were an acknowledgment that the stranger's confession had been heard. Joe might as well have said, "Go in peace."

"It was an act of kindness," says Weisman. "It made people feel good."

NBC WAS a great gig for Joe. There was little pressure, and a lot of time to stay home with the family. That was the cure, of course, domestic tranquility. It wouldn't mend his joints, but it soothed wounds he suffered as a boy at the top of the stairs. All he had deferred—from his wages to his wedding—was for this: to be a father, to have a family, to keep it healthy and whole.

The Namaths decided to raise a family in Tequesta, Fla., a quiet, affluent town in northernmost Palm Beach County. The home was four bedrooms, 6,813 square feet, with a pool, on the banks of the Loxahatchee River. Orange and mango trees dotted the property, but Deborah decorated with rustic European touches. "With an English garden for me," she said. For Joe, the water was filled with flounder and snook. He fished off his dock, and off his boat. He bought a new 25-foot Boston Whaler, naming it *Team Game Too.*

On Dec. 11, 1990, Joe and Deborah had a second daughter, Olivia Rose. She looked like her daddy.

Joe taught his girls to handle live bait, shrimp from the bucket. Before she was nine, Jessica had caught a ladyfish just north of Jupiter Inlet. The ladyfish broke the water four times before Jessica got it to the side of the boat. Olivia was four when she caught her first snook. "Reel," said Joe. "Reel!" It was, recalled the proud father, "the prettiest snook we had ever seen." Joe threw it back.

What was love? What would you die for? What would save you?

"Just having those little arms wrapped around you," he once said.

Bathing. Wiping. Feeding. Reading the stories. Tucking them in. Waking them up. Later, hobbling into the kitchen before dawn to make their lunch. Driving them to school. Picking them up. There were tennis lessons and soccer practices and ballet recitals. He helped with their homework. Broadway Joe became Mr. Mom.

What could the kingdom of television bestow upon him now? What did he care if he had a hard time using the telestrator? Why would he ever need a drink? "He was with those kids every day, every morning, every night," says Hoot Owl. "The happiest thing in his life was his kids."

Those were happy years, through the mid-1990s. Everybody seemed to notice his glow when he was around the family. "So content," says Tom Werblin, the son of the late Jets owner, Sonny, who would visit the Namaths while vacationing with his own family in nearby Jupiter. In Deborah, he saw "a sweet girl, totally devoted to Joe." Olivia and Jessica clearly worshipped their father. "You could see it in their eyes," says Werblin. Meanwhile, Joe had become someone Sonny's son had never imagined: frolicking with the kids in the pool, bringing them by Jet Ski to a tiny island in the inlet, taking them to the movies.

What Deborah sought in Fiji, Joe found on his dock, harbor to his private paradise, where his own stars were harmoniously aligned.

IN DECEMBER 1991, Joe was assembling a swing set for the kids when his left knee gave out. The left was supposed to be his good knee, but it had been the one doing most of the buckling lately. Finally, the very notion of a good knee, however relative, had become as obsolete as the joints themselves. He fell by the swing set, in the backyard. He had never fallen before. For years, the doctors had been warning him that artificial knees were an inevitability. But only now, with his younger daughter a year old, did he opt for surgery. "I didn't want to take any chances when I was carrying Olivia," he said. "I had to have this done."

The rehabilitation lasted for months, during which time Namath learned to use a walker. But now as ever, his physical state had no bearing on his ability to move merchandise. He had reached a new level of ubiquitousness as the relentlessly cheery face behind Flexall 454, an analgesic balm, and the Wiz, a New York City–based consumer electronics chain. In 1992 Namath became the first corporate spokesman for NFL Properties Inc., the league's licensing arm. Jimmy Walsh, now with six kids of his own, was keeping busy. Later that year, Walsh cut a deal for Namath to endorse Ambervision sunglasses, guaranteeing a minimum of $1.25 million over the next decade. Like his contract with NFL Properties, it would provide a steady six-figure income into the next millennium—enough to help Namath take it in stride when NBC let him go the following year, after six seasons with the network. "Had I been a younger guy, I'd have been angry," he said. Finally, he knew better. At 50, he had learned who he was, and what he wanted.

Unfortunately, the same could not be said for his wife, who found that being Mrs. Joe Namath came with its own set of complications. "It's not easy being married to someone who's as big a legend as Joe," says Shirley Mays. "Not because he isn't nice and wonderful and everything else. But you kind of lose your identity."

Deborah was 21 when they met, 22 when they were married, and 23 when Jessica was born. Her own ambitions went into abeyance, melding with a legend that people regarded as public property. Still, she became far more than just Mrs. Joe Namath; she became his driving force. She wanted him to be well-spoken. She wanted him off the booze. And she got what she wanted, for hers was the approval he sought. "She had great influence over him," says Howard Felsher, a producer who offered the genial Namath a job as host of *Family Feud*. "Every time he made a comment, he looked to her for approbation." When the deal suddenly collapsed, Deborah couldn't have spent too long mourning. While the money might have been good, being the wife of a game show host was not what she had envisioned when she married Joe Namath. She had other aspirations.

"I was stunned when I first saw her," says Al Hassan, Joe's old friend. Without makeup and without that Nordic shimmer, she belied her husband's famously advertised preference for blondes. But she was gorgeous, and more than that, Hassan found her knowledgeable about art-house movies and theater, as she spoke Chekhov and O'Neill. "She wanted to be an actress," he says.

Actually, she wanted to be a serious actress, and that was a problem. For while her husband could be a game show host or a football announcer or a pitchman for the Wiz, her own role—played in a quiet town 90 miles from Miami—remained the same. She would always be cast as Mrs. Joe Namath. Or, as some people still insisted on calling her, "Debbie."

How she hated that name. On April 1, 1992, she changed it, legally, dropping "Deborah" in favor of "May." Still, "May" did not achieve the desired effect, as a name or an identity. So on July 8, 1993, she again petitioned the court, and became "May Tatiana Namath," or, as she preferred to be known, Tatiana.

Whatever her reasons, says Shirley Mays, "it's her God-given right." Tatiana's husband agreed, informing friends of her preference matter-of-factly, offering no explanation. Her name was her business; her happiness was his.

In January 1995, the Namaths bought a two-bedroom apartment in the Dakota, one of Manhattan's most exclusive addresses. Florida remained the family's primary residence, where Joe did his fishing and golfing and where the kids went to school. But Tatiana's acting lessons were in New York City, and she commuted there regularly.

In a city fueled by ambition, however, her aspirations remained unfulfilled. Among her teachers was E. Katherine Kerr, who found her to be a trying student. Tatiana—who asked that Kerr call her "Anna" for a while—did not lack talent. Rather, the problem was "this enormous tension she walked around with," says Kerr. "When it comes to acting you have to be open and vulnerable. She was shut down."

The notable exception came in an autobiographical monologue she prepared, "a beautifully written piece," as Kerr recalls. It was all there, a series of emotional dislocations: her brother's disappearance, her mother's denial and her parents' eventual divorce. It was clear that Tatiana had issues with her mother. Just as clear was her profound sense of loss, undiminished by the passage of time. She idolized her brother. And as Kerr got to know her better, she couldn't help but think that Joe had become something of a brother figure to Tatiana.

AT 152 West 71st Street, the Church of the Blessed Sacrament houses two tenants in its basement. One is a transitional residence for men who have tested HIV-positive and proven themselves clean and sober. The other, with a seating capacity of 100, is the ArcLight Theater, managed by Michael Griffiths, an actor who played safety for the University of Tulsa. In the spring of 1997, Tatiana paid him a visit and told him, at some length, of her plans to produce and star in a production of Chekhov's *The Seagull*.

The family came to New York City in preparation for the show, a run of four performances in late June. In addition to her duties as producer, Tatiana would play Nina, a young actress victimized by her own illusory ideals of romance and art. The role of Arkadina, also an actress, went to Kerr, who doubled as the director. Joe, at the request of both Tatiana and Katherine, played Dr. Dorn. Chekhov's character was 55, a year older than Namath. He was, like Joe, a handsome, worldly ladies' man now leading a contented, reflective life. For the role, Namath grew a beard, which came in white. Other than that, recalls Griffiths, "he looked like any other Upper West Side dad." He always seemed to be taking his daughters somewhere. "He was Mr. Mom. And he liked it. You could see he definitely liked it."

One day Joe poked his head into the men's shelter, asked if anybody needed anything.

"Yeah. A TV," came the response.

The next day Blessed Sacrament's transitional residence received a delivery from the Wiz, a 37-inch Sharp with a VCR.

Namath seemed determined to create an atmosphere of harmony on the set. His concern wasn't for Chekhov, but for Tatiana. "I felt he could give a s--- how the play was going as long as she was happy," says Griffiths.

But Tatiana's happiness, like Deborah's, was a complicated proposition. Where Kerr saw an actress who was tense and blocked, Griffiths saw a beautiful woman "searching for something. I think she wanted to have a real experience as an artist," he says. "She [also] had a will to be a celebrity on her own, not just Mrs. Joe Namath."

For Tatiana, the production was a supremely serious matter. She rehearsed. She argued with her director. She seemed preoccupied with her husband's performance. "Do you think he'll be all right?" she asked.

As it happened, Joe was just fine. He made a very good Dorn, and it was arguably the finest performance of his dramatic career. After all, at this point in his life, playing Dr. Dorn was less of a stretch than playing Broadway Joe. Still, that's who people came to see, the ex-quarterback; the theater was packed for the four performances. "Joe got the attention. Joe got the affirmation," says Kerr. "I almost think [Tatiana] was jealous. She wasn't expecting him to be that good; I don't think anybody was."

Kerr never saw Tatiana again. She called a couple of times but got no response. Perhaps there had been too many disagreements between the two. Or perhaps Kerr's closed-down student had finally opened up. One morning while they were in rehearsal for *The Seagull,* the two were having breakfast on Columbus Avenue when Tatiana announced that she had met someone.

JOE AND the girls went back home a couple of months after *The Seagull.* But Tatiana stayed behind in New York City, returning to Tequesta only briefly the following summer. Then she left for California. "The Wife," as she was called in Joe's eventual petition for divorce, "left Florida in September of 1998, and except for infrequent visits to Florida to visit the parties' children, she has remained in California. To the best of her Husband's knowledge, it is the Wife's intent to remain in California."

Namath didn't file divorce papers until March 19, 1999, and the action didn't become public knowledge until the April 13 issue of the *National Enquirer.* The tabloid paid for a tip that yielded a photograph of Tatiana with her love interest, the man about whom she had spoken with Kerr. He was Dr. Brian Novack, a Beverly Hills plastic surgeon who specialized in the enhancement of breasts and penises. "The tip came from someone who knew the plastic surgeon," says *Enquirer* reporter John South. "We caught them driving down the street. It was after that, that I spoke with them."

As South quoted Tatiana: "Joe loves being out on the golf course all day, or watching sports on TV, while I love museums, art galleries and the theater. Florida was too boring for me.

"After I moved to Los Angeles, I met Brian Novack. Now I'm in love with him. Brian is totally different from Joe. Joe's a jock and Brian's more of an artist than a surgeon. He wears his hair long for a doctor and he's very sensitive."

Tatiana described case #99-4051, now on the docket in Broward County, as "a friendly divorce."

After his account of Broadway Joe being "sacked" by a plastic surgeon, South noticed that women around the office—the *Enquirer* was based in Palm Beach County—seemed particularly saddened by the news. "They would see him dropping the girls off for soccer practice," says South. "Total family man. Quite the doting father."

Namath sought custody as "primary residential parent." Tatiana never contested the divorce.

The legal papers cited a Latin term: *a vinculo matrimonii.* Namath had been released from the bonds of marriage. The dissolution left him in a position much like his mother had once been in. A vinculo matrimonii. The worst was yet to come.

Joe was awarded custody of the two girls and the house in Florida. He had been the primary parent since Tatiana left in 1998. But by 2000, his daughters, now 14 and 9, came to him with a request. They wanted to join their mother in Beverly Hills. Here was irony in its cruelest form. He loved the girls more than anything, but after all that had happened, did he love them enough to let them go?

Namath would call his daughters' departure "the most devastating thing I've ever gone through." The pain could not be considered in relation to mere football injuries. It was beyond calibration, beyond metaphor, almost beyond words. "I can't compare family to athletics," he said. "There's a lot more . . . boy, I don't know . . . love."

Love. He let the girls go because he loved them. That was about as much love as he could survive.

Now he couldn't sleep. He'd wake in the middle of the night unable to breathe. "First thing in the morning, it's on your mind," he said. "You're consumed." Then came the pressure on his sternum. Once, the chest pains lasted for two straight days.

Not long after the kids left, Joe received a visitor. His old friend Sal Marchiano, the New York City sportscaster, had been in Florida, palling around with some of the old crew; he pulled up in a rental car. Though Sal can't remember the time, it felt late. Sundial shadows cut across the Loxahatchee River and all through the house in Tequesta. The new millennium had just begun, and here they were: a couple of guys in their 50s comparing notes on daughters and divorce. Sal had been through his some years earlier, and survived it. "One day," he told Joe, "you'll be sitting with your daughters in Paris, laughing about all this."

That was not a day Joe could envision. His devastation was plain to see. They were sitting in the kitchen with a counter between them. Sal was struck by how neat everything was, meticulously clean, unnaturally quiet.

"Do you want a drink?" asked Joe.

"Ice water."

Joe served Sal, and then pulled out a bottle of vodka, pouring one over ice for himself. Everybody reaches for something, thought Sal. He'd been there.

"I know it's not good for me," said Joe, shrugging with the peculiar insouciance of a condemned man.

"Well, since you brought it up," said Sal, "you better be careful."

Careful? What did they think of careful when they were young? They remembered a lot of late nights, some of them funny, some risky and not as funny. "Every time I fly into New York and see the skyline, I think about how lucky we are to be alive," said Joe.

He didn't look so lucky, drinking in the shadows. Joe couldn't understand how it had happened, his daughters leaving.

"You know what the answer is," said Sal. "You got to go there, live near them."

"I hate Beverly Hills," said Joe. "That's why I got out of there. I don't want them growing up there."

They talked some more, then Joe walked him to his car. "If you ever need anything, call me," said Sal. "You can't be sitting alone in this house. Don't do this to yourself."

Joe nodded.

"C'mon," Sal said, finally. *You're Broadway Joe.*

Namath smirked, signaling contempt for his own mythic self.

"Joe!" said Sal, trying to get his attention. "Everybody loves you, Joe."

Sal got in his rental and started to drive. He was approaching the Intracoastal Waterway when he thought to look back. Who'd have thought it would be like this, Joe Namath alone, drinking in the shadows. So there were no guarantees, after all.

"DEPRESSION," NAMATH would say, "has a way of sneaking up on you." Eventually, a doctor would prescribe an antidepressant. In the meantime, Joe did what he knew how to do. He had been medicating himself for most of his adult life.

On Aug. 23, 2000, the Miami Dolphins hosted a tribute to Dan Marino at Pro Player Stadium, where Namath was scheduled to speak. But just minutes before he was to go on, 52,000 fans were told that he had run into "transportation problems." In fact, according to the Fort Lauderdale *Sun-Sentinel*, Namath "was so disoriented he could barely stand up or talk."

A man named Kevin Barry saw him in the VIP room before the festivities. Barry had wanted to tell him that he had been a Jets ball boy at Peekskill Military Academy, but Joe didn't look to be in a conversational mood. He sat near a corner of the room, a good-looking middle-aged blonde behind him. Joe was slumped in his chair, head down, a glass in his hand.

Sadly, such Namath sightings became commonplace. Tank Passuello, who counted Joe as a regular when he ran a bar near the Jets' training camp, saw him at a banquet. "He was a little woozy, to say the least," says Passuello. "He came up and started babbling, but nobody gave a s--- because they all loved him."

Everybody still loved him. Everybody wanted to help. But he was deaf to the best of wishes. He had become like a fugitive to some of his oldest friends, always changing his phone number. Finally, Al Hassan called Walsh's office in Manhattan, and asked Jimmy's secretary for the new number, which she gave him. Al left three messages, none of them returned.

"I can take a hint," he says, trying to hide his hurt. "But the next time I see Joe, it will be like it never happened."

After 15 years, Mort Fishman had heard enough to stop waiting for an apology. "How could I hold a grudge?" asks Mort. "Joe has a good heart. He was probably just embarrassed." With two recently replaced hips, Mort drove to the camp, and Joe greeted him with a big hug. They talked golf and even made a tee time. But when Mort came to pick him up the next day, he discovered that Joe and his daughters had left town earlier that morning.

"I remember thinking: What would he do now?" says Mort. "I mean, a guy his age."

ON NOV. 9, 2000, a crew from ESPN Classic showed up in Tequesta to interview Namath for the network's series on the outstanding sports figures of the 20th century. One subject Namath would not talk about was the divorce. "He made it clear that he didn't want to get into that," says Craig Mortali, the producer.

Mortali had been apprised of Joe's drinking and depression, but saw signs of neither. Still, Mortali found himself slightly disappointed to discover that the house in Tequesta contained no evidence of the cool life. There wasn't even a pool table. Rather, the playroom had dolls and a kitchen set. "It was still very much a home for children," he says.

At the producer's request, Namath thumbed through a box of old photographs. He stopped cold on an image of the whole family—himself, Tatiana and the kids. He made a face and mumbled something; then, gathering himself, he moved on.

The shoot went smoothly, pausing only to change film and, once, when the phone rang. It was Olivia on the answering machine. "Daddy," she was heard to say, "I was just thinking about you."

As requested, Mortali didn't ask about the divorce. Instead, he tried another approach, asking Joe to tell him about his daughters.

"What else would you give your life up for?" asked Namath. On most subjects he already had his lines down pat: Old Joe was in the third quarter of his life and planned on living to be a hundred. He got goose bumps just thinking about the Super Bowl. It was his version of a soft-shoe act, the latest rendition of Broadway Joe. But this answer about his daughters cut through all that; he had chosen to frame it as a matter of life and death.

"You don't flinch, right?" he said, his eyes suddenly glassy and his voice thick, as if something had lodged in his throat. "You'd sacrifice your life for your children."

The interview concluded shortly thereafter. The crew packed up and left, but Mortali lagged behind. There was something he was still curious about, a rooting interest he wanted to satisfy. His rented Taurus was still in park when Joe's next visitor arrived.

He could make out the silhouette: beautiful, blonde, very leggy.

"Good boy, Joe," he said, addressing the rearview mirror. "You still got it."

ALMOST A year later, Namath received the Arthritis Foundation's Freedom of Movement Award. Joe was no stranger to charity work, having given freely of his time and his likeness to the March of Dimes. But arthritis was more than a charitable mission. Namath landed a deal with Boehringer Ingelheim pharmaceuticals and Abbott Laboratories to promote an osteoarthritis medication, Mobic. His appearances were well-attended by senior citizens as he traveled the country, urging his fellow Americans to join him in the "Arthritis Huddle." The erstwhile poster-boy of booze and broads now advocated a "winning game plan" that included proper diet, exercise and consulting with your doctor. This was one celebrity spokesman who knew whereof he spoke. Artificial knees were the least of his problems; osteoarthritis had wedged into joints traumatized by years in the game—his spine and his thumbs. He could no longer make a fist. He was often irritable. "It was never—never—out of your mind." Chronic pain, Namath warned, "can damage some relationships, not only with friends but even with family. When you're always grumpy or when you're always tied up with pain, it's a tough deal on everyone around you."

To hear him speak of the disease's emotional toll was to wonder how much his arthritic aches had contributed to the breakup of the marriage. On the other hand, if he had to suffer, he might as well get paid for it.

NAMATH'S 40TH high school reunion was held on Saturday, Aug. 11, 2001, at the Beaver Falls (Pa.) Holiday Inn out on Route 18. Rumor had it that Joe would finally attend. He had been in Pittsburgh the day before, promoting his arthritis medicine. "There were probably 20 people who stayed late at the bar," recalls Cathie Smith, the hotel's lounge supervisor. "They were all waiting for Joe Namath. They all kept saying he was going to show. And then he didn't."

Namath might have had a good time. Despite the divorce, he could have counted himself lucky to still be a prince in a room full of bad toupees and missing fingers (the telltale sign of a life spent in the mill). But reunions were curious propositions for him, as he was the one through whom everybody summoned dormant memories. He had to be *on*. He had to be Broadway Joe. The act was more difficult to pull off with old friends than strangers.

The good old days and the good old guys had little hold on him. A couple of years after Namath's divorce, Ray Abruzzese became ill with Parkinson's disease. He suffered tremors and anxiety attacks. Word got around, and friends called with best wishes. But not Joe.

"I'm shocked," says Bobby Van, Joe's partner in the Bachelors III night clubs. "They were comrades."

Tim Secor knew how it felt. Some years before, he had been hit by a truck, an accident that left him a paraplegic. Some guys visited in the hospital. Others called. Again, not Joe. Tim never once heard from Joe.

Namath's friendships didn't have second acts. Whatever his old pals meant to him, they had one thing in common: They weren't blood.

Everything came down to blood, even the money. But hadn't Joe always known that? Going back to the first big deal, Sonny Werblin's concern was publicity, while Joe's was providing for his family. The Super Bowl, and the myths it spawned, made him a good living. But his life—what made Joe Namath weep and tingle—was the two girls.

The money helped, but it didn't cure anything. Joe still had to negotiate his own kind of truce with the bottle. He had to learn how to be a divorced dad. "Some pain never goes completely away," he said. "But you learn to deal with it."

After the girls left, he began flying out to the coast "every couple of weeks or so." Then, in January 2002, he bought a condo in Brentwood and began spending more and more time in Los Angeles with his daughters.

He was a better man when they were around. He even went back to school that fall, taking tutorials to finally earn his degree at Alabama. Namath hadn't forgotten the promise he made to his mother, but even more compelling was a remark he had made to Jessica. She said she would be the first college graduate in the family.

"You want to bet?" said Joe.

IT WAS right around that time when Tad Dowd ran into them in Century City, Calif. It was a Friday, early evening. Tad had stopped at Johnny Rockets, a hamburger joint in the mall. He was ready to sit down and study the *The Racing Form* when he spotted Joe in a baseball cap. Joe introduced him to his daughter as "Mr. Dowd." The two men had seen each other perhaps a half dozen times over the last two decades. Still, they talked for the better part of an hour before Joe said goodbye. "Make sure to call the office and leave your number," he told him.

He was taking Jessica to a movie, a big picture with a handsome young star his daughter liked. Going back all those years, Tad had never seen any woman have this effect on Joe. "There was a lightness to him," he says. "A glow."

Tad made a point to watch them as they walked toward the multiplex, father and daughter, blood and light, dissolving into the crowd at the mall. Then he spread out his *Racing Form*, ready to ponder the odds.

IN ANOTHER year's time, Namath's daughters would return to live with him in Tequesta. But by then he couldn't seem to stay sober for long. Old friends would hear things through the grapevine. He drank too much wine at Michael's in Santa Monica. He was pounding vodka tonics at Clarke's in

Manhattan. Early one morning at Reagan National Airport in Washington, D.C., he was seen wearing a baseball cap and sunglasses, nursing a beer at the bar.

An appearance for College Sports Network—a new venture from the creators of *Classic Sports*—was cut short after too many vodka tonics. Producers of a promotional interview featuring Namath complained that their footage was useless, as he wasn't making much sense. "He was definitely pretty soused," says Christian Red, a New York *Daily News* sportswriter who attended the event. During the taping, a bloodshot Namath even asked Red's girlfriend to fetch him a drink. "More vodka than tonic," he said.

Twelve days later, on Dec. 20, 2003, Namath attended a game as a member of the Jets' Four Decades Team. It was a night game, and he had been drinking steadily since that afternoon. Before the first half ended, ESPN sideline reporter Suzy Kolber asked him for a few words about the struggling Jets. "I want to kiss you," slurred Namath. "I couldn't care less about the team struggling."

Within a month Namath was an outpatient at Hanley-Hazelden, a West Palm Beach rehabilitation facility specializing in the treatment of older adults. "I've embarrassed my family," he told Jeremy Schaap, his first biographer's son, now a reporter for ESPN. "Every time in my life that something has gone askew, alcohol has been involved. . . . I'm convinced that I need help."

Namath's request for a smooch quickly became fodder for late-night monologues and drive-time rants. Just as inevitable were references to the sideline incident as a "wake-up call." Perhaps it was a curious bit of good fortune for Sonny Werblin's creation to be seen drunk on national television. Maybe that was the only place for him to hit rock bottom, there in the vast wasteland.

SO WHAT about Joe Namath? What becomes of him?

The clues, the signs of his ever-potent magic, are there on the morning of June 25, 2003, some six months before the incident on ESPN. The Jets are hosting a press conference at the Renaissance Hotel in Times Square. Its ostensible purpose is to announce that Joe Namath has been named the team's "ambassador-at-large." As such, he would shill for a new stadium in Manhattan. "Four decades of Jets football, absolutely wonderful," says Namath. "I get goose bumps thinking about it."

He speaks from a lectern. Behind him, beyond the wraparound window: Broadway. "I was standing right outside, there," he says, referring to the famous nighttime shot on the cover of SPORTS ILLUSTRATED. From there to here, night to day, then to now, Broadway is transformed. It is not unlike the Super Bowl: well-lit, huge, homogeneous, a corporate theme park. The Olive Garden chain of restaurants, one of them situated directly below Namath, now provides the universally accepted standard for Italian cuisine. Broadway's small-time hustlers have been replaced with big-time ones: Morgan Stanley, McDonald's, Budweiser and, of course, Disney.

The sportswriters remain obediently enthralled for the better part of two hours. Some of them were there way back when; others were just kids. But Joe appears to have aged better than them all: tanned, energized, healthy. He's wearing a green tie with a gray double-breasted suit. His teeth are as white as his shirt.

"We're gonna bring them a stadium somehow," he says. Now, at the age of 60, he is finally leading a pep rally. So what if he's hustling? It's *his* hustle, in furtherance of a higher purpose. It has become part of his patrimony.

"The Jets are a family," he says.

He knows better. Family is blood, the ones you would die for. His daughters are in the audience. Olivia is 12. She has big, bright eyes, and braces on her teeth. Jessica is slim, 17. Joe doesn't always approve of her taste in music—the lyrics these days. "I can hear that kind of stuff in the locker room," says Joe. The sportswriters laugh.

"Daddy," says Jessica. "Daddy." She is attentive, practiced at reading her father's body language. She hands him a soft drink. He's been talking for so long. He's still twinkling, though. Joe Namath is happy. He now spends more days with his daughters than away from them. Soon, they will come back to Florida for good.

It has rained steadily for almost a month. But today sunlight washes over everything. One imagines the father and his daughters strolling down Broadway, the distant fabled land now cleansed of all shadow, every trace of nocturnal life.

| | | | | |

Almost Perfect

BY JOHN ED BRADLEY

Arkansas lineman Brandon Burlsworth dedicated himself to doing everything flawlessly. When something finally went wrong, it cost him a bright NFL future—and his life.

E NEVER LOAFED. HE NEVER CURSED. HE NEVER complained. Everything was "Yes sir" and "No sir." He was a man of routine who resisted change as if it were an affliction without a cure, who believed you stuck with what got you there. "How bad do you want it?" Brandon Burlsworth asked his Arkansas teammates every time the offense came within 20 yards of the end zone. "O.K., guys," and now his voice got as loud as he ever let it, *"how bad do you want it?"*

He knew, as they say, only one speed. If at practice a coach made the mistake of lining up against Burlsworth to demonstrate something, the coach got punished. "First you felt his forearm, then the back of your head hitting the ground," says Tommy Tice, his coach at Harrison (Ark.) High.

Four years after he walked on at Arkansas in the fall of 1994, Burlsworth was one of the most dominant interior linemen in the country, a *Football News* All-America at guard, "the best to play the offensive line in Arkansas history," says Mike Bender, a former lineman who played on the Razorbacks' 1964 national championship team and, as an assistant in Fayetteville, coached Burlsworth from '95 to '97. "There has never been one like Brandon Burlsworth, and there never will be again."

"If God ever made the perfect person, it was that guy," says Razorbacks defensive lineman Sacha Lancaster. Which is why Burlsworth's death on April 28, only 11 days after the Indianapolis Colts took him in the third round of the NFL draft, left people in Arkansas in shock and asking questions that will remain unanswered. Burlsworth allowed so little room for error that the car crash that claimed his life seems inconceivable. He was driving east from Fayetteville to Harrison when he drifted over the center line, clipped the fender of an oncoming semitruck and then swerved into the path of another tractor-trailer rig, which hit his car head-on and threw it back 168 feet. Burlsworth, 22, died on a piece of road he'd traveled a thousand times. He was 15 miles from home, where he had planned to go to church and have a quiet dinner with his mother.

"Brandon just didn't make mistakes," says Don Decker, the Arkansas strength and conditioning coach, "and this is why the accident is so hard to accept. When I heard the news, I thought, Well, it had to be someone else's fault, because Brandon was definitely driving 55, and he had his seat belt on."

Burlsworth seemed destined for big things in the NFL. The Colts wanted him to start immediately. Team president Bill Polian says, "Brandon promised to be one of those players we point to and say, 'This is how it's done.' " At the NFL scouting combine in February he ran 40 yards in 4.88 seconds, best among offensive linemen, and bench-pressed 225 pounds 28 times. He weighed in at 308 pounds and measured just shy of 6' 4", yet he could stuff a basketball with two hands from a standing start. As awesome as he was physically, however, it was in private interviews that NFL scouts and coaches really fell for him. Polite almost to a fault, Burlsworth seemed too good to be true. Some called him a throwback, but he was better than that. He was the future. "He always did everything exactly right," says Arkansas coach Houston Nutt, "and I've never known anyone to work as hard. At the end of last season he said, 'Coach, I want to thank you for the best year of my life in football.' I said, 'Brandon, you made it happen.' He said, 'No, it was my teammates and coaches. Y'all made it.' "

When Burlsworth began his senior year at Harrison High, in 1993, he stood only six feet tall and weighed 200 pounds. A couple of small colleges showed interest in him, but he was one of those homegrown kids whose loyalty to the university in Fayetteville forbade him to pursue any fate but one in Razorback red.

Louis Campbell, then an assistant at Arkansas, made the hour-and-a-half drive to Harrison only because Tice kept hounding the Razorbacks coaches about his "big rascal," as Tice liked to call Burlsworth. Campbell met the player in Tice's office, and Burlsworth, as was his way, had little to say beyond the usual courtesies. "We sat there for about 30 minutes looking at each other and not saying a whole lot," says Campbell, now Arkansas's director of football operations. "I was thinking, 'If you want to come, come. But there ain't no way you're ever going to play.' What I couldn't see was what was brewing inside of Brandon. A lot of kids, about 35 a year, walk on here, but most quit in the first year. Some make it to the second. How many stay four years and start? I can think of only two or three in the last 10 years."

By the spring of '94 Burlsworth had put on 30 pounds and grown nearly three inches. He made a return visit to Fayetteville, and coaches were impressed by his growth but told him he needed to gain still more weight if he expected to play major college football. By summer's end he weighed 311 pounds. "You had to be careful what you told Brandon," says Tice. "You'd better be real specific and tell him just how much you wanted him to gain. Brandon believed that whatever his coach told him was right, whatever his mother told him was right and whatever his preacher told him was right. At Arkansas the coaches told him one day that his legs could be stronger. Well, he ends up squatting 700 pounds."

Burlsworth was so focused on becoming a better player that he seemed willing to make any sacrifice, and his behavior bordered on the obsessive-compulsive. Until late in his senior year at Arkansas he didn't date, fearing that a romantic relationship would interfere with football. He refused to move into an off-campus apartment because he liked his dorm's proximity to the stadium and to his classes. Besides, he figured, the dorm had been fine for him when he was an unknown, so why should that change now that he was the most recognized athlete on campus?

During his five years in Fayetteville, Burlsworth always parked his car, a '93 Subaru, in the same spot in a parking lot by the stadium. In his room his bed was always made except for when he slept in it. He so liked things in their place that friends say you could drive him half crazy by moving a pencil an inch on his desk. Every night he copied his notes from the day's classes, practicing perfect penmanship, whiting out mistakes and writing over them. He maintained a 3.4 grade point average and earned a bachelor's degree in marketing management and a master's in business administration in his years at Arkansas.

His haircut was never any length but short. Unlike others of his generation, he didn't abide tattoos, body piercing or facial hair. His clothes were always clean and neatly pressed. A style of glasses last popular in 1958 suited him best; people said they made him look like Drew Carey. Walking to class or the cafeteria, he never strayed from the sidewalk, never cut across the grass even when he was running late. "If you told the team to keep things neat around the locker room," says Nutt, "you'd catch Brandon picking up gum wrappers and Coke cans all over the building."

Burlsworth carried his single-mindedness even further. Once he stepped on the practice field, he refused to remove his helmet, even during breaks. He kept his chin strap buttoned, too, and when his comrades on the offensive line, goofing on him, reached over and unsnapped it, he immediately resnapped it. For five years he sat in the same chair during team meetings. Once, when Burlsworth was a junior, an underclassman sat in his chair. Burlsworth quietly stood behind him, saying nothing. "That one belongs to Burls," teammates told the player. The boy grew so uncomfortable that he hopped to his feet and found someplace else to sit.

"When the coaches reported to work at six in the morning, Brandon would already be there," says Nutt. "One night during Alabama week we're leaving a meeting at 10:30, 11 o'clock, and you can hear shuffling, feet against the turf. We go down to the indoor practice field, and it's Brandon. 'Brandon, what are you doing, son?' 'Coach, we didn't have too good a practice today. I just wanted to make sure I had my steps right.' This wasn't Eddie Haskell, either. He was almost embarrassed. He didn't want us to know he was down there."

It was a rare day that Burlsworth didn't lead his group in conditioning drills at the end of practice. If the team was running wind sprints, he routinely finished first, even when he wasn't feeling well. One afternoon Burlsworth, suffering from diarrhea and dehydration, refused to sit out a mandatory 440-yard run. "The strength coach said to me, 'I don't think Brandon can do it,'" recalls Bender, the former line coach. "Well, tell Burls that. He got sick on the run and messed all over himself, but he still beat everybody by 20 or 30 yards. He wouldn't quit for anything."

Every chance he got, Burlsworth went home to Harrison, a town of about 10,000 in the Ozarks, near the Missouri state line. He slept either in his little room at his mother's house or at his brother Marty's, to be close to his three nephews. Even after away games, when the Razorbacks returned to Fayetteville late at night, Burlsworth packed a bag and drove home. "He wanted to be with Mama and go to church in the morning," says Marty, who owns a photography business and was 16 years older than Brandon. "He'd play a game on Saturday in South Carolina, say, then on Sunday he's at my son's flag football game. Half the time there were so many fans around him that he couldn't watch the game."

Brandon and Marty's parents divorced when Brandon was two years old, in large part because Leo Burlsworth, a musician who traveled a lot with a country band, had a serious drinking problem. When Brandon was 10, his father, having undergone successful rehab, came back into his life. Abandoning his music career, Leo found work at a die-cast plant in Green Forest, 20 miles away, and he got together with his three children—Marty, Brandon and middle son Grady—for holidays and special occasions. Years later he made trips to Fayetteville to attend some of Brandon's games, but he seemed embarrassed to let people know that he was the father of a star player. "Dad had a button that said MY SON IS NUMBER 77, and he had a shirt we gave him one Father's Day that said BURLSWORTH 77 ARKANSAS RAZORBACKS," says Marty, "but most of the time he wouldn't wear either of them. He'd say he wanted to hear what the people around him were saying."

After Leo was out of the picture, Barbara made ends meet by running a day-care center. (She now sells real estate.) She and Leo bought Brandon his Subaru when he went off to Fayetteville, and Barbara and Brandon developed a routine every time he headed back to school. She would walk out on the porch and watch him as he backed into the street. "Watch for old big trucks and pray," she'd say. (When Brandon was a little boy, "old big trucks" were what he called 18-wheelers.)

"Mom, I love you," he always said quietly, then drove away.

"He was the biggest family guy I've ever met," says Razorbacks fullback Nathan Norman, Burlsworth's former suitemate in Bud Walton Hall. "Most guys go a long time without talking to their families, but Brandon would call every day, sometimes several times a day, just to check in."

During spring practice two years ago, Burlsworth appeared in the doorway of Bender's office. "Coach, my dad's real sick," Burlsworth said. "It looks like he's going to die before spring training's over. What should I do, Coach?"

"You need to go home, son," Bender answered. "You need to spend as much time with your daddy as you possibly can."

"But Coach," Burlsworth said, "he wouldn't want me to miss any practice."

"Brandon, that's just something you're going to have to do."

A couple of weeks later Burlsworth reappeared in Bender's office. "Coach, my father died today, but if it's all right with you, I want to go ahead and practice."

"Brandon, you need to go home."

"Coach, my dad would want me to practice today. And it would help me get my mind off things a little."

Bender wasn't sure what to tell him. Many kids look for any excuse to skip practice. "O.K., Brandon," he said at last. "If you want to practice, then you go ahead. But as soon as it's over, I'm going to walk you out to your car, and you're going home to be with your mama."

After practice the team huddled around Burlsworth and offered up a prayer for Leo. "It wasn't that Brandon wasn't caring," says Marty. "He was just doing what Dad wanted him to do. In the months before, just to get us off the subject of his dying, Dad would say, 'O.K., let's take care of football now.' He knew he wouldn't see the next season, and I think he felt he was letting Brandon down."

Although Brandon loved his father, he rarely talked about Leo to his coaches or teammates. Perhaps out of respect for Barbara, he didn't write Leo's name in the questionnaire the sports information department gave him to fill out each year. He left the space beside "Father" blank. After the question, "Where you would most like to spend a day?" Burlsworth once wrote, "Harrison, because it's a nice town."

"You fixin' to take care of your mama?" Mike Markuson, the Razorbacks offensive line coach, asked Burlsworth shortly after the NFL draft.

"Yes sir," Burlsworth answered.

His plan was to lease a town house in Indianapolis large enough to accommodate Barbara, Marty and Marty's family during the season. Once that was taken care of, Brandon wanted to buy a house for Barbara and later perhaps one for himself, both in Harrison. He didn't need a fancy neighborhood or a mansion, he told Marty, because no place was better than where he came from.

Though courted by any number of agents, Brandon chose Marty to represent him. At the time of the accident, Marty and the Colts were a week from beginning contract negotiations. Marty says Brandon most likely would have received a three-year deal worth about $1.2 million, including a $450,000 signing bonus. The NFL's collective bargaining agreement provides $100,000 in life insurance to each signed rookie, but Brandon had yet to reach an agreement with Indianapolis. Polian, the Colts' president, says that the team nonetheless intends to help Burlsworth's family.

While many rookies flush with NFL money run out and buy expensive sports cars, Burlsworth hoped to cut an endorsement deal that would put him in a sport utility vehicle. "Brandon wasn't going to waste anything," says Decker, the Arkansas strength coach. "We used to go to a movie every Friday night when we played on the road, and everybody but Brandon would be blowing his per diem check on Cokes and popcorn and everything else. We'd be like, 'Brandon, aren't you going to get something?' The guys would tease him about it, and he'd just shake his head. Later, at the Citrus Bowl, I asked him why he didn't spend the per diem money, and he said he was using it to buy Wal-Mart stock."

At Burlsworth's first minicamp after the draft, Howard Mudd, the Colts offensive line coach, was so impressed with his new guard that he penciled him in as a starter. The camp lasted four days, and after the last practice Mudd approached Burlsworth in the locker room. "Brandon," he said, "are you prepared to run through the goalposts at the first game of the year when they introduce the starting lineup?"

"Yes sir," Burlsworth answered.

"Brandon, you've been outstanding," Mudd continued.

"Yes sir."

"Now, Brandon, I've got to tell you something. This is the NFL. We're in an adult world here. I want you to understand that I'm very comfortable when players call me by my first name. My dad named me Howard, and you can call me that."

Burlsworth thought about it for a moment. "Yes sir," he said.

His last day was a beautiful day in Fayetteville. The sky was big and clear, and a spring breeze blew. Burlsworth joined Mike Bender's son Brent for lunch at Ryan's steak house. Brent said, "Burls, guess what? You're famous."

"No," Burlsworth replied softly, "I'm just me."

Bender's face lit up with a smile. "Brandon, you're going to be very, very rich. Think of that."

Burlsworth shrugged his big shoulders and lowered his head, as if it were of no great importance.

When they got up to leave, Burlsworth offered to pay, but Bender had a firm grasp on the check. "When I go up to see you play in Indianapolis, I'm going to make you take me to a place better than Ryan's," Bender told him.

"Brandon was happier that day than I'd ever seen him," Bender says, "and it made me feel good. He told me he couldn't believe how everything in his life had come together."

Burlsworth said goodbye to Bender at 1:30 p.m. That afternoon the Razorbacks football team was receiving SEC Western Division title rings in a private ceremony at the stadium, but Burlsworth, determined to have dinner with his mother and attend the Wednesday-night service at the Faith Assembly of God church in Harrison, decided to forgo the event. He piled into his little Subaru and started for home.

"The last thing Brandon said to me was, 'Mom, I love you,' " says Barbara. "The last thing I told him was, 'Sweetie, watch for old big trucks and pray.' It was always easy being Brandon's mother. He made it easy."

"I keep remembering something," says Mike Bender, his coach for three years. "I told him once, 'Burls, promise me you'll never change.' He looked at me for a long time and said, 'I won't, Coach.' 'Never change,' I said again. 'Coach,' he said, 'I promise.' "

They buried him in a small cemetery just outside Harrison, in a place called Gass that you drive right by unless you're looking for it. One day Tice went out to visit but didn't stay long. The coach, his heart heavy in his chest, stepped out of his car and looked around. The little yard, overlooking a hilly ridge, couldn't have been more peaceful. But Tice understood that Burlsworth wasn't there after all. After a minute he got back in his car and left.

"Brandon Burlsworth probably represents more good things in this world than I thought existed," says Tice. "I loved that big rascal, but we all loved him. You know what he leaves behind? I think I have it figured out. Brandon leaves behind a way of doing things that we can all point to and say, 'Once upon a time we actually knew somebody like that.' "

GAME TIME

| | | | | | |

A Matter of Life and
Sudden Death

BY RICK REILLY

The 1982 playoff between the Chargers and Dolphins wasn't just a football game and wasn't a war, exactly, but it did change a few people's lives.

NE PLAYER SAT SLUMPED ON A METAL BENCH UNDER a cold shower, too exhausted to take off his blood-caked uniform. Four were sprawled on the floor, IVs dripping into their arms. One of them tried to answer a reporter's questions, but no words would come out of his parched, chalky mouth. And that was the winning locker room.

On Jan. 2, 1982, a sticky, soaked-shirt South Florida night, the Miami Dolphins and the San Diego Chargers played a magnificent, horrible, gripping, preposterous NFL playoff game. For four hours and five minutes, 90 men took themselves to the limit of human endurance. They cramped. They staggered. They wilted. Then they played on, until it was no longer a game but a test of will. "People remember all kinds of details from that game," says San Diego tight end Kellen Winslow, "but they can't remember who won, because it wasn't about who won or who lost." It was about effort and failure and heroics. Each team's quarterback threw for more than 400 yards.

Combined the two teams lost four fumbles and missed three easy field goals. They also scored 79 points and gained 1,036 yards. Miami coach Don Shula called it "a great game, maybe the greatest ever." San Diego coach Don Coryell said, "There has never been a game like this." Years later Miami fans voted it the greatest game in franchise history. And their team lost.

FOR HIS first 24 years Rolf Benirschke may not have had the perfect life, but it was at least in the class photo. Handsome. Gorgeous smile. Son of an internationally acclaimed pathologist. Honor student. Stud of the UC Davis soccer team. Star kicker on the school's football team. Beloved San Diego Chargers kicker—by 1979, he was on course to set the career NFL record for field goal accuracy. Wheel of Fortune host. Spokesman for the San Diego Zoo, best zoo in the country. It was all blue skies and tables by the window.

Looking back, maybe he should have seen trouble coming.

IT ALL started with bananas.

Squalls had just blown through Miami, and the weather report called for nasty heat with humidity to match by game time, so Coryell ordered his players to eat bananas to ward off cramps. Lots and lots of bananas.

Problem was, it was New Year's Day in Miami Beach, and except for those being worn by the Carmen Miranda impersonators, bananas were a little hard to come by. Chargers' business manager Pat Curran had to go from hotel to hotel rounding them up at one dollar apiece. Not everybody got enough. "I think I had a couple beers instead," says San Diego quarterback Dan Fouts.

The Dolphins were three-point favorites, what with their Killer B's defense and their home field advantage—the dingy, rickety Orange Bowl, where Fouts remembers fans "blowing their nose on you as you walked out of the tunnel." Fouts was the brilliant, belligerent boss of the turbocharged Chargers offense that knocked pro football on its ear. But the team had started that '81 season 6–5, and was routinely dismissed as a bunch of underachievers. Even Winslow, who led the league in catches for the second straight year, was hearing catcalls. "They call me the sissy, the San Diego chicken," he said the week before the game. "I'm the tight end who won't block. They say I need a heart transplant . . . that our whole team has no heart. But I know what I can do."

All of which set the game up as a barn burner: the unstoppable San Diego

O versus the immovable Miami D, and the two highest-ranked kickers in the AFC—Miami's Uwe von Schamann and San Diego's Benirschke.

On San Diego's opening drive Benirschke hit a 32-yard field goal, which figured. The guy hadn't missed a road kick on grass all year. Then San Diego wideout Wes Chandler returned a short punt for a touchdown to make it 10–0. Benirschke wedged the ensuing kickoff high into the wind, and when it hit the ground, it bounced backward into Chargers hands. That set up a one-yard touchdown run by bespectacled halfback Chuck Muncie. Three plays later the Dolphins' wunderkind 23-year-old quarterback, David Woodley, fired a beauty straight into the arms of Chargers free safety Glen Edwards, who ran the interception back far enough to set up another easy score—24–zip. And how's *your* Sunday going?

"I wanted to dig a hole and crawl in it," says Miami tight end Joe Rose.

Across the sideline the Chargers' veteran receiver, Charlie Joiner, had his head in his hands. "What's wrong?" Winslow asked.

"Man, you just don't *do* this to a Don Shula team," Joiner moaned.

"He's gonna pull Woodley, put in [backup veteran Don] Strock, start throwing the ball, and we're gonna be here all damn day."

Joiner was wrong. Strock kept them there all night.

THE YEAR he nearly died, Benirschke was perfect. He opened the 1979 season with 4 for 4 field goals in four games, then spent the rest of the season in area hospitals. He had what the doctors originally thought was a demon intestinal virus that they eventually identified as ulcerative colitis. Basically, it was eating up his intestines, microscopic bite by bite.

Two surgeries, 78 units of blood and 60 lost pounds later, Benirschke wasn't dead, but he was a reasonable facsimile. "After the second surgery," he recalls, "I knew that if I had another, I wouldn't make it."

Three days later the doctors told him he needed a third operation.

EVERYTHING CHANGED the instant Don Strock, with his mod-squad haircut and double-hinged arm, strode on the field three minutes into the second quarter. "You could just sense the difference," says Chargers linebacker Linden King. "Strock had a real presence out there." Calling his own plays, with nothing to lose, Strock drove the Dolphins to a quick field goal, then a touchdown.

The Chargers' O, meanwhile, was suddenly getting battered. The Killer B's strategy was to turn Winslow into a complicated collection of lumps, so on every pass play the defensive end would take a lick at him, linebacker A.J. Duhe would say a quick hello with his forearm, and then one of the defensive backs would take a shot at him. Early in the second quarter Duhe opened up a cut in Winslow's lip that needed three stitches.

Winslow had been a one-man outpatient clinic coming into the game: bruised left shoulder, strained rotator cuff in his right, sore neck from trying to compensate for both. It was so bad that Sid Brooks, the Chargers' equipment guy, had to help him put on his shoulder pads before the game. Brooks would get good at it—Winslow went through three pairs that night.

Ahead 24–10 with just 36 seconds left in the half, Benirschke attempted a 55-yarder that was plenty long, but right. His first miss since November. With good field position off the miss, Strock came back sizzling. In three plays he took Miami to its 40-yard line with six seconds left in the half—too far out for a field goal. Just for fun, Miami called timeout and tried to dream something up. "What about the hook-and-ladder?" said Shula. Interesting idea. *Dumb* idea, but interesting. The Dolphins hadn't tried that play all year, possibly because it hadn't worked once in practice all year.

So they tried it. Strock hit wideout Duriel Harris on a 15-yard curl on the right wing. Nothing fancy. In fact the pass was underthrown, so Harris had to dive to catch it. Every Chargers defensive back on that side rushed to finish Harris off . . . except that when they got there, Harris was missing one thing: the ball. He'd lateraled to running back Tony Nathan while falling down. Nathan had come straight out of the backfield, cut right and tucked Harris's lateral under his arm without breaking stride. It was the alltime sucker play. "I never saw him," says San Diego corner Willie Buchanon.

Neither did Harris, but buried under the pile of duped Chargers, he could hear a roar. When he finally sat up, he saw Nathan in the end zone, lonely as an IRS auditor, holding the ball over his head. Touchdown. The lead was suddenly just seven.

The Chargers' sideline froze in shock. "It was a beautiful, beautiful play," remembers Coryell. "Perfectly executed."

Said Fouts, to no one in particular: "Aw, f---! Here we go again." Then he went into the locker room and set new records for swearing, punctuated by a heaved helmet that nearly decapitated Chandler.

Not that anybody could hear Fouts ranting. The schoolyard flea-flicker had so inflamed the Orange Bowl crowd that Shula could not deliver his half-time speech in the Dolphins' locker room because of the din. "I've never heard anything like it," says Strock. "It was like we were still on the field. It was that loud. We were in the locker room, what—10, 15 minutes?—and it never stopped!"

It would get only louder.

BENIRSCHKE NEVER had that third operation. While looking at a pre-op X-ray, doctors noticed that the abscess in his abdomen had disappeared. They couldn't figure it out. Benirschke's father couldn't figure it out. Benirschke, now a devout Christian, calls it a miracle.

Still, the stud college hero was down to 123 pounds and the approximate shape of a rake, and was going to have to learn to live with two tubes coming out of his abdomen for his ostomy pouch. Kick again? He was hoping just to walk again.

He asked the Chargers' conditioning coach, Phil Tyne, to help him get back some strength. Tyne started him on weights—a dumbbell bar with nothing on it. Benirschke couldn't even lift that.

Still he made his way back. By 1980 he not only was a spokesman for sufferers of ulcerative colitis (Von Schamann eventually became both a sufferer and a spokesman) and the 120,000 Americans who have ostomy surgery each year, but was also back playing football.

He showed his "bags" to his teammates one day in the shower. It was a little awkward, explaining it all, until special teams captain Hank Bauer finally said, "Hey, Rolf, do you have shoes to match?"

WHEN THE second half started, the Orange Bowl fans were still roaring, and Strock was still firing, throwing another touchdown to Rose on the Dolphins' first possession. The game was now tied at 24 and starting to look like the ultimate no-heart loss for a no-heart team. Except to Winslow. "*No*," he said to himself on the sideline. "No. We are *not* going to be the team that blew a 24–0 lead in the playoffs."

A whole bunch of Chargers must've felt the same way because this is when the game *really* got good. "Never in my life," says Eric Sievers, the second San Diego tight end, "have I been in a game like that, when no-body took a single play off."

Back came the Chargers. Winslow took a 25-yard touchdown pass from Fouts to give them the lead again, 31–24. Returning to the bench, Winslow started to cramp—first in his thighs, then in his calves. "And I ate my bananas," Winslow says.

Back came the Dolphins. Strock hit reserve tight end Bruce Hardy for a 50-yard touchdown. Now the noise in the Orange Bowl sounded like a DC-11. "It made my ears pop," recalls Ric McDonald, the Chargers' overworked trainer that day. "It would be at this incredibly loud level and then it would go *up* about 10 decibels. Guys were coming up to me and screaming, 'My ears are popping!' You could stand two feet from a guy and not hear him."

Maybe that's why a Fouts pass was picked off by Lyle Blackwood, who lateraled to Gerald Small, who ran it to the San Diego 15 to set up another easy touchdown run by Nathan and a 38–31 Miami lead less than a minute into the fourth quarter.

That score seemed to kill the Chargers. They tried to put together a drive on their next possession but had to punt after seven plays, and Strock, starting on his own 20-yard line, led a brutal, clock-munching drive that put the Dolphins on the San Diego 21 with five minutes to play. A three-pointer by Von Schamann, the AFC leader in field goal percentage, would ice it. "We thought they were dead," Rose told NFL Films. "It was like, C'mon, throw in the towel! It's hot, we're tired. Let us win the game."

On first down, Nathan ran right for a short gain. On second down and seven, Andra Franklin took a safe handoff and plunged up the middle, where he got tortillaed by Gary (Big Hands) Johnson, and the ball was ripped out of his grip by San Diego's 280-pound lineman Louie Kelcher. Safety Pete Shaw fell on it. San Diego lived.

San Diego, the city, however, had no idea. Right around then a storm there caused a huge power outage. It was as if half a million people were simultaneously stabbed in the knee. All over town, in the wind and rain, fans huddled in their cars listening to the game on the radio. One caller to a TV station threatened to shoot the president of San Diego Gas and Electric if the game didn't come back on. This was the *playoffs*.

Back came the Chargers. Fouts connected with Joiner for 14 yards, Chandler for 6, Joiner for 5 and then 15 more, Winslow for 7 and Chandler for 19. "It seemed so easy," says Fouts. "There was just no pass rush from Miami. They were gassed."

Winslow was really cramping now—his thigh, his calves and now his lower back. If you ever get your choice of cramps, do not pick the lower back. A cramp there means you can't stand and you can't bend over either. "Kind of like paralysis," Winslow remembers. Each time Winslow was helped to the bench by teammates, the San Diego trainers surrounded him like a NASCAR pit crew: one working on his calves, another stretching his shoulder, a third massaging his back, a fourth trying to pour fluids into his mouth through his face mask. Somehow, Winslow got up each time and got back into the game.

First-and-goal from the nine. Fouts dropped back, scrambled and lobbed one toward the corner of the end zone to Winslow, who jumped for it but couldn't get high enough. Fouts had cursed his overthrow the instant he released it, but then something strange happened. James Brooks, the Chargers' sensational rookie running back, had the ball and the grin and the tying touchdown. On his own initiative Brooks had run the back line of the end zone—behind Winslow—just in case.

"That was one of the alltime brilliant heads-up plays I've ever seen," Fouts says. "In all the hundreds of times we'd run that play, I'd never thrown to anybody back there."

When Benirschke added the pressurized extra point, the game was tied at 38. Fifty-eight seconds left. For the first time in more than two hours, the Orange Bowl crowd was silent.

JUST WHEN Benirschke figured he had his problems licked, his insides attacked him again. During the 1981 season, the small section of colon the doctors hadn't removed in the previous two surgeries began sloughing blood. More tests. More hospitals. More surgery. More impressions of a rake. And yet he built himself back up—again. He didn't miss a single game that year. "You discover within yourself a greater courage," he says, "a greater perseverance than you ever knew you had."

It would turn out to be a handy trait.

FOUTS IS still ticked off that Coryell had Benirschke squib the ensuing kickoff. The Dolphins took over at their 40, 52 seconds on the clock. Strock's first pass was nearly intercepted by Edwards. His second pass was intercepted, by Buchanon, who fumbled it right back. First-and-10, 34 seconds left, Strock hit Nathan for 17, then running back Tommy Vigorito picked up six yards, to the San Diego 26. Miami let the clock run down; Shula called timeout with four seconds to go, and Von Schamann ran out to kick a 43-yard field goal that would bring this game to an unforgettable end. It was as good as over—Von Schamann had already won three games this season with last-second kicks. Winslow, who was slumped on the bench trying to hold down some liquids, ran back onto the field to try to block the kick. He was on the "desperation" team. Never in his career had he blocked one, and now he could hardly stand, much less leap, but he went in anyway. Why not? It was the last play of the season. "Get me some penetration, guys," Winslow yelled to Kelcher and Johnson, "so I can have a chance at the block."

They did. The snap was a little high, but Strock's hold was good. Winslow summoned everything that was left in him, heaved his 6' 6" body as high as it would go and blocked von Schamann's kick with the pinkie finger on his right hand. "To get as high as he did after all he'd been through?" Fouts says. "Amazing."

When Winslow hit the ground, he got history's first all-body cramp. He lay on the field, spasming from his calves to his neck. He was carried off again. He would return again.

Overtime.

BENIRSCHKE IS a humble man who has spent half his life raising cash for critters and blood for people, but he seems to have Trouble on his speed dial. He nearly lost his wife, Mary, in childbirth after she'd spent the last five months of her pregnancy in bed. He nearly lost his newborn daughter, Kari, that same day—the nurses woke him up in the hospital at 4 a.m. so he could say goodbye to her. Somehow she survived. She has cerebral palsy, but she's alive and she's happy.

He and Mary adopted a second daughter, Christina, in 1995 and were beside themselves with joy. Eight days later, the biological mother rang their doorbell and took Christina away.

He flew to Russia to bring home an orphan, only to be told he also had to take the boy's brother, who had a cleft lip, refused to eat, was malnourished and infected with scabies. Benirschke was given no health reports. He couldn't reach his wife. He ran out of time. He brought home two orphans.

"We never ask, 'Why us?' " Benirschke says. "We just try to build our pa-
tience and resolve as deep as they'll go."
He'd need more.

THE IDEA of overtime on this thick, broiled night was about as appetiz-
ing to the players as a bowl of hot soup. Still, the marathon ran on. "You hear
coaches say, 'Leave everything on the field,' " says Miami lineman Ed Newman, now a judge. "Well, that actually happened that day. Both teams. We
really did give it all we had. Everything."

Even Benirschke was exhausted. Not physically, *mentally.* All game he'd
been stretching, running, kicking—always averting his eyes from his teammates. He was the one apart, the one man on the team with the clean jersey, getting himself ready for the moment he knew was coming: when all
the gazelles and gorillas would leave the field and ask him to finish what
they could not.

San Diego won the flip, took the kickoff and cut through Miami. In five
minutes they were at the Miami eight-yard line, second down. Coryell called
for Benirschke to kick a 27-yarder. On the sideline, San Diego's Shaw started pulling the tape off his wrists. Rolf just doesn't miss from there, he
thought. No lie. Benirschke hadn't missed from inside the 30 all year, and
two of those kicks had given the team last-second wins. Come to think of
it, Benirschke had kicked a 28-yarder to beat Miami in the Orange Bowl in
overtime last season.

But a field goal unit is not one man, it's 11, and some of the sapped men
on San Diego's field goal team were getting water and didn't hear the coach's
call. They were late getting onto the field and didn't even make the huddle. "Eddie," Benirschke called to his holder, Ed Luther, "We're not set!"

"We're O.K.," Luther said. "Just kick it."

Benirschke prepared for the snap, but his rhythm was off. The ball was
snapped, Luther put it down, and Benirschke hooked his kick just left of the
goalpost.

Benirschke was nearly sick with regret. "I knew I'd never get a second
chance," he remembers. "I thought, How long will I have to live with this?"

That miss was, strangely, a blow to *both* teams. The players were now
on a death march. Men in both huddles leaned on one another for support. "Guys would refuse to come out of the game just so they didn't have

to run all the way to the sideline," says Sievers. Whatever side of the huddle receivers happened to be on was the side they lined up on, formations be damned.

Neither offense was able to sustain a drive, and the two clubs staggered through what seemed to be a pointless, hopeless, endless dance. There was a punt, a lost San Diego fumble, two more punts. "I remember Kellen had his eyes closed in the huddle, mouth hanging open," Sievers says. "He looked like a slow-motion picture of a boxer—his mouthpiece falling out, saliva dripping from his lip."

Shula was hot that his players were helping Winslow up after a play only to see him beat them with another great catch. (He had 13 in all, for 166 yards.) "Let him get up by himself!" Shula kept yelling.

At one point in this blast furnace of noise and sweat and exhaustion, Winslow was blocking Miami cornerback Gerald Small. When the play ended, both men tried to get off the field for the punt, but they couldn't move. They just leaned on each other for a few seconds, too tired to get out of each other's way. They shoot horses, don't they? "I'd never come that close to death before," Winslow says.

Finally, nine minutes into overtime, Miami made one last Jell-O-legged breakaway. Strock hit wideout Jimmy Cefalo for a big gain, and Von Schamann set up for a 34-yarder to win it. Across the field Benirschke looked like a man about to get fitted for a lifetime of goathood. He knelt on the sideline, "waiting for the inevitable," he says. "It was like watching your own execution. Only in slow motion."

"I wanted to get the kick up right away," said Von Schamann later, thinking of Winslow's block earlier. He tried too hard. His shoe scuffed the painted green dirt and the ball went straight into the right arm of defensive end Leroy Jones. It was the only NFL field goal attempt Jones ever blocked.

Three times Strock had prepared to ride off into the sunset at the end of the movie—and three times his horse had broken a leg.

IN 1998, 19 years after his last surgery, Benirschke took a standard physical for a life insurance policy. Doctors said his blood showed elevated levels of liver enzymes. This time, Benirschke had hepatitis C, which causes an inflammation of the liver that can lead to cancer and, often, death. Doctors told him that one of those 78 units of blood he received during his surgery in 1979 had probably been infected with the hepatitis virus.

Benirschke dug in. Again. As he'd done with the ulcerative colitis, he decided to make himself an expert on hepatitis C. There were days he wished he hadn't.

BACK CAME the Chargers. "You find something deep down inside you," says Winslow, "and you push on." Almost robotically Fouts drove his team again. He hit Brooks and Chandler and Chandler again, and then Joiner for 39 yards, down to the Miami 10.

Fate, in a forgiving mood, presented Benirschke with a second chance. Guard Doug Wilkerson approached Benirschke on the sideline. "You know that giraffe at your zoo?" he asked.

"Yeah?" said Benirschke, warily.

"Well, if you miss this, I'm gonna go down there and cut its throat."

The giraffe lived. This time San Diego's field goal unit was ready and the rhythm was fine. Benirschke says he didn't even have butterflies. The snap was sweet, and the kick perfect. Wasn't it? "There was just this silence," Benirschke remembers. The linemen for both teams were still lying on the ground. Nobody was celebrating. Benirschke turned to Luther and said, "Didn't it go through?"

"Yes!" Luther said, and Benirschke was mobbed by his teammates. "Hold on! Hold on!" Benirschke yelled. Not every hero has to watch out for his ostomy pouch.

San Diego 41, Miami 38. Sudden death.

At the bottom of the pile Winslow felt a spoonful of joy and a truckful of pain. As players from both teams struggled to their feet, a Miami player gave Winslow a hand up. Winslow took three or four wobbly steps, then fell, wracked by spasms. Sievers and tackle Billy Shields helped Winslow up and carried him off.

At the line of scrimmage, the massive Kelcher and 270-pound Chargers guard Ed White hadn't moved. The photographers and the reporters and Winslow were long gone, and still they lay there. "Louie, you know we're gonna have to get up and walk," White groaned. "They don't carry fat guys off the field."

Both locker rooms looked like field hospitals. Miami's Newman wept.

Wilkerson was so overheated, he sat under a shower fully clothed. Despite the IV in his arm, White had no color and couldn't connect his brain to his mouth. "I really thought Ed was gonna go," says McDonald, the trainer. "I'm not kidding. I thought we might lose him."

Winslow's body temperature was up to 105°, and he'd lost 13 pounds. Pretty much everything on the sissy had stopped working—except his heart.

Kelcher, hair matted with sweat, blood caked on his hands, needed someone to cut the socks off his feet. He could not stand. An hour later, he said, "I feel like I just rode a horse from Texas to California."

Said White, "I feel like the horse."

Reporters mobbed Benirschke, who had scored the first and last points in this epic game. Is this your biggest thrill? they asked him. "Yes," he said with a little smile. "In a football game."

No player on either team would ever take himself that far or that high again. There would be more misery: San Diego went to Cincinnati the next week and lost the coldest playoff game in NFL history—a –59° windchill. There would be payback: Miami beat San Diego in the playoffs the next year. There would be sorrow: Miami linebacker Larry Gordon would die the next year jogging; Muncie would be arrested for cocaine trafficking; Woodley would have a liver transplant. And there would be honor: Shula, Coryell, Fouts, Joiner and Winslow all were inducted into the Hall of Fame. But there would never be another game like the one they played that night.

"People come up to me sometimes and say, 'Too bad you never went to the big one,' " says Fouts. "And I say, Really? Well, do you remember who played in Super Bowl XIV? And they'll say, No. Super Bowl XXII? And they'll go, No. How about our playoff game with Miami in 1982? And they all go, Oh, yeeeah!"

Winslow retired six years later at 30 with a bum knee and an aura of glory that just won't fade. "Not a day goes by that somebody doesn't bring up that game," he says. "It's wonderful and it's humbling to be remembered for something people see as so heroic."

A motivational speaker now, Winslow has two enduring memories from that day. One is his permanently sore shoulder. The other is a shoebox filled with pictures of kids named after him. Winslow's count was up to 129, until the author showed him a picture of his son, and made it an even 130.

REACH FOR a can of beer in Benirschke's fridge these days and what you will mostly find are the needles he uses to inject the drugs he hopes will save his life. "There's a chance I'll die," he says, "but we're not focusing on that." Instead, he's a spokesman on hepatitis C. Five million Americans have it, he'll tell you, but only 250,000 are being treated for it. Some people think there's a reason God gave Benirschke all these diseases. Who would handle them better?

Doctors say the virus is undetectable in his system, but he'll be tested again in six months because 65% of those who get rid of it get it back. He may need a liver transplant.

Whatever happens, Benirschke is ready for it. His wife, Mary, says, "People don't realize what you can go through."

Funny, isn't it, how much of Rolf Benirschke's life has been like that game? Up, down, joy, woe, win, lose and start all over again? Would it be asking too much for him to get one more second chance?

| | | | | |

All the Way with O.J.

BY DAN JENKINS

The game of the year, and very likely the national championship, went to USC
when its peerless runner finally outshone UCLA's matchless quarterback.

ERE IS THE WAY IT WAS IN THAT COLLEGE FOOTBALL
game for the championship of the earth, Saturn, Pluto
and Los Angeles: UCLA's Gary Beban had a rib cage
that looked like an abstract painting in purples and
pinks, and USC's O.J. Simpson had a foot that looked like it belonged in a
museum of natural history, but they kept getting up from these knockout
blows, gasping, coming back and doing all of their outrageously heroic things.
So, do you know what? In the end, the difference in the biggest game of the
1967 season and one of the best since the ears of helmets stopped flapping,
was that this guy with a name like a Russian poet, Zenon Andrusyshyn,
couldn't placekick the ball over this other guy with a name like the president
of the Van Nuys Jaycees—Bill Hayhoe. And that was the contest. Andrusyshyn
would try to side-boot a field goal or extra point for UCLA, and Hayhoe, who
happens to be 6' 8", would raise up. The ball would go *splat, plink* or *karang*.
The last time Hayhoe did it, he tipped the leather just enough to make the
Bruins fail on a precious conversion, and USC got away with a 21–20 victory in a spectacle that will surely be remembered for ages, for at least as long

as German-born, Ukrainian, Canadian-bred soccer-style kickers play the game.

Of course, it is not exactly fair to insinuate that Zenon Andrusyshyn, the German-Ukrainian-Canadian, was the goat of the whole desperate afternoon. Though only a sophomore, he is a splendid kicker who boomed punts into the California heavens all day, and it appears that if the ball is given time to rise, he is capable of placekicking one more than 60 yards. Rather, it is more accurate to give credit to USC's John McKay for one of those little coaching touches that sometimes supplies a subtle edge. This time it proved to be a subtle edge that gave McKay the most important game of his life. "We knew he kicked it low, so we just put the tallest guy we had in there on defense," said McKay later, in what may have been the happiest dressing room since showers were invented. "We told the kids it wasn't so important that they bust through and make him rush the kicks as it was just getting to the scrimmage line and raising their arms high."

In his wry, twinkling way, McKay then lit a cigar and said, "I call that brilliant coaching."

Everything about the day was brilliant, of course—as more than 90,000 limp souls in the Los Angeles Memorial Coliseum certainly noted, and as millions of others watching on national television must have, too. Led by those folklore characters, Gary Beban and O.J. Simpson, both teams played extremely well, considering the slightly barbaric circumstances. Not only was the national championship quite probably at stake, but so were a few other odds and ends, such as the Rose Bowl bid, the Pacific Eight title, the Heisman Trophy, some All-America trinkets and a couple of coaching reputations. That both squads and staffs went into the gnawing pressure of this kind of Saturday with such poise was unique enough. But that they also managed to litter the premises with so much brilliant play was downright against the rules for games of the century, era, decade, year (choose one). There can only be one reason why the Trojans and Bruins responded so well to the occasion, and it is that they are, quite simply, the two best teams in the U.S. this season.

Some of the big stakes in the game were indeed decided by that one-point margin, which is growing fatter by the hour. USC's 9–1 record measured against the quality of its schedule makes the Trojans the most deserving team for all the No. 1 cups and saucers. The Trojans are also in the Rose Bowl. Some things obviously were not settled last Saturday, however, like, for instance, the individual duel between UCLA's Beban and USC's Simpson.

Although neither player was 100% perfect physically, both were superb in clutch after clutch. While he practically had to crawl to the sideline no less than five times to regain his breath because of his injured ribs, Beban whirled the Bruins to three touchdowns, passing for more than 300 yards, giving his team a 7–0 lead in the first quarter, a 14–14 tie in the third and a 20–14 lead in the fourth.

Meanwhile, Simpson, his right foot throbbing inside a shoe with a special sponge cover, wearily hobbled away from piles of brutal tacklers and eventually managed to race for 177 yards, including the touchdowns that put the Trojans ahead 14–7 and finally 21–20.

Had a Heisman Trophy award, therefore, really been decided by a couple of young men named Zenon Andrusyshyn and Bill Hayhoe? As Jim Murray of the *Los Angeles Times* said, "They should send the Heisman out here with two straws."

There had been an agonizing wait for this game. It began when USC climbed to No. 1 after its third win, and the agony increased when the Bruins eased up to No. 2 for a few weeks. Ironically, big-game time found Tommy Prothro's Bruins in No. 1 and McKay's Trojans two deep breaths below. Oregon State had caught USC sagging under the burden of No. 1, and on a muddy field at a perfect psychological time and—with not too bad a team, of course—had scored a 3–0 upset. All this made last week's pregame rituals of special significance. As unusual as anything else was the fact that UCLA was on top of the polls but USC was a three-point favorite.

McKay and Prothro honed their teams quite differently for the big one. The Bruins worked shorter hours, for one thing. Zip, zip, zip. It was as if Prothro was trying to conserve their energy. On the last warmup day, Friday, his team was out only seven minutes in contrast to USC's hour and a half. Across town, the Trojans ran more. Lots of wind sprints at what McKay calls "party time," which is a sort of postpractice session. The defense especially ran more than normal, and it is worth noting that USC's defense was fresher at the end of the game. All of those Trojans who were chasing, and catching, Gary Beban there at the finish looked capable of playing another two quarters.

It was obvious that USC needed this win more than UCLA did. Prothro had beaten McKay the last two years, for one thing. Not only that, a feeling had emerged in the minds of many, much to McKay's anger, that Prothro had won with guile, wisdom and genius rather than athletes. "Well," said McKay sharply one day, "we pushed 'em all over the field in 1965, but we fumbled on their one, seven and 17. I guess he planned that."

Anyhow, McKay was grim. Uncharacteristically grim. And USC, the team that is normally loose, was grim and quiet, right up to an hour before the start. The Trojans looked tense enough to fumble at least 10 times, but O.J. Simpson argued differently. "We're just mad," he said.

Nor was UCLA in the emotional frenzy that has been its most commonly displayed trait. The Bruins were quiet, too, concentrating. Gary Beban was told that O.J. said USC was mad, and Gary, Mister Cool, said, "Anger doesn't win football games."

For almost the first 20 minutes it looked as if UCLA was the only team in the Coliseum. The Bruins were a lot quicker in the line, niftier in execution, more confident in their game plan and more inventive in their attack. At the same time, the Trojans had not been able to move. In five possessions they had not scratched out a first down. On his first 10 carries, even behind an occasional and surprising eight-man line that McKay thought would unsettle Prothro, O.J. Simpson had gained only 11 measly yards. He had come no closer to breaking clear than Andy Williams, who was there to sing at halftime.

The situation looked normal; Prothro had McKay's number, just as everyone had been saying at The Daisy, The Factory, La Scala and Stefanino's before diverting conversation back to who got which part in what TV series. It was normal except for one thing: USC did not have any yards or first downs, but it had seven points.

On the last play of the first quarter, just as it looked like Beban was cranking up the Bruins again, the UCLA quarterback threw a pass at midfield into the wide left flat. The receiver was open, as Bruin receivers were all day, but the ball hung. It may have hung because Beban's side, injured in the Washington game the previous week prevented him from slinging the ball hard when he had to. It may have hung because he misjudged the risk of an interception. Whatever the reason, USC's Pat Cashman saw it coming. He darted in front of Greg Jones, leaped and took the ball with nothing but 55 yards of beautiful, unpopulated Coliseum turf before him.

"I called the play," Prothro drawled later on. "It's a new one. He's supposed to roll one direction, turn and throw blind, hoping no defender's there. It's a stupid play. I'll never use it again."

While Pat Cashman's interception perked up the USC rooters—hundreds of whom, like UCLA's, had been in the stands since dawn to get good seats—it did not seem at the time to be all that important; it might hold down the score, maybe. Sure enough, after a wiggly, 42-yard punt return by UCLA's Mark Gustafson, the Bruins were quickly threatening again, with a first down on the 15.

But now a series of strange things happened that changed the game for the rest of the day. In three plays the Bruins got nowhere, and on the third one Beban got the first of the deadly blows in the ribs, which would send him writhing toward the sideline. Andrusyshyn came in and missed a field goal from the 20. The kick was not one of those molested by Bill Hayhoe; Zenon simply side-winded if off to the left. And on USC's first play from its own 20, the game suddenly had another offensive team. Earl the Pearl McCullouch started it by streaking down the sideline off a daring reverse for 52 yards. McCullouch then caught a 13-yard pass. And now Simpson was warmed up. From 13 yards out, O.J. burst over the guard for the touchdown—one that was especially vital, for it proved to the USC offense that it could move the ball.

Still, if UCLA was impressed it did not act it. The Bruins took the kickoff amid the most noise since D Day, and Beban promptly threw a 48-yard pass to Nuttall. It was first down on the Trojan 15 again. But, just like the time before, USC's defense got riled. Beban was smacked by everybody but USC president Norman Topping, one of nine losses he would suffer, and he had to retreat to the bench again. In came Andrusyshyn for the first of two field-goal tries that Bill Hayhoe would block.

As has been said so many times about Beban, he learns from mistakes. He could hardly wait for the second half to start to take advantage of Pat Cashman, who had intercepted him and who had buried his red USC headgear into Beban's lung. With only two minutes gone in the third quarter, Beban laid a perfect 47-yard pass into the hands of halfback George Farmer for the tying touchdown. "Cashman had been waiting for another of those flat passes, so we sent Farmer straight down, right past him," said Gary afterward. "It balanced out—Cashman's interception was really responsible for our second touchdown."

Between this score and the one that put UCLA ahead early in the fourth quarter, Prothro's team blew another excellent opportunity. The combination of a poor punt by USC's Rikki Aldridge, who redeemed himself for this and all other misdeeds of a lifetime by ultimately kicking the game-winning conversion, and a Beban pass put UCLA on the Trojan 17. It was here that Hayhoe, a junior from Van Nuys who weighs 254 along with his 6' 8", lumbered through to drop Beban for a whopping loss, and two plays later he blocked another field goal attempt by the Ukrainian. "Those things somehow weren't as discouraging then as they are now," said Beban later as he wandered around in the USC locker room, sipping a canned Coke, smiling and congratulating the Trojans. "We knew we would score again."

They did. Beban hit four passes in a brisk seven-play drive covering 65 yards, the last one going to Nuttall for 20 yards and the touchdown that made it 20–14 with only 11 minutes remaining. Andrusyshyn missed the point because Hayhoe had gotten a finger on it, and while it occurred to everybody in the Western world that this could be a pretty unfortunate point to miss, UCLA still looked like the better team. The Trojans had not seriously threatened. Junior Steve Sogge had given way to senior Toby Page at quarterback, and it was no Los Angeles secret that John McKay's wife Corky was a better passer than Page. Nor had O.J. really busted loose.

But now it was time for Simpson to get back in the Heisman derby, thanks to a thing called 23-Blast. UCLA's tough tacklers had been kindly helping O.J. back up on his feet all day, a fine sporting gesture with the subtle-design of keeping Simpson from resting. And at last it was time for O.J. to knock them down. And out.

It was third down at his own 36 when Toby Page saw UCLA's linebacker move out, anticipating the play Page had called in the huddle. Page checked signals and called another play at the line. It was 23-Blast. As it unfolded, it looked like a five-yard gain; then Simpson veered out toward the left sideline. Oh, well, a 15-yard gain and a first down. But end Ron Drake screened off UCLA's halfback, and the safety sucked over, and, hey, what's this? O.J. angled back to the middle, to his right, and a great glob of daylight became visible. And then he was running like the 9.4 sprinter he is, despite that sore foot and that funny shoe, and there was not anybody down there for the rest of the 64 yards who was about to catch him.

Of the remarkable 1,415 yards Simpson gained this season, those 64 were the most impressive of all, for they came after two hours of the toughest punishment he had endured—and they stretched all the way to Pasadena and Number Onesville.

About an hour and a half after the game, down in the USC dressing room, which had finally emptied and grown as quiet as it had been before the kickoff, a brief scene was enacted that served as a fitting epilogue. Dressed now, blazers on, hair combed, refreshed, Gary Beban and O.J. Simpson met, looking like two young men anticipating a fraternity council meeting.

"Gary, you're the greatest," said O.J. "It's too bad one of us had to lose."

"O.J., you're the best," said Beban. "Go get 'em in the Rose Bowl."

O.J. grinned, then ambled down the hall, through a door and up a walkway to an exit gate where clusters of USC fans were still gathered. It was roughly, oh, about 64 yards.

| | | | | |

Getting There the Hard Way

BY RICK TELANDER

*The Broncos were goners until John Elway led them upfield on
what will forever be known as the Drive.*

AVE YOU EVER BEEN MEAN TO A NICE OLD DOG?
Did you sit there with a tail-wagging mongrel at your
knee and kindly offer him a meaty bone, hold it barely
in front of the pooch's eager snout and at the last in-
stant, just after his head lunged forward but before his teeth clicked shut, pull
the bone away? Have you? Just for fun?

Then you've been John Elway, the Denver Broncos quarterback who
yanked the bone from the mouth of the Cleveland Dawgs, er, Browns, 23–20
in overtime, for the AFC Championship before 79,915 stunned fans in Cleveland Stadium on Sunday. No, let's clarify this metaphor. Elway didn't just
pull victory from the Browns' mouth. He ripped the thing from halfway
down their throat.

The game was over. The Browns had won and the Broncos had lost. It
was that simple. But then, with 5:32 remaining and Denver trailing 20–13,
Elway led his team 98 yards down the field on as dramatic a game-saving
drive as you'll ever see. It was the way Elway must have dreamed it while
growing up the son of a football coach, the rifle-armed youngster and his dot-

339

ing father talking over the breakfast table about how to pick defenses apart.

Playing on unfriendly turf, generating offense where there had been precious little before, Elway ran, passed, coaxed and exhorted his team in magnificent style. Finally, with 39 seconds left and the ball on the Browns' five-yard line, he found Mark Jackson slanting over the middle in the end zone and hit him with a touchdown bullet. After that the overtime was a mere formality. Elway took the Broncos 60 yards this time, giving Rich Karlis field goal position at the Cleveland 15-yard line and a sweet piece of advice: "It's like practice." Karlis's 33-yard field goal, his third of the afternoon, cut through the Browns like a knife.

Only a few minutes earlier, back in regulation, when the home team still had that big seven-point lead, nobody in the delirious Cleveland throng could have imagined such a nightmarish turn of events. Browns wide receiver Brian Brennan had just made it 20–13 by twisting safety Dennis Smith into a bow tie on a 48-yard touchdown reception from quarterback Bernie Kosar, a play that seemed destined to go straight into the NFL archives. Super slow motion, voice of doom narrating: *On a frigid afternoon a short, curly-haired young Catholic lad from Boston College snatched glory from the ominous skies over Lake Erie and presented it to this desperate city of rust and steel. . . .* Brennan was Dwight Clark making The Catch against the Dallas Cowboys to send the 49ers on to Super Bowl XVI. He was a vivid canvas to be placed in the Cleveland Museum of Art. Hell, he was the glue-fingered kid who caught the Hail Mary bomb against the University of Miami in 1984 to earn Doug Flutie a Heisman Trophy, wasn't he? Well, no, that was Gerard Phelan.

Nonetheless, Brennan sure looked to be the hero of this game. The Broncos misplayed Mark Moseley's ensuing knuckleball kickoff and downed it at their own two-yard line. There was no way they were going to drive 98 yards and score a touchdown. No way. On its two previous fourth-quarter possessions Denver had moved just nine and six yards, respectively.

The Broncos' only touchdown drive had been a mere 37-yarder set up by a fumble recovery. Otherwise they had gotten only two short-range field goals from Karlis, a 19-yarder in the second quarter following an interception and a 24-yarder late in the third. To make matters infinitely worse, Elway had a bad left ankle, and the Browns had a ferocious, yapping defense. And straight behind them was the Dawg Pound, the east end-zone section where fans wore doghouses on their heads and bellowed for their Dawgs to treat Denver like a fire hydrant. Even from this distance the Broncos were amazed at the insane howling of the Pound.

"I just waited for guys to run into me," said left tackle Dave Studdard. "I could not hear."

It didn't matter. Using hand signals and a silent count, Elway began moving his team.

Now, the image of John Elway—blond, 6' 3", 210 pounds, fourth year out of Stanford—conjures up different things to different people. Some see a hot-tempered California beachboy type who runs all over the place throwing heaters without ever winning big games, at least not on the road. (Denver scored only three touchdowns while losing its last three road games of the regular season, to the Giants, Chiefs and Seahawks.) Others see a still-developing athletic prodigy, surrounded by not too much offensive talent, almost ready to take his place at the table of Graham, Unitas and Staubach. His teammates see a leader.

"In the huddle after that kickoff to the two he smiled—I couldn't believe it—and he said, 'If you work hard, good things are going to happen,' " says wide receiver Steve Watson. "And then he smiled again."

The only other people smiling just then were the Browns and everybody else in northern Ohio. "We're a city that's been kicked around a lot," owner Art Modell said earlier in the week, obviously tired of hearing all those Cleveland jokes over the years. "And winning on the football field does something for our spirit. It binds this city, black and white, rich and poor. Hey, everybody needs a love affair."

And the biggest object of Clevelandic affection was Kosar, the storklike helmsman whose work afield reminds one of a gangling surgeon methodically carving some poor chap to shreds. So skilled had the 23-year-old Boardman, Ohio, native become in just his second NFL season that he seemed to have received a brain transplant from someone much older than he—a Hall of Fame quarterback, for instance. Indeed, it was hard to believe that Kosar was two weeks *younger* than Vinny Testaverde, the kid who replaced him at the University of Miami and is a senior there.

In this game, however, Kosar was to suffer the same fate that Testaverde did against Penn State in the Fiesta Bowl, when another championship was on the line. The man who led the NFL in interception avoidance this season threw two balls that were picked off and had a couple more bad passes dropped by defenders. Broncos assistant head coach Joe Collier had prepared a special defensive strategy to use against Kosar, a sneaky one that differed from the accepted method of attacking a young QB. In midweek reporters had tried to get Broncos defensive end Rulon Jones to spill the beans on the plan. "I can't tell you," he said. Would the plan be obvious during the game? "I don't want to say any more about it," quoth Jones.

After the game Jones confirmed what had become obvious. "We decided we wouldn't blitz," he said.

Indeed, Denver dropped seven or eight defenders into pass coverage and let its stunting linemen harass the relatively immobile Kosar. "We didn't get sacks," said Jones, who snared his team's only one. "But we got pressure."

They did, and Kosar quite often had nowhere to throw. "He was rattled because we had everybody covered," said Denver linebacker Ricky Hunley, who picked off a Kosar pass in the first quarter. "For him it was like knocking on a door and nobody's home."

Still—despite Kosar's shakiness, just four rushing first downs and a lost fumble—Cleveland had the game won. Running back Herman Fontenot had scored on a nifty six-yard pass reception in the first quarter, in which he left Denver safety Tony Lilly grasping at his shoelaces, and Moseley had added field goals in the second and fourth quarters. Then came Brennan's miracle catch for the 20-13 lead late in the fourth, and the rest was up to the Dawgs, the Cleveland defense that got its name by barking at opponents. Until Denver's final drive the Dawgs had allowed the Broncos just 216 yards in total offense.

But now it was Elway's turn to growl. At midweek back in Denver, Elway had stood in a lightly falling snow at the Broncos' practice facility, casually eating an ice-cream bar, and shrugging off worries about his sprained ankle and the Cleveland defense. "I could play now if I had to," he said. And the defense? "There are no dominating teams in the NFL." What about the Giants? "Anybody can be beat." And the potential for bad weather in Cleveland? "The weather is all in your mind."

Indeed, as Elway set the Broncos forth on that fateful fourth-quarter drive, the swirling snow had stopped, and the cold, while real enough, didn't matter. The game was on the line. The season, too. Elway completed a short pass to Sammy Winder. Three plays later he broke from the pocket and ran for 11 yards and a first down. He sent a 22-yarder to Steve Sewell and followed with one for 12 yards to Watson. Three plays, three first downs and all of a sudden Denver had the ball on Cleveland's 40-yard line with 1:59 to go.

Hey, this was almost too easy. The old pass master, Jack Elway, now the head guy at John's alma mater, couldn't in his wildest dreams have plotted a better scenario for his boy. But not so fast. After an incompletion on first down and an eight-yard sack on second, Denver had to call timeout. Third-and-long. So here's the play: Shotgun formation, Watson goes in motion, Jackson goes far enough down the left side to turn in for a first down. What actually happened: Watson went in motion, all right, and the snap deflected off him—three crucial plays, three crucial miscues—but Elway saved the day by getting control of the ball and passing 20 yards to Jackson for a first down at the Browns' 28.

Elway had entered the magic realm that few athletes enter. He was doing whatever he wanted. "We shut him down the whole game," said Browns defensive end Sam Clancy afterward, "and then in the last minutes he showed what he was made of."

Elway had shown flashes of his skill earlier in the game. Even on his bad ankle he had scrambled for 34 yards on one play, setting up Gerald Willhite's scoring plunge from the one when Cleveland had only 10 men on the field. Before that, Elway had punted from the shotgun. And, of course, there was his arm, the slingshot that nearly blew holes through his receivers. Now on this drive he was keeping his troublesome inner fire under control. "As a quarterback you have to remain calm," he said, smiling in the locker room afterward. "You can't be like a linebacker and go a hundred miles an hour."

Denver was approaching the goal line and the awesome din of the Dawg Pound. Biscuits thrown by fans coated that part of the field. "You could feel the things crunching under your feet when you ran," said receiver Vance Johnson. "Bones and everything were flying through the air. I've never, ever, seen so many biscuits."

A 14-yard pass to Sewell put the ball on the 14 and, after an incompletion, Elway broke cover and rushed for nine yards to the five. On third-and-one with 39 seconds left, he delivered the crusher. Dropping back, he fired a rocket to Jackson angling across from the left side into the end zone. "They were in a zone and the corner let Mark go," said Elway. "I tried to put it in the hole." In the process, he nearly drilled a hole in Jackson's belly. "I felt like a baseball catcher," the 174-pound receiver said later. "That was a John Elway fastball, outside and low."

It was also a touchdown, and after the extra point the score was tied 20–20. The drive, one of the finest ever engineered in a championship game, had been performed directly in the Browns' faces. There was no sneakiness about it; John Elway had simply shown what a man with all the tools could do. It was what everybody who had watched him enter the league as perhaps the most heralded quarterback since Joe Namath knew he could do. One was left with the distinct feeling that Elway would have marched his team down a 200-yard- or 300-yard- or five-mile-long field to pay dirt.

The Bronco drive left the city of Cleveland, the future home of the Rock and Roll Hall of Fame, in shock. If the stadium could have tuned in an appropriate rock number, it would have been *It's All Over Now* by the Rolling Stones.

Kosar could do nothing in overtime, and when the Browns punted after their first possession, everybody knew what was going to happen. Phil Collins should have provided the melody: *In the Air Tonight.*

Elway hit tight end Orson Mobley for 22 yards, and two plays later nailed Watson for 28 more. After three runs by Winder centered the ball at the Cleveland 15, Karlis came on and blasted the game-winning, dream-shattering field goal. The Broncos made a flesh pile of joy on the field while the Browns fans applauded bravely for Bernie and the Dawgs, who, after all, had given folks a good ride this season. Hatred for John Elway was almost palpable as people filed into the streets.

The Golden Boy had just led two final scoring drives of 98 and 60 yards. He had rushed for 20 yards and completed eight of 12 passes for 128 yards during the possessions. He had arrived.

"You know how you'll think, the night before, about how you'd like to do great things in the game?" Elway said in the locker room. "Well, this is the kind of game you dream about."

| | | | | |

No Team Was Ever Higher

BY JOHN UNDERWOOD

*Stoked-up Miami climbed all over mighty Nebraska in the Orange Bowl
to lay claim to the national championship.*

N THE MORNING BEFORE HE SENT HIS SACRIFICIAL
lambs out to slaughter the butcher, University of Miami
coach Howard Schnellenberger gazed out a picture window in his hotel suite high above downtown Miami and
wondered aloud if the Nebraska Cornhuskers realized "what a bunch of alley
cats they're about to run into." He said he doubted it. He said he doubted a
number of things about No.1–ranked, 12–0 Nebraska, including whether it
was as unbeatable as everybody thought. The bookies, for example, had made
the Huskers an 11-point favorite. Looking lordly in his Oriental smoking jacket and red felt slippers, Schnellenberger bit down on a bagel and wondered, too,
if the Huskers realized they were about to get hit from the heavens by a round-
eyed, curly-haired freshman quarterback who talks as if he's 30, thinks as if he's
40 and may not be spacy but is definitely from another world. "I doubt it,"
said Schnellenberger.

What he didn't doubt was his Hurricanes. "The only thing that worried
me," he said, "is that they're so high I have to walk among them like a zom-
bie so they won't get any higher. I mean they are *high*." He pointed out that

the Hurricanes were "about to face the Russian Army, and they don't care. They think they're going to win. And I'm the silly bastard who has everybody around here thinking they will." Schnellenberger smiled. "That's O.K. I think so, too."

It's unlikely that any team in the history of college football ever got higher for a game than Miami did for Nebraska, and if you missed Monday night's Orange Bowl, you missed an emergence. Before a crowd bleating with passion, the hometown Hurricanes dealt themselves the national championship by pulling it from the hands and from under the nose of a Husker team to which many honored observers, including those with names like Parseghian, Paterno and Devaney, had already conceded supernal status. In the end, the bitten-fingernail-thin margin of a batted-away two-point conversion attempt with less than a minute to play was the difference in Miami's 31–30 victory. The win, combined with Georgia's 10–9 Cotton Bowl defeat of previously unbeaten Texas, locked up the No.1 spot for the Hurricanes.

When the two-point pass failed, the 72,549 Orange Bowl fans—a lot of them, anyway—poured onto the field like a wave of green and orange lemmings even before the game was finally and mercifully over, mercifully because the crowd couldn't have taken much more. Down went Nebraska's 22-game winning streak, and up went the burgee of a team that may well be the next great name in the game. For this is no flashdance Schnellenberger has choreographed in Miami; it's a precision chorus line of young, tough, talented and cocky-loud high-steppers, and they look and act as if they might be around for a while.

What made the upset all the more stunning is that Miami was rebuilt from slag by Schnellenberger in five short years. When he took the Hurricane job in 1979, the university wasn't even sure it wanted a football team and had a pretty good idea it couldn't afford it. But now it's stuck with the best. Said Schnellenberger as the sweat dripped from his mustache in the Miami locker room, "No words can describe it."

Well, some words can and should. *Bernie Kosar* are a couple that will do for starters. Kosar has what Hurricane quarterback coach Marc Trestman calls "the gift." It almost need not be said that the gift includes the ability to pass—all good quarterbacks can do that. What distinguishes this gawky-looking post-adolescent is a mind Trestman calls "razor-sharp" and the uncanny ability, says Schnellenberger, "to find the right receiver 18 out of 20 times." Completion records are often deceiving. A quarterback who connects on 10 of 12 passes might have thrown half of those to the wrong man and thus gotten only half the yards he could have. Kosar, says Trestman, "picks up the subtleties and is so icy cool under fire that he not only amazes his coaches but astounds his fellow players as well. "They tell me they'd protect me with their lives," Kosar says. And they do.

In the final hours before the Orange Bowl, Trestman said he knew Kosar was ready for Nebraska because "he was going around like he was bopping, loose and relaxed. But I could see the wheels turning. We run a very sophisticated offense, and he makes it go. Inside, his mind was going wild."

Against the would-be champions, Kosar did indeed go wild. Schnellenberger said if Kosar had any kind of day at all, the Cornhuskers were in for it "because in their conference [the Big Eight] they haven't seen a dropback passer all season to compare with Bernie." The first time Miami got the ball, Kosar announced the kind of day he was going to have: three completions in three attempts on a 57-yard touchdown drive, climaxed by a two-yard toss in the right flat to tight end Glenn Dennison. Another Hurricane march ended in a field goal, and before the first quarter was over, Kosar found Dennison again, this time over the middle on a 22-yard pass play that put Miami ahead 17–0. In all, Kosar completed 19 of 35 passes for 300 yards. No quarterback had a better day this season against the Huskers, but more crucial was this: Kosar's passing canceled the Nebraska ground attack, which had accounted for 401.7 yards a game. Against the smallish Miami defense, which gave up 36 pounds per man on the line of scrimmage, Nebraska runners had to settle for 287.

To offset the Huskers' tonnage, the Hurricanes chose to forgo the reckless chances—safety blitzes and the like—other teams had taken against Nebraska. Instead, Miami combined its natural tenacity with a bewildering number of looks, which defensive coordinator Tom Olivadotti had devised in hopes of getting the Cornhuskers into a "second-and-15 situation" at least once every time they had the ball. Certainly the Hurricanes weren't wholly successful, but Olivadotti's tactics worked frequently enough. Before the game Schnellenberger had said, "Weight only works against you if it's leaning on you. If it's not, if it has to stop to figure out where to lean, it's not a factor."

Looking at the films the Miami coaches had picked up a vital key: Nebraska center Mark Traynowicz snapped the ball on his own count—that is, whenever he was ready. The Miami linemen, like the Husker blockers, keyed off Traynowicz, which gave the Hurricanes a crucial split second they wouldn't have had if Nebraska had gone on a snap count determined in the huddle. Further, the Hurricane front five and linebackers seemed to strike from every possible angle, which saved them the wear and tear of straight-on confrontations with the Huskers' beefy line. Finally, the Miami linemen got a stunning variety of support from the secondary. "I'd give my left ear if I could get them to pass," Schnellenberger had said, and he tempted the Huskers by sending his irrepressible cornerbacks, Rodney Bellinger and Reggie Sutton, flying up to meet the dreaded Nebraska option plays. As often as not, Bellinger and Sutton were playing like linebackers, and as a result, every Husker TD drive, save the last, consumed at least 10 plays. In other words, Miami denied Nebraska the big play.

The Hurricanes had Nebraska's 52-points-a-game offense misfiring for a quarter and a half. They didn't give up a score until Huskers coach Tom Osborne dusted off an old hidden-ball play that had 270-pound guard Dean Steinkuhler pick up a deliberate fumble by quarterback Turner Gill and, running against the direction of the play, pound 19 yards to a touchdown. For the remainder of the half Miami went overly pass-happy, and the Cornhuskers effectively mixed up their coverages and, for the time being, shut down Kosar. Meanwhile, I-back Mike Rozier, the Heisman winner, broke loose on a couple of options, and Nebraska pulled even. A Gill sneak late in the second quarter and a 34-yard field goal after a fumble recovery a minute-plus into the second half made the score 17–17.

At this point, it seemed that Miami's jig was up and the inevitable rout on—were it not for two things Schnellenberger had emphasized in his pregame analysis: 1) that the Hurricanes could move on Nebraska whenever they got their pass-run act in proper balance and 2) that as long as Miami kept the score close, the Huskers would have to play their starters. "With the season they had, blowing everybody out, their regulars aren't used to playing so much," he'd said. "If it's hot, they'll wear out. Their size will work against them."

The weather wasn't hot (66° at kickoff), but Miami *was* on two well-designed third-quarter drives. The first covered 75 yards in 10 plays. It was made up of three Kosar completions—the first to his best receiver, Eddie Brown, who wound up with a game-high six catches—and an assortment of traps and counters that featured freshman fullback Alonzo Highsmith. Highsmith scored on a one-yard dive to put Miami ahead for good.

Miami drove to another touchdown and took a 31–17 lead into the fourth quarter. If a rout was on, the wrong team was doing the routing. Miami was getting superior blocking from its "rejects and retreads," as Schnellenberger calls his linemen, and equally important, from fullbacks Highsmith and Albert Bentley. The Cornhuskers realized from the start that given time Kosar would pick them apart, so early in the second quarter they started sending their safeties and cornerbacks crashing in—as often as not to be met by crushing blocks from Bentley or Highsmith. Kosar seldom was pressured and never was sacked.

Schnellenberger doesn't worry about falling behind because, he says, "our entire offense is a two-minute drill." The ploys used to offset Nebraska's size and rush included quick screens and sprint draws. Indeed, the Hurricanes were much more successful on the ground than expected. On the night, Highsmith gained 50 yards on just seven carries, Bentley picked up 46 on 10, and Keith Griffin added 41 on nine.

If Schnellenberger's forecast regarding the Nebraska regulars was correct, the Hurricanes were in the clubhouse with their 14-point lead with less than 12 minutes remaining. But Nebraska had saved something for the last hole. With Jeff Smith spelling Rozier, who had left the game with a twisted left ankle in the third quarter after having gained 147 yards on 25 carries, the Cornhuskers marched 76 yards—the last yard coming on a Smith plunge—to make the score 31–24. Then, after a Miami field goal attempt went wide, Nebraska got the ball back with 1:47 to play.

One-forty-seven was an extravagance. Gill needed only 59 seconds to take the Huskers 74 yards, but he nearly ran out of downs. On fourth-and-eight from the Miami 24-yard line Smith took a Gill pitch, swept right and dived into the end zone. Suddenly it was 31–30; a point to tie and still gain the national title, two to win. "I knew they'd go for two," said Hurricane roverback Kenny Calhoun. "They're champions. They had to."

Schnellenberger was so sure of it he ordered up a two-point defense even before he observed which conversion unit Nebraska had on the field. Gill rolled right, and Calhoun's man, wingback Irving Fryar, released to the inside. "When I saw that, I went out to pick him [Smith] up," said Calhoun. "[Gill] threw a little behind [Smith], and I got three fingers of my left hand on the ball." The pass fluttered away, and with it, Nebraska's No. 1 ranking. "I do that kind of thing all the time," Calhoun said, and winked.

The victory, the Hurricanes' 11th in a row, gave Miami the longest winning streak in major-college football. This was also the Hurricanes' first appearance in the Orange Bowl in 33 years, and it's worth noting that they, with the freewheeling Schnellenberger conducting, treated themselves to every pregame entertainment available. "Join the Hurricanes and see Miami," said middle guard Tony Fitzpatrick. The Cornhuskers, meanwhile, kept their noses to the grindstone and their practices off-limits—Miami even invited Nebraska reporters to its workouts. On press day Schnellenberger arrived in a helicopter. Osborne came in a Volkswagen bus.

A few nights later, at a private dinner during which the shrapnel from the stone crabs was flying and the football conversation more or less centered on the way the Hurricanes were conducting themselves—enjoyably, for the most part—Osborne asked a friend if Schnellenberger "always did things like that." No, he was told, "but he looks like he would like to get used to it."

| | | | | |

The Immaculate Reception And Other Miracles

BY MYRON COPE

The Pittsburgh Steelers arose from the slag heap in 1972 by the agency of such assorted wonders as a providential catch by Franco Harris and the groovy benediction of Frank Sinatra.

I N THE SPACE OF 40 YEARS, INFANTS HAVE GROWN TO BECOME Watergate plotters, beauty queens have been retired to nursing homes, and Norman Thomas has become for many a name they might identify as that of a San Diego Padres first baseman. So 40 years is a long time, and unless you were one of us—that is to say, a part or partisan of the Pittsburgh Steelers, who after four desolate decades in the NFL won their first divisional title—you cannot possibly know the sweetness. Sweetness, did I say? More, it was the *ne plus ultra* of fruition when, as if to compensate for the lost years, everything fell into place. Even Frank Sinatra came around, and I shall begin by telling you about him in the event there exists any doubt that to get hot after 40 years is to be *hot*.

It is December 1972. We are in Palm Springs (I as the color man for Steelers radio broadcasts) to acclimate ourselves for the upcoming title-clinching game in San Diego. Dinner the second evening is at Lord Fletcher's, well out beyond Frank Sinatra Drive. Over cocktails I say to traveling secretary Buff Boston, "I'm giving up on the Sinatra project. I've had it." During our short stay, at least six local Italians have represented themselves to me as Sinatra's No. 1 *compáre* and guaranteed to put him in touch with me at once. "All phonies," I say. "I'm not wasting any more of my time."

"Waste a little more," says Boston, who is facing the front door. "There's your man."

In the flesh, to be sure. He goes to a table in an adjoining room, followed by a toothsome girl, Leo Durocher and Ken Venturi. I write a note on a napkin:

Dear Frank:

We are press and front-office bums traveling with the Steelers. We do not wish to disturb your dinner except to say this: Franco Harris, who as you probably know is a cinch for Rookie of the Year, has a fan club called Franco's Italian Army. Franco is half-black, half-Italian. So a baker named Tony Stagno started Franco's Italian Army and is its four-star general. The Army hopes you will come out to practice tomorrow to be commissioned a one-star general. There will, of course, be an appropriate ceremony in which you will be given a general's battle helmet, and there will be ritual dago red and provolone cheese and prosciutto, and there will be much Italian hugging and kissing.

And then, reaching back to Sinatra's origins, I tell a small lie: "P.S. Franco's from Hoboken."

He's really from Mt. Holly, N.J., but my artful approach—supported, in retrospect, by the fact that quarterback Terry Bradshaw has a dislocated finger and Sinatra the earmarks of a man who bets football—does the trick. His first words, after making a beeline to our table, are, "How's the quarterback's finger?"

In Pittsburgh, Four-Star General Stagno, summoned by my urgent phone call, tumbles out of bed to learn that Sinatra has agreed—"groovy" is the way he put it—to present himself approximately 15 hours hence. Never in his 34 years has Tony Stagno been able to screw up the courage to board an airplane, but within the hour he and Three-Star General Al Vento are talking to an airline clerk. "Economy or first class?" asks the clerk. Tony replies, "Always the Italian Army travels first class." With that, the two generals peel off close to $500 apiece for round-trip tickets that will land them in Palm Springs at two p.m. and six hours later fly them back to their bakery and pizza establishments in Pittsburgh.

So right there along the sideline at practice with Italian flags flying, the whole thing comes off—the wine, the cheese, the embracing and kissing, the cries of *compáre*. Franco Harris stands there beaming, the first player in the history of the league to drink during practice. Sinatra, after giving his ear the familiar tug and saying "Groovy, groovy," inquires of Franco, "How's the quarterback's finger?"

Before boarding his return flight, General Stagno telephones his wife and tells her, "It was like kissing God."

SO I ask you, can you doubt the sweetness of that 40th year? Perceive it you may but, again, unless you were part or partisan of the Steelers, you cannot fully comprehend. I am 13, walking, sometimes skipping, down the hill to the foot of Bouquet Street, heading for the bowels of old Forbes Field. I pass through a narrow entrance into the vendors' hole, a dungeon furnished with two battered picnic tables and a few benches. No problem gaining entrance, for during the baseball season I had appeared regularly for the shape-up. On days when big crowds were expected and a great many vendors needed, boss Myron O'Brisky would force himself to look my way. He would sigh, distressed at having run out of strong backs, and say, "O.K., kid, *soo-vaneers*."

But this was football season and I had no intention of working. An iron gate separated the vendors' hole from a ramp leading into the park to keep the no-goods among us from sneaking off to spend the day as spectators. I had learned that if I arrived early enough one of the bosses going to and fro would leave the gate unlocked for a few moments. I would dash through, sprint clear to the top of the ball park in rightfield and hide in a restroom. It would be 2½ hours till the ball park gates opened, but I passed the cold mornings memorizing the rosters I had torn from the Sunday sports section. At 11 a.m. I would be in position for a front-row space amid the standing-room crowd. The standees, who came in thick, lowing herds, seemed to outnumber the people holding tickets for seats. The reason was that they consisted of men who had walked in free or for four bits, courtesy of pals working the turnstiles. In those days, as Steelers owner Art

Rooney knew full well, Pittsburgh ticket-takers had large circles of friends.

We came knowing we would suffer. Picture, if you will, a chunky man named Fran Rogel who, if given a football and told to run through a wall, would say "On what count?" It is 1955, and the Steelers have a splendid passer named Jim Finks, and a limber receiver named Goose McClairen. They also have Fran Rogel at fullback, and a head coach named Walt Kiesling, who in training camp a few months before cut a rookie named John Unitas. A big, narrow-eyed German, Kiesling wears the expression of a man suffering from indigestion and has the view that there is only one way to start a football game. On the first Steelers play from scrimmage, Sunday after Sunday, rain or shine, he sends Frank Rogel plowing up the middle.

The word having gotten around, the enemy is stacked in what might be called an 11-0-0 defense. From the farthest reaches of Forbes field 25,000 voices send down a thunderous chant, hoping ridicule will dissuade Kiesling. "Hi-diddle-diddle, Rogel up the middle!"

And up the middle he goes, disappearing in a welter of opponents battling like starved wolves for a piece of his flesh.

From his seat in the press box Art Rooney—the Chief—tightens the grip on his cigar till his knuckles whiten. Never has he interfered with a coach. But he has absorbed all he can bear, so for the next game, he furnishes an opening play. "Kies," he tells the coach, "we are going to have Jim Finks throw a long pass to Goose McClairen. That's an order."

McClairen breezes into the open field, there being nobody in the 11-0-0 defense remotely concerned about him, takes Finks's pass at a casual lope and trots into the end zone. The touchdown is called back. A Steeler lineman was offside. After the game Rooney confronts the offender, only to learn from the poor fellow that Kiesling ordered him to lurch offside. "If that pass play works," Kies hissed at the lineman, "that club owner will be down here every week giving us plays." A philosophical man, the Chief never again makes the attempt.

So you see, it was not that we always had the worst talent in all the league. On the contrary, Jim Brown used to say, "you'll usually find a way to beat the Steelers, but on Monday you'll ache as you haven't ached all season." Heroes we always had. They thrived in the black pall that rose from the steel mills along the Monongahela; they perfected the brand of football the working people loved. After all, why was the incomparable Ernie Stautner wrapping all that tape around his fists and forearms? Could he, as some suspected, have been soaking it in cold water, so that when it dried it would set like plaster of Paris? From Johnny Blood to Bullet Bill Dudley (who as a rookie complained of being driven from the huddle by the whiskey on his teammates' breath) to Bobby Layne and John Henry Johnson, we had football players to cheer but usually not enough of them. Even when there were, something invariably went wrong. For two years we had a great tyrant of a coach, Jock Sutherland, who was building a juggernaut. He died of a brain tumor.

Our ascent to glory began on a gray winter's afternoon 4½ years ago in an upstairs suite of the Roosevelt, an aging downtown hotel where the Steelers had their headquarters. Don Rooney, then 36, the Chief's eldest son, for several years had been easing into command of the club's day-to-day operation, and now he was presenting the Steelers' 16th head coach to the press.

Chuck Noll, 36, defensive backfield coach at Baltimore under Don Shula, scarcely cut a figure to trigger excitement. Vaguely handsome with an F.D.R. chin and the sloping shoulders of a linebacker, he wore a tweed jacket and in a light voice evaded pointed questions. He did it with the same tactful smile he would employ four years later when, barring cameramen from practice, he explained, "Fellas, it's icy out here. You might slip and break your expensive equipment."

During his first season in Pittsburgh Noll would look into the stands and say to himself, "My goodness! What strange football crowds." He thought back to his first pro coaching stint with the Chargers in Los Angeles and San Diego, where he had seen brightly frocked women on the arms of their husbands and often, too, the little ones tagging along from Sunday School. Here he saw middle-aged boisterous men wearing their old high school football jackets, their faces grown beefy on Polish sausage or Italian bread or corned beef and cabbage. These men invariably showed up in high humor only to plunge, as often as not, into teeth-gnashing rage. The previous season, under coach Bill Austin, the Steelers had won but two games; now they won but one. If all those ex-high school tackles form the river towns of Aliquippa and Beaver Falls and McKees Rocks had known that the new coach frequently tied on an apron to prepare gourmet dishes, that he religiously attended concerts of the Pittsburgh Symphony or that his fondest wish (granted by his wife last Christmas) was to putter among Martha Washington geraniums in his very own greenhouse, they might have passed up the deer season for an armed assault on Steelers headquarters.

"The problem we had," says Noll of that first year, "was to find out about our players. And the only way was to play them."

Noll is, beyond anything, resolute. While a low-salaried linebacker and messenger guard for Paul Brown's Cleveland Browns, he completed three years of a four-year night-school law course, with no intention of every practicing law. "I felt that just playing football and doing nothing else was a waste of time, so I went to law school simply with the idea of gaining background," he says. Always a superior student and once described by Jim Brown as the only player who could score 100% on Paul Brown's playbook examinations, Noll sees nothing incongruous in his having studied Blackstone in the casual spirit of a suburban housewife taking classes in ceramics. When he coached in Baltimore, the newspapermen there dubbed him, not entirely without envy, "Knowledge," and when Pittsburgh sportswriters assayed his efforts he privately objected less strenuously to pieces that pained him than to those written without style.

The son of a Cleveland laboring man who died in his 40s of Parkinson's disease, Chuck Noll had come poor to football and culture. He thinks of himself not so much as a coach as a teacher, and is totally confident of his ability. Steelers crowds booed him and critics panned him when he refused to call plays for Terry Bradshaw who, after having quarterbacked at Louisiana Tech, was finding the transition to the NFL roughly equivalent to trying to trying to fly a lunar rocket after having six lessons in a Piper Cub, but Noll was serene.

"Chuck feels," says Dan Rooney, "that if the quarterback is totally involved, even to the point of helping form the game plan, he'll feel freer to audibilize and to consider a story from a receiver who says he can get clear. I don't think our quarterbacks draw up the game plan, but I think that's what Chuck would like it to come to."

So the teacher brought up his young pupils quickly and somewhat sternly. "I have never had an extended conversation with the man," said one Steeler the day the team clinched the Central Division title. Noll's premise, no doubt, was that attachment to players destroys objectivity. "On Monday morning he'll smile passing you in the hall and say, 'Good morning,' and just from the way he smiles you're damn sure he's telling you you played a terrible game yesterday.' The feeling you get is not that you're only as good as your last game, it's that you're only as good as your next game. You never know where you stand with Noll, so you're always working like hell to keep your job. But he is so knowledgeable, so cool under fire, that you have tremendous respect for him."

During the recent off-season, players who dropped into Steelers head-quarters observed unprecedented signs of warm—and fatal?—loquaciousness in Noll, who previously had restricted such impulses to haranguing the Steelers into believing they were better than their opponents. Not long ago, pressed to assess the Steelers' difficult 1973 schedule, Noll finally said, "We have an easy schedule. We don't have to play the Steelers."

Yes, having risen, our Steelers are given to flippancy, for they have the look of an express still gathering steam. One afternoon last November, Joe Gordon, the publicist, looked up from a sheaf of statistics and said, "Hey, listen to this." Of the 40 men on the club's active roster, no fewer than 24 were 24 years old or younger. Twelve were second-year men from the 1971 draft, and six of those were starters. Let George Allen chew on that while he's turning up the thermostat to keep his old folks warm.

IN THE the spacious lobby of the new Steelers offices on the ground level of Three Rivers Stadium, a brilliant hand-stitched tapestry covered the right-hand wall. Avant-garde and dazzling, it depicted a football-play diagram exploding into meteors of black and gold. The Chief frowned over his cigar as he studied the spectacular work. It was the summer of 1970 and this was his first visit to the new offices. At last he pronounced his verdict on the artist's creation. "It looks," he said, "like a hockey play."

The past seemed to have been obliterated by one fell swoop of decorators, except that one anachronistic note remained. Each day the Chief would enter the vast, lavishly appointed new dressing room, pause inside the doorway to get his bearings and then wander from locker to locker. To players dressing for practice he would offer his hand and say, in a dialect surviving Pittsburgh's long-gone Irish First Ward, "How ahr ya?" To his favorites he would proffer an expensive cigar.

They had every right, these young studs collected by Chuck Noll, to won-der what is it with this old man whose history of failure lies upon us like a millstone, perpetuating our ridicule. He had, in fact, been a great all-round athlete, one who knew football as well as any owner, but he had run the Steelers as a sportsman torn between two loves, the other being horse racing. More often that not he hired coaches who shared his feelings for the track, and he let them run their teams unencumbered, clear through to making all trades. "I think that was my whole mistake, letting the coaches have a free hand," he has said. "I was able. I was competent."

At Three Rivers now, his personal attentions to Noll's players, rather than causing him to appear the fumbling fool, dissolved the athletes' worldly veneer to reveal them as boys far from home. Their cynicism crumbled in his presence, for what other owner in the whole of the league knew the names of the lowliest rookies? Black quarterback Joe Gilliam, an 11th-round draft choice who in December would save a vital win over Houston, had entered a four-way fight for three jobs, pessimistic that he would receive an impartial evaluation. Briefed, however, by his soul brothers, he said, "I'm not worried about Mr. Rooney."

"THE WAY I see it, we've got to win two of the first four to have a chance," Dan Rooney said last summer. A young team needing time to congeal, the Steelers faced a difficult first month—their opener against the strong Oakland Raiders, then three straight road games. But they pulled it of by winning two of the four, whereupon the first sign of euphoria appeared. It was a banner that hung from the bottom deck of the south end zone and it said, "Gerela's Gorillas." In a city that would soon embrace the mad notion that the Steelers could win a title, what could be more appropriately senseless than the emergence of the team's first fan club as a claque for, of all people, placekicker Roy Gerela.

Victories accumulated—three in a row—and suddenly, on my morning radio show, I found myself hollering, "Attention, Gerela's Gorillas!" Cincinnati kicker Horst Muhlmann was coming to town only two weeks after blowing three crucial field goals in a game at Los Angeles. "Attention Gerela's Gorillas! Hang out an end-zone banner that says, 'Hey, Horst! Remember L.A.!'" Next, Kansas City's Jan Stenerud was heading our way. Had he not cost the Chiefs a possible trip to the Super Bowl by blowing a field goal against Miami in the 1971 playoffs? "Attention, Gerela's Gorillas! The banner for this week is 'Hey, Stenerud! Remember the Miami playoff!' " Next,

Minnesota's Fred Cox presented an emotional problem: local boy from nearby Mon City, ex-University of Pittsburgh halfback, highly popular in Pittsburgh. O.K. "Mon City Freddy, we love you. But Choke!" The Gorillas, however, had no time for sentiment. Their banner simply read, "Mon City Freddy, choke!" Don Cockroft was having a super season with the Browns, but it came back to me that during his horrible slump of 1971 the insiders were whispering, "He thinks too much." So for Don Cockroft, the Gorillas' banner cried out, "Hey, Cockroft! Think!"

The Steelers tore through the Bengals, Chiefs, Vikings and Browns, and all the while the Gorillas dangled perilously over the grandstand façade, jabbing their fingers at their art as Horst, Jan, Freddy and Don ruefully looked up. Among them the kickers managed to put just two field goals between the uprights, and one of those a meaningless boot that came after the Steelers had a 26-point lead. Lord, this was more fun than the time fat old Bobby Layne led a jazz band till three in the morning, then went out on a treacherously icy field to establish a Steeler record by passing for 409 yards.

As the Italian Army general staff danced on the dugout roof, Franco Harris was running over cornerbacks, laying them as flat as so many slices of capocollo. Count Frenchy Fuqua, his natty running mate, was now wearing two watches (one on a gold fob across his vest), and defensive end L. C. Greenwood was hanging in there week after week on one healthy leg. One Sunday the congregation of St. Bernard's Roman Catholic Church arose in the middle of mass to give a lusty cheer for linebacker Jack Ham. But it was in the Astrodome at Houston the next to last week of the regular season that our troops, striving to protect a one-game lead over surprising Cleveland, proved what they were made of.

Flu struck five players the morning of the game, but they played. Thirteen Steelers went down with injuries but played on till doctors forbade them. Joe Gilliam, the team's last functioning quarterback, saw his first (and last) action of the season and had his knee torn apart. "Ready to surrender?" said an Oiler, but gimpy Joe, now a black McAuliffe at Bastogne, replied, "Nuts!" The score was tied 3–3 when our stupendous, defensive tackle, Mean Joe Greene, told himself, "I have not come this close to a title to see it slip away." Five times he singlehandedly sacked the Houston quarterback; on another play he jarred loose the ball from an Oilers running back and recovered the fumble to set up a field goal. All told, Gerela kicked three and, amid the rubble of a 9–3 Steeler victory passions overwhelmed their normally self-composed coach. "We had guys out there bleeding," Noll said. Bleeding but simply gutting it out." His thoughts turned to Greene and summoning the encomium he believed said it all, declared, "That's a class football player."

How then can anyone insinuate that the Steelers were anything less than deserving of the now-famous Franco Harris miracle, the Terry Bradshaw fourth-down pass that in the first playoff game ricocheted from the shoulder of Oakland defensive back Jack Tatum to be gobbled up on a shoestring catch by Franco? To be sure, as Harris galloped to a touchdown with just five seconds left on the clock our team stood guilty of receiving 12th-man assistance. While Bradshaw had barked signals, General Tony Stagno had extracted from a small case an ivory fetish and fixed the Oakland Raiders defense with the Italian evil eye. But perhaps an even higher power had ordained the astonishing play, and provided a fillip to ensure that Pittsburghers, in obedience to a decree immediately issued by a 50-yard-line fan named Sharon Levosky, forever more shall celebrate Dec. 23 as the feast of the Immaculate Reception.

Alas, there was to be no Super Bowl trip, owing to the fact that in the second playoff game, after our men had jumped off to a 7–0 lead over Miami, our peerless coach had one inspiration too many. Judging that Dolphins punter Larry Seiple, coming off a leg injury, would kick as quickly as possible, Noll rushed only one man, peeling the others back to block. Seiple astutely perceived the goings-on; instead of punting he fell right in behind Steelers going his way, running three yards to set up a touchdown that brought the Dolphins to life and ultimately to victory.

So, now we must try again, but our hearts are lifted by the knowledge that ours is a team that is surely meant to taste the best of life. Lest anyone doubt it, let him be told the Battle of the Soft Drink Cooler.

It is last Dec. 3, and the Steelers have just broken a first-place deadlock with Cleveland by lathering the Browns 30–0—obviously an occasion for great dressing-room jubilation. At the height of it equipment manager Jack Hart, a wiry, brush-cut man, comes upon several small children. To the adult accompanying them he says, "No kids in the dressing room."

"They're O.K.," says Art Rooney Jr., the club's 37-year-old vice president in charge of personnel. "They're friends."

"No kids," reiterates Hart.

One word leads to another, whereupon Rooney seizes Hart and deposits him in a soft-drink cooler. From his seat among the Cokes and Dr Peppers, Hart reaches out and pops the vice president two stiff shots to the eye. A while later, after Hart has climbed out of the cooler to ponder prospects for unemployed equipment managers and after the vice president has had his eyes attended to, the vice president goes to the equipment manager and says, "You did right, Jack." And then the other vice president, Dan Rooney seeks him out and says, "It's all right, Jack."

So there you have it, the enduring flavor of the Pittsburgh Steelers. And maybe that is why so many good things came to them in the 40th year and why there are surely more in store.

| | | | | |

Seven Up

BY MICHAEL SILVER

Showing more grit than prowess, John Elway executed a brilliant game plan in the Broncos' stunning Super Bowl win over the Packers.

E SPENT 15 YEARS PUSHING THE PHYSICAL LIMITS of football, making jaws drop and decorating highlight clips with bursts of brilliance. Then, with one fearless thrust of his 37-year-old body late in the third quarter of Super Bowl XXXII, John Elway finally lifted himself and the Denver Broncos to the top. In the greatest Super Bowl ever, the pivotal moment, fittingly, belonged to one of the NFL's alltime greats.

For all the importance of coach Mike Shanahan's dazzling game plan, of running back Terrell Davis's MVP performance and of the game-ending stand by Denver's oft-slighted defense, it was Elway, with his self-described "three-inch vertical leap," who elevated himself into immortality and his franchise into the realm of champions with the Broncos' 31–24 upset of the Green Bay Packers.

The play said everything about the defiant Broncos and their unlikely march to the title: With the game tied at 17 and Denver facing third-and-six at the Green Bay 12, Elway dropped back to pass, found no open receivers and took off down the middle of the field. He darted right and was met near the first-down marker by Packers strong safety LeRoy Butler, who ducked his head and prepared to unload on the quarterback. Elway took to the air, and Butler's hit spun him around so that he came down feet-forward as he was absorbing another shot from defensive back Mike Prior.

When Elway hit the ground at the four, an adrenaline rush surged through the Broncos. Denver scored two plays later, and though the Packers came back to tie the score again, Green Bay was a depleted team fighting a losing battle against an opponent that had been recharged. When the Broncos launched their game-winning drive from the Packers' 49 with 3:27 remaining, it was like watching a battle of the bands between Pearl Jam and the Kingston Trio. "When Elway, instead of running out of bounds, turned it up and got spun around like a helicopter, it energized us beyond belief," Denver defensive lineman Mike Lodish said after the game. Added Shannon Sharpe, the Broncos' All-Pro tight end, "When I saw him do that and then get up pumping his fist, I said, 'It's on.' That's when I was sure we were going to win."

Though only an infinitesimal slice of the earth's football-viewing population believed Denver would dethrone Green Bay, the Broncos carried a confidence into this game that belied their status as a double-digit underdog. More than two hours after the game, as Shanahan rode from the stadium in a stretch limousine with Denver owner Pat Bowlen and their families, the third-year Broncos coach raised his champagne glass and said, without being brash, "This was just the way we planned it."

While the AFC's 13-year Super Bowl losing streak and Denver's 0–4 record in the big game helped convince many experts that a Green Bay blowout was inevitable, Shanahan saw no cause for panic. As early as eight days before the game, he began telling people he trusted that the Broncos were poised for victory, saying to one reporter, "Just between you and me, we're going to win the game. With all this hype Green Bay's getting, the whole AFC inferiority thing, how Denver has played in the Super Bowl and how the Packers played against the 49ers [in Green Bay's 23–10 NFC Championship Game victory on Jan. 11], everybody will be stroking them. It will all work in our favor, and our guys are pretty determined."

Shanahan and Elway could barely contain their excitement the evening before the Super Bowl as they reviewed the game plan in Elway's hotel room. While much was being made of the quarterback showdown between

Elway and three-time NFL MVP Brett Favre, the battle of wits between Shanahan and Packers coach Mike Holmgren—probably the game's two shrewdest offensive strategists—would prove to be even more compelling. One coach who worked with Shanahan and Holmgren during their respective stints as San Francisco's offensive coordinator noted a key distinction: Whereas Holmgren is a master at crafting a strategy that will work against any team, Shanahan takes his preparation a step further to create a plan aimed at exploiting specific defensive weaknesses.

In this case Shanahan was convinced he could get inside the head of Packers defensive coordinator Fritz Shurmur, who relies on the versatile Butler for frequent blitzing and run support. Shanahan believed that when Denver lined up in a slot formation—an alignment with two receivers to one side of the line and the tight end to the other—he could predict Butler's assignment based on the safety's positioning. Denver had spent the season running out of its base alignment and passing from the slot, but on this day all of its runs came from the latter formation. Green Bay never adjusted. The Broncos gained 179 yards on the ground, even though they ran for no yards in the second quarter while Davis (30 carries, 157 yards, three touchdowns for the game) sat out with blurred vision after getting kicked in the helmet during a first-quarter run. "The Packers were outcoached, pure and simple," Sharpe said. "LeRoy Butler and [end] Reggie White are their two best defensive players. Where were they today?" Butler had no big plays among his nine tackles, most of which came downfield, and White had only one tackle, on Denver's second play of the game.

Meanwhile, Broncos defensive coordinator Greg Robinson rattled the normally unflappable Favre, throwing blitzes at him like right-wingers flinging sex rumors at President Clinton. Favre threw for three touchdowns, including an ominous 22-yard strike to wideout Antonio Freeman on the game's first possession, but he never found his rhythm. Denver did what few observers believed it could—survive an instant Green Bay score, get away with daring Favre to beat its cornerbacks in man-to-man coverage and, unlike so many AFC patsies of recent years, win the turnover battle, which the Broncos did, 3–2. The Packers eventually adjusted to the blitzes, and Robinson backed off for a while. But on Green Bay's last gasp, a fourth-and-six play from the Denver 31 with 32 seconds remaining, Robinson threw an eight-man rush at Favre, whose pass across the middle to tight end Mark Chmura was broken up by lunging linebacker John Mobley.

That triggered a Rocky Mountain high from San Diego to Colorado and completed one of the most impressive runs in NFL playoff history. In becoming only the second wild-card team to win a Super Bowl—the 1980 Oakland Raiders were the other—the Broncos, after a 12–4 regular season, crushed the Jacksonville Jaguars at home, avenging their shocking divisional-playoff defeat of the previous season. Then they gutted out road victories against the Kansas City Chiefs and the Pittsburgh Steelers. After Denver won the AFC title at Three Rivers Stadium, Shanahan had little trouble persuading his players that, by comparison, playing the Packers at a neutral site was no cause for a coronary. He also worked the old bulletin-board ploy to perfection, spending 45 minutes each morning in San Diego scanning newspapers for usable nuggets and saving the best ones for the team meeting the night before the Super Bowl.

Green Bay manufactured some incentive of its own, most of it derived from the media's focusing on Elway's quest to win a Super Bowl after three washouts. Just as they had seethed over the media attention surrounding New England Patriots coach Bill Parcells's impending move to the New York Jets before last year's Super Bowl, the Packers again convinced themselves they were being overshadowed. "We've heard all about poor John Elway," defensive tackle Santana Dotson scoffed three days before the game. "We're all very touched. But, hey, that's the classic pregame story. As long as we're the focus of the postgame story, that's cool."

Sorry, Santana. History will show that this was Elway's week of glory. Sure, his stats were wimpy. He threw for only 123 yards, didn't complete a pass to a wideout until Ed McCaffrey's 36-yard catch-and-run midway through the third quarter and blew a chance to build on a seven-point lead by throwing an end zone interception to free safety Eugene Robinson with 11 seconds left in the third quarter. But Elway carried the day with his poise. "That was the ultimate win, there's no question," he said. "There have been a lot of things that go along with losing three Super Bowls and playing for 14 years and being labeled as a guy who has never been on a winning Super Bowl team."

Remember how shaky Elway had looked at the beginning of his last Super Bowl appearance, against the 49ers in January 1990, when he threw his first pass into the ground and the Broncos went on to lose 55–10? After that game he and wide receiver Michael Young, now Denver's director of corporate sales, were the last players to leave the locker room. When Young asked Elway if he was O.K., Elway shook his head no. "They'll never, ever forgive me for this," he said, referring to the fans in Colorado.

This time Elway was as steady as the jets that buzzed the stadium during his introduction. He dismissed the Robinson interception from his mind immediately, and when he strutted onto the field with 3:27 left, the score tied at 24 and the ball on the Green Bay 49, he was in control and confident. "I looked at John before he took the field, and he had this huge smile on his face," Jeff Lewis, Denver's third-string quarterback, said after the game. "You could see it in his eyes; he was ready. It was one of those times you just have to stop yourself and watch the best quarterback ever do his thing."

It helped that the Broncos' offensive line, despite being the league's lightest, had worn down the Packers defenders—particularly mammoth nose-tackle Gilbert Brown, who was being moved around like a giant beanbag chair. "He was lying down out there," Denver center Tom Nalen said of Brown. "We thought he was hurt. But he was just tired." Tired of watching Davis whiz past him, no doubt. Still, it was Elway's game to pull out, a chance for the quarterback with the most victories in NFL history to win the big one, finally. Put some points on the board, have them hold up, and all would be forgiven and forgotten.

On his biggest pass of the game, Elway made a perfect delivery, throwing a quick toss to fullback Howard Griffith that went for 23 yards and gave Denver a first-and-goal at the eight with two minutes remaining. That set up Davis's winning one-yard touchdown run, which the Pack conceded on a second-down play with 1:45 left in a futile attempt to get the ball back with enough time to win. (Mistakenly thinking it was first down, Holmgren, with only two timeouts left, feared the Broncos might run down the clock and kick a field goal in the closing seconds.) "John makes mistakes; he is human after all," Broncos receiver Rod Smith would say later. "But you never see fear in his eyes. He's like a linebacker with a good arm."

Even when that golden right arm was being used to hoist a few beers, Elway was zeroed in on the upcoming game. On the first two nights after the Broncos arrived in San Diego, Elway, Lewis and Bubby Brister, Denver's No. 2 quarterback, commandeered a limousine to take them around town.

At several bars Elway elected to remain in the limo, alone with his thoughts. "One time I stayed in the car with him," Lewis said, "and he was so focused, it was amazing. He said, 'I can't wait for this game. Before the other Super Bowls, I really didn't grasp how big they were. But I've never been this ready for a game in my life.' "

He was so loose that his wife, Janet, was unnerved. "I keep waiting for him to snap at me, to end a conversation abruptly, but he's still so loose and happy," she said four days before the game. "That's not like him; he usually saves his happiness for afterward. One of his former teammates, Keith Bishop, was looking for Super Bowl tickets, and a radio station in Texas was giving away tickets to whoever could get the most famous person to call. So John called the radio station for Keith, and Keith won the contest because John's probably the most famous person there is this week."

It's a measure of how far Denver has come that Elway, who once had to carry his team, didn't have to be spectacular in his finest hour. Shanahan built these Broncos to reflect his own personality—resilient, businesslike and fearless. Strong safety Tyrone Braxton, whose first-quarter interception set up Denver's second touchdown, knew the significance of the victory extended beyond the realm of Elway. "It means everything," Braxton said, "not only for this team but for the past Broncos teams, all the way back to 1960 [the year the franchise played its first season in the AFL]. We're not a city of losers anymore, and we won one for the AFC. It's been a long, hard road for all of us."

Later Shanahan celebrated with Bowlen in the limo while the coach's 18-year-old son, Kyle, discussed how relaxed his father had been in the hours before the game. "He got one of my friends a field pass, and he gave another one money to buy a ticket," Kyle said. "He was ultramellow. We were sitting in his hotel room watching *White Men Can't Jump*, and he was laughing his head off."

Funny how things work out. White men can't jump? Don't try telling that to the Packers—not after Elway's leap into history.

| | | | | |

The Best Football Game Ever Played

BY TEX MAULE

In the pros' first brush with sudden death, the Baltimore Colts
won the world championship in hair-raising style.

EVER HAS THERE BEEN A GAME LIKE THIS ONE. When there are so many high points, it is not easy to pick the highest. But for the 60,000 fans who packed Yankee Stadium, the moment they will never forget—the moment with which they will eternally bore their grandchildren—came with less than 10 seconds to play, when the Baltimore Colts kicked a field goal that put the professional football championship in a 17–17 tie and necessitated a historic sudden-death overtime period. Although it was far from apparent at the time, this was the end of the line for the fabulous New York Giants, Eastern titleholders by virtue of three stunning victories over a great Cleveland Browns team (the last a bruising extra game to settle the tie in which they had finished their regular season), and the heroes of one of the most courageous comebacks in the memory of the oldest fans.

This was a game that had everything. And when it was all over, the best football team in the world had won the world's championship. The Baltimore Colts needed all their varied and impressive talent to get the 17–17 tie at the end of the regular four quarters. Then, for eight and one quarter minutes of the sudden-death extra period, all of the pressure and all of the frenzy of an entire season of play was concentrated on the misty football field at Yankee Stadium. The fans kept up a steady, high roar. Tension grew and grew until it was nearly unbearable. But on the field itself, where the two teams now staked the pro championship and a personal winner's share of $4,700 on each play, coldly precise football prevailed. With each team playing as well as it was possible for it to play, the better team finally won. The Colts, ticking off the yards with sure strength under the magnificent direction of quarterback Johnny Unitas, scored the touchdown that brought sudden death to New York and the first championship to hungry Baltimore.

The Colts won because they are a superbly well-armed football team. They spent the first half picking at the small flaws in the Giants defense, doing it surely and competently under the guidance of Unitas. The Giants line, which had put destructive pressure on Cleveland quarterbacks for two successive weeks, found it much more difficult to reach Unitas. Andy Robustelli, the fine Giants end, was blocked beautifully by Jim Parker, a second-year tackle with the Colts. Unitas, a tall, thin man who looks a little stooped in his uniform, took his time throwing, and when he threw, the passes were flat and hard as a frozen rope, and on target. He varied the Baltimore attack from time to time by sending Alan Ameche thumping into the line.

The Giants defense, unable to overpower the Colts as it had the Browns, shifted and changed and tried tricks, and Unitas, more often than not, switched his signal at the last possible second to take advantage of weaknesses. Once, in the first quarter, when the New Yorkers tried to cover the very fast Lenny Moore with one man, Unitas waited coolly while Moore sprinted down the sideline, then whipped a long, flat pass that Moore caught on the Giants' 40 and carried to the 25.

The Giants blocked the field goal attempt that followed, and then Charley Conerly, the 37-year-old quarterback who played one of the finest games of his long career, caught the Colts linebackers coming in on him too recklessly. He underhanded a quick pitchout to Frank Gifford, and Gifford went 38 yards to the Colts' 31; a couple of plays later the Giants led 3–0 on a 36-yard field goal by Pat Summerall.

In the second quarter, with the probing and testing over, the Colts asserted a clear superiority. They had gone into the game reasonably sure that their running would work inside the Giants tackles, and sure, too, that the quick, accurate passes of Unitas to receivers like Moore and Ray Berry could be completed. The first quarter reinforced that opinion, and the second quarter implemented it. A Giants fumble recovered on their 20 by Gene Lipscomb, the 288-pound Colts tackle, set up the first touchdown. Unitas punctured the Giant line with Ameche and Moore, and sent Moore outside end once when the Giants center clogged up, and then Ameche scored from the two and it all looked easy.

It looked easy on the next Colts foray, too. This one started on the Baltimore 14 and moved inevitably downfield. The backs, following the quick, vicious thrust of the big line, went five and six yards at a time, the plays ending in a quick-settling swirl of dust as the Giants line, swept back in a flashing surge of white Colts uniforms, then slipped the blocks to make the belated tackles. Unitas passed twice to Berry, the second time for 15 yards and the second Colts touchdown. The Giants, now 11 points behind, looked well whipped.

The feeling of the game changed suddenly and dramatically late in the third quarter on the one accomplishment that most often reverses the trend in a football game—the denial of a sure touchdown. The Colts had moved almost contemptuously to the Giants three-yard line. After the half the Baltimore team, which had manhandled the New York defense to gain on the ground for most of the first half, switched to passing. Unitas, given marvelous blocking by his offensive line, picked apart the Giants' secondary with passes thrown so accurately that receivers often snatched the ball from between two defenders who were only a half step out of position. When the irresistible passing attack carried the Colts to the Giants three-yard line, first down and goal to go, even the most optimistic Giants fans in the stands must have given up.

But the Giants defense, which, more than anything else, brought this team to the championship game, again coped with crisis and stopped Baltimore cold.

Now, for the rest of this quarter and most of the fourth, the Colts were surprisingly limp. The Giants' stand keyed the collapse, but an odd play, which set up the first Giants touchdown, underlined it and so demoralized the Baltimore team that for some time it was nearly ineffectual. Conerly, quick to capitalize on the letdown, sent Kyle Rote, who usually spends his afternoon catching short passes, rocketing far downfield. Rote, starting down the left sideline, cut sharply to his right, and Conerly's pass intersected his course at the Colts 40. Rote carried on down to the 25 and ran into a two-man tackle, which made him fumble. There was a paralyzed second when a little group of players from both teams watched the ball bounding free without making a move, then the still life broke into violent motion and Giants halfback Alex Webster picked up the fumble and carried it to the Colts' one-yard line. Mel Triplett hurdled in for a touchdown, and the Giants, fans and all, were back in the game. The crowd roared as if the Giants had taken the lead. And they did, quickly.

The Colts offense, until now clean and quick and precise, began to dodder. The protection broke down, and Robustelli and Dick Modzelewski ran through weak blocks to dump the Colts quarterback for long losses. The Giants, on the other hand, were operating with the assurance of experience and a long intimacy with the uses of adversity.

They took the lead on the second play of the fourth quarter. Conerly, who had been throwing to Rote and Gifford, suddenly zeroed in on end Bob Schnelker once for 17 yards and repeated on the next play for 46 more and a first down on the Baltimore 15. Then Conerly befuddled the Colts secondary with Schnelker and threw to Gifford on the right sideline, and Gifford ran through a spaghetti-arm tackle on the five to score, sending the Giants into a 17–14 lead.

The Colts now seemed as thoroughly beaten as the Giants had been at the half. Unitas's protection leaked woefully. Only a Giants fumble slowed the New York attack, and when the Giants punted with barely two minutes left in the game, not even the most optimistic of the 20-odd thousand Colts fans who had come from Baltimore would have bet on victory.

Baltimore started from its 14, and the hero of this sequence was, of all the fine players on the field this warm winter day, the most unlikely. He has a bad back and one leg is shorter than the other so he wears mud cleats on that shoe to equalize them. His eyes are so bad that he must wear contact lenses when he plays. He is not very fast and, although he was a good college end, he was far from a great one. On this march, he caught three passes in a row for a total of 62 yards, the last one for 22 yards to the New York 13-yard line. His name is Ray Berry, and he has the surest hands in professional football. He caught the three passes with two defenders guarding him each time. He caught 12 passes for 178 yards in this football game, and without him the Colts would surely have lost.

After Berry had picked the ball out of the hands of two defenders on the New York 13-yard line, Steve Myhra kicked a 20-yard field goal with seven seconds left to play for a 17–17 tie, which sent the game into the sudden-death overtime period. The teams rested for three minutes, flipped a coin to see which would kick and which receive, and the Giants won and took the kickoff.

The tremendous tension held the crowd in massing excitement. But the Giants, the fine fervor of their rally gone, could not respond to the last challenge. They were forced to punt, and the Colts took over on their own 20. Unitas, mixing runs and passes carefully and throwing the ball wonderfully under this pressure, moved them downfield surely. The big maneuver sent Ameche up the middle on a trap play that broke him through the overanxious Giants line for 23 yards to the Giants 20. From there Unitas threw to the ubiquitous Berry for a first down on the eight, and three plays later Ameche scored to end the game, 23–17. Just before the touchdown a deliriously happy Baltimore football fan raced onto the field during a time-out and sailed 80 yards, bound for the Baltimore huddle, before the police secondary intercepted him and hauled him to the sidelines. He was grinning with idiot glee, and the whole city of Baltimore sympathized with him. One Baltimore fan, listening on his auto radio, ran into a telephone pole when Myhra kicked the tying field goal, and 30,000 others waited to greet the returning heroes.

Berry, a thin, tired-looking youngster still dazed with the victory, seemed to speak for the team and for fans everywhere after the game.

"It's the greatest thing that ever happened," he said.

HIGHER
POWERS

| | | | | |

The Making of a Coach

BY DAVID HALBERSTAM

Patriots coach Bill Belichick learned his trade at his father's knee, breaking down game film and annotating playbooks at the Naval Academy when most boys his age were just learning to ride a bike.

HEN THE CLOCK WAS FINALLY WINDING down, the seconds ticking off, with the Philadelphia Eagles unconscionably slow in getting their plays off, Steve Belichick, always in the background whenever there were television cameras around, left his place behind some of the New England Patriots, back around the 35-yard line. Moving quickly, he headed toward the 50, wanting to share this glorious moment with his son, Bill, the New England coach, about to win his third Super Bowl in four years. Bill himself was puzzled by the almost languid way the Eagles were running their plays, as if they were the ones with the lead and they wanted to burn the clock. He kept checking the scoreboard, which said 24–14, as if perhaps he was the one who had the score wrong. He called his assistants, Romeo Crennel and Eric Mangini, on the headphones to make sure the Patriots did indeed enjoy a 10-point lead. "Have I got the score right?" he asked, and they assured him he did. "Then what the hell are they trying to do?" His assistants did not know, either. The long, slow drive finally culminated in a Philadelphia score, on a 30-yard pass play, because of a blown defensive cov-

erage. Seeing that his players were in the wrong coverage, Belichick had tried desperately to call time out, but he had been too late. Belichick was momentarily furious, mostly at himself, because he demanded perfection first and foremost of himself. But the Eagles' touchdown would not affect the final outcome.

Steve got to his son's side just in time to be soaked by Gatorade in the ritual shower of the victorious. That gave him his first great moment of celebrity, at the end of a six-decade career of playing and coaching football, and that moment was witnessed by much of the nation, live and in color. It was easy to imagine one of those Disney World commercials, generally accorded the young and instantly famous at moments like these, when a voice would ask, "Steve Belichick, you've been coaching and playing for 60 years. Where are you going now that your son has won his third Super Bowl in four years?"

It was one of the best moments of the entire Super Bowl extravaganza, filled as it so often is with moments of artificial emotion, but this moment was absolutely genuine, father and son drenched together, the feelings finally showing on the face of the son, usually so reticent, as if to show emotion was to give away some precious bit of control, to fall at least momentarily into the modern media trap. Father and son were bonded in this instant by the joy of victory and by the shared experience of a lifetime of coaching.

Steve Belichick was a lifer, viewed by his peers as a coach's coach. He had never made much money and never enjoyed much fame outside the small, hermetically sealed world of coaching. Like most coaches he had lived, especially in the early part of his career, with the special uncertainty of the profession, a world without guarantees, except for the one ensuring that no matter how well things were going, they would surely turn around soon. There would be a bad recruiting year or a prize recruit who said he would come to your school and then decided at the last moment to sign with your archrival; there would be too many good players injured in the preseason (but only after the national magazines had looked at your roster and predicted a conference championship) or a change in athletic directors, the new one with a favorite whom he hoped to install in what was now his program. In the end, the head coach would be fired and the assistant coaches would have to leave with him.

BILL BELICHICK was born in Nashville in 1952, when Steve, already considered an exceptional coach—tough and smart, original and demanding, way ahead of the curve in the drills he devised and, in addition to everything else, a brilliant scout—was in the process of being fired as an assistant coach at Vanderbilt, even though the team he was part of had done reasonably well.

Thus Bill Belichick entered a world rather typical for the son of a lifer. By the time he was a toddler, his parents had already given up the lease on their house and put their furniture in storage, and his father was waiting for word on a next job. The head coach they had followed to Vanderbilt, an immensely popular man named Bill Edwards (William Stephen Belichick was named both for Bill Edwards and for his father), was well connected in the world of coaching, liked by almost everyone, but it was late in the year, and there were not a lot of openings.

It was a difficult moment. On Steve's tiny salary the Belichicks had not been able to save any money. The phone, which was supposed to be ringing with job offers, did not ring. There was talk that Bill Edwards might be offered an assistant's job at North Carolina and that if he were, Steve Belichick might become a part of his team, but it was still just talk. Time was running out. Finally, with Jeannette Belichick's help, a game plan was formulated: They would pile everything they had into the car and drive east. Somewhere along the way they would stop and call the Carolina people. If the job was there, they would continue on to Chapel Hill; if there was no word, they would leave the uncertain world of college coaching, and Steve would try to find a job in Florida coaching high school football.

In Knoxville, not quite halfway to Chapel Hill, the Belichicks pulled up alongside a restaurant, and Steve got out and called from a pay phone. The Carolina job was his. So they went to Chapel Hill, and the idea of coaching high school football was put aside, at least for the moment. The Belichick family loved Chapel Hill, and the job there lasted three years, 1953 to '55, before they were all once again fired.

From there Steve Belichick managed to get a job as an assistant coach at Navy. Bill was three years old when they went to Annapolis, Md. Steve loved it there, loved coaching the Midshipmen, and decided he would stay there permanently if he could. He did not long to be a head coach—he had seen how quickly they came and went, even when they were talented, like his friend Bill Edwards. He did not need the title or the power. He decided everything he needed was right there: a solid program (Navy still had nationally ranked teams in those days), great young men, an attractive community, wonderful colleagues.

Steve Belichick was one of those rare Americans who, though ambitious and exceptionally hardworking, knew when he had a deal that suited him, and he had no urge for greener pastures, which in his shrewd estimate might in fact not be greener. Over the years he turned down countless job offers from other colleges and from the pros. And he did another shrewd thing: At Chapel Hill he had become close to the Carolina basketball coach, the legendary Frank McGuire, who had taken a special liking to the Belichick family and especially to its three-year-old son. Basketball practice always stopped when Steve and Bill showed up, and someone was ordered to find a ball, always brand new, to roll out to Bill. When McGuire heard that the Belichicks were going to Navy, he told Steve to do what his friend Ben Carnevale, the basketball coach there, had done, which was to try and move up on a tenure track as a physical education instructor in addition to coaching. This would protect him from the volatility and uncertainty of the coach's life. Steve took the advice and became an assistant professor and then a tenured associate professor. That gave him something rare in the world of coaching, job security, and he ended up staying at Navy for 33 years, under eight head coaches. Coaching at Annapolis, he said, "was like dying and going to heaven."

Steve Belichick was an original teacher, and he had a rare skill in preparing players for a game, because he had no equal as a scout. "The best scout I've ever seen—the amount of detail and knowledge was unmatched," said Mac Robinson, who had played for him at Vanderbilt. "If Steve said something was going to happen in a game, then it was going to happen in a game." Other players agreed. "Best scout in the precomputer age that football ever had," said Don Gleisner, who played defensive back at Vanderbilt. "Nothing was left to chance." Steve did not prepare with broad generalities but with minutiae, detail after detail. Each player, he felt, should go into a game feeling he had a distinct advantage over the player he was matched up against.

Years later Bill Belichick would understand what made his father such a good scout: the absolute dedication to his craft, the belief that it was important and the fact that so many people—the people who paid his salary, his colleagues and the young men who played for him—were depending on him. "What I learned," Steve's son would say years later, "was that it was not just a game, it was a job."

STEVE BELICHICK also passed on to his son—a far more privileged young man, operating in an infinitely more affluent America—a relentless work ethic, one that had been part of his own boyhood as the son of Croatian immigrants who had settled in Youngstown, Ohio, and had survived the Depression. The lessons of that difficult childhood and young manhood were never forgotten. If you were new in the country and your name was Belichick (or Bilicic, as it had been until it was changed by a first-grade teacher in Monessen, Pa., who had trouble spelling it), you were likely to get the worst jobs available. But you always worked hard. You always did your best. You did not complain. You wasted nothing. You had to be careful in good times because bad times would surely follow. Nothing was to be bought on credit. As a high school fullback Steve had earned a scholarship at Western Reserve, but just to remind himself how lucky he was, he had taken a job in the mills during the months after graduation, turning coal into coke for 49 cents an hour, unbearably hot, unpleasant and dangerous work. Nothing else in his life would ever seem hard again.

Steve's son would eventually have two childhoods: a normal American childhood and then a football childhood. As a boy he spoke two languages: English and coach-speak, football version. (At 13, he would talk to his coach about whether his team should use a wide-tackle-six defense—that is, a six-man balanced front, with two linebackers—or, against teams that had a better passing attack, the Oklahoma, a five-man front with two linebackers and four defensive backs arrayed like an umbrella.) Other kids had their hobbies: Some collected postage stamps, and others had baseball cards. Bill studied football film. It seemed natural to him, and he had a great aptitude for it—plus, it allowed him to spend a good deal of time with his father. He was about five when he saw his first game, and when he was taken at that age to what he was told was the William and Mary game, he wondered aloud if William would beat Mary.

He started hanging out with Steve at Navy practices when he was six or seven, and by the time he was nine he would make a scouting trip with

Steve once a year—compensation for the fact that his father was away so much on weekends scouting. Bill loved making that annual trip; his father seemed so important a figure in a world that the boy admired and was gradually coming to understand. On Monday nights, after his father had scouted an opponent, Bill was allowed to go with him (if his homework was finished) to do the breakdown of the upcoming opponent for the whole Navy team. He would sit there, transfixed by the serious way these wonderful athletes listened to his father and the respect they showed him.

In a way it was as if Bill were part of a larger family. When Ernie Jorge, the Navy line coach, did the final game plan on Friday night, he always made an extra copy and put it in an envelope with Bill Belichick's name on it. "He'd get the report and go up to his room and study the plays," Steve Belichick said years later. "I think he was nine at the time, but he knew 28 was a sweep, 26 was off tackle. He knew all the pass plays, the banana and the down-and-out." What Bill remembered best about his father in those years, perhaps the most important thing of all, was that he seemed to come home from work happy each night and always seemed eager to go to work, and that the men he worked with obviously respected him greatly.

Very early on, Bill Belichick, not surprisingly, started seeing the game through the eyes of a coach. Studying the game and scouting off film is exhausting, repetitive work that can quickly turn into drudgery, as there is no shortcut: You have to run the film forward, run it back, run it forward again and run it back again two or three more times. To most people, a quick view of what another team did was enough. But for Steve Belichick and soon enough for his son, that quick view was a ticket into a secret world, in which you could find so much more than what was on the surface: the way players lined up for different plays, the difference in cadences for running and passing plays—all the things that might give you an edge.

Football was always on young Bill's mind. When he was in class—and he generally got good grades—he was thinking football and drawing up plays. Some 35 years after he left Annapolis High, Jeannette Belichick found some of her son's old notebooks, including one from French class. She opened it to find not very much in the way of French verbs, but a lot of football plays that had been diagrammed, his secret world of X's and O's.

Steve Belichick taught thousands of players and younger coaches, many of whom went on to prominent jobs, but in the end his greatest pupil was his son. He taught him many things, including how to scout and to study film and what position to play—center—because the boy was smart and strong for his size but was not going to be very big, not on a football-player scale, and because, even more important, he was not going to be particularly fast. Steve knew that early on because Bill had heavy ankles. That was the first thing he looked for when he was recruiting, the ankles, because they were a tip-off on speed. Center was the right position for Bill because he would know the game, and a smart center who knew how to read a defense was always valuable. So, as a result, a particular repetitive sound, a kind of thud, filled the Belichick house in Bill's teenage years: the sound of him centering the ball against a mat hanging on a wall in the basement. If anyone had helped create the extraordinary coach who stood there, soaked in Gatorade, that evening of his third Super Bowl win, it was Steve Belichick. At that moment his son stood at the pinnacle of his profession.

WHAT FOOTBALL men—coaches and players alike—admire about Bill Belichick more than anything else is his ability to create a team in an age when the outside forces working against it seem more powerful every year and often the more talented a player is, the more he needs to display his ego, to celebrate his own deeds rather than team deeds. A fan can now watch truly bizarre scenes on Sunday: a player, his team down by four touchdowns, making a good catch and dancing as if he'd just won a championship. Belichick, as much as anyone in football, tries to limit that and to make New England win and behave at all times like a team.

The most obvious example of that old-fashioned emphasis on team came before the first of New England's three Super Bowl victories. The league asked Belichick, according to tradition, whether he wanted to introduce his offensive or defensive team to the crowd and the nation at the start of the game, and he said, Neither—he wanted to introduce the entire team. The league officials argued against it, because that was not the way it had been done, and they told him he had to choose. Belichick is nothing if not stubborn—stubborn when he is right and sometimes just as stubborn when he is wrong—and he refused to budge, so, finally, the league caved.

Out they came, all the Patriots, joyously and confidently, and it was not just other players and coaches who got it immediately, that this introduction was something different, designed to show that this was a team and everyone was a part of it. It was also undoubtedly understood by much of the vast television audience, exhausted not merely by players' excessive egos but also by broadcasters who failed to blow the whistle on them. The Patriots were not necessarily America's Team, but they were an easy team for ordinary football fans to like in the new era of football.

Bill Belichick was a star who did not want to be a star, a celebrity in search of privacy and the right to do his job without any public interference. He feared the celebrity culture, which was particularly dangerous to football, a sport based entirely on the concept of team, for which as many as 40 players might play important roles in any given victory but the television camera might celebrate the deeds of only one or two. Thus a great deal of time and energy in the world of the New England Patriots went into selecting players who were not prone to displays of ego and self. This did not mean Belichick was without ego—far from it. His ego was exceptional, and it was reflected by his almost unique determination. He liked being the best and wanted credit for being the best. But his ego was about the doing, it was fused into a larger purpose, that of his team winning. It was never about the narcissistic celebration of self.

He was about coaching; he did not exist in a world of 100 new friendships, created instantly by his success, or friendships with other celebrities. His friends were people he had known in grade school, high school, college and his early coaching days. His friendships were based on trust, and they were kept private if at all possible. He shielded family and friends alike from public scrutiny. He did not do particularly well with the media, lacking the desire and skill to create artificial intimacy. He did not do small talk well. He did substance much better.

Belichick had done very well academically at Annapolis High and had been the starting center on the football team. He wanted to play some college ball, but he and his father were well aware of Bill's physical limitations, so they decided that he should go to a good, small private school. A lot of hard work and planning had gone into putting aside the money for his college expenses, and the game plan was this: In his senior year he would apply to four colleges—Yale, Dartmouth, Amherst and Williams. If he got into one of them, he would go to college immediately. If he didn't, he would do a fifth, or postgraduate, year of high school at either Lawrenceville in New Jersey or Andover in Massachusetts, where the family had connections. It turned out he did not get into any of the four colleges, so he set out for Andover, his choice because one of the assistant coaches at Navy, Dick Duden, had been a great player at Andover and then Annapolis, and because the head coach at Andover was Steve Sorota, a man who was himself a quiet kind of legend.

Steve Sorota coached for 41 years at Andover and was much loved by several generations of men who competed under him in football and in track. He had been a blue-collar kid, growing up in the nearby mill town of Lowell, Mass. His family roots were in Poland. Sorota's father had worked in the Gillette factory in Andover, and the family had been quite poor. But, like Steve Belichick, Sorota was fast and strong, and he was a talented, if not very big, running back at Lowell High. His services had been coveted by several college scouts, including one working for Jim Crowley, the coach at Fordham, then a rising football power. In those days—the early 1930s— Crowley had put together several great teams which played before sellout crowds in the vast Polo Grounds in New York City. Sorota's time at Fordham overlapped with that of Vince Lombardi, who would be a star on teams that featured the famed Seven Blocks of Granite.

SOROTA GRADUATED from Fordham in 1936, and in the spring of his senior year Phillips Academy in Andover, near his hometown, was looking for an assistant football coach. Those were the worst days of the Depression, and jobs were hard to come by. Sorota went up to Andover that spring, stayed for a week and in effect auditioned for the job before they finally gave it to him. The offer was thrilling because it meant that Sorota and his fiancée could get married. He started at the school in the fall of 1936 at, she remembered, a salary of about $1,000 a year, and he became head coach three years later. He coached there through three wars: World War II, Korea and Vietnam. In that time the school changed dramatically, and perhaps more important, so did the attitude of the young men toward authority. By the late 1960s, when a dean or a coach made the rules, it was no longer a given that the young men would automatically obey them. In those years Steve Sorota barely changed at all; he had always been a formidable authority figure, but luckily, given the dramatic social changes taking place around him, he wore his authority lightly. His power came from his intelligence, his subtlety and his kindness. He was uncommonly sensitive to the emotional vulnerability of adolescent boys, who were often dealing with all kinds of problems and doubts, almost none of them readily visible to a coach. He tried to lessen the pressure that competing in football might bring. He coached by persuasion, not orders and yelling. He would always explain to his players, in a calm voice, what they needed to do in a given game, and which part of their mission he expected them to figure out and execute on their own.

When he had first arrived at Andover, the school's headmaster, Claude Moore Fuess, had given him marching orders very different from those given to most new coaches: "Your job is to teach, not to win a lot of football games." That, Sorota would later say, was the perfect message for a young coach, because it meant that his job depended not on his won-lost record, which actually turned out to be exceptional, but on his teaching, which he did with great skill, and on his effect on the young men, which was exemplary, for he reached into the deepest part of them, their character, and helped shape it. The headmaster's challenge allowed him to let his young players find their own way. He did not, like so many high school coaches, call the plays for his quarterbacks; instead he allowed them to make these decisions on the field. That was something that might have gotten him fired elsewhere.

In the years right after the war he received a tantalizing offer from one of the area's better colleges to become the head coach. It was a big program, and it would mean more than twice as much money as he was making, and he spoke of it at some length with his wife, but, in the end, he turned the offer down. He already had everything he needed, he told her.

He was protective of his kids; he did not want college recruiters or scouts or media people around. There was, he suspected, already enough pressure on them. He wanted to create an atmosphere in which football was played well, where excellence was valued, but where the game was always fun. There was never to be too heavy a price to be paid if you made a mistake.

His practices reflected his personality. His players did not do a lot of hitting. His philosophy was that a great deal of the hitting in high school ball was wasted, that you only wore the kids down and detracted from their ability by having too many scrimmages. Why increase the possibility of injuries? He expected his players to be in good shape and to listen to their coaches—if they did, they would do it right. He never belittled a player and never, as far as many of his assistants and former players could remember, needed to discipline one. The rules were set, they were clear, and no one fooled around on Steve Sorota's time.

None of this escaped Bill Belichick, who was already intent on coaching. As one of his Andover teammates, Bruce Bruckmann says, "You could tell from the start that he lived and breathed football, nothing less than 24 hours a day, seven days a week."

INDEED, BELICHICK was determined to reach the pinnacle of his profession, and in that lifelong journey the victory against the St. Louis Rams in Super Bowl XXXVI on Feb. 3, 2002, was the high-water mark, the best job of coaching he had ever done, Belichick would later say. It is important to remember the context of that victory: The Rams were already the Rams, one of the NFL's golden teams. They had won Super Bowl XXXIV in 2000. They had a brilliant quarterback in Kurt Warner and a group of shockingly fast receivers—Isaac Bruce, Torry Holt, Az Hakim and Ricky Proehl—who seemed wired to Warner by some kind of extrasensory perception. And they had Marshall Faulk, a great running back at the height of his game, with power and speed, balance and excellent hands, which made him a multiple threat in a dangerous and unpredictable offense.

The Patriots, by contrast, were not yet the Patriots, a dynasty in the making, and Belichick was not yet the genius that he was later accused of being. (The genius talk made everyone in the Belichick family a little nervous. When writers began to suggest in print that Bill might be a genius, Steve Belichick wisely demurred. "You are," he said, "talking about someone who walks up and down a football field.") Serious football fans simply did not think the Patriots belonged in the Super Bowl, that most sacrosanct of games—it was almost as if they were seen as intruders. For those making bets, the spread was two touchdowns.

When Belichick flew to New Orleans for the game, he was accompanied by his assistant Ernie Adams, an enigmatic, almost mysterious figure in football circles. He had been a close friend and adviser of Belichick's since 1970, when they were both seniors at Andover. Not even all the people who understood the Belichick operation knew exactly what Adams did, and that included some of the Patriots' players. Once during a team meeting, a giant photo of Adams had been punched up on the immense screen, and under it was written, WHAT DOES THIS MAN DO?

The answer, of course, was that Ernie Adams was Belichick's Belichick, the film master's master of film. He was supremely knowledgeable about the history of the game, no play ever forgotten, and his brain was like a football computer, always clicking away, remembering which defense had stopped which offense, and who the coaches and the players had been. He was in a class with his boss in breaking down film and finding little things that no one else saw, and just as good at understanding the conceptual process that drove another team. He shared Belichick's views and his passion.

He was one of the very few men against whom Bill Belichick liked to test his own view of a game, trusting completely Adams's original mind and his encyclopedic knowledge of the game; if they differed on a strategy—which happened rarely—then Belichick took Adams's dissent seriously. He might not ultimately adopt Adams's view, but he would always weigh it carefully. They had been through a great deal together, playing next to each other on an unbeaten Andover team (for which, as his senior project, Adams did a study breaking down Andover's tendencies on offense) and then coaching together with the Giants, Browns and Patriots.

Adams, the son of a career Navy officer, was in his fourth year at Andover when Belichick arrived. Adams was already as advanced a football junkie as Belichick; he had an exceptional collection of books on coaching, including *Football Scouting Methods*, the only book written by one Steve Belichick, assistant coach at the Naval Academy. It was a very dry description of how to scout an opponent, and, being chock-full of diagrams of complicated plays, it was probably bought only by other scouts and the 14-year-old Ernie Adams.

That year, just as the first football practice was about to start, coach Sorota posted a list of the new players trying out for the varsity, among them Bill Belichick. Ernie Adams was thrilled. That first day Adams looked at the young man with a strip of tape on his helmet that said BELICHICK and asked if he was from Annapolis and if he was related to the famed writer-coach-scout Steve Belichick. Bill said yes, he was his son. Thus began a lifelong friendship on the playing fields of Andover.

Adams had already befriended another football-crazed classmate, Evan Bonds, with whom he talked football constantly and with whom he endlessly diagrammed football plays. Bonds had also read Steve Belichick's book and was thrilled that the scion of such a distinguished football family was about to become a teammate. "Because we were such football nerds, it was absolutely amazing that Bill had come to play at Andover, because [Ernie and I] were probably the only two people in the entire state of Massachusetts who had read his father's book," Bonds said years later. Bonds felt that although his own life revolved completely around football, Adams was even more advanced in his football obsessions: "Ernie already had an exceptional football film collection, 16-millimeter stuff, the great Packers-Cowboys games, Raiders-Jets, films like that, which he somehow found out about through sports magazines, and had sent away for and for which he had enough primitive equipment so that he could show the films," Bonds said. "It's hard to explain just how football-crazed we were."

The connection among the three of them—Belichick, Adams and Bonds—was immediate and lasting; they were a club, although it became increasingly clear that Belichick and Adams were more committed to becoming football coaches and that Bonds, by their standards, was a bit soft and given over to interests in other things. They were inseparable that year. "Others would be at the library doing trig or history, and the two or the three of them would be off to the side in a corner, and you'd look and they'd be X-ing and O-ing," said Bruckmann, the halfback on that Andover team. For a time Bonds thought about trying some coaching. When he graduated, he went off to Duke, but he discovered that he was just as passionate about music as he was about football. Eventually he became a music professor at nearby Chapel Hill.

Adams went to Northwestern, a Big Ten program then enjoying some of its better years under famed coach Alex Agase. Agase was a little surprised when he received in the mail, unsolicited, an unusual document, beautifully bound as if it were a college senior thesis. It turned out to be a treatise on the importance of the drop-back quarterback in T formation football. It was written by a young man then 18 years old named Ernest Adams, who had been one of the team's managers earlier that fall. He mentioned in the letter that he would like to help coach at Northwestern in some form or other. Most coaches would have thrown it away, but Agase gave it a quick glance and then handed it to Jay Robertson, a young assistant on his staff, who read it and thought it could have been written by any number of rather distinguished college or professional coaches. When Agase told Robertson that it had been written by one of the managers, Robertson remembered a very young-looking freshman with curly hair who always seemed to edge his way close to the huddles so he could hear everything that Robertson said. Agase told Robertson to go out and talk to the kid and find out the depth of his knowledge. "That was 33 years ago, and he was 18, I think, and I still don't know what it is, what the bottom of his knowledge is, what it is that he doesn't know, because he knows so much," Robertson said recently.

They decided to let him break down film, which he did with great skill in the catacombs of the football offices in a dark, grim little converted ticket room they called the Dungeon. But it was one thing to analyze film in the Dungeon with the luxury of time and quite another to scout a game live. Soon they sent him out on the road to scout an upcoming opponent and found, to their delight, that he could get it all down quickly, accurately and perceptively. That made Adams, at only 18, a full-fledged scout for a big-time team. For the Andover trio it was a marvelous moment: The first one of them had gotten his foot in the door in coaching. Adams was a very successful scout and was soon a de facto coach as well, coaching the scout team as it ran opponents' plays in practice—in effect coaching his classmates.

BY HIS senior year it was clear that all Adams wanted to do was be a football coach, that nothing else interested him. In those days it was part of the Northwestern assistants' responsibility to do some recruiting in the Chicago region, and something that Robertson sensed the shy Adams was extremely uncomfortable with. He was not a person who liked to go around selling anything, particularly himself or his school. Football to him was a great chess match. One Friday they had visited a local high school, and, driving back to Evanston, Robertson saw that Adams, normally quite ebullient, seemed rather depressed. Robertson finally said, "It's the pro game or nothing, isn't it, Ernie?"

"Yes," Adams answered.

Adams finally landed a job in New England, even though it was without pay. The Patriots' head coach at the time was Chuck Fairbanks. The way Steve Belichick, with his ear to the ground in the coaching world, understood it, someone had told Fairbanks that Adams was really smart, and he would work for free, and Fairbanks had replied that he had coached for some 30 years and that anyone who would do anything for no pay was not worth a goddam. But what Fairbanks told Adams was that they were glad to have him, and while they were not going to pay him, they were not going to carry him either. If he could do the work, he could stay; if not, he would be out of there very quickly, because no one had the time to teach him.

By chance it was mid-June, the one time in pro football when almost everyone takes a vacation. Adams had the Patriots' facilities all to himself and spent the next two weeks studying their playbook and their films, so that by the time they returned, he knew it all, as if he had photographed it and then computerized it. Soon after, Fairbanks called Adams up to the blackboard and asked him to draw up one of their more arcane coverages. He did it flawlessly, of course.

When Adams was hired by the Patriots, he immediately called his pal Bill Belichick. At that moment Belichick, newly graduated from Wesleyan, was living with his parents and hoping to get a job as a graduate assistant in the college ranks. Adams suggested that Belichick try for a professional job, which he did, ending up as a virtually unpaid assistant with the Baltimore Colts.

NOW, 30 years later, Adams and Belichick were flying south to play the Rams in the biggest game of the year. The two teams had met earlier in the season, and the Rams had handled the Patriots easily. The score was relatively close, 24–17, but the game was not.

Afterward Belichick believed that he had coached badly. He had been preoccupied with too many other issues that week, his game plan had been flawed, and the Rams had parried it all too easily. The Patriots had blitzed, but because the Rams had picked up the blitzes, nothing had broken Warner's rhythm, and he had enjoyed something of a free-fire zone. Belichick had gone back and looked endlessly at the film of that game and of all the other Rams games, looking for a way to throw them off stride. Forty-two Patriots blitzes, he saw, and they had handled them all.

This time Belichick intended to make it different. He was all too aware of the vast imbalance in talent between the two teams. The key, both he and Adams decided independently, was stopping Faulk. That Adams agreed with him was comforting to Belichick, but stopping Faulk was much easier said than done. The game plan was to key on him on every play and wear him down. They were going to hit him every time he had the ball and hit him every time he didn't have the ball. The phrase they used was "butch the back," which meant, as Belichick later said, "knock the s--- out of him."

And so that single week of preparation was given over to practicing how to stop Faulk. It began with Belichick's telling his players that he had screwed up and done a poor job of coaching the last time. "I'm not going to screw up again," he promised them. The first and most important thing they were going to do, he said, was know where Faulk was at all times. So all week the scout team lined up and ran Rams plays and a player would imitate Faulk, and there would be Belichick standing behind his defense and yelling, "Where is he? Where is he?" It was a constant all week, that yell before every practice play: "Where is he?" Finally one of the defensive players turned around and yelled, "Shut the f--- up!" which even Belichick appreciated, because it meant that they had it down.

There were other things the Patriots worked on, but the primary one was dealing with the Rams' speed, so Belichick lined the scout-team receivers about three yards ahead of the normal line of scrimmage to give his defensive backs a sense of how quickly it all would happen.

The X's and O's are fine, but the X's and O's don't always work like they do on a blackboard. The X's don't get to where they're supposed to get to, and the O's turn out to be smarter than you thought. But on game day it all worked for New England. Faulk gained only 76 yards. The Patriots' X's stopped the Rams' O's when they were supposed to. New England led for almost the entire game, then held off a late St. Louis charge just enough for Adam Vinatieri to kick a field goal in the final seconds for a 20–17 win.

Watching that day was Stan White, a talented linebacker who had been just three years into the pro game in 1975 when he worked with Belichick, newly arrived at his first job with the Colts. "I was sure he was going to try and take Marshall Faulk out of the game," White said. "He would want to stop Faulk and throw the timing of those great receivers off just a bit. Make Warner throw to places where the receivers had not yet arrived. Even back in Baltimore, when he was a kid, he was thinking of what the offensive teams were going to do and how to stop them."

Of the media people covering the Super Bowl that day, the person who understood most clearly what Belichick and his staff had done was ESPN's Ron Jaworski, who had spent 15 years as an NFL quarterback. After eight hours of screening the Patriots-Rams film, he said Belichick had done "the best coaching job I've ever seen." Not just that season, not just in a Super Bowl, Jaworski said, but in his 29 years of playing and watching football.

Jaworski also broke down the Rams-Patriots game of the regular season and was fascinated by the difference between it and the championship game. By his count (which was slightly different from Belichick's), in the first game the Patriots had sent five or more players after Warner 38 times, or 56% of the time. In the Super Bowl they had done it only four times. "I've never seen anything like it," said Jaworski. "Here's the key: The Rams rely on timing and rhythm, but everyone thinks that rhythm runs through Warner. Belichick and [defensive coordinator] Romeo Crennel decided that the Rams' rhythm depended on Faulk. So they hit him and kept hitting him."

The Patriots, Jaworski also noted, had used five or more defensive backs 74% of the time. Sometimes they used seven defensive backs. "Think about that— there are teams that don't carry seven defensive backs," he said. With all those defensive backs out there, the Rams would have had better success running the ball more at the smaller backs, but they had failed to do that. In that sense, Jaworski believed, Belichick had outsmarted the very bright Rams coach, Mike Martz. "I talked with Ricky Proehl after the game," Jaworski said, "and he told me that the Rams players were all on the sideline during the second half, screaming at the coaches that the Patriots were playing five and six defensive backs, that they had to run the ball, that the run was there every time. But Martz was telling them, 'F--- it, I'm going to win it my way.' Chalk that one up for Belichick."

What had happened, Jaworski added, was not a fluke. "Belichick is the best in the game today, maybe the best ever."

| | | | | |

Moment of Truth

BY GARY SMITH

*There was no action in the TCU locker room before the 1957 Cotton Bowl,
but what Marvin Newman photographed there is as close to the essence
of sports as anything that happens on a playing field.*

OU HEARD ME RIGHT: COME IN. NO, YOU WON'T DISTURB
a soul in this locker room. They're all lost in that place
most folks go maybe once or twice in a lifetime, when
their mamas or daddies die or their children are born, a
place they don't go nearly as often as they should. Trust me, these boys will
never know you're here. All right, maybe that fellow in white will notice,
the one looking your way, but Willard McClung would be the last to make
a peep.

See, that's one reason we picked this, out of all the crackerjack sports pictures the editors at SI might've chosen, as our favorite of the century. Not
claiming it's better than that famous one of Muhammad Ali standing and
snarling over Sonny Liston laid out like a cockroach the morning after the
bug man comes. Or that picture of Willie Mays catching the ball over his
shoulder in the '54 World Series, or any number of others. But you can
walk around inside this picture in a way you can't in those others, peer
right inside the tunnel these boys have entered. Their boxer shorts are hanging right there, on the hooks behind their heads, but their faces are show-

ing something even more personal than that. Almost reminds you of a painting by Norman Rockwell.

Can you smell it? No, not the jockstrap sweat, or the cigar reek wafting off the coach, Orthol Martin—better known as Abe, or Honest Abe—in the brown hat. It's the smell of men about to go to war. What I'm inviting you into is 12:50 p.m. at the Cotton Bowl on Jan. 1, 1957, just a few minutes after the boys have returned from pregame warmups, just a quarter of an hour before a legend is born. A roomful of young men from Texas Christian University are about to try and stop the best football player in history, a fellow from Syracuse by the name of Jim Brown, in his last college game— but only his second in front of the entire nation, thanks to the NBC cameras waiting outside.

No denying it, a lot of folks might whip right past this in a collection of sports pictures, rushing to get to those slam-bang plays at home plate or those high-flying Michael Jordan circus shots. But it's funny. The older you get, the more you realize that *this* is what sports are most about: the moments *before*, the times when a person takes a flashlight to his soul and inspects himself for will and courage and spirit, the stuff that separates men such as Jordan and Ali from the rest more than anything in their forearms or their fingers or their feet. *Who am I?* And, *Is that going to be enough?* That's what you're peeking at through the door, and believe me, those are two big and scary questions, the two best reasons for all of god's children to play sports, so they can start chewing on them early. Because once the whistle blows and a game begins, everything's just a blur, a crazy ricochet of ball and bodies that springs—inevitably, you might say—from whatever it is that these boys are discovering right here, right now.

But you're still hesitating, a little intimidated by all those cleats and helmets and knees. Come on, there are things I want to show you.

MAYBE IT was like this for you, too, back when you played. All the posturing and bluffing and the silly airs that human beings put on get demolished in a moment like this. A team is never more a team than it is now, yet look at the looks on the Horned Frogs! Ever see so many guys look so alone?

Look at Buddy Dike, number 38, just behind old Abe. He's the Frogs' starting fullback and inside linebacker, and he's just gotten a good look at

Jim Brown's 46-inch chest and 32-inch waist in warmups. Doctors advised Buddy never to play football again after he ruptured a kidney tackling another phenom of the era, Penn State's Lenny Moore, two years earlier. The kidney healed but hemorrhaged four more times, doubling Buddy over with pain, making blood gush out his urethra, bringing him within a whisker of bleeding to death, yet here he is, with a look on his face that might not be seen again until the day he loses his 18-year-old son in a car wreck.

There are 32 more young men suited up in this room, besides the 17 you're looking at. Almost every one's a kid from a small town or ranch or farm in west or south Texas, where all his life he's watched everyone drop everything, climb into automobiles and form caravans for only two occasions: funerals and football games. Nine of the 11 TCU starters—remember, they have to play both ways—are seniors, most of them staring into the biggest and last football game of their lives. Eleven wars are about to burst out on every play, because that's what football is, and what those wars hinge on, more than most folks realize, is the question lurking in the shadows of this room: Who has the most tolerance for pain?

That's a loaded question about manhood, and a matter of geography too. Jim Brown be damned, the Southwest Conference team that loses to an Eastern school in the Cotton Bowl in the 1950s might as well run right past the locker room door at the end of the game, exit the stadium and just keep going, till it's lost in the prairie.

Let's take a good look at old Abe. Country boy from Jacksboro, Texas, who played end at TCU in the late 1920s and kept to the grass on campus, claiming the sidewalk was too hard for his feet. Some folks take him for a hick, but be careful, every shut eye isn't asleep. Notice, Abe's not working the boys into one of those tent-preacher lathers. Not his style. The season after this one, just before the Horned Frogs take the field at Ohio State with 80,000-plus fans licking their fangs, all Abe will tell his boys is "Laddies, you're playin' the best team in *the* United States of America"—then walk away. Another game, what he'll say is, "These are big guys. Hope you don't get hurt." He's a master of the subtle psychological ploy, a man who lacks both the strategic genius and the double-knotted sphincter of your other big football honchos, but who maneuvers a college of 4,700 students, most of them female, into three Cotton Bowls in four seasons between '55 and '58 and humbles elephants such as Southern Cal and Penn State and Texas along the way. "You just believe in human beings, that they're all pretty good folks, and you just try to keep 'em that way"—that's how Abe sums up his coaching philosophy in the Cotton Bowl program they're hawking outside that locker room right now.

In practice he'll drop to his hands and knees and crawl into the huddle, gaze up at his gang like a gopher and declare, "Boys, run a 34." Late in a game, when the Froggies are driving for a score they need desperately, old Abe will come down off the chair he always sits on—fanny on the seat back, feet on the seat—take another chomp of the unlit cigar he alternately sucks and rolls between his palms until it disintegrates, and walk down the sideline murmuring to his troops, "Hold your left nut, laddies—we need this one."

Oh, sure, Abe can get riled. But the vilest oath he ever musters—with his fist clenched and his thumb in an odd place, on top of his index finger instead of around his knuckles—is "Shistol pot!" which is a spoonerism for *pistol shot*, in case you need a translation. Usually Abe just walks a player away from the group with an arm around the boy's shoulders and quietly says, "Now, you know better 'n that." You know what troubles the fellows most at a moment like this, 15 minutes before kickoff? The thought that they might let Abe down.

All right, let's be honest, not everyone's dying to please the boss, not in any locker room in the world. See number 67, Norman Ashley, sitting third from the left against the back wall? He's in Abe's doghouse for late hits in practice and for tackling quarterback Chuck Curtis so hard one day that Curtis peed blood. Ashley will never play a lick, and he knows it. He'll end up spending four decades in Alaska flying a Piper Super Cub just big enough for him, his rifle, his rod and his hunting dog, searching for places where there are no whistles and no quarterbacks to flatten. And over on the other side, second from your right, that's center Jim Ozee, who started all season, till today. Damn near half a century later, when he's a grandpa tossing raisins to the mockingbird that visits him in his backyard in Fort Worth each day, he'll still remember, "That's despair on my face. I'm offended by Abe at this moment. I couldn't figure why I wasn't starting. I didn't hear anything he said. . . . "

"*. . . wanna thank you fellas. Seniors in this room . . . no need to tell you how I feel 'bout you. You were my first recruitin' class, came in green just like me,* *and accomplished some great things. Now you're 'bout to split up, go your separate ways, and this'll be the game you remember the rest of your days. Life's about to change, laddies. You're never gonna capture this moment again. . . . "*

Two in this room will end up in early coffins when their hearts quit: Dick Finney, on your far right, and John Mitchell, second from your left, the lad inspecting the fingernails he's just chewed. Two other players will lose sons in car accidents, which is worse than a heart attack. Another, Jack Webb, seated in the deep corner just to the left of the youngster holding his chin in his hand, will relish the tension of moments like this so much that he'll become a fighter pilot, only to lose his life when his jet crashes in the Philippines. Two will get rich, then go bankrupt. Allen Garrard, number 84, the guy seated on the floor near the corner, will get multiple sclerosis and draw on moments like this 40 years from now, when his car blows a tire in a rainstorm in the dead of night and he has to hobble painfully on his cane far beyond the 200 feet he's usually able to walk. Of course, Abe himself, when he's in his 70s, will be found draped across his bed by his wife one morning when his ticker quits.

See that fellow on the floor behind Abe, number 53, Joe Williams? Can you tell? A year ago he lost his mom, who attended every game he ever played, in a car accident, and he's worried sick about his dad, sleepwalking awake ever since she died, who's somewhere in the stands high above this room. Here's what Joe will say 42 years from now, when his hair's as white as snow and arthritis has racked his joints with pain and stolen his right hand: "I should've expressed my gratitude to Abe. I'm still living by the principles he taught us. I'm not gonna give in. I'm still coming out of bed swinging even though I might not hit a thing. He guided us through those years. He looked out for us the way our parents presumed he would.

"You know something? Nothing ever again will match the intensity, the passion of moments like this. What it takes to overcome yourself—because if you listen to your body, you'll always be a coward. Don't get me wrong, I love my wife and kids, but I'd give anything to go back. More than who you're looking at now, that guy in the picture, *that's* me. *That's* who I really am."

" . . . HASN'T BEEN an easy road for us this season, laddies. Stubbed our toe real bad, and a lot of folks started calling us a second-rate team. But we didn't roll up in a ball, and by going through what we did and coming to-

gether, we're more a team now 'n we've ever been. . . . "

This is how the boys will recollect Abe's speech four decades later. The coach doesn't dwell on details, but here are the facts: You're listening to a coach who was hung in effigy and made it to the Cotton Bowl in the same season. Right now, as Possum Elenburg, the fellow gnawing his knuckles on your far left, puts it, "Abe's done a rare thing—got all his coons up the same tree." He's got them all ruminating on a season that began with the Horned Frogs as heavy favorites in the Southwest Conference, returning a slew of starters from the nation's sixth-ranked team the year before, busting out to a 3–0 start with a 32–0 blitzing of Kansas, a 41–6 crushing of Arkansas and a 23–6 spanking of Alabama. Next came TCU's blood enemy, Texas A&M, with Bear Bryant at the wheel, the team that had handed the Frogs their only regular-season defeat the year before.

So now it was payback time, a gorgeous Saturday in College Station, the Aggies' stadium jammed and the 3–0 Frogs cross-eyed crazy in their locker room. And what happened? Sometime during the first quarter, all the friction between the two squads was more than the sky could hold, and the ugliest wall of black clouds you ever saw came rolling in from the north. The wind began to howl so hard that flagpoles bent into upside-down L's, and the ref had to put a foot on the ball between plays to keep it from sailing to Mexico. The rain came in sheets so thick that the subs on the sideline couldn't see the starters on the field, and then the rain turned to hail so helmet-drumming heavy that the linemen couldn't hear the signals from the quarterback screeching at their butts. Postpone the game? This is Texas, y'all! This is football!

The Frogs knifed through winds that gusted up to 90 mph, penetrated the A&M two-yard line on three drives behind their All-America running back, Jim Swink—and couldn't get it in! On one series Swink crossed the goal line twice—the Frogs had the film to prove it—but either the refs couldn't see or it was too slippery to get a good grip on your left nut in a monsoon. TCU finally scored in the third quarter but missed the extra point, and the Aggies stole the game with a fourth-quarter touchdown, 7–6.

Ever drive a car into the exit of a drive-in theater when you were 16, not knowing about those metal teeth? That's the sound that leaked out of the Froggies after that. Miami rocked them 14–0 the next week, Baylor scared the daylights out of them before succumbing 7–6, and then Texas Tech, a team that didn't belong in the same county with the Frogs, pasted them 21–7. Another ferocious storm fell on the team bus on the way home from Lubbock, and the Frogs crawled through it, wondering if their senior-laden squad had lost focus, become more concerned with the honeys they were fixing to marry and the careers they were fixing to start than with the mission at hand.

Back on campus, there dangled poor Abe from a rope lashed to a tree not far from the athletic dorm, brown hat and sport coat over a pillow head and sheet body. It was a startling sight at a university that many players had chosen because it had the homey feel of a big high school, a cow-town college where guys felt at home wearing cowboy hats and boots, or jeans rolled up at the cuffs and penny loafers. Just like that, the dispirited Frogs had a cause. Their starting quarterback, Chuck Curtis—that's him, number 46, sitting two to the left of Abe—along with end O'Day Williams and backup end Neil Hoskins, the youngster two to the left of Curtis, with his chin in his hand, went out to do a little rectifyin'. Curtis slashed down the effigy with a pocket knife, then led his mates, rumor by rumor, to the perpetrator, who turned tail after a little shouting and shoving. Two days later the Frogs called a players-only meeting at the dining hall, where the subs vented their frustration over lack of playing time, and Cotton Eye Joe Williams, the captain, promised to take their beef to Abe. The players all agreed that an attack on Abe was like an attack on their daddies, and they closed ranks.

To Cotton Eye's suggestion that the second fiddlers fiddle more, Abe said, Great idea. To the notion that the boys were steamed about the hanging effigy, Abe said, Couldn't've been me—I'm a lot better lookin' than that. To the proposition that the Froggies might still make it to the Cotton Bowl (A&M had been hit with NCAA sanctions for recruiting violations and wouldn't be eligible), Abe said, Let's go make hay. That's what the Frogs did, slapping Texas in the face 46–0, elbowing a ripsnorting Rice squad by three and thumping SMU 21–6 to finish 7–3, second to A&M, and scoop up the Aggies' fumbled Cotton Bowl bid. Then came a month to heal and prepare, a half-hour Greyhound bus ride to Dallas a few days before the big one, the formal dance and then the downtown parade on the fire engine, eyeing that big load on the other fire truck, the one who scored a record-breaking 43 points against Colgate: Jim Brown.

FINALLY ALL the buildup is over. The Southwest Conference princess-
es in convertibles and the high-stepping high school bands are drumming
up one last buzz among the 68,000 waiting outside the locker room. But
here inside there's only quiet, broken by a soft sob just outside the frame,
from the Frogs' All-America lineman Norman Hamilton—who'll swear
decades later that no matter what his teammates recollect, he didn't cry
before games.

Quiet, broken by the calm drawl of Honest Abe. Whose calm is a lie, so
keep your eye on him, because any minute he might just sneak off to the
john and throw up. That's what Virgil Miller—he's number 18, the little
guy in the dark corner with his head down—will find Abe doing before a
game a few years later, when Virgil returns to visit the coach. "Ever get
nervous like that?" Abe will ask Virgil. It's safe, since Virgil has graduated
and gone.

It's almost like going to church, being here, isn't it? Nope, it's more religious than church, because half of the people here aren't faking it. Maybe
folks who never played can't understand how you can be 15 minutes from
tearing somebody's head off, 15 seconds from vomiting and a half inch
from God, all at the same time. But Chuck Curtis knows. Forty-two years
from now, when this picture is placed under his eyes, he'll say, "Look at
us. Compared to players today? We weren't great athletes. But we were a
team from top to bottom, all giving entire respect to our leader and wanting the same thing wholeheartedly. A sincere group of young men. It'd take
a miracle to get the feeling we had in that moment again. With that attitude,
there's not a sin that's not erased." When he looks up, there will be tears
in his eyes.

Henry B. (Doc) Hardt, he'd understand. He's the old-timer wearing his
brown Sunday best and that purple-and-white ribbon on his left arm, so lost
in his meditation that he doesn't know that his pants leg is climbing up
his calf and that three decades have vanished since he last suited up for a
football game—he'd snatch a helmet and storm through that door if Abe
would just say the word. That's reverence, the look of a man with four
Methodist minister brothers and a missionary sister. Doc's the head of the
TCU chemistry department and the Frogs' NCAA faculty representative,
the man who makes sure the flunkers aren't playing and the boosters aren't
paying, and he's so good at it that he'll become president of the NCAA a

few years after this game. Huge hands, grip like a vise and a kind word for everyone, even when he hobbles on a cane to Frogs games a quarter century later. Nice to know he'll make it to 90.

But you need to meet the rest of the boys. Just behind Doc's left shoulder is Mr. Clean: Willard McClung, the quiet assistant to renowned trainer Elmer Brown. Brown's busy right now shooting up guard Vernon Uecker's ankle with novocaine, but Willard would be glad to go fetch a glass of Elmer's concoction for those whose steak and eggs are about to come up, a cocktail the boys call "the green s---." Trouble is, Elmer's green s--- usually comes up along with everything else.

Willard's the only man here who never played, the only one not crawled inside himself—no coincidence there. His ankles were too weak for him to play ball, but he was determined to jimmy his way into moments like this, so he climbed aboard a train his senior year of high school, a fuzzy-cheeked kid from Minden, La., and rode all day to reach the National Trainers' Convention, in Kansas City. Trainers were so thrilled to see a kid show up that Elmer Brown finagled him a scholarship at TCU.

That's Frankie Hyde just behind Doc Hardt's right shoulder, the blond studying the hairs on his left calf. He's the Frogs' scout-team quarterback and an all-around good guy. Doesn't know that he'll hurt his shoulder a few months from now in spring training, that he'll never suit up for a football game again. Doesn't know that Abe's steering his rudder, that he'll end up coaching football just like six of the 17 players in the picture. That he'll end up guiding wave after wave of teenage boys through this moment, some who'll start chattering like monkeys, some who'll go quieter than the dead, some who'll slam their shoulder pads into lockers and poles, some who'll pray like a priest on his third cup of coffee, some who'll get too sick to play. Take it from Frankie: "People who don't experience this don't know themselves like they should."

Or take it from Hunter Enis, the handsome raven-haired boy leaning forward in the dark corner, the one who'll make a bundle in oil: "Sure, there's times in business when you'll work together with a group of men to meet a goal. But that's not about anything as important as this. It's just about money."

Or Possum Elenburg, the sub on the far left, sitting there thinking, Heck, yes, it'd be nice to get in and quarterback a few plays on national TV, but heck, no, I don't want to have to play defense and risk getting burned deep like I did against Texas Tech. Forty-two years later, here's Possum: "This is reality stripped to its nakedness. There's no place to hide. Time is standing still. It's funny, but all your life people tell you that football's just a game, that so many things more important will happen to you in life that'll make sports seem insignificant." Listen to Possum. He's a man who came within a quarter inch of losing his life in '60 when an oil rig crashed into his skull and paralyzed his right side for a year, a man who lost a fortune overnight when oil prices crashed on his head two decades later. "But it's not true, what people tell ya," he says. "I'm fixing to be tested in this moment, and I'm gonna be tested again and again in my life, and I'm gonna get nervous and wonder about myself every single time. Your priorities as a kid are just as important to you as your priorities as a 60-year-old man, because all your aspirations and goals are on the line. At any age, each thing that's important to you . . . is important to you, and each fight needs to be fought with every effort."

WE'RE LOOKING at a roomful of bladders fixing to bust, but it's just a hoax—any doctor could explain the phenomenon. It's just anxiety sending a surge of adrenaline to the nerve endings in the bladder, causing it to tighten and creating the feeling that you gotta go. These boys are like a pack of hunting dogs spraying all over the place just before the hunt, only dogs are lucky enough not to have all those laces and hip pads and jockstraps to fumble with.

"... *don't need to remind you, laddies, what happened to us in the Cotton Bowl last year, and what that felt like. Not many folks in life get a second chance, but we've got it right here, today . . . the chance to redeem ourselves . . . .*"

Redemption. That's all that thumps through the hearts and heads of two players who happen to be sitting elbow to elbow: Chuck Curtis and, on his right, Harold (Toad) Pollard, number 16, with the dirty-blond crew cut and the eye black. See, Toad's missed extra point was the margin of defeat in TCU's 14–13 Cotton Bowl loss to Mississippi last year. And Toad's missed extra point in the monsoon at A&M cost the Frogs that 7–6 heartache. Before you get the idea that Toad's a lost cause, you need to know that he led the nation's kickers in scoring last season and that his nickname is Abe's bungled version of Toad's true moniker, the Golden Toe. But ever since that wide-right boot in the Cotton Bowl, Toad has walked around imagining that the entire campus is thinking or saying, "There goes the guy who missed the extra point." Every morning last summer, before his 3-to-11 shift as a roughneck in the oil fields, he toted a tee to a high school field and kicked 40 through the pipes, alone, to prepare for his redemption. "It's a lot more hurt," he'll admit years later, "than a person would realize." Especially since Toad always seems to be clowning, doing that dead-on Donald Duck imitation. But right now he's more nervous than he's ever been, trying to swallow back the notion that he could bungle another critical extra point and be stuck with seeing himself in the mirror every time his hair needs combing the rest of his life.

It's a double-wide hot seat over there, cooking Chuck Curtis's fanny too. Because it was in this very room, at this very moment at the Cotton Bowl last year, that Abe concluded his pregame talk by reminding Chuck-a-luck, as he was fond of calling his quarterback, that he was absolutely *not* to run back the kickoff, that he was to pitch it back to Swink. But Chuck-a-luck, who believed fiercely in his ability to perform or charm his way out of any fix, walked out of this room and fielded that kickoff on the run, down near his shins, and decided that all that forward momentum shouldn't be wasted on a backward lateral, and actually traveled a few yards before—*crunch!*—he took a lick that cracked three ribs and partially dislocated his shoulder, and the Frogs' star quarterback was gone on the game's first play.

Of course, Dick Finney, the backup quarterback—that's him on your farthest right, the one who used to call audibles with fruits instead of numbers ("Apples! Oranges! *Bananas!*")—came trotting into the huddle with that bird-eating grin of his and declared, "Have no fear, Finney's here." But fear truly was in order, because although Diamond Dick ran like a jackrabbit, he also passed like one, and Ole Miss stacked everybody but the trombone players on the line to create a terrible constipation.

Imagine what that did to Chuck Curtis, a strapping 6' 4", 200-pound All-Conference signal-caller, a Pentecostal preacher's son who could sell a bikini to an Eskimo. In a few years he'll be buying cattle like crazy, owning a bank, winning three state championships as a high school coach and selling automobiles to boot, joking with a former Frogs teammate who protests that he can't afford to pay for a car, "Hey, ol' buddy, I didn't ask you to pay for a car—I just wanna sell you a car." In the '70s, when he comes up on charges of making false statements on bank-loan applications, there will be preachers preaching in his favor on the courthouse steps, alongside his Jacksboro High football team, cheerleaders and band, all crooning the school's alma mater, and he'll get off with a $500 fine. But no amount of preaching or singing or selling can hide the fact that Chuck-a-luck's ego, more than Toad's blown extra point, cost his teammates the '56 Cotton Bowl, and that he'll have to wear that around like a stained pair of chaps for the rest of his life . . . unless, in about 10 minutes, he can maneuver the Frogs past Jim Brown.

NOW TURN around. It's long past time you met Marvin Newman, the well-groomed fellow with the side of his snout pressed against that camera. Nearly forgot about him, he's been so quiet, but none of this would've been possible without him. Funny guy, Marvin: your classic pushy New Yorker when there's something he really wants, but when what he really wants is to disappear into the woodwork—presto, Marvin's a mouse. You can barely hear the click of that Leica he's pointing toward Abe.

He can't use a flash—that would be like taking a hammer to a moment like this. So he has to spread his legs, brace his knees, lock his elbows against his sides and hold his breath to keep that camera stone still. He has to become the tripod, because the quarter second that the shutter needs to be open to drink in enough light is enough to turn Chuck-a-luck and Toad and Buddy and Joe into a purple smear if Marvin's paws move even a hair. Doesn't hurt that he's only 29, because the hands won't let you do that at, say, 59. Doesn't hurt that he rarely drinks, either, because more than a few magazine shooters would still have the shakes at 10 minutes to one in the afternoon on New Year's Day.

He's a Bronx kid, a baker's only son who knew at 19 that he wasn't going to keep burying his arms to the elbows in a wooden vat of rye dough, wasn't going to do what his father and grandfather and great-grandfather had done, even if his old man nearly blew a fuse when that first $90 camera was delivered to the door. Marvin was too brainy, having jumped two grades before he finished high school, and too hungry for something he couldn't even give a name to, so he surprised his old man again, telling him he'd go to Chicago and study art at the Illinois Institute of Technology on his own dime, not that he owned one. Crawled right out on the limb and then had to prove to his dad that he could dance on it.

Who knows, maybe that's why he lies in hotel beds for hours, boiling with plans A, B, C and Z on the night before an assignment, brainstorming about how to come home with an image nobody else would have thought of. Maybe that's why his gut's already working on that ulcer. Could be why he hangs around the photo department at SPORTS ILLUSTRATED, promoting ideas that might snag him a color spread worth $600, till finally the photo editor nods, or maybe his head just sags in exhausted surrender. See, Marvin was one of the first to figure this out: If you're technically sound and willing to invest in the best equipment on the shelf—all those long lenses and motor drives just coming out—and if you played some ball and can anticipate where the next play might go, you're a hundred miles ahead of the posse of freelancers dying to land an assignment from SI.

But a tack-sharp action shot won't be enough to satisfy Marvin. He has to come up with something at this Cotton Bowl as heart-touching as the picture he nailed at last year's, that classic shot of Ole Miss's Billy Kinnard coming off the field after beating TCU by one point and planting a kiss on Ole Miss cheerleader Kay Kinnard, who just happened to be his new bride. So, recollecting from last New Year's Day how mouthwatering the light was in that locker room, Marvin made it his first item of business when he saw Abe in Dallas to start schmoozing, start persuading Abe how discreet he'd be, how lickety-split he'd get in and get out, and how much his boss was counting on him . . . so could he *please* slip into the Frogs' locker room just before kickoff? Heck, Abe didn't need schmoozing. *Sure, Marvin! Why not drop by at halftime too?*

Guarantee you, Marvin can smell and taste his own pregame heebie-jeebies from that year he played end on the Brooklyn College football team at a preposterous 125 pounds, and from all those times just before he ran the 800 when he'd start hacking so much that he even tried sucking on a pebble, and he cut a deal with his gut not to bring up breakfast and lunch until he was just past the finish line, first more often than not.

Sure, he'll take snaps more famous than this. He'll bag that black-and-white shot of the World Series-winning homer soaring off Bill Mazeroski's bat as the scoreboard shows all the pertinent facts—3:36 p.m, ninth inning, score tied—of Game 7 between the Pittsburgh Pirates and the New York Yankees in 1960. He'll catch eyes all over the country with his picture of the newly widowed Jackie Kennedy clutching John-John's hand as they watch JFK's coffin go by. But 40-plus years after this New Year's Day in Dallas, long after his knees and hips have grown weary of all the kneeling and contorting and camera-bag banging, long after he's left sports photography to specialize in travel and city-skyline shots, and even after his pictures have been exhibited in all sorts of important places, he'll remember this picture almost as if he took it yesterday.

"They completely forgot about me," he'll say, sitting over the photo in his Manhattan apartment at age 71. "When photography works well, you can go inside the psyche of the people in the picture. You can see beyond the moment. I always loved this picture. I knew it was special. There hadn't been many photographs taken inside locker rooms, so I knew I was privileged. I couldn't have been standing more than 10 feet from Abe Martin. . . . "

" . . . *but we're not gonna shut down Jim Brown, boys. Not with one tackler. We're gonna have to swarm him. We'll slow him down. We'll go right at him when we've got the ball. He's not a great defensive player. We'll tire him out. We won't stop him. We'll outscore him. This game can put us right back where we belong, with the best teams in the country. Look inside yourselves and ask, Do I really want it? If you do, laddies, the goose hangs high. Now let's have the prayer.*"

SOME OF you might not quite grasp what's sitting and waiting for the Frogs in the room down the hall. Jim Brown stands 6' 2" and weighs 225 pounds, which is at least 35 pounds more than the average halfback of his day, not to mention 22 pounds heavier than the average player on the biggest line in the country, Notre Dame's. He runs 100 yards in 10 seconds flat, high-jumps 6' 3", hurls the discus 155 feet and once won six events for Syracuse in a track meet, which gave him the notion that it might be fun to enter the national decathlon championship, which he did on 10 days' practice and placed fifth. He scored 33 in a Syracuse basketball game and will be drafted by the NBA's Syracuse Nationals, not bad for a fellow who at the time was considered to have been the greatest lacrosse player in U.S. history. He's just finishing up a senior season in which he averaged 6.2 yards per carry, and he will average a record 5.2 yards per carry for the Cleveland Browns over the next nine years, leading the NFL in rushing in eight of those, before he'll hang it up, as

MVP, at age 30. Forgive me if you knew all that, but some legends get so large, the particulars get lost.

Now, some of the Frogs are deeply worried about Brown. Others have been fooled by the three game films they've seen, because Brown looks slower on celluloid than he does when you're reaching for his heels. Still others think he's very good, but he can't possibly be better than John David Crow of Texas A&M.

Brown's sitting very still and silent right now. He's the sort of man who contains a lot more than he lets out, till he steps on the field, and maybe some of what he's holding in has to do with a question that's struck you already, looking around the TCU locker room: Where are all the black folks? There's not one playing football in the Southwest Conference, and there won't be one on scholarship till nine years down the road, after Chuck Curtis becomes an SMU assistant coach and recruits Jerry Levias. In fact, it was only two years before this that the first blacks played in TCU's stadium, when Penn State brought Lenny Moore and Rosey Grier to town and they had to sleep at a motel way out on Jacksboro Highway, because the team couldn't find a downtown Fort Worth hotel that would have them.

That wasn't going to happen to Brown. He decided before the Orangemen arrived in Dallas that he'd refuse to be separated from his teammates, but it hadn't come to that. Syracuse was staying in a hotel on the edge of Dallas that accepted the whole squad.

Sure, Brown's thoughts are fixed on football right now, 15 minutes before kickoff, but it would be a lie to say that another question isn't nibbling on his mind: What's going to happen when he's circled by nearly 70,000 white Texans, some of them wearing cleats? Abe hasn't said a thing to his boys about color. Before the game against Moore and Grier in '54, all he said was, "They're darn good football players, so it wouldn't make much sense to say something to get 'em mad."

Brown will never be the sort to live on the fumes of his past, or reminisce much. But even at 63, when he's running across America directing Amer-I-Can—an organization he founded to tackle gang problems and help prisoners get ready for life outside the walls—some of what coursed through him in that Cotton Bowl locker room will still be with him.

"I was concerned how their players would carry themselves, if there'd be any epithets," he'll say. "But I wasn't going to make that any kind of extra motive, or try to prove something. Racism is sickness, and I'm not gonna prove something to sickness. I was a performer with my own standards, and living up to them was all I worried about. For me, the time just before a game was always tense, like going to war without death. I always felt humbled. It's a very spiritual moment. I'd try to go into a pure state. No negative thoughts, even toward the other team. No rah-rah, because rah-rah's for show. Your butt's on the line, and you either stand up and deal with it, or . . . or you can't. You become a very difficult opponent for anyone or anything when you know that you can."

LET ME tell you what happened that day, right after Marvin's last click. Chuck Curtis went wild. He called a run-pitch sprint-out series that no one expected from a drop-back quarterback without much foot speed, and he threw two touchdown passes to stake the Frogs to a 14–0 lead.

Then it was Brown's turn. The tip that TCU coaches had passed on to the Frogs after studying film—that just before the snap Brown leaned in the direction he was about to go—was accurate, but it wasn't worth a Chinese nickel. As Brown carried a couple of more Frogs for rides, Abe spun toward his boys on the sideline and nearly swallowed his cigar, then howled, "Shistol pot! Can't anybody tackle him?"

Against Brown, everything the Frogs had learned about hitting a man in the thighs and wrapping him up went down the sewer—there was just too much power there. First tackler to reach him had to hit him high, delay him for a second, take some of the forward momentum out of those thighs, then wait for reinforcements to hit him low.

Brown bashed in from the two for Syracuse's first touchdown, kicked the extra point, then hurled a 20-yard pass that set up his own four-yard touchdown run and booted another point after to tie the ball game 14–14 just before intermission. Lonnie Leatherman, a backup end for the Frogs, would shake his head from here to the year 2000, yelping, "He ran through the whole stinkin' team! That man was bad to the bone! He was unbelievable! These are great football players, and they couldn't tackle him. Norman Hamilton was an All-America and couldn't tackle him."

A savage moment came early in the second half. Syracuse was on the TCU 40 and rolling—Brown had just made another first down on a fourth-down plunge—when Buddy Dike, with his battered kidney, threw caution to the wind. He hit Brown head-on, producing a sound Hamilton would never forget. "Like thunder," he'd recall. "Never heard a sound that loud from two men colliding. I thought, How can they ever get up?"

Dike's face mask snapped in two, the pigskin burst from Brown's grasp and TCU recovered it. Brown would not miss a play. The inspired Froggies again targeted Brown when he was on defense, flooding his side of the field with three receivers. Years later Leatherman would make no bones about it. "Brown was horrible on defense," he'd say. Joe Williams would be a trifle kinder: "Maybe their coaches didn't want to offend him by teaching him defense."

Curtis closed a drive by sweeping around the left end for a score, and Jim Swink found paydirt for the Frogs a few minutes later. Toad Pollard stepped on the field for the extra point. He was 3 for 3, and his side was up 27–14, but with nearly 12 minutes left and Brown yet to be corralled, the kicker's gut quivered with evil memories. To Jim Ozee, finally getting a few minutes at center, it seemed like eternity between his snap and the thud of Toad's toe against the ball. "What took you so long?" Ozee demanded seconds after the kick sailed true.

"I wanted to be sure," Toad said, breathing heavily—as if he knew that Brown would rip off a 46-yard return on the kickoff, then slam in from the one and bust open Toad's lip a few moments later. As if he knew that Syracuse would roar right down the field on its next possession, finally figuring a way to reach the end zone without Brown, on a touchdown pass with 1:16 left. As if he knew that Chico Mendoza, the lone Mexican-American on the Frogs' roster, would storm in from right end just after Syracuse's third touchdown and block Brown's point-after try, making the team that lost by one extra point in the Cotton Bowl in 1956 the winner by one extra point in 1957, by a score of 28–27. "All those white boys out there," Leatherman would point out, "and the Mexican and the black were the key players."

Brown would finish with 132 yards on 26 carries, three kickoff returns for 96 more yards, three extra points, the whole country's admiration . . . and no slurs. "They were nice human beings," he'd say of the Frogs. But Chuck-a-luck, who finished 12 of 15 through the air, would see Brown speak at the University of Texas–Arlington years later and leave sniffing that "he sounded like one of those Black Panthers."

Toad would remember "floating" at the postgame banquet, thinking he was saved from a lifetime of negative thoughts, but in his 60s that extra point he missed in the '56 Cotton Bowl would still occupy his mind more than the four he made in '57, and every kick he watched on TV would make his foot twitch up, as if the kick were his.

TCU? The Frogs wouldn't win another bowl game for 41 years. The rules changed on Abe: Free substitution and the end of the two-way player meant that a college needed at least 22 studs, and that a small school with a scrawny budget and even less national TV exposure had almost no prayer, no matter how sincere its players were 15 minutes before kickoff. When Abe quit nine years later, people said the game had passed him by.

Come 1999, that bare locker room would no longer be a locker room, that Southwest Conference would no longer exist, and that New Year's Day game would be known as the Southwestern Bell Cotton Bowl Classic.

One last thing. There's a saying Texans used to share about men in locker rooms awaiting battle, and pardon my French, but it goes like this: Brave men piss, cowards s---.

Which were you? Which was I? Guess I just can't walk out of this picture without asking questions like that. But I'll shut up now, in case you want to go back and catch Chuck-a-luck going watery-eyed as he leads the team prayer. Hurry, though. It's going hard on nine minutes to one.

| | | | | |

Barry's Back

BY SALLY JENKINS

Five years after Oklahoma forced out Barry Switzer in an ugly swirl of scandal,
he was suddenly hired to coach the world-champion Dallas Cowboys.

BARRY SWITZER LOOKED LIKE A MAN WHO HAD JUST been pulled from the wreckage of his own life. He had slept about five hours in the previous 72. He was sitting last Thursday night in Norman, Okla., at Othello's restaurant, a low building radiating five shades of neon. Othello's is the home of the Table of Truth, a red Leatherette booth in which Switzer has dined nearly every night for 10 years. A tiny brass plaque adorns the wall of the booth, placed there in Switzer's honor. It says, OLD COACHES NEVER DIE, THEY JUST FORGET THE SCORE.

Switzer had driven three hours from Dallas at the end of his first full day as the Dallas Cowboys' coach. At Othello's a party of 30 was gathered around a banquet table for a lobster dinner prepared by the restaurant's owner and Switzer's good friend, Pasquale Benso. Surrounding Switzer were family and friends wearing T-shirts in Cowboy blue and gray. BARRY'S BACK, they read.

That's right. Switzer, 56, the banished king of college football, the guy with the image tarnished nearly black, is the new conservator of America's

Team. During the March 30 news conference at the Cowboys' Valley Ranch complex announcing his appointment, Switzer held forth like a carnival barker. But a moment after the session ended he stood in a hallway, seemingly dazed by the week's events. "I feel like I just won the lottery," he said. "Pinch me."

The day before, Cowboy owner Jerry Jones had accepted the resignation of Jimmy Johnson, the coach who had guided his team to two straight Super Bowl wins, and replaced him with Switzer. Out of coaching since his forced resignation from Oklahoma in 1989, Switzer suddenly had a five-year contract worth a reported $1 million annually to take a job that few thought he could handle. This was a man whose coaching prospects had appeared to be nonexistent. To NCAA schools he is a pariah for having presided over one of the college game's most unsavory programs, and his favored brand of offense, the wishbone, made him ill-suited to coach a pro team. "I know people doubt it," Switzer says. "But let me tell you, I can do this."

Switzer went right to work, striding the halls of the Cowboys' office complex, doing his best to win over the skeptics with his considerable charm. Switzer assured all within earshot that the Dallas offense would rest in the hands of new coordinator Ernie Zampese, Johnson's last hire. Switzer ran into All-Pro wideout Michael Irvin, who in the wake of Johnson's resignation had declared that he wouldn't play for Switzer. "Hey, Michael, who you going to play for?" Switzer boomed, grabbing Irvin's hand. "Don't worry, I won't make you throw any of those crackback blocks. I'll get you the ball." Irvin, disarmed, winked at Switzer and promised to come by to get acquainted.

The trouble with getting to know Switzer is that there are at least two of him. His penchant for self-destructive behavior is matched by a genius for survival. Switzer has been accused of many things and has done quite a few of them.

The son of a Crossett, Ark., bootlegger who did time in prison and a mother who committed suicide in 1972, Switzer got to the University of Arkansas on a football scholarship. Though he had never been a head coach, he succeeded Chuck Fairbanks at Oklahoma in 1973 and went on to win three national championships, amassing 157 victories in 16 seasons. While the Big Eight slowly integrated its teams in the mid- and late '60s,

Switzer eagerly recruited black players, and he gave several blacks an opportunity to coach as his assistants. At the same time he thumbed his nose at the NCAA, an organization he considered insensitive in its treatment of athletes, especially those from poor backgrounds, and his program was regarded as one of college football's outlaws.

"The best team money could buy, right?" Switzer says, groaning and laughing at the same time. "Look, I never bought players. It didn't work that way. I took care of them when they were there and so did my assistant coaches, probably. I had a hard time saying no to players. But I never bought them. I didn't have to."

Switzer survived a brush with the Securities and Exchange Commission, which in 1983 investigated and subsequently exonerated him in connection with an insider-trading scheme. However, Switzer resigned as the Sooners' coach in June '89 after a series of events that included a shooting and a gang rape in the athletic dormitory and the arrest of his starting quarterback, Charles Thompson, for selling cocaine. Six months earlier the program had been placed on probation for violations that included players' receiving cars and cash.

Though reviled by his critics, Switzer has inspired loyalty in most of his former players and associates, among them Cowboys quarterback Troy Aikman, who started for Switzer at Oklahoma in 1985 before breaking his ankle against Johnson's Miami Hurricanes in the season's fourth game. Later that year Aikman and Switzer agreed that, as a dropback passer, Aikman was miscast at Oklahoma, and Switzer called UCLA coach Terry Donahue on the quarterback's behalf. Last week Aikman was a valuable public ally for his past and present coach. "I feel like I'm stuck in *Groundhog Day*," he said.

People who know Switzer contend that he is quieter these days than he was as Oklahoma's coach. He says that he has given up red meat and hard liquor, preferring pasta and red wine. He has made several visits to Italy in recent years with Benso, whose family is from the town of Mola di Bari on the Adriatic coast, and with his children: Greg, 25, a former Arkansas linebacker who is now in graduate school there studying to be a concert pianist ("He can bench-press a piano, but he'd rather play it," says his father); Kathy Rutz, 24, an Oklahoma senior who has studied in Rome and lived with her husband for a year in Singapore; and Doug, 21, an aspiring quarterback at Missouri Southern who recently applied for a White House internship. Divorced since 1981, Switzer is the steady companion of Becky Buwick, the women's gymnastics coach at Oklahoma.

In his five years away from coaching, Switzer was involved in several businesses, including a meat-and-produce packaging company, a group of physical rehabilitation centers, a couple of restaurants and an insurance company. He also served as a front man in failed negotiations to bring an Arena Football League team to Oklahoma City and exerted considerable effort to persuade the Comanche, Creek and Seminole Indian tribes in Oklahoma to build gaming facilities on their land, though he met with little success.

Switzer was well-off financially, but Jones's first phone call to him about the Cowboys job was like a bucket of water to a thirsty man. "I needed it," Switzer says. "Not to prove something. I needed it because I missed coaching. I didn't know how much until the last few days."

It is not surprising that Jones called upon Switzer, whom Jones has known since his college days at Arkansas. In 1961 Switzer was a young Razorback assistant supervising freshman recruits, including Jones and Johnson, who went on to become roommates and teammates on the '64 national championship team.

While Jones headed off to make millions in oil and gas, Switzer and Johnson moved through the college coaching ranks, often recommending each other for jobs. From 1970 to '72 Switzer and Johnson served at Oklahoma under Fairbanks, along with yet another Arkansan, Larry Lacewell, who is currently the Cowboys' director of college scouting. Today, Johnson's former wife, Linda Kay, and Switzer's ex, Kay, remain close friends, but not all the personal and professional entanglements of the Arkansas clan have been so pleasant. Lacewell left Oklahoma in 1977 after his wife, Criss, became involved with Switzer. "I won't skirt the issue; I got mad and left," says Lacewell. "But it was blown out of proportion; it wasn't what people thought." After a separation, the Lacewells reconciled, but Lacewell told one Cowboy that the idea of working with Switzer again had put a knot in his stomach.

Yet when Jones asked for Lacewell's opinion of Switzer, Lacewell's recommendation was instrumental in bringing Switzer to Dallas. "I don't think he ever set out to be a bad guy," Lacewell says. "He doesn't get up saying, 'I'm going to do something bad today.' He falls into a trap and does-n't know how to get out of it. Maybe he should have handled a lot of things differently, but he has handled the most important thing superbly, and that's his relationships with his players."

For his part, Switzer says, "I wouldn't be here if it wasn't for Larry."

Jones said that his first phone call to Switzer was on March 28, six days after the incident at the NFL owners' meeting that irreparably damaged the Jones-Johnson partnership. Switzer casually contradicted his new boss, saying it was around March 24. As Switzer lay on his couch at home, Jones called and said, "Are you interested in coaching again, and are you interested in coaching the Cowboys?" The answer was an emphatic yes.

Only Switzer's children and a couple of confidants, including his lawyer, Larry Derryberry, knew of his call from Jones. At one point Derryberry called Kathy, who was keeping a vigil at her father's duplex apartment. "How's he doing?" Derryberry asked. "He needs to chill out," she replied.

At 10:30 a.m. on Tuesday the 29th, Switzer's phone rang again. He was in the shower. He stood dripping, a towel wrapped around him, as Jones of-fered him the job. The towel fell off. "I was standing there buck naked," Switzer says. Jones asked him to come to Dallas for negotiations. Switzer chatted with Jones for another minute and then hung up. "I won the lottery," he told Kathy.

Switzer and Jones and their lawyers met at the home of a friend of Jones's in Plano, Texas. Derryberry began the negotiations by telling Jones, "If this is a take-it-or-leave-it deal, he'll take it." The lawyers worked until 2:30 a.m. At that point Switzer and Derryberry sat alone for a while, and Switzer suddenly turned contemplative. "I don't know that I deserve this," he said. Twelve hours later he faced a blaze of TV lights as the new Cowboys coach.

It was at the end of the next day that Switzer drove back across the Red River for his farewell party at Othello's. Over the restaurant, above the neon, a new sign in blue lettering had been raised. It said, HOME OF BARRY SWITZER, COACH OF THE DALLAS COWBOYS. Inside, Benso was talking on the phone. "So," he was saying, "you want Super Bowl tickets?"

| | | | | |

The Toughest Coach
There Ever Was

BY FRANK DEFORD

Bull Sullivan drove his players to astonishing extremes,
molding generations of boys into men while creating a legend
that transcends the tiny place where he lived and worked.

OBERT VICTOR SULLIVAN, WHOM YOU'VE SURELY
never heard of, was the toughest coach of them all. He
was so tough he had to have two tough nicknames, Bull
and Cyclone, and his name was usually recorded this way:
Coach Bob "Bull" "Cyclone" Sullivan or Coach Bob (Bull) (Cyclone) Sullivan.
Also, at times he was known as Big Bob or Shotgun. He was the most uncommon of men, and yet he remains utterly representative of a time that has
vanished, from the gridiron and from these United States.

Coach Bob "Bull" (Cyclone) Sullivan was a legend in his place. That place
was Scooba, Mississippi, in Kemper County, hard by the Alabama line, hard
to the rear of everywhere else. He was the football coach there, for East
Mississippi Junior College, ruling this, his dominion, for most of the '50s and
'60s with a passing attack that was a quarter-century ahead of its time and
a kind of discipline that was on its last legs. He was the very paradigm of that
singular American figure, the coach—*corch*, as they say in backwater Dixie—

who loved his boys as he dominated them, drove off the weak and molded the survivors, making the game of football an equivalency test for life.

Bull Cyclone had spent his own years struggling through a hungry childhood before fighting as a Marine and then coming home to raise a family and till a tiny plot of American soil. Once that would have meant working 40 acres with a mule and a plow. What Bull Cyclone turned was a parcel of earth 100 yards long and about half as wide, scratching out boys as his crop. "There are two reasons people play football," he was heard to declare. "One is love of the game. The other is out of fear. I like the second reason a helluva lot better."

RANDALL BRADBERRY, who is now the football coach at East Mississippi—most people just call it Scooba—was a quarterback there in 1967. One day a Buckeye jet trainer from the nearby Meridian Naval Auxiliary Air Station went out of control. The pilot bailed out, and the empty plane winged in dead over the campus, missing the boys' dorm by 40 feet before plowing into the ground, miraculously doing no damage to edifice or person, except for muddying N.J. Smith, an agriculture teacher, whose outdoor laboratory—"Mr. Smith's pasture"—abutted the football practice field. But what a God-awful noise! Bradberry heard the jet skim over and then explode. "The only thing that crossed through my mind was that the Russians were attacking us," he recalls, "and that they had decided they had to go after corch Sullivan first. I mean that."

Except possibly for the story about how he made his team scrimmage in a pond full of man-eating alligators, none of the tales about Sullivan have been exaggerated. "I mean, everything you hear is true," says Joe Bradshaw, who played guard for him in the early '50s. Bull Cyclone did sometimes run scrimmages in the pond, except the only gator certified to have been in it was an itty-bitty one the coach's family had brought back from Florida as a souvenir. And maybe it did grow up.

Few of the stories were written down. Instead, as if from some other age, an oral history of the coach developed, and whenever old players or other Scooba minstrels gathered, they would share Bull Cyclone stores, telling the same ones over and over, word for word, liturgically, as the wives drifted to the corners and shook their heads. Nobody even knows how many games Bull Cyclone won, although the best detective effort puts his record at 97-62-3. That was over the sixteen seasons, his life's work. However, he never had any real fame outside of Scooba and environs, he never won a national championship, never even won a Mississippi Junior College Association title, and he was too ornery, too cussed independent, for any big school to take a chance on him.

A lot of folks recall that Bear Bryant himself was on record, way back when, as saying he wasn't near so tough as Bull Cyclone. As early as 1959, Jim Minter, now the editor of *The Atlanta Constitution* and *The Atlanta Journal*, wrote in fascination about the growing Scooba fable. Minter had heard some coaches talking about tough. Their opinion, wrote Minter, was that Wally Butts, "The Little Spartan . . . was left at the gate . . . Bear Bryant failed to win, place or show . . . General Bob Neyland was not even mentioned." Instead, when it came to old-fashioned tough, "without dissent . . . Shotgun Sullivan." And Minter's story went on: " 'I can tell you one thing,' offered one college coach who has seen Shotgun Sullivan in action. 'If you get a boy who has survived him for two years, I can guarantee he will make your team.' "

Though many football people acclaimed him as a genius, and everyone accepted him as a man of integrity, no one would dare hire him in the big time, because Bull Cyclone sure as shooting wasn't going to be a football *assistant* for any mother's son. It's apparently true that Norm Van Brocklin, an old pal of his, did once ask him to take over the Atlanta Falcons' offense when Van Brocklin was head coach, but Bull Cyclone declined, saying, "Now, Norm, why should I come up there and work for you when I already know more football than you do?" So he stayed in Scooba, eking out a living for his family, hunting and fishing, developing offenses that big-city coaches would make fashionable a generation later, and driving his players, whom he tricked out in skull-and-crossbones helmets and short-sleeved jerseys he designed himself. The shirts were known as star jerseys because below the black shoulder trim and above the numerals, there across the chest, were arrayed five stars. As far as anybody knew, no one, not even his wife and children, had any idea what the stars signified, and, of course, no one dared ask Bull Cyclone prying question such as that. He was some coach. Curiously, as you shall see, he was also beloved.

HE WAS 32-years-old, a veteran, husband and father, when he returned to the Deep South in 1950 to assume his first head coaching job. East Mississippi had gone winless the autumn before and, for that matter, had in previous seasons seldom won a game. Even as the years wore on, as he produced 31 J.C. All-Americas, Bull Cyclone would tell his players they were suiting up for the smallest football-playing college in America. That might well have been true. Scooba had only about 250 to 300 kids then, a third of them girls. So in any given year, a substantial proportion of the male enrollment was playing football for coach Sullivan.

The hamlet of Scooba (Choctaw for "reed brake") then boasted 734 souls, which made it a metropolis in Kemper County. The county must look exactly the same now, only less so; when Bull Cyclone arrived in Kemper in 1950, the population was 16,000; today only 10,000 remain, planting a little cotton or soybeans, cutting pulpwood—"pu'pwood," as everybody says. Even into the '60s Scooba's main street had hitching posts, and it still has a big faded sign that reads SERVE COKE AT HOME. For more substantial spirits, the folks would go out to what were known as "jig joints," illegal roadhouses in a state of Baptists and bootleggers that nevertheless winked at Prohibition, which remained the law in Mississippi until 1966. More than that, of course, Appomattox had yet to be acknowledged anywhere in Mississippi, especially not in Kemper, its most antediluvian, impoverished outpost.

Bull Cyclone had been reared nearby—"So far out in the country you could still smell pu'pwood on his breath," according to his old friend Carlton Fleming. Sullivan moved his wife, Virginia, and two daughters—another daughter and a son would come later—onto campus into what was known as the Alamo, a broken-down dormitory that housed the football players. It was reputed to be the only three-story public building in the county. The old place as so ramshackle that the Sullivans had to practice "leak drills," but it was home, and Christmastime they'd set up the tree out where the boys on the team could share it.

Getting those quarters in the Alamo was crucial because all Bull Cyclone was paid for being the football coach—and the baseball coach and athletic director—was $3,600 a year, plus $75 for every game he won. Most of the latter went for gas so he could go on recruiting trips. Bull Cyclone couldn't do much work over the phone inasmuch as there were only three in all of Scooba, one at the drugstore, and one each at the president's house and the president's office.

What Scooba had above all was homogeneity. The students were all the same, bound together in a way that most of today's diverse student bodies couldn't conceive. The girls were only allowed out one night a week, and on the Sabbath girls and boys alike were "urged" to attend both Sunday school and church and then, for good measure, to observe a "quiet hour" from two to three in the afternoon. "At this time," the school catalog explained, "students are to be in their rooms. It is suggested that they write their parents during quiet hour and that they spend some of this time in meditation." The college library had only 4,500 volumes. A football coach could be a gigantic personage in that sort of place.

And he was. For amusement Scooba had jig joints and bad girls, hunting and fishing, and, in season, football. It has always been Dixie's game. Bradberry, who was raised close by in the little town of Sturgis, says, "If you were a boy and grew up in Sturgis, Mississippi, and didn't play football for the high school, your daddy didn't get credit at the grocery store."

Said the East Mississippi catalog the year that Bull Cyclone arrived, "Athletics may be justified as part of the physical culture program, as a recreational feature and as disciplinary measure. . . . We also teach good sportsmanship and self-denial in habits and attitudes."

Armed with that mandate, Bull Cyclone got in his old station wagon and, like some preacher or salesman, hit the highways and byways in search of football players. He had only one returning from the winless '49 season. Sullivan ranged far and wide and, brandishing the GI Bill, even induced some soldiers at various posts to abandon service for their country to play for Scooba. Tales of such outlanders arriving on motorsickles can still be heard. "They'd put 'em in jail for tearing up, then they'd tear up the jail," Fleming recalls with a guffaw. But on his field, Bull Cyclone, who peaked out at around 6' 5" and 285 pounds, brooked no backtalk.

His first team assembled, coach Sullivan called up and got a game with Little Rock J.C. to open the season. And what was Little Rock J.C.? Only the '49 winner of the Junior Rose Bowl, the junior college champion of America. Bull Cyclone was scared of no one, and he would prove it.

When the Scooba team arrived in Little Rock, it was told to practice at the stadium itself. Bull Cyclone, who was especially attuned to spies, suspected that some would be hidden in the stands, so he had his players run all sorts of goofy plays. After a while, Bull Cyclone called over his manager, instructed him to play dumb and to go over to the Little Rock J.C. locker room and tell the coach that Scooba had forgotten to bring kicking tees. He then was to ask whether he could borrow some. Sure enough, the manager saw that the Little Rock coach was drawing all the ridiculous East Mississippi plays on the blackboard for his players.

Bull Cyclone was pretty sure, then, that his first game as a head coach would be "like taking candy from a baby." One of his major tenets was to strike fast with surprise. He knew Little Rock wouldn't know what hit it.

Back in Scooba that night, the postmistress, who had a good radio, picked up the game all the way from Little Rock. Bull Cyclone had promised that he would call in the outcome to the phone at the president's house, but during the game the lady with the radio soon started going around town giving everybody updates. Pretty soon a lot of townspeople were congregated around her radio in the Sullivans' apartment at the Alamo, listening to the game. This was the biggest thing that had ever happened to Scooba, and Bull Cyclone had only just come to town.

He beat the defending national champions 34–14, and his legend was in the making in that grateful little crossroads. As best we can tell, Bull Cyclone went 8–3 that first season, and 21–9 for three years, which was more victories than Scooba had enjoyed in its entire previous history since the college had been chartered in 1927. However, in 1953 Bull Cyclone departed Scooba, taking his family up to Nashville, where he wanted to finish up work for his bachelor's degree in physical education at Peabody College.

Once he had his degree in hand, though, he planned to return to Scooba. And he did—for the '56 season. East Mississippi had taken on a new president in the interim, a local man familiar with Bull Cyclone's exploits, and he hired him back. The president was a little red-haired fellow named R.A. Harbour. He always went by his initials, hoping that no one would remember that his square name was Ritzi Algeine. Unfortunately, behind his back he was called Stumpy, for he was as small a man as Bull Cyclone was big.

STILL, IT'S fair to say that Stumpy wanted as much for the college he ran as Bull Cyclone did for the football team, and the new president was delighted to get Sullivan back in '56. The team had again fallen on hard times, and the fans had grown resentful, as all fans do, at the lack of success. When Stumpy hired Bull Cyclone, the *Kemper County Messenger* ("This is the only newspaper in the world whose sole interest is in Kemper county") exulted: "He is considered one of the best offensive coaches in existence, including senior college. . . . Sullivan's teams didn't always win, but they always put on a show for the spectators. When you saw Sullivan's boys play, you saw a jam-up scoring, razzle-dazzle game that left you breathless and sometimes mad also. But you saw a football game."

But it was just like 1950 all over again. Scooba had only two players back from the '55 squad, so Bull Cyclone had to scour the territory for live bodies. The way it worked then, at Scooba and at a lot of other places, a coach would rope in so many players, weed out the losers during summer practice, and then "dress out" the survivors. Bull Cyclone didn't disguise what he was doing. Just the opposite. A candidate he was recruiting would ask, "Corch, are you giving me a scholarship?"

"Yeah," Bull Cyclone would grumble, "I'm giving you a scholarship *if* you don't quit or *if* I don't run you off." It was customary for a Scooba player—freshman or sophomore—to sign his scholarship form as he boarded the team bus to go to the first game.

Understand, "running off" was a fairly common gridiron practice in those days. It was, for example, what cemented Bryant's reputation as a martinet when he started coaching at Texas A&M in '54. You didn't get cut, you got run off the team. Or perhaps, more often, you chose to run yourself off. "Bull ran off more All-Americans than he kept," says Don Edwards, who played quarterback at Scooba in the late fifties. Players can remember hearing suitcases banging down the stairs of the Alamo just before dawn as boys decided not to go through another two-a-day. Others would leave surreptitiously in the black of night. They'd sneak down the stairs and then push their cars out of earshot before starting them up, lest Bull Cyclone wake up and come after them and make them stay on the team.

When Sullivan's old players get together, they often wonder about the ones that quit. It wasn't exactly dishonorable to get run off. After all, a lot did, and damn near everybody *almost* did. Edwards, for example, left six times before ultimately deciding to stay. Still, the survivors wonder what ever happened to the others. Well, here's one report, from C. R. Gilliam of Carrollton, Alabama: "We'd practice four hours in the morning and then four more hours in the afternoon. I was playing defensive guard and got my nose broken. It was bleeding real bad and pushed around to the side, but Bull just kicked my butt and told me to get back in there.

"That night, I'm laying on that pillow, my nose is aching, I'm feeling real sorry for myself, and I'm thinking, 'I don't have to take this.' I got up and met Bull in the hall the next morning and told him I was going home. 'How?' Bull asked me. 'Walkin',' I told him. I started out and must have gotten four or five miles, to near Geiger, when here come that red Pontiac station wagon of his. He picked me up and took me on home to Carrollton. I never did go to the doctor about that nose."

Something like 200 of Bull Cyclone's players became coaches, and he'd tell them, "Son, don't never worry about a player who leaves. The only thing for you to do is find out why he left and work on it for the next one comes along like that."

Coaching, at least as it was practiced then, in the good old days, wasn't exactly like the ministry. The idea wasn't to save all the souls. The ones that got run off were on their own, but the ones who stayed would be affected far out of proportion. Bull Cyclone, like a lot of coaches, especially football coaches, had more impact on many boys' lives than did their fathers. It was all very basic, really. "You either loved him or you didn't stay," says Bill Buckner, Scooba's best quarterback, who is now the coach at Hinds J.C. "He pushed everyone to the point where they either left him or they gave him what they were capable of."

Edwards remembers the year he was captain and a big lineman complained that Sullivan was slugging him. "Nobody hits me, not even my daddy," the lineman said. But Edwards wasn't about to get involved. "Besides, Bull wasn't really hitting the boy," he says. "Just in the solar plexus."

"Yeah," says Bill (Sweet William) Gore, a retired postman who was Bull Cyclone's good friend. "They'd think he was killing a boy out there when all he was doin' was gettin' his attention."

Bull Cyclone's attention-getting took varied forms. One of his favorite tactics was to have his players practice hitting one-on-one, head-on, right before a game or, when he was especially irritated, at halftime, or even during time-outs. More often than not, this was very disconcerting to the wide-eyed opposition, not to mention what it did to the bodies of the Scooba players. Before such drills, Bull Cyclone also had the habit of saying, "Now,

I don't want to see any of you bastards standing up, and I don't want to see any of you bastards on the ground."

L.C. Jeffries, who played on one of Bull Cyclone's early teams after having seen combat with the Second Infantry in Korea, says, "Sure, we broke some ribs and noses going one-on-one with ourselves at halftime, but understand that what Bill did didn't come out of cruel rural ignorance. He was a smart man and he was playing on the psyche."

Although Bull Cyclone would line up all his players in their star jerseys for the pregame head-ons, he often made sure that his best ones, especially the quarterbacks, who were inviolate in his scheme, never took a lick. When they neared the front of the line, one of the eight or nine scrubs would jump ahead and replace them in the rotation. These unfortunates Sullivan called the "gook squad." Hence when the opposition looked over to see Scooba banging heads, what it unknowingly saw for the most part was the gook-squadders repeatedly laying into each other.

Bull Cyclone made sure, though, that no one on the team felt safe. Sometimes he would advise his players, "I've killed more men than I can *stack* on this football field." That usually got their attention. One time, when he was mad at Bradberry, he said, "Bradberry, I killed seven gooks with a foxhole shovel. One more sonofabitch like you won't matter."

If these remarks were hyperbolic, their substance was real enough. Sergeant Sullivan had fought the last battles of the Pacific with the First Marines, ending up on Okinawa, where he was wounded on June 16, 1945. Maybe that's why he thought he could demand so much of his players, whose sacrifices couldn't compare with those of the good Americans he had fought alongside, and left behind—and finally, as we shall see, honored. He never quite separated war and football. Flipping through what seems to be a scrapbook dedicated entirely to football, one suddenly comes to a long clipping about Okinawa, with a huge headline: BLOODIEST BATTLE OF THE PACIFIC. Once at halftime, Bull Cyclone spread his players along the 50-yard line—"Team! A-ten-shun!"—and marched them to the end zone, military style, to reacquaint them with that foreign terrain.

BULL CYCLONE didn't always need a whistle to get his players' attention. He just hollered "Whoaaa!" and everything screeched to a halt. His language, especially in the earlier years, could wilt the blossoms in Mr. Smith's pasture. Grown men listened in awe when he cursed—"Unbelievably vile," says Charlie Box, who was a fullback and no prude. One time, Dick Potter, a referee, felt obliged to penalize Scooba 15 yards for unsportsmanlike conduct because of how grossly Bull Cyclone had yelled at one of his *own* players.

But more frightening was his mere presence. He was big all over—hamlike arms, huge feet, a melon head so large that when he decided to change his game ensemble, switching from a 10-gallon hat to a baseball cap, he had to split the cap in back to get it comfortably on his head. Virginia, a lovely woman, his second wife, who was at his side all the years in Scooba, remembers a player telling her, "Miz Sullivan, we're not afraid of Corch. Why, we reckon 10 or 12 of us together could whip him." Players commonly took off their shoes as they passed his room, fearful that they might awaken him from a nap. A lot of times he would tear off his coat in the middle of a game, throw it down, stomp on it and then sort of hurl it back to the bench. Whatever player got in front of it would quickly pass it along, because nobody wanted to be holding it when Bull Cyclone started looking for his coat again. And, to be sure, nobody dared put it on the ground. So the coat would go up and down the bench like a hot potato.

To spice up practices he would sometimes have the managers wrap old mattresses around pine trees to make blocking targets. The idea was to see if anybody could smack into a tree hard enough to knock off a pinecone. Try it. Or, if he thought things were slack during a scrimmage, he would scream, "Get after it!" and the linemen were automatically obliged to choose up and start fighting one another.

From his Parris Island days, Bull Cyclone borrowed the idea of an obstacle course, adding a wrinkle of his own—a trip wire in the tall grass that the managers yanked as the weary players came through. From another part of the course, Bull Cyclone would hurl bricks at the players as they tried to regain their balance after clambering over a wall. He would miss, but barely. He did, however get their attention.

Probably his most famous gambit was to hold scrimmages at the edge of the pond, which is located at the bottom of a gentle slope, down from where Mr. Smith's pasture used to be. Bull Cyclone came up with the scheme in order to test goal-line defenses. He took his defensive unit and lined it up in the shallow water, which came up to about the players' knees. Then he had the offense storm down the hill. It "scored" if the running back could make it into the water.

Gerald Poole, who's still on the faculty at Scooba, was Bull Cyclone's defensive assistant the day he dreamed up the pond scrimmage. "You think your f------ defense is tough?" Bull Cyclone roared, and then had coach Poole station his players in the water. The first two goal-line plays, off-tackle, failed to get a splashdown. On the third and last shot, Poole told his middle linebacker that he thought the ballcarrier would come right over the middle on the next assault. "If he does, I'm gonna shoot him like an old dove," the linebacker said. Sure enough, the runner took the handoff and tried to leap into the pond over center. The linebacker popped up, met him at the height of his dive, and the two players crashed into the mud, headfirst. It wasn't uncommon for defenders to lose their cleats in that Mississippi mud.

The reference to dove shooting wasn't unusual, either. Most Scooba players were country boys who had, like the coach, grown up with guns. Because Bull Cyclone was almost paranoid about opponents spying, he outfitted his managers with rifles. On at least two occasions it's documented that Bull Cyclone grabbed a rifle from a manager and fired at a private airplane that had strayed into his practice airspace. Another time he bade the manager to open fire on a plane, but the boy panicked, threw down the gun and, so the story goes, ran off the field, never to show his face again in Scooba. On another occasion, a succession of shots were heard from where a manager was stationed with a shotgun and order to shoot to kill any suspected spies.

"Oh my Lord!" Bull Cyclone screamed. "Who did he shoot?"

Mercifully, no one. The manager was just another old country boy, and when he saw a covey of quail nearby, he had blasted away.

Scooba boys were the last in the country to eschew leather helmets, because Bull Cyclone believed that the hard modern helmets caused more injuries than they prevented. He thought his players would be better off with the nice, soft leather helmets—especially if they were decked out with skull and crossbones. No sooner had he thought of the skull-and-crossbones idea than he dispatched a manager with a bunch of helmets for Mrs. Sullivan to start painting. "Bob thought the skull and crossbones would kind of rattle the other team," she says. "He told the players, 'Now, you don't have to make faces. But don't smile.'"

Traditionally, when the Scooba players came out before a game, they didn't make a sound. Most teams scream and shout and carry on to prove they're *ready to play*, but Bull Cyclone thought that was a waste of good energy. His charges came out as silent as the fog. Imagine being a player on the other team, and here comes the bunch you're going to play, togged out in star jerseys—and now in skull-and-bones helmets—quiet as mice, and then on the sideline, they start going one-on-one. That was likely to get your attention.

Bull Cyclone had some kind of temper. Because he was a man of his word, remarks he made while in a rage were not disregarded. He often drove the team bus, a rattly, broken-down vehicle that was known as Night Train because it seemed to function better after the sun went down. After one defeat, Bull Cyclone climbed behind the wheel and announced that he was so mad he was going to run the bus off the road and kill the whole team. Box, who was aboard, says, "I don't know how many of us believed him—most of us believed everything he ever said—but the manager sure did, because he started crying. "Well, let me off first, Corch, because I'm just the manager, and I didn't have a thing to do with us losing this game."

Bull Cyclone's tempestuous hijinks didn't go unnoticed. People would come out just to watch him carry on, throw his coat down, stomp on his hat. One time at Holmes the crowd got so abusive that Bull Cyclone called time and had his players pick up their benches and march to the other side of the field. Robert McGraw, now an assistant at Ole Miss, recalls seeing Bull Cyclone storm onto the field because a wide receiver had run the wrong route. He picked up the player by his jersey and sort of flung him aside. The boy scurried to the bench and hid under it, quaking, while the coach stormed back, the fans all the while chanting, "Give 'em hell, Bull!"

At his maddest, he could really kick a ball. Langston Rogers, who served as Bull Cyclone's aide-de-camp and is now the sports information director at Ole Miss, swears that on one occasion when the coach got mad at the officials, he blustered onto the field between plays, right up to the line of scrimmage, and booted the ball 30 yards, soccer style, dead through the uprights. Another time he went out and kicked the ball into the stands. As a result the Mississippi Junior College Association required him to spend the whole next game in a chair on the sideline. Stumpy Harbour was infuriated. He acted as if Bull Cyclone had embarrassed him in front of the other presidents. None of them had a football coach kicking game balls into the stands, did they?

A lot of people thought Bull Cyclone would never be able to sit still in the chair the entire game, but wouldn't you know it, Bull Cyclone stayed put, barely even rising from his seat. That might have made Stumpy even madder. Bull Cyclone could control himself when he had to. Why to this day, you'd have a hard time find a lady in Kemper County who ever heard coach Bob Bull (Cyclone) Sullivan utter a curse word.

For that matter, although he constantly fought with officials, he never argued just to dispute a call. Bull Cyclone only let the officials have it when he thought they had misinterpreted a rule. "You stink, Billbo!" he screamed when Billbo Mitchell made a call that Sullivan didn't agree with. Mitchell stepped off 15 before saying, "Can you still smell me, Bull?" Bull Cyclone was a stickler about the rules. He knew the book so well and cared so passionately for it that General Neyland, the revered Tennessee coach, eventually got Bull Cyclone from Scooba appointed to the NCAA rules committee, even though his unknown little school wasn't even a member of that august national body.

This isn't to say that Bull Cyclone was above taking the rules as far as they could go. At least one time, in the rain, he taped thumbtacks to his quarterbacks' fingers so they could get a better grip on the ball. That worked just fine until the tacks started scratching up the pigskin. Another time, Bull Cyclone got to thinking about how his linemen pulled out to block. He was using the split T then, and most of the plays came off the quarterback rolling right. So Coach thought, "Well now, if my guard and tackle are going to pull on just about every play and everybody figures this, I might as well get them headed in the right direction to start with." So he had them come up to the line of scrimmage and take their three-point stances facing the other way, with their rear ends staring the opposing linemen in the face.

And on a most memorable occasion, just as Scooba was about to score against Southwest, the officials called a holding penalty, citing the number of a player who wasn't in the game. Enraged by this breach, Bull Cyclone ran onto the field to get his point across better. That's an automatic 15 on top of the fifteen for holding. First-and-forty, Potter, the referee said, "You gotta go back, Corch," but Bull Cyclone kept on coming. Another 15. First-

and-55. "C'mon, Bull," Potter pleaded. He liked him. "Go on back, or I gotta give you 15 more."

"I don't give a damn!" Bull Cyclone thundered. "You're wrong!" Potter stepped off 15 more. First-and-70. Then, as soon as Potter placed the ball down once again, Bull Cyclone went into his patented kicking phase. He booted the bejesus out of the ball. By the time they retrieved it, it was first-and-85.

BECAUSE THEY had nearly run out of acreage and he had made his point, Bull Cyclone returned to the sideline, pausing only to tell his quarterback to call a Z-out, Z-in. This was only one play, mind you. Southwest was still laughing and, needless to say, wasn't looking for Bull Cyclone to try to get the whole 85 back on one play. But he was. Z-out, Z-in. TD.

"Wooo, that did it," Poole says.

Bull Cyclone enjoyed matching wits with other coaches. Dobie Holden down at Pearl River was his favorite rival. Pearl River was often the top team in the conference. It was a much larger school than Scooba and always well coached. One year Pearl River was an overwhelming favorite against Scooba and was at home, to boot. This brought out the best in Bull Cyclone. He really put on his thinking cap. Scooba would normally arrive for a Saturday night game around 4 p.m., after stopping along the way for a typical training meal that the players referred to as "the four Ts"—tea, taters, toast and tough meat. This time, however, as old Night Train rattled through Hattiesburg on the way to Pearl River, Bull Cyclone had the bus pull up to one of the fanciest restaurants in all of Mississippi and treated the boys to the finest of repasts. Then, as Night Train rolled into the Poplarville area, where Pearl River is located, Bull Cyclone diverted it to a roadside park. Everybody in Pearl River was wondering what was up as game time approached. Where were Bull Cyclone and the Scooba team? Finally, just in time for the players to dress, Night Train arrived.

In the locker room, Bull Cyclone told them not to utter a sound until right before the kickoff, whereupon they were to "go crazy." Pearl River, already discombobulated by the late arrival, was put off even more by these antics, and the home team left the field at halftime down 3–0. Unfortunately, Bull Cyclone didn't have any more psychological tricks up his sleeve, and Pearl

River won something like 42–3. Edwards, who was a sophomore, remembers saying to him afterward, "Well, that kinda backfired."

"Oh, we got a half out of 'em," said Bull Cyclone, with equanimity. He never had any difficulty accepting defeat—or even losing seasons—as long as he thought he was outmanned and everybody had done his best.

Most of Bull Cyclone's players still maintain that the public never really saw him at this best—at halftime. Even with one-on-ones awaiting them, Scooba players were wont to say, "It's safer on the field than in the locker room." As Poole remembers, chuckling, the players would "draw up" during halftime. Among other things, Bull Cyclone threw a lot of objects, from salt tablets up to and including a huge axle-grease drum. To give the devil his due, Sullivan thought the drum was empty. It wasn't. It had been used as a trash container, and when he flung it at a post, the top flew off and the garbage poured over the poor lad who had chosen to sit against the post. Petrified, the player never budged, just letting the trash spill on him and his star jersey, while the coach raved on. Other times, Bull Cyclone destroyed a chair by smashing it against a table, kicked any number of things, drove his fist clear through a blackboard and, to use the singular Mississippi expression, "forearmed" a variety of stationary objects.

But halftimes weren't just pyrotechnic displays. Indeed, to add to the air of uncertainty, Sullivan would always leave his boys alone at first, letting them unwind with Cokes and Hershey bars. Because he favored wing-tip brogues that always seemed to squeak, everyone could hear him approaching. The first game Bradberry played for Scooba, Bull Cyclone came in and squatted on the floor in front of the quarterback. He didn't say a word until it was time to go back onto the field. Then, staring straight through poor Bradberry, he snarled, "Come on, young lady," and got up and departed. The performance so unnerved some of the veteran sophomores that a couple of them threw Bradberry against a wall and advised him he damn well better not screw up and get the coach down on the whole team. Terrified, Bradberry brought Scooba home 29–3.

During another memorable halftime, Bull Cyclone suddenly materialized in the locker room on his hands and knees, with his overcoat collar pulled up around his ears. He gave no explanation for this bizarre posture but merely crawled from player to player, stopping before each one, staring him dead in the face, like a mad dog. This caught their attention.

Bull Cyclone usually started at halftime by walking the length of the locker room. Then he'd shorten the span until eventually he wasn't taking steps, but just sort of doing an about-face. It was mesmerizing. Next he would talk. To hear him was a hypnotic experience, for he would blink a lot—an aftereffect of his war experiences—or his eyes would sort of roll back up in his head. When he spoke with emphasis, which he invariably did, his jaw would shake, so that his gruff voice resonated all the more. Edwards recalls one halftime when Bull Cyclone went through this routine, but without saying a word, until, at the last, he spun on his heels and screamed, "I was on an island with five thousand Japs! Now, get out of here!" The players all but stampeded in an effort to escape him, and then destroyed an unsuspecting opponent.

Box remembers when Bull Cyclone gave his finest Knute Rockne oration. He spoke very softly, recounting how he was in a foxhole with a buddy who had just been hit by shrapnel. Blood was pouring out of the Marine, and he obviously wasn't going to make it. "Anything I can do for you?" Bull Cyclone whispered. The locker room was still and reverent.

"Yeah, Big Bob, just win one for me sometime." Well, this was the sometime. And Scooba won, too. Apparently, that was the only time Bull Cyclone invoked his friend's dying wish. But he always wanted to do something for the ones he left back in the Pacific. Sometimes, when he was really furious, out of the blue he would holler, "You c----------, you're out here playin', breathin' this f-----' free air because a heap of people died for you."

That was the way men were made. Maybe it was the wrong way, but it was the way back then. "He'd ride you to just before he got you to the ground, and only then he'd let you up . . . some," Bradberry says. "Then he had you in his hip pocket."

"Yeah, he was tough," Edwards says. "But I loved him like a father. And I'll tell you: Any player who ever stayed with him will say that."

"That was the way it was. That was the way people let it be. The players were all the same sort, they were in it together, and football and Okinawa were very much the same. Football doesn't mean near as much as it used to," Bradberry says. And no, he goes on, there's no way in the world that he—or anybody else—could coach Scooba the way coach Sullivan did. "The ones playing now look at football differently," says Bradberry. "They've got more to do. There's nowhere near as many dedicated people."

Bull Cyclone's family remembers the first time he saw the Beatles, and, recalls Royce Tucker, one of his daughters, "he thought the world had come to an end." Still, everybody could see that at least he made some accommodations as the '60s came to an end and a new type of player evolved. Nonetheless, as Royce says, "Yeah, he changed some. He changed, but he liked the old ways best. You could see he was under some stress."

One time he told Royce flat out, "You can't coach in the same way."

"Why," she asked.

"Because it doesn't work anymore." And that was all there was to that.

AT A very early age the boy who would become Bull Cyclone realized that the best chance he had on this earth was with football. That doesn't mean he was dumb. Mrs. Elizabeth Cunningham, one of his high school teachers, remembers that he was an "excellent" student, and all through his life he loved such un-pigskin things as writing and anthropology. But the Sullivans were the poorest of poor whites in the poorest of times in the poorest part of the country. Mrs. Sullivan had to support six children by herself because her husband, Wild Bill, dropped dead one day, down at the creek, fishing for dinner. Mrs. Sullivan barely got by, working at the cotton mill in Aliceville. That's just up from Scooba, only on the Alabama side.

Bull Cyclone was born in Echola, in Tuscaloosa County, Alabama, in 1918, and the family moved to Aliceville when he was 10. Mrs. Sullivan moved the family again when young Bob was 16. She went down to Mobile, hoping to find a better paycheck in the big city, but Bob stayed behind to play football for Aliceville High. He got a room in back of a store by the cotton mill, paying for it by sweeping out the place. Years later, as a coach, no matter how badly Bull Cyclone would embarrass a player, he'd never let a boy be embarrassed by his clothes. Whenever possible, he'd try to get the youngster some better duds.

He also learned to abide almost any sort of person except someone who put on airs. It especially irritated Bull Cyclone that Stumpy Harbour had come to be more interested in the trappings of his office than in the substance. According to Bull Cyclone, Stumpy would rather gussy up the president's expanding mansion than improve the curriculum. Bull Cyclone never could tolerate Kemper County's self-proclaimed social elite, which dismissed the Sullivans as boorish newcomers even after they'd lived in Scooba for 15 years.

ONE SPRING Sunday, Bull Cyclone took his family out to lunch over at the old Five Points Restaurant. It had a fine reputation, although its owners closed down with the onset of integration rather than serve the colored on white tablecloths. But on this particular Sunday, one of the pillars of Scooba society was also dining there, and she kept casting sideways looks at the Sullivans. Bull Cyclone stared back at the dowager, and out of the corner of his mouth, to his family, he whispered, "Don't anyone dare laugh." Then, while smiling at the matron, he reached over, picked up one of the daffodils that decorated the table and most conspicuously, ate it, stem and all.

Staying alone back in Aliceville paid off for Bull Cyclone. He captained the football team in '37 and was its biggest and best player, a barreling fullback in the old short punt formation. On defense he was a linebacker. His play gained him passage to Union University up in Jackson, Tenn. By then he had married a hometown girl named Thelma. The marriage didn't work, except for the three children it produced. One of the two sons was named Vic. Later on, when Bull Cyclone married Virginia, they named *their* only son Vic, too. The two half brothers are known as Big Vic and Little Vic. Few people knew that the father's middle name was Victor, and if you ask anyone why Bull Cyclone gave two sons the same name, he'll say, "Corch always wanted to have a victory around." That isn't as farfetched as it seems; he and Virginia named their third daughter Gael because he wanted to have a Little Cyclone.

In 1942 Union was a football powerhouse, going undefeated and outscoring the opposition 211–75 behind a fabled back known as Casey Jones. Sullivan, big number 41, was settled at center by then and was good enough to get an offer from the Detroit Lions. But he joined the Marines instead.

Bull Cyclone probably decided to be a coach while in the service. Certainly, his experience at Parris Island, where he became a DI, relates to Scooba. "The recruits hated you so much it was hard to take," he once told Virginia. "But by the end of the training cycle they had come to love you. They'd even buy you a little something, and then they'd leave, and the awful part of it was, there was a whole new group in there the next day, hating you all over again."

The members of that great '42 Union team had vowed to come back and finish school together. But when Bull Cyclone returned late in '45, shrapnel in his right leg, blinking nervously from all the gunfire, jumping at unexpected noises, he discovered that the Union administration had eliminated football. For one of the few times in his life he was bitter. In the college paper he wrote this in his sports-page column, which was entitled *by* **S**ullivan *on* **S**ports:

"Then the matter of a war came along and the boys left the football field for the battle field only [to] return and find what they fought for [had been] taken from them by people who slept between clean sheets while the boys made themselves cozy in a muddy foxhole."

Before departing Union at the end of the school year, Bull Cyclone got his first real coaching experience and crowned it by marrying one of his players. His marriage to Thelma had been dissolved by now, and when Bull Cyclone took over a girls' softball team on campus, he took a shine to the shortstop. He named the team the Terrapins because he thought the players were so slow. He shifted the shortstop, Virginia Dale, to first (and later tabbed her All-League in his column) and led the club to an undefeated season. The first big game he ever coached was a showdown between the Terrapins and their main rival, which boasted the league's fastest pitcher. To prepare his girls Bull Cyclone brought in his roommate, a softball pitcher, to throw batting practice. The first two days, they didn't get a bat on the ball, but by the time they had to face the female fireballer her vaunted offerings looked like changeups, and she was quickly driven out of the box. Not long afterward, Sullivan married his first-sacker, and they headed to Reno so he could play football at the University of Nevada, where a coach named Whistlin' Jim Aiken was assembling a postwar juggernaut.

Nevada set national offensive records that stood for years, and Bull Cyclone was a standout at center and linebacker, good enough to make the Shrine All-Star game in Honolulu, where he intercepted three passes. The Baltimore Colts of the old All-American Conference offered him a contract. But when Whistlin' Jim went north to take over as coach at the University of Oregon in 1947, he asked Bull Cyclone to come along as an assistant, and he did. Sullivan had decided it was time to stop playing and get on with his calling in life, which was to coach football.

When Bull Cyclone arrived in Scooba in '50, the split T, a grind-'em-out power offense, was in fashion, but he favored a wide-open passing game, so he operated from the I formation. Jimmy Jobe, who played and coached against Bull Cyclone, says, "Things you saw last Sunday for the first time on TV, well, I guarantee he was doing them 20 years ago. All that motion and then reverse—Bull was doing that in the late '50s."

"I had to laugh when Bill Walsh won the Super Bowl and everybody discovered a genius," says Bradberry. "Corch Walsh may be a genius, but Corch Sullivan was doing the same thing when I played for him in the '60s. I don't believe we ever ran a play that didn't have five receivers."

Adds Poole, "Every play was pass action. I don't know how anybody prepared for us. He'd make up at least six plays for every game."

He conjured them up at all waking hours. Around the house, plays would be sketched on newspapers, napkins, books, calendars; they were found on church programs and high school prom dance cards. One morning Bobbie discovered that her father had absentmindedly scribbled plays all over the margins of a term paper she was turning in that day.

Box remembers being awakened in his room in the Alamo at 3 a.m. by Little Vic. Instructing Box to follow, the boy took him downstairs to the Sullivan apartment and then right into his parents' bedroom. Virginia was sound asleep in her half of the bed. But Bull Cyclone was sitting up next to her, running a projector, staring at films on the far wall. He ran a play and asked Box if he thought a new variation involving him would work. Flabbergasted, Box said, "Yes, sir, I don't see why not."

"O.K.," Bull Cyclone said. "Go back to bed." He promptly began to diagram the play on an index card. He usually had all his special plays for that week's game designed by Monday.

Bull Cyclone would take the basic stuff he planned to use and make a deck of plays that he flipped through on the sidelines. Says Bradberry, "I can see him now, wiping the blood off my face with one hand, shuffling through his deck with the other to find me the play he wanted." Purists maintain that one quarterback must be deputized to be in charge of a team, but if Bull Cyclone didn't believe he had an outstanding player, he'd use two or even three quarterbacks during a game, alternating these paragons of leadership after each play. And it worked just fine.

For example, as a freshman Bradberry alternated with a stringbean named Ricky Garner. In one game, Bull Cyclone got furious with Bradberry for citing some wrong information about a linebacker and yanked him. "You little sonofabitch," he screamed, "don't you ever open your mouth again. The only way you'll ever take another snap for me is if Garner breaks both his legs." But out of the blue late in the first quarter, Bull Cyclone summoned Bradberry from the bench, riffled through the deck, and dispatched him to run one play. It wasn't exactly a vote of confidence, for the call was a rare halfback sweep, in which the quarterback was supposed to block. Bradberry ran the play, and, on another possession midway through the second quarter, Bull Cyclone sent him back in to run the same punishing sweep.

Then, right before the half ended, the coach yelled for Bradberry again, shuffled through his deck and like a magician, pulled out a card and showed it to the quarterback. "See this," Bull Cyclone said. "Hit the tight end, and it'll be a f-----' touchdown.

Telling the story, Bradberry merely smiles, then shrugs and says, "And hey. . . " and raises his arms in the TD salute.

Defense bored Bull Cyclone, so he let his assistant handle that. Of course, from carefully studying the passing game, he became an expert at pass defense. Scooba played man-to-man and stunted constantly. "Forty-four red dog," was his favorite defensive alignment: four-man line, four others up close, blitz. Against running attacks, which were what he usually faced, Sullivan's basic concept—again presaging the future—was to have his linemen "mess things up" so that the linebackers could dash up and make jarring tackles. A wiry little demon of a linebacker named Bob Wilson is reputed to have made as many as 25 stops in a game, 150 in one season.

In practice, though, Bull Cyclone would spend almost all of his time working on passing—seven-on-eight—exiling the interior linemen to the sidelines, where they could get at it among themselves all day. Nowadays, major schools have so many assistants that a head football coach primarily has to be an administrator just to keep practices running effectively. But Bull Cyclone was always in the midst of things, and when he ran his beloved passing drills, he'd move right along with the team. Most coaches stand in one spot and shout "Bring it back." Bull Cyclone's players would practice up and down the field, simulating a real drive. No one was allowed to disturb this routine, and, or course, no outsiders were present, lest they be shot as spies.

One thing Bull Cyclone had going for him was that few other teams concentrated on the pass—and none in all of America as much as he—so that opponents weren't geared to stopping a promiscuous aerial game. On the other hand, Scooba was invariably the runt of the litter. The Mississippi Junior College Conference had 15 teams then, and the rules limited recruiting to certain areas. Bull Cyclone, like Bradberry today, was left with slim pickings in his six backwoods counties. Big as he was himself, Bull Cyclone came to admire the tiny farmers' sons he had to make do with—"Little itty-bitty boys," says Box, who played fullback at 160 pounds. Smith was a 150-pound quarterback, and Garner didn't weigh even that much. Wilson, the best linebacker Scooba ever had, barely went 135. You've heard of baseball players who can't hit their weight. The year Wilson supposedly made 150 tackles he might have been the only college football player in history to *tackle* more than his weight.

For all the great quarterbacks Bull Cyclone had—at one stretch four in a row went on to star at four-year colleges—the only uniform number he ever retired was 31. It belonged to a halfback named Clyde Pierce, who was always described as "Baby Doll Pierce, 124 pounds soaking wet, from West Point, Miss." Bull Cyclone even had a reel of film made up just of Baby Doll to show the big guys what tough really was. One time Baby Doll got hurt, and as the call went out for a stretcher, Bull Cyclone just scooped up the limp little form and carried Baby Doll of the field in his massive arms.

Though quarterbacks enjoyed an exalted status in Bull Cyclone's cosmos, they suffered much more for their sins than other players. Smith was brought to Scooba two weeks before school opened in 1962, and he moved in with the Sullivans. As he studied the offense with Bull Cyclone, he became a member of the family. But in the first quarter of his opening game, after he had marched Scooba to a touchdown, he muffed the two-point conversion pass attempt. Smith turned around to find Bull Cyclone running at him, screaming, "You traitor, Smith! You're a traitor!" Smith couldn't believe what had come over the man. "I was fixin' to go over the hill right then," he says.

Smith stayed, however, and Scooba went on to qualify for something known as the Magnolia Bowl. Shortly before that game, Bull Cyclone saw quarterback Billy Wade of the Chicago Bears play on TV with tiny shoulder pads, and he figured Smith would profit from the same gear. Only Sullivan didn't have any tiny pads, so he asked Smith if he'd go padless. Smith quickly agreed. "You must understand, he had enough effect on me that I wouldn't even question him when he asked me to play without shoulder pads," Smith says. Bull Cyclone didn't let the rest of the players know what was up until just before the game. "Fellows," he said, "Lester's not going to wear any shoulder pads tonight." Long pause. To let that sink in. "*And . . . he . . . better . . . not . . . get . . . hit.*" Smith didn't, either, except on two occasions when he lost his head, checked off the coach's plays, and ran the ball on sneaks.

ALTHOUGH SCOOBA won and Smith escaped the coach's wrath, Bull Cyclone usually went berserk when a quarterback of his risked getting tackled. A perfect game wasn't a quarterback completing every pass. A perfect game was a quarterback not having his star jersey touched. The first thing Bull Cyclone taught any quarterback wasn't how to throw a complete pass but how to throw an incomplete one. Bradberry well remembers the time Bull Cyclone ripped off his jersey and another time when he yanked off his helmet and chucked it clear into Mr. Smith's pasture to illustrate how you threw a ball away with proficiency.

Once that art was mastered, Bull Cyclone's quarterbacks got down to completing passes. He required them to come out an hour before practice and half an hour before games and throw to each other "on a knee"— that is, kneeling—a drill that improves form and increases arm strength. Buckner threw so many passes that, for a while, he had to keep his arm in a sling when off the field. Over and over the quarterbacks would work on the same precise patterns, learning to release the ball before the receiver broke. And if a quarterback did anything incorrectly—or worse, stupidly— a terrible wrath was visited upon him. "Get out of my f-----' huddle! Get out of my f------' life!" Sullivan would bellow. The quarterbacks were different, and everybody knew it. Even now, the quarterbacks talk about Bull Cyclone in a more intimate way than do the other players. The quarterbacks were really the only ones who were back with him, alone, on Okinawa.

Bradberry says the most memorable moment of his life came in the first game of his second season. To this point, he'd never been anything but a 'f-----' idiot' who did what he was told off the index cards. Suddenly, while standing on the sidelines before one play, Bull Cyclone turned to him and said, "Well, what do you think?" Bradberry's knees turned to jelly. He had been ordained. The rest of the season he was junior partner, and afterward, Bull Cyclone highly recommended him to Delta State. He was awarded a scholarship, and he broke the records Buckner had set there.

But Buckner was undoubtedly Bull Cyclone's best quarterback. He was the one who almost got everything for Coach. With his little itty-bitty boys, only twice did Bull Cyclone have enough to win it all. The last time was in '69. Looking forward to that season, he told Virginia, "It's going to be like taking candy from a baby." To others, more worldly than she, he advised that he was "holding a royal flush." The other time he could have won a championship was in '64, Buckner's final season.

In '63, when Buckner was a freshman, Scooba went 10-1-1 and was ranked seventh in the national J.C. rankings, although, wouldn't you know it, Pearl River still won the conference. But with Buckner back in '64, Scooba was even more formidable, winning its first eight games and climbing all the way to No. 3 in the country. Scooba was a lock to be invited to the Junior Rose Bowl if it kept winning. Scooba was going to come out of nowhere and show California football that Scooba was 15 to 20 years ahead of its time. Buckner was already a J.C. All-America. He had thrown for 39 touchdowns and almost 5,000 yards in 20 games. Further, he was Mr. Everything: president of the student body, head of the local branch of the Fellowship of Christian Athletes.

Scooba's ninth opponent was Jones Junior College, the top defensive team in the conference. With a 6–1 record, Jones had lost only to Pearl River, by 6–0. It was homecoming at Scooba, and the festive crowd of 4,000 overflowed the stands, whose normal capacity was 3,000. Buckner didn't disappoint anyone, either. On the game's first offensive series, second-and-one on his own 40, he called an audible and struck with a touchdown pass to George Belvin. Sixty yards, just like that, for his 40th TD toss. Only 2:11 gone, and Scooba was up by seven. On to Pasadena!

Not only that, but Scooba held Jones and got the ball right back. Buckner had had such an outstanding career that all week Mississippi had been buzzing with rumors that Jones was out to get Buckner. However, Bull Cyclone had his charges ready. He put them through the toughest week of practices any of them had ever experienced. One day, he even lashed out at Buckner, and pulled him from the starting lineup. Benching the greatest quarterback in junior college ball was ludicrous, of course, but Bull Cyclone was bringing everything to a boil. "That man had a gift to know," Buckner says now.

But at the time Buckner was simply distraught. That night he left his room in the Alamo and went outside, thinking he might keep right on going. A mattress was airing out on a fence, and Buckner lit into it, pummeling it, harder, harder, harder, all his anger and frustrations pouring out. A man has to wonder if Bull Cyclone might not have heard all the commotion and come out his window and watched, smiling, content.

The next day, Buckner was still second-string. Only as soon as the other quarterback made an error, Bull Cyclone was all over him—"Get out of my f-----' huddle! Get out of my f-----' life!"—and Buckner was back in the saddle. They were getting ready for Jones and then the Junior Rose Bowl. Coach Sullivan didn't have much more to tell Buckner, except throw the ball and throw it away if pressured.

So it was 7–0 Scooba. Buckner was back to pass again, and the Jones defenders rushed in. Instead of lobbing the ball far away, he thought he saw a way to salvage the play and scrambled. He ducked this way and that, but two Jones linemen were still closing in on him. "Throw it away!" Bull Cyclone hollered. "Throw the sonofabitch away! Get rid of it!"

Buckner was trapped now; it was too late. He was hit low, and as he went down, another defender caught him with his fist, solid, square on the cheek. As he buckled, Buckner could feel his whole face cave in as if it were papier-mâché. The man who took the game films for Bull Cyclone told him he'd caught it all. But the films had to be developed in Jackson, which is Jones territory. When they came back that one play had been spliced out. Bull Cyclone didn't care. He'd seen it all himself. He vowed never to play Jones again, and he never did.

Buckner struggled to his feet and staggered to the sideline. He didn't lose consciousness, but he knew his jaw was broken the instant the blow landed. Now he was bleeding so much he had difficulty talking. His face was all splintered. He went over to Bull Cyclone, and he mumbled, "Corch, I believe my jaw is broken."

BULL CYCLONE just stared at Buckner, dead on, for the longest kind of time. Finally, he balled his fists and screamed, "You damn idiot! I told you not to run that f-----' football!" Then he turned away from Buckner and sent in the No. 2 quarterback. They would retire Baby Doll's number, but not Bruckner's. Jones won the game.

Bull Cyclone's youngest daughter, Gael, Little Cyclone, was 12 then. She used to race her friends onto the field after games, all of them trying to see who could get to her daddy first. This time Gael won, but as soon as she reached him, she froze. "Right away, I knew something terrible had happened," she says. "This time I could tell he was sad, not angry."

Scooba was in shock and lost the next week, too, finishing 9-2. Buckner never again wore his star jersey. Somebody else got invited to the Junior Rose Bowl. Somebody else was national champion. Scooba fell in the polls. It didn't even win the conference. Bull Cyclone never won it.

A few days after the Jones game, Sullivan went to the hospital in Meridian to visit Buckner. He was carrying flowers. A lot of times he would yank up some black-eyed Susans and have the managers take them over to Mrs. Sullivan, but now he was carrying a real bouquet. Buckner has never forgotten any of it. Bull Cyclone came in, laid down the flowers, and just stood there at the end of the bed. Buckner was waiting to say something after Bull Cyclone spoke, but Bull Cyclone never said a word. For 10 minutes he just stood there, until, at last, bereft of voice and dreams, he turned and walked away, going back to Scooba.

FINALLY, IN 1966, the Sullivans got their own house, a neat and sturdy red brick just beyond the end zone. President Harbour thought that respectable faculty housing was good for the campus. But that was the coach's only perquisite, and for his $5,600 salary, Bull Cyclone wasn't only football coach and athletic director but dean of men as well. A friend gave him a partnership in a little local franchise known as Chicken Chef, even though Bull Cyclone never had the cash to invest in the deal. "If Bull lived to be 200 years old, he'd never have had any money," says his old buddy Fleming. Friends say letters would come in from his former players, down on their luck, between jobs, and old coach Sullivan would pull out his last five-dollar bill and send it on.

The best way to sum up Bull Cyclone was what a boy named Bernard Rush heard from an old-timer after Rush quit the team and went back home. "Son," the old fellow said, "you ought to get yourself back over to Scooba. Corch Sullivan will do anything *to* you on the football field, but then he'll do anything *for* you once you left." Rush went back.

Then, too, some said he even mellowed a bit in the '60s. During each Religious Emphasis Week, it was Bull Cyclone, the toughest coach there ever was, that the girls wanted to come to their dorm and talk to them about boys and morals and sex. He was a Methodist, but the Baptists wanted him to address them. He began to take to religion seriously and to punish himself. If he let loose a "goddam" during practice, the whole team was permitted to go in early. Finally, says Gael, one night in '67 he went to the front of his church and fell to his knees "in unashamed prayer." Scooba had telephones now, and the cynics in town burned up the wires questioning Bull Cyclone's sincerity. However, it was real, and it was true.

A few months later, Bull Cyclone brought a black player onto the team. Nineteen sixty-eight: Now that may not sound especially progressive, but it was three more years before Bryant integrated his Alabama squad and a year before any of the major Mississippi teams welcomed blacks. And Kemper County was the deepest part of Dixie.

Sylvester Harris wasn't just the first black player on the Scooba team; he was the first black to attend the college. In fact East Mississippi had lost a lot of federal funds because President Harbour hadn't let in blacks. Sullivan's action made a good many people around Scooba mad; Kemper wasn't called Bloody Kemper for nothing. Not long before, when a company bought some timberland and began enforcing no-hunting regulations, forest fires were set all though those lands. One day, one of the big shots in the county offered the coach $500 to run Harris off.

It would've been easy, too because Harris wasn't all that good a player. But Bull Cyclone just told the man to clear out, and he went on treating Harris like any other player. Bull Cyclone once said to Tommy Atkins, a player who became a career Marine, "Tommy, there are two kinds of young men—those you have to kick in the pants to get their potential and those you have to pat on the back. If you, as a leader, make a mistake, you've done a great injustice. So be very careful and decide as accurately as you can whether to kick or to pat."

Away from the field Bull Cyclone could be a different character altogether. In his classroom, where he taught sociology and anthropology, he was, his students said, "like a Sunday school teacher." He spent more and more time working in that discipline. He exchanged a lot of correspondence with Sen. John Stennis, who came from down the road in DeKalb, about archeological work in Kemper. A 1968 photo shows Bull Cyclone with three of his students following a dig. In a caption he's quoted as saying, "The only significant find seemed to be a complex of single-shouldered projectile points, found in lower-strata kitter midden. The people who populated this site probably belonged to a Woodland Culture some 2,000 years ago."

Says Fleming, "Yeah, Bull had an old skeleton head and all." Otherwise, he devoted his spare time to studying the Good Book and watching football film. Praise the Lord, and pass the ammunition.

At home, for relaxation, he loved to listen to *Stardust*. Bull Cyclone could never get enough of *Stardust*. His other musical favorites included *Harbor Lights*, *Somewhere My Love* and *Easter Parade*, which he enjoyed 12 months a year. His daughters were musical, and often he would cry out, "You can be a second Lennon Sisters!" Then he would fall asleep while Bobbie played *Stardust* for him on the piano.

When he'd first get home from practice, "we'd just lay back for a while," Gael says. The family cat was used as litmus paper. If the cat spied Bull Cyclone and ducked away, the practice hadn't gone well. Sometimes he'd line the family up, as if he were back at Parris Island, and make them fall in and count off. But it was fun. Their favorite order was "Get in the car!" because nobody knew whether he was going to take them for a drive, flying off the bumps in the road, or just go around in little circles in the driveway. One time, when they came to a Howard Johnson's, he pulled in and ordered 28 scoops of ice cream, one of each flavor. "We thought everybody had a family like ours," Bobbie says, laughing. His kids still refer to him as Bull.

STILL, NO bigger school would touch Bull Cyclone. The word that traveled before him was that he was a thug, the meanest football coach that ever walked the land. Buckner remembers getting an offer to play quarterback at a major school "up north in Virginia." The backfield coaching job was vacant, and he said he'd come if Bull Cyclone was hired. Buckner tried to explain what a genius the man was. The head coach told him to save his breath. "Hey, I'm afraid of that man," he said.

Clois Cheatham, who is now the president of Scooba, shakes his head. "Off the field, no one was more compassionate," says Cheatham. "But the name was right. He was bullheaded, and he couldn't always make the right transition to others after dealing with players."

At Perkinston J.C., they used to fire a cannon right behind the visitor's bench to stir up the crowd. Bull Cyclone, who could still get nervous when he heard loud noises—"You didn't sneak up on Dad," Bobbie says—protested to the president of Perkinston, but the reply came back that the cannon was tradition. Bull Cyclone then wrote that "my managers and I will bring shotguns to Perkinston, and if there is one tradition I learned in the military it was to retaliate." The president agreed to silence the guns of Perkinston. And so the tales of rough, tough Bull Cyclone spread, and Stumpy Harbour simmered.

By now, too, Bull Cyclone had been pretty much his own football boss for a long time. Maybe he never could work well under someone else. Virginia recalls sitting in the press box with Bull when he was a lowly assistant at Oregon. Over the phone he kept imploring Whistlin' Jim Aiken to employ a certain strategy. After a while, when the head coach didn't, Bull Cyclone just sat back, folded his arms, and watched the game, refusing to answer the phone for the balance of the half.

Without question he would have delighted in a larger stage, for even his family agrees that he loved recognition. But he had to learn to take refuge in his pride. "He knew he was a great coach," Bobbie says, and that had to be enough for him. Besides, he had come to believe that Scooba was his destiny, that that little stretch of nothing on the one hand and pu'pwood on the other was his realm. That was where he would teach football players to be men, and everybody else he could to be patriots and Christians. If the world was changing, at least the gridiron was a rectangular verity.

Around campus he came to be an amalgam of Mr. Chips and Mr. Roberts. In 1967, *The Lion*, the Scooba yearbook, was dedicated to Bull Cyclone, with this inscription: "We respect your strong will, strength and spirit. We admire your nature, loyalty and competence. You are just, you are fair, you are great." The coach who had spent a lifetime hewing grown-ups out of pu'pwood had shaped himself into a whole man, too. This may be the best thing about the best coaches—not what they make of others in a couple of years but what, in the long run, they make of themselves.

Bull Cyclone was comfortable now. His family was growing up; two of the girls were already in college. He had completed his studies, and he was at peace with his God. The rest of the football world was even beginning to catch up to his wide-open style. All that eluded him was a championship, the one that had been wrenched from his grasp when Buckner ran with the damn ball in '64. And the '69 squad was going to give him that. Already, by that spring, Virginia says, he had so many index cards that he had "a whole new box of offense." It was a lock. It was, as we know, "going to be like taking candy from a baby."

School was out, so the players and students who loved Bull Cyclone were away from Scooba when Stumpy Harbour convened the board of trustees to fire him on June 29, 1969. Three of the coach's strongest supporters weren't on hand. Still, word of the meeting and what the president had in mind leaked out. Joe Bradshaw, one of Bull Cyclone's former players, distributed petitions in his support that were signed by every high school coach in the Scooba district. Stumpy refused to admit the petitions. Neither did he admit friends of Bull Cyclone's who gathered outside the meeting room.

Bull Cyclone couldn't speak in his own behalf, but he wrote a letter to the board. His desperation was obvious, his supplicant's tone almost pitiful: "I have heard through the grapevine that you have been called together to take up my contract as coach as East Mississippi Junior College. I beg you not to do this. This school is part of my life and I am a part of it; as a matter of fact, this school is my life."

He was dictating to Virginia. "If you put me out now it will be just like killing a man, for I know that I wouldn't live six weeks." When she finished typing the draft, she told him that that last sentence was overwrought. He took out his pen and scratched this instead: "If you put me out now I won't live long." But the letter went on, pleading—he had only four more years to retirement; he was working 16 to 20 hours a day at a summer job to help put his kids through college. "I have given of myself to this school so diligently and so long and so completely that now I have nowhere to turn. . . . Thank you and God bless you."

Harbour and his cohorts weren't moved. Bull Cyclone was a disgrace to a respectable institution. He was a Neanderthal man, more backward than his Woodland Culture people. Why, he'd been forced to sit in a chair for a *whole game*. No, he was fired. All he got was a 30-day eviction notice to clear his family off campus and a deal to keep his mouth shut or forfeit 18 months' severance. "Our entire lives, value systems and hearts were ripped out and we were cast to an unknown destiny," recalls Royce. "Being young and having been raised to believe in justice, honor, patriotism and love made our pain and confusion indefinable."

THE FAMILY found an old house up in Columbus, where the Chicken Chef franchise was. A radio station there hired Bull Cyclone to do some sports commentary, and he got a job selling insurance. All his friends bought a little, and that helped. That the situation was so desperate was good in a way, because he didn't have the time to dwell on football when the season started. "Still," Bobbie says, "you can't imagine what it did to him after the leaves started to fall, and he knew he was supposed to be on a football field, and everybody knew he was supposed to be on a football field, and he didn't have his field."

Under its new coach, Scooba had a fine year. He installed a conventional attack—you established the run before you dared pass—and he went 9–1. Nonetheless, Pearl River won the conference, and there wasn't any national championship. The 9–1 finish kept the pressure off Stumpy for a while, but he had signed his own notice when he got Bull Cyclone fired. The coach's friends began to mobilize, and on April 10, 1970, the board summarily fired Harbour. The school comptroller was ordered to change the lock on the school safe.

But all that was small beer for Bull Cyclone. "The firing of Harbour does not restore my wrecked life," he wrote shortly afterward. "I came to Scooba when I was 30 years old and left when I was 50. If ever a person gave his life for anything, I have mine to EMJC."

His anguish increased as another football season approached. A few schools had talked to him about coaching positions, but when they asked Scooba for a reference, the academic dean, operating on orders from Harbour, responded with a scurrilous letter, defaming Bull Cyclone with false charges. The new president, Earl Stennis, fired the dean when he learned about the letter, but that was no consolation for Bull Cyclone. The first game in Mississippi that year was an NFL exhibition over in Jackson in early August. Bull Cyclone was given a couple of tickets, and he invited Gael to join him. He enjoyed the game, but driving home he told her that he prayed every day for Stumpy, and that she must do so as well.

Then it was September again, and the season was upon him in earnest.

Some friends in the Lions Club invited him to speak the next Tuesday. The subject was to be how best to watch football on television, and Bull Cyclone got some old blank index cards and made notes for his talk.

While he was getting dressed, Bobbie called from Tulsa, where she had moved a few days earlier to take a job as a junior high physical education teacher. He chatted with her and told her how much he missed and loved her, and then he handed the phone to Virginia and went to finish dressing for the Lions Club meeting. In the bathroom, Bull Cyclone had just slapped some cologne on his face when he dropped dead without a sound.

Nobody in the family, or any friends, or anybody who ever played for coach Sullivan doubts that he died of a broken heart. Everyone who ever knew him says that unequivocally. It was football time again, and Bull Cyclone didn't have a field.

When they buried him, cradling a pigskin, Little Vic didn't want to leave his father. Finally, he snatched off his jacket, took a shovel from one of the workmen and began to toss dirt on the casket. Without anyone saying anything, one by one, all the men there, so many of them Bull Cyclone's old players, removed their coats and took turns shoveling the grave full. A rose fell and someone tried to pluck it out of the dirt. Little Vic stopped him. "No," he said, "it's over his heart. That's where it belongs."

A couple of years later Little Vic was on the varsity at New Hope High in Columbus, and he was playing a good game. The referee was old Billbo Mitchell—*Can you still smell me, Bull?*—and when he kept hearing the name Sullivan on the P.A. for making tackles, he came over and peered closely at the rangy boy. Little Vic thought maybe he was being assessed a penalty for something or other, but he couldn't figure out why. Finally, Billbo said, "You wouldn't be any kin of the late Bull Sullivan, would you?"

"He was my daddy," Vic said.

And then, right there, right in the middle of the game he was refereeing impartially, Billbo put the ball down and stuck out his hand and made Little Vic shake it. "I loved that man," he said.

Years before, coach Poole had been sitting with Bull Cyclone in Bull's office in Scooba. Bull Cyclone put aside his index cards, pulled out a piece of paper, and started doodling. Before long, Poole could tell he was drawing football jerseys, because he could see their general form and the big numbers. Of course, he didn't say anything. He just watched.

Then Bull Cyclone started on about the war and about the time he was with five soldiers with whom he had grown close. But when the island was secure, Bull Cyclone was the only one of them who came home. "There must be a reason," he said.

Coach Poole nodded

"I've been searching for a way to honor them," he said, and then he doodled some more. He passed the drawing to Poole. "There, Corch," he said. It was a rough draft of the star jersey, with the five stars across the breast for the five boys who didn't get out in '45.

Bull Cyclone would live another 25 years, changing the autumns and the lives of Scooba football players he didn't run off in the summers.

| | | | | |

His Own Way

BY S.L. PRICE

Never afraid to speak his mind and always happy to whip his rivals,
Steve Spurrier is the man his opponents most love to hate.

VERYWHERE HE GOES, THEY HATE HIM. IN KNOXVILLE, before his Florida Gators came in to beat No. 2 Tennessee in September for the fourth year in a row, a local pub invited its patrons to throw a football at a poster that depicted him in his usual pose: mouth agape, white Gators visor across his brow. There was no subtlety involved; you didn't have to toss the ball through a hoop or anything. The point was simply to rear back and inflict serious pain on Steve Spurrier—if only in a photo—to throw the pigskin so hard that the poster dimpled.

In Nashville, Vanderbilt loyalists still gnash their teeth over Spurrier's dismissive comment before November's game against the Commodores that he'd gladly run up the score. In Auburn, they still steam over his 1994 crack about the Tigers' soft schedule, not to mention Florida's 49–38 destruction of Auburn, which ended the Tigers' national title hopes in '95. In Georgia, they still talk about the time in '95 when Bulldogs coach Ray Goff, tired of Spurrier's yapping, growled that he would like to get him alone in an alley for half an hour. In North Carolina, they haven't forgotten how Spurrier was quite happy to encourage his 1988 Duke team, which led the Tar Heels 34–0, to humiliate them with another score. As his former coach, colleague and opponent Pepper Rodgers once said of Spurrier, "Embarrassment is part of the game to him."

Oh, yes, they loathe him all over the South. But nowhere as much as they do today in Tallahassee. It wasn't enough that three summers ago Spurrier heckled the players involved in FSU's notorious Foot Locker buying spree by calling their school Free Shoes University. Or that he refused to recant, instead wondering aloud about the shine on all those new cars in the Florida State players' parking lot. "I'm not saying anybody broke any rules; I'm just saying there was a feeling of, well, those kids are driving awfully nice cars," Spurrier said innocently. "How's it happen?"

No, this year he compounded that transgression by publicly accusing the Seminoles of taking cheap shots at his quarterback, Danny Wuerffel, in Florida State's 24–21 win over Florida. He went so far as to send a videotape of the alleged illegal blows to the SEC office. To top it all off, five weeks later he beat the Seminoles when it counted most, with a national championship on the line, topping off a mouthy and spectacular rise to the top of college football with a masterful 52–20 demolition of his archrival.

The Gators have, after 56 years of nothing, won five SEC championships since Spurrier came back to Gainesville—six if you count the 1990 season, when they would have won the title but were ineligible because of NCAA violations committed during the tenure of previous coach Galen Hall. Under Spurrier, Florida has gone 73-14-1 and become a perennial power. And now the Gators have their first national championship.

But it's not just that Spurrier wins; it's *how* he wins. Two years ago, an LSU fan in Baton Rouge screamed at him, in a bayou twang thickened by liquor and envy, "You're lucky, Spurrier! You ain't that good!" But the coach couldn't hear; he was busy watching his team finish its calm dismissal of the Tigers for the eighth straight time (he made it nine with a 56–13 drubbing this season), watching from the sidelines as his Gators put the lie to LSU's faith in its once awesome home field advantage. He was too far away, and when the voice came down again, it had lost something. "You're lucky. . . . " it said, and then there was just this insecure silence, because the screamer was realizing it's not true—and everyone knows it.

And that's what is so galling. Look at him! He's tall, lean and, at 51, still has his hair, and, damn it, he nails his putts and has a Heisman Trophy and a 30-year marriage and loyal children and. . . . You ain't that good!

Worse, Spurrier pretends no modesty. "I don't look at him as overly arrogant," says Terry Dean, the former Florida quarterback whose benching in 1994 led to a bitter and public rupture with Spurrier. "Maybe egomaniacal." Legendary Auburn coach Shug Jordan used to call him Steve Superior when Spurrier was a Heisman-winning quarterback for Florida in the mid-1960s.

"Arrogant . . . cocky . . . loudmouth—well, what else could they say?" Spurrier says, voice rising into his oft-imitated squawk. "Teams are not supposed to like their opponents if the opponents are beatin' 'em. And I am a little different. I read something once that I think is so true: If you want to be successful, you have to do it the way everybody does it and do it a lot better—or you have to do it differently. I can't outwork anybody, and I can't coach the off-tackle play better than anybody else. So I figured I'd try to coach some different ball plays, and instead of poor-mouthing my team, I'd try to build it up to the point where the players think, Coach believes we're pretty good; by golly, let's go prove it."

"He says a lot of things a lot of us think but only wish we could say," Florida State coach and Spurrier nemesis Bobby Bowden has said. "I might be thinking it, but I don't have guts enough to say it." Spurrier, understand, is a Florida loyalist who savaged his own fans early in the '95 season for booing and is a father who took his namesake, Steve Jr., aside in high school nine years ago and told him he would never make it playing quarterback.

"Steve's a brat," says his wife, Jerri, laughing. "He doesn't take everything in this world so seriously. Sarcasm, teasing, digging: He loves that kind of stuff. He's great at it." Growing up, Spurrier says with something close to pride, "we used to call it being a s--- disturber."

Dishing it out is one thing; taking it is another. Hit him where he lives—his golf game, his tightfistedness, his handling of quarterbacks—and Spurrier gets defensive. Once, some friends gave him a picture of himself cringing after a blown putt. "That wasn't funny," Jerri says. "But if he gave it to somebody else? That's funny."

When Spurrier demoted Dean in 1994, he took the first serious heat of his coaching career, for trashing his quarterback's confidence. Three weeks later, receiver Jack Jackson, who had been benched for skipping a team meeting and for lackluster play, also blasted Spurrier in the media. When the coach came into his weekly press conference three days afterward, he pulled a piece of paper from his pocket. Before saying a word, Spurrier began sniffling and breathing hard, his eyes filling with tears. Then he began a 15-minute tirade against the media, some members of which, he insists now, threatened him with criticism if he didn't provide inside information. It was like watching Nixon in full paranoid bloom, complete with talk of secret threats and enemies and the certainty that some reporters were out to get him. Said Spurrier a few months later, "If you can hurt me, give it your best shot. I'm not going to give inside scoop to anybody. Nobody owns me and never will."

WHERE DOES Spurrier's complex nature come from? "I think everything is competitive," the Reverend Graham Spurrier says. "You want to be as successful as you can possibly be." Steve's father is 82, retired now, but still preaches on occasion. He found his Presbyterian faith during high school in North Carolina and fondly remembers the day when fellow preacher Billy Graham came by and the two knelt in the Spurrier house. "I am a great admirer of Billy Graham because Billy has gone all out," he says.

Graham Spurrier often uprooted his family: They lasted a year in Miami Beach—where he and his wife, Marjorie, had Steve, the youngest of their three children—before going to Charlotte and then to the hills of eastern Tennessee, alighting in Athens and then Newport before settling in Johnson City. He coached Steve's Little League and Babe Ruth baseball teams, opening one season by telling the kids, "Those who think the object is not to win or lose but how you play the game, raise your hand." Most of the kids did. Steve didn't; he knew his father. "They wouldn't keep score if the object isn't to win," Graham told the children. "You might as well stay home if you don't come to win." He still gives coaching tips to Steve and Steve Jr., who was a graduate assistant at Florida under his father from 1994 to '96. Steve says Graham "was never overpraising me. He would say, 'How about that shot you missed in the corner? How about that incomplete pass?' You always could've done a little better."

"Graham was Steve's coach, and whatever Steve did was never good enough," says Jerri, who married Steve in 1966. "He pushed and pushed and pushed. That doesn't work with everybody, but Steve could handle it."

Graham may have pushed his son, but Steve's talent and, more important, his confidence and ability to see plays develop were gifts he uncovered on his own. In 1966, when his 6–0 Florida team was tied with Auburn 27–27, the Gators had a chance to kick a game-winning 40-yard field goal— out of range for their regular kicker but not for their quarterback. Spurrier, who hadn't attempted a kick all season, persuaded coach Ray Graves to let him try. He nailed the field goal, and with it the Heisman Trophy.

But when Spurrier hit the NFL, everything changed. He spent most of the next decade backing up John Brodie on the San Francisco 49ers and then earned the ignominious distinction of piloting the only 0–14 team in NFL history: the 1976 expansion Tampa Bay Buccaneers. He wasn't, by his own admission, a hard worker, but his time spent staring from the sidelines made him the coach he is now. "Coach Spurrier can stand on the sidelines, with or without a headset, and look at the defense, and 95 percent of the time he'll pick a play that's going to work for us," says Gators backup quarterback Brian Schottenheimer, son of Kansas City Chiefs coach Marty Schottenheimer. "The way he sees the whole field is amazing."

But when he came to work at Florida the first time, in 1978, Spurrier lasted only a year; head coach Charley Pell didn't like the fact that Spurrier, his quarterbacks coach, wasn't interested in 20-hour workdays and marathon film sessions. Spurrier moved on to Georgia Tech the next season to tutor the quarterbacks for Rodgers before becoming offensive coordinator at Duke under Red Wilson in 1980. Wilson quickly found that he was relying on Spurrier; during games Wilson would ask him what play he had decided to call. "Touchdown, Coach," Spurrier would reply. "And, dadgummit," Wilson says, "it *was* a touchdown."

But scoring wasn't what really pushed Spurrier. Mention how much he loves to win and he instantly corrects, "No, I hate to lose." And all along the way, Spurrier has remembered every slight, every insult. "See that?" he says, pointing to a newspaper clip on the wall in his office. "I was released by three NFL teams; I wasn't kept by Charley Pell or Bill Curry [at Georgia Tech]. I was cut loose five times in 2½ years."

Spurrier's tenure at Tech ended shortly after the Yellow Jackets lost their '79 season finale 16–3 to Georgia. Rodgers was fired, and when Curry was hired, he elected not to retain Spurrier. Every time he faces Curry, he remembers. Every time he faces Georgia Tech, he remembers. And he remembers that it was Georgia that handed Rodgers—the guy who gave Spurrier his first break—a loss in his last college game 17 years ago. In November, Spurrier had Doug Johnson, a backup quarterback, throw into the end zone with 2:23 left to tack on a meaningless touchdown in a 47–7 rout of the Bulldogs. After the game, Spurrier presented Rodgers with a game ball. "He dislikes [Georgia], just like all of us Gators," Spurrier offered as an explanation. Spurrier is now 7–0 against Georgia. He remembers.

"I'll show those people they were wrong, the ones who didn't keep me as a coach," he says. "We all like to prove people wrong who say we're no good."

THERE ARE signs, however, that Steve Spurrier has begun to mellow. He still flings his visor when his team blows a play, but Jerri says that he's making the kind of effort to help raise their nine-year-old adopted son, Scotty, that he never made with their three older kids. One autumn night, as he sat in an icy TV studio doing his weekly call-in show, someone called to tell him he's a "wizard," and Spurrier mumbled, "Well . . . not really."

And nowadays he tells stories like this: In 1994, he says, a Gators fan in Georgia faxed him, begging him to refrain from making incendiary comments because it hurt recruiting. "I wrote him back saying it's not a big deal," Spurrier says. "The next day he called and said, 'Coach, please disregard what I wrote. I was listening to the wrong people. I was listening to people who are jealous of our success.'

"I said, 'Well, I appreciate it, but if somebody doesn't like you. . . . ' " Spurrier pauses here, because maybe he's not getting his point across. He tries one more story: "A Tennessee writer wrote an article up there a couple of years ago saying, 'If Spurrier was coaching at Tennessee and we won the SEC, we'd love him, and Florida fans . . . Florida fans wouldn't like him very well at all.'"

ALL-
EVERYTHING

| | | | | |

The Roots of Greatness

BY BRUCE NEWMAN

Motivated by the preachings of a noble mama and propelled by his mighty legs,
Earl Campbell left plank-shack poverty far behind. But the man who was the
NFL's rushing leader as a rookie never forgot to look back.

ERE IS WHAT WE KNOW ABOUT THE STATE OF POVERTY: Its boundaries do not appear on any map; it has no flag or official song, but once you are there it is difficult to get your zip code changed; as a character-building experience it is overrated by the rich and overpopulated by the poor; and it's a place where nobody goes for the weekend.

Earl Campbell had never given much thought to being poor, had never really realized how deprived his family had been, until—in the space of a single year—he won the Heisman Trophy, signed a contract worth $1.4 million to play for the Houston Oilers and became the hottest thing to hit the NFL since *Monday Night Football.* When the full weight of his family's privation hit him, Campbell decided to take some of his NFL greenbacks and build a spacious new house for his mother and then turn the rundown plank shack where he had grown up into a museum where other underprivileged kids could come see firsthand that the NFL was, indeed, the land of opportunity.

And so, as Campbell's fortunes soared on football fields across America last season, his mama's new house went up. And lest the contrast between his past and his present would be too subtle to grasp, Campbell had the new house built about 25 feet from the old one, with only a large gray septic tank between them.

If anyone ever deserved to have a shrine of his very own after only one year in the NFL, that person surely is Earl Campbell. Last year as a rookie he rushed for 1,450 yards—more than O.J., more than Walter Payton, more than Tony Dorsett, more than any other running back in the league—and he led the Oilers, who had had an 8–6 season in 1977, to the AFC championship game against the Pittsburgh Steelers, who then put an end to Campbell's spectacular season.

The Steelers, who had lost to the Oilers in Pittsburgh during the regular season when Campbell ran for three touchdowns, were glad to have seen the last of Campbell. "He can inflict more damage on a team than any back I know of," says Mean Joe Greene. "O.J. did it with speed, Campbell does it with power. He's a punishing runner. He hurts you. There are very few tacklers in the league who will bring Earl Campbell down one-on-one. When we're preparing for the Oilers, we emphasize the importance of gang-tackling Campbell. We work on it."

For Campbell, there was no period of transition as there had been for Simpson, no bow to the depth chart as Dorsett had been obliged to make with the Cowboys the year before. From the moment Campbell touched the ball for Houston, the Oilers were the Earlers. On his third professional carry he took a pitchout and thundered 73 yards for a touchdown against the Atlanta Falcons. Campbell became the first rookie to lead the NFL in rushing since Jim Brown did it in 1957, and Campbell led the Oilers to a 10–6 record—and their first playoff berth in 12 seasons.

"Houston could always move the ball with the passing game and the quick screens and the gimmicks," says coach Don Shula of the Miami Dolphins, who lost to the Oilers in the Astrodome in a game in which Campbell scored four touchdowns and rushed for 199 yards, and then lost a playoff game to the Oilers in Miami. "When the Oilers got Campbell it made Dan Pastorini that much more effective at all the things he's been doing through the years. I don't think it's any coincidence that Pastorini came into his own as an NFL quarterback at the same time the Oilers got Campbell. He's the guy Pastorini was always looking for and never had."

Among the 29 awards Campbell won were NFL Rookie of the Year and NFL Player of the Year. Bum Phillips, the Oilers coach and maybe the only clipboard toter in the league who refuses to take himself seriously, says of Campbell that no one in the past 20 years had a greater impact on the NFL in his first season "except Pete Rozelle."

The Oilers had gone 9–33 for the previous three years when Phillips, wearing his lizard-skin, zircon-encrusted, needle-nosed cowboy boots, took over in 1975. In those days you could fire a cannon into the Astrodome's stands without hitting anybody and fire the same cannon at the Oilers with only a 50–50 chance of hitting a real football player. Bum had a 10–4 record in '75, a 5–9 season in 1976, the 8–6 record in 1977, and the big juicy No. 1 pick in May of 1978.

Soon Houstonians took to saying, "Since Earl came. . . . " Well, for one thing, since Earl came, the Oilers have played to sellout crowds in the As-trodome; average attendance rose to a capacity 51,573 in 1978, and all tick-ets for this season's 10 games, including exhibitions, were sold out last March.

Elvin Bethea, Houston's standout defensive end the past 11 years, recalls the grim pre-Campbell days. "Before Earl came along," Bethea says, "this was just a stopover for a lot of players. We'd show up on Sunday and give the other team a good fight, but we knew all along what the outcome was going to be. Earl put us at the watering hole; now we're going to drink with everybody else."

Until Campbell arrived, the quarterback had long been the Oilers' most visible player. Dante Pastorini had earned a reputation as a hell-raiser by racing jet dragboats and by crashing cars, and it seemed that if anyone was likely to have a personality clash with Campbell, a Baptist Bible–thumper, it would be the infernal Dante. Instead, Campbell and Pas-torini soon came to hold one another in a kind of awe. Pastorini can't get over Campbell's attitude. "It would be easy for a guy coming into the game with all those accolades and all that publicity to be cocky or arrogant," says Pastorini, "but Earl's not that way. He does his job, and if he hasn't got something good to say, he doesn't say anything. You hear a lot of backbit-ing in this league, but I've never heard anyone say a bad word about Earl."

When Phillips talks about Campbell you could swear those tiny hairs on top of the coach's great granite head are standing straight up, out of sheer excitement. "Earl has gotten nine million compliments without letting them swell his head," Phillips says. "I said if he got by last year without changing, he'd survive. I don't believe he'll ever change now. Earl's mama did a heck of a job raising him."

There may be no greater tribute one Texan can pay another than telling him he must have a wonderful mama. Nowhere are mamas held in greater esteem, and nowhere are the things that mama don't 'low held in lower repute. When Campbell was going through the hazing that veterans traditionally inflict upon rookies in training camp, he was required to stand up during one meal and sing a song from soup to nuts. Campbell sang *Mamas Don't Let Your Babies Grow Up To Be Cowboys*, a country-and-western anthem to the Texas matriarchy that was made popular by his good friends Willie Nelson and Waylon Jennings.

Like all but three of his 10 brothers and sisters, Earl Christian Campbell was born at home in the same bed where he was conceived. From the time she was pregnant with Earl until he was a sophomore at the University of Texas, Ann Campbell worked as a cleaning lady for some of the wealthiest families in Tyler, Texas. She did floors, polished other people's silver for their fine parties, and at Christmas she gratefully accepted the hams they gave her. When her famous son signed with the Oilers, Ann Campbell didn't do cartwheels. "All this money don't make me nervous," she said. "I was always in fine places, beautiful homes. They may not have been mine, but I could enjoy them just the same."

There is a prevailing roundness about Mama (it is no use calling her Ann, this being among the things that Mama most assuredly don't 'low), a pleasing full-bodiedness that makes her seem to be built implausibly close to the ground. Mama's face is expressive but she doesn't give away anything she isn't ready for you to know. One of her front teeth has a gold jacket, giving a certain unassailable value to just about everything she says.

Ann and Burk Campbell were married in June 1942, soon after the U.S. entered World War II, and she spent the war years living with her parents while he served in the Army in France. After five years of marriage, they inherited a 14-acre plot in Tyler, on which they began to grow peas and corn, and eventually roses.

Now and then Willie Nelson sings *Stardust*, which contains this lyric.

The nightingale tells his fairy tale
Of paradise where roses grew.

Tyler grows more than half of the rosebushes sold in the U.S., as many as 20 million bushes a year. There are small wooden roadside stands all over Tyler at which a dozen roses sell for a dollar, and there are 2,000 people who depend upon the Tyler rose industry for their living. Though the Campbells couldn't hope to compete with the larger nurseries, they scratched out a living.

"I've been on this corner for 32 years," Mama said the other day, "and all my life I never had to file an income tax return, never had no money in a bank. What little we made on the roses we spent right here. We had to take a lot of our clothes from the Salvation Army, stuff we could get for 25 cents or so. My kids were never crazy about it, though. They refused to wear other people's old clothes. We grew all the food we needed. In the spring I'd slaughter a calf or a hog and we'd have our beef and pork for the year."

As the Campbell family grew in size, more spacious quarters were needed. When Earl was 10 years old, the family moved a few hundred feet to another house on the same property. Mama recalls that the family completed the move just in time to celebrate Christmas of 1965 in their new house. "But the whole time we were moving, my husband was always complaining he didn't feel right," she says. "We'd only been in the new house for four months when he died of a heart attack."

The house that was so new and full of promise in 1965 now is abandoned. Perhaps because it is raised on concrete blocks, it has something of the look of an old jalopy. In fact, there is the front seat of a car on its porch.

On summer days the tar on Country Road 492 blisters where it passes these two Texas monuments, and small bubbles percolate to the surface. At noon on sunny days, trees strain themselves to produce a few feet of shade. All around the Campbell house the wind holds its breath, and the sky is the purest blue. The new house is made of brick and seems to catch the full brunt of the sunlight; the old house gets the same light, but its gray, weatherbeaten pallor makes it look like the big house's shadow.

Last spring when the new house was finished, Earl Campbell's mama couldn't shed the old shack that had been like a second skin to her for

13½ years, so she asked Earl to leave it standing. That is when he began to consider the idea of turning the old place into a museum.

"When they told me I could start moving everything into the new house," Mama says, "I was kind of sad about it, you know. It took me quite a while to get everything moved in, and I kept my bed in the old house for a long time. One day my daughter asked me why I did that, and I just told her I wanted to take my time. If I was moving and night was to catch me in the old house, why I'd just spend the night there. And if it caught me in the new house, I'd sleep there. I wasn't particular."

When Earl was growing up, he shared a room as well as a bed in the old plank house with his brothers Herbert and Alfred Ray. It was the first room you saw when you opened the front door.

The Campbells in residence varied from one year to the next, depending upon the intercession of natural disasters. When Ann Campbell's mother and sister lost their home in a fire, they packed up three children and moved in, temporarily swelling the ranks to 15. The air above the peeling linoleum floorboards always was close and clammy during the long Texas summers. In the winter the family sometimes used space heaters to keep warm, but the body heat of several Campbells to a bed provided warmth enough even on the coldest nights.

Ann Campbell always told her children, "If you want to be someplace safe, be in church." And every Sunday from the time he was christened until he went away to college, that is where Earl was, front and center at the Hopewell Baptist No. 1. For four years he sang in the church choir.

"I never paid a fine for any of my children and never bailed any of them out of jail," Mama says proudly. "We always had a lot of love, and I think that's why they all turned out so well. We worked together in the fields during the day, and we all slept together at night."

It seems odd, given his extreme rectitude now, that Earl was his mama's only real problem child, the one who came the closest to real trouble with the law. When Earl was in the sixth grade at Griffin Elementary School, he began smoking a pack and a half of cigarettes a day, a habit he maintained for three years. "I used to be a thug from about the time I was in the sixth grade until I went into high school," Earl says. "I lived the street life for a while. I gambled and stole, and I used to make a pretty good living shooting pool. I did just about everything there was except get mixed up with drugs."

Naturally, this type of behavior didn't win him his mama's gratitude. "She's the onlyest person in life I would steal for, or lie for, or kill for," Campbell says now. "She's a great lady, but she's a terrible person to be on the bad side of. I'm her son and it took me a *long* time to get on her good side."

That ascent to grace didn't occur until Campbell was nearly 14. One evening, as he set out upon the road to one of Tyler's iniquitous downtown street corners, probably for a crap game, Earl abruptly decided to change his ways. "I never really liked the country life when I was growing up," he says. "I was always searching for something else. Then that day out on the black tar road that passed by where we lived, I said, 'Lord, lift me up.' "

Once set upon the path of righteousness, Campbell found football. He was so strong and so gifted that in his senior year at John Tyler High School he scored 28 touchdowns, leading his team to a 15–0 season and the state 4A title.

"You just knew every time he got the ball he was going to get you three or four yards, even if there was no blocking at all," says Miami Dolphins rookie tight end Ron Lee, a teammate of Campbell's at John Tyler. "And at each level he's advanced—and made it look easy. I guess you could say that Earl's just a person who was born to be great."

After Campbell had scored two touchdowns in the state championship game, the coach of the losing team said, "I always thought Superman was white and wore an *S*, but now I know he's black and wears number 20."

When Campbell left home for the first time in his life, to attend the University of Texas, 200 miles away in Austin, he became so homesick that, as former Longhorn coach Darrell Royal recalls, he "would sit on the curb and face in the direction of Tyler."

In college Campbell took every opportunity to spread the credit for his rushing feats among his teammates. "If it were up to Earl," wrote David Casstevens in *The Houston Post*, "he would probably change the name of his 'I' formation to the 'We.' "

Last year, after Billy Sims of Oklahoma had won the Heisman Trophy that Campbell had won the year before, Sooners coach Barry Switzer offered this comparison: "Earl Campbell is the greatest player who ever suited up. He's the greatest football player I've ever seen. Billy Sims is human. Campbell isn't."

When the Oilers, desperate for both a quality football player and a box office attraction, acquired the No. 1 pick in the 1978 draft from Tampa Bay and then used it to select Campbell, former Texas assistant coach Pat Patterson warned Bum Phillips what to expect. "When you meet Earl," Patterson said, "You're not going to believe anybody can be that honest and sincere. So you're going to be waiting for him to make a slip, for his true temperament to show through. But you can stop waiting because it's not going to happen. Earl is exactly what he seems to be, one of the nicest people you'll ever meet."

In college Campbell never shied away from hard work, and, when pressed, he wasn't diffident about assessing his own worth. Worth, as it happens, is a concept dear to his heart. Once, when someone implied that Earl would be picking up easy money when he signed with the pros, the 5' 11" Campbell drew himself up to his full height and said coolly, "There isn't a check big enough to pay me back."

As Campbell has discovered, it's much easier to leave the state of poverty than it is to get rid of the poor man's state of mind. When he purchased a comfortable three-bedroom house on Houston's southwest side last year, he asked a contract landscaper to quote him a price for cutting, weeding and trimming the lawn. When the contractor told him it would be $150 a month, which he could easily afford, Campbell whistled softly and thanked the man for his time. Then he went out and bought himself a power mower. "Earl isn't going to waste any money," says Oilers offensive backfield coach Andy Bourgeois. "He's a most frugal young man."

Campbell dislikes signing autographs, probably because he finds the attention embarrassing. Whatever his reasons, he avoids such situations. Yet when he ran out of candy last Halloween, rather than go out and buy more, he gave each kid who came to his door an autograph. A heartwarming instance of generosity, or just plain old tightfistedness?

Consider this. Shortly before the Oilers' training camp opened in July, Campbell threw a small party for a few of his close friends in Houston. When he stopped by a liquor store near his home, he was amazed and somewhat horrified to learn that it would cost him $60 or $70 to stock his bar for the evening's roistering. Rather than cough up that kind of money, Campbell identified himself to the owner of the store, and then proceeded to talk the man into supplying the liquor for the party in exchange for four autographed pictures. When Campbell tells this story, he does so without irony, trying to make a point about the high cost of hooch.

None of this is meant to imply that Earl Campbell is cheap. His thriftiness is punctuated by occasional bursts of generosity, or in the case of his Earl Campbell Crusade for Kids, a longstanding commitment to making life a little more pleasant for underprivileged children in the Houston area. This summer he went on local television in Houston and asked the community to donate old books, school supplies and toys to the crusade. Campbell's fans came through with a truckload of gifts, and Earl kicked in with some lunchboxes and notebooks of his own, then handed the swag out to kids in several Houston parks.

Though he doesn't own an expensive car, Campbell recently bought a $34,000 Mercedes 450 SEL for Reuna Smith, his girlfriend of the past 10 years, "just for putting up with me all that time." As training camp got under way at San Angelo State, Campbell gathered his offensive linemen around him and gave each of them a gold money clip in the shape of a spur, engraved with the words 1,000 YARDS. An act of simple gratitude, or a rite of self-preservation? "If I took all the credit all the time," Campbell says, "maybe someday our offensive linemen and Pastorini will say, 'O.K., this time we're going to let Earl really do it alone.' I'm nothing without them."

And, he might truthfully add, they without him. He has the speed and quickness of a great running back, as well as a marvelous sense of invention that can turn a routine off-tackle play into a big gainer. The power he generates by his enormous thighs and prodigious backside makes it nearly impossible for a single tackler to bring Campbell down.

Toni Fritsch, the Oilers' placekicker, was at Campbell's home recently when, without warning, he grabbed his host around the thighs—"ties," as Fritsch calls them in his Austrian-accented English—and began imploring Campbell to protect his massive assets. Fritsch is 5' 7", weighs 200 pounds and is balding; he looks more like a cabdriver than a pro football player. But he has Super Bowl rings on both his hands, thanks to five years' employment with the Dallas Cowboys, and they give his monologues a lift they might otherwise lack.

Fritsch looked up into Campbell's face and shouted, "Watch out, please, Mr. Oohl. These are your capital. You can buy a new house, a new car but, excuse me, please, these you cannot get back."

It seems that all of Campbell's teammates are protective of him. Last season Pastorini passed for more touchdowns and yardage than he ever had before and also had the second-best completion percentage in his eight-year career—hats off, he says, to Campbell. "Earl made us the best play-action team in football," Pastorini says. "We were on the verge of becoming a good team even without him. Earl can make us great."

Freezing onrushing linemen dead in their tracks by faking to Campbell, Pastorini has time to wait for his receivers to get open. The quarterback had often been booed in Houston, especially on the several occasions he had publicly requested to be traded, but with Campbell alongside him, he suddenly was being called a "field general." Campbell's presence also seemed to have a tonic effect on Bethea, who had grown tired of Houston. "Nobody had worked harder than Elvin," says Pastorini, "but he had lost some of his enthusiasm for playing in a losing situation year after year. When you're losing, you wonder when it's going to end and where your career is headed."

Says Bethea, "It's hard to go out and play when you lack confidence that the offense is going to do anything with the ball when you get it for them. With Earl, the defense isn't constantly on the field. A thing like that makes a big difference."

The Oilers gave the ball to the Tyler Rose an average of 19 times a game in 1978, and he responded with an average gain of 4.8 yards and 13 touchdowns, while fumbling only seven times. With a number of talented wide receivers—notably Ken Burrough, Rich Caster and Mike Renfro—the Oilers rarely threw to Campbell; he caught only 12 passes. But if Pastorini calls on him to run pass patterns this season, or to become a blocking back, or, for that matter, to wallpaper the Astrodome, no doubt Campbell will.

"Anything you ask him to do," says Phillips, clearly impressed, "he's going to do it. It's very important to have a player of Earl Campbell's caliber, but it's even more important to have him be the kind of kid he is."

One authority on the subject of running in the NFL believes it is an instinct for leadership that makes Campbell such a surpassing talent. "Earl's physical talents are considerable, of course," says O.J. Simpson, "but he has inspirational quality far beyond those talents. He provides a certain lift to a team; everything will be going along normally, then all of a sudden he takes over. I tell you, I'm inspired by his kind of performance."

Campbell's running style is markedly different from the way Simpson ran when he was in his prime, though the result are often the same. More often Campbell, who carries 225 pounds, is compared to the Cleveland Browns' superstar of 1957 to '65, Jim Brown. But Brown's old coach, Paul Brown, and Simpson both feel the comparison is not entirely apt. "Earl jukes as many as he runs over," Juice points out. "He's a true halfback, and Jim was a fullback. I was amazed how short Earl is. He sure looks bigger on the TV."

Paul Brown is right when he says Campbell will have to put together a string of outstanding seasons before he can be meaningfully compared with Jim Brown. "Brown didn't take an intense physical pounding for his yardage," says Paul Brown. "Campbell does it the physical way. He's not as good a pass receiver as Jim was, and I don't think he has the same straightaway speed. But Brown never liked the blocking aspects of football, and I think Campbell tries to do his part. The only thing you can question about Campbell is whether his style is the type that will allow him to have a long career."

THERE ARE a few incandescent moments in any great athlete's career when muscle seems more tightly joined to bone, and when his body crackles like a summer cloud with heat lightening. When one of those moments coincides with desperate necessity, it is advisable not to stand too near, for the brilliance can be blinding.

Last November, Campbell had just such a moment—really an entire game of such moments—on a Monday night in the Astrodome against Miami on national TV, churning through and around the Dolphins, as previously noted, for four touchdowns and 199 yards. Campbell can remember thinking after his third touchdown that he couldn't move anymore, that he was so exhausted his legs felt like concrete piles—the kind that hold bridges up. Late in the fourth period the Oilers were holding a 28–23 lead and facing second-and-long at their own 19. Pastorini could see that Campbell was breathing heavily, but when he knelt down in the huddle he called, almost automatically, "Pitch 28".

"Before Pastorini tossed me the ball," says Campbell, "I would have sworn I couldn't run anymore at all. Even after I was through the hole and I saw [running mate] Tim Wilson hit his man, I didn't think I could make it to the other end of the field. Then I saw pure sideline, and I decided to keep running until somebody knocked me down."

Nobody did. Campbell swept right end, his body leaning hard to the left, and then straightened and rumbled down the sideline 81 yards to the end zone, ensuring a 35–30 Oiler victory.

"He gave them what they had to have," acknowledges Miami's Shula. "He had some head-on collisions with our players and I think he won them all. We had some people get run over that don't get run over." Dolphin linebacker Steve Towle, a friend of Campbell's, was similarly impressed. "When he sees his spot, he's into it before the hole can be filled," Towle says. "He had two tremendous games against the Dolphins in one season, and I can't recall anybody else I could say that about."

After the Monday night game, Campbell lay wide awake until nearly dawn, just as he does after every game. The buzz in his ears wouldn't go away, and the lightening in his body he had not used up was now flashing behind his eyes. "I usually lie there in bed, tossing and turning, until about 4 a.m.," Campbell says. "Most of the time I have flashbacks from the game, mental pictures in which I can see holes forming in front of me, and then see the defensive linemen fill them up as they charge at me. But I'm never scared. It's just like in the game, fear doesn't enter into it."

Earl Campbell put down a pool cue in his game room, and his face tried to break into a smile, but his lower lip was so full of snuff he couldn't. "Waylon says cowboys are like smoky old pool rooms," he said. "You clear 'em all out in the morning."

And with that, he began to sing in an affecting falsetto.

Cowboys ain't easy to love and they're harder to hold,
They'd rather give you a song than diamonds or gold . . .
Mamas, don't let your babies grow up to be cowboys
'Cause they'll never stay home and they're always alone,
Even with someone they love.

| | | | | |

Let's Hand It to Him

BY RICK TELANDER

*Jerry Rice's dedication to his craft has made him
the finest receiver in the game's history.*

HE BEST? ❡ HE'S HERE, IN BLUE TIGHTS AND RED
windbreaker, bitchy as a diva with a headache. ❡ The best
ever? ❡ He's right here, sitting at his locker, taking off his
rain gear after practice, edgy as a cat in a sawmill.

Around him swirls the clamor of big men winding down, messing around,
acting like fools. Two bare-chested linemen lock up and start to grapple,
rasslin' each other and snorting like trash-talking sumos. Other players
laugh, but not the best ever.

"Guys," he says irritably. "Hey, guys!" Someone could get hurt.

The two wrestlers slowly come apart, his voice bringing them to their sens-
es. They've heard that voice before; it's their fourth-grade teacher scolding
them for rolling spitballs. It's the voice of San Francisco 49er Jerry Rice, the
best wide receiver ever to play football. The 6-foot, 2-inch, tightly braided
coil of nerves, fast-twitch fibers, delicate grasping skills and unadulterated
want-to is setting such high standards for the position that they will probably never be approached again, and he can't stand distractions while he works.

Rice does not fool around. Ever. He works so hard at his conditioning that during the off-season he virtually exits his body and studies his physical package the way a potter studies clay. "I mess with it," he says. "I like to do different things to motivate myself. I set goals and go after them."

As a rookie in 1985 he came to the 49ers at a muscular 208 pounds, but now he weighs 196. He is so lean that you wonder if he's sick. He likes to mess with his body fat, wants it to know that he is its master. For Rice, fat is a cornerback in man coverage with no safety in sight, a minor and ultimately irrelevant nuisance. Eschewing dietary fat, he got down to 189 a year or so ago, but the weight loss was too much. His starved body was eating up his muscles. His trainer ordered him to start eating things like ice cream. "Under four percent body fat and I don't feel good," Rice states. "I'm a health-food fanatic, but getting that low really hurt my performance. I'm at 4.8 percent now, and I feel good."

Well, not really *good*. Not the way you or I might feel good if we knew that not only were we certifiably the best receiver in the history of football but, perhaps, the greatest offensive player ever. That argument can be made. Rice already has more receiving touchdowns (130) and more total touchdowns (138) than anyone in NFL history. He has more 1,000-yard seasons (nine) than any other receiver, more touchdown catches in a Super Bowl (three) than anyone and more consecutive games with a touchdown reception (13) than anyone.

Was he this good in college? Imagine, for a moment, that it's September 1984, and you are in sweltering Itta Bena, Miss., watching Mississippi Valley State coach Archie (Gunslinger) Cooley direct his Satellite Express offense, with quarterback Willie Totten flinging passes to a senior wideout named Rice, who races out of a stacked receiver formation that looks something like a Motown chorus line. In the first four games of that season Rice caught 64 passes for 917 yards and 12 touchdowns. As a junior he caught 24 passes in one game, an all-division record. He left school with 18 NCAA I-AA records. Yes, he was good.

Rice never missed a game in college, nor has he missed one as a pro. Since he joined the 49ers the team has gone 126-45-1 (the best record in the NFL during that period) and won two Super Bowls. And at the seemingly advanced age of 32, he is still in his prime. Heading into the final game of the regular season, he has 108 catches for 1,446 yards and 12 touchdowns, plus 93 yards and two more touchdowns on seven rushing attempts. "He's in his 10th year," says 49ers player personnel director Dwight Clark, a former star receiver himself, "and he's better than he was in his first."

On a Wednesday one might expect Rice to be civil, but in this case he's already badly game-faced. Usually that doesn't happen until Thursday, but here's the reason: The 49ers are playing on Saturday. Rice's schedule has been moved ahead 24 hours. The gold earring sparkles in his left ear; the gold-flecked tattoo of a 49er helmet on his right deltoid flashes. Rice is miserable. "I'm so grouchy," he says with a tight grin, "my wife is going to move out."

He showers. Earlier in the season he had talked about his compulsion to prove himself, to never let up even for an instant out of fear that everything might come apart. He had started at the bottom, and he could be back there in a heartbeat; people would forget him, and if that happened . . . would he even exist?

"There's always doubt about me," he says. "I was disappointed coming out of college that Al Toon and Eddie Brown were drafted ahead of me, but they went to major colleges. You would think that in my 10th season there wouldn't be any doubt, but it's still out there." It is? Both Toon, who played with the New York Jets, and Brown, who played with the Cincinnati Bengals, are long gone.

There was an article last year, he explains, that ranked him as the third-best receiver in the league at the time, behind Michael Irvin of the Dallas Cowboys and Sterling Sharpe of the Green Bay Packers. "I read that," he says. "You have to have confidence, and guys like that, they're prolonging my career."

Rodney Knox, the 49ers publicist, remembers the article too. "After that," Knox says, "Jerry just exploded."

Rice felt he had stumbled into Oz when he arrived in San Francisco. "I stepped off the plane, and I wanted to turn right around and go home," he says. "I'm still trying to deal with it. There were guys who felt like they were gods at Mississippi Valley State, but it never went to my head. I've never put myself above anyone else. I can get the job done, but I don't see myself as a natural. I'm shy. The pressure is every second. I *have* to perform."

Afield, as in life, Rice is evasive. He almost never takes a direct, crushing blow after catching a pass. He controls his body like a master puppeteer working a marionette. A one-handed grab here, a tiptoe up the sideline there, an unscathed sprint through two closing safeties when it seems de-capitation is imminent. "I don't think I've ever seen him all stretched out," says 49er quarterback Steve Young of Rice's ability to avoid big hits. Rice jumps only when he has to, and unlike almost all other receivers, he catch-es passes in mid-stride and effortlessly continues running, the ball like a sprinter's baton in his hand. It's almost certain that no one has run for more yardage after catching the ball than Rice. Though he's not particu-larly fast, Rice has a fluid stride and a sudden burst that, as Young says, "is a speed you can't clock."

And the hands. Clad in gloves, the hands are so supple and sure that last year they snared a touchdown pass by latching onto the *tail end* of a fading ball. "That was not giving up on the ball," explains Rice. Sounds simple. In reality it's like grabbing the back end of a greased pig.

Rice's hands and agility allow him to catch the ball comfortably no mat-ter where it's thrown. "He makes a lot of catches around his ankles," says Young. At a practice before the 1992 Pro Bowl, Cowboys quarterback Troy Aikman saw from a different perspective just what he and his teammates are up against when they play the 49ers. "We were running a quick out," says Aikman, "and I guess at San Francisco they run it different than we do, which is I drop back five steps and fire it. My arm was strong because I hadn't thrown in a while, and the ball was in the air, and I was sure I was going to kill him. He was still making moves, and the ball was almost at his head, and it wasn't so much that he just reached up and caught it. It was that he didn't even *flinch*."

Rice's dad, Joe Nathan, was a bricklayer, and much has been made of the fact that as a teenager Jerry worked eight-hour shifts with his dad and his brothers on scorching summer days back in Starkville, Miss., hoisting mor-tar and catching the bricks tossed up to him on the scaffold. This repeti-tive action, it has been written, is what forged Rice into the greatest pass catcher ever. The story is nice but probably not true. At least not in the way people would believe. After all, catching bricks is to catching footballs as sawing logs is to slicing sushi. "Catching bricks," says Rice, "taught me the meaning of hard work."

His dad was "very strict and demanding," Rice explains in a way that leaves one with the sense that his father was considerably more than that. Still, after work Rice would jog to the high school football field and exercise for two hours, then jog home—in his work clothes. "I didn't know anything about workout gear," he says.

After he got to the NFL, Rice had difficulty turning down his competitive flame when it wasn't needed. "My first five years I had a hard time turning it off," he says. "If things didn't go right for me in football, I'd find myself not turning it off at home." His wife, Jackie, is a strong woman, but even she had had enough of his intensity. Rice forced himself to let up as best he could. "You hear about stereotypes, about football players being very abusive off the field," he says. "I'd seen things when I was growing up, and I decided I wouldn't be like that."

What had he seen?

"I really don't want to go into that."

Now it is the rainy season in San Francisco, and Rice has limited opportunity to hit golf balls or ride his Harley—the two things he does to keep from coming apart at the seams. It's pouring on this Wednesday, adding to the pressure of the buildup to Saturday's game. He'll watch TV at home and play with his two children, seven-year-old Jaqui and three-year-old Jerry Jr., but he won't be at ease. "People come up to me and say, 'I'd love to be in your shoes,'" he says with a sigh. "I say, 'No, you wouldn't.' They don't know what it's like. The pressure. Before games I can't sleep. Before Super Bowl XXIII I woke up at 4 a.m. and just paced. I can't relax. I should be able to enjoy it, but I can't. The table can turn."

Someday Rice will probably score his 200th touchdown, which will be 74 more than his closest competitor, Jim Brown, who has been retired for almost 30 years. It's a figure so high, it's crazy. But it may not be enough for this most graceful and obsessive of men. "It's a lot of wear and tear on me," he says needlessly of his intensity down the stretch. Don't forget the playoffs coming up, or the Super Bowl itself. Or years to come. "I might not survive," he grimaces.

Constant vigilance is required. The table must not move.

| | | | | |

Thanks, Your Honor

BY STEVE RUSHIN

*Twenty-five years after their first meeting, the author finds
he chose a worthy childhood idol in Alan Page.*

HE NATIONAL FOOTBALL LEAGUE WAS BORN IN AN
automobile showroom in Canton, Ohio, on Sept. 17, 1920.
Alan Page was born in that city nearly 25 years later—
on Aug. 7, 1945, in the 72 hours between the bombings
of Hiroshima and Nagasaki. He entered the world 22 days after the first
atomic bomb was exploded near Alamogordo, N.Mex., and the world he
entered was defined by that explosion. "We knew the world would not be the
same," the bomb's father, J. Robert Oppenheimer, said of that first A-test.
"A few people laughed, a few people cried. Most people were silent. I remembered the line from the Hindu scripture, the *Bhagavad-Gita*: 'I am become
Death, the destroyer of worlds.' "

"Born between the bombs," affirms Page, the former Minnesota Vikings
and Chicago Bears defensive tackle and 1971's NFL Most Valuable Player,
now seated in his office in St. Paul, contemplating the era of his birth. "It's
interesting, isn't it, given the significance of those bombs? I have thought on
occasion about what it all means. I haven't yet come to any conclusions."

Page has the disarming habit of saying "I don't know" when he doesn't know the answer to a question. It's a quality rare among star athletes and unheard of in elected officials. For most of his adult life Page has been one or the other: a gridiron luminary enshrined in 1988 in the Pro Football Hall of Fame—which was under construction in Canton when Page attended Central Catholic High there—and an off-the-field overachiever elected in November 1992 to the Supreme Court of Minnesota, on which he still sits. "There's a danger for judges to assume they have all the answers," says Page, who seldom submits to interviews, explaining his reluctance to pontificate. "There's a saying one of my former colleagues used quite a bit in talking about this court: 'We're not last because we're right. We're only right because we're last.' I think that's something that you have to keep remembering."

When Page does speak, his words carry greater moral authority than those of more heliocentric celebrities, the balls of hot gas around whom the world turns. He has the aura of an oracle, an effect heightened by his soft voice (the listener leans on every word) and black robe (from beneath which peeks a pair of Doc Martens). Page tackles subjects, as he did ball-carriers, from unexpected angles. To his way of thinking, the more unsavory NFL players of today—Rae Carruth, Ray Lewis, Mark Chmura, et al.—are quite useful role models for American youth. "One of the frustrations for me is that this whole role-model business works two ways," he says. "There are models to look up to and models who demonstrate clearly what we should not aspire to. But we don't use those latter models for that purpose. In fact, there's an odd transference: We end up *glorifying* those people."

I haven't yet told Page that he was my childhood hero, or that we have met before, nearly 26 years earlier, but I have come here to do just that—to St. Paul, hometown of F. Scott Fitzgerald, who wrote, "Show me a hero and I'll write you a tragedy."

"I've never understood the phenomenon of athlete worship, of how we get our athletic heroes," says Page, 54, when Fitzgerald's line is recited to him. "I can remember from the beginning, by which I mean my sophomore or junior year in high school, being looked on as a good football player, yes, but it went beyond my ability as a football player." People who had never met Page nonetheless began to admire him, and he found this profoundly disquieting. "I like to think that I was a good human being," he continues, "but people couldn't know that from watching me play football. So I kind of rejected the whole hero notion early on.

"There were times," he adds, a trifle unnecessarily, "when I didn't sign autographs."

YOU COULDN'T buy a number 88 Vikings jersey in Minnesota in 1974. You could buy the 10 of Fran Tarkenton or the 44 of Chuck Foreman, but if you wanted the 88 of Alan Page your parents had to find a blank purple football shirt and have the numbers ironed on. As far as I know, my parents were the only ones who ever did. The jersey became my security blanket— what psychologists call a "transition object," the item that sustains a child in moments away from his mother. I wore the shirt until it disintegrated in the wash and blew away one day like dandelion spores.

I grew up in the town in which the Vikings played their home games, in the decade in which they played in four Super Bowls. Yet even in Bloomington, Minn., in the 1970s, I was alone among my schoolmates in worshipping Page, who was fearsome and had a reputation for brooding silence, a reputation that I scarcely knew of as an eight-year-old. I knew only that Page had gone to Notre Dame, that he was genuinely great—the first defensive player to be named MVP of the NFL—and that his Afro sometimes resembled Mickey Mouse ears when he removed his helmet. I at once loved Alan Page and knew nothing whatsoever about him.

Then one unfathomable day in September '74, the month in which I turned eight, a second-grade classmate named Troy Chaika invited me to a Saturday night sleepover at the Airport Holiday Inn, which his father managed and where the Vikings, as everyone knew, bivouacked on the night before each home game. I could meet the players when they checked in and, if I asked politely and addressed each of them as "Mister," get their autographs, a prospect that thrilled and terrified me in equal measure. So every night for two weeks, toothbrush in hand, I practiced my pitch to the bathroom mirror: "Please, Mr. Page, may I have your autograph?"

Time crawled, clocks ticked backward, but, after an eternity, Saturday came. My mom—God bless her, for it must have pained her beyond words— allowed me to leave the house in my 88 jersey, now literally in tatters, the kind of shirt worn by men in comic strips who have been marooned on a tiny desert island with one palm tree.

So I took my place in the Holiday Inn lobby—Bic pen in one damp hand, spiral notebook in the other—and recited my mantra rapid-fire to myself, like Hail Marys on a rosary: *"PleaseMr.PagemayIhaveyour autograph? PleaseMr.PagemayIhaveyour autograph?PleaseMr.Page. . . ."*

Moments before the Vikings' 8 p.m. arrival, my friend's father, the innkeeper, cheerily reminded me to be polite and that the players would in turn oblige me. "Except Page," he added off-handedly, in the oblivious way of adults. "Don't ask him. He doesn't sign autographs."

Which is how I came to be blinking back tears when the Vikings walked into the Holiday Inn, wearing Stetsons and suede pants and sideburns like shag-carpet samples. Their shirt collars flapped like pterodactyl wings. They were truly terrifying men, none more so than Page, whose entrance— alone, an overnight bag slung over his shoulder—cleaved a group of bell-hops and veteran teenage autograph hounds, who apparently knew to give the man a wide berth.

Page strode purposefully toward the stairwell. I choked as he breezed past; I was unable to speak, a small and insignificant speck whose cheeks, armpits and tear ducts were suddenly bursting into flames. It was to be an early lesson in life's manifold disappointments: two weeks of excruciating anticipation dashed in as many seconds. Still, I had never seen Page outside a television set and couldn't quite believe he was incarnate, so—my chicken chest heaving, hyperventilation setting in—I continued to watch as he paused at the stairs, turned and looked back at the lobby, evidently having forgotten to pick up his room key.

But he hadn't forgotten any such thing. No, Page walked directly toward me, took the Bic from my trembling hand and signed his name in one grand flourish. He smiled and put his hand on top of my head, as if palming a grapefruit. Then he disappeared into the stairwell, leaving me to stand there in the lobby, slack-jawed, forming a small puddle of admiration and urine.

PAGE LISTENS to the story in some suspense, visibly relieved at the outcome. "My sense, for a period, was that it's mostly an intrusion," Page says of autograph requests. "It's never at the right time or the right place for me. The problem is, for the person seeking the autograph, it's the only time."

He pauses in judicial repose, folding his enormous hands in a church and steeple. "But I came to a conclusion," he says at last. "What I figured out is this: *Just sign 'em*. Sign 'em all. It's just easier to sign. Somebody told me, 'Nothing bad ever comes from being nice to somebody.' You know what? For some people, it makes their day. Absolutely makes their day! They're adults, kids, football fans, people interested in law—all of the above. Some of it is simply any-hero-will-do. But some of it is a need, and I don't know where it springs from, but there is a *need* among a lot of people to be part of something, or someone, they perceive as important. And signing an autograph is a pretty simple thing to do to make someone happy.

"Sometimes," he adds, "it makes me happy too."

NOW THAT I have introduced Page to the eight-year-old that I was in 1974, he acquaints me with the three-dimensional, 29-year-old human being who encountered me in the lobby of that Holiday Inn. Page didn't play football until ninth grade, and only then because his older brother, Howard, did. Alan was instantly great, a prodigy of sorts, earning a scholarship to Notre Dame. Four years later the Vikings selected him with the 15th pick in the draft. "The conventional wisdom when I entered the league was, you've got this little square plot of ground to cover," recalls Page, "and if you take care of it, we'll love you forever. Well, that wasn't very interesting to me. Or very challenging."

Lithe and almost feline, Page went wherever the ballcarrier was, often pulling the runner down with one hand. He won his MVP award in his fifth year. "By the end of the '74 season I had been in the league eight years," says Page, "and there are only so many things you can do on the football field. I'd done most of them. I was bored. Plus, you know you're not going to play forever. So for me, it was time to go get the law degree."

His office is bereft of football memorabilia, crammed instead with Jim Crow collectibles—a COLORED WAITING ROOM sign and other reminders that everyone is equal under the law. "Long before I had an interest in football, I had an interest in law," he says. "My earliest recollections are from fourth grade, back when you don't have any idea what the law is about. It was probably a little to do with Perry Mason, but also a sense, without knowing any lawyers, that, viewed from the 11-year-old's eyes, the law is an easy life, you make lots of money, you play golf every afternoon. That looked a lot more interesting than the steel mill.

"There's also the component that the law is about helping people, about fairness, this concept we have of *justice*," says Page. "I was a teenager in the late '50s and early '60s, and as a nation we were going through tremendous upheaval related to issues at the heart of fairness: issues of race. That was a catalyst—not that I could have articulated any of this back then."

In his second year in the NFL, Page attended three weeks of night classes at William Mitchell College of Law in St. Paul. "It was clear after a couple of days that I was in over my head," he says. "But it took me another three weeks just to figure out how to drop out."

It was around the time of our wordless meeting in the Holiday Inn that Page resolved to return to law school. He did so the following year, spending 13 weeks in a summer program at Texas, then enrolling at Minnesota during the 1975 season. (He would graduate in '78 and practice law for seven years before joining the state attorney general's office.) Page read law books in the locker room. He prepared for exams on team buses. If he appeared to be "silent" and "brooding" to fans or sportswriters, he was in fact merely quiet and contemplative. He didn't refrain from signing autographs because, as I had assumed, the seeker wasn't worthy, but rather because the *signer* wasn't worthy. "The fact that one has an athletic ability," Page says, "doesn't mean you don't have the same problems that every other person has."

On the other hand, as he discovered, nothing bad ever came from being nice to somebody. So while the 29-year-old Page entered the Holiday Inn that Saturday evening in '74, thinking only about the numbing routine ahead—"check-in at eight, followed by team meeting, curfew at 10, 7:30 wake-up, nine o'clock breakfast, we go to the stadium at 10 o'clock for a one o'clock game"—he paused on his way to the stairwell. He spent five seconds signing my notebook and palming my noggin. Then he wearily climbed the stairs to his usual room, never to think of the moment for another quarter century.

Whereas I was so smitten by the one small act of kindness that I *still* wait on athletes in hotel lobbies and stadiums, hoping they'll deign to speak to me. That's what sportswriters do. It is a blessed existence—nice work if you can get it—and it's high time I thank Page for keeping an introverted eight-year-old interested in sports at a time when neither of us was entirely sure if his heart was in it for the long haul.

PAGE TOOK up marathon running in his 30s, as have I. (He still logs 60 miles a week and weighs 225 pounds, the playing weight at which he retired in 1981.) He finds the NFL largely unwatchable, as do I. ("It's like watching paint dry," he says. "It's just not me. I loved playing, but watching? I just can't do it.") And, like me—like most of us, one hopes—he finds *Jerry Springer* an alarming reflection of American society.

"In this day and age," Page says, "when we have TV programs devoted to people yelling and screaming and fighting to no end, I think we, as a society, have changed. The more you see of that, the more it appears that that kind of behavior is acceptable, then the more people engage in it. Athletes are no different.

"We see everything here," he says of the highest court in Minnesota. "The worst of the worst of the criminal cases. It can be ugly. Some days you don't go home with a very good impression of the human condition."

Other days he goes home awestruck by "the resilience of the human spirit." In 1988 he established the Page Education Foundation, which has helped more than 1,100 minority students attend colleges in Minnesota. This past academic year 405 students received more than half a million dollars in financial aid. One of those kids is a 20-year-old graduate of Minneapolis's Roosevelt High; on his grant application, he listed his parents' address as "Somewhere in Somalia."

"He came to the United States four years ago," says Page. "He said his parents are constantly on the move as circumstances change in Somalia. You've got to be pretty tough to deal with that at age 16. My heroes are a lot of young people who have worked their way out of circumstances other people would succumb to.

"Every one of our scholarship recipients commits to going back into their community and working with young children. They must act as mentors to kids, kindergarten through eighth grade, through community-based organizations, and send the message to young people that education is important. They serve as examples of successful students—the perfect role model for young children. Here is somebody who is going to school, who can say, 'You can do what I've done.' *They're* the real heroes in this world."

My hero's other heroes are more predictable: His walls are filled with pictures of Paul Robeson, Thurgood Marshall and Robert F. Kennedy, whom Page honored at his first Supreme Court swearing-in. He received, in return, a long, handwritten thank-you letter from Kennedy's widow, Ethel. Its first heartfelt sentence reads, "Hallelujah!"

"My father was a bartender, not educated beyond high school," says Page, one of four children. "But he and my mother understood the importance of education: Go to school, do your homework, be a good citizen."

Page and his wife of 27 years, Diane, passed that simple edict on to their four children, all of whom are grown and successful. More than athletics, more than the law, education is what *really* interests Page—the way one good role model can have an outsized effect on an impressionable child. "I think, if I can drum up the courage, I'd like to teach one day," Page says, his mind far from his Supreme Court chamber. "When I say teach, my inclination is elementary school."

He looks me in the eye and says, "A class full of 30 eight-year-olds could be challenging, don't you think?"

"You'd do fine," this eight-year-old replies.

| | | | | | |

Born to Be a Quarterback

BY PAUL ZIMMERMAN

Schooled in the fundamentals from the time he could walk, Joe Montana
showed early that he was a gifted passer, and football fans from the
Monongahela Valley to San Francisco have marveled at his abilities ever since.

I T'S A NORMAL MINICAMP LUNCH BREAK AT THE SAN FRANCISCO 49ers training facility. The players are unwrapping their sandwiches in the locker room, and Joe Montana is giving an interview upstairs in p.r. director Jerry Walker's office. Well, most of Joe Montana is concentrating on the interview. His right hand is busy with something else, as if it has a life of its own, a mechanized life of autograph production.

A steady stream of objects appears on the table in front of him—hats, jerseys, photos, posters—and Montana's right hand automatically rises, then lowers, producing a large sweeping *J* and tailing off to an almost illegible *ana*. Then his hand rises again, and another item is moved into place. Secretaries, p.r. people, coaches, players all present offerings at this ritual.

"A book to sign," says Walker. "Two pictures," says tight end Jamie Williams. "A ball," says p.r. assistant Dave Rahn. "Make this one out to 'a Nevada sports fan,' " says defensive coordinator Bill McPherson, sliding in a picture.

Rise and fall, rise and fall; the big *J*, the scribbled *ana*. Most of the time Montana doesn't even look at what he's signing. You get the feeling that someone could slip in a small child, a hamburger bun, a fish. It's all the same. At 34, the world's most famous quarterback has turned into an autograph machine.

Secretary Darla Maeda brings a hat. Walker is back with a toy rabbit. Guard Guy McIntyre is next with a jersey. "Oh, no, not you too," Montana says, rolling his eyes.

"He'll come up here once or twice a week to sign stuff," says p.r. assistant Al Barba. "We use the real Joe pictures until they run out, then we send the ones with the printed autograph. Everyone will get something—eventually."

Since he blistered the Denver Broncos in last January's Super Bowl, Montana is hot again, just as he was after the 49ers' Super Bowl victory in '82 and the one in '85, having been voted the game's Most Valuable Player each time. The first success represented the thrill of discovery, the potential star who blossomed, and it carried a healthy round of commercial endorsements with it. The second one reestablished him after Miami Dolphins quarterback Dan Marino had captured most of the headlines in '84. But then, in the 1985 season, the adulation for Montana cooled.

There were drug rumors, all unsubstantiated. Montana in his Ferrari reportedly stopped by police, even though the car was in his garage at the time. Montana seen in a bar, when he happened to be in a team meeting. In '86 there was the back operation two weeks into the season. Doctors said Montana might never play again. He was back in 55 days. The '87 season was his best statistically at that time, but the year ended with a loss in an NFC divisional playoff. When Montana was lifted for Steve Young in that game, it was the first time since he had reached football maturity that San Francisco coach Bill Walsh had given him the hook. The fans cheered when Young entered the game. Trade Joe now, they said, while you can still get something for him.

Walsh started Young a few times in '88, saying he was giving Montana time to get over nagging injuries and "general fatigue." Montana says it was a lack of confidence, tracing back to the end of '87. "It's tearing my guts out," Montana told his wife, Jennifer. But the exclamation point on the '88 season was the terrific 92-yard drive in the final minutes to beat Cincinnati in Super Bowl XXIII, and Montana came into '89 riding the crest. He put together a remarkable season, the best any quarterback has ever had. And he was even better in the playoffs and Super Bowl XXIV, reaching a level of brilliance that had never been seen in postseason football. Which leaves only one question to ask about this remarkable 11-year veteran: Is he the greatest quarterback ever to play the game?

MONTANA'S ROOTS are in western Pennsylvania, the cradle of quarterbacks. Soft coal and quarterbacks. Steel mills and quarterbacks. Johnny Lujack from Connellsville, Joe Namath from Beaver Falls, George Blanda from Youngwood, Dan Marino from Pittsburgh, Montana from Monongahela, Terry Hanratty from Butler—he was Montana's idol as a kid. Terry Hanratty of Notre Dame, the Golden Domer. Montana would throw footballs through a swinging tire in the backyard, just like Terry did. Why do so many of them come from western Pennsylvania? "Toughness, dedication, hard work and competitiveness; a no-nonsense, blue-collar background," says John Unitas, from Pittsburgh.

But there are a lot of no-nonsense, blue-collar places in the country. What is it about western Pennsylvania and quarterbacks? "Maybe it's the Iron City beer," says Montana.

The most logical answer is tradition—and focus. If you're a kid with athletic ability in western Pennsylvania, you've probably got a picture of Montana or Marino on your wall. Montana had the athletic gift. You could see it right away. "He used to wreck his crib by standing up and rocking," his mother, Theresa, says. "Then he'd climb up on the side and jump to our bed. You'd hear a thump in the middle of the night and know he hit the bed and went on the floor."

And he had the focus, supplied by his father, Joseph Sr., who put a ball in his son's hands when the kid was big enough to walk and said, "Throw it."

"I played all sports in the service, but when I was a kid I never had anyone to take me in the backyard and throw a ball to me," says Joe Sr., who moved to California with his wife in '86. "Maybe that's why I got Joe started in sports. Once he got started, he was always waiting at the door with a ball when I came home from work. What I really wanted to do was make it fun for him. And I wanted to make sure he got the right fundamentals. I read books. You watch some quarterbacks, sometimes they need two steps to get away from the line of scrimmage. I felt the first step should be straight back, not to the side. We worked on techniques—sprint out, run right, run left, pivot and throw the ball. I've been accused of pushing him. I don't think that's right. It's just that he loved it so much, and I loved watching him. And I wanted to make sure he learned the right way."

Joe Jr. was an only child, a pampered child, perhaps, but he didn't see it that way. The family lived in a two-story frame house in a middle-class neighborhood. He was shy with strangers, outgoing at home. He had a few friends, but no one was as close to him as his father and his mother. His fondest childhood memory? Playing ball in the backyard with his dad, then coming into the kitchen, where his mother would have a steaming pot of ravioli on the stove.

Montana started playing peewee football when he was eight, one year younger than the legal limit. His father listed his age as nine. His first coach on the Little Wildcats was Carl Crawley, a defensive lineman in college and now an NCAA referee. "We ran a pro offense, with a lot of the underneath stuff he's doing now," Crawley says. "Joe would roll out. If the cornerback came off, he'd dump it off; if he stayed back, he'd keep going and pick up five or six yards. He was an amazingly accurate passer for a kid."

Crawley remembers Montana as an "exuberant kid who had stardom written all over him, but nobody ever resented it because it came so naturally. And there was no show-off in him. He wanted to win, and he'd do whatever it took, and that's another thing the kids liked about him. With Joe on the field, they knew they were never out of any game."

In the spring it was baseball, and Montana played all the positions. As a pitcher in Little League, he threw three perfect games. In the winter it was basketball, for which there was no organized program for kids until Joe Sr. started one. The team practiced and played in the local armory, and the kids paid a dollar a piece for a janitor to clean up after them. The practices were five nights a week, and there were always tournaments to play in. Montana has always said that his favorite sport was basketball. He loved the practices. "I could practice basketball all day," he says. Practicing football was work.

He came to Ringgold High with a reputation for being something of a wunderkind. When coach Chuck Abramski took his first look at Montana on the football field, he saw an agile, 6-foot, 165-pound sophomore who was too skinny and too immature to stand up to the rigors of western Pennsylvania Class AAA football. Abramski gave Montana a seat on the bench and told him to watch and learn. And to be sure to report to the summer weight program before his junior year. Montana had other ideas.

"For me competing in sports was a 365-day-a-year thing," he says. "I was playing American Legion baseball, summer basketball. It was hard for Coach Abramski to accept that. Chuck was a great coach in a lot of ways, but he never got over the fact that I didn't take part in his summer weight program. The man's all football."

The weight program was Abramski's baby, his joy. It was part of the toughening-up process. Here was Abramski's junior quarterback, a guy who had superstar written all over him—hell, everyone knew it—and he wasn't there. It ate Abramski up. When the season started, Montana was on the bench. Abramski's starting quarterback was a big, rough youngster who splattered defenders when he ran the option play but had a throwing arm like a tackle's. In scrimmages he would line up at defensive end and take dead aim at Montana, the guy who was trying to take his job. "Every day he just beat the hell out of me," Montana said. "I'd be dead when I came home. Football wasn't much fun at that point."

The Ringgold Rams were blown out by Elizabeth Forward 34–6 in the 1972 opener. They won the next two games by forfeit, but lost the two practice games that were played to fill in the schedule. During this time Montana was finally moved up to be the starter for their next game, against Monessen.

Keith Bassi, who was the Ringgold fullback, says the scene that night at Monessen was like nothing he has ever seen before or since. "Monessen had some players," he says. "Bubba Holmes, who went to Minnesota; Tony Benjamin, who went to Duke. The rumor was that guys there had been held back a year in nursery school so they'd be more mature when they hit high school. We were doing our calisthenics, and there was this big roar, and here they came, 120 of them, in single file from the top of that concrete stadium, biggest stadium in the [Monongahela] Valley. It was like Custer's Last Stand."

The final score was 34–34, Holmes scoring for Monessen in the last moments. "We call it our 34–34 win," Bassi says. Montana's passing numbers read 12 for 22, 223 yards and four touchdowns.

"They played a three-deep, where they give you the short stuff," said Frank Lawrence, who had been the Rams offensive line coach. "Joe just killed 'em with timed patterns. It was eerie, seeing Montana drop back from center, set and throw. All his 49er mechanics were there, the quick setup, the nifty glide to the outside, scrambling but under control, buying time, looking for a receiver underneath. It seemed as if he had been doing it all his life, and this was a kid in his first high school start."

By his senior year the somewhat slender kid was gradually filling out, standing taller in the pocket, almost 6' 2" now, up to 180 pounds—the makings of a superstar. He was all-everything his senior year—including *Parade* All-America as a quarterback—a gifted athlete who starred on a league championship basketball team ("He could stand flat-footed and dunk with two hands," says Fran LaMendola, his basketball coach), a baseball player good enough to get invited back to a major league tryout camp, a potential standout in sports in which he merely filled in—a victory in his only tennis match, an informal 6' 9" high jump, a junior high record in his only attempt at the discus.

North Carolina State offered him a basketball scholarship. Notre Dame basketball coach Digger Phelps said he would try to arrange it so Montana could play football and basketball. A few dozen college offers came in. Georgia was one of the schools Montana visited, along with Boston College, Minnesota and Notre Dame. His parents had taken him for a look around Penn State, and he had been to Pitt many times to watch the Panthers play.

It was all window dressing. His mind was already made up. It would be Notre Dame, where his idol, Hanratty, had played.

Montana left the Monongahela Valley in the fall of 1974 for a strange sojourn at Notre Dame that mirrored his entire athletic career—lows, moments of despair, followed by glorious highs.

He was 18 when he arrived in South Bend, still skinny, still shy, a bit at sea so far away from his hometown and his parents. At Notre Dame he found himself amid an incredible collection of talent. He was a high school hotshot surrounded by hotshots. Forty-six players who played for Notre Dame during the Montana years would be drafted by the NFL, eight in the first round. The Irish won a national championship under Ara Parseghian the year before Montana arrived in South Bend, and they would win another one, under Dan Devine, in '77, Montana's junior year.

Montana saw no varsity action his first year and got only minimal playing time in the freshman games. He would call his dad three, four times a week. Joe Sr. told him to hang in. On a whim Montana once drove home in the middle of the night. Joe Sr. occasionally would make the eight-hour drive from Monongahela to watch Joe Jr. in an afternoon scrimmage, grab a bite to eat with his son, and then drive home to be at work the next day. "His dad would sometimes show up in the middle of the night, and we'd all go out at 1 a.m. for a stack of pancakes," says Montana's freshman roommate, Nick DeCicco. "It was crazy."

Montana came off the bench as a sophomore to pull out two games in the fourth quarter, and then did it again as a junior. The players couldn't figure out why it was taking the coach so long to grasp something they already knew, that this skinny, sleepy-eyed kid from Monongahela was the man, the guy who could get it done when he had to. "When the pressure came," says 49ers free safety Dave Waymer, who started his Notre Dame career as a wideout, "we knew he was the guy who wouldn't overheat."

The time Montana spent on the bench at Notre Dame still bothers him. Walsh, the former 49er coach, says there's something about Montana when you first see him on the practice field, "an almost blase look, although actually he's anything but that. I could see a college coach being put off by the fact that he's not responding overtly, so he'd say, 'Well, this guy's not motivated, he's not with the program.' "

There is a stat sheet compiled by the Notre Dame sports information department entitled "Joe Montana's Comeback Statistics," which lists six games. The Irish won five of those games in the fourth quarter, and they almost won the sixth—the 1978 game at Southern Cal in which Montana brought the Irish back from a 24–6 deficit to a 25–24 lead before USC pulled it out with a field goal. At the top of the list is a game at North Carolina in his sophomore season. The Irish were down 14–6 with 5:11 to play, when Montana came off the bench and led them to a 21–14 win with 129 yards passing in his minute and two seconds on the field. That's the kind of list it is, and there probably isn't another one like it.

The legend was born; Montana was the Comeback Kid.

The 1979 Cotton Bowl against Houston, the famous Chicken Soup game, was, of course, the one that put the capper on the Comeback Kid's collegiate career. A freak ice storm had hit Dallas, and "all you heard as you came in was, bam, bam, bam, people knocking ice off the seats," Waymer says. By the fourth quarter, Montana was in the locker room with hypothermia, his temperature down to 96 degrees, and the medical staff was pumping bouillon (not chicken soup) into him to warm him up. Houston was building a 34–12 lead, while Montana lay in the locker room covered with blankets. Oh, yes, it's a story, all right.

With 7:37 to go, Montana came running onto the field, and a mighty roar went up. "Uh, no, not exactly a mighty roar," recalls Dave Huffman, the Notre Dame center. "More like a feeble, frozen roar, since there were only a few people left in the stands, and ice was falling out of their mouths. Actually, I didn't even know Joe was out there until I felt his hands taking the snap. I thought, Wait a minute, these are different hands."

With six seconds left, the Irish were down by six points. "I told Joe to run a 91, a quick out," Devine says, "and if it wasn't there, to throw it away. Kris Haines, our wideout, slipped, and Joe threw it away. Now there were two seconds left. I turned my back on the field. That meant Joe could call his own play. He called the 91 again, the noseguard came through, Haines broke to the flag, and with the noseguard staring him in the face Joe threw a perfect pass, low and outside, a bullet—under all that pressure, with terrible conditions. He was so calm. I swear to God he was no different than he would have been in practice."

You look for clues to help you understand Montana's ability to bring his team back from the brink. It would become his trademark in the NFL, too. "I don't think the guy ever feels pressure" says Ken MacAfee, a Notre Dame tight end who is now a dentist in the Philadelphia area. "I don't think he knows what it is. To him it's just football. He doesn't change. I can't remember Joe ever missing a read. Even watching him on TV now, he knows the system so perfectly, he knows so well where everything's going to go."

When the 1979 draft was approaching and the Cotton Bowl glow had worn off, the NFL scouts started putting down numbers for Montana. One combine gave him a grade of 6½ with 9 being the top of the scale and 1 the bottom. Washington State's Jack Thompson got the highest grade among the quarterbacks—8. Montana's arm was rated a 6, or average. "He can thread the needle," the report said, "but usually goes with his primary receiver and forces the ball to him even when he's in a crowd. He's a gutty, gambling, cocky type. Doesn't have great tools but could eventually start." The dumb teams believed the report. The smart one has won four Super Bowls.

HERE'S THE thing about scouting college football players for the NFL draft: It's based on fear. Scouts hedge their bets. Their evaluations all read, "Yes . . . but. . . ." *Yes,* he can move the team down the field, *but* he doesn't have an NFL arm. If the player makes it, the scout will say, "Well, I told you he had potential," or if he's a bust, the scout will shake his head and say, "See, the arm didn't hold up, just like I said."

Intangibles, the look scouts see in a player's eye or a certain feeling about him, are for late-night, third-drink talk at the hotel bar. Unless a scout feels very secure in his employment, he won't load up his reports with intangibles. It's too easy to be wrong. And that's what terrorizes scouts—the fear of being wrong all by themselves, the big error, the No. 1 pick that was a total bust. And on draft day 1979, a lot of scouts were wrong about Joe Montana.

Eighty-one choices were made before the San Francisco 49ers took him near the end of the third round. What were the negatives on Montana when he was coming out of college? Strength of arm? Sure, he couldn't knock down buildings. So what? The Hall of Fame is filled with quarterbacks who didn't have a cannon. But there was something else, an undercurrent. He had trouble with his coach at Notre Dame. Uh-oh, look out. A warning light went off.

For a while the Bears were very close to drafting Montana. "Notre Dame is right down the road, and my wife and children loved Joe Montana," Bears player personnel director Bill Tobin says. "When I left the house, I told them, 'If he's there on the third round, he's ours.' "

Montana *was* there when the Bears picked in the third round, but the team took Willie McClendon, a running back out of Georgia. "I had a lot of explaining to do to three young kids and my wife," Tobin says. "But who knows, if he came here, that he would have had the career that he's had in San Francisco?"

"What if a Tampa Bay or a New Orleans would have taken him?" says Abramski, Montana's high school coach. "What if, instead of having Bill Walsh to work with all those years in San Francisco, he had been in a system where he had to drop back seven steps and throw 50 yards downfield?"

Montana has reflected on that many times. "There's no coach I could have played for who would have been better for my career," he says. "Absolutely none."

"We were coming off a 2–14 year," Walsh says. "We were in dire straits everywhere. I investigated every viable college quarterback. I first became aware of Montana the previous year, my second year coaching at Stanford. We were so proud of our 25–22 comeback win over Georgia in the Blue-bonnet Bowl, and then I looked in the paper and read about Notre Dame and Joe's even more spectacular comeback in the Cotton Bowl—under impossible conditions. That was just so impressive.

"Joe was the last quarterback we looked at. The minute I saw him drop back—his quick movement, those quick, nimble, Joe Namath–type feet—I got very serious. As much as I wanted Steve Dils, who'd been my quarter-back at Stanford, who knew my system, I knew I had to forgo that for Joe. Joe was bigger and quicker, and he threw better."

The first thing people noticed about Montana when he reported to 49er training camp was how skinny he was. The team's media guide listed him as 6' 3", 200 pounds. (The guide has since dropped an inch off his height and five pounds from his weight.) Actually, he stood 6' 2" and weighed barely 185.

"I was sitting next to him at the counter in Howard Johnson's," says Dwight Clark, a 10th-round pick who would become Montana's favorite receiver. "Long blond hair, Fu Manchu mustache, skinny legs. I thought, This guy must be a kicker. Then he introduced himself, and I couldn't believe this was the guy who brought Notre Dame back to beat us in the fourth quarter when I was at Clemson."

Montana started one game in his rookie year, saw brief action in two games and made spot appearances in the other 13. Walsh, who had developed quarterbacks Ken Anderson at Cincinnati and Dan Fouts at San Diego, was in no hurry to push Montana. "There were those in our organization who didn't think Joe would be an NFL starter," Walsh says. "He was a little in awe of everything, like all first-year quarterbacks. At his best, though, when he was in sync, he had an instinctive nature rarely equaled by any athlete in any sport. Magic Johnson has it.

"Even watching Joe warm up, there was something hypnotic about him. That look when he was dropping back; he was poetic in his movements, al-most sensuous, everything so fluid, so much under control. But you couldn't lose sight of the fact that he was still a young player, and in game situations every play is almost crisis-like to a young player."

BY 1980 the 49er offense was beginning to come into focus. The short, controlled pass became much of the running game. Clark, who began to emerge as a serious mid-range threat, had a thing going with Montana, who started seven of the last 10 games that year. "We'd stay after practice and work on our own stuff," Clark says. "I don't know how much it helped him, but it helped me. I didn't have a clue about reading defenses, about making adjustments. That's the thing about Bill's system. You could do your own adjusting as long as it was in the guidelines. A lot of times, say, I'd run a 10-yard hook. If the guy was inside me, I'd kind of push off and run a breakout. Joe could read that. He was good at it."

Steve DeBerg, who had shared the starting quarterback job with Montana, was traded before the '81 season. No one had yet called Walsh a genius. Nothing had been written about Walsh's system, which is now the standard for offensive football. But it was coming into focus. He had had to go slowly with Montana. He couldn't give him the full package at first, but now he felt Montana was ready. "There was a lot of time spent studying," Montana says. "Coach Sam Wyche helped me a lot with the little keys, the knowledge of what a defense was or was not capable of in a certain situation—pre-reads we call it, knowing where not to go before the ball is even snapped. You'd learn to work on individuals. We'd see a film, and Sam would say, 'See, this guy can't cover that far, but he tries to.' "

When Walsh talks about offensive football, he eventually mentions the "quick, slashing strokes" of attack. He'll use analogies with tennis and boxing, even warfare, which was why he was so taken with Montana's nimble feet. A quick, slashing attack needs a quick-footed quarterback. The statuesque quarterback who can throw the ball 60 yards downfield has never been Walsh's type. And when he refined his offense to blend with Montana's skills, Walsh introduced the X factor, which was the great escape talent of his quarterback—elusiveness, body control, the ability to throw while in the grasp of an opponent.

"A lot of our offense was play-action," Walsh says, "and I learned that on a play-pass you have to expect an unblocked man just when you're trying to throw the ball. Your linemen have blocked aggressively. You can't expect them to hold their guys. Joe had to understand that. You're going to fool somebody downfield, but also you're going to have someone unblocked bearing right down on you. Here he comes. If you can throw and take the hit, TD. If you can avoid him, so much the better. We were on the cutting edge of Joe's ability. He was gifted at avoiding and throwing. We practiced the scrambling, off-balance throw. It wasn't accidental when he did it. It was a carefully practiced thing."

Finally it all came into focus in the '81 postseason, in one momentous play, the last-minute touchdown pass to Clark that buried Dallas in the NFC championship. The play will always be known as The Catch: Montana scrambling to his right, with three Cowboys clutching at him; the off-balance throw; and finally Clark, on a break-off route, ducking inside, then cutting back, just the way he and Joe had practiced on their own so many times. "On the touchdown play my concentration level was never so high," Montana says. "I remember pump-faking to get those guys chasing me off the ground, just like when I was playing basketball with my dad. I remember trying to get the ball to Dwight high, so no one else could get it. I never saw the catch. I heard the crowd roar."

The Super Bowl was an anticlimax. Montana was facing the consensus All-Pro quarterback, Ken Anderson of the Bengals. The 49ers beat the Bengals 26–21, with Montana taking MVP honors. In each of the 49ers' next two Super Bowls, he again was matched with a consensus All-Pro, Dan Marino of Miami in '85 and Boomer Esiason of Cincinnati in '89.

Montana had gone in as the second-best quarterback each time and won. By the time of the 49ers' fourth Super Bowl, in 1990, everyone had learned, and the question was only how badly would Montana and the 49ers beat John Elway and the Denver Broncos?

The first talk of Montana being the greatest of all came in Bay Area circles after the '82 Super Bowl, as put forth by a couple of old 49er quarterbacks. John Brodie said it, flat out, and people laughed. Frankie Albert said, "At 25, he's ahead of Unitas, Van Brocklin, Waterfield . . . all the immortals."

The '83 season was a good year statistically for Montana, even though the 49ers lost to the Washington Redskins in the NFC Championship Game, but '84 was his best up to that point. In that season he received his highest NFL quarterback rating (102.9), his second Pro Bowl selection and the MVP award for leading San Francisco to a crushing 38–16 victory over the Miami Dolphins in the Super Bowl.

The 49ers were bruised and banged up when they faced the New York Giants at Giants Stadium in the NFC wild-card game. San Francisco lost 17–3.

Montana injured a shoulder on a blind-side hit by Lawrence Taylor after an interception, but he remained in the game. It was a preview of things to come.

In the '86 season opener at Tampa Bay, Montana twisted in the air while throwing a pass, and his back went out. An examination showed a ruptured disk and, worse than that, a congenital narrowing of the spinal cavity. He would need an operation. Doctors told Montana he might play again, but he would be crazy if he tried it.

Crazy? His whole life had been football. He was 30 and at the peak of his game. After two marriages, the first to hometown sweetheart Kim Moses in college and the second to flight attendant Cass Castillo from 1981 to '84, he had found a woman he could be happy with. Football had brought him to the absolute crest, and now doctors were telling him to give it up?

"I thought he was finished," his mother, Theresa, says. "I was in his hospital room the day after the operation. They wheeled him in, sat him up, or at least tried to. I could see the pain in his eyes. I wanted to cry, but not in front of him. Ronnie Lott was in the room, Dwight Clark, Wendell Tyler. They couldn't hold the tears back. A day later I asked him, 'What do you want to do?' He said, 'I want to play football again.' The next day he was up doing exercises, the day after that he was working with weights, small stuff mostly, but at least he was doing something."

Montana was out for 55 days. The 49ers were 5-3-1 when he returned, but he led them to five victories in the last seven games and into the playoffs. They faced the Giants in Giants Stadium again, and lost again, 49–3. Montana was knocked out in the second quarter when noseguard Jim Burt buried his helmet under Montana's chin. But the back held up.

The 49ers were the sweethearts of the NFL in '87, going 13–2 in the regular season, and Montana had a career high for touchdown passes (31), all of which made it tough for everyone to take when Minnesota beat them 36–24 in an NFC divisional playoff in San Francisco. By the third quarter of that game it was clear that the 49er offense was going nowhere, and Montana was benched for Young. That's all the fans and the media needed to start talk of trading Montana, who would be 32 that June. Young was 26. There was the future.

In '88, Young started three times and came off the bench to play in eight other games as Montana was slowed by nagging injuries to his elbow, ribs, back and knees. Montana said he could have played; he was bitter about

Walsh's not playing him. "One bad pass, one bad series, and I'm out of there," he said.

The '89 Super Bowl, the final drive against the Bengals—92 yards to win it 20–16 with 34 seconds left (actually 102 yards if you count an ineligible receiver penalty)—cured everything. It was the 19th time as a pro that Montana had brought his team from behind in the fourth quarter. There were four more in the '89 season. Has any quarterback had more? Does anyone keep track of those things? Add six as a collegian, one more in the Big 33 Pennsylvania-Ohio high school all-star game, and Montana has a total of 30. Is it a record? Who knows? But it's impressive.

That last drive against the Bengals in the '89 Super Bowl has been well-documented. Montana completed eight of nine passes for 97 yards en route to the winning throw. "I was kind of wild on the sidelines before we took the field for that drive," says right tackle Harris Barton. "I was worried about the penalty on the kickoff that set us back to the eight. I was yelling at somebody, can't remember who. Joe came over to me and said, 'Hey, check it out.'

"I said, 'Check what out?'

"He said, 'There in the stands, standing near the exit ramp, there's John Candy.'

"I looked. Sure enough, it was him. I grabbed John Frank, our tight end. 'Hey, John,' I said. 'There's John Candy.'

"Then I got hold of myself. What the hell was I doing? Fifteen seconds later we're in the huddle and Joe's clapping his hands and saying, 'Hey, you guys want it? Let's go.' "

The scariest moment in the drive came with a minute and a half left, first- and-10 on the Bengal 35. Montana had been yelling, calling signals, and he began to hyperventilate. He couldn't catch his breath. "He signaled to me that he wanted a timeout," Walsh says. "He didn't know if he could go on. I waved it off. I didn't realize what was happening to him. He came up to the line, and the next pass he threw went over Jerry Rice's hand. It was his only incompletion of the drive. Later he said he threw it away because he didn't want to risk an interception. He told me that as he was coming to the line he felt himself getting his breath back. He didn't panic. Joe functioned in a clear-headed manner, even in distress. He didn't lose it. It's like the soldier taking two in the belly and still finishing in charge."

Based on the NFL quarterback rating system, Montana's '89 season was the best anyone has ever had—the highest rating (112.4) and third-highest completion percentage (70.2) in history. But those are just numbers. The 49ers swept through the playoffs and Super Bowl, trouncing Denver 55–10 to repeat as NFL champions. Their efficiency was frightening, and Montana was the master. If you want to highlight one game that season, try Philadelphia on Sept. 24. Some people call it the finest Montana has ever played.

For three quarters the 49er offense was falling apart. Montana had been sacked seven times, with one more to come. He had tripped twice while setting up and had fallen down in the end zone for a safety. The Eagles were coming at him like crazy, and the 49ers were down 21–10 with 10 seconds gone in the fourth quarter. Then Montana threw four touchdown passes into the teeth of the Eagle rush to pull out a 38–28 victory. His fourth-quarter stats read 11 completions in 12 pass attempts for 227 yards, and he scrambled for 19 more.

"Worried? Oh, hell, yes, we were worried," Barton says of the Eagle assault on Montana. "Joe gets that glazed look in his eyes, and you know he's been shellacked. Then three guys try to help him up. That's the first thing you think of. Let's get him on his feet right away, then maybe everyone will miss what happened. We'd get to the sidelines and Joe would say, 'O.K., let's get this thing settled down.' I was just amazed that he could line up at all after getting smacked in the head by [Eagles end] Reggie White."

If you want to make a case for Montana as the greatest quarterback who ever played the game, there it is. Toughness. The great ones all had it—Unitas, Graham, Baugh, Waterfield, Tittle, Bradshaw. When you add Montana's finesse, the sensuous and fluid qualities that Walsh saw at the beginning, plus his uncanny accuracy—no one has ever thrown the short crossing pattern with a better touch—you've got a special package.

The numbers declare him the best of all time: highest career quarterback rating (94.0), highest career completion percentage (63.9; no one else is above 60), second to Bernie Kosar of the Cleveland Browns in lowest lifetime interception rate. Here are a few more. Among quarterbacks with a minimum of 1,500 passes, Montana is the only one to have thrown twice as many career touchdowns (216) as interceptions (107). In the 150 games in which he has thrown at least one pass, including the playoffs, his completion percentage has been under .500 only five times, and he once went five seasons (1980–84) without having a sub-.500 game. In three playoff games after the '89 season, he threw 11 touchdown passes and no interceptions. Had enough? The best stat of all, of course, is his feat of 23 fourth-quarter comeback NFL victories.

Teammates and coaches have talked about Montana's almost mystical calmness in the midst of turmoil, when everything's on the line in the fourth quarter. How does he describe it, this ability to elevate his performance? "I don't really know," he says. "It seems like your concentration level goes up and things get a little clearer because of that. Maybe it's because ever since I was little I was involved in pressure situations, plus winning traditions."

Everyone who has come into contact with Montana has tried to figure out the source of his greatness. Wyche said that no quarterback ever re-acted as fast to changing situations, no one ever absorbed coaching so readily and immediately put it into execution. "When I'd tell him some-thing," Wyche says, "it was almost like he'd lean in and pull the words out of my mouth."

Perhaps Jeff Petrucci, Montana's high school quarterback coach, has the best answer to the secret of Montana's greatness. "Joe was born to be a quarterback," Petrucci says. "You saw it in the midget leagues, in high school, even in the Big 33 all-star game—the electricity in the huddle when he was in there. How many people are there in the world, three billion? And how many guys are there who can do what he can do? Him, maybe Marino on a good day. Perhaps God had a hand in this thing."

So is he the greatest quarterback of all time or not? A large body of play-ers and coaches, including Walsh, votes yes. The ones who say no say that a Johnny Unitas or a Norm Van Brocklin playing in this era would do the same things Montana does. "Yeah, I know. I've heard it," Petrucci says. Well, in my mind, he'd be the greatest in any era because he's the ultimate winner. Somehow he finds a way to get it done."

| | | | | |

Passing Marks

BY MICHAEL SILVER

While leading one of the most prolific offenses in the history of the NFL, Colts quarterback Peyton Manning was poised to break a hallowed record by throwing for more touchdowns than one of his idols.

OWNSTAIRS IN PEYTON MANNING'S HOUSE, WHERE the world's hottest quarterback regularly hosts parties for teammates after Indianapolis Colts home games, it's tough to take two steps without stumbling upon an exceptionally cool memento. Near the bar there's the large wicker basket overflowing with game balls; the *Caddyshack* poster signed by the film's stars is in the home theater (used exclusively, alas, for watching game video); and in the weight room, a wall is lined with framed photographs of the proprietor schmoozing with some of football's most recognizable faces.

"It's my Quarterback Wall," Manning proudly explained as he surveyed a cast of majestic passers that includes Johnny Unitas, Brett Favre and Michael Vick. Then, pointing to a shot of his father, Archie, the longtime New Orleans Saint, standing next to a young, excessively tan and bushy-haired Dan Marino in a Miami Dolphins uniform, Peyton lowered his voice to a reverential tone and added, "This one right here's my favorite. My dad, of course, was my idol, but when he retired in 1984, I needed a new favorite player, and Marino kind of took over." The photo was snapped hours before a 1986 game between the Dolphins and the Saints at the Superdome when Archie, then a radio broadcaster for the home team, walked onto the field with his second-oldest son to say hello to Dan the Man. Peyton, who was 10, remembers everything about the interaction, most notably the "big ol' Skoal can Marino was holding."

Now chew on this: No NFL passer, not even the great Marino, has had as productive a season as Manning's magical 2004 campaign seems destined to turn out. On Sunday at Reliant Stadium, Manning threw a pair of first-quarter touchdown passes to lead Indianapolis to a 23–14 victory over the Houston Texans, giving him 46 for the year—two shy of the single-season record Marino set two decades ago. With their sixth consecutive victory the Colts (10–3) clinched a second straight AFC South title, meaning the most suspenseful storyline heading into their home game against the Baltimore Ravens this Sunday night is if and when one of football's most hallowed milestones will be surpassed.

Or *matched.* "I'm telling you, it would be kind of neat to tie it," said Manning, who completed 26 of 33 passes for 298 yards against the Texans. "People don't understand the respect I have for Marino. But I think if I got to 48 and shut it down, our receivers would be out there changing plays for me."

You can bet that the ball Manning tosses for TD number 49 will be displayed more prominently than those in the wicker basket. Of course, first there is the small matter of retrieving it from whoever makes the historic catch. "We've been talking about selling it on eBay," running back Edgerrin James said while dining with four teammates at a downtown Indianapolis restaurant. "I'll tell you this—if he's at 48 and I get a little swing pass, I'm going in punt-return mode and taking that thing to the crib."

"If it's me," wideout Reggie Wayne chimed in, "I'm gonna drift *all the way* across the field and put my hand up, like P-Dub [Peter Warrick] used to do at Florida State, and then be gone."

These are giddy times for the Colts, who are on pace to surpass the record 556 points produced by the 1998 Minnesota Vikings. Not only is Manning, at 28, playing at an uncharted level, but Indy's other skill-position players have also stepped up their games. James, in his third year removed from major knee surgery, is back to his All-Pro form—he had 104 yards on 28 carries against the Texans, giving him 1,395 for the season, and added seven catches for 54 yards. Star wideout Marvin Harrison now gets significant help from Wayne, slot receiver Brandon Stokley and tight ends Marcus Pollard and Dallas Clark.

"This is a once-in-a-career kind of situation," Colts coach Tony Dungy says. "Everything is falling into place for us—the way Peyton's playing and the weaponry we have. It's not so much the passes he's throwing as the way he's running the offense and the decisions he's making."

SITTING IN the club seats outside of suite 279 at Reliant Stadium on Sunday, Colts owner Jim Irsay was equally effusive in his praise of the seventh-year veteran, whom the team drafted first overall in 1998. "Success comes from hard work and preparation, but sometimes you're blessed, and the stars seem to align," Irsay said. "I remember the last Sunday of the '97 season. Arizona was down 12 [to the Atlanta Falcons] with eight or nine minutes to go, and I was thinking, Well, it looks like we're going to have the second pick of the draft. Then they come back, and with five seconds left Jake Plummer throws a touchdown pass to win it and give us the first pick, and I just went berserk. The kids came running in saying, 'What is wrong with Dad?' "

As Irsay spoke, Manning was in the process of directing his second touchdown drive in the game's first 11 minutes, giving Indy a 14–0 lead. Twice Manning went to his first read for scores: On third-and-goal from the three the Colts lined up with an empty backfield, and Manning noticed outside linebacker Kailee Wong in single coverage against Harrison. Practically scoffing at a weakside blitz, Manning turned to his right and zipped the ball to Harrison for a 7–0 lead.

Later, on second-and-five from the Houston 12, Manning called 6 R Slant Inside and looked for the ever-improving Wayne, who lined up to the left, slipped inside of rookie cornerback Dunta Robinson and flashed open while cutting across the front of the end zone. "The safety [Glenn Earl] was on the inside and was looking at Reggie," Manning said. "He was so concerned with not looking into the backfield—which happens a lot—that I was able to throw the ball right past his ear before he knew what hit him."

Like that, one of Marino's records went out the window: It was Manning's 13th consecutive game with at least two touchdown tosses, breaking an NFL mark shared by Marino, Unitas, Favre and Don Meredith. Manning worships quarterbacks in general and is especially awed by Marino because of the unmatched consistency displayed by the future first-ballot Hall of Famer. The two faced off four times before Marino retired in March 2000—Manning went 1–3—and last February in South Florida they became playing partners on the golf course. "I went down there to play in his tournament, and I wanted to hide out for a few days afterward while my contract was being worked out," Manning says. "Dan told me I could stay in his guesthouse. Some people feel you can be too old to have heroes, but I'm 28, and I don't think so."

So, while Manning was in the midst of becoming the NFL's richest man (ultimately signing a seven-year, $98 million contract extension with a record $34.5 million signing bonus), he really got in touch with his inner fan. Call it the M&M Show: Though Manning never serenaded Marino's wife, Claire, with chants of "Cut that meat," the signature line from his funny MasterCard commercial, he thoroughly enjoyed his stay in Casa Marino. The two quarterbacks played rounds of golf at elite courses, sipped vintage red wine and had a grand old time.

"My kids just loved sitting around with him talking after dinner," Marino recalls. "They're Peyton Manning fans. [Around me] he wasn't nervous or anything like that. Or if he was, I didn't notice it. He's cool."

THE SAME can't necessarily be said about Manning's receivers in 2004. "Things are tense," James acknowledges. "When you do get the ball, you know you have to do something with it because you might not see it for a while. Somebody's going to be mad every week; it's just a question of who."

Earlier this year Harrison was frustrated by his lack of involvement, at one point voicing his displeasure to ABC's Michele Tafoya in an off-camera interview. Having caught an NFL-record 143 passes in 2002, Harrison has seen a steady reduction in opportunities as Manning has grown more comfortable with Wayne, Stokley and Clark. "I know it's been an adjustment for Marvin," Manning said last Friday while sitting in his home office. "Hey, it's a good thing we don't huddle, because otherwise I'd hear a lot of griping from everyone." Then, gesturing to his Labradors, Manning added, "Colt and Rookie here are my two favorite receivers because they don't talk back."

The quarterback laughed, then predicted that the touchdown-pass record might not come as easily as people expect it will. "I'm telling you, it's hard to throw for a touchdown, and I have a feeling it's going to get harder," he said. "I think defenses are going to start dropping everybody into coverage in the red zone, thinking, He's not getting the record on us. And I'm telling you, if they do, I'll hand it off to Edgerrin *every single play*. It'll make you sick how much we'll run it if they dare us to. Heck, I'll call a quarterback draw."

After getting burned on the first two drives, Texans defensive coordinator Vic Fangio changed up coverages, mixing in man-to-man schemes behind the Texans' usual zones. "They threw a lot of junk at us," Wayne said, "and that's what we're going to get the rest of the way—junk."

It all looked good enough to Manning, who left the locker room nearly an hour after the game with a black 2004 AFC SOUTH CHAMPIONS hat on his head and a huge grin on his face. He emerged from a tunnel and slowly walked across the field with his wife, Ashley, his older brother, Cooper, and the only quarterback he worships more than Marino. It had been a bittersweet day for Archie and the Manning family—Peyton's younger brother, Eli, the New York Giants' rookie quarterback, had played miserably in a 37–14 loss to the Ravens—but this had been another memorable moment in an extraordinary season.

As Irsay, the admiring owner, had said earlier, "To do the things Peyton's been doing week in and week out, it's kind of like when a Bob Dylan comes along—you don't see someone like that very often."

Blame it on a simple twist of fate.

| | | | | | |

Emmitt's Domain

BY S.L. PRICE

*Stiff-arming his opponents and critics, Emmitt Smith
became the leading rusher in NFL history.*

S UDDENLY, LATE ON SUNDAY AFTERNOON, HE HAD NOTHING left to explain. It was all coming back: The line kept opening holes, and Emmitt Smith kept hitting them hard and gliding through, getting closer. Thirteen years ago he had vowed that he would get here, to this moment in football history, and now it was as if the intervening seasons had barely left a mark. He spun. He juked. He ground out yard after yard against the Seattle Seahawks, 55 in the first quarter alone, each step taking him closer to Walter Payton's NFL rushing record, each step taking the sellout crowd at Texas Stadium back to his prime. Smith wanted it no other way, of course—for Payton's family, for the Dallas Cowboys, for himself most of all. He had struggled all season to find his game, feeling the city turning on him bit by bit, feeling for the first time the sting of words like *old* and *finished* and *selfish*.

All season Smith had tried to pretend that this didn't hurt. In his calmer moments before Sunday he would smile and take the long view, because Emmitt Smith is a religious man, and it is an article of his faith that each blessing brings a curse. Or he would just shrug, as if to say, *What can I do?*

for the Scriptures preach forbearance, and Lord knows he tries to live a righteous life. Still, there's a limit to his patience, and at times the shrug would turn to rage. Then the magnanimous Emmitt Smith was a 33-year-old bear swiping at the hounds at his heels, off and running about "couch potatoes who sit on their asses" and "idiots that've got these so-called sports shows" and "media chumps." Running behind an injury-riddled line that's still learning a new blocking scheme, playing on a mediocre team for a city and franchise happy only with supremacy, Smith has this season entered that paradoxical zone inhabited by so many great athletes nearing endgame: Even as he was being celebrated for his march into history, teammates and coaches said he was not the force he used to be, fans insisted that his back-up was better, commentators wondered if he was hurting the team. Nice career, Legend. Now isn't it time you stepped aside?

"You can just look at my age and say, 'Yeah, he's 33, he should go,' " Smith says. "But how about looking at my five guys up front? They've already been beat to heck, and it's not going to get easier. We've got young quarterbacks, trying to learn on the fly. Yeah, I am 33. But have I lost my step? Have I lost my vision? Have I lost my power? Have I lost my ability to make a person miss? If I answer yes to those questions, then you might be right. But don't tell me I should quit just because of my age. That's what makes this frustrating. You have to know who you are. I know who I am."

Indeed, long before Sunday, Smith could always look up from his desk at home and see a wood-carved reminder: EMMITT SMITH #22, WORLD'S ALLTIME GREATEST RUSHER. Finally, against a notoriously porous Seattle defense, he set the notion in stone. Averaging only 63.9 yards entering the game—and needing 93 to break Payton's mark of 16,726 yards—Smith heard Seahawks defensive lineman Chad Eaton say during the coin toss, "You're not going to get it today on us," then saw him flail helplessly as Smith uncorked his best effort of the year. By the fourth quarter, with Dallas down 14–7 and flashbulbs popping, he stood just 13 yards short of the record. Not for a moment did he seem surprised. The Cowboys' next two games are on the road. Smith wanted to grab history at home.

Yes, Smith knows who he is, and he knows where he is too. More than speed or power or balance, awareness has been his greatest asset. He's always been able to read the men shifting in front of him, anticipate where and when a hole would open, when to make that famous cutback. So it was:

On first-and-10 at Dallas's 27-yard line Smith churned for three yards. On second down he took the ball from rookie quarterback Chad Hutchinson, cut left, found a seam, stumbled over a defender's arm, placed his right hand on the turf, kept his balance and kept on chugging until he had caught Payton and passed him by. Then Smith bounced to his feet, face alight, knowing without being told that the record was his. The game stopped, he saw his mother's face and wept, kissed his wife, Pat, and their three kids, hugged former teammate Daryl Johnston and wept again. After a five-minute break, he returned to the game, capping the Cowboys' drive with a one-yard burst that extended his NFL record for rushing TDs to 150. He finished the day with a season-high 109 yards on 24 carries, including six of at least 10 yards.

He didn't look like a man about to go away; he won't do that until he's good and ready. Should anyone be surprised? Smith is, after all, pro football's ultimate survivor. Passed over by 16 teams on draft day in 1990, considered too small and too slow, he has outlasted all competition. Over the past five years at least a half-dozen backs have been more highly regarded than him: The list of those who began their careers after Smith, rose to stardom and then vanished is long and distinguished. Terrell Davis, Robert Smith and Jamal Anderson are gone. Barry Sanders, whom even Emmitt regards as more talented than himself, retired mysteriously in 1999 at age 31, just 1,458 yards short of Payton's record. Those are the vagaries in the life of an NFL running back—for everyone but Smith. He has endured concussions, bone chips, a broken hand. He is still here.

"By all the laws of nature and careers, he shouldn't be sitting in this locker room," says Cowboys owner Jerry Jones. "Every time I look over there, something inside me smiles."

Admittedly, Jones has little else to smile about. His offense is a mess, his quarterbacks still raw, and after losing 17–14 on Seattle's last-minute field goal, his team was 3–5. Smith has certainly had moments when he's looked vulnerable and slow, especially early in the season, but he has been the Cowboys' lone highlight. All they have is his season-high performance on Sunday, his 82-yard effort the week before against the Arizona Cardinals, and the hope that he is only getting warmed up.

"I can still play the game," Smith says. "There's no doubt in my mind I can still play."

This is vital, because Smith knows that doubt is all around him. Last season his backup, Troy Hambrick, had a higher rushing average (5.1 yards) than Smith's (3.9). He's hypersensitive to charges that his run to the record, the cornerstone of the Cowboys' marketing campaign this year, has retarded the team's rebuilding process. A few weeks ago Smith read a column in a Dallas newspaper, "and it really got to me," he says. Never mind that part of the offending sentence—"No one is suggesting that the Cowboys have Edgerrin James and Ricky Williams wasting away on the bench while Smith selfishly pursues a personal goal"—could be read as defending Smith. Those last six words left him so depressed that, the next day Pat called his cellphone and recited Scripture about Saint Peter's failing to walk on water because he lacked faith.

"I've been playing football in a Dallas uniform for 13 years now, and I don't ever recall anybody telling me I was selfish," Smith says. "When it comes to the game, I don't know how any man can fix his lips to say I'm selfish."

Part of the hurt arises from the fact that Smith's reputation is beyond reproach. But more than that, Smith regarded his pursuit of Payton as anything but a one-man grind toward a cold number. No, it was a mission to make good, something personal and pure. He first met Payton in 1995, during the Doak Walker Awards in Dallas, when Payton made a point of sitting with him, talking about the game, workouts, life. Payton told Smith that only he and Sanders would have a shot at his record. "Yo, I'm with the man who done *did* it," Smith says. "And he's just pouring into me, and I'm soaking it up like a sponge soaking up water."

The following fall Smith began what would turn out to be his most injury-stricken season, against the Bears in Chicago, by hurtling over a fourth-quarter pile and landing on his neck. He lost feeling in his left side and was carried off the field on a stretcher, wondering if his career was over. And then, out of nowhere, there was Payton looming above him, telling him everything would be fine. The men kept in touch, and after Payton learned he needed a liver transplant in February 1999, the calls became more frequent. Smith couldn't believe how strong Payton was in facing death, how he refused to be bitter. "He showed me how to be a man," Smith says.

During that last year, Payton asked Smith to keep tabs on his son, Jarrett, a running back about to start his college career at Miami. Smith called

Jarrett a few times, but that was the extent of their communication. Then, not long before Walter died in 1999, he spoke with Smith for the last time.

"I'm going to be O.K. It's in God's hands," Payton said.

"O.K.," Smith said. "If you need me, I'm here for you."

"Just keep praying for me and my family," Payton said. "Check on my boy every now and then."

Payton died on Nov. 1, at 45. A memorial service was held that Friday, and three nights later in Minneapolis, Dallas played the Vikings. There was a moment of silence before the game, and "I felt his presence so strong," Smith says. He wept before the kickoff and then had the greatest half of his career, rushing for 140 yards and two touchdowns, scoring them just 18 seconds apart. He had never experienced anything like that night, not even in his three Super Bowl wins, and then he broke his hand after 24 minutes. What did it all mean?

Smith and Jarrett kept in touch, but it wasn't until two years ago, at Dan Marino's golf tournament in Miami, that the two finally saw each other in person. After they'd met, Jarrett stepped back and watched Smith greet his peers and fans, then turned to a friend and marveled at the similarities between Smith and his dad.

"He reminds me a lot of my father," says Jarrett, now a junior. "They have the same personality; they're both really nice people. Both are big in the community, helping out kids. So if anybody's going to break the record, I'm glad it'll be him. I've learned a lot from Emmitt—the kind of person he is, the kind of husband he is, the kind of father he is. When I get to be that age, I want to be the same way."

Smith met Payton's widow, Connie, on Sept. 10, 2001, when she flew to Dallas to help kick off Emmitt's foundation for kids. The next morning, after the planes had hit the World Trade Center and the Pentagon, Connie couldn't get back to Chicago. She sat watching the TV in her hotel room when the phone rang. Pat and Emmitt insisted she come to the house. She stayed all that day, scared but secure, eating dinner and staring at the news. "I couldn't think of anybody else I would want to break the record but Emmitt," Connie says.

This past summer the Paytons invited Smith to the family restaurant in Aurora, Ill., to present him with the first Spirit of Sweetness award. Film clips of Payton and Smith were shown, and Jarrett spoke before Smith took the podium. All at once, as tears rolled down Smith's cheeks, everything he knew in the abstract became concrete: Payton was dead, he was going to break the record, and he had been given something precious. He felt Jarrett staring at him. "Right then I realized what I was about to embark upon," Smith says. "And what it meant to me."

On Sunday, with Payton's mother, Alyne, and brother, Eddie, in the Texas Stadium stands, Smith wept again. In a videotaped message, Connie told him and 63,854 fans how proud she was and how "truly blessed" she felt to have him as a friend. This is why there was no shame in Smith's protracted pursuit of the record. Too often, in the past few years, the news concerning the league's greatest backs has been sad or strange or appalling. Smith knows that a man's life can be measured by how much he learns from those who came before, and how much he gives to those who come after, and without some purity of purpose, all those yards add up to nothing more than a cold number on the page. The record? Lord, yes, he wanted it, blessing, curse and all.

"But what really means more to me," he says, "is not letting that kid down."

OUTSIDE
THE LINES

| | | | | |

The Wrecking Yard

BY WILLIAM NACK

SPECIAL REPORTING BY LESTER MUNSON

As they limp into the sunset, retired NFL players struggle with the game's grim legacy: a lifetime of disability and pain.

hen I came to my first NFL camp, it was like I was a tall, cold can of beer. They popped the top, and all that energy and desire and ability poured out. I gave of myself with the same passion that I had in high school and college. When I was empty, when I had no more to give, they just crumpled me up and threw me on the garbage heap. Then they grabbed another new can and popped him open, and he flowed out until he was empty.
—Curt Marsh, NFL lineman 1981–86

THEY ARE THE WINCING, HOBBLING WOUNDED: THE MEN who played professional football, a notoriously joint-shearing, disk-popping, nerve-numbing exercise that has grown only more dangerous since Curt Marsh last crashed into a defensive lineman as a Los Angeles Raider. "If you go to a retired players' convention, there are older retirees who walk around like Maryland crabs," says Miki Yaras-Davis, director of benefits for the NFL Players Association. "It's an orthopedic surgeon's dream. I'm surprised the doctors aren't standing outside the door handing out their cards. Hardly one [former player] you see doesn't need a hip replacement. Everybody comes out of pro football with some injury. It's only the degree that separates them."

A 1990 Ball State study, commissioned by the NFLPA and covering the previous 50 years of league history, revealed that among 870 former players responding to a survey, 65% had suffered a "major injury" while playing—that is, an injury that either required surgery or forced them to miss at least eight games. The study also reported that the percentage of players incurring such injuries had increased alarmingly: from 42% before 1959 to 72% in the 1980s, after many stadiums had switched from grass to artificial turf. Two of every three former players disclosed that their football injuries had limited their ability to participate in sports and other recreation in retirement, and more than half of them also had a curtailed ability to do physical labor. Of those who played during the '70s and '80s, nearly half (50% and 48%, respectively) reported that they had retired because of injury—up from 30% in the years before 1959.

There's little doubt, based on a follow-up survey in 1994 and on considerable anecdotal evidence, that injuries in the NFL are becoming more serious and frequent as the colliding bodies grow bigger and stronger. The 300-pound-plus lineman, a rarity 40 years ago, is today as common as the soccer-style kicker. James Andrews, a leading orthopedic surgeon who has been operating on pro football players for almost 30 years, sees a correlation between the worsening of injuries and the size and power of the modern player. In fact, Andrews is witnessing the rise of a phenomenon that was almost unheard of only 15 years ago. "The incidence of serious, *noncontact* knee injuries is much higher than it used to be," he says. Artificial turf is only part of the problem. "These athletes are bigger, stronger and running faster, and they're tearing up knees from cutting, changing direction on a dime," Andrews says. "In fact, the incidence of anterior cruciate ligament injuries is higher from noncontact than contact. I've seen guys get significant injuries just falling on the football. It's like a big tree falling."

The New Age tyrannosaurs battling in the trenches have become so large and powerful that injuries have risen alarmingly in their hand-to-hand combat. "They are exerting forces strong enough to dislocate their elbows and shoulders forward and backward," Andrews says. "With the blocking techniques we're seeing, there's an increased incidence of offensive linemen's shoulders being dislocated."

Some players have quit rather than court more pain. A teary-eyed John Elway, claiming he still had a passion for the game at age 38, retired because his body could no longer take the punishment. Minnesota Vikings running back Robert Smith, 28, an unrestricted free agent at the height of his game, astounded the NFL by retiring without explanation, turning his back on what was expected to be a lively bidding war, with offers likely to exceed $30 million for five years. Smith had already had three knee surgeries, and while his agent, Neil Cornrich, denied that the on-the-job pounding played any part in the running back's decision to leave the game, Smith had implied as much to reporters.

No matter how young they are when they retire, a great many NFL players face a visit in middle age from that most pernicious of postfootball afflictions, degenerative arthritis. An athlete who suffers an injury to a major weight-bearing joint, such as the hip or knee, is five to seven times more likely to develop degenerative arthritis than an average member of the population. Repeated pounding and jarring of the joints—even in the absence of injury—all but guarantee that former players will be caught in the ganglia of serious and chronic pain. The 1994 NFLPA-Ball State survey said that arthritis is the most commonly reported health problem among retired players, affecting 47% of respondents. "A lot of ex-players with terribly arthritic spines say, 'But I never had a back injury!'" Andrews says. "That doesn't matter. There's no way to heal those cartilage lesions. They heal with scar tissue and are never as good again. What you end up with is a bunch of ex-NFL players, in their 40s and 50s, who shouldn't have arthritis but have degenerated knees and need total replacement done at an early age."

This, then, is not about a few casualties wandering off the playing field into retirement, their bells rung and still chiming in their heads, but rather about a whole society of broken men hounded through their lives by pain and injury, and all the psychological problems that often attend them.

JOHNNY UNITAS once owned the most dangerous right arm in the NFL. Today he barely has use of the hand attached to it. Unitas, who is considered by many to be the greatest field general to play the game, is still paying for a hit he took more than three decades ago as a Baltimore Colt. That day in 1968, Unitas was drawing back his arm to throw a pass when a Dallas Cowboy mashed the inside of his elbow. Unitas came back to play again—the arm seemed fine up through his retirement in 1974—but by the mid-1990s he was having problems with the nerves that controlled his hand and fingers. He lost strength and feeling in the hand and became unable to rotate the thumb back and grasp objects. The symptoms only got worse. Now Unitas cannot close the hand that made Raymond Berry famous.

Unitas's two knee replacements work perfectly well—cartilage and ligaments in the right knee were torn in a collision with two Bears in 1963, while the left wore out from years of favoring the right—but when he plays golf, which is about all the exercise he can get with those knees, he has to use his left hand to close the fingers of his gloved right hand around the grip, then strap the hand to the shaft with a Velcro strip. He goes through this tedium on every shot. "I do it putting, too," says Johnny U, who's 68.

Forty years ago Unitas was the toughest and smartest quarterback in the game, calling the plays and running the show in a way that inspired both fear and awe among teammates and opponents alike. Mentally, he always seemed a step ahead of everyone else. Unitas perfected the two-minute drill, and no one since—not Montana, not Elway—has run it better. Setting an NFL record that seems as unassailable as Joe DiMaggio's 56-game hitting streak, Unitas threw a touchdown pass in 47 consecutive games between 1956 and '60. In the years since, only Dan Marino has come anywhere close to that mark, throwing scoring passes in 30 straight games from '85 to '87.

Unitas has demanded disability compensation from the league but says he has been turned down for various reasons, among them that he didn't apply by age 55—though his right hand didn't fail him until he was 60—and that the league pays him a pension of $4,000 a month. The NFL adds that, in its opinion, Unitas is not "totally and permanently disabled."

Meanwhile, of that magical hand that spun footballs like strands of gold, Unitas says, "I have no strength in the fingers. I can't use a hammer or saw around the house. I can't button buttons. I can't use zippers. Very difficult to tie shoes. I can't brush my teeth with it, because I can't hold a brush. I can't hold a fork with the right hand. I can't pick this phone up. . . . You give me a full cup of coffee, and I can't hold it. I can't comb my hair."

BILL STANFILL never thought it would come to this. Never conceived, through all his years as a rampaging defensive end for the Miami Dolphins, that he would be reduced to what he is now. Never imagined that at 54, he would be navigating his house in Georgia with a metal walker—step-shuffle, step-shuffle—as he recovered from hip-replacement surgery. Or still feeling the consequences of that near-fatal injury he suffered when, during a pre-season game against the Bengals in 1975, he cracked heads with a teammate and almost severed his spinal cord between vertebrae C-4 and C-3.

It was like nothing he had ever felt. "I'd had stingers, but this was entirely different," Stanfill recalls. "I just numbed up. Could not move my arms or feel myself breathing." Stanfill had subluxed the joint in his cervical spine; that is, a disk and the surrounding bone had slipped nearly far enough to damage the cord. He would never be the same player again, and by the end of the next year he would be out of football. Two decades later, the disks began herniating, and he has had four vertebrae fused in his cervical spine.

"I can't tip my head back at all," says Stanfill, an avid bird hunter, "so I can't shoot dove anymore. I feel like I swallowed a Viagra pill and it got stuck in my throat. My neck is stiff as hell. The neurosurgeons have told me that if another disk goes [in my cervical spine], I will be totally disabled."

Stanfill was an old-fashioned football gladiator, a 6' 5½", 255-pound country boy who won the Outland Trophy, as the college game's best interior lineman, in his senior year at Georgia; helped Miami win two Super Bowls, after the 1972 and '73 seasons; and was named to four Pro Bowls. He relished the battle in the trenches, mano a mano. "All I wanted to do was play," he says.

All those wars left all those scars, however, and not only to his spine. In late January, while sitting next to the fireplace in his five-bedroom redbrick house outside Albany, Ga., Stanfill pointed out a glass jar sitting on the mantel. At the bottom of the jar, immersed in a clear solution, was a mysterious white ball. "I'm gonna see if I can donate it for auction," he said. " 'Who wants a piece of Bill Stanfill?' That's part of me. The price I paid for playing pro football."

It was the ball of his left hip, and it had been sawed off his skeleton three weeks earlier. Stanfill had been suffering from avascular necrosis (AVN)—in which blood circulation is cut off to the hip bone, causing it to die—because of repeated trauma and, possibly, repeated injection of the anti-inflammatory drug cortisone when he was in pro ball. ("I was like a pincushion," he says.) Stanfill sells agricultural real estate, but he has worked little since March 2000, when a disk in his lower back ruptured. Doctors have told him that his right hip also has AVN and will have to be replaced.

Stanfill's football days have left him a physical wreck, making him wonder what his life will be like in five years. Still, he expresses neither rancor nor self-pity. "Just wish I'd made some of the money they're making today," he says wryly. "It would make this a lot easier to live with."

EARL CAMPBELL has a dazzling assortment of rings that were given to him in honor of his storied accomplishments as a college and pro running back: the Heisman Trophy ring, the NFL Rookie of the Year ring, one MVP ring (though he was MVP three times) and the NFL Hall of Fame ring, but he wears none of them because of arthritis in both his hands, the ones that he used to push away tacklers. "Jim Brown and I were the best at the stiff-arm," says Campbell. "Now I can barely close my left fist—the arthritis and the soreness and the pain."

Campbell was a complete force as a running back, fast enough to turn the corner and race upfield, strong enough to crash through the line. He always seemed to be running out of his clothes; it was as if he invented the tear-away jersey. It was easy to imagine him in the end zone dressed in nothing more than his jockstrap and shoulder pads, standing there with a quizzical smile on his face and various large bodies scattered behind him, each clutching a remnant of his uniform. As his Houston Oilers coach, Bum Phillips, said, "Earl Campbell may not be in a class by himself, but whatever class he's in, it doesn't take long to call roll."

Now 46 and the owner of a barbecue restaurant and a sausage-making business in Austin, Campbell winces at more than his swollen digits. His knees and back ache ceaselessly. He also has a condition called drop foot: As a result of nerve damage to his legs, he cannot raise the front of his feet when he lifts them off the ground to take a step. The feet flop along loosely when he walks. To use the bathroom upstairs from his home office, Campbell—unable to grip with his hands or bend his knees—must lean his forearms on the railings and drag himself up the eight or 10 steps. The process is as painful to watch as it must be for Campbell to complete.

"I realize that every time you get something in life, you've got to give up something," he says. He likes to hunt deer and wild boar in south Texas, and he is reminded of what he gave the game whenever he is home on the range. "Sometimes it gets to the point that I can't stand the pain, like when I've got to walk a lot," he says. "Thank God I'm with people who understand me: 'Take all the time you need.' It's embarrassing when I've got to hop onto the back of a pickup and I need help. Or I need help climbing into deer blinds.

"Sometimes I tell my wife, 'Shoot, if I knew it was going to hurt like this, I don't know if I'd have [played football].' It's a hell of a price to pay."

FOR MOST NFL players, especially linemen, weight training is as much a part of the daily regimen as stretching exercises—and the weight room works its own form of wickedness. Hoisting iron, players rupture the patella tendons in their knees, put enormous strain on their lower backs and cause ligament injuries to the lumbar spine. They even damage their shoulders by doing something the joint was not designed to do: bench-pressing huge weights.

Joe Jacoby, a former Washington Redskins offensive lineman, was a habitue of the Skins' weight room, squat lifting his afternoons away. He dare not lift weights anymore, for fear it will accelerate the deterioration of his ankles, knees, wrists, elbows and back. Jacoby still feels the reverberations of years spent snatching iron and leaning his sequoia body into snot-blowing defensive linemen who drove shuddering forces down his spine and onto his lower joints.

At 6' 7", 305 pounds, Jacoby was a giant among the Hogs, a 13-year veteran who retired in 1993, the year he collapsed in his bathroom at home and could not get up. "My lower back went out," he says. "I dropped to my knees on the floor. The pain was that sharp. I crawled out of the bathroom to the bed." Like Stanfill, imbued with the ethic to play in pain, Jacoby played again later that year. Then, against the Kansas City Chiefs, his back went out again. He ended up spending three days in a hospital.

"I never wanted to go out that way," says Jacoby, 41. "I wanted to keep playing, even though I was hurting. I felt like I was letting down the team. You've been brought up that way since high school. It's *ingrained* in you. I had a wife. I had a family. A business I was starting. But I kept hearing those little things in the back of my mind: *You're letting your team down.*" He was in traction, shot up with cortisone, when the thought finally struck him: I can't keep doing this. I have a life to live after this.

Jacoby had blown out his left knee earlier in his career, when his leg got wrenched in a pileup. "The kneecap was way over on the side of the knee," he recalls. "I still hear the crunching and popping." Another old wound—vintage for linemen, who are forever getting their fingers caught and dislocated in face masks and shoulder pads—is the busted knuckle on Jacoby's wedding-band finger, as gnarled as a tree root. He has won many wagers in bars, claiming he can get the ring over that knuckle. His wife, Irene, had the band made with a clasp, so he can take it off like a bracelet.

Jacoby owns an auto dealership in Warrenton, Va. He and Irene had the sinks in the kitchen and master bathroom of their house installed higher than normal, "so he doesn't have to bend down," she says. He often walks about sockless in loafers. "It's too painful for him to bend over and put on socks or lace up shoes," Irene says.

Jacoby walks stiffly on his damaged ankles, but he endures the discomforts with stoic grace. He still remembers vividly the pounding he took year after year, through 170 games, including four Super Bowls—a career that left him unable to do any exercise other than walking. "Some days the back gets unbearable," he says. "It's really deep in the lower back and goes down to my left buttock and hamstring. Sometimes it gets so bad it hurts my nuts. There's pain down my left leg now. My left foot has been numb for two months. The bone's pressing on the nerve. Too many years of abuse, using the back to block."

Like so many other hobbled former players, Jacoby says he would do it all again if he had the chance. He knew what he was getting into. "Football players know the risk and the consequences," he says. "They know they will pay for it later in life. If they don't, they are misleading themselves."

AS MUCH as Jacoby has gone through, he looks fortunate when compared with Chris Washington. Only 39, Washington seems old beyond his years. He was an NFL linebacker for seven seasons, most of them with the Tampa Bay Buccaneers, and he has had 21 operations. He suffers from severe arthritis in both knees—he has had six surgeries on the right, five on the left—and his right thigh and calf are atrophying. He endures his days with help from a pharmacopia in a kitchen cabinet: one pill for sleep, two for pain (including double-strength codeine) and two to reduce inflammation.

Washington was a zealous weightlifter, but now his home looks like a

Gold's Gym after closing, with everything racked and idle: the stationary bike, the treadmill, the stair-climber and tons of barbells. He won't use any of them for fear of inflaming his diseased joints. Not only is he virtually crippled by ailing knees, but he also suffers hand tremors from pinched nerves; he shakes too much to fasten a necklace around his wife's neck. Although he has upper arms like ham shanks, he experiences periodic loss of strength in the right one and has back spasms as well. Washington carries his 10-month-old daughter, Taylor, in a Snugli, but not simply for convenience. He fears he will be seized by a shooting pain in his back or arm or suffer the sudden collapse of a knee and drop her.

Washington, who has worked as an insurance salesman and a data-entry clerk after retiring from the NFL in 1992, has been unable to hold a job since 1996. He draws disability payments to help support his family and is seeing his worst fears slide before his eyes. "Not being able to run around and play with my daughter," he says, giving one example. "I tried coaching [as a volunteer at the high school level], but my body couldn't take it; I can't stay on my feet that long. What kind of an example am I setting for kids if I'm walking around with a cane? I don't go to a lot of NFL functions. I would like to hang out with those guys, but I don't want them to see me like this."

None of this comes in the tone of a complaint. Washington wishes only that when he played he had known more about what he was doing to his body and had taken better care of it. He wishes that he had not allowed himself to be shot up with painkillers and cortisone so he could play hurt. Like the other former players who have been down that tortuous road, he assumes his share of the blame. "It was my choice to do what I did," he says. "I guess I didn't expect to be in this kind of shape."

NOR DID Harry Carson, for 13 years a crushing, headfirst inside linebacker of the New York Giants. Carson's injury is to an organ that is still little understood. By his own count he suffered at least 15 concussions while playing pro football, from 1976 to '88, and he is afflicted by what Yaras-Davis, of the NFLPA, believes is one of the most common and troublesome maladies among former players: postconcussion syndrome, which is marked by headaches, forgetfulness, blurred vision and difficulty tracking mentally.

Former Cowboys quarterback Troy Aikman and former 49ers quarterback Steve Young, each of whom suffered repeated bell-ringers on the field, are the players most closely associated with concussions. Carson, however, was one of the first former players to go public with the debilitating aftershocks of concussions, in an attempt to broaden understanding of the problem. Carson had his share of other injuries, but none quite as stunning as the concussion he suffered in 1985 when he crashed head-on into his favorite opponent, Redskins fullback John Riggins. "It was pretty much my power against his power," Carson says. "I remember hitting John and going back to the huddle . . . everything faded to black. I was literally out on my feet."

Carson would find that such blows had long-term effects. In 1991, three years after he retired, he wrote in his journal, "I don't think as clearly as I used to. Nor is my speech, diction, selection of vocabulary as good as it used to be, and I don't know why." As a TV broadcaster with the MSG Network in New York City, he would occasionally misspeak. "I would mispronounce words and lose my train of thought," he says. "Things would happen, and I'd think I was going crazy. I'd go to the store to get something and forget what."

Like Yaras-Davis, Carson believes the syndrome is far more common than is generally thought. "One problem is that a lot of players who suffer from it have no clue what they're dealing with," says Carson. "I've talked to players I've played with and against. Once I went public with this concussion thing, they were looking at me as being sort of brain-damaged, drooling and all this stuff. But it is an injury just like one to your knee or hip."

WHAT AILS Curt Marsh is far less elusive. The 41-year-old former offensive lineman for the Raiders could serve as a poster boy for crippled NFL veterans who ache in all the usual places: neck, back, knees, hips, ankles. Bone by bone, Marsh's body is gradually being replaced. He has had more than 20 operations, including one in '96 to replace his left hip, which had developed AVN, and he expects soon to undergo surgery to replace his right hip, which also has been damaged by AVN.

Like Stanfill, Marsh allowed team doctors to shoot him up repeatedly with painkillers and cortisone. By the time he retired, after seven years in the league, Marsh had a scoped knee, bulging disks and a right ankle that had been destroyed when the Raiders' team physician, Robert Rosenfeld, who died in 1994, apparently misdiagnosed and mistreated a broken talus bone. By '94, after the 13th operation on it, the ankle was a hopeless ruin, and doctors cut off Marsh's leg eight inches below the knee.

Marsh is not shy about being an amputee. While attending a 1998 hearing of the California Senate's Industrial Relations Committee in Sacramento, Marsh, all 350 pounds of him, heard one agitated senator, Ross Johnson of Irvine, excoriate pro athletes who had taken advantage of the state's generous workers' compensation laws by filing their claims there, even if they lived in other states and had played only road games in California. Johnson, backing a bill that would have limited workers' comp payments for pro athletes, declared that he was "outraged" that "professional athletes, who earn huge sums of money, wind up abusing a system that was created for the benefit of average working men and women."

Moments later Marsh, in a move as memorable as any he ever made with the Raiders, pounced on Johnson, saying he was "offended" to see athletes being treated "as if they were a piece of meat" because they were well paid for their labors. "And that makes [what happens to them] O.K.? That really bothers me. We have families that go through the pain. We have. . . . "

Here Marsh reached both hands down to his right leg, pressed a button on the side of his black boot and, to gasps from the audience, removed the prosthesis from his stump and raised it in the air. "Fact of the matter is, you cannot pay me enough money to make this worth my while," he said, holding the boot aloft. "This is a real issue. . . . Seventy times a game you run into a human being as big as you are. They say that's like a traffic accident. . . . What is that, 1,400 traffic accidents a year? And we're gonna say it's O.K. because we pay 'em a lot of money. . . . but they don't deserve to get the same thing that we give everyone else?"

The bill was never enacted.

For all that he has been through, Marsh is remarkably free of bitterness, even though he believes his amputation was the result of poor medical care. "I'm not looking for pity," he says. "That's just the way it is." For him and for countless other veterans of pro football's trench warfare.

There is a whole battalion of Curt Marshes and Chris Washingtons and Earl Campbells out there, enough of them to fill an NFL Old Soldiers' Home and dodder arthritically around the grounds. Busted knees, numb and bulbous ankles, sawed-off hips and all.

| | | | | |

The Nightmare of Steroids

BY TOMMY CHAIKIN WITH RICK TELANDER

South Carolina lineman Tommy Chaikin used bodybuilding drugs for three years. They drove him to violence and nearly to suicide.

I WAS SITTING IN MY ROOM AT THE ROOST, THE ATHLETIC DORM at the University of South Carolina, with the barrel of a loaded .357 Magnum pressed under my chin. A .357 is a man's gun, and I knew what it would do to me. My finger twitched on the trigger. I was in bad shape, very bad shape. From the steroids. It had all come down from the steroids, the crap I'd taken to get big and strong and aggressive so I could play this game that I love.

I felt as though I were sitting next to my body, watching myself, and yet I was in my body too. I was trying to get up that final bit of courage to end it all. Every nerve inside me was on fire. My mind was racing. I couldn't get a grip on anything. The anxiety attacks I'd been having for the last five months had become so intense that I couldn't stand them anymore. I'd lost control of everything—it's impossible to describe the horror I felt, the fear, the anxiety over that loss of control.

I could hear my teammates outside my room. They were walking back and forth, listening at the door. They talked in low voices, and they sounded very concerned. Every now and then someone would try opening the door, but I'd locked it. "Tommy," someone would say quietly. "You O.K.?"

"Yeah."

"You sure?"

"Yeah." I was definitely going crazy, but not in a wild way. I answered in a very calm voice. I knew I was history—it was just a matter of time. I thought about the explosion and the bullet, about how it could take away this pain.

And then I heard my father's voice. He was banging on the door. "Tommy, open up!" he said.

It was a Friday morning, the day before our game against Clemson, and my dad and my older brother, Mark, had arrived from our home in Bethesda, Md. They were going to come down for the game anyway, but they arrived ahead of schedule because I'd called my sister, Dawn, early that week and told her I was sick and needed help. My father flew down on Wednesday, but he really had no idea what bad shape I was in. On Thursday night I went to see my girlfriend, and mentally I was already gone. I'd lost it. I started crying, and I hadn't cried since way back when I was a kid. "Please don't think of me as a coward if I do something wrong," I sobbed to her.

"What are you talking about?" she asked. She was scared.

"I can't take it anymore," I kept saying. "Please don't think of me as a coward."

I was a 23-year-old football player at a big-time school, 6' 1", 250 pounds, a senior defensive lineman who could bench-press 500 pounds. I was ready to kill myself, but I couldn't stand the thought of being seen as a coward. That's all I cared about.

Somehow I got back to the Roost that night and fell asleep. I don't know how that happened, since I hadn't been able to sleep right for months. But when I woke up Friday morning, I felt O.K., and the first thing I said to myself was, "I'm going to play against Clemson. I'll *play*, goddammit!" We were 7–2, having a great season. I wanted to continue to be a part of it.

But then I started feeling bad again. The waves of anxiety washed over me, I started to tremble, and then I got my gun. And now my dad was pounding on the door. On reflex, like a dutiful son, I hid the gun and let him in. He looked at me and said, "Tommy, let's go home." He took me to the airport, and we flew to Washington. I tried to compose myself on the flight, but it was horrible. I felt I was suffocating. My mom was waiting at the airport. "We're taking you to the hospital," she said.

All I said was, "I hope it isn't the psych ward, because I'm not going to the psych ward."

In the waiting room at Sibley Memorial Hospital in Washington, I started to have spasms. My body was having a reaction to Stelazine, the drug that a psychiatrist had prescribed for me a few weeks earlier when I'd first come home from South Carolina to get some professional help. That was right after our game against North Carolina State, which we won 48–0. I played well, too. I had six tackles. But off the field I was lost, erratic. Suicide was always on my mind. Suicide and football. The fact that I could play at all in my condition seems strange to me now. The Stelazine was supposed to reduce my anxiety attacks, but it just seemed to intensify them.

Finally my psychiatrist arrived at Sibley. He tried to explain what was happening to me, and I said, "I don't care about any of that. Give me something to help me now, or it's all over."

All of a sudden two guys in white jackets appeared. "We're just going to take you to the top floor of the hospital," one of them said. "You'll be fine." We all got into the elevator, and I thought: *One Flew Over the Cuckoo's Nest*. I was in a movie. I was Jack Nicholson. I was Randle McMurphy. But nothing was funny. I couldn't believe any of it. My mind was on fire.

We got off on the seventh floor, and there in front of us was a big door with a lock on it. I freaked. I turned to my dad and screamed, "What the hell are you doing, man! I told you I'm not going to this place! I'm not crazy! I don't belong here!"

Then the attendants grabbed my arms. I looked at them and said, "No." I was very powerful at the time, my adrenaline was flowing and my mind was reeling. I said to the men, very quietly, "You won't last 10 seconds with me right now." I could have broken their necks like clicking my fingers. They knew it. They let go of my arms.

"Do not touch me," I said. "I'll walk in myself."

I looked straight ahead. They opened the door, and I walked in. The door closed, and my parents and the rest of my life were locked out. In front of me I saw people milling around, some of them blank and silent. Suddenly, everything caved in. This was how far I had fallen. This was how far I'd gone since I'd enrolled at South Carolina four and a half years earlier to chase the American dream.

I OFTEN sit and wonder how it all happened, how I let anabolic steroids lead me into this mess. I feel there's something in me—a flaw maybe, a personality trait—that brought me down. Oh, yeah, I take responsibility for my actions. I'm headstrong, and I've got a temper. I can't blame others for my mistakes, certainly not for making me take dangerous drugs. But I still think of myself as someone who started out as just a normal guy, a hard worker, a studier, a kid who loved sports. And I feel part of the trouble comes from things outside of me—the pressures of college football, the attitudes of overzealous coaches and our just-take-a-pill-to-cure-anything society.

As I recover from my steroid use, I wish I could have amnesia, to tell you the truth. It's very painful for me to reflect on what happened. It's like having to watch game films of yourself where you get chop-blocked over and over. But it's how you learn, too.

I had a normal childhood, I suppose. I grew up in Bethesda, the youngest of three kids in an upper-middle-class family. My dad runs his own window-replacement business, and my mom is a housewife. My dad always wanted us kids to be successful, but he didn't put pressure on us to excel in sports. All my drive was self-motivated.

I started playing soccer when I was seven, but I got bored with it and picked up tennis a few years later. I was pretty quick and I worked hard, and before long I was ranked fairly high in local junior tennis. I had always wanted to play football, though, and in my junior year at Walt Whitman High, I decided I was going to. But my dad wasn't big on contact sports—Mark had blown his knee out playing high school football—so it was a battle for me to get permission to play. Finally my mom signed my release without telling my father, and I joined the team as a split end.

I wanted to play because all the popular guys played football. And I wanted to excel. During that first year of high school ball, I was about 6 feet, 185 pounds, and I did all right as an end. But then our noseguard got hurt, and I switched to that position. I started spending a lot of time lifting weights, and I came back for my senior season weighing about 220. My teammates were amazed at how much I'd progressed. But the reason was simple—I'd worked real hard. I was named all-area, all-county and all-metro, and I knew I wanted to play big-time college ball. But I also knew I was no blue-chipper. Not at my size.

A few schools recruited me, but the coaches at South Carolina showed the most interest. They sent up the defensive line coach, Jim Washburn, and he came to see me in the hospital in the spring of '83, my senior year. I was recovering from having a prolapsed rectum wall repaired, fairly serious work. I was in a lot of pain, but I remember he told me that my bench press of 350 pounds would make me one of the strongest guys on the S.C. team. And he said that after the Gamecocks' annual spring game, the winners always ate lobster and the losers got steak. He was a good salesman.

All the time he was talking, he was checking me out, walking up and down the side of the bed to see how tall I was. I'd said I was 6' 2", but I'm more like 6' 1". He saw the tattoo of a star on my arm and the stretch marks around my pecs from lifting, and I guess he liked those things. Anyway, I wanted to play college ball so bad that I would've played anywhere at all. I'd never been to Columbia, S.C., but I didn't care where the school was. When they offered me a full ride, I snapped it up.

So I showed up in Columbia in the fall of 1983, a naive, easygoing but ambitious 19-year-old, ready to make his mark. The first thing I found out was that Washburn had fed me a line. I wasn't even close to being one of the strongest players on the team. There were a lot of monstrous guys in the weight room. And I found out later that the spring game winners didn't get lobster, either. They got little steaks, and the losers ate hot dogs. Basically, what I discovered was that I couldn't trust this man, my position coach.

I also discovered that Columbia was one of the hottest places on earth. For the first few days of double sessions Washburn ran me and the two other freshman defensive linemen half to death. Then one of the linemen, Ray Bingham, went to offense, and the other, Ricky Daniels, blew out his knee. That left me and Washburn, one-on-one in the heat, until the upperclassmen reported a few days later.

Washburn never stopped screaming at me. I was dehydrated, my electrolytes were screwed up, and my legs cramped all night. I actually prayed for a serious injury. One day I was standing in the huddle, and my eyes rolled up and I just keeled over. I'd stopped sweating, my skin was cold, I was delirious. They packed me in ice and gave me fluids. And the next day I was back at practice. All this—and I was sure they'd redshirt me anyway. I wouldn't even play for a year.

So I held a dummy for the scout team and got knocked around all fall. I didn't like it, but it was no big deal. Already guys had asked me if I wanted to take steroids—they called the stuff "juice"—so I could beef up and fight back. They were big guys, on steroids themselves, and they were trying to help me, but I always said no. I'd smoked pot a couple of times in high school, but I didn't like drugs. And I'd heard stories about the side effects of steroids, which can include cancer, liver damage, heart disease and sex problems. No way was I going to mess with something as risky as steroids. I was going to build myself up naturally.

In fact I'd decided that I wanted to be a defensive end, and I figured I wouldn't have to build myself up at all. Over Christmas break I ran and ran and ran, and actually *dropped* my weight down to 205. I wanted to be lean and quick as a cat for spring practice. I get obsessed when I put my mind to something, and I was obsessed with being a fast defensive end.

That spring I got the crap knocked out of me. I got pushed all over the field. I also got a lot of muscle pulls in my legs, and Tom Gadd, the defensive coordinator at the time, reacted to that by saying, "Dianabol abuse! Dianabol abuse!" to me. He was referring to a type of steroid, but I hadn't taken any yet, so he didn't know what he was talking about. But neither did I—at least as far as being a defensive lineman was concerned. It turned out that being light and quick meant nothing. I found out the hard way that you've got to be *big* and quick.

I finally said to myself, I've had enough of this, and I started looking hard at those guys who were using steroids. They looked fine to me: They were happy; they were going out drinking, they seemed to have normal sex lives, and they were a hell of a lot bigger than I was. Maybe it was time for me to join the crowd.

At that point I was so laid-back that guys on the team were calling me the Mild-Mannered Man from Maryland. I thought I was fairly intense, but I was nothing compared with some of the others. In fact, the aggression level and the intensity of the players were the things that shocked me the most about college ball. There were fights all the time in practice, a lot of them instigated by coaches. They would always let the fights go, too, let guys beat the hell out of each other. If you showed a violent nature, regardless of your athletic ability, it definitely swayed the coaches' opinions in your favor.

Coach Gadd was big on drills that promoted fighting. Gadd was a dictatorial type, a little man with a little mustache, who had never played major college ball. We called him Little Hitler. One of his favorite drills was called Escape from Saigon. It involved three blockers, a ballcarrier and a defender. The defender would try to get to the runner, who was darting around while the blockers beat the hell out of the defender. Sometimes the defender would get his helmet knocked off and the three guys would keep hitting him. He'd be on his knees, dazed, and they'd keep sticking him with their helmets. A lot of guys took a beating in that drill. Gadd did it to get our aggression level up. We did it because if you didn't, you were a pussy, and if you were a pussy, you didn't play. You always hit the guy when he was down. Definitely. Your instinct as a human being was to have compassion. But then you just said, "Oh well, this is football." You suppressed your humanity to succeed.

In another drill one of my friends, George Hyder, was going one-on-one with a player who was very passive, and George ripped the guy's helmet off and smashed him in the face with it, chipping some of his teeth. It was uncalled-for, but the coaches liked it.

Joe Morrison, our head coach, might have been the one guy who *didn't* like it. In fact he was against fighting. But he thought we were pussies if we couldn't handle the August heat. One practice it was close to 120 degrees on the field and unbelievably humid, and guys were passing out left and right. Players were ripping off all their pads and running to get in the little bit of shade under this old dead tree. Morrison went nuts. He said we were mentally weak for letting the heat get to us. "If I had a chain saw, I'd cut that damn tree down!" he yelled.

He would just stand there in the heat in black pants, a black vinyl windbreaker and a baseball cap, smoking cigarettes like crazy, and he'd never sweat a bead. He was unbelievable. He had heart problems in the spring of '85, after my first varsity season, but he still smoked like a chimney all during practices and games.

As a team, we must have run and hit in practice more than any other team in college football. Gadd was a Lombardi disciple. We had what he called Packer Days, even in the 100 degrees heat, when we'd do conditioning drills that seemed like they'd never end. Guys would just drop from exhaustion. Washburn liked contact drills, including one where two linemen would grab each other's shoulder pads and butt heads until one of them dropped. Washburn would watch us and yell encouragement. He loved it.

He was a pretty big guy—6' 3", 245 pounds—with red hair. He'd played offensive lineman at a small college, and he used to tell us, "I would've loved to play defense, but I wasn't good enough." So our drills were a reflection of what he couldn't do himself. Washburn was hung up on being macho, and he'd say bizarre things to us about manhood and being tough and big and mean. "Ever think about just ripping someone's head off?" he'd ask us. And, I swear, he was serious.

The coaches definitely had the ability to draw out the viciousness in players. On defense, for instance, most of the guys were black—my sophomore year, there were only two or three white starters—and before we'd go up against the offensive line, Washburn would get the black guys together and say, "Those honkies are calling you niggers." Of course the black guys knew he was just trying to get them riled, but they also knew there were some offensive linemen who were very Southern and anti-black.

Anyway, the coaches wanted us to be as aggressive as possible, and it didn't matter where that aggression came from. That's the thing about football—once you whip up anger, you can twist it, channel it, aim it, just like a water hose. Coaches got me to respond by going after my ego, my pride. If they said I was a bum, I had to prove I wasn't.

So that spring of my freshman year I decided I was going to take steroids to get big and strong and aggressive. There was no one thing, really, that led to the decision. Gadd always preached about the big, violent guys he'd seen in the Western Athletic Conference when he coached at Utah. He made those guys sound like animals, killers, and it made us feel we didn't measure up.

That affected me. I took it as a challenge to my manhood, and I'm sure that's exactly how Gadd wanted me to take it. Then, too, I saw how well the guys already on steroids were doing—maybe 30 of them at that time. There was also the fact that I was young and felt nothing bad could happen to me, combined with the fact that I was part of a drug-oriented society. In addition to all of that, I felt I had the coaches' encouragement. I'm told

531

that Washburn says he opposes steroid use, but he told me, "Do what you have to do, take what you have to take."

Another thing that had gotten to me was trying to compete with the black guys. I hadn't played against many blacks, and they intimidated me with their strength and speed. I'd say that all but a couple of the guys on my team who used steroids were white, and the reason they did was to keep up with other guys on steroids and with black athletes.

I made my decision, and the funny thing is, I felt good about it. I was looking forward to the adventure of it and the chance to perform at my best. The thing people often don't understand is that college athletes feel tremendous pressure to succeed. Some guys have parents who are pushing them real hard. Other guys are just very competitive and have great pride. Nobody wants to sit on the bench and be a failure.

After I'd made my decision, getting the stuff was no big deal. I had spent a lot of time back home at a gym where serious lifters worked out, and I think by now everybody knows that the majority of bodybuilders and powerlifters use steroids. I had a friend there, and I knew he could get me what I wanted or tell me where to go for it. He got me some steroids, and I told him I also wanted hGH, human growth hormone. He told me where I could get it.

I knew hGH was expensive, but I'd read in a muscle magazine that it was safer than steroids, and I wanted to believe that. I also knew that hGH could cause acromegaly—the enlargement of the brow, hands and feet that's sometimes called "Frankenstein's syndrome"—but that you'd have to take megadoses for it to happen. Some bodybuilders take $10,000 worth of hGH per cycle—that's a bodybuilding term for a series of drugs in varying doses—but I only got $800 worth, enough for 10 injections over eight weeks. Tunnel vision had set in. My attitude was: Just give me what it takes to get big.

Still, I was pretty scared because I'd heard all the horror stories about the drugs. My supplier told me that if I didn't get too crazy with this stuff, didn't abuse it, I'd be O.K. Then we went down into his basement at home, and he gave me my first injection, in the top of my butt. I went right to the weight room and had a great workout. I was pumped, but, of course, it was all psychological.

I had a lot of injections that summer, and after a while the spots I had to hit on my rear end got so callused from shots that at times I couldn't even get a needle in. You don't inject steroids into a vein. You shoot it deep into a muscle, and it gradually disperses through the body. It's very hard to shoot yourself up in the butt, and sometimes when I did, I hit spots that hurt so bad I could barely sit down the next day. Other times I'd shoot myself in the quad, the front of my thigh. It's dangerous because you have to go in an inch or so, and you can cause nerve damage if you're not careful.

You can take most steroids in pill form, but you have to take them every day, and certain pills can be harder on the liver. With shots you don't need to do it as often—12 times a month, in my case—and the drug stays in your system longer. At first I was very worried about needles, but after a while my concern went away—mainly because my body was changing so fast.

People who say steroids don't work don't know what they're talking about. You've got to experience it to know what I mean. Your muscles swell; they retain water and they just grow. You can work out much harder than before, and your muscles don't get as sore. You're more motivated in the weight room and you've got more energy because of the psychological effects of the drug.

I went from about 210 pounds to a lean 235 in eight weeks. My bench press went from the upper 300s to 420, and my squat from 400 to 520. I watched my diet and I was really cut—big arms, chest and legs, great definition. I went back to Columbia in the summer of '84, before my first varsity season, for the Iron Cocks meet, a lifting competition for football players. A bunch of guys who were already on steroids saw me and said, "Aha, so you bent to the pressure."

I said, "Yeah, I've begun the chemical warfare." And we laughed. Washburn saw me and said, "You look great!" He must have known I was using juice.

Besides the muscle growth, there were other things happening to me. I got real bad acne on my back, my hair started to come out, I was having trouble sleeping, and my testicles began to shrink—all the side effects you hear about. But my mind was set. I didn't care about that other stuff.

In fact my sex drive during the cycles was phenomenal, especially when I was charged up from all the testosterone I was taking. I also had this strange, edgy feeling—I could drink all night, sleep two hours and then go work out. In certain ways I was becoming like an animal.

And I was developing an aggressiveness that was scary. That summer I was working as a bouncer at this bar in D.C., and one night a Marine bumped into a girl I was dancing with. Words were exchanged, then I followed him to where he was sitting and said, "I didn't appreciate that." He put his beer down and came up hard under my chin with his hands, and a slice off my tongue about an inch long went flying out of my mouth. I didn't even notice it. I saw red. I felt an aggression I'd never felt before. I hit him so hard that he went right to the floor. He was semiconscious, and I got him in a head-lock and started hitting him in the ribs and kneeing him in the back. I want-ed to hurt him real bad. I could literally feel the hair standing up on the back of my neck, like I was a wolf or something. If I hadn't been on steroids, I would've walked away in the first place. But I had that cocky attitude. I wanted to try out my new size. I was beginning to feel like a killer. It was like football: a test of manhood between two people—you or me, all the way.

Back at school that fall, when I took the football physical, a doctor said, "Have you ever had high blood pressure and a heart murmur?" I said no. He said, "Well, you do now." I brushed it off. No big deal. I never heard a word about it from the coaches. Nobody seemed to care. I certainly didn't. A lot of guys were using more steroids than I was, and they were fine. Besides, I was in great shape. I ran the mile in 5:45, faster than a lot of linebackers.

I brought a bagful of stuff I'd gotten from my connection to school—bottles of Deca-Durabolin, 100 syringes, some vials of vitamin B-12—and I started selling it to teammates. We thought the B-12 would help us get through two-a-days. We wanted it for the energy, the placebo effect, what-ever. Our team doctor, Paul Akers, injected B-12 into anybody who wanted it before games. And our orthopedic surgeon, Robert Peele, would shoot up guys who had injured ankles or whatever with Xylocaine, a local anes-thetic. So what we were doing wasn't much different from what the doc-tors were doing; it was all done to enhance our performance.

Back in the spring I'd used some other drugs, too. I snorted cocaine with a couple of other players one night, but it was a bad experience for me. Coke was sort of circulating through the team then. I'd say about a third of the players had used it occasionally. But some guys used it the night be-fore games, and a few drank before we played. That's just how it was.

Then one night some of the guys on the team took microdots of LSD. That was interesting but intense; I don't know how anybody could take it very often. But some of my teammates had done it a lot. My buddy George Hyder said he had taken acid about 300 times. He could ingest anything. He was a very hyper person, and other guys on the team were too. The word was that one of them got into a fight on a recruiting trip and bit somebody's ear off.

These guys were my friends, and they were remarkably aggressive. I admired them because they had a mean streak I didn't have. They got on steroids about the same time I did, which heightened their aggression. One of my teammates hit a guy in a bar one time, and after the guy fell to the floor with his jaw collapsed and some teeth knocked out, the player kicked him in the head. Blood was everywhere. I'd say steroids had something to do with it.

I really feel that under certain conditions some of the guys who were on steroids would have been perfectly willing to beat someone to death. One time during the middle of a cycle George and another guy punched out the windshield of George's car, an old Toyota Tercel, and head-butted the windshields of some others. Then they came and got me and said, "Let's go kill somebody." I knew this was trouble, but I went anyway, for the hell of it. We drove for a while in George's Toyota, then they got out and started head-butting cars, breaking windshields. If anybody looked at them funny, they'd intimidate the guy until he ran away.

During two-a-days in August, I started a new cycle, taking Deca-Durabolin to help me keep pumped up. The coaches liked my new size and aggressiveness, and they moved me up to second-string defensive end, where I knew I'd play a lot. This was in 1984, and we didn't have to take drug tests yet, so there was nothing to worry about. Even after the NCAA instituted tests in '86, they were a sham. A lot of guys would just say, "Doc, I can't urinate in front of you," and they'd go into a stall where they'd hidden a vial of someone else's urine, and pour that in the cup. Some guys would pour salt or vinegar into the cup, which was supposed to mask any traces of drugs. Even when guys tested positive, nothing happened to them.

The trouble for some of us was that we couldn't sleep—that's one of the things steroids did to me—so we drank a lot at night because there wasn't anything better to do. I could drink a dozen beers and maybe eight or nine shots of vodka or bourbon in a few hours, easy. And because of the steroids and the booze, I'd get into fights.

Five nights before our first game of the season, against The Citadel, I was in a bar, and I got into an argument with this guy. I told him if he wanted to fight, to come out into the alley, which he did, and when he pulled his arm from behind his back, he was holding a 12-inch deer knife. He swung at me and I blocked it. Then he swung lower, and I couldn't tell if he got me or not. Just then one of my teammates, Woody Myers, came into the alley, and the guy tried to stab him. Woody and I jumped behind a car, but when I looked over my shoulder, I saw that the whole back of my shirt was soaked with blood. I put my finger in a hole under my right arm. The guy ran away and, before too long, the paramedics came. They were shocked at how high my blood pressure was, particularly after I'd lost so much blood. They asked if I was on steroids, and I said yes. At the hospital I told the doctor to stitch me up tight because I had a game that week.

The coaches were very upset when they found out what had happened, but they told me not to discuss it with anybody. "It's not what we want to talk to the press about," Morrison said. So nobody found out. And I played against The Citadel, my first college game, with a stab wound under my pads.

After a few games our nosetackle got hurt, and I moved from defensive end to nose and played a lot. I did pretty well, but I was still going against guys who weighed 280 or 290 pounds. I ordered some rhesus monkey hormones from back home—two bottles, 20 injections, for $800. It was supposed to be great stuff, able to build muscle without a lot of the water retention steroids cause. But I didn't get any size off it, so I think it was fake.

I was getting steroids for a lot of guys now through my source. He had a close friend who was a doctor, and he could get anything we wanted. I'd sell the stuff, but I didn't make a profit from it. I knew it was wrong, but I rationalized that the guys wanted the steroids and I could get high quality juice instead of the junk some guys were getting from Mexico and other places, stuff with no labels or anything on it.

By my junior year I'd say about 50 guys out of the 100 on the team were using steroids—almost all the offensive linemen and a lot of other players. And I'm convinced that we weren't much different from other major college teams. Believe me, players can tell. I'd say the majority of recent All-America offensive linemen have used steroids. You can tell what steroid users look like; pink and puffy skin, swollen faces and necks, but very tight skin wherever there's muscle. I'd play against these guys and they'd be huffing and puffing, and we'd look at each other and one of us would say, "How's that blood pressure?"

Before the North Carolina State game in '84, I tore ligaments in my right big toe in a pileup in practice. We were undefeated at the time, 7–0, and Washburn said he needed me. I couldn't push off on the foot and it hurt tremendously, but I wanted to play. So the day of the game I went into the back room with Dr. Peele, Washburn and Morrison. Morrison told somebody to lock the door because he didn't want the referees walking in on this. Washburn held my hand while Dr. Peele injected my toe joint with Xylocaine. When he was done I couldn't feel my foot at all. It wasn't till the painkiller wore off during the bus ride home that I was in agony.

I played in the next two games, against Florida State and Navy, but missed the Clemson game because of problems with my toe and back. We finished the regular season 10–1 and went to the Gator Bowl, where we lost to Oklahoma State.

It had been a successful season for me, so being the kind of obsessive guy I am, I went even harder into steroids. Real hard. During the spring I was taking two cc's of testosterone every third day and 10 Dianabol tablets daily, a huge amount. Washburn looked at me and said, "Wow, what did you take? Everything but the kitchen sink?"

I liked being on the edge; most athletes do. We're thrill-seekers. Athletics itself is a high. Football players will do wild things because it keeps them on the edge. At South Carolina, when we had time off, some of us would take our guns and go out and shoot—at anything—to keep from getting bored. Taking steroids was just another way of living on the edge. And it became a big social thing. Seven or eight of us heavy users would get in a dorm room together and start shooting each other up. Guys would show up with their bottles, and there'd be a lot of chatter: I shoot you, you shoot me. We all enjoyed it. I had boxes of syringes that I got from certain pharmacies in Columbia for 20 bucks for 100. We'd say it was for B-12 shots, but those needles are shorter and you need an inch or so to do steroids intramuscularly. They would give us the longer needles as long as we signed "B-12" in the book.

We never used the same needle twice. We tried to be careful how we injected each other, too, but sometimes you'd hit the sciatic nerve or something, and the guy's legs would buckle. I mean, none of us were doctors or anything. But we were needle-happy. We would have injected ourselves with anything, if we thought it would make us big.

A lot of times, if we were really getting bigger, we'd increase our dosage to gain bulk even faster—just fill the syringe to the end. We'd occasionally read the paperwork that came with the bottles, trying to figure out what a dosage should be for someone with anemia or a guy whose body can't produce enough testosterone, which is what the stuff is usually used for. Then we'd take 2, 3, 4, 10, 20 times that amount. Sometimes we'd take our needles and pull half a cc from one bottle and half from another, just mix them up. The more the better.

By the fall of '87, my senior season, there was one guy who was taking so many tabs of a steroid called Anadrol that he developed liver problems. At one point during the summer of '85, there were guys so heavily on steroids that they couldn't make it once around the track without getting back cramps from being so bloated. This alarmed Keith Kephart, our strength coach, so he took all the linemen in a room and said, "I want to know who's on Anadrol. I'm hearing horror stories. This is the strongest stuff around. It can be lethal. Now, who's using?"

A lot of guys raised their hands. Kephart wanted guys to cut back on their intake. I don't remember him telling us to stop, but he did say, "If you want counseling, come to me." I really think he cared, but he didn't think he could change us.

It was common knowledge that we were using the stuff. I had bottles of juice all over the place. We threw the used syringes into the waste cans in our rooms. I mean, we even had syringes sticking in the walls. Coaches would walk in and see the stuff, but nobody gave a damn. One of the coaches came in for a room check once, saw a vial with a skull and crossbones on the label and said, "I used to use Dianabol. What's this stuff?" We laughed and said, "It's a great new product from Germany. Look at the instructions. They're in German." He just laughed.

Players would stop by my room, as if it were a store, and ask if they could get some steroids. There was just this sort of no-big-deal attitude about it all.

The spring of '84, I bulked up some more, and people were in awe of my strength. I was benching close to 500 pounds, squatting more than 600. I could do 30 one-armed presses with a 100-pound dumbbell. I weighed about 260, and I looked like a steroid user. I took all kinds of stuff, including Equipoise, a horse steroid designed to make thoroughbreds leaner and more muscular. It was tough on me—I got colitis and was bleeding rectally—so I switched to other stuff. Guys started calling me Quasibloato and the Experiment, because they thought I'd take anything.

My aggression level was so high that I got into an argument with the team trainer during spring practice and went to my locker, put my hand through the metal mesh and ripped the door off its hinges. Then I went back to the Roost and took a baseball bat and demolished my refrigerator, smashed it to pieces, and then ripped the phone off the wall. My nerves were on edge like they'd never been before. At practice one day I got into a fight with a linebacker because he cut in front of me in line for a drill. I threw him down, pulled his helmet up far enough so I could get my fist in there and smashed him in the eye. As he got up, bleeding and humiliated, I felt sympathy for him. But then the steroids kicked in and I said to myself, "All right! You're a tough guy!"

I went home for spring break, and my mom took one look at me and said, "My God! What have you done to yourself?" I tried to deny everything, but my dad looked in my bag and found two vials of testosterone. He got very upset. He called our family doctor and had him try to convince me to get off steroids. My dad tried to talk me into quitting football and told me that he'd pay for my schooling. My sister called me constantly, trying to get me off the stuff. But I wouldn't listen. "I'm sorry," I said to my parents, "but it's a decision I've made, and I'll try not to abuse the steroids."

I don't know if you can call steroids addictive, but there's a vicious cycle involved with using them. The growth of the muscles enhances the aggression and other psychological changes caused by the drug, and those changes, in turn, make you want to get bigger and take more steroids. Plus, there is a terrible letdown when you come off them. I would be very high and then there'd be this extreme depression. And after each cycle, the comedown itself would get worse, plus, I'd get sick. I got walking pneumonia, bronchitis, exhaustion to the point where I had to sleep 12 to 14 hours at a time. Steroids were definitely wrecking my body.

I was also going through a personality change. I was becoming a hard-ass, one of the meanest guys on the team. It was a dramatic change, and the coaches loved it. So did I, in a way, because being passive hadn't done anything for me. But I also knew my behavior was becoming erratic, and that frightened me. Images of violence often filled my mind. I'd drive along and find myself thinking about sick things like crushing people to death, tearing off their limbs. I'd be grinding my teeth and gripping the wheel so hard that my arms would hurt.

Because of the tension at my house, I started spending a lot of time at my supplier's place in the summer of '85. Hyder and Myers came up from school, and we sat around injecting ourselves with all kinds of steroids, whatever was there.

One night we all injected each other, then went out drinking and got crazy. George had a pistol and we picked up a friend who had a shotgun, and I drove everybody out into the country in George's pickup. As we went past signs, those guys would blast away at them. They blew out the spotlight and security camera in front of an estate, and then shot the windows out of a bus parked in front of a church. One of the bullets went through the bus and killed a cow in the nearby pasture, and the cow slumped over the fence and rolled into the road. Blood was dripping from its head. I freaked, but the other guys were laughing. One of them wanted to shoot the cow again. Right then a cop car started chasing us, but we drove down some paths in the woods and lost the cop.

This hadn't been my way, but it had become my way. Steroids ruled my life.

THAT FALL, my second varsity season, I played pretty well, but we finished with a 5–6 record. The high point for me came when we played Michigan, a team I'd dreamed about playing against since I was a little kid. Ohio State–Michigan, that was what college football was all about. And if I played for South Carolina against Michigan—well, that was pretty damn close.

To get really fired up, I started taking a steroid called Halotestin a couple of weeks before the game. Its only effect, as far as I could tell, was that it enhanced aggression. It should have been called Holocaust, judging by what it did to me. My aggressiveness was out of control. I was cheapshotting people in practice, clotheslining them, ripping scout team quarterbacks' helmets off in noncontact drills. The coaches liked my enthusiasm, but they had to sit me down a few times for being a little too wild. I played great against Michigan, even though we got our butts kicked. Against Georgia the next week, we lost again, 13–6, but I was named defensive player of the game.

I started getting sick toward the end of the season, though. During the game against East Carolina in late October, I had bad chest pains, numbness in my arm and chills, and I had to come out in the second half. I thought I was dying. They cut off my jersey and took me to the hospital in an ambulance. The doctor said my cholesterol level and blood pressure were off the charts, probably because of the steroids. The pain was from angina, a pre-heart attack condition. Still, the coaches didn't seem to notice. My dad told Washburn he wanted me tested weekly for steroid use, but nothing came of it. And me—all I could think of was football. I was obsessed. We players even had a motto: "Bury me massive, or don't bury me at all."

I stopped taking steroids for a while because I'd been so sick, and after the season I had knee surgery. Then, over spring break, I went down to Fort Lauderdale. I was back on steroids and was very big and cocky, and after a few drinks one night, I got into a hassle with two cops in front of a bar. They told me to move, and I told them that if it wasn't for their guns and badges, I'd beat their asses. The next thing I knew, they'd clubbed me across the neck and legs, beat me up pretty good, and taken me to the station. When I went in front of the judge the next day, though, he just looked at me and said, "Trying to be a Fighting Gamecock, huh?" Then he let me go.

Not long after that I had a pain in my side, which I thought was from the beating. But when I went to a doctor I found out I had a swollen liver from the steroids. About this time Dr. Akers asked me if I was on steroids. I told him I was but asked him not to tell anybody. He turned right around and told Morrison, who called me in to find out who else was taking them. I told him I wouldn't talk about anybody else. Morrison looked at me and said, "Don't do it anymore." That was it. He's very quiet, not real communicative. He played for the New York Giants for 14 years, and he's very old school and tough: *You hurt? Put a little dirt on it.* So the whole thing just sort of went away.

Just the same, I vowed to turn over a new leaf. I was going to watch what I ate and if I used drugs at all, it would be very little. I was getting sick a lot, and even though I'd been doing O.K. academically, I was having a hard time concentrating on school. I'd either be up all night or I'd be listless and sleep a lot. Also, the way my sex drive came and went was bizarre. And when I got drunk—oh brother! One night in my dorm room, I pulled a shotgun on the pizza delivery boy, threw him down and put the gun in his face. It was loaded and I could have blown the kid all over the floor, but I was just fooling around. It was the kind of thing I thought was funny.

In 1986, my third varsity season, we lost some close games and finished a miserable 3-6-2. I moved around from nose to tackle and even played a little linebacker. After the season, though, I developed a tumor on my chest and it grew to the size of a handball. I was in bed coughing up mucus, and I was very depressed and fighting bouts of severe anxiety. Right before spring ball, I started another steroid cycle and, *boom!*, my blood pressure shot right up. I was sweating and had hot flashes. I knew my body was rejecting the drugs, so I stopped taking them.

I went to Dr. Akers and showed him the tumor, and he said, "Don't worry about it, it'll go away." But I didn't trust him, so I went to another doctor, and he said I needed surgery right away. I also had a tumor on my right hand that he said needed to come out. The tumors, he said, were caused by steroids, but the athletic department said they weren't football-related injuries, so the school wouldn't pay the medical bills. My dad's insurance paid for the surgery, which was performed in February of '87. As I lay in bed recovering, I began to wonder what this was all about. I was very depressed and I needed time for rehab, but spring drills would begin soon. Since the school hadn't paid for the surgery, it was as if it hadn't happened. *You're fine, get your ass out there, boy*—that was their attitude.

I said, "Screw it, screw all of you," and I quit the team and moved out of the Roost. I was sick, but I still had the desire to play, to excel. I couldn't kill that. I was reading a lot of philosophy, and I started thinking that this mindless aggression and physical self-destruction wasn't what life was all about. But I couldn't quit football before my senior season—I just couldn't come to terms with that. So I wrote a letter of apology to Morrison, and he took me back. It was a phony apology, but I would have done whatever was necessary to get back on the team. My sense of self-worth was tied up in the game.

About this time I was starting to battle anxiety attacks that I was sure were caused by the steroids. I can't really describe an attack, except to say that it's like your mind is a car engine stuck in neutral with the gas pedal to the floor, just screaming. There is terror mixed in, and you think that you're going to explode. The anxiety attacks were the worst mental pain I'd ever experienced.

By the end of the summer of '87, though, I was getting a handle on things, feeling better, working out a lot, doing it the natural way. I had vowed never to touch steroids again, but I couldn't stop. Just before I went back to school, I did a shot of Parabolin, yet another steroid. I blew up to 270. I couldn't bench much because of a shoulder injury, but I could squat 650 pounds. I also started to get that edgy feeling again. My mind started racing, and I felt out of control. The night before two-a-days began, I went out drinking with the other players, and we got crazy, head-butting each other, getting ready.

The next morning I had an anxiety attack, a big one. I sat in my room for hours, just trying to hold on to reality. I had another attack a few days later. I didn't think anybody could help me. I had tried to explain the feeling to my parents, but they couldn't understand. They didn't think I was doing steroids anymore, and so they tried to reassure me. "Don't worry, you're just tired and worn-out," they said.

But the attacks got worse and worse. Somehow, I was still a starter. I spent a lot of time in my room because I was so afraid, so paranoid. I'd wake up in the morning and everything was gray, everything had lost its colors. There was a roaring in my ears, and I saw trails behind moving objects. I couldn't read, because I couldn't concentrate. One minute I would think the mental illness was over with, and the next minute it would come racing back. Thoughts of suicide came into my mind. Every day was torture, and I started saying, "Please, God, let me make it through one more practice." I had to make it through practice so I could play in the games. That was all that mattered. I didn't care about my health, just football. I wasn't going to quit, by God, and I didn't want anyone to take my position. I didn't care if I died, as long as I completed the season, as long as I finished like a man.

I had a good game against Nebraska, but I don't know how. On the plane to Lincoln I'd had an anxiety attack and had to lock myself in the bathroom to try to calm down. In the game, though, my technique was almost flawless, and I had a lot of tackles. But I was like a fist, ready to squeeze myself to death.

Then in the sixth game of the year, at home against Virginia, I was overwhelmed with anxiety, almost panic. The crowd seemed like it was closing in. Except for that one shot of Parabolin, I hadn't used drugs for five months, and I kept wondering what was happening to me. I finally just walked off the field in the third quarter of the game and took my pads off and sat on the bench. The doctor asked me what was wrong, and I just said, "I don't feel good."

The coaches let me go home to see a psychiatrist, who agreed that steroids were to blame. That's when I got on Stelazine, which was supposed to help me. It didn't, and I saw another psychiatrist in Columbia, who put me on an antidepressant to go with the Stelazine. One day in class I felt the room start to sway. I staggered out of the class and down the stairs, even though they seemed to be moving. I weaved past people, but I couldn't hear anything. I got outside and I lost control of my bladder and my bowels. I urinated and defecated all over myself. I was praying to God I could make it to my car. Somehow I got there, drove back to the dorm, showered and lay down in bed. That was the end. I couldn't do anything. I couldn't practice. It was over.

MY FATHER came soon after that, and I went back home with him. I got out of Sibley in seven days, and after several more weeks at home, I went down to visit the team in Jacksonville, where they were beating their heads in while preparing for the Gator Bowl game against LSU.

The guys looked pretty ragged because they'd been going through two-a-days, but my friends saw me walk in and invited me to eat with them. The coaches saw me, too, but none of them came over to say hello. The players had suggested to the coaches that the Clemson game—the one right after I left—should be dedicated to me. Some of the guys wore my number on their helmets, but apparently Morrison didn't even mention it to the press. He tried to keep it quiet. He never called me in the hospital, either. And neither did Washburn.

When I returned to school the next semester and told Morrison I wanted to live off campus, he said the school wouldn't pay for it. Fortunately, my dad called and said, "Listen, if you don't pay for his housing, we'll go right to the papers about it." I got a check in the mail real fast. I don't think the coaches thought I was a bad guy. They were just scared that I'd say something about my steroid problem, and probably wanted to sweep it all under the carpet. It seems to me that if a guy has given himself to the team for 4½ years, they should be a little more concerned about his welfare.

People ask me if I hate Morrison and the other coaches. I feel sorry for them because they have so little compassion, but I don't hate them. I'm not out to get them—that's not the point of this article. I just want people to know that steroids change you in many ways, and that the psychological changes are the most drastic of all. I've seen so many players become brutal and mindless from steroid use. Look what happened to me.

I love football, but I am worried about the course it is on right now. Most coaches are hypocrites. They don't really care about their players. They only care about winning, and that's because of the pressures put on them— I understand that. But once you start using people as commodities, you've lost your integrity. And it's hard to get that back.

I don't know if our coaches could have stopped our steroid abuse, but they could have helped us act more rationally. They know that they're dealing with 19-year-old boys who need guidance, not pounding and brainwashing and hypocrisy.

I don't want to see another player go through the living hell I went through the last few years, and that's why I'm speaking out on this. I'm embarrassed by what I did. But if I can help someone else, maybe I can help myself, too.

I take no drugs now, not even aspirin. I still have problems with my vision, but the doctor says that should pass with time. The whooshing in my ears is probably there forever. I can't deal with physical stress the way I used to, and I can't exercise too aggressively or I get terrible headaches. My balance isn't what it used to be, and I still feel edgy. I can't work full-time, because some days I have to rest. I'm not well. Steroids screwed me up pretty good. Maybe you have to be a little crazy to play football. But you shouldn't take steroids. You *can't* take them.

And yet, there I was in the weight room at South Carolina last spring, and I could tell a lot of guys were still on the stuff. I saw an old teammate, a guard, a big country boy who's heavily into steroids, and I said, "Look in the mirror, man. All you're going to see is my reflection."

"I don't give a damn," he said. "It won't hurt me, Tom. It just affects you a whole lot worse than it affects other people."

Maybe that's true, maybe not. God help those who find out.

| | | | | |

It's All a Part of the Game

BY JOHN M. BARRY

The author reflects on his days as a football player and coach, and on an ever-present but seldom discussed aspect of the sport—the threat of serious injury.

THIS IS ABOUT FOOTBALL, ABOUT A PART OF FOOTBALL that happens to every team on every level. Recently I watched Patriots quarterback Jim Plunkett go down with an injury that required surgery, and then listened as one of his teammates was asked about it. "It's part of the game," he said. "You know? You can't worry about going down. It's part of the game."

I used to coach some football. Football coaches become inured to players getting hurt, even though the coaches are as vulnerable to injuries as the players. After all, it can mean coaches' jobs and coaches' careers. When I coached, I waved aside images of players undergoing the knife. I had to. But now, when a player lies on the ground I go get a hot dog, or turn away from the television set for one or two or three minutes, and try not to think about the one boy I saw get really hurt. I'm not a coach anymore and I do think about it.

I went down myself as a player; pain shot up my leg and I was wincing instead of running. My recovery progressed slowly. I believed the coaches all thought I was dogging it, but, damn it, I wasn't. At first the sideways glances the coaches shot at me made me feel guilty, but later I grew so angry that I decided never to play again.

The next season found me in the stands, but watching gnawed and gnawed at me. Not so much the not playing. It was more that I felt like a quitter, which is far worse than being just a loser. That feeling continued to haunt me after graduation until I scrapped my Ivy League degree and graduate-school fellowship and nascent doctoral dissertation to coach a high school team. Of course, I swore always to give a player the benefit of the doubt on any injury.

Like every other high school coach, when a boy went down I would run onto the field and order players to move back and ask, "Where's it hurt?" and hope someone who actually knew something about injuries would come out on the field. Quick.

During one game at a private school in the South the smallest player on the field, one of those fast, tough kids you always see in high school athletics, the kind of kid you love, went down. Out cold. I ran out there with a doctor. The boy was not badly hurt, the doctor said, and could even return to the game, so after he rested I sent him back in. We needed him in there. In the locker room after the game the boy collapsed. Unconscious, his eyes glassy, sweating profusely. I raced out to find the doctor. While waiting for the ambulance—the one at the game had left already—I slammed my fist against the lockers and shouted, "That *doctor* said he could play! Where's that *doctor*?" I felt guilt and wanted to transfer that guilt to him; I felt hate and wanted to kill him. The boy, as it turned out, was fine and later in the season even played again.

I was successful in high school, then coached club football at a small college and then became a coaching aide at a major college. National ranking. Television. An 80,000-seat stadium. Fantasyland for someone who didn't even play three years of Ivy League football. But it wasn't the sauna in the locker room or the giant stadium that struck me as so different. It was the zippers. So many athletes had zippers down the side of their knee, or knees; they thought nothing of it and called this or that a "Band-Aid" operation. I just kept looking at where the knife had cut and shaking my head. There were so many.

In college the coaches don't deal directly with injuries. There are trainers for that. In college the coaches receive injury reports and worry about them.

"Oh, Christ," they mutter when someone lies a little too long on the ground. "Get up. You're not hurt. Damn it, don't be hurt."

"It's not too bad," the trainer says. "Have to cut sometime, but not right now. You never know. He might make it through the whole season."

When the college season ends, those injured players who did make it through the year check into the hospital for surgery. The sooner the better for all concerned. The players are as anxious as the coaches; spring practice is not that far away. It was funny; one freshman had made the varsity that more than half a million adults had paid to cheer. He was under 18 so the hospital put him in the kiddies' ward and decorated his walls with flappy-eared purple elephants. He did not take kindly to his surroundings.

I don't want to identify the major college I was affiliated with. Identifying it could hurt its football program, and unfairly. It's not hard to envision rival recruiters showing copies of an article like this to a high school star and his parents and saying, "Now, ma'am, you don't want to send your boy to a school where the coaches treat folks like that, do you?" Yet the coaches there show as much concern as any about their players, and more than most.

In preseason we were running a game-type scrimmage inside our huge empty stadium, referees and all. A wide receiver runs an out. The quarterback ducks a rushing linebacker and starts to run, is chased, crosses the line of scrimmage. The receiver's eyes gleam, a pursuing defensive tackle suddenly in his crosshairs, and he sets himself to unload a blind-side shot. Except it isn't blind side. The defensive tackle sees him coming and—WHAM!—the receiver goes down, stumbles to his feet, goes down again and stays. Out run the trainers. Out runs a substitute receiver. The boy went down in front of the defensive bench. The defensive coaches ignore him. Hell, he's a receiver. He's not one of theirs. The offensive coaches are huddled, engrossed in play selection. The trainers help the boy off the field.

The head coach approaches the offensive coaches, beckons one of them closer. "Don't you *ever*," he says, "don't you *ever* let a boy lie on the ground again without a coach going over to him."

The season started and the team was doing well, winning games and staying pretty healthy. One starter did get hurt, though, and had to have his knee operated on, for the third time. He'd have been a pro prospect but for those operations. A couple of days after the surgery we were playing a night game at home. I knew no players would visit him that day—on game days the players had to stay in the athletic dorm for meetings and taping and eating and just being together. I thought the player would feel like the forgotten man, so in the afternoon, when I had nothing much to do but watch whatever game was on TV, I decided to visit him. Another visitor was there when I arrived. The head coach. You wouldn't catch many head coaches out visiting a player, except maybe a high school All-America, the day of a game. I always liked that man.

WHEN I think of football injuries I like to think of incidents like that. And to forget a day I can't forget. I was coaching club football at a small college, very small-time football. But for our level the team was excellent. Even though it was November, we had not lost a game. Naturally the team we were playing was up, whooping and hollering and jumping up and down and in general doing all sorts of carrying-on before the game. We went through our warmups with a minimum of screeching, poised as always. The other team was screaming louder than ever at the opening kickoff, which our 200-pound return man took out to about the 30, near our sideline. I saw the hit that brought him down. It was not a particularly hard tackle, but the other team shouted, "Good stick! Good stick!" just the same, and a couple of their players hustled over to pat the tackler as he got up. Except he didn't get up. He had gone down.

Our trainer was out there, with his coaches, talking to him.

"For Chrissakes," I was thinking. "Get up, kid."

Our head coach came over to me. "Really playing the role out there, huh?"

"Yeah."

Then the other team's trainer yelled for the doctor.

The doctor? Maybe the kid was hurt after all. We looked for the doctor. No doctor. The boy had been on the field for close to five minutes now. The trainer asked a cop to call the rescue squad. Where the hell was an ambulance? No doctor, no ambulance.

The doctor arrived. He had volunteered to be there but thought it was a two o'clock game, not 1:30. Sorry.

Now rumors spread along our bench that the kid was dead. I turned around and tongue-lashed a player who said that. "Don't be a jerk. Look at him. He's talking to the doctor."

Sirens. The rescue truck digging tracks in the moist field. Ten minutes had passed since the kid went down. I finally decided to join the huddle around the boy and see if we could get things moving.

With his helmet off, he looked shrunken and fragile in his equipment, his head sticking out of the massive shoulder pads like that of a small boy from his father's much-too-large jacket. He looked frightened. The doctor leaned over him.

"Am I going to be all right? I'm going to be all right, aren't I?"

"Just relax now."

"I can't feel anything. My legs. I can't feel anything." His voice, a scared child's voice. A lost child's voice. Wanting to be found. His face was handsome, almost pretty. The trainer took the boy's cleats and socks off.

"Can you move your toes?"

The boy's face strained and tensed, his teeth grated and his eyes closed as he bore down, and a little sweat appeared on his face. The toes did not move.

"Can you feel this?" The trainer jabbed a scissors' tip into his foot.

"What did you say?" the boy asked.

The trainer looked up, as if appealing to me. "Oh . . . nothing," he told the boy.

And all the people bustled around the boy. "Am I going to be all right?" he said again. "I can't feel my legs."

The doctor said they were taking him to the hospital, that one of the best neurosurgeons in the country, from Brown University, would see him, as if the boy should feel honored, as if the fact that the neurosurgeon taught at Brown University made him omniscient and omnipotent.

Our offensive team was on the field running through plays. The defense was doing calisthenics. It was not cold for the season, but it was November, and they had to stay warm or risk muscle pulls. I looked at the boy's face, at the wonderment in it, and felt sick. Sick of football. It couldn't be worth it. His eyes were open wide, as if absorbing this world never seen before. They started cutting off his equipment and he closed his eyes briefly, then reopened them.

"Am I going to be all right?" he asked the doctor one last time.

"Yes," the doctor answered him, "you're going to be fine."

Although he was already lying on the ground he seemed to lean back then, or sort of settle. I stood off to the side with our head coach, watching knives slash through pads. We had loaned our opponents some equipment before the game; their managers had made a mistake in packing. "With our luck," somebody said, "those are our pads they're cutting through."

I laughed. It was funny. I turned away from the semi-circle of people gathered around the boy and tried not to laugh; put my hand over my mouth and still laughed. It was funny. We had had budget problems all year.

They weren't our pads. We won the game easily, our fifth shutout of the season. The boy was paralyzed. I continued to coach for another three years before I quit. During that time I had players in the hospital and never got around to visiting them. Too busy planning practices. And after all, you can't worry about going down. It's part of the game.

Acknowledgments

THIS COLLECTION REPRESENTS THE CUMULATIVE EFFORTS OF DOZENS of SPORTS ILLUSTRATED writers and editors, representing every generation of the magazine's staff and distinguished outside contributors. Editors generally toil in anonymity, but several of them deserve recognition here, especially those of recent vintage who helped inform the selection of these stories and bring this book to completion: Bob Roe, Kevin Kerr, Dick Friedman and Mark Godich. Also indispensible to this project were Steve Hoffman and Josh Denkin. Other members of SI's staff somehow found time, despite the rigors of producing a weekly magazine, to make invaluable contributions: Linda Verigan, Sarah Thurmond, Natasha Simon, Joy Birdsong, Helen Stauder, Barbara Fox and the tireless SI imaging department. And special thanks to Terry McDonell, who played the game, and can still bring it.

We are also grateful for permission to reprint the following copyrighted material:

It's All a Part of the Game © 1975 by John M. Barry

The Game That Was © 1969 by Myron Cope

My Career (So to Speak) © 1970 by Myron Cope. Originally published as *How I Went from Fleet Breakaway Threat to Hard-Running Blond to Solid-Socking Blond to Loose and Fun-Loving off the Field* and *How Intangible Can You Get*, in SPORTS ILLUSTRATED, Nov. 16 & 23, 1970.

The Immaculate Reception and Other Miracles © 1973 by Myron Cope

Bang, You're Dead © 1972 by Don DeLillo. Originally published as *Pop, Pop, Hit Those People*, in SPORTS ILLUSTRATED, April 17, 1972.

The Making of a Coach © 2005 The Amateurs Ltd. Excerpted from *The Education of a Coach* by David Halberstam. Reprinted with permission of The Amateurs Ltd. and David Halberstam.

Vanity on the Gridiron © 1968 by Jack Kerouac. Reprinted with the permission of John Sampas, literary representative of The Estate of Jack Kerouac.

Where Have You Gone, Joe Namath? from *Namath: A Biography* by Mark Kriegel, © 2004 by Mark Kriegel. Used by permission of Viking Penguin, a division of Penguin Group (USA) Inc.

The Tackle by John O'Hara. © 1984 by Louise Erdrich, permission of The Wylie Agency